THE JOURNEY
BACK FROM HELL

ANTON GILL

THE JOURNEY BACK FROM HELL

Conversations with
Concentration Camp Survivors

GRAFTON BOOKS

A Division of the Collins Publishing Group

LONDON GLASGOW
TORONTO SYDNEY AUCKLAND

Grafton Books
A Division of the Collins Publishing Group
8 Grafton Street, London WIX 3LA

Published by Grafton Books 1988

British Library Cataloguing in Publication Data
Gill, Anton
The journey back from hell: conversations
with concentration camp survivors.
1. Europe. German concentration camps,
1939–1945 – Biographies
I. Title
940.54′72′43090922

ISBN 0-246-12897-6

Photoset in Trump Medieval by
Rowland Phototypesetting Ltd, Bury St Edmunds, Suffolk
Printed and bound in Great Britain by
William Collins Sons & Co. Ltd, Glasgow

The maps of Auschwitz-Birkenau and the Auschwitz Complex
are based on maps copyright © Martin Gilbert 1986.

This book is dedicated to all those who went through the ordeal of the German concentration camps, but especially to those whose courage and generosity of spirit enabled me to write it.

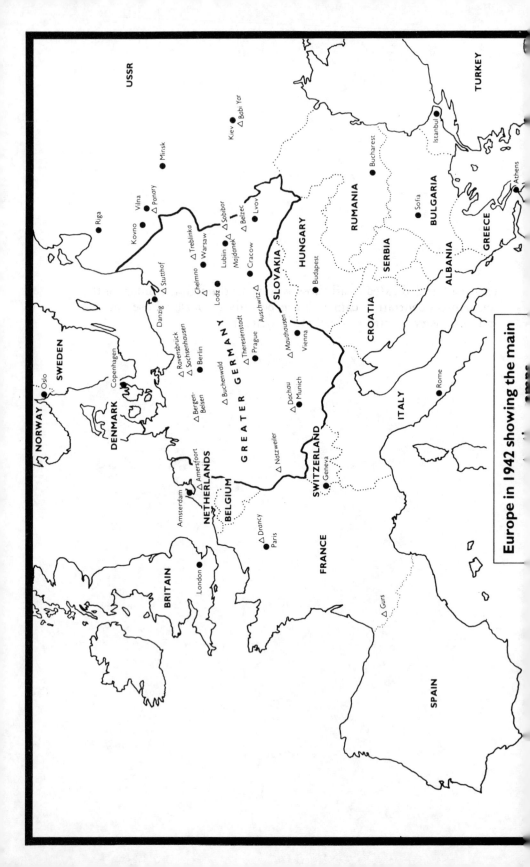

Europe in 1942 showing the main

Auschwitz-Birkenau

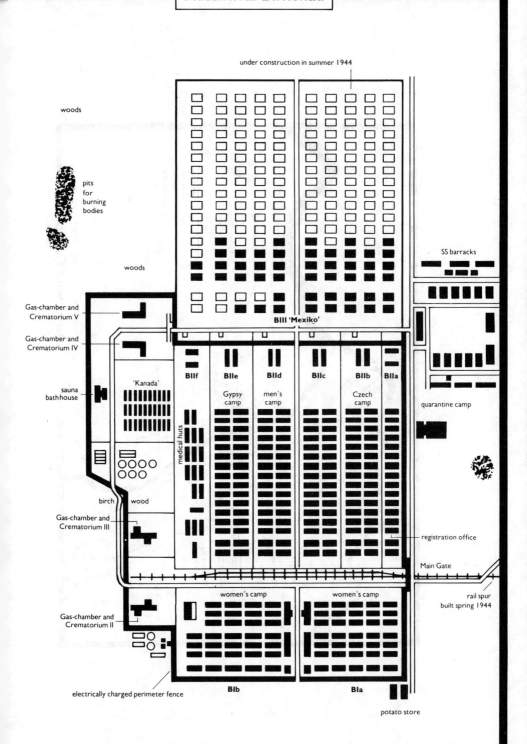

under construction in summer 1944

woods

pits for burning bodies

woods

SS barracks

Gas-chamber and Crematorium V

Gas-chamber and Crematorium IV

sauna bathhouse

'Kanada'

quarantine camp

BIII 'Mexiko'

BIIf   BIIe   BIId   BIIc   BIIb   BIIa

Gypsy camp   men's camp   Czech camp

medical huts

birch wood

Gas-chamber and Crematorium III

registration office

Main Gate

rail spur built spring 1944

women's camp   women's camp

Gas-chamber and Crematorium II

electrically charged perimeter fence

BIb   BIa

potato store

0   yards   660

0   metres   500

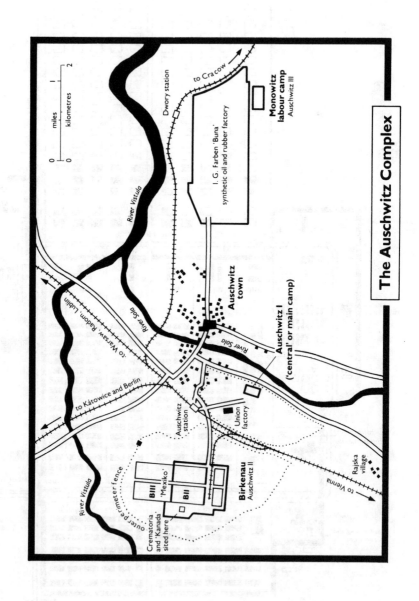

The Auschwitz Complex

Contents

CONTENTS

Acknowledgements

During the time taken to research this book, I have talked to over 120 survivors of the German concentration camps now living in Austria, Denmark, France, Great Britain, Israel, the Netherlands, Northern Ireland, Norway, the United States of America and West Germany, and have corresponded with many more in further countries still. Since it depends so much on oral testimony, the work would have been impossible without the generous help of these survivors; but I also have to thank the physicians, psychologists and psychiatrists concerned with their physical and mental recovery after the concentration camp experience, and the historians who have recorded their fate. A few contributors prefer to remain anonymous, and some further omissions are inevitable – for these I apologize.

First of all, I thank those most directly involved: the vast majority of the names that follow belong to survivors themselves. Those that do not, belong to people very closely concerned with them: Dr Yitzhak Arad (Chairman of the Directorate, Yad Vashem); 'AB'; Yehuda Bacon; Prof. Dr Jan Bastiaans; Fela Bernstein (née Drybus); Edith Birkin; Rabbi Abraham Brysh; Dr Elie A. Cohen; Gilbert Coquempot; the late Prof. Shamai Davidson; Robert Deneri; Ludwig Eder; Prof. Dr Leo Eitinger; Arie and Gila Fatran; Zenon Frank; Rabbi Dr Albert Friedlander; Prof. Saul Friedländer; Valerie Jakober Furth; Mag. Brigitta Galanda; Max R. Garcia; Martin Gilbert (without whose exhaustive work on the Jewish Holocaust any subsequent student of the period would be lost); Bertrand Ghibaudo; Dr Wanda Grabinska; Rabbi Hugo Gryn; Dr le Général le Comte Albert-Marie Guérisse, GC, DSO; Lina Haag; Dr Albert Haas; Kitty Hart; Prof. Eugene Heimler; Hans Heiss (Vice-President, Lagergemeinschaft Dachau eV); Ben Helfgott (Chairman, 45 Aid Society); Zenta Herker; Antonin Horcicka; Witold Huml; Karl Ibach (President, Fédération Internationale Libre des Deportés et Internés de la Résistance, and Federal Chairman, Zentralverband demokratischer Widerstandskämpfer- und Verfolgtenorganisationen); Feliciya

Karay; Prof. Dr Robert M. W. Kempner; Eugen Kessler (President, Lagergemeinschaft Dachau eV); Dr Jørgen Kieler; Dr Dennis B. Klein (Director, Center for Holocaust Studies, Anti-Defamation League of B'nai B'rith, New York); Freddie Knoller; Stanislaw Kocyan; Eugeniusz Konecki; Dr Edith Kramer-Freund; Erich Kulka; Jean Kuntz; Antonina Laniewska; Anita Lasker-Wallfisch; Benon Lastowski; Hofrat Dr Ivan Hacker Lederer (President, Israelitische Kultusgemeinde, Vienna); Dr Dov Levin; Revd Dr Isaac Levy, OBE, TD; Hanna Lévy-Hass; Helen Lewis; Madeleine Mallet; Denise McAdam Clark; Benjamin Meed (President, the American Gathering of Jewish Survivors of the Holocaust); Ernest Michel (Organizer of the World Gathering of Jewish Survivors of the Holocaust, and Executive Vice-President of the United States Jewish Appeal-Federation of Jewish Philanthropies of New York, Inc.); Zygmunt Modelski; Hadassa Modlinger; Denise Morel; Joachim Müller; Alec and Maria Ossowski; Dr Colin Murray Parkes; Myriam Pfeffer; Jean Piaud; Gisèle Probst; Stefan Przybylski; Dr Hadassah Rosensaft; Menachem Z. Rosensaft (Founding Chairman, International Network of Children of Jewish Holocaust Survivors); Jack Santcross; Kurt Schmidt; Edith Sklar; Dr Ludwig Soswinski (Chairman, Bundesverband österreichischer Widerstandskämpfer und Opfer des Faschismus); Ludwig Stark; Prof. Dr Herbert A. Strauss; Dr Halina Szwarc; Prof. Paul Thygesen; Richard Titze; the late Frode Toft; Michael Tregenza; Pierre Volmer; Dr Rudolf Vrba; Henry Wermeuth; Bernhard W. Wette; Simon Wiesenthal; Charlotte and Norbert Wollheim; Eli Zamek.

I also thank the following people: Prof. Dr H. G. Adler; Zbigniew Bako (Embassy of the Polish People's Republic, London); Rabbi Tony Bayfield; Chris and J. de Berg; Rex Bloomstein; Jean-Noël de Bouillane de Lacoste (French Embassy, London); Birgit Brandau; Dr Harald Braun (Embassy of the Federal Republic of Germany, London); Eva Brewster; Rabbi Balfour Brickner; Dr E. Chigier; Elizabeth Cross; Irena Czarnecka (Secretary-General, the Polish Government in Exile, Department of Foreign Affairs, London); Tony Dinner; Meira Edelstein; Annegret Ehmann; John Felsteiner; Joachim Fest; Bonny Fetterman; Helga Funken (of WDR Cologne); Dr Jozef Garlinski; Richard Gauld; Mrs E. L. Gill, MA (London) (for sharing the load of background and historical research); Geoffrey Goldberg; Martin Goldenberg; Charles Golding; Dr Gideon Hausner; Dr Adrian Hodge; Vladimir Ivanov (of Novosti Press Agency, London); Greville Janner, QC, MP; Fr Paul Jasinski, MIC; Dominique Jubien; Dr Christine E. King; Millie Kingsland; Peter Kingsland; Aleksandr Kodintsev (late of Novosti Press Agency, London); Xavier Kreiss; John L. Libson; the late Harry Loshak; Georg Menzel (Embassy of the German Democratic Republic, London); Christopher Moller; Mathias Mossberg (Swedish Embassy, London); Pamela Mulcaire (US Embassy, London); Jakob Murkes; the Very Revd Archimandrite

Nicanor; Hayim Pinner (Secretary-General, The Board of Deputies of British Jews); Victor Price; Peter Razzell; Dr E. Rosen (Embassy of Israel, London); Steve Savage; Gitta Sereny; John Stevenson; Robert Thorne; Ingeborg Traupe (ZDF, London); Dr Robert Paul Ullrich; Zdenek Vanicek (Embassy of the Czechoslovak Socialist Republic, London); Pastor Alexander Varga; Anthony Vivis; Peter Wickham; Patrick Whinney. Additionally, I wish to thank three Jewish members of the British Armed Forces who were in German POW camps: Dr Julius Cohen; Ivan Kayes and Mr I. Shine.

I would have been at a great disadvantage without the help of several organizations and institutions. These were: Aktion Sühnezeichen (Action Reconciliation); American Ex-Prisoners of War (Clydie J. Morgan); the American Jewish Committee, the William E. Wiener Oral History Library (Irma Kopp Krents, Milton E. Krents, Muriel Robbins) and the National Endowment for the Humanities, USA; the American Jewish Joint Distribution Committee (Denise Gluck, archivist); l'Association de Flossenbürg et Kommandos (President, Henri Lerognon; Secretary, Mme Péchiney); the Association of Jewish Refugees in Great Britain; l'Association Nationale des Anciennes Deportées et Internées de la Résistance; the Association of Ukrainians in Great Britain Ltd (I. Rawluk); the Australian High Commission, London (V. W. Davies); the Australian Jewish Historical Society (Sophie Caplan); the Australian War Memorial (M. G. Piggott); the British Library; Bundesverband österreichisher Widerstandskämpfer und Opfer des Faschismus (Ing K. Pordes); Bund Sozialistischer Freiheitskämpfer und Opfer des Faschismus, Austria (Eduard Schlesinger); CBF World Jewish Relief (Michele Williams); the Imperial War Museum, London; Institut für Zeitegeschichte, Munich; Institut d'Histoire du Temps Présent, Paris (Michael Pollak); International Tracing Service of the Red Cross, Arolsen (H. Siebel); the Jehovah's Witnesses; the *Jewish Chonicle*, London; the Jews' College, London (Simon Caplan); Judiska Församlingen i Stockholm (Gabriel Stein); Komitee der Antifaschistischen Widerstandskämpfer der Deutschen Demokratischen Republik (Otto Funke); KZ-Gedenkstätte Dachau (Barbara Distel); Lagergemeinschaft Dachau, eV; the Library of the Royal College of Psychiatrists (Susan Floate); Maximilian-Kolbe-Werk (Elisabeth Erb, Dr Gisela Armbruster); the Polish Association of Concentration Camp Prisoners; the Polish Air Force Association in Great Britain (I. J. Kedzierski); the Polish Committee for Refugees (Z. Janik); the *Polish Daily*; the Polish ex-Combattants' Association, London; the Polish ex-Servicemen's Association in Australia (J. Jaskiewicz); the Polish Institute and Sikorski Museum (T. Bialostocki); The Ray D. Wolfe Centre for Study of Psychological Stress, University of Haifa (Miriam Rieck, MA); Sociéte Française de Bienfaisance (Mlle J. Aliventi); Stiftung Dokumentationsarchiv des österreichischen Widerstandes; the Union of Polish War-Disabled ex-Servicemen (E. Nowak); the Video Archive for Holocaust Testimonies at Yale (Prof. Geoffrey Hartman, Dr Dori Laub, Joanne Rudof, Sandra Rosenstock); VVN, Munich; the Wiener Library, London (Christa Wichmann, Alexandra Wiessler, Tony Wells – especial thanks are due to these people, for there were times when I practically lived at the Wiener Library, and received incalculable help from them); Yad Vashem (Iris Berlatzky); Zentrale Stelle der Landesjustizverwaltungen, Ludwigsburg; Zwiazek Bojonikow o Wolnosc i Demokracje.

For the chapter on reparation I am especially indebted to the Amt für Wiedergutmachung in Saarburg; Amt der Wiener Landesregierung (Dr Brettbauer); Bundesministerium der Finanzen, Bonn, Dept VI A 4 (Dr Kraus); Bundesministerium für soziale Verwaltung, Vienna (Dr Karl Ernst); Conference on Jewish Material Claims Against Germany, Frankfurt-am-Main (Dr E. Katzenstein); Richard Saper.

Several people expressed interest in and support for my work, and among these I thank Prof. Yehuda Bauer; Suzanne Heffez Berensohn; Dr Jan Cibula (of the Romani Union, Bern); Frank Collins (Franz Wrobel); Mr Duraj; Eberhard Fechner; Franz Forster (öVP Kameradschaft der politisch Verfolgten, Vienna); Liv Frankel; Jozef Gresko; Eva Gross; Dr E. Hlwya; Prof. Henry R. Huttenbach; Revd J. Lang, SJ; Rabbi Robert Lehman; Gerda Mayer; M. L. Meyer; Ernest Mitchell; Teofil Modelski; Fred Pagel; Mr K. Podgorski; Janina Romanska; Kazimierz Sabbat (Prime Minister of the Polish Republic Government in Exile, London); Shimon Samuels and Leon Abramowicz (of the Anti-Defamation League of B'nai B'rith, European Foundation, Paris); Dr Rosa Scheuer-Karpin; Dr Antoni Slupik; Zygmunt C. Szkopiak (Undersecretary of State, the Polish Republic Government in Exile, London); Italo Tibaldi; Malka Vered; Prof. Elie Wiesel; Nico Wijnen; Mr O. Winter; Dr Wolynec; Janina Wysocki; Yechiel Yanai (of Beit Lohamei Haghetaot, Asherat, Israel).

Finally, I acknowledge the support and encouragement at every stage of Richard Johnson of Grafton Books; of my agent, Mark Lucas; and of my wife, Nicola, who helped me enormously, with her patience and understanding, through work which has often, by reason of its nature, caused me stress.

Author's Note

The face of Central and Eastern Europe was fundamentally changed by the two world wars of the twentieth century; in a lifetime, a person born before 1914 might find his birthplace change nationality and name three times. In the text of this book I have generally used the names that towns had during the Second World War, and have put the modern name and nationality in brackets afterwards. Exceptions are Auschwitz (Polish name: Oswiecim; the town is now once again properly part of Poland), and Theresienstadt (Czech name: Terezin) where I use only the German, because these names occur frequently in the book and it seems appropriate to use the names the camps went by.

Readers will find at the back of the book a short glossary of terms related to the concentration camps; one or two are used throughout the text, and it will be helpful to know them at the outset:

KZ, pronounced 'katzet', is the unofficial abbreviation of *Konzentrationslager* (concentration camp) – the official one is *KL*. Inmates of a KZ were known as KZlers or KZniks.

Prisoners in charge of work squads of other inmates were known as **kapos** (sometimes spelt 'capo'). Kapos were nearly always criminal or political prisoners, and although some were 'good', the majority were brutal thugs who earned precarious privileges for themselves by doing the Germans' dirty work – precarious because a kapo's power ended once he was put on transport to another camp.

Prisoners who had lost the will to live, who had lost half their original body-weight and more and who, effectively, were walking corpses, were known as **Mussulmen**. The origin of this nickname is obscure, though there is a theory that Himmler coined it, since the starving prisoners reminded him of eastern ascetics, or perhaps simply of starving Indians.

To obtain extra food, clothing, anything at all, by unauthorized means in the KZ was known as '**organizing**'. Some survivors hold that by definition 'organizing' did not harm fellow-sufferers.

Inmates of the KZ were of three main 'racial' types, according to the precepts of the SS. The **Reichsdeutsche**, born in Germany, Austria or those parts of neighbouring Europe that had formerly belonged to either of those countries, of pure Germanic stock: these were generally treated less harshly than other prisoners, especially after 1939, and were at the upper end of the scale of the camps' pecking order. **Volksdeutsche** were those born in Germany's neighbouring countries who could claim some 'pure' German ancestry – many Poles and even Ukrainians got themselves attested as *volksdeutsch*. At the bottom of the scale were the **Untermenschen** – the 'subhumans' – Jews, Slavs and Gypsies. Racial distinctions were, however, made among different Gypsy tribes, and many Slavs later became members of the SS.

For reasons of space, I regret that not all of the testimonies given me could be included.

French and German proper names and expressions in the text are accentuated. Those in Eastern European languages (mainly Czech, Hungarian and Polish) are not.

I have checked historical facts as carefully as possible. For any inaccuracies that remain I apologize, and take full responsibility for them. The faults in this book, whatever they may be, are my own, and should not be taken as a reflection upon anyone who has helped me with it.

Prologue

I

Any writer approaching the subject of the German concentration camps of the Second World War is faced with two main problems: that of scope, and that of the emotions and reactions that treatment of the subject evokes. As far as scope is concerned, one may as well accept that no one is ever going to produce a single work which encompasses every aspect of the camps, from the moment of their inception to their effect on European history and thinking, at least, up to now and into the future. Even though I am limiting myself to the story of KZ survivors' post-war experiences, I can tell only a fraction of what I have heard. As for the emotions they evoke – we are familiar with them. The camps have a fascination in their revoltingness. We are repelled and attracted – but the attraction (and I am not talking about the perverted titillation which some people feel, to which the trash literature and films relating to the camps testify) lies in an attempt to understand why they came about. Reactions, not least of survivors, to books about the camps are highly sensitive. As a writer on the subject, I seek not to offend; but I accept that there will be passages in this book that are bound to distress or anger somebody. I have kept my own comments to a minimum, noting my reactions and thoughts only where I think it appropriate to do so. I have seen my job as building a bridge between the survivors and the readers of this book. The readers must draw their own conclusions from what the survivors tell them.

The survivors of the concentration camps in this book are all Jews, or former political prisoners of the Nazis, or resistance fighters. They live now in Western Europe, the USA and Israel. For the most part they were born in central and Eastern Europe. Because some of the people I spoke to expressed surprise that I was not going to deal exclusively with the Jewish tragedy, I think I must now say why I have not. It is quite correct that the bulk of attention given to the concentration camps should have centred upon the attempt by the Third Reich to eradicate the Jews, because there is no doubt that no other victims of the camps were so inexorably slated for death. The war Hitler waged against them was the one in which he was all but victor, and the one which he personally continued to press with unabated vigour, without regard for the practical considerations of defending his country, to the bitter end. In September 1939 the Jewish population of the Europe that Germany was to occupy and control for the next five years was 8,301,000. It was long established: the community in Greece was 2,200 years old; in Bulgaria, France, Hungary, Italy and Rumania the communities were not much younger. There had been Jews in Germany for 1,600 years, in Poland for 800. Jew-hatred was nothing new, and there had been three pogroms of increasing severity in Russia, in 1881–4, 1903–6 and 1917–21, leading to a migration westward; but what was to come was beyond the bounds of anyone's imagination. In the course of five years, 5,978,000 Jews were killed – 72 per cent of the pre-war population. In Poland, where the Jews numbered 3,300,000 (a tenth of the total population of the country and the second largest community in the Diaspora) 2,800,000 were killed – 85 per cent of the original total.[1] Today, there are barely 5,000 Jews in Poland; they are mainly old. It is hard for a local community to make up a minyan. There has been only one bar-mitzvah since 1945.[2] The reason for this decay is not due to the actions of the SS alone. Many returning Polish Jews, survivors of the concentration camps, were murdered by anti-Semitic Poles in the years immediately following the war, and again in the wake of the Six-Day War and the Yom Kippur War. About half the Jewish survivor population of Poland, and predominantly the young ones, emigrated in the years following the Second World War, and the trend has continued. It is likely that there will soon be no Jews in Poland at all.

In remembering what happened to the Jews, it is still important not to forget that other, much smaller groups were scheduled for death – the Gypsies, of whom at least 500,000 were killed; Russian prisoners-of-war; homosexuals. To them one must add the numbers of political prisoners of all those nations occupied by Germany; captured resistance fighters; religious dissidents and other groups to be mentioned in Chapter 2. So that to the appalling figure of six million Jews, with which everyone is familiar, must be added at least a further six million people who met their deaths in the camps. I do not consider that discussion of the degrees of brutality meted out to prisoners who survived will be necessary, since readers will be able to make their own comparisons (as far as these are desirable) and draw their own conclusions; but it should be stated that generally the Jews were treated much more brutally than the non-Jews. Nor should it ever be forgotten that the Jews were abandoned by the rest of the world. Two inter-national conferences (at Evian in 1938 and in Bermuda in 1943) were convened to discuss ways of helping them. Only Holland and Denmark discharged themselves with any credit at Evian.[3] In 1938 there might have been some slight excuse for believing that the danger threatening the Jews was exaggerated; but the lack of interest displayed by Western nations in general was interpreted by Hitler as a green light for his plans. In 1943, in Bermuda, there was no excuse at all, as plenty of reports of what was going on had reached the Allies by then. But attitudes had not softened. By a bitter irony, the Bermuda conference was taking place at precisely the time of the Warsaw Ghetto Uprising.[4]

That the suffering of others should not be forgotten, however, is demonstrated by the story (told in Chapter 11) of Karl Ibach, a German Social Democrat who was first imprisoned in the tiny, short-life concen-tration camp of Kemna, in Wuppertal, at the age of 18 in 1933. He did not see his home again until he was released from the Russian POW camp of Mariupol in November 1947. Those political prisoners, deemed dangerous opponents of Nazism, were condemned to *Nacht und Nebel* – 'night and mist'. In other words, they were to be made to disappear, either to be worked to death, shot or gassed.

This is a book mainly concerned with the survivors' lives after liberation. It is a subject that has occupied specialists – physicians and psychiatrists – for decades,[5] but one which has had relatively little attention in the vast corpus of literature about the concentration camps themselves, and life in them.[6] That is one reason for writing it. Another is that the preconception that the prisoners' suffering ends when they are liberated must be dispensed with. For many survivors of the KZ, the trials continued, not least because there was no home to return to. Here again a distinction may be drawn between the returning political prisoners or resistance fighters, who were able to come back to an intact house, family, society and even job in their own country, and the tens of thousands of East European Jews (and anti-Communists, but overwhelmingly the people most affected were Jewish) who after years of torment had to gather up what remained of their strength and use it to carve a new home and career in a new country, with a new language and a radically different culture – a country moreover which, while accommodating them, might not otherwise be especially friendly or sympathetic.

The third principal reason is that time is running out. The youngest survivor I interviewed was born in 1934; but the oldest was born in 1898 (Jack Santcross experienced Bergen-Belsen as an 11-year-old; Edith Kramer-Freund was a doctor in Auschwitz and Theresienstadt in her forties) and it will not be long before it will no longer be possible to gain direct testimony from those with adult memories of the camps.

Thus this book will be one of the last of its kind, and one of the few ever. Inevitably the disaster of the German concentration camps will become part of history – a scar rather than a wound – but where the scar is, the skin should remain thin, the nerves more sensitive. We must not forget the 12-year-long slaughter and rape of the senses that Nazi Germany perpetrated in its concentration camps, nor that it was premeditated, deliberate, systematic and sustained. If we did forget it, it would be to our eventual peril. There have been massacres of people before and since, but nothing quite like this; and we must never, by indifference or moral laziness, let it happen again.

There is a revived interest in the camps now, originally sparked by the 40th-anniversary celebrations of the end of the war, and by the number of survivors who, previously silent, have now chosen to speak out. This last aspect, and why it may have come about, will be discussed in more detail in Chapter 6. Partly, too, we have reached a point where we can at last look at the concentration camps. There was little interest in the Fifties: people wanted to forget, to get on with rebuilding the world. Economic considerations crushed moral obligations, and only the lonely voices of such people as Elie Wiesel were raised in remembrance, admonishing us, crying in the wilderness; though doctors, faced with the job of trying to heal people whose suffering was without precedent, began research work immediately after the war.

With the trial of Adolf Eichmann in Israel at the beginning of the Sixties, the lid was taken off, the cupboard door opened. Now we have reached a crucial point. East Germany has for long declined any responsibility for the KZ;[7] though one should add that in the course of a long speech delivered on 31 December 1966 Walter Ulbricht mentioned the subject of former Nazis in the DDR. He said, 'Many millions of people were organized in the Nazi Party and other Nazi organizations. We have passed just sentence on those who committed crimes; but for the others we have provided the opportunity for them to overcome the past in work for peace and the community.'[8]

The East German courts imposed heavier sentences on former Nazis than their West German counterparts who were sometimes lenient to the point of embarrassment; but that did not prevent former Nazis from holding high office in the DDR.[9] Only recently has the DDR decided to compensate Jewish victims of the KZ living in the DDR. (After 43 years few potential beneficiaries remain.)

In West Germany, the mood now is to try to forget, or at least to reduce the impact of the KZ episode in their history. Only a very small number of the youth of West Germany involved themselves in 'reconciliation' work, and a third generation has grown up. When I was at school in West Germany for a term on an exchange scheme in 1965, my 17-year-old contemporaries' first question was always, 'What do you think of us in England? Do you still hate us? Have you forgiven us?' But in 1987 a

4

21-year-old West German girl told me with something amounting to resentment of the *Schadenfreude* with which other tourists viewed German tourists visiting the Hall of Remembrance at Yad Vashem. Dennis B. Klein, Director of the Center for Holocaust Studies at the Anti-Defamation League of B'nai B'rith, New York, also makes a point about young Germans now aged about 20 who say, 'The Second World War has absolutely nothing to do with us and we're fed up with having it rammed down our throats.'[10]

I sympathize with them; but against this may be set what Menachem Rosensaft told me. He is the son of Josef and Hadassah Rosensaft, both survivors, and was born to them in 1948 in Bergen-Belsen Displaced Persons' Camp, where he spent the first two years of his life: 'Of the criminal Nazis, many are still around, and very few regret anything more than not winning – or being caught out, if you prefer. And these were and are the parents of our generation – and the crimes of the Second World War have not been especially highlighted in German education up to now. Only a few – Manfred Rommel (Mayor of Stuttgart, and son of the famous general), Johannes Rau (Minister-Präsident, Nordrhein-Westfalen, whose father was a prisoner in Dachau), Richard von Weizsäcker (Federal President of West Germany) – do not shrink from the subject, and square up to Germany's moral and ethical responsibility. But many Germans want to paper over it or consign it to the past. I certainly don't harbour a sense of hatred towards Germans and I actively admire such people as Willy Brandt, for example. But for me one thing is crucial: one's heritage is the good as well as the bad. If a German tells me today that he wants to repudiate his entire heritage and start off anew from 1945, that's fine with me. But if he wants to have his cake and eat it – that is, he wants Goethe and Bach, Beethoven and Schiller, but he doesn't want to accept that the same nation was responsible for the Holocaust, then I have no time for him. The Third Reich is part of every German's heritage, and they must accept it, however hard or unpleasant that is to live with. Equally, no one has the right to forgive the Germans, except on his or her own behalf, and no one has the right to say, "Let's forget it," apart from those who suffered, if that's what they want. Whether any nation would have been capable of doing what the Germans did is a debatable point, though I believe that it is possible. No one has the right to regard Germans visiting Yad Vashem with *Schadenfreude*. Equally, however, no German has the right to resent being thus regarded. It is the German political dissidents who suffered at the hands of the Nazis themselves, often terribly, who are the first to admit this.'

The fact remains that the general feeling in West Germany is that they've had enough of it, and have had enough of being treated as the moral lepers of Europe. My own sense is that if they had shown a little more generosity in the question of investigating reparation claims and a little less leniency in the sentences handed down to former Nazis, they might by now have earned a part of the forgiveness some of them think is their right. This seems an appropriate moment to dismiss the so-called 'revisionist' historians – those who claim either that the camps never existed, or that nobody was ever gassed in them. As they retreated, the SS desperately tried to destroy the evidence of what they'd done; but they were conscientious about their paperwork (one example of the lunatic criminality of the KZ was that death-certificates giving false but 'respectable' reasons for death, such as heart failure, were issued for those gassed, tortured, or simply worked to death) and the Allies captured no fewer than 3,000 tons of documents and photographs relating to the camps.[11] This documentation alone is enough to crush the insidious suggestion that the KZ never was. One of the most moving things that happened to me occurred during the early stages of an interview with a couple who had both been in Auschwitz and later married. They were suspicious of me at first because they had recently talked to a journalist who subsequently wrote a 'revisionist' article. 'But Auschwitz did exist,' they said to me. 'We went back to see it again. Look – here are photographs. And here is a piece of fern that we picked, which we found growing near the ramp at Birkenau.'

Against the German desire to consign the concentration camps to history and hopefully bury them there, there are the voices that have been raised not only by the survivors themselves but by those who are interested in them – and who realize that their experiences are not only of a moral, ethical and philosophical interest, but are of practical application too. The concentration camp syndrome identified by Eitinger, Thygesen and others soon after the war, to take one example (see Chapter 6), has provided a model for and the basis of the post-traumatic stress syndrome, identifiable in the victims of hijack, terrorists' hostages, and soldiers;[12] but if the emphasis shifts, as it must with time, we should not forget the origins. Similarly, courageous work by Jewish doctors in the Warsaw Ghetto, who conducted a clinical study of the effects of starvation there (all but one of them died there themselves), and the pioneering work on semi-starvation by a team of Danish doctors, many of whom were themselves former inmates of the KZ, immediately after the war, have contributed to our ability to understand and aid famine victims in the Third World today.[13]

From what has been said it may be inferred that anyone writing about the concentration camps at the end of the twentieth century is writing at a unique time: at a moment of heightened interest in them, and at a moment when one has a last opportunity to illuminate one's work through personal contact with survivors. There are great difficulties. I cannot convey a tone of voice beyond describing it; I can say that someone cried; but can I convey what it feels like to sit in a comfortable office in Munich with a woman who stood across a desk from Himmler and pleaded with him for her husband's life? Can I describe how I felt when, sitting in an armchair in a large drawing-room in Harrow, a vigorous 58-year-old told me how, in Buchenwald, he had awoken on his wooden bunk, disturbed by a stone that was digging into him? 'But how could a stone be there? I reached around and found that it was my pelvis; there was no flesh between it and the nerves of my skin; my buttocks had disappeared.' I am deeply aware of the responsibility I have to those who have trusted me. In his Foreword to Eitinger and Krell's *Psychological and Medical Effects of Concentration Camps and Related Persecutions on Survivors of the Holocaust* Shlomo Breznitz writes: 'No longer personally painful, yet not entirely distant, the Holocaust experience is situated in that grey no man's land which makes it for the first time in many years accessible to the objective investigation and mind. However, this may turn out to be a short-lived interest, just as the candle, before dying, flickers intensely just one more time.' I am not sure that the experience is 'no longer personally painful', but I take the point of the caveat. The hope is that the material generated by the interest will be so stimulating that the candle will in fact go on burning, to illuminate future generations.

Part One of this book aims to provide a background of information against which Part Two, which is the body of the book, can be read, thus avoiding the need to pepper Part Two with quantities of explanatory notes. In relating the survivors' stories, if I have dealt not only with their post-war experiences but also with their lives in the camp, it is because the two are inseparable: one cannot be understood without the other. Jørgen Kieler suggested to me that the number of reactions human beings can master is limited, but the number of stresses they can be exposed to is possibly limitless. I make no apology for any repetition of experience or reaction in the stories related in Part Two, because I believe that the repetitions set up resonances, and such resonances, such similarities of experience and reaction, will enable the reader to draw whatever conclusions about survival in and after the camps he chooses.

Each interview took the survivor through his or her life, from pre-war days and family background, through the camps to the present. There were thus three phases in each conversation. Many survivors, especially Jews, came out of the KZ to find new homes in Israel, the USA and the United Kingdom. Often, where they had hoped to find sympathetic interest in their stories, which they were eager to tell, in order to externalize the experiences and so attempt to exorcize them, they found instead indifference or even hostility. Relatives who had got away in time, or those who had long lived away from mainland Europe, adopted an attitude of 'don't tell me – it's too horrible – I don't want to hear it', which deeply wounded the survivors and drove some into a silence which lasted decades. I was the first person many people had told their experiences to; and their need to talk was reflected by the extraordinary detail in which they remembered their time in the KZ, a time which they frequently described as being more real, more vivid to them still, than the decades which have passed since. The reasons for this will become apparent as the stories unfold. Interviews might take seven hours or more, and one French Resistance survivor told me, 'It would take me a day to really describe a day in Flossenburg.' The need to tell of the KZ experience, over and over again, is important. Just as you or I, in the wake of a lost job or a broken marriage, will lean on our friends and exorcize our woes by telling and retelling the story of what went wrong, until we have talked it out of ourselves, so a survivor will try to tell his story repeatedly. But we know people who understand completely what it is like to lose a job, or a lover, and we know that they will be able to sympathize because they have shared the experience. The KZ survivor can turn with confidence only to other survivors, and the enormity of his experience is such that it can never be truly talked out.

That is only one reaction. Some former KZ inmates have reacted by blocking or suppressing the memory; one or two who have only recently broken their silence told me that they were made to feel so alien by others who had not been in the KZ and who did not want to hear about it that they kept quiet in order to get a place back in the fold of the 'normal'. 'I kept quiet, once I'd got the message, because I wanted to blend into the crowd, to be unnoticed, to carry on as if nothing had happened.' Many survivors remain silent; but it is impossible to suppress the memories for ever, especially with retirement, the departure of grown children, and the onset of old age. It is at that time, and it is happening now, in the late twentieth century, that the silent survivors are at their greatest danger. They are not the only ones affected, either. In recent years a number of creative writers and historians, themselves former KZ inmates, have committed suicide, among them Paul Celan, Piotr Rawicz, Uri Tal and Primo Levi. This propensity to suicide emerged in a conversation with Albert Friedlander which took place before Primo Levi's death; but at the time Dr Friedlander, himself a survivor, not of the camps but of the *St Louis*,[14] expressed a fear that more suicides would follow.

Something which I hope will emerge in these pages is a picture not of martyrs or heroes (though I think they are both) but of ordinary people who, subjected to extreme and sustained stress, more or less managed to cope with it, get through it, and afterwards find a way of coming to terms with the wound it left. This book is not a history, not even an interpretation of facts, but a presentation of true stories, of recollections, and a relation of incredible courage in the face of continuing pain. A point that must be stressed at the outset, however, is that the people I have talked to belong to an elite group: they have made a sufficient recovery to talk about what has happened to them. There are many, many more survivors whose spirits were permanently broken, or who were driven mad.

One could make a shortlist of the attributes essential for survival in the camps: a sense of humour, adaptability, the ability to form small self-help groups, the ability to keep your head down, to get 'soft' jobs whenever possible, to maintain your own sense of dignity and decency. It is more difficult to make a similar list of what you need to adapt back to normal life. One thing seems clear to me: for the concentration camp survivor, there is no return to the person he or she formerly was, nor is there any final laying of the ghost, no matter how well adapted once again the survivor may appear to be; and many, possibly most, of them would not even wish there to be. The journey back from hell is not one that is achieved for any former camp inmate – it is a journey each one is still making, with pain, with continuous effort, with courage, with varying degrees of success – some striding, some limping. It is not even a question of putting a greater distance between oneself and the KZ – rather it is a question of coming to an accommodation with the memory, with the person the KZ has made one. If you lose your hand, the impression of it lingers long after it has gone. Ultimately you become used to its absence, and you get along without it. For hours on end you might not even think about its absence. But never a day passes when you are not aware that it has gone. Survivors cannot escape their past, or what was done to them, or what they have lost. The physical and mental scars are there for good; one's life-expectancy is reduced. But if they are lucky, and strong enough, they can live, and that is a triumph.

II

In approaching survivors, one must take a number of considerations into account. In the camps, they were exposed to unimaginable horrors and humiliations. The effect of this exposure has many aspects, and one of them is the formation of a protective shell. Herbert Strauss, who has worked widely with survivors, suggests that they dissimulate instinctively – a protective device they learned in the camps: 'Don't be deceived by an apparently calm and collected exterior appearance – underneath, their emotions are seething.'[15] This has not entirely been my experience, but his reaction bears out my sense that no survivor ever fully recovers.

Another element, already mentioned but constantly to be borne in mind, is the different treatment handed out to different categories of KZ inmate – a German Communist might spend 13 years in Dachau, a Polish Jew three years in Auschwitz-Birkenau. Given that both survive, the Jew will have almost certainly suffered more physical and mental hardship than the Communist; but how can one say that the German, incarcerated for 13 years, suffered less – except that, possibly within himself, because he knew why he was there, he was better able to withstand the injustice by rising above it.

Further, there is the question of various individual reactions to the same kind of assault. Although arguably standards of education have a bearing on the degree of success with which a survivor readapts after liberation, it is common knowledge that social and educational advantage were overwhelmingly not a factor in the camps. In that totally alien world, where all normal received civilization was torn inside out, people lost the bearings that had been defined for them by all they had acquired culturally, and became quite other. One is reminded of the legend of the mirror that shows, not the reflection of the person's face, but his personality. A reward is offered by the king who owns the mirror to anyone who can look into it for one whole minute without turning away, and no one can. Thus the survivors who could remain true to their own standards of decency were surrounded not only by the bestiality of the Germans and their henchmen, but by morally and ethically broken fellow-prisoners. There are people who survived at any price – at the price of other inmates' lives – but they survived at the cost of their own souls, if I may use so imprecise a word to denote the ability to live decently with oneself. Of course, as Strauss said, 'No ex-kapo is going to tell you that he survived by being a kapo. He will have invented his own cover-story and he will have repeated it so often that now he will believe it himself. The truth will be buried so deep he will no longer recognize it.'

The question also arises of the effect on the survivor of the degree of attention paid to the concentration camps in recent years. Referring to the resurgence of interest in the wake of the 40th anniversary of the end of the war, Strauss suggested that the survivors, because of this attention, might either become more defensive about their unexorcizable past, or go the other way and become a sort of 'actor' – constantly repeating their KZ experiences 'to the camera', and thus distancing themselves from the reality of these experiences, screening them off by turning them into a performance, rather than confronting them. 'In West Germany today not a week goes by without there being something on TV about the concentration camps. The Germans are trying to make up for what happened, but they are overdoing it . . . In fact the current reaction of German Jews living in West Germany to the Holocaust is remote: "Let Yad Vashem deal with it" – but maybe they're compensating for the guilt they feel about living in Germany.' Whatever the truth of the suggestion about screening off, I have met one or two Jewish survivors, usually high up in American survivor organizations, who have given me a set speech rather than a personal interview; but I would argue that this is because they are public figures publicly associated with keeping the memory of the Holocaust alive; from the eyes, faces and gestures of those whom I spoke with, it was apparent that any attempt to screen off was not successful. If living openly with the KZ experience, making it your job, is one survivor's way of coming to terms with it, then that seems valid. On a purely human level, it should be added in fairness that any kind of public figure is less prepared to expose areas of their private personality in an interview with someone who is a relative stranger than is a person who lives privately: how much more so, perhaps, when the subject under discussion is the concentration camps.

Many survivors lecture to students and schoolchildren; some conduct tours of the camps in which they were prisoners. Brigitta Galanda of the Stiftung Dokumentationsarchiv des österreichischen Widerstandes in Vienna does not believe that those who do so under the auspices of the SDöW become inured to the impact of their experience through repeatedly telling it. 'They relive it with real pain every time they talk about it.' My own impression too has been that those survivors who lecture do not do so because they want to talk about it in any compulsive sense (indeed, the decision to do so at all often comes at the end of a long and painful deliberation) but because they feel strongly that the young especially must be taught about the camps, and that they have a duty as living witnesses of it to pass their story on directly; they owe it to the young, and to those who did not survive. I came across only one German ex-political prisoner who had been unable ever to leave Dachau, mentally and even physically. Being taken round the camp by him reminded one of an old soldier reliving his battles – the finest moments of his life.

It is important that we should not surround the survivors with too much mystique. If we constantly handle them with a kind of reverence that keeps them at one remove from us (and therefore a selfish, self-indulgent reverence) or alternatively regard them as simply other-than-us by virtue of what they have been through, we reinforce the barrier between them and us and increase the isolation, the loneliness which is the principal cause of most survivors' unhappiness. Those who have adapted back most successfully seem to be not necessarily those who have had the most fulfilled lives in terms of career or material success, but those who from the first have been surrounded by loving and caring people who are interested in them, and who provide a warm and secure atmosphere.

There is another side to the coin which, for completeness, must be mentioned here – not so much to discuss it but as food for thought. Professor Strauss has pointed out to me that there is one type of survivor who relates all the suffering imposed on concentration camp victims to himself: 'I bear the suffering of the world on my shoulders.' 'But he expects his experience to exempt him from the norms of usual ethical, social and moral behaviour.' I have myself spoken to survivors in Central Europe who are engaged in criminal activity but who were not, I am sure, of a criminal nature while actually in the camps. The justification they give is one which has been remarked by others, but which I was surprised to find confirmed: 'Who is anybody to criticize me for what I do for a living? Were they in the camps?' These particular people were German Jews who had elected to return and live in West Germany after the war. I am not for a moment saying that they are typical of modern German Jews; rather the contrary is true; but they displayed toughness, adaptability and a willingness to take any road to provide the material success that affords the bastion against insecurity – all prerequisites of survival in the KZ. Why had they gone back? One had started a small business in the Displaced Persons' Camp and, as it was successful, he'd continued it in conjunction with his German contacts. Another had met and married a Gentile German girl. Both, however, lived embattled lives, mistrustful of everyone around them ('Your German's too good for an Englishman: are you sure you're who you say you are?') and yet at the same time quite prepared to cheat any German: the fact that they were getting the better of Germans justified the dishonesty; they hadn't, I think, moved on from a wartime outlook.

Related reactions have been observed by Rabbi Balfour Brickner in New York:[16] 'By and large they are an impossible bunch ... they consider themselves sanctified by the KZ and they think it gives them a right of precedence over everyone else.' Brickner's general view of survivor organizations may be thought controversial: 'A friend of mine was PR on the Holocaust Memorial Committee, which is the classically typical one: first of all, it's riddled by the ugliest petty in-fighting, which neutralizes its effectiveness. Secondly, it is interested in keeping itself alive and to do that it keeps the memory of the Holocaust alive: I think the work done is important, but I think in general the Holocaust organizations are petty, hard to work with, on occasion extremely aggressive. The Holocaust museum is a-building, next to the Smithsonian in Washington. It'll be like Yad Vashem, which thank God was done tastefully. But it won't make any real difference to whether the Holocaust will happen again.'

These comments however seem perfectly valid and not even surprising; I include them to demonstrate the humanness of KZ survivors. Having survived a KZ does not make anyone into a saint automatically, or even at all. In support of this one can turn to Helen Epstein, who writes: 'The term "survival syndrome" did not address itself to . . . beneficent changes in personality. It seemed to imply that a defective human mutant had been created, intrinsically different from you and me. Novels and films had elaborated on this characterization, portraying survivors either as saints or martyrs, people who had survived the worst and could do no wrong; or alternatively, as little more than shells of their former selves, near-criminals, who had stooped to inhuman measures in order to prolong their lives.'[17] The KZ had the power to change a person's nature fundamentally and permanently: but it did not permanently change people into angels or devils.

Among the survivors I met, all sorts of attitudes were represented, all classes, all degrees of education, and most of the nationalities involved. The group I eventually saw was put together at random. Very few of the people I met gave me any reason to doubt their integrity or the truth of what they were telling me (which in any case I was able to cross-check, if necessary, with other survivors as the work progressed). Contrary to the findings of many far more qualified and experienced workers in the field than I am, I generally had the impression that the people I met looked younger than they actually were and showed far greater vitality and mental liveliness than other people of their age. When I was talking to Dennis Klein about this, he suggested that the vitality might have something to do with the nature of survivors. 'Also, they have confronted their mortality, which radically changes their outlook on life from then on; and no one who hasn't been there really knows it.' But I must stress again that I was talking to a very select group. My concern is that their success should not lead people to the conclusion that perhaps the KZ wasn't as bad as all that.

The survivors whose stories appear in this book are ennobled – but not so much because of what they went through as by their efforts to come to terms with it, to live with it. And it is never very far away. The 'journey' of my title is not one across distance away, but towards a point of control over the uncontrollable. 'In the camps I was afraid when I woke up,' one survivor said to me. 'Now I am afraid when I go to sleep.'

To understand the achievement of survivors who are making the journey back from hell, one must understand specifically what they underwent. Psychiatric studies report significant fears continuing or resurfacing. Niederland[18] tells of fear of noises, even of the telephone bell; of fireworks; of letting young children speak too loudly at home. One survivor treated by him, waking out of dreams at night, doesn't remember for a long time whether she's really in the USA now or back then in Poland at the time of the persecution. The effect of her nightmares is so terrible that her husband used to have to take her round the apartment and show her the view of New York from the windows, to convince her that she wasn't back in the camps. Another survivor describes a terrible moment: after months of hiding out in the woods, living like beasts, she flees westwards with her husband, leading one child by the hand, the other at her breast. A stray bullet strikes the baby at her breast and kills it. It is winter 1944, in Poland. The ground is too hard to bury the baby. She has to leave it lying on the hard ground. Its body stopped a bullet that would otherwise have killed her. Professor Niederland identifies what he calls *Seelenmord* (the death of the soul): the state you are reduced to when you can no longer recover from the outrage committed to your psyche, when you are cut off from 'normal' people and cannot get away from your memories. 'Many saved from the clutches of the SS at the last moment are living corpses today.'[19]

The problem of those Jewish survivors who have to make the transition to a new culture and a new country frequently centres on their identity. Saul Friedländer says that 'the Nazi persecutions were the first encounter for assimilated Jews like my family actually with Judaism – it was Hitler who made them Jews again, if you wish.'[20] Those who came out of the camps alive had to make a decision for themselves about their identity. They didn't bring their identity with them from home. Previously, they may have been Communists or, and this applies especially to those in German-speaking areas, culturally totally assimilated.[21] The same was true of Jews in France. The brutal encounter with identification brought many of them to a crucial choice: would they continue thereafter to identify themselves racially and religiously with Judaism, or would they eliminate it completely? Friedländer is aware of several people he has encountered in the course of the 30 or so years that he has been teaching in Switzerland 'in university life at least who for years I didn't suspect of being of Jewish origin. Until they told me, after a certain degree of friendship had grown up between us; and they explained that they had wanted, after the concentration camp experience, to bury their identity as Jews for their own sake and that of their children, so that if anything similar should ever happen again, their children or grandchildren would never have to suffer.' Such people frequently changed their names to blend in with the ordinary non-Jewish names of their adopted country. This phenomenon is commonest among people who came originally from pretty well assimilated families, and who came out of Central and Eastern Europe, but who now want to feel themselves to be British, Swiss, French, American, rather than Jewish at all. I have not met many such survivors, but I think it likely that such people will also be inclined to repress their memory of the KZ and not talk about it. However, because the erasing of Jewishness has been consciously engineered, the awareness of that sooner or later leads to a desire to discuss it, to confess it, to defend it – and frequently the interlocutor has to be someone like Friedländer who himself came within an ace, not only of converting to Roman Catholicism, but of studying to become a Jesuit. But Friedländer redis-covered his Jewishness as part of his being. He is judged by the 'secret' Jews to be worthy of being taken into their confidence – someone to whom they can unburden themselves of what (for want of a better word) is guilt at hiding an identity which perhaps ultimately they cannot deny.

The crucial problem comes back to identity. No Jew has come out of the Holocaust unharmed in terms of self-image; but this applies specifically to those who went through the war in Europe, either in hiding, in the camps, in the resistance or the ghettos – as opposed to those who managed to escape before 1939 from what would eventually be German-occupied Europe. This damaged self-image may also con-tribute to the guilt that many survivors (especially Jewish ones, who frequently lost their whole families) feel at having lived: 'I don't think this can be dissociated from the shame which they were branded with: they were so profoundly humiliated that it's difficult for them ever to shake it off.'[22] Not that survivor guilt is peculiar to KZ survivors; but it is such a profound syndrome that it can put them at odds with their own identity.

To use pretence as a means of escape is not usually a defence in the long run. The shoring-up of artificial defences against the inroads of guilt, or ghastly memories, can last only so long, and it is a common occurrence that what survivors have assiduously been trying to sup-press will ultimately have to come out. The breaking point usually occurs between 20 and 40 years after the event, and often coincides with the onset of old age. In terms of the breakdown, the carefully constructed new persona disintegrates and the survivor is mentally back in Poland or Hungary or wherever the trauma occurred. The new identity can only be synthetic; it's a shell, not solid. Inside, little has changed. These survivors will not talk, they haven't confronted their past, but they have attempted to rebuild their lives, on the surface often very successfully. There are others who have never been able to make the attempt at any level: the permanently depressed; those who cannot settle; those whose inability to concentrate any more makes any kind of serious work impossible; those who are in mental hospitals. They must not be forgotten.

I have stated my belief that no prisoner (with the possible exception of some non-Jewish political prisoners who spent a relatively short period in the KZ, probably before the outbreak of the war) ever fully recovers from the concentration camp experience. Friedländer supports this with the image of the fissure. 'There is a crack in the wall – despite it, the wall has stood, the house has been built; but the crack is there, never filled, constitutes a weakness in the structure, and may widen. It may even be that the very aggressiveness of the achievement of some survivors is the result of a counter-measure to the inherent weakness that they know to be within them; a defence against their vulnerability.' And there is an example of how the fissure can manifest itself. A man came to Israel from the camps, rebuilt his life, became materially successful. His marriage was also apparently successful, and he had two daughters. But he would constantly punish himself in little ways. On a very hot day, for example, he might buy ice-creams for his family, but not for himself. He identified this tendency within him, and could talk about it in therapy, but nevertheless his life continued to be littered with similar small symbols of punishment, to no ill-effect. But one day, relatively late in life, he again met a woman whom he had originally encountered on the boat coming to Israel and had liked at the time, though they hadn't seen each other now for ten years. They met by chance and, just as in a bad novel, they clicked: he fell deeply in love with her and was overwhelmed and overjoyed at the sudden rush of feelings he had been unable to express before, or for so long. But together with these released feelings, the whole camp experience came back too, and the horror of that affected him to such an extent that he had to leave the woman and return to his family, to that mode of life which had protected him before, and would again. The rush of liberated emotions widened the fissure to such an extent that the house threatened to fall. The best thing a survivor can hope for is a recognition of the fissure and an accommodation with it.

As for the 'shell' method of defence, its relative success is complex. For some people the shell may last and be effective all their lives, so that it is impossible to say for certain that there has to be catharsis to free one from the KZ experience. And if the shell does break, then the survivor may or may not be able to weather the ensuing trauma; but it is doubtful whether anyone would come out on the other side whole. There is no tidy formula for coming to terms.

PART ONE

1

The KZ System

This will be no more than a brief description of the events and thinking that led up to the establishment of the concentration camp system, and of the system itself. (The Select Bibliography [see p. 461] suggests a number of books on the subject.) For present purposes, it is important only to establish the structure of the hell to which KZ inmates were condemned, without entering into a profound discussion of it; this aspect has already been dealt with in many works of which it is the central theme.

One of the questions put to survivors was: 'Why do you think it happened?' This is a question that will never be fully answered. Hatred, envy and suspicion of the Jews is as old as the Diaspora, and in the past Jews either have not been allowed or have not chosen to integrate into the communities of their host countries in very many instances. That this was not the case in Germany makes the question more difficult, and its possible answers more frightening, for within a generation the Jews there ceased not only to be Germans, but even to be regarded as human. Men who had fought bravely for their country in 1914–18 were, 17 years later, stripped of their rights; and within a matter of another seven years they had seen their families and friends slaughtered and, in the majority of cases, had succumbed themselves. The speed with which the Nazis moved once in power is one of the most daunting facts of the whole history of the period.

In the nineteenth century there was a good deal of pseudo-scientific and mystical thinking and writing about racial purity, and this went hand in hand with anti-Semitism. One stumbling-block was of course the fact that the non-integrated Jews were themselves racially pure, but this was seen as having a sinister purpose. Houston Stewart Chamberlain, a German-naturalized Englishman and (as Richard Wagner's son-in-law) a prominent member of the *Bayreuther Kreis*,[1] in 1899 had published a book called *Die Grundlagen des Neunzehnten Jahrhunderts* ('The Foundations of the Nineteenth Century') which was widely read and ran through eight editions in ten years. Chamberlain was in the forefront of those who believed in the superiority of the Germanic peoples above all others, and his work must be regarded as a major influence on Hitler, who visited Chamberlain on his death-bed in 1927.

The Jews' sinister purpose, Chamberlain shakily argues, was to dominate the world with their money, and to 'infect' the Aryan peoples with their blood. In the midst of the 'chaos of the peoples' (*Volkerchaos*) were the Jews, *the one race which had chosen purity of blood*, states Chamberlain. The Teutonic race entered history as an opposing force to the diminutive but influential Jews. To a modern reader the book seems almost impossibly turgid, and its arguments are intemperate to the point of lunacy – not one has internal or cohesive logic. But Chamberlain and, after him, Hitler were able to play on fear; and, once fear and its frequent comcomitant, hatred, have been aroused, there is no further need for reason. The Jews were branded as sub-human under Hitler, literally believed to be vermin, infectious, unfit even to be buried in German soil; and yet their poor corpses were turned into fertilizer to grow food for Germany,[2] their hair was woven into matting for U-boats, and their blood was taken for transfusion use at the Front. Yet the tactics ascribed to the Jews in the film *Jud Süss* (premiered in Berlin in September 1940) are those actually used by the Germans against the Jews, and even Süss' pleading, designed to make him look ridiculous and craven, at his trial and on the gibbet before he is hanged, is an ironic foretaste of what would be heard coming from the mouths of the Nazis at their own trials exactly five years later: 'I only followed orders.'

To anti-Semitism and preoccupation with Teutonic racial purity must be added German militarism, recently reawakened by Bismarck and Wilhelm II. Two later examples of how the Germans sought to influence their own children's thinking seem relevant here. The first is a problem taken from a school mathematics textbook published in 1936 and widely distributed and used, running to several editions:

Problem 200: According to statements of the Draeger Works in Lübeck in the gassing of a city only 50 per cent of the evaporated poison gas is effective. The atmosphere must be poisoned up to a height of 20 metres in a concentration of 45 mg/m^3. How much phosgene is needed to poison a city of 50,000 inhabitants who live in an area of four square kilometres? How much phosgene would the population inhale with the air they breathe in ten minutes without protection against gas, if one person uses 30 litres of breathing air per minute? Compare this quantity with the quantity of poison gas used.

More chilling still, perhaps, is the children's rhyme mentioned by Adler in his massive history of Theresienstadt:

Händchen falten, Köpfchen senken,
Und an Adolf Hitler denken!

which I give in German as it is impossible for a translation to carry the flavour, but which means:

Fold your little hands, lower your little head,
And think of Adolf Hitler![3]

The concentration camps themselves were not originally designed for Jews, and although the thought of using poison gas against them was formulated very early on,[4] Hitler's original idea seems to have been simply to get them out of Germany and the German empire he envisaged. If the world powers at Evian had opened their doors to the Jews, they would have been saved. There was another plan to exile them *en masse* to Madagascar;[5] but while the Nuremberg Laws were not promulgated until towards the end of 1935,[6] to be followed quickly by a whole series of gradually escalating restrictions against Jews including their not being allowed to own pets, the concentration camps were started almost immediately after Hitler had come to official power as Chancellor. He moved with great speed against his political opponents. The Reichstag Fire occurred on 27 February 1933, and Dachau was opened barely a month later. Many political prisoners had been in Dachau for seven years before the war started, and Karl Ibach, in his memoir of Kemna concentration camp in which he was incarcerated in 1933, tells of a Jewish political prisoner of that time who was treated no worse than the others – though, as we shall see, the tiny and short-lived concentration camp on the outskirts of Wuppertal already had the full range of tortures that were to become the stock-in-trade of its successors. All it lacked was gas chambers.

The development of the camps is complex. During the period leading up to the war, elements other than political dissidents were deemed to be enemies of the people and sent to the KZ. Dachau remained primarily for political prisoners, but Sachsenhausen, as early as 1937, contained a large number of homosexuals, Jehovah's Witnesses and common criminals – all lumped together as 'antisocial elements'. Buchenwald was opened on 19 July 1937 as a camp for criminals, where they held sway until they lost power to the political 'red triangles'. Flossenburg was opened in June 1938 for politicals and Jews from the Sudetenland. It was ultimately to house a significant number of members of the French Resistance. The politicals were subjected to 'protective custody'. Each activity had its euphemistic label. Slave labour was known as *produktive Vernichtung* ('productive annihilation'); execution by gas was *Sonderbehandlung* ('special treatment'). Despite their size and proximity, no inmate of Auschwitz-Birkenau was supposed to know what the function of the crematoria was. Corpses were not described as such, but as *Stücke* ('pieces').

A report to SS Obersturmbannführer Walter Rauff concerning redesigning the trucks (built by Saurer; the firm is still in operation) used for gassing in Chelmno refers to the van's 'load':

Since December 1941, 97,000 have been processed [*verarbeitet*] by the three vehicles in service, with no major incidents . . . The van's normal load is usually nine per square yard. In Saurer vehicles, which are very spacious, maximum use of space is impossible, not because of any possible overload, but because loading to full capacity would affect the vehicles' stability. So reduction of the load-space seems necessary. It must absolutely be reduced by a yard, instead of trying to solve the problem, as hitherto, by reducing the number of pieces loaded. Besides, this extends the operating time, as the empty void must also be filled with carbon monoxide. On the other hand, if the load-space is reduced, and the vehicle is packed solid, the operating time can be considerably shortened. The manufacturers told us during a discussion that reducing the size of the van's rear would throw it badly off balance. The front axle, they claim, would be overloaded. In fact, the balance is automatically restored, because the merchandise aboard displays during the operation a natural tendency to rush to the rear doors, and is mainly found lying there at the end of the operation. So the front axle is not overloaded.[7]

Administration of the camps was in the hands of the SS *Totenkopfverbände* (Death's Head Brigades), extermination and imprisonment being the responsibility of the RSHA (*Reichssicherheitshauptamt*, or Main Reich Security Bureau), and exploitation of slave labour the responsibility of the WVHA (*Wirtschafts- und Verwaltungshauptamt* – the Economic and Administrative Main Office, under Oswald Pohl). The role of the WVHA became increasingly important as the war progressed and Germany – particularly at the very end – depended on slave labour to keep its war-machine going, and *produktive Vernichtung* replaced gassing. By then, however, the terrible damage was done.

Camps were notionally divided into categories representing degrees of severity. Class I was the mildest form, on paper at least, and was supposed to denote a labour camp. But Dachau was designated a Class I camp! Class II indicated harder working and living conditions, and Class III meant death-camps. The reality was that conditions in all the camps were brutal and harsh beyond imagination, that death was the prisoners' daily companion, and the only difference was one of size and numbers. The extermination camps, discussed below, were different from the others in that they were specifically operated to kill Jews in large numbers. Only a small squad of prisoners was spared to run these camps and sort out the plunder. All the others arriving at them were gassed as soon as possible after arrival. There was no element of labour at these camps.

Immediately after the German invasion of Poland in September 1939, and immediately after Hitler's invasion of Russia and the end of the Molotov–Ribbentrop Non-Aggression Pact, when German troops poured across the Brest-Litovsk line into Russian-occupied Poland (until then a place of precarious safety for Polish Jews able to reach it from the west) on 22 June 1941, ghettos and concentration camps were established. The ghettos were set up in nearly every town and they were administered by Jewish Councils (*Judenräte*), answerable to the SS. These places, not seen in Europe since the Middle Ages, were in the poorest parts of towns. Jews were forced to leave their own homes and were crammed into these near-slums, often several families to a room. Food was so severely rationed that, without the ability to get extra provisions clandestinely, people would die; and they did, in their thousands, of starvation and disease. Walls were built around the ghettos, for the construction of which the Jews had to pay. They also had to pay for the yellow stars they were forced to wear, which were collected from the local police stations. There were occasions when they even had to pay for their railway journeys to the camps. In any case their fares were taken into account by the *Ostbahn*.[8] Some industry was carried out in the ghettos but, as the programme of extermination progressed, more and more ghettos were liquidated, for they were essentially holding-places for Jews until the camps were ready to receive them, and the *Judenräte* would be required to deliver up 'consignments' of thousands of people daily, rounded up by the Jewish ghetto police, to the SS. Lodz had the first ghetto, and it was the last to be liquidated, in August 1944, when the remaining population of 68,500 were transported to Auschwitz. Its existence had been prolonged because of a row between Himmler and Speer over the disposition of its industries.[9]

The decision to implement the Final Solution (the very word 'final' betokens the long tradition of anti-Semitism of which this was the ghastly culmination) was taken formally after the Wannsee Conference of January 1942, but the extermination of the Jews had started before that. Behind the eastward-advancing Wehrmacht came the *Einsatz-gruppen* ('task forces'). Their duty was 'the suppression of all elements hostile to the Reich and to Germany behind the fighting line'.[10] These

were in fact killing squads, whose victims were the Polish intelligent-
sia, political dissidents likely to foment resistance, Gypsies and, overwhelmingly, Jews. A squad would arrive at a town or village and round
up the people they sought, sometimes assisted by the local police. They
would then take them to the outskirts, or to a nearby wood or open
land. The victims would then be forced to dig a pit, which would
become their grave after they had been shot. That the *Einsatzgruppen*
did their work with a vengeance is borne out by one statistical report
from Group A, which on 29 August 1941 slaughtered 1,469 Jewish
children in Moletai and Utena. In the period between June 1941 and
April 1942 the four main groups were responsible for the following
numbers of deaths:

Group A:	250,000
Group B:	70,000
Group C:	150,000
Group D:	90,000

Each force numbered between 500 and 1,000 men, including back-up
and technical staff. For the ten-month period mentioned above, each
'executioner' member of Group A would have had to kill two people a
day, every day. The figures are conservative.[11]

For all their zeal, however, this method of slaughter was too cumber-
some, too slow and too expensive (in terms of ammunition and transport costs). Another way had to be found.

Four camps[12] were established in remote parts of Poland. Chelmno-
on-the-Ner, where gas-vans were used, was operational from 7 December 1941 to spring 1943 (the 'castle' period), and again from June
1944 to January 1945 (the 'church' period – these names derive from
the buildings where the victims were housed). The other three camps,
which also used carbon monoxide gas, but from stationary engines
which pumped the gas into the chambers, were Belzec, Sobibor and
Treblinka. They were smaller and less efficient than Auschwitz-
Birkenau was ultimately to be, since gassing by carbon monoxide takes
about 40 minutes, as opposed to the 15 minutes or so needed for
Zyklon-B, the highly volatile hydrogen cyanide preparation, supplied
by the firm of Tesch & Stabenow of Hamburg for use at Auschwitz, to
take effect. Nevertheless, their record speaks for itself. Belzec was
operational from March to November 1942. Between 400,000 and
600,000 people were killed, and perhaps only one survived.[13] Between
April 1942 and 14 October 1943, when the inmates rebelled and escaped,
Sobibor's gas chamber accounted for 250,000 people. The number of
eventual survivors, including those who escaped (most of whom were
hunted down), was 50. Treblinka was the largest extermination camp.
Its life spanned the period from 22 July 1942 to September 1943. In just

over a year, a million people perished there. About 60 survived the camp which, like Sobibor, was hastened to its end by an uprising among the inmates – under such extreme circumstances, a testimony to human courage and endurance. In the period August to December 1942, 864,000 people were killed at Treblinka: 6,000 a day for 144 days. 'At the end of August [1942] there was a hiatus of one week because too many corpses and too much clothing had accumulated and the camp staff was unable to cope with the work-load.'[14] The last commandant of Treblinka, Kurt Franz, was finally tracked down in 1965 to his home town of Düsseldorf, where he was living under his own name. Albums of photographs of the camp found in his flat had the words 'The Best Years of My Life' embossed in gold on their covers.

The majority of the other concentration camps were places of extreme hard labour, designed to result in death, under conditions of great cruelty. Many of them, though not all, were equipped with gas chambers, though slaughter by gassing was on a smaller scale than that practised at the camps described above and at Auschwitz-Birkenau. Work at Stutthof involved flattening sand-dunes to make airstrips; Flossenburg and Mauthausen were the sites of quarries. Each camp had a number of sub-camps, which could be as many as 40 or 50, or even more. These satellites were factories of one kind or another devoted to the German war effort, where the KZ-inmates might work alongside ordinary civilian workers (though the conditions they lived under were no less harsh than in the main camps); or they might be quarries, or logging camps.

Dominating them all was Auschwitz.[15] There were three 'core' camps here. Auschwitz-I, sometimes known as Auschwitz-Central, was the original camp. It was based on 'some old Austrian artillery barracks consisting of 20 brick buildings'.[16] They stood in Zasole, a suburb of Auschwitz, a bleak town in a marshy area of south-western Poland, but with the advantage of being at an important railway junction. The very first occupants arrived in May 1940, and the first transport of 728 Polish political prisoners arrived on 14 June.[17] The camp was built up and transports of Jews arrived. Block 10 became the place where experiments were conducted on women. Block 11 was the *Bunker*, or punishment block. Between these two buildings was the black wall, against which people were shot. There was also a crematorium and gas chamber. These were in operation for a total of 24 months, with a monthly corpse-burning capacity of 9,000. In the course of its life, the gas chamber destroyed 215,000 people.[18]

A few kilometres to the east, across the River Sola, was Auschwitz-III, the industrial complex at Monowice, dominated by the firm of I. G. Farben, and also known as the Buna-Werke.

It is, however, to Auschwitz-II, Birkenau (Brzezinka), that people are usually referring when they speak loosely of 'Auschwitz'. This town of a camp, which was to become the greatest death-factory of all, unique in human history, was sited about two kilometres north-west of Auschwitz-I. Work began on it at the end of 1941, and it was fully operational by the end of the following year. It was built in sections, first of brick barracks, then of wood,[19] and was to house a population of at least 200,000 at any one time. It was divided into sections for men and women; there was a Gypsy camp, and a Czech family camp, so called because families there were not broken up.[20] A section called *Kanada* housed those *Kommandos* (work-squads) whose job it was to sort through the effects of those sent to the gas chambers. Another large section, *Mexiko*, was begun in anticipation of the transportation of Hungarian Jews in 1944, but was never completed. Block 25 of the women's camp served as a collecting point for women *selected* for the gas chambers. This was truly a place of horror, since the women would simply be abandoned there – sometimes for days – without food or water, until they were taken to the gas chamber.

Until near the very end, up to 90 per cent of every transport arriving at Birkenau would be sent straight to the gas chambers. People selected to go into the camp and be attached to *Kommandos* were men and women who were young and fit, without dependent children. Life-expectancy in the camp was three weeks. If you could survive that time, your chances of survival (all other things being equal) improved. The old, the sick, children, nursing mothers, pregnant women: all these went straight to the gas. Children were people generally under 14; the old were those over 40.

There were four main crematoria at Birkenau, with their attached gas chambers. These were large, each covering a total area of about 300 square yards. About 2,000 people at a time could be gassed. Once full of people, small children were pushed in above the heads of the adults. The furnaces, designed by J. A. Topf & Sons of Erfurt as early as 1937, could each burn three bodies every 20 minutes. The two larger crematoria were capable of burning 6,500 bodies every 24 hours. Each of them was in operation for approximately 18 months, and in that time accounted for about 1,800,000 corpses.[21] It is estimated that four million people lost their lives at Auschwitz, half of them Jews. The gassing ceased towards the end of 1944 on Himmler's orders; but during that summer, in an orgy of killing of which Adolf Eichmann was the principal organizer, 400,000 Hungarian Jews were gassed, following Germany's occupation of Hungary in March. The furnaces in the crematoria became so hot that firebricks cracked, and additional burning pits had to be dug. Once started, the flames were fuelled with the fat that had run off the burning bodies. The hot fat was channelled into concrete gutters which ran along the bottoms of the pits, at the sides, into vats, from which prisoners on this particular *Kommando* scooped it up with long-handled ladles, to pour over the bodies burning in the pits. The pits were designed by the 29-year-old SS Hauptscharführer, Otto Moll. As at this period it was not considered worth gassing babies and small children, Moll would throw them live into the gutters of boiling human fat.

For those who survived, life in the camp was hedged about with impossibly complicated and pointless regulations, infringing any of which could mean death, or a flogging of at least 25 lashes. There was one main street in Birkenau, the *Lagerstrasse*, which was the only one to be paved. Only SS were allowed to walk on it. The other streets were ploughed-up mud. Vrba[22] presents an image of the streets of Auschwitz-I. They had names like Cherry Street and Camp Street, and each sign was garnished with a 'comical' carved vignette – for example, of an SS-man kicking a prisoner, who falls on to another prisoner and makes him topple.

Some of the survivors whose stories appear in this book were at one time or another inmates of Theresienstadt.[23] Theresienstadt, a little garrison town to the north of Prague, was taken over in its entirety for housing Jews only. It was supposed to be a 'model' camp – the Jews ran their own affairs within it, and if ever Red Cross dignitaries should visit it, the visit would be preceded by a clean-up operation to give the place the appearance of being well organized and happy.

This was not the only place to which the Germans applied deceitful set-dressing. Treblinka boasted the façade of a large railway station and junction, with signs directing you where to change for your onward train, and a station clock, to deceive those who were arriving there to die. The clock's face was painted; its hands stood permanently at four o'clock.

It was to Treblinka and Birkenau that large transports of Jews from Theresienstadt were sent to their deaths. Near the town was the 'little fortress', on the other bank of the River Eger, where recalcitrant prisoners were tortured and killed. Inmates of Theresienstadt lived in the old eighteenth-century military barracks. Conditions were overcrowded and unhygienic. There were camp banknotes, probably printed in Berlin, which showed a caricature Moses holding the Commandments.[24]

The SS allowed great breadth of freedom in artistic expression in Theresienstadt, and cultural life flourished – which is not surprising, in view of the talent shut up there.[25] A succinct poem from a cabaret there sums up the spirit of the place, however:

Ein Meer von Tränen
Unendliches Sehnen
Niemals satt –
Theresienstadt.[26]

Many of the survivors interviewed in this book were liberated from Bergen-Belsen, most of them having been transported there from the Auschwitz camps in the face of the Russian advance early in 1945. It was never an extermination camp; indeed it had been designated a 'recuperation camp' (*Erholungslager*) and a 'preference camp' (*Vorzugslager*). It was never either; but it was not until its last months of operation, when it gained a new command brought in from Auschwitz and became appallingly overcrowded with evacuees from other liquidated camps to the east, that it became a death-camp in every sense of the word. Typhus was rife, and there was no food. 'I think if the British had arrived even a fortnight later, they would have found no one left alive.' Belsen was liberated by the British 8th Corps on 15 April 1945.[27]

Those Who Suffered

The Germans identified their concentration camp prisoners with a marking system based on coloured triangles of cloth, apex downwards, usually sewn on to the right trouser-leg and the left breast of the wearer's jacket or 'dress'. A Jewish prisoner would additionally have a yellow triangle, base downwards, beneath the triangle whose colour denoted his 'crime' (usually red, as a catch-all), the two superimposed triangles thus forming a Star of David. Political prisoners would have the first letter of their nation's name printed as a black capital on their triangle. German politicals had no letter 'D' on their triangles. The colours of these triangles were as follows:

> black: asocial
> blue: émigré
> brown: Gypsy (sometimes designated 'black')
> green: criminal
> mauve: Jehovah's Witness
> pink: homosexual
> red: political

These are only the basic markings. There were variations for such categories as 'Jewish race defiler', 'labour disciplinary prisoner' and 'punishment squad assignee',[1] among others. All prisoners had a serial number, peculiar to the particular camp they happened to be in at the time; but only at the Auschwitz complex were incoming inmates tattooed. The marking of KZ inmates was a matter of discussion. One idea, later abandoned, was to tattoo a number on the prisoner's forehead. Several Jews in the ghettos were in fact branded on the forehead with the Star of David or the swastika. The tattoo is on the left forearm, but its exact size and location depended upon how lucky you were with the prisoner who tattooed you. Usually the number is on the inner side of the forearm, and is relatively small and neat; but I have seen the number on the outer side of the forearm, in figures nearly an inch high.[2] Early numbers belonging to Jews also had an inverted triangle tattooed beneath them, but this practice was discontinued as the numbers of prisoners passing through the camp rose. Only prisoners admitted to the camp were tattooed. Those who were sent to the gas chambers immediately were not. The Germans developed a very precise and structured system of numbering, and kept complex files and card indices.

A prisoner with an 'early' number, a low number, would enjoy a better status, even with the SS, by virtue of his or her survival. All other things being equal, one's chances of getting through increased, the longer one managed to hold on, not least because one had learnt the ways of the camp and how to exploit them. Prisoners of this type were known as 'old' numbers.[3] Jewish 'old' numbers were also accorded respect. As will be seen, the mentality of the SS defies logic; theoretically, the Jews were sub-human, and yet Jewish talent within the camps, both technical and artistic, was exploited and even admired. Because they had absolute power within the KZ, the SS were whimsical, which made them even more dangerous.

The Germans relied upon an infrastructure of prisoner administration for the smooth running of the camps. The two most dominant groups were the criminals – the 'greens', and the politicals – the 'reds'. Frequently one or other group would be in control, or power would be wrested by one from the other, as happened in Buchenwald. Political prisoners had the advantage of solidarity within their particular group, be it Communist, Social Democrat or Conservative, and there are examples of differing ideological groups working together against the common enemy, or at least to alleviate conditions generally. Also, while politicals in control would tend to make sure that their fellow party-members got the best jobs, a prisoner in a camp where they held sway would usually find overall conditions marginally better. Criminals had no solidarity, and could retain their power only by demonstrating to the Germans how zealously brutal they could be in their service. Without solidarity, or any ideals to cling to, 'greens' tended not to be survivors, unless they attained positions of considerable security and privilege.[4] The Jews, also numerically dominant, were never in a position to join in any power-struggle. Most of those arriving were immediately gassed, as has been seen, and those within the camps had to endure harsher conditions and smaller rations than the other prisoners. They were not, for example, allowed food parcels. They had no solidarity other than that offered by a common language and nationality: Polish Jews stuck together, Czech Jews stuck together. Crucially, their deaths were a direct aim of the SS. All considerations of a practical kind were laid aside when it came to the treatment of the Jews. 'For many generations, the Jews of Salonica had serviced the port as stevedores and dockworkers: the smooth working of the port depended upon them. But the Nazi design would allow no exceptions, no logic, no special pleading.'[5]

The political prisoners comprised a very wide group, from committed Communist MPs to men who had merely criticized Hitler casually in a pub. Red triangles were also worn by captured resistance fighters from the occupied nations. Criminals, too, covered a broad spectrum: from pickpockets, through the ranks of 'professional' criminals, to psychopaths who in any conventional society would be cared for in mental institutions. Pickpockets crossed the definition boundary, as some qualified for the black triangle, a group made up of tramps, prostitutes, even gigolos, but also of men whose crime had simply been to be late for work a couple of times. Black triangles were a pathetic group of people. The women were frequently exploited as prostitutes within the camps and were physically ruined. The men, belonging to no defined group outside the context of their triangle colour, might either simply die, or seek escape by volunteering for army duty, when it was requested of them as the war progressed and Germany had to start scouting around for more manpower wherever it could.

There were several thousand priests, and members of religious orders of both sexes, in the camps; but because they would neither vote nor fight, the Jehovah's Witnesses attracted the especial enmity of the Nazis. They were stripped of their civil rights, and sacked from government posts. In October 1934 they declared their opposition to Hitler's regime, and a year later 500 of them were already prisoners in Sachsenhausen. In the minds of the Nazis, they became increasingly linked with Bolshevism and Judaism, though Himmler was inclined to consider them potential first settlers for the East, once it had been conquered. By 1939 there were 6,000 of them in the KZ. Although the dependability and equanimity required of them by their teaching led them to better jobs within the camps, their steadfast refusal to acknowledge Hitler led to bitter reprisals against them. Despite their generally low social and economic standing, however, their group integrity and solidarity helped them through the KZ. So strong was their faith that they even managed to proselytize in the camps, to the extent of distributing clandestinely produced leaflets.[6]

The question of the Gypsies' status in the Third Reich is a complicated one. Edicts of 13 October 1942 and 11 January 1943 defined those exempted from imprisonment: those married to 'pure-blooded' Germans; those with permanent jobs and fixed abodes; those on military service (in certain circumstances), and those with bona fide foreign (non-German) papers.[7] However, the regulations governing their arrest were not drawn up with great precision, and 'many men were arrested while on leave from the front, despite high decorations and several wounds, simply because their father or mother or grandfather had been a Gypsy half-caste. Even a very senior [Nazi] Party member, whose Gypsy grandfather had settled in Leipzig, was among them. He himself had a large business in Leipzig, and had been decorated more than once during the First World War. Another was a girl student who had been a leader in the Berlin League of German Girls.'[8] Gypsies were subjected to medical experiments, to enforced sterilization, and to the gas chambers. Like the Jews, they were unified only by their race, and they had no country of their own to represent them. Unlike Israel, they have never received any general compensation, though latterly their case has been taken up by the Green Party in the Bundestag[9] and their case has been put in a letter from Dr Jan Cibula of the International Romani-Union to the Chancellor.[10]

The Gypsies certainly occupied an anomalous position in Nazi thinking. Rosenberg admired their Aryan racial purity,[11] but 'in their commentaries on the Race Laws of 1935, (Wilhelm) Stuckart and (Hans) Globke place Jews and Gypsies on the same footing: they were of a blood foreign to Europe and as such inferior'.[12] Hans Günther, another race 'specialist', argued that although Gypsies started out pure Aryan, in the course of their wanderings they polluted their blood by interbreeding with the inhabitants of the countries they passed through. In Birkenau, they were theoretically not prisoners but 'internees' – and as such not set to work until the period April–June 1944, but even then they never entered the camp's work-lists. They were housed in 32 *Blocks* comprising Camp B II e, and were mainly Czechs and Germans. They did not wear camp uniform, though they were tattooed, their number prefixed with a 'Z'. The richest of them were the Germans, many of whom were circus-people, musicians and dance-hall proprietors. On the night of 1 August (some sources give 6 August) 1944, at 8 pm, on Mengele's orders the Gypsy Family Camp at Birkenau was liquidated and its occupants gassed. The operation lasted four hours. Some 3,200 people died on that occasion, but Gypsies were killed throughout the KZ system in their hundreds of thousands.

'The fate of the homosexuals in the concentration camps,' writes Kogon,[13]

can only be described as ghastly. They were often segregated in special barracks and work details. Such segregation offered ample opportunity to unscrupulous elements in positions of power to engage in extortion and maltreatment. Until the fall of 1938 the homosexuals at Buchenwald were divided up among the barracks occupied by political prisoners, where they led a rather inconspicuous life. In

32

October 1938, they were transferred to the penal company in a body and had to slave in the quarry. This consigned them to the lowest caste in the camp during the most difficult years. In shipments to extermination [sic.] camps, such as Nordhausen, Natzweiler, and Gross-Rosen, they furnished the highest proportionate share, for the camp [i.e. Buchenwald] had an understandable tendency to slough off all elements considered least valuable or worthless. If anything could save them at all, it was to enter into sordid relationships within the camp, but this was as likely to endanger their lives as to save them. Theirs was an insoluble problem and virtually all of them perished.

At a ceremony at the memorial site to Sachsenhausen concentration camp on 27 June 1985, a wreath was laid to the memory of the 15,000 homosexual men who died in the KZ. The only paper to report it was the West German homosexual magazine, *Siegessäule*.[14] Sachsenhausen camp contained a brickworks; the homosexual prisoners were condemned to work at the clay-pit attached to the works, some six kilometres from the camp. One of the few homosexual survivors to talk about his experience has described this clay-pit as the 'Auschwitz of homosexuals'.[15] The death rate for the *Kommando* working here was up to 30 a day.

One of the central problems for the homosexual prisoners was lack of solidarity: apart from his sexual tastes, a homosexual would have nothing in common with his fellow 'pink triangles'. Male and female prisoners in the concentration camps were segregated, and were in any case in a permanent condition of high anxiety and semi-starvation. Most inmates had no interest in sex. Women prisoners virtually all ceased to menstruate from the moment of their being rounded up for transport, and did not do so again until after liberation. Men's fantasies centred exclusively on food. Masturbation was negligible, though some male survivors have said that they turned to it for comfort in the conventional prison where they were confined in their home country before being transported to the KZ.[16] Only well-fed kapos and collaborators had the energy and sense of security needed for sexual activity. These, in circumstances of sexual segregation (brothels in the camps were sporadic), would turn to homosexuality. In the camps, however, a distinction was drawn between these opportunistic homosexuals and the men who wore the pink triangle. The first group was 'respectable'. The second group, who in any case stood in the shadow of the disgraced and murdered homosexual Nazi, Ernst Röhm, were segregated and condemned to the hardest and most demeaning work. They were used for medical experiments and, on one occasion at Sachsenhausen, with Jewish prisoners were forced to build an earthwork on a firing-range while the range was still in use. At Flossenburg, in the 'queers' wing', the lights were left on all night and anyone caught sleeping with his hands under the blanket received the standard punishment for minor offences: 25 lashes. Himmler had his own ideas for 'curing' homosexuality – by forcing homosexual men to use the camp brothel; though by the end of 1943 he was offering freedom to any 'pink triangle' volunteering for castration. The Austrian protagonist[17] of Heinz Heger's book, *The Men With The Pink Triangle*, managed to survive by taking 'protector' kapos as lovers; and finally became a kapo himself, with the softening of SS attitudes towards *Reichsdeutsch* prisoners. His survivor symptoms are typical of anyone else who got through the camps alive: he complains of an inability to concentrate, and familiar sights and events can trigger ghastly memories. A Christmas tree was erected at Flossenburg and decorated. Then the SS hanged six recaptured Russian escapers at its foot. He can now never look at a Christmas tree without thinking of them.

Homosexuals were also known as '175ers' after the paragraph in the Penal Code defining homosexuality as a criminal act. This had been introduced in 1871, and a recommendation to reform it in 1929 was interrupted by Hitler's rise to power. In 1935 (after the fall of Ernst Röhm), Paragraph 175 was tightened up considerably. The pink triangle was introduced in 1937, but, like the red triangle, it was used to cover people for whose arrest no other excuse suggested itself. Several priests, who were unwise enough to criticize the Nazis openly, found themselves in the camps wearing the pink triangle, for example.

Paragraph 175 (or Paragraph 175a of the Nazi Penal Code) was to have an effect on the homosexual survivor which explains why so very few have told their story. After the war, and after Germany split into two nations, East Germany reverted to the original Paragraph of 1871, and kept it on the statute books until 1968, when homosexuality ceased to be a crime. West Germany, however, retained the Paragraph as revised by the Nazis in 1935, and did not legalize homosexuality until 1969. Thus until the end of the Sixties former KZ-inmates who were homosexuals could do nothing but keep a low profile and say nothing about their sufferings, although a few anonymous voices were raised. Worse still, by the time the Paragraph was repealed, possible reparation applications by homosexual victims had been overtaken by the statute of limitations on such claims. Only in 1980 did homosexual pressure-groups succeed in getting reparation made available for the 'pink triangles'; but by then, 35 years on, the victims were no longer prepared to undergo the investigation necessary for them to be able to claim.

Conditions for all but the most privileged prisoners – the kapos and the *Prominenten* (who might be doctors, skilled mechanics, craftsmen and clerks needed by the SS to help them run the camp administration)

– were filthy, unhygienic and overcrowded to a degree which cannot be described adequately. A barrack typically[18] consisted of a large hut, called a *Block*, measuring 44.20 metres by 8.50 metres. There would be a primitive washroom and a privy. There would also be a private room for the *Blockälteste* (Block leader). Bunks (*koje*) were in tiers of three, with not enough space between them for a person to sit up. They were made of coarse wood, and measured about 180 × 75 centimetres each. 'The bed boards were covered by straw mattresses or loose straw. In each berth there were generally two blankets. Blankets and straw mattresses were filthy, e.g. with the blood and pus from phlegmon patients. In addition, faeces and urine often dripped from one storey to another from prisoners suffering from hunger, diarrhoea and polyuria.'[19] A bunk designed to be occupied by one person would often be used by four, and it was not unusual for a *Block* designed to hold 600–700 to have more than 2,000 people crammed into it. Those who could not get a place on a bunk would be forced to sleep under them – and the earth floor would be a mire of excrement.

Overcrowding was similarly intense on the transports. Prisoners would be sealed in, a hundred and more to each cattle-waggon, and taken across Europe on train journeys that, however short they might be in terms of distance, would always be long in time. Journeys would last six days, and during that time no food might be issued, nor even water; and the prisoners might not even be allowed to empty the single latrine bucket. Everyone, without exception, travelled in this way, from women of 80 to month-old babies. These transports were an instrument of death, too; and those who survived them were too dazed or bewildered when they arrived at the camp to do anything but believe what they were told. They had no time to react, in any case. Transports usually arrived at night, and the shouted orders, the hail of blows, the snarling dogs and the blinding searchlights left one's mind able to do nothing but whimper. 'You wouldn't have thought it possible that any of us would believe the lies they told us after a journey like that; but we did. Perhaps we just wanted to believe that things would be better now.'

Conditions of overcrowding were worse for women than for men, and women, being regarded as useless because they were not thought to be strong enough even to be useful slave labourers, were sent to logging or rock-breaking *Kommandos*, in order to kill them off as fast as possible. The fortunate ones got jobs as clerks or messengers, or worked in factories attached to the camps. The women's camps and camp-sections were run by SS-women and female kapos, not a whit less brutal than their male counterparts.

Excremental assault[20] has been correctly defined as one of the central lines of attack by the SS on the inmates. Diarrhoea was universal and unavoidable; but privies were small and primitive, and could be used only at certain times of the day, or with permission. 'Otherwise you just had to go where you stood, and let it run down your legs.' A torture in context was *Zählappell*, or roll-call. The SS were obsessed by numbers – everything had to tally. Told off in fives, KZ-inmates had to be counted *Block* by *Block* twice a day, before and after work. If there was a discrepancy, the roll-call could go on for hours – all night – even in freezing conditions; 'I remember once a fellow-prisoner who had no clogs; his feet froze to the parade-ground. They had to tear him loose. But of course his feet were ruined, and that was the end of him.' At Stutthof, the *Zählappell* was used deliberately as an instrument of death; but in every KZ the number of deaths due to exposure and exhaustion during roll-call ran into thousands.

The standard KZ uniform was the familiar striped costume, which consisted of a shirt, jacket, trousers, cap and clogs for the men, and a dress for the women. This uniform was not consistently issued, however, and was by no means worn by every prisoner in every camp. It was usually made of thin, cheap cotton material, to be worn in all weathers, and for those who worked in the heavy-labour *Kommandos* it was soon in shreds, at which time new clothes had to be organized, for none would be issued. The uniforms were given out with no regard for size, and at Birkenau they were not cleaned; if a prisoner died, his body was stripped and his uniform was reissued in the state he'd left it.[21] Footwear was the greatest problem, as the clogs were coarsely made and caused sores; and to have damaged feet was fatal. Anyone unable to walk would be unfit for work. Anyone unfit for work would go to the 'hospital', which almost always meant death, so dreadful were the conditions, and so frequently were the *selections* (for the gas chambers) made from them. Or the prisoner might simply be shot where he stood, or sent directly to the gas. Possession of a cap was of major importance. While a prisoner[22] was not allowed to look at an SS-man, he had to doff his cap whenever he encountered one. If he'd lost his cap and therefore could not show this sign of respect, he could be shot.

KZ-inmates ate three times a day. A diet has been reconstructed, and what follows is a summary of it. This should be taken as a relatively generous ration, since it is based on that given to political prisoners and resistance fighters at Neuengamme.[23] Many survivors suspect that the ersatz tea or coffee (a thin, lukewarm fluid probably based on crushed acorns or herbs, and made with unsterilized water) and the soup were sprinkled with a bromide derivative, or even a poison.[24] 'Soup' was the KZ staple, and was generally based on turnips, swedes or cabbage – all of cattle-fodder quality, and all encouraging diarrhoea.

The first meal was taken at about 5am, and consisted of half a litre of unsweetened thin black ersatz tea or coffee; 125 grammes of black bread (made up with sawdust content), and perhaps 10 grammes of 'margarine' or 'marmalade'. The second meal, at noon, for which half an hour was allowed, consisted of one litre of soup, made up of 200 grammes of turnip, 50 grammes of potato, 25 grammes of cabbage, 10 grammes of flour, and 2 grammes of margarine. Once a week traces of meat or peas might be added, of the poorest quality. The last meal of the day, taken after return to camp from the work-sites, was 125 grammes of bread, 20 grammes of margarine, half a litre of tea or coffee, with, once a week, a small piece of sausage or cheese. Meals could be withheld as a reprisal for any number of infringements of camp rules. The nutritional value of this diet, on top of hard labour for at least 12 hours a day, is so low that without supplement the healthiest prisoner would be dead within three months. At Birkenau, even non-Jewish inmates were not allowed food-parcels for the first three months.[25] Parcels were frequently pilfered by the SS and prominent prisoners for use as barter at the 'top end' of the KZ black market, where astonishing delicacies, such as caviar, were to be had. The ordinary KZ prisoner had to organize extra food, and he would also have to provide his own eating utensils.

But even the food supply officially provided was subject to abuse: 'in the concentration camp Neuengamme Robert Darnau, in November 1944, "found in his soup a human jaw". When this was reported to the commander, "investigation revealed that the kitchen kapo and the crematory kapo had agreed to sell the meat from the kitchen and feed the prisoners on corpses."'[26]

Displaced Persons

As has been seen, once the camps had been liberated, most of those imprisoned in them for reasons other than being Jewish were able to make their way home, not without difficulty and often with anguish, but nevertheless in the majority of cases to an intact and continuing life containing the same people, places, jobs and social structure as they had left. Further, the former political prisoners and resistance fighters had known exactly why they were in the camps, whereas the Jews had been put there simply because of their birth; many were assimilated, many only part-Jewish, and even unaware of their Jewish origins. They considered themselves to belong to their nation first, and to the Jewish race second. Those born in Germany and Austria had fought valiantly for their countries in the First World War, and many were highly decorated officers. Some had welcomed Hitler in his early days for his reforming zeal on behalf of Germany. Their sense of betrayal by their own countrymen and their bewilderment at it can be imagined. 'I spent some time in South Africa after the war, and remember a man I'd met there was suddenly "reclassified" black. He committed suicide. I left South Africa soon after; my own memories, and my conscience, had been stirred.'

Returning non-Jews could go back to their own country, language and culture. The Jews of Eastern Europe, Germany and Austria either did not have this option or did not choose to take it. Poland remained anti-Semitic, often violently so, and the redivision of Europe after the war meant that German Jews born in, for example, Breslau, found that their home was now called Wroclaw, and was in Poland. But it is unlikely that they would have wished to return anyway: their homes had been taken away from them, their whole families and even their entire community had been slaughtered. There was nothing to return for, to return to.

For these people, liberation from the KZ was followed by a period of time in a Displaced Persons' camp. This period might last for years, for there was no rush in Australia, Canada, the UK or the USA to provide new homes for them. 'The last chapter in the Nazi persecution of the Jews was written in the DP camps and in the emigration of survivors during the years after the war in Europe.'[1] There was an irrational fear of being swamped by Jewish immigrants which matched and even outstripped the sentiments which had informed the reluctance of the same countries to accept them at the Evian and Bermuda conferences.

While they waited, the survivors found themselves having to battle for that Jewish identity and sense of solidarity which they had attained through suffering in conditions and under administrations that were often not much better than they had been in the KZ.[2] In one DP centre, Rentzschmule, an ex-Nazi was actually in charge of the Jewish former KZ-inmates. He paid no attention to their needs, and they had to walk 16 miles to a US Army base to protest about him. Austrian Jews generally received no help from the United Nations Relief and Rehabilitation Administration (UNRRA) 'because they were not citizens of UN nations, while the Austrian government refused aid to Jews because they had *only* been racially, and not politically, persecuted'.[3] And while one can sympathize with the plight of the Allied armies, faced with a job for which there was no precedent, in the complete chaos of post-war Europe and on a scale of vast proportions, there is no excuse for some of the behaviour encountered: 'Faced with such conditions, officials fell back upon the things they knew best: maintenance of law and order and rigid discipline within the more than 500 hastily set up assembly centers ...'[4] 'The [US] Seventh Army in northern Germany attempted to deal with DPs in a humane fashion ... In the Third Army in southern Germany, which contained most of the DPs in the United States zones, General George S. Patton, Jr, insisted that every camp be surrounded by barbed wire and manned by armed guards to watch over the detainees as if they were prisoners. Patton's behaviour cannot be attributed solely to crowded conditions and a shortage of soldiers. He wrote in his diary on 15 September 1945, that others "believe that the Displaced Person is a human being, which he is not, and this applies particularly to the Jews, who are lower than animals".'[5] There is, of course, no excuse at all for such an attitude; but liberators and victims were trying to handle a situation that no one had any precedent for. No one could know even approximately what effect the KZ experience had had on the psyche. The rape of the senses perpetrated by the SS, the deliberate undermining of all acquired values of culture and civilization, dislocated such fundamental aspects of behaviour as being able to use a privy privately, or even whenever one wanted to. A frustrated US Army major who, unlike Patton, was sympathetic to the DPs in their plight and was not anti-Semitic commented: 'Even after concentration camp life it is not too much to expect people to flush toilets that are in working order. Is it too demanding to ask that they use the urinals in the latrines and not the floors? When a garbage can is provided, is it reasonable to expect them to put the garbage into the can and not on the floor next to the can?'[5] The DP camp in question was Landsberg, a good camp, well equipped, with a theatre and even a radio station. But more important than physical comfort was a recognition of the psychological disturbance, and this was lacking at the outset.

Immediately after completing her work for UNRRA in France, Germany, Austria and Yugoslavia in 1945 and 1946, Francesca Wilson wrote of the DP camp Feldafing, which had previously been a luxuriously equipped Hitler Youth school:

> As for the inmates of the camp – at first it was hard to look at them without repulsion. I have seen victims of famine before: Bulgarian prisoners in Serbia, Russians in the Volga area in 1922, children in Vienna in 1919 and in Spain in the Civil War – but this was worse, for these people were the victims of more than famine, they were the victims of cruelty . . . They had the furtive look and gestures of hunted animals. By years of brutal treatment, by the murder of relatives, by the constant fear of death, all that was human had been taken away from them . . . nothing would persuade them to eat in communal dining rooms. I noticed an old man who was trying to eat but was too weak to finish his food. Three boys were staring at his plate. I had once seen the same look of burning yet cautious intentness on the face of a wolf that was following my sleigh on the Russian steppes.[6]

She goes on to describe a group of Greek Jews smashing up enough musical instruments for three orchestras found at the former Hitler Youth school, 'because they were German'.[7] She comments on the DPs' refusal to wash, flush lavatories, or pay the slightest attention to hygiene, and notices their obsession with food. 'I was reminded of some of our evacuee children, who, their families gone and every known tie severed, had, by smashing and soiling and burning and stealing, revenged themselves on a society which had hounded them into the hideous void of the countryside and made them feel outcasts.'[8] Of the children in the DP camps she writes: 'Most . . . described with complete indifference their blood-curdling experiences – even the murder of their parents – but would storm over some trifling incident: having to wait a week before having their hair cut again, or a Red Cross parcel without a pot of honey in it. It was clear that their rehabilitation would be difficult.'[9]

Not all former KZ-inmates regressed to infantilism, and not all who did were Jews. The Jewish DP camp at Bergen-Belsen was a triumph. But the DPs had to be heroes to withstand the pressures put on them, through nothing other than understandable ignorance. And this ignorance was born of another factor:

Our troops came across the Mediterranean Sea and across the English Channel to fight their way through Italy, France, Belgium and Holland, through the shattered and crumbling remains of cities, towns and villages. We were dirty but we met people who were dirtier, who were disease-ridden and starving, who grubbed in garbage cans for our waste, and who smelled like the holes in which they existed.

But we saw and understood the reasons for the dirt, disease, filth and squalor. The American soldier offered his strength, his assistance, his kindness, his rations, clothing, and medicine – and to millions of unfortunates this was the first kindness, the first human act, that had been extended to them in ten or more years.

As the Allied Armies thrust toward Germany, the tide of liberated Displaced Persons swelled from hundreds to thousands and finally to 30 million. As the Germans fled toward Berlin the liberated persons began to move in wild disorder toward their homelands . . .

Then most of the soldiers who had experienced combat were redeployed to the United States in the fall of 1945 and the spring of 1946. Fresh American military personnel, who had just left the solid, clean and substantial comforts of our fine homes and towns, arrived in Europe and Germany. Their understanding of the results of the many forces that had been at work in Europe over the several preceding years, naturally, was limited.

The new GIs found it difficult to understand and like people who pushed, screamed, clawed for food, smelled bad, who couldn't and didn't want to obey orders, who sat with dull faces and vacant staring eyes in a cellar, or concentration camp barrack, or within a primitive cave, and refused to come out at their command.

When people are reduced to the animal level their reaction to suggestion and situations is on that level. When some of the Displaced Persons were liberated they gave first priority to retaliation against their one-time masters rather than to cooperation with the Allied civil affairs authorities. Thus, in later months, when American soldiers compared the law-and-order attitude of the Germans with the lawlessness of some Displaced Persons, their attitude toward Displaced Persons was not improved. They failed to make the essential distinction between a people disciplined in defeat and these others, most of whom might properly hope to be treated as friends and allies.[10]

In this atmosphere, DPs found themselves subject to a series of indignities amounting to mental cruelty. They were fed on a diet of bread and coffee; they were treated worse than the Germans, and the Jewish DPs were treated worst of all. Anti-Semitism unfortunately existed among Allied troops, and it went unmonitored and unchecked. Its effect was to make Jewish survivors feel more isolated and threatened than ever, the more so since they were at the end of their tether, and might indeed have expected warm and sympathetic treatment after their ordeal. It is small wonder that suicide became a more frequent occurrence than it had been in the KZ where, in the words of one survivor, 'we at least had liberation to hope for, to keep us going. Now what was there?' In the absence of other clothing, DPs were even expected to wear salvaged SS uniforms.

In the USA, Truman, who 'came from Missouri, a state where Jewish opinions did not carry much weight',[11] tried to do a balancing act with the 'we'll-be-swamped-by-them-if-we-let-them-in' lobby. At the same time he sought to get Attlee to allow 100,000 Jews into Palestine. Attlee prevaricated, not wanting to attract the anger of the already simmering Arab states. Meanwhile, the DPs waited and their numbers built up – there were a million of them in camps at the end of 1945. Then, in Kielce, in Poland, early in July 1946, 75 Jews were beaten up and another 41 murdered by locals, the result – after all that had gone before – of a made-up story by a nine-year-old boy who'd gone missing (he'd been with relatives) for three days. He said that he'd been abducted by Jews and had seen other Christian children murdered in a cellar. Over 100,000 Jews left Poland before the autumn.

The Jews continued to get short shrift. 'The entire yearly quota [to the end of 1945 for the USA] for all of the East European nations, the source of most DPs, amounted to only 13,000; another 26,000 quota places were reserved exclusively for Germans.'[12] Many former SS members, especially those of Baltic States' origin, had been able to get into DP camps incognito and, with the help of forged documents and good contacts, managed to be accepted for immigration. One at least was able to pass off his SS blood-group tattoo as an Auschwitz tattoo. Because of the number of papers required to be presented to the authorities in order to qualify for consideration for immigration, a healthy forging industry grew up in the camps.[13] As large as little towns, and self-contained, their inmates gave in to institutionalization. Elsewhere, on Cyprus, the British maintained internment camps for Jews who had attempted to emigrate to Palestine illegally, while the Central British Fund negotiated doggedly with the British government to allow refugees to make a home in the UK.

There were 850,000 Displaced Persons still in Europe in 1947, 20 per cent of them Jewish. Despite this small percentage, mistrust of Jewish

Communist DPs hindered the passage of a Bill to admit them to the USA. The Jewish Socialist Party of Poland, the *Bund*, was anti-Communist, but unfortunately American right-wing elements either could not or were not prepared to make a distinction. The 1948 Displaced Persons' Act was described by William Haber, Jewish Advisor to the US Army in Europe, as 'the most anti-Semitic Bill in US history',[14] but fortunately it contained sufficient loopholes to be utilized to good effect *vis-à-vis* the Jews when it was implemented. It provided for allowing entry to the USA to 200,000 DPs by 30 June 1950. In the end, about 450,000 DPs made new homes in the USA, at an estimated cost of $100,600,000. The USA, albeit with initial reluctance, did more than any other nation to help the bereft of the war; though it may be argued that in terms of space and money she was better able to, and that smaller nations were proportionately as generous.

Upon arrival in the United States, refugees were helped principally by HIAS (the Hebrew Sheltering and Immigrant Aid Society) and NYANA (the New York Association for New Americans). In Europe, throughout and after the war, it was the American Jewish Joint Distribution Committee, usually referred to as the JDC, or JOINT, that beyond any other voluntary organization, of any denomination, aimed to help refugees. It was founded on 27 November 1914, and its name derives from the three separate commissions for assistance which joined together to form it. Its original finance derived from 'a tremendous fund-raising effort that yielded a total of $33.4 million for 1919–21'.[15] During 1939–45 it spent $78,878,000 in Europe, mainly on relief and rescue operations. It parachuted $300,000 to the Jewish underground in Poland in 1943–4 and, after the war, in 1945–52, it spent $342,000,000 on the feeding, clothing and rehabilitation of 250,000 DPs, and on the remnants of Jewish communities in Europe. Without its efforts, there would be no Jewish community in Europe at all any more, and the cultural and economic boost given the USA by Jewish immigrants there would not have happened. With Israel, the USA is now the custodian and beneficiary of a heritage which Europe, through Hitler and through indifference, threw away. As far as the USA is concerned, however, that may be more by luck than judgment. Earl G. Harrison, sent to report on the standards of DP camps in the US zones in 1945, wrote in his report, delivered in the autumn: 'as matters now stand, we appear to be treating the Jews as the Nazis treated them, except that we do not exterminate them'.

There are mitigating circumstances for disorganization, but not for cruelty or prevarication. For too long *Realpolitik* dominated ethical considerations. Soon the fate of the DPs was accorded only scant attention anyway; the Western Allies and the Russians, muscling up for the Cold War, were more concerned with former Nazi rocket scientists, who in any case ran willingly to the Americans. Werner von Braun was comfortably ensconced in El Paso on a salary of $750 per month by October 1945. The last DP camp to close, at Föhrenwald, did so on 28 February 1957.

4

Reparation

Before granting an entry permit, security in the form of an affidavit from a citizen of the granting country had to be acquired. Generally, that citizen was a relative of the applicant, but he or she could also be a friend – one, for example, who had got out before the war, or a soldier present at the liberation of the camp with whom bonds had been established. Affidavits were available only up to the number defined by the quota for any given year.[1] Frequently the country of refuge was determined for the KZ survivor by the presence of such a friend or relative there. Alternatively, there was the possibility of emigrating – legally or illegally – to Palestine. When Palestine gained independence and became the State of Israel in 1948, many more people went there. But a significant number of the soldiers in the battle against the Arabs for Israel's independence and thereafter were former KZ-inmates.

For many survivors this was the beginning of another struggle. The world was unable to comprehend at first that for these people liberation did not mean immediate recovery from what had happened to them, and the initial euphoria which stemmed from being free and the excitement of a new environment caused the mainly young survivors to give the impression of being healed. The desire to make up for lost time, to get on with the interrupted business of education or career, was strong. Strong too was the impulse to start a family – a replacement for the one that had been lost, and for many Jews especially an instinctive imperative to continue and reassert the race. However, the after-effects of the KZ experience soon made themselves apparent both physically and mentally. Additionally, the outrage of arbitrarily robbing people of years of their lives demanded compensation. There was also the question of the vast sums that had been stolen from the Jews, in terms of property, business and liquid cash and jewellery. It was not long before the case for reparation was made and acknowledged.

'Nothing happened at first because Germany was bankrupt, but with the help of the Allies laws were promulgated which started by awarding compensation for time spent under unjust imprisonment – laws which related to pre-Third Reich German legislation. But this affected only people who had been resident in Germany before; the others had no legal standing in this respect. So, the different regional governments of West Germany promulgated new legislation – rather grudgingly – and with them individual indemnification laws for damage to health, mental health, economic standing, and family – for the death of a family member. Those who could claim were exclusively those who could prove that they were survivors of the concentration camps, and each case was dealt with on an individual basis. Apart from this, there were laws governing restitution for loss of property, from land to jewellery, and in the majority of cases the government repaid a nominal sum. In the case of lost businesses, compensation was paid by the new owner.'[2]

Several volumes would be needed to cover the whole subject, and Richard Saper, a lawyer based in London who has specialized in presenting claims in West Germany since 1962, admits that he hasn't fathomed all the ramifications of the reparation laws yet.[3] It is not simply a question of West Germany paying pensions or lump-sum indemnifications. Individual countries, such as Denmark, France, the Netherlands and Norway, set their own scales of compensation for returning nationals, according to different standards, and these standards can and have changed, reflected in changes in the laws of those countries as physicians, psychiatrists and psychologists have identified illnesses arising from the KZ experience which have manifested themselves only 30 or 40 years later. That West German psychiatry has been at variance with the view that there is a connection between these 'late effects' and the KZ experience complicates the issue still further. West German law on the subject of the *Bundesentschädigungsgesetz* (or BEG) covers nine books, if one takes into account the many revisions and the distinction made between such factors as damage to or loss of property; physical ability; mental ability; freedom, and so on. Reparation further can differ quantitatively as it affects former political or former Jewish KZ-inmates. Also, although there is a department of the Finance Ministry in Bonn (Department VI A 4) which provides the umbrella administration, actual cases are dealt with autonomously by the various regional reparation bureaux, tied to the Regional Presidents' offices. The discretion of these bureaux varies considerably.[4]

Taxation on pensions received from West Germany or Austria in the adopted country of the recipient is another factor to be aware of. In the UK, for example, full relief from British income tax on such pensions was extended only in the Budget of March 1986, costing the Treasury about £1 million per year. Prior to that time, only half the pension had enjoyed tax relief; while the same pension paid to recipients in West Germany and Austria has always been tax-free.[5]

In the context of this summary, it will be clearest to cover certain areas one by one. Reparation is a vexed and little-aired question, but the impression gained is that while West Germany has done a lot, it has not done enough, and it has hedged the acquisition of a pension about with a formidable bureaucracy. The impression, equally, is that Austria and East Germany have not met their obligations adequately in this area.

The history of reparation[6] in West Germany dates from 1949, the result of representations made by the Chairman of the German Social Democratic Party, Dr Kurt Schumacher, himself a former KZ-inmate. Originally, reparation developed in the hands of the regional governments, and related to property and freedom lost. The Federal Republic was constituted in September 1949, and on 27 September 1951 Konrad Adenauer, then Chancellor, spoke to the Bundestag: 'The government, and with it the great majority of the German people, are very conscious of the appalling suffering brought to the Jews in Germany and the occupied territories during the National Socialist period. The German people in their overwhelming majority were disgusted by the crimes perpetrated against the Jews and took no part in them. During the National Socialist period many Germans put themselves in danger, motivated either by religious feelings, by conscience, or by a sense of shame at the profanation of the German name, to help their Jewish fellow-citizens. But in the name of the German people appalling crimes were committed, that demand from us moral and material reparation,[7] not only as far as damages to the individual are concerned, but also with regard to Jewish property.'

The Transition Agreement of 26 May 1952, whereby the German state occupied by the Western Allies (France, Great Britain and the USA) became a sovereign state, included a clause recognizing an obligation to make amends. The Luxemburg Accord between West Germany and the Government of Israel, together with many Jewish organizations represented by the Conference of Jewish Material Claims Against Germany, chaired by the influential negotiator Nahum Goldmann, established principles on which future reparation legislation should be based. 'According to the terms of the Accord, negotiated in Luxemburg and The Hague, and signed on 10 September 1952 in Luxemburg, West Germany undertook to pay DM3 billion to the State of Israel, and DM450 million to Jewish organizations. The payments to Israel were principally to take the form of goods, in recognition of the material burden that the young State had taken upon itself through accepting and assimilating Jewish European victims of National Socialist persecution.' (See Note 6.) The money paid to the Claims Conference was to be used for the support and settlement of Jews living outside Israel.

In implementation of the Transition Agreement and the Luxemburg Accord, a number of compensation regulations were drawn up. Briefly, they were the so-called *Bundesergänzungsgesetz für die Entschädigung der Opfer der nationalsozialistischen Verfolgung* (the Federal Restoration Law for the Compensation of Victims of National Socialist Persecution) of 1 October 1953; followed by the *Bundesgesetz zur Entschädigung für Opfer der nationalsozialistischen Verfolgung* (the Federal Law to Indemnify Victims of National Socialist Persecution) of 29 June 1956. This law, known by legislators, lawyers and survivors as BEG, is the central influence on the machinery by which reparation is made. It substantially extended the 1953 law, and was itself expanded through the BEG (*Bundesentschädigungsgesetz*) of 14 September 1965, whereby 'once more the circle of persons entitled to claim was significantly widened, and whereby certain forms of payment were substantially improved'. BEG is designed to compensate people who were persecuted on political, racial or religious grounds, or by reason of their philosophical outlook; and who suffered physical or mental damage, or loss of freedom, property, health, or career potential. It also applies to artists and scholars whose work was banned or destroyed by the Nazis, as well as people implicated in the persecution by virtue of being related by blood or friendship to those directly involved; and to the families or bereft dependants of those persecuted. 'For items compulsorily taken by the German regime [the Third Reich] or its agents, which are no longer in existence and can therefore *rerum naturalum* not be returned, the Federal Restitution Law [*Bundesrückerstattungsgesetz*, known as BRüG] of 19 July 1957 ultimately amended by the Fourth Amendment Law [*4. Änderungsgesetz*] of 4 September 1969' obliges the West German government to make good the value of such items to their notional value as calculated at 1 April 1965.

The matter is much more complex than that because there are so many eventualities to cover, but these are the bones.

Between 1959 and 1964, West Germany reached so-called Global Accords with 11 European countries over reparation payments for those countries to administer and pay over to those of their citizens who had suffered at the hands of the Nazis, but whose cases were not covered by BEG, or to their surviving dependants. To take three examples from the list, Greece was paid DM115 million on 18 March 1960; France DM400 million on 15 July of the same year, and Great Britain and Northern Ireland DM11 million on 6 June 1964. The other countries affected were: Belgium, Denmark, Italy, Luxemburg, the Netherlands, Norway, Sweden and Switzerland. Similar 'global' payments have been made to Hungary (DM6.5 million), Poland (DM100 million), Russia (DM7.5 million), and Yugoslavia (DM8 million).

Austria presented a special case, since at the time of the discriminatory measures taken by the Nazis it was an integral part of the German
Reich, and therefore had to honour reparation claims for injustices
committed on its soil. Notwithstanding that, the West German government contributed DM102 million to Austria for reparation payments,
DM96 million of which were to establish a fund to compensate political
victims at home and abroad for loss of assets. The remaining DM6
million were to be earmarked for restitution claims.

Despite the payments made, the official attitude remains cautious:
'The West German government, her western Allies and the relevant
victims' organizations have always been aware that despite [their]
considerable efforts it is impossible to make full restitution for the
National Socialist persecution because of the extent of the damage
inflicted and the limited economic potential of West Germany, which
cannot, of course, draw on the resources of a united Germany.'[8]

'It should, however, not be overlooked that the West German government has had to and still must give priority over other urgent tasks –
in coming to terms with the bequest of the Hitler regime – to restitution
for National Socialist injustices, and to the removal of the consequences
of the Second World War, started by the National Socialists; and among
these tasks is the care of the victims of the war and their surviving
dependants, as well as the re-assimilation and compensation of refugees, and those driven from their homes.'

As matters stood on 1 January 1986, monies already paid out under
BEG stood at DM59,878 billion, plus DM3,923 billion under BRüG.
Foreseen future payments stand at DM15,122 billion and DM327
billion respectively – it must be borne in mind that payments overall
will cease with the eventual deaths of all the survivors and their
pension-entitled dependants, and that these outgoings for West
Germany decrease with every year that passes.

Responsibility for assessment of applications and subsequent payment of reparation based on those assessments rests with the individual
regional Administration Offices for Reparation (Ämte für Wiedergutmachung). It is at the individual level that the survivor can suffer most,
both spiritually and materially. This is a very difficult area. Some
survivors refused altogether to accept reparation from Germany, view-
ing it as unwelcome charity. 'How can I accept some German's assessment of how much my wife and children's lives were worth?' Others
were hurt by the attitude of individual German investigators and
officials who made them feel like freeloaders. Others still found themselves regarded with actual suspicion – as if they were criminals trying
by false pretences to get a pension they had no right to. Added to this
was the question of 'compensation neurosis', where the sufferer will
try to milk a disability to get as much as possible out of the paying

authority. This last has been found barely to exist among survivors of the camps, but it was taken into account sternly by the German investigating authorities. Another factor is the disagreement that existed initially between German and other psychiatrists over the need to establish 'bridge symptoms' – provable links between, say, a neurosis appearing in the Sixties or Seventies, and the KZ experience. The applicant would have to have shown symptoms treated at the time of liberation and since. 'Late effects' were not in fact fully recognized by the German authorities until the Seventies. Germans also originally held that those few people who survived the camps as small children did not qualify for compensation since their minds, it was argued, would not have been sufficiently developed at the time to be permanently or profoundly affected by the KZ. This view has since been discredited.

Overall, the burden was on the survivor to prove, most exactingly, that he had been in the camps and had suffered there, and many forwent the chance of a pension rather than put themselves into the hands of German or German-appointed doctors and, as they saw them, interrogators – both of whom KZ survivors had reason to fear.

Initially, it was through the agencies, both Jewish and non-Jewish, which looked after survivors that news of the availability of reparation was disseminated, and compensation claims were usually made through such organizations, or survivor groups, though, as each case was treated as an individual claim against West Germany, each was investigated and judged on its individual merits, just like a criminal case, and so many survivors pursued their claims through specialist lawyers.[9] Nearly all survivors whose claims were accepted did not start drawing a pension until the Sixties. To be fair, the date of commencement of payment depended somewhat upon the date of application; but, as will be seen, the process was not one designed to be speedy or easy for the applicant. Given too that the survivors who contributed to this book represent a broad cross-section, the reaction of the West German authorities to enquiries is interesting:

Naturally reparation payments could only be paid after the respective regulation had come into force, and after the execution of related procedure. In individual cases the payment depended upon the date of application, the state of proof, the duration of procedure, etc. As far as the relatively late payments mentioned by you are concerned, these must have normally concerned complicated cases, in which a decision was only possible after long deliberation. But then there were also, for example, many cases in which an application was only made very late, or where owing to a lack of cooperation on the part of the applicant, a quicker result was made impossible. Also to be taken into consideration in this context is that the unusually high number of applications dealt with confronted the German Federal regional Reparation Authorities with a hardly-to-be-resolved workload.[10]

Richard Saper has a large walk-in cupboard in his office piled high with 250 bulky files of concluded cases. Near the cupboard stand two four-drawer filing cabinets overflowing with the files of those cases still in train. Reparation payment is based on percentage disability. The minimum disablement required by German law is 25 per cent. However, Saper explains, even if somebody is 80 per cent disabled, it has to be determined what percentage of that was due to Nazi persecution. 'The German authorities require proof of incarceration, and proof of damaged health, such as hospital depositions. Once those have been satisfied, an investigation is set in motion.' The responsible bureau in West Germany instructs the West German embassy of the country in which the applicant now resides to arrange an examination by a *Vertrauensarzt* – a doctor, not necessarily German himself, but on a list of doctors willing to undertake the necessary tests on behalf of the West German government. Initially, there is a general examination which will, if necessary, lead to further examinations by specialists. Those usually involved at this later stage are psychiatrists and neurologists. The resultant reports are delivered to the embassy which in turn passes them to the bureau. The bureau has the reports read and commented on by doctors in West Germany who, on the strength of them, will recommend or reject the application. If they choose to reject, they must state why. The percentage of disability is reckoned by reference to predetermined lists. These lists were prepared long after the event, of course, and while it is easy to give rough values to the degree of disability occasioned by, say, the loss of a hand or a foot, it is much harder to evaluate psychological damage.

Should an application be turned down – that is, the applicant has failed to convince the West German authorities that his or her disability is more than 25 per cent of a notional 100 per cent 'unfitness', or the authorities deem that the extent of total disability actually occasioned by the time spent in the camps is less than 25 per cent, the applicant may appeal. This involves producing new evidence of 'damage' in the form of further medical documentation from doctors and hospitals. If that appeal fails, and the applicant lives in Europe, he or she may within three months bring a suit against the region[11] in which the relevant reparation bureau is. For example, if one's application was rejected by the Cologne bureau, one would sue in the *Düsseldorfer Landesgericht*. This regional court could however demand yet more new proofs, or get a new doctor to peruse the existing files and evaluate them without a further medical examination. Alternatively, a new examination might be required. Richard Saper has had many clients who have had to travel to their respective regional bureaux[12] to undergo such examinations, in some cases years after the event.

If this appeal were rejected, further appeal could be made to the superior court (*Oberlandesgericht*), but only specified West German lawyers could represent the appeal at this stage. Rejected again, the determined applicant would have two final courses of action: first, to take the case to the federal court at Karlsruhe; and, failing that, to swear a deposition against the reliability of the bureau's decision. This rarely taken step is the very last. The whole process could take a decade or more.

On the positive side, if the application is successful, it is passed to the indemnification authorities to determine the level of pension to be paid.[13] If the applicant was financially independent before 1939 for at least three years, reparation would be calculated on the basis of his earnings then and the potential earnings his career would have promised had it not been interrupted. If the former KZ-inmate was a minor at the time, the material status of his parents would be taken into account. Four classes of pension, related to material standing, were defined carefully in tabular form, and correspond to the following grades of management: upper, executive, middle and lower.[14] Also taken into account was the applicant's material standing from 1953 until the time his application came to be considered (at any level, should it initially have been rejected and thus set out on the ladder of appeals described above), as well as his or her age in 1948. The older the applicant was, the greater the reparation. To complicate things further, the factor of 'reduced capacity for work'[15] was taken into account. Without going into detail here, it is important to mention because it played a role when the indemnification authorities were calculating the effect of one's ordinary job-pension on one's pension *as a victim*. It will be seen how hedged about with bureaucracy the system of reparation is. Many survivors have expressed a wish that West Germany had simply paid a flat-rate pension and left it at that. 'The cost of administering the reparation system alone makes my mind reel.'

'Every year since 1953 the pension has been calculated on a sliding scale against the income of the victim. Every victim gets a form each year, very similar to an income tax form, on which he or she must declare his or her earnings. The only people exempted from this are those on a minimum pension.'[16] This is borne out by the authorities themselves: 'The calculation [of the pensions] is concerned with the personal and material standing of the recipient in so far as the level of the pension can alter in relation to increase or decrease of otherwise received income in the course of the years.'[17] An illogicality immediately appears: that the receipt of a conventional pension at, say, 55 can adversely affect the level of the 'KZ' pension. And a materially successful survivor – one who prospers through business acumen, the successful application of a craft, or by other talent or marriage – is penalized for that success by a reduction of pension. In all their calculations it seems that the West Germans have forgotten that reparation paid to victims of the concentration camps should be in respect of what they suffered there, and thus not be dependent for its size upon the current material status of the recipient. In fact, after a survivor has passed the age of 60, the 'KZ' pension cannot be changed any more. Unfortunately, I have heard directly of the cases (of which more later) of two women survivors (of different national origins, one now living in New York and the other in London) who have both had attempts made by the two principal separate reparation bureaux to reduce their pensions as they approached their 60th birthday. In another case, that of a survivor who came to the UK, trained as a woodcarver, and now runs a highly specialized, expensive and successful business where he reproduces and restores the work of such masters as Grinling Gibbons, the relevant bureau attempted to reduce his pension on the technical grounds that his earned income was not solely gained through the use of his acquired skill. Saper believes that the argument the West Germans would produce in defence of reducing the pension of a materially successful person is, 'they can't be that badly affected if they are capable now of doing well'.

The four 'grades' of status already referred to relate to income levels in the German civil service, and it is upon these that the pensions are calculated. If, for example, an applicant is assessed at 25–39 per cent disabled, he will draw as his pension between 15 per cent and 40 per cent of the income of a civil servant of the level he has been assessed at. Additional pension may be paid on account of dependants.

Deadlines were set for applications to be in by, but these were relaxed as it was realized that former KZ-inmates were still returning from behind the Iron Curtain as late as the early Sixties.

The pitfalls and the horrors of such a process for an applicant can be imagined; and the standards by which an application was considered were frequently so strict as to be harsh.[18] Small wonder that some survivors fought shy of the whole operation! And it will be seen that those Jews especially who spent the war in hiding or as partisans would not be able to claim any reparation at all,[19] though their suffering was as great through hardship and stress as that of anyone in the camps.

The East German government has not associated itself or its country's past with responsibility for the Third Reich, though 'victims of fascism', in which category Jews are included, enjoy a generous state pension and additional allowances. Despite representations from Israel, at the time of writing East Germany does not pay individual indemnifications.

Although the head of the Jewish community of East Berlin estimates that there may be ten times as many Jews in the country as
are registered with the eight communities, the official number is 350,
having shrunk from 1,500 or so in 1961, when the Berlin Wall was
erected, and the administration of the communities today can be
sustained only with government help. There is still a significant number of Jews active in the upper echelons of East German cultural and
political life, but as their children marry non-Jews, 'total absorption
into the general community is only a matter of time'.[20] The community
members are nearly all over 70 years old.

As far as reparation in general is concerned, the Committee of
Anti-Fascist Resistance Fighters gave this response:

> The then Russian-occupied zone, now the German Democratic
> Republic,[21] has already, decades ago, thoroughly and completely
> fulfilled all the requirements of the Potsdam Conference. Those
> imperialistic monopolies and great landowners responsible for the
> war were stripped of their power and their property given over to the
> people. As far as the fighters against fascism and those persecuted by
> the Nazi regime are concerned, they have been excellently cared for,
> both with regard to their material security through high honorary
> pensions, which they receive in addition to other allowances, and to
> the support given to them culturally, socially, and concerning their
> physical health. To these ends there are welfare units within every
> district advisory centre. Organization is the responsibility of our
> central administration. With this as our starting point, we are con-
> vinced that in its widest sense 'reparation' means that a state does
> everything to ensure that never again will it be possible for fascism
> and militarism to recur. The German Democratic Republic is consti-
> tutionally bound to this aim, and she will do justice to it through
> the politics of peace.[22]

In Austria[23] The Law Covering Succour to Victims (*Opferfürsorge-
gesetz* or OFG) was introduced in its first version by 27 July 1945.
Supplementary laws were soon added, and availability of reparation
advertised in the official legal gazette. Reparation could be claimed
from the date of the promulgation of the original law. The three
resistance-fighter organizations, which are affiliated to the major political parties and which were formed immediately after the war and played
a significant role in the re-establishment of democracy in Austria, were
involved in the drawing-up of the OFG from the start, as was the Jewish
community. Under the Act, a guaranteed monthly income for single
people stood at S.7,034 (1986) and S.8,855 for married couples, or
couples living together, where 30 per cent of the partner's income is
taken into account when calculating pension. No distinction is drawn

between the grounds – racial or political – on which a victim was persecuted. Once-and-for-all payments to compensate for imprisonment (S.860 per month in prison), loss of income (S.10,000), interruption of education (S.6,000), and obligation to wear the Yellow Star (S.6,000) are reckoned additionally to any assessed pension. Applications are assessed in the first instance by the regional president (Landeshauptmann), in the second by the Federal Minister for Social Services. Where pensions are to be decided upon, this is done by a committee at both regional and national levels, on which sit representatives of the resistance-fighter organizations and the Jewish community. Any appeal against an adverse decision can be made in the courts.

This summary should not give the impression that the Austrian system is much less bureaucratic than that of West Germany; and by insisting on its status as a formerly occupied country, rather than one which was allied to Hitler's Germany and abetted its policies, it is arguable that Austria has evaded many of its post-war responsibilities with regard to reparation.

Political prisoners returned to their home countries as resistance heroes, and reparation was provided for them by their governments in addition to any restitution they may have been able to claim from Germany. In Scandinavia, through the efforts of such men as Leo Eitinger in Norway and Paul Thygesen in Denmark, and through the work of, among others, Jan Bastiaans and Elie Cohen in the Netherlands, reparation laws were revised to cover survivors whose disabilities began to show themselves only many years after the end of the war, so that they could claim compensation long after the originally set deadlines for such claims. There were, however, whole groups of people who were not covered by the various reparation statutes: those, for example, who had worked as slave-labourers for the great German industrial concerns such as Farben and Flick;[24] those who had been in hiding; Jewish partisans; homosexuals. Of these groups one of the worst hit was the Gypsies.[25]

Gypsies received nothing as a people. Indeed, owing to lack of advice and too precipitate action, many of them settled for less as individuals than might have been their due. 'In 1952, when the West German government offered to pay survivors DM5 for every day they had spent in the camps, many ... Gypsies simply signed away their claims for compensation in exchange for trifling sums. Gypsy activists have uncovered one case of a woman who received the equivalent of $10 for the death of her baby at Auschwitz.'[26] A similar case is reported by Josef Schmidt[27] who writes of a Gypsy woman called Hedwig Strauss, a survivor of Ravensbrück, Treblinka and Bergen-Belsen. She underwent medical experiments and nearly died. After the war she lived in Hanover, but didn't apply for reparation until 1957. There followed a

27-year-long battle for compensation, at the end of which she received a pension of DM480 a month, and a once-and-for-all payment of DM20,000. However, the Hanover welfare authority immediately demanded payment from her of DM6,538.70 in respect of money spent on renovating her flat. The Christian Democrat President of Lower Saxony, Ernst Albrecht, caused the local law, whereby the welfare authority could take the money away from her, to be changed – but it came too late for Frau Strauss, who by that time had died.

In general terms, too, the Gypsies have found themselves in a cleft stick as far as reparation is concerned. According to the so-called Auschwitz Decree of 1 March 1943, Gypsies became racially 'subhuman'. If they had been imprisoned in the camps before that date, it was technically on account of criminal activity. Thus Gypsies sent to the KZ up to the end of February 1943 'frequently had their applications for reparation automatically turned down on the grounds that they had . . . not been racially persecuted, but "only" been the objects of more stringent police measures'.[28]

Against these examples, it is hard to reflect that many former Nazis and even SS were able to pick up civil and military pensions with no trouble at all. The Nazi criminal and SS mass-murderer Werner Braune, executed by decree of the US Military Court in Landsberg on 8 June 1951, was elevated to the status of 'war victim' by the Bavarian welfare authorities, thus qualifying his widow for an automatic pension. Braune had been a member of the *Einsatzgruppen*. In February of the same year (1985), the widow of *Oberblutrichter* Freisler had also received a pension from Bavaria, on the grounds that, had he lived, he would have been able to accept a high position in post-war West Germany. 'The Bavarian government also made a six-figure [DM] sum available to Freisler's widow to enable her to buy into the Employees' Insurance Scheme.'[29]

5

The Survivor and Society,
the Family, Age and Grief

The development of concentration camp survivors as they try to come to terms with the past has many aspects. Ordinary daily events, and even sights and sounds and smells, can be frightening by association with the past, or can trigger dreadful memories. These reactions are not always understood by other people; survivors themselves may try to suppress them in an effort to become 'like other people'. Nevertheless, in life after the KZ, relationships with other people are marked by the experience. Inevitably the people most affected are those closest to the survivor, and it is not surprising that, of those people whose post-war family lives have been most affected, the Jews constitute the highest number. After the war, the urge to marry, both as a flight from loneliness and from a desire to replace the people who had been lost, was very strong. Marriages and indeed births in the DP camps were many: there was a great sense of regeneration. However, marriages were often made in haste and outside any normal social context, and thus 'disregarded differences in pre-war socio-economic and educational status, lifestyle, age or other ordinary criteria'.[1] Yael Danieli, who has researched this area in depth, calls these 'marriages of despair'.

To the united pair of survivors, a child would soon be born, and the child would be named after someone related to one or other of the parents who had died in the camps. The new child would carry a heavy burden: in him, all the lost, but now renewed, hopes of the parents would be vested, and he would be expected to live on behalf of the lost child whose name he carried. Additionally, the lost child would be an idealized ghost, constantly hovering in the background;[2] and the post-war world would also be idealized by the parents, whose attitude would be that after what they had been through the world *had* to be changed for the better. Another problem, encountered by virtually all survivors but which was to have an understandable effect on certain survivors' families, was the disinclination of anyone who had not been through the camps to listen to the accounts of them which the survivors wanted – often desperately – initially to give, in an attempt to external-ize them. 'Even people who were consciously and compassionately interested played down their interest, partly rationalizing their avoid-ance with the belief that their questions would inflict further hurt.'[3] The apparent lack of interest was also due to a fear on the part of those who had not been through the camps that they might, if they heard the worst, not be able to shut off the feeling of guilt at having stood by and done nothing while the destruction was going on – or indeed a guilt at having escaped the KZ altogether. Whatever the motives of those who refused to listen, the impression made on the survivor (at its worst) was one of indifference, even of callousness, which caused them to withdraw into their own society: their family, and fellow survivors. Where they had moved to a new country, the situation was worse, because they had a new language and a new culture to learn. Unfamiliar food, customs, buildings, scenery and even weather sur-rounded them. I have talked with many who have spoken bitterly of their reception by the local communities – and again, especially Jewish communities – in their new home countries. 'The one thing I wasn't prepared for was the intense loneliness I felt' . . . 'I was more miserable in the years immediately after the war – actually miserable – than I ever was in the camps.' After so long, I was also surprised to find that for several people I was the first person to have shown an interest in a survivor's story; though I think it is fair to add that some people found it easier to talk to me as a stranger than to a close member of the family – with me, the door could open and then shut again: I would not be around every day. Nevertheless, every survivor whom I met with that intention wanted to talk about their concentration camp experience, and some were grateful for the opportunity.

Those turned in upon their own company by the apparent rejection of the world[4] would react in different ways. In a new, foreign environ-ment, new, voluntary ghettos would spring up as survivors sought to live in their own communities. As far as family life was concerned, the child became the focus of the parents' attention. Four main types of 'troubled' survivor family have been identified.[5] The first tended to cling very closely together, united by a mistrust of the outside world inculcated in the child by the parents 'for its own good', but actually geared to bind the child more closely to its parents, thus underpinning their egocentrically demanding sense of security. Equally, even the slightest illness manifested by the child was treated to near-hysterical overreaction. The children of such survivors were further bound to their parents by emotional blackmail: 'You're all I have to live for'; and yet great things were expected of them, especially if the parents' own lives and marriages did not turn out particularly well, which, in the psychological circumstances, was not infrequent. Joy, or pleasure, were regarded as luxuries. Security was the main aim in life, and the sole source of satisfaction. It is not within the scope of this book to deal with the effects KZ survivor parents had upon their children, except tangentially, but the effect of such parental control as that described can be imagined.

In contrast to the so-called 'victim' family is that of the 'fighter'. Danieli, whose term it is, concedes that it is not perfect, used as it is to identify survivors who either lived their post-war lives in the role that had got them through the camps, or took up a posture 'to counteract the role of victimized Jew'. The term is only misleading in so far as 'fighting' in the KZ would not be a factor in survival, whereas luck, the ability not to draw attention to oneself, and a talent for *organization*, would – though these last two could be construed as 'fighting' for life. In such families, great stress was laid on achievement. Constant activity was utilized, perhaps to keep unpleasant memories at bay,[6] and illness, far from being responded to at its slightest manifestation, was only noticed when it had gone so far that it could not be ignored; exactly the situation as it would have been in the camps. Similarly, any expression of weakness, from tears to self-pity, was taboo. Enforced ebullience was the order of the day. The outside world, still regarded as alien and unfriendly, was there to be exploited rather than avoided.

A third type of family was that in which physical and emotional silence reigned. 'Both parents were frequently the sole survivors of their individual families',[7] and had cut themselves off from any form of emotional attitude, or social responsibility, towards the world they still had to live in, and this extended even to the children they had created in the euphoria and desperation of the first months of liberation.

While the marriages themselves in the three groups just described may not be particularly happy or successful, by virtue of the psychological processes behind them, they rarely end in divorce, for the couple is isolated from or fighting against the outside world. In a fourth group, some interlocking action is sought with the outside world, which can disunite the couple. People in this category tried to make up for what they had lost, and to make up for lost time. They wanted to be 'high achievers', and they desired the security represented for them by money, fame, and a recognized place in society. Nothing was denied their children, who were given every opportunity through education to go even further than their parents, and thus create an unbridgeable gap between the threat of the KZ and themselves. Many such survivors had their tattoos removed, and suppressed their memories, thereby hoping to shed them altogether and remove the stain on the soul they felt the KZ had placed there. The innocent victims of rape, or even of burglary, feel unclean because they have been 'invaded'. How much more so will someone who was subjected to years of humiliation and vilification? But suppression is rarely the answer for survivors, and the long-term effect on this kind of former inmate, who wishes to give the impression that he got through unscathed, is harmful.

Jan Bastiaans, whose pioneering work using LSD-25 in conjunction with psychotherapy in aiding concentration camp survivors and other severely traumatized patients has enabled them to express within a relatively short space of time what might otherwise have taken years to come out, has also had experience of their relationships with their post-war families. The two dominant roles in KZ society are those of master and slave.[8] 'Many victims continued their post-war life in the role of the slave. They remain too submissive, too slavish towards the outside world, even towards their own children. Others identified themselves in an act of defence too much with the role of master. In the post-war era they could be very strict and sometimes cruel [towards] their own family or the wider environment. A third group was marked by an irritating oscillation between the two roles. For many it seemed as if no other roles than these two were possible in daily human contact.'[9] The problem of the therapist in dealing with such patients (a problem encountered by teams supervised both by Bastiaans and by Danieli) is their own reaction to what they are told, so emotionally charged is it. Care has to be taken too with the role the therapists themselves assume in relation to their patients.

The case-histories of two of Bastiaans' patients serve as illustrations of how the survivor, marrying a 'non-survivor', may react in the master/ slave context.

In 1971 a 52-year-old married man was admitted to the Leyden Department of Psychiatry. He was a KZ survivor. Already for some years he had suffered from untreatable malignant hypertension ... During the war he had been in Buchenwald. Already in 1941 he was in a so-called *Mussulman* state. He saved his life by working in a dissection room where he had to make lampshades out of human skin; he did this work in a state of chronic depersonalization. During the LSD therapy, he once again went through the horrible camp experiences, especially the horrors of the dissection room. In therapy it was the first time he could express his feelings of guilt about what he had been required to do in the camp. The mere fact that he was able to express these guilt feelings led to a remarkable reduction of his blood pressure already after the first session. In the next sessions all the camp experiences came to the fore. He sat on the floor, leaned on the knees of the therapist and cried like a child. He had the feeling that the therapist was his good father. For the first time in his life he experienced that his 'father' understood what he had gone through in the camp and in his very unhappy childhood. Ten weeks after the start of the treatment, including three LSD sessions, the blood pressure had been reduced to normal values.

His wife and children had suffered a great deal from his chronic nervousness and dominant behaviour. Sometimes in the contact with his wife and children he had behaved as a real psychopath. Apparently this behaviour had been the result of overidentification with the 'masters' in the camp.

Treatment was continued with marriage counselling and family therapy. Unfortunately six years later his wife committed suicide, partially because she had not forgotten how she had been ill-treated by him. Again he had to be admitted to a hospital for an intensive elevation of his blood pressure. Again this elevation of the blood pressure predominantly was determined by his guilt feelings about the death of his wife. This time the blood pressure could be kept under control with the aid of normal psychotherapy in which a free discussion took place about these guilt feelings, his aggressive tendencies and his feelings of frustration and abandonment.[10]

In the second case, Bastiaans treated a 44-year-old Dutch Jewess, who had become a nurse in Israel after the war. Her father had been a rabbi, highly thought of before the war for his brave efforts in helping Jewish refugees from Germany. But the parents had been so engrossed in these activities that they had hardly any time for their own children. In the middle of the war, the whole family was arrested and taken to the KZ, where the woman, then aged 11 or 12, saw her father beaten to death by the Germans. 'Already before the war she was very much attached to a younger brother who suffered from mental deficiency. Still he was the only source of warmth for his sister. At the age of 13 [she] was transported to another camp which was liberated by Russian troops soon after. The greatest trauma for her was that the dying brother had to stay in the first camp. Later on she suffered from terrible guilt feelings that she had not been able to take him with her.' She was a nurse in Israel from 1951 until 1969. During this time she was

married to a sadist, an Israeli, who had the mentality of a German SS-man. Under most unfavourable circumstances she got three children. She was constantly ill-treated by the husband. In retrospect it became clear that the unhappy marriage was closely linked to her war experiences and to her guilt feelings towards her parents who had not paid enough attention to her before the war. In Israel, also later on in Holland, she functioned as a head nurse. In this way she could identify herself with the role of good parents. Progressively she decompensated in the mid-Seventies. Finally she had the greatest problems with the consequences of the divorce and with her children.

During intensive LSD therapy it became clear that she was fixated as well in the most terrible camp experiences with the loss of the beloved brother, as in the pre-war period which subconsciously fixated her in the situation of a child crying for attention she in fact had not received at all.

The transference situation was most difficult. The therapist became the good father and also the rejecting father. If she could only hear his voice by phone in between the sessions she felt relaxed. As soon as the contact had to be reduced an intensive relapse of many months occurred because now the therapist was identified with an SS-man who tortured her by rejection. Up to now this case is a striking example of the great effort that has to be invested in the treatment of a severe masked hysterical character neurosis which expressed itself for many years in pseudo-adapted overactivity, psychosomatic symptoms, additional and intensive masochism.[11]

What often makes it difficult for any therapist or researcher in this field is that survivors' 'longing to talk about their experience is tempered with reluctance to do so. So even if they're confronted with a sympathetic listener, they may not want to present themselves openly – unless the listener is a fellow-sufferer.'[12] After contact has been established, it is important to sustain it, if that is what the survivor wishes. In terms of passing on the impressions of the KZ experience to their children, the survivors employ various means.[13] Israel, with 100,000 survivors among its population, has presented a unique opportunity to study the effect of these means.

Shamai Davidson was a psychiatrist living and practising in Israel; he specialized in the treatment of survivors of the concentration camps and their children.[14] The brutal treatment in the KZ left permanently scarred the minds of those who underwent it, and the scars showed themselves in the ways already described, and through lack of concentration, fear of committing oneself to love, inability to obtain real satisfaction or enjoyment from anything. The mere act of living with people so affected would be bound to rub off on anyone, let alone on their children. Davidson, however, viewed the survivors' ability to adapt back to normal life with optimism:

Since the early 1960s the children of survivors have increasingly concerned us. From our study of the second generation our orientation has evolved from an emphasis on the individual survivor to that of the survivor family. We now see that the concept of the survivor syndrome[15] was a construct based on medical models of symptomatology and psychopathology, and was thus related to prevailing attitudes in society that viewed the survivor as a damaged, disabled person who was entitled to compensation payments. The considerable adaptive capacity shown by many survivors in their reintegration into society despite the massive trauma they suffered did not receive sufficient attention and has become a central topic in our studies.

Studying the families and children of survivors gives us the opportunity to study the emergence from massive trauma, the reintegration of individuals into normal society with the reconstruction of families and the birth of a new generation. Here we can observe the meeting of traumatized and damaged processes with coping and adaptive processes in response to psychological forces.

It is interesting that this optimism exists in the face of work which reveals the continuing need for psychiatric support among survivors over 30 years and more after the event. I introduce it here as a corrective to the impression that survivors are generally 'different' from the rest of us. Man is a remarkably adaptable creature; that is one of the secrets of his success; and the same adaptive ability that helped people survive in the KZ itself may in many cases have helped them find their way back to a normal role in society and life. Again the question arises, not of shutting out or confronting and conquering what had been done to them, but of coming to terms with it.

Davidson has identified seven 'specific vulnerabilities arising from . . . traumatization' which usefully summarize the problems confronting the survivor:

1. External, often trivial, stimuli of great variety in daily life which arouse deeply imprinted memories of persecutory experiences in a flash-back way and causing acute exacerbation of anxiety. Some examples are the sound of a dog barking, the sight of tall chimneys, certain smells, etc., or even hearing certain words. Likewise, events such as Nazi war crime trials, Holocaust memorial days, visiting the country of origin, the wars, security crises and terrorist incidents in Israel [the country with whose survivor population Davidson was concerned] can serve to arouse memories and precipitate a re-experiencing of the horrors of the traumatization resulting in considerable distress.

2. Confrontation with physical illness including hospitalization and surgical operations in the survivor himself, members of his family and friends.

3. Disappointments and crises in relationships, especially marital and with children, e.g. when they fail to live up to certain expectations.

4. Separations in relation to spouse, friends and children.

5. Deaths of friends, relatives, neighbours.

6. Loss of activity from any cause, e.g. accidents, illness, loss of job.

7. The ageing process – leading to reduction in adaptive capacity, physical powers and activity.[16]

Davidson would have been the first to add the caveat that these are generally true points, but do not all apply to all survivors all the time. Survivors, like any other group of human beings, are a collection of individuals, and perhaps they are more heterogeneous than most by virtue of having been so arbitrarily lumped together by their common fate.

Some of Davidson's findings counterbalance and augment those already mentioned: discussing general clinical experience with children of survivors seen in psychiatric outpatient clinics and hospitals in Israel, he reports:

The parents of most of these children belonged to the age group of concentration camp survivors (people in their twenties and thirties) who married soon after their release from the camps and many of them had lost previous spouses and children. Marriage and the birth of children in these groups took place very soon after their Holocaust experiences and insufficient time had elapsed for them to work through and come to terms with their traumatic experiences and massive losses. The children of these survivors were thus intensely involved by the parents in their parents' early attempts at recovery. On the other hand, survivors who were late adolescents or young adults at the time of their liberation from the camps often married only some years later after they had resumed their development and achieved some degree of integration of the massive trauma they had undergone. The latter group of survivor parents have thus had less need to use the family situation and their children to work through their Holocaust experiences and losses. As a result, the directness of the impact of the Holocaust on the children in these age groups has been much less, and the effects of their parents' Holocaust experiences on their children, many of whom are only now [1980] reaching adolescence, seem to be of a more subtle nature.

It may be, as he himself points out, that the majority of survivors and their children achieved a positive sense of identity in Israel.[17] Danieli's work was done amongst Jewish survivors in the USA, mainly in New York.

Despite his optimism, it is fair to point out also that his findings about the types of survivor family defined by Danieli are very similar to hers. Only children were prone to be more seriously affected than those with siblings, who could share the burden of their parents' maimed emotional or social outlook placed on them.

Two other ways in which survivors' children were affected were: the use by the parents of a secret language – that is, their native one, and not the English or Hebrew the child had grown up speaking, in order to discuss the child; and the intrusion of concentration camp imagery into family and social life. Thus a parent might overreact enormously at wasted food. Even the use of an innocent word in a modern context might cause an 'inexplicable' reaction in the parent because of the way the parent understood it in the context of the KZ. 'For example, a mother on being told that her teenage daughter was "deteriorating" in her studies became violently distressed because of her compulsive association to the word "deteriorating", with memories of the heaps of corpses she had seen in Auschwitz.'

There are many examples of such behaviour. To return for a moment to the identification of a parent with the 'master' or 'slave' dominant types of the camps, a child's ordinary misbehaviour could be given an altogether exaggerated significance, and the reaction to it could be inadequate, in terms of either too much or too little discipline. In extreme cases the child, in any case disorientated by the parents' reactions, might take on the role of 'master'. One example is of a boy who in early adolescence tortured his mother by greeting her with 'Heil Hitler'.[18] The British psychiatrist, Colin Murray Parkes, recalls treating survivor parents who know they are being 'bad' parents, but who can do nothing about it.[19]

That the curse of the concentration camps, so far from being one which is petering out or diffusing in time, is still very much present, in its effect on the second generation and even, arguably, on the third, may be seen in one final example: 'A 32-year-old man agreed to be present during the birth of his first child. The labour was a very difficult one and his wife's screams, associated on the one hand with his desire to help her and on the other hand with his feeling of overwhelming helplessness, resulted in a severe panic state, fear of death, and horrifying, destructive death imagery with torturing guilt feelings of unusual intensity. His mother, an Auschwitz survivor, had overwhelmed him in his adolescence with stories of her Holocaust experiences, including her feelings of helplessness when her entire family was sent to the gas chambers. The man's relationship with his mother contained overtones of dependency.' His reaction to the childbirth required emergency psychiatric treatment and hospitalization.

The onset of old age presents another set of potential problems to the survivor. As we have seen, activity is one way in which survivors are able to keep painful memories at bay. If these memories have merely been kept at bay and not dealt with, or if help has not been sought in accommodating them, then retirement alone can create an unpleasant vacuum into which they can rush. Even in the case of a person who has not been subjected to the stresses experienced by a survivor, the transition from an active life, where every day has been spent with a number of other people and in which a position of responsibility may have been held, to one of inactivity, possibly isolation and lack of responsibility can be very difficult unless it has been prepared for and substitute interests supplied. At its worst, the departure of children from home, and the inevitable death of contemporaries, can represent for survivors a repeat of their experiences of loss in the camps. If they have to move to a smaller house, or, possibly worse, to an old people's home, the disruption to their lives may be interpreted as the earlier disruption, when they were plucked from a secure environment and transported in the most unpleasant circumstances to one where not the slightest thing was certain. If the onset of old age brings with it an inability to continue work, that can be equated in the mind with what such an inability brought in the camps: death.[20]

Edith Sklar traced her aunt, Laura Schmidt – a survivor of the Warsaw Ghetto, Majdanek, and subsequently of forced labour in factories in Leipzig – to Berlin immediately after the war. Edith herself had been lucky: she and her parents had got out of Germany just before war was declared. Laura had married a Polish Jew, from Lodz, and was living in Warsaw when the Germans invaded. Before her marriage she had been a bookseller in Berlin and had been a prominent figure in the city's literary circles, being on friendly terms with such figures as Kurt Tucholsky. Her response to Hitler's rise to power was to involve herself with the publication of Zionist works. She met her future husband in Warsaw and they married there, but soon after they had to go to the ghetto, where she ran a laundry. When her husband was shot for going to look for bread after the curfew and his body dumped on her doorstep, she lost her nerve and volunteered for transportation 'to the East'. At Majdanek, her fluent Polish and German saved her, as she was taken into the camp administration.

Her first job after liberation was to work at a DP camp in Belgium for child survivors. It was a post arranged for her by relatives, and it seems to have been of great therapeutic value. When the camp was closed, she returned to Berlin, but the Berlin she had known belonged only to the past, and she agreed to come to England to join her sister's family.

At the time, the cut-off age for immigrants to the UK was 50. Laura was 54, but looked younger than her age and was able to slip through because all her original papers had been lost in the war, and there was no documentary proof of when she had been born. In preparation for her journey and her new life, she went to the milliner and the dressmaker whose customer she had been before the war, and ordered clothes – but in pre-war style. 'She looked so out of place when she arrived – so old-fashioned. It was almost as if she was trying to convince herself that the war hadn't taken place.'[21]

Attempts by the family in London to get her to give up these clothes met with an aggressive reaction. She never quite got on with the adults of the family and, although she was at ease with Edith as a teenager, she became increasingly reserved towards her as she grew up.

Laura's attitude towards the rest of the family didn't relax with time. She was more comfortable with outsiders, once she had got to know them, though initially she was very ill at ease with them. She wouldn't speak to people who weren't Jews. Her one social pleasure was playing bridge, the discipline of which appealed to her intellect. At the same time, a bridge evening provided a ritual, formal social structure in which nothing dangerously personal needed to be said.

Inside the family, her attitudes were paradoxical. 'Every move you made she took the wrong way. One day she was asked to watch over a chicken that was cooking, but she let it burn and spoil, and when we asked her why, she said: "There's no need for chicken – there's no need even to eat."' She loved her relatives to distraction, despite being unable to confide in them, and, paradoxically, as time passed, the only way she could express her affection was to cook them meals, which were always enormous – far too big – 'We couldn't eat them, and that offended her.'

A turning point seemed to come when Edith's mother contracted cancer. Laura nursed her sister through her illness and, it appeared, ceased being concerned with the problems created for her by her own past. For a period after her sister's death, there was no further mention of the concentration camps, though she started to assume the role of Edith's mother, and to overplay it. At moments of high tension in life, such as the birth of Edith's son, which happened after her mother's death, Laura would have severe nervous attacks, manifesting anger, and involving violent fits of screaming, followed by physical collapse. She had reacted in a similar way when Edith married. 'I think it was because she thought she was losing control of me. She saw herself as my protector, but also, I think, as my guard. There was another time when an older cousin of mine came over from the States to stay with my aunt – she had her own flat by then. Laura looked forward to the visit eagerly, and the preparation went on for weeks. But when it happened it lasted for two days. My cousin phoned me to say she couldn't stand it. Every move she made was watched; she had mountains of food pressed on her every half-hour, but at the same time she was rigorously cross-questioned if she wanted to leave the flat on her own.'

In order to have her reparation claims ratified, Laura twice had to go to West Germany. She had to steel herself to do this, since she couldn't stand Germans. She used the pension she received to travel all over Europe, and she visited the USA and Israel, but she always travelled alone, and never established new relations with anybody during her post-war life. Though she travelled so widely, she would never go in a car or a taxi, and would go to any lengths to avoid having to use a lift, or entering any enclosed space.

Laura refused to have any possessions, but she was persuaded to rent a flat, which she did reluctantly; though when she did, she chose a very large place – far bigger than she needed. Nevertheless, she had to be forced to buy even the most basic furniture for it. There was, however, a significant exception to her opposition to belongings. 'The only thing she had a mania about was overcoats; an overcoat was a vital piece of equipment for her, and everyone she cared about had to have one too. She had several herself – many, many overcoats: ten or fifteen. Otherwise she was totally uncaring about clothes.'

When she was in her late seventies, she went out shopping one day and crossed the road without looking. She broke her hip in the ensuing car accident. When she came round she was not in hospital in North London, but in the Majdanek *Revier*. The nurses were SS-women. She refused to speak to them. Somehow, miraculously, the hip healed and she returned to her flat, but her mind had crossed a final boundary. 'The hallucinations were intermittent, but one day when she had turned 80 she came to see me and told me that the SS were shooting all the babies in her block of flats in Hampstead. Her neighbours had already been complaining to us about her screaming in the middle of the night.' The family engaged private nurses to look after her day and night, but when they arrived at the flat she took them to be Gestapo and refused to let them in. Accepting the inevitable, they arranged for her to be admitted to a private clinic. 'But when we broke the news to her she refused to go – shouting obscenities that I'd no idea she even knew.' In the end, Laura had to be sectioned. Once in hospital, she would speak only in French, German or Polish. She died there in 1983, aged 87.

Although this is a particularly tragic story, elements of Laura Schmidt's reactions are present in many survivors as they attempt to find a way of coping. An emphasis on food, indeed on food as a means of expressing love which can find no other outlet, is not unusual, nor is the difficulty found in trusting people, and the perhaps consequent sense of ease with children and young people. But it is important to be wary of taking any survivor as typical. There is no such thing as a typical survivor; only certain features of reaction, which may show themselves more or less, according to the stress the survivor is under.

Mourning is a vital element in coming to terms with grief. To grieve one needs time, however, and no more urgent call on the mind, such as the necessity to ensure one's own immediate survival.[22] Survivors had no time to mourn loved ones at the moment when they lost them. In the concentration camp, the overriding instinct was to survive oneself, a process which did not permit energy to be used up on grieving or mourning. Only much later, after liberation, did former KZ-inmates find themselves in a position psychologically to accommodate grief; but this delayed grief could also be a contributory source of the feelings of guilt many survivors carry with them. That this general rule has its exceptions will quickly be seen in reading the survivors' individual stories, but it is worth bearing in mind nevertheless:

> . . . 'serious matters like the death of relatives or close friends often met with only superficial sympathy, whereas trifles or small quarrels . . . would lead to severe temper outbursts'. In this situation imprisonment without guilt, hopelessness, sexual segregation, lack of privacy, forced labour, semi-starvation, and the constant threat of being sent to an extermination camp were ever-present stresses. Grief and depression in such circumstances could well have tipped the scales against survival, and it may be that psychic defences come into operation to protect people in extreme conditions such as these. After the liberation a number of the survivors had severe depressive reactions: 'A strong feeling of guilt for having survived where relatives and friends succumbed was one of the outstanding features.' The grief was sometimes expressed in a prolonged search for the graves of beloved persons as if it was possible in this way to get them back.[23]

Parkes sets out seven major aspects of the many reactions to bereavement:

> a process of realization; . . . an alarm reaction – anxiety, restlessness and the physiological accompaniments of fear; an urge to search for and find the lost person in some form; anger and guilt . . .; feelings of internal loss of self or mutilation; identification phenomena – the adoption of traits, mannerisms, or symptoms of the lost person, with or without a sense of his presence within the self; pathological variants of grief, i.e. the reaction may be excessive and prolonged, or inhibited and inclined to emerge in distorted form.[24]

It is clear that any KZ-inmate bereaved at the moment of imprisonment would not have the time to work through these stages, so their process would be frozen until there was. An important additional factor is that grief did not strike the isolated individual. 'When I realized that my wife and child had been killed, 100 men in my *Block*, sitting near me, were realizing exactly the same about their loved-ones – it hit us all together' . . . 'There was nothing to do but go on.'

For some survivors, the inability to mourn has never been resolved. Some have told me additionally that not only are they no longer able to express love ('I did love, once, but it seems a strange memory: I can remember the emotion quite vividly, but I am detached from it') for whatever reason; they are also unable to feel sympathy, though they are not unfeeling people. They regret the loss, but it seems there is nothing they can do about it. Such people, among the survivors I have met, are in the minority; the great majority have declared that their experience has left them more sympathetic to the plight of others suffering today than they might otherwise have been. To attempt to make a hypothesis about the kind of person one might have been had it not been for the camps, however, is to attempt the impossible.

If stress has been laid on the problems encountered and created by survivors, this has been done in the interests of completeness. There is another side to the coin, concerning those survivors who achieved readaption to normal life with great success. Speaking of his own experiences in well over 20 years of working with survivors in Israel, Shamai Davidson said: 'I am very aware that a distorted impression can be arrived at by generalizing from . . . clinical observations to the entire survivor population, which constitutes several hundred thousand people. An uprooted heterogeneous group from all the countries of Europe, they have made a remarkably successful social adjustment in the countries where they were permitted to settle after the war, creating new homes and new lives . . .'[25] To this should be added – though by no means in mitigation of life in the camps – that even there, ordinary, decent humanity persisted and even flourished. Examples of it abound in the stories that follow; but as the ultimate testing ground of human integrity the KZ system has had no equal, and it is important to record that mankind was not broken by it. The people who betrayed the aspirations of being human, if not the realities, were the SS and those who threw in their lot with them, not the prisoners whom they sought to dehumanize.

6

Some Effects of the
KZ on the Mind

In taking a more detailed look at the long-term effects of the concentration camp experience on the survivor's psyche, the work of two psychiatrists will be examined. The first is Jan Bastiaans, whose work in psychotherapy assisted by the use of LSD-25 has already been mentioned. The account with which this chapter begins deals with a survivor of Westerbork and Bergen-Belsen, talking first to the author of this book, then some months later during an LSD-assisted therapy session. There follows a discussion with Professor Bastiaans and a short review of his work in this field.

MAY, LONDON

I was born in December 1934 in an inner suburb of Amsterdam. My mother worked as an administrator in a big department store, and my father was a diamond polisher. Both my parents' families were in the diamond business. They were badly hit by the recession in the Thirties, but they got through it.

Measures against Jews didn't really start to affect us until 1941; but I had barely started my education before I was moved from a regular state school to one within the Jewish community. I was an only child, and home seemed a relatively warm place, though looking back I don't think we were happy. I think my parents had been too much influenced by the difficulties of the Thirties. Still, we lived reasonably well, and we had a modern, three-bedroomed flat in a 1920s development.

I can't recall any childhood friends, or any real contentment because practically as far back as I can remember people were starting to disappear, and the atmosphere I lived in was one of uncertainty. At the beginning of 1943 all Jewish people had to move into the east end of

Amsterdam, which was very run-down. Of course we had to leave our flat. But we weren't in our new place long, because in April there was the inevitable knock on the door in the middle of the night, and we were taken to a theatre in Amsterdam that the Germans were using as a collection point for Jews. From there we were taken to Westerbork[1] in the north-east of the country, where we remained until January 1944, with the exception of a month in Amersfoort, where I think we were sent because Westerbork became overcrowded. That January they took us to Bergen-Belsen by train, where we stayed until early April 1945, when they cleared some of us out of it because the camp had become so overcrowded by then. The family was not split up at any stage.

There were a couple of train transports out of Bergen-Belsen that April. The one we were on wandered aimlessly through Germany – I think the train just went wherever the track was still open, trying to head south. Finally it came to a halt in a village near Leipzig, and we woke up in the morning to find our guards gone and the train surrounded by Russian soldiers. That was my liberation, but I honestly have no recollection of feeling anything. I was ten years old, we'd been in those cattle-waggons for two weeks. People were dying all around me. The floor was awash with diarrhoea. I don't think any of us had enough energy left to feel glad. Some of the intellectuals, who could immediately see the historical significance of the moment, might have felt glad – but even they lost their intellectual energy in the camp. You had to think of one thing only: how to get from one day to the next. Of course, people wrote books later and probably thought they remembered having great thoughts at the time, which they only actually had afterwards.

After the Russian soldiers had liberated us, those of us who were able to were allowed to leave the train. We fled to the village and looted the shops for food and clothing. My parents and I were lucky to have been spared typhus, but the Russians set up a field-hospital for those who had got it. After a month or so we Dutch were handed over to the Americans in Leipzig, who arranged transport for us back to the Netherlands, though we didn't get home until the end of June. Once there, we children had proper medical examinations at an orphanage, and I was sent to a hospital for three months, after which I went to Switzerland to convalesce. They kept me there until January 1946, when I went back to Amsterdam and was reunited with my parents.

By then my parents had decided to leave, because the reception back home had been so frightful. The authorities had promised us the moon when we got home, but what we had in fact was the curtained-off corner of a large room in a flat. Much later I asked my father why he hadn't gone and repossessed our old flat which had been taken over by

Nazi sympathizers. You know what he said? 'One mustn't make trouble.' I'd have made trouble! I'm still angry about that.

Apart from the indignity, there was another reason why my parents wanted to leave. They couldn't bear the memories that Amsterdam held for them. So few Jews came back from the camps, and many of them were leaving for the USA and Israel. In March 1946 my father came over to London, and after he'd found a flat my mother and I followed in April.

The reason they chose England, and the reason we'd stayed together as a family, was because my paternal grandfather had been born in London and we were therefore able to claim British nationality. Some of those Jews with foreign ancestry from neutral or unoccupied countries – such as Britain, Portugal, Spain, Switzerland – were kept together by the Germans for possible exchange purposes. Bergen-Belsen was originally a camp for holding people like us – of potential value to the Germans while the war was still on. I guess that's why we were moved out when it became a reception camp for transports evacuated from the east, and conditions there became impossibly insanitary. But it was no holiday camp at the best of times, and the tension and insecurity made for great suffering. Still, we were alive and together. Others of the family were not so fortunate. Since we come from a Sephardic background, my paternal grandmother had the possibility not only of claiming British nationality, but Portuguese too, and it was because she tried to cover herself by claiming both that she died. The Swiss were looking after British affairs in the Netherlands after the occupation, and her two applications had caused confusion. After the Germans had arrested her we went to the Swiss Embassy to try to get her British citizenship attested, but they only said, 'Come back after the war.' She was sent to Sobibor. On my mother's side of the family, everyone was sent to the extermination camps. I am glad her father was spared that. He died in 1938. He used to take me to the zoo.

My parents are not religious. I wasn't brought up observant, though there was just a little trace of Zionist influence in my mother's house, where there was a collection box on the chimney-piece. But I wasn't brought up as a Jewish child, and I think that has created enormous difficulties for me in some areas of my life since. One of the things that has worried me about the history of the whole concentration camp system is the emphasis that's put on the Jewish aspect of it. I know that it's justified, but it's also created a reaction of 'We don't want to go on and on hearing about how much the Jews suffered; other people suffered as well, then and since.' In other words, I think the Jews have reached a stage in their discussion of the Holocaust where other people, among them Jews too, are beginning to think that they are protesting too much. But there was a TV drama series about Englishwomen in a

Japanese internment camp during the war, and I think that was good because it showed English non-Jews people like themselves in a situation just a little bit similar to that which the Jews found themselves in in the KZ. Through a programme like that I think ordinary people can become more receptive to the idea of the Holocaust. It ceases to be as remote as those sallow-looking people in Eastern Europe make it, staring out of grainy black-and-white photographs at you from a distant world in time and space.

For many years I think I must have been a naïve and innocent child. What I remember of Westerbork and even of Bergen-Belsen was the sheer monotony of passing the days, because there was nothing at all to do. In Westerbork I remember the railway line by which people arrived and left.[2] There were small trucks on the sidings, and we children would get hold of iron bars and by levering them under the trucks' wheels make them move along the lines and even stage modest collisions – that was our play. There were some workshops in the camp as well, and in one of them they made toys, which meant that they used plywood and fretsaws, and we were allowed a little wood and the use of saws to make things – there was quite a vogue for fretwork at the time. There were also some warehouses set aside to receive the goods which were pilfered from the houses of the Jews, and within those buildings people were employed to dismantle radio sets to get the aluminium foil out of them, and we would sometimes go in and mess about with the bits and pieces, and there was the possibility of making small stamp collections. There were a lot of discarded letters and envelopes. I think we children tried to maintain a degree of normality in the camp. Certainly, in my case, I was totally unaware of what it was all really all about. I was eight years old. I'd had a lonely and isolated childhood; both my parents worked before we were taken away, and they used to dump me with my grandparents.

I think the thing I remember most about the camps is how crowded the barracks[3] were, and being in contact with all sorts of people who behaved in the most peculiar way. People behaved like lunatics; they couldn't control their emotions at all. When one's a child, surrounded by adults who aren't behaving the way adults should behave – who aren't reliable, but who squabble and shriek and weep – well, I think that's something that's still got to come out, for me, in an LSD session: the impression grown-ups make on a child when they are desperate and lost themselves. It was simply frightening. But then gradually you became aware that the quarrels were about food, about not having fair shares of the rations. Someone would shout that she had three grammes of margarine less than the next person, and I think that the amount of energy that was expended over things like that would have been much better conserved.

None of us survived because of our cleverness. It was a matter of luck. Some people will spin yarns about how cunning they were, but it's not true.

In one sense the camp was a fascinating experience. There were people from all over Europe. From Albania, Greece, Italy. I remember a party of Italians coming. They were people from a different world. I went to their part of the camp once: the food they'd brought with them: pasta, salami, things I hadn't seen. And to hear all those different languages. It was a fascinating place, like I imagine it might be in a North African *souk* – all the strange people, sights and smells. But of course there wasn't much energy; people came in worn out from transports. And I am remembering what a child saw. Snapshots: a slice of white bread with sugar on it as a treat; a Hungarian trading a potato with me for a gold ring my father had given me to give him. People made sick from eating frost-bitten swedes.

Certainly I don't remember how many other children there were, not even roughly. There was a number of them, but I can't remember any particular friends. I was with my parents all the time, except when they worked in the camp. My father worked in the laundry at Westerbork, though I don't think my mother worked at all there. In Belsen, they both worked in the kitchens, which meant that they could smuggle food back to the barrack from time to time. I remember the tedium of Belsen. In the winter it was worse, it was cold, there was never enough food; and there were endless roll-calls where you had to stand in the rain for hours on end in a big square with the officers in the middle. The question was always, would the numbers tally, or would we have to go through the whole thing again? However, I don't think one was aware of making an effort to get through it, or of any kind of inner strength. People of my age reacted instinctively; we weren't equipped intellectually to do anything but just get through the days. It was the state of things, and don't forget that we were the lucky ones – we were not under actual threat of death.

Nobody bothered to tell me what was going on, and I didn't bother to ask. I have found it almost an experience in retrospect, by reading in adulthood the diaries of people who were in Belsen as adults – those of Renate Laqueur and Hannah Lévy-Hass, for example.[4] However, I didn't start reading about the concentration camps until around 1980, about the same time as I started LSD therapy. Now I don't read so much, simply because I think I know all I can know about the subject.

When my father came to the UK to work as a diamond polisher he found some rooms in Willesden, a north-western suburb of London, where we all lived for a couple of months before we moved to Wembley. There was a lot of anti-Semitism, and a lot of xenophobia. I found it better not to talk about the concentration camps, and not to do or say anything that would make me appear different from anyone else. People simply didn't understand what we'd been through, and they didn't make allowances for anything. I just thought it was safer to say nothing. I felt so threatened. I am very angry about what happened to me. From the time I left the camp I was shunted about, and there was nothing solid, nothing firm in my life; and I am angry when I look back and consider how we were treated when we came to England. Of course I was too young to know properly all that was happening at the time, but we lived among Jewish people, indeed our landlady and her daughter were observant Jews, and they all knew that we had come out of the camps, and yet not one of them lifted a finger to help us, to offer a word of friendship. Not one! I could strangle the Jewish community in this country. I don't know why they reacted like that – but one reason may be that our surname gives away our Sephardic origins, and another is that we were not religious. They took the attitude that if you weren't Ashkenazim and you didn't go to the *shul*, you weren't one of them at all. I'm still bitter and angry about it. It wasn't that we needed financial help. My father started to earn money quite quickly because his trade was in demand, so materially our position became secure within a very short time; the problem was that my parents couldn't speak English and didn't know what kind of education would be best for me here after my wartime background. These people were in a position to advise my parents, and they didn't. Nobody lifted a finger! All I got was an invitation to dinner with the people across the street once. Their boy was about the same age as me, and he had a superb stamp collection, which he showed off to me. But apart from that, nothing. No rabbi even paid us a visit. Even today, although our neighbours see us socially – the wife was in hiding in a convent during the war – their Jewish friends won't, because my wife is a Roman Catholic. Quite recently, when one of my sons had just turned 12, he went to a party given by the daughter of a rabbi; the rabbi asked a friend of my son a few questions about his background, and when he found out that my son was only half-Jewish, he said to the friend, 'I don't want to see that boy in my house again.' That is one reason why I've never been to Israel. The dissension between the groups of Jews is pathetic, after all they've suffered. And the ones in England are disgusting! And yet they complain about being discriminated against, and persecuted.

When I was about 12 I was sent to a secondary modern school in Kensal Rise. I was ridiculed; I was made to stand in front of the class and repeat certain words that I had difficulty pronouncing, like 'desk' and 'chair', and the class laughed at me. At the same time I was used as a scapegoat for misdemeanours by the other children because I couldn't speak English well enough to defend myself, and the teachers didn't even think of taking that into account, or considering what I'd been through – though of course none of them knew, exactly. They caned me once for letting off caps on a wall: something many of the others had been doing, but I took the punishment because the others pointed at me. That caning was the first physical assault I'd ever experienced in my life. In all the camps, no one had offered me any physical violence. So it had to happen to me in England.

In July 1946 my parents moved and I went to a different school, but it wasn't any different from the first one. I was very self-conscious because I was made to feel like an outsider. I didn't like singing stupid songs like 'I love sixpence, pretty little sixpence', and I was painfully aware of my accent, and of the fact that I couldn't sing anyway. There was no joy in my heart. I skived off with some other boys. Some of the classrooms were in wooden huts, rather like barracks, and there was room to hide underneath them; we'd go there and have the odd cigarette. But of course instead of finding out why I was behaving like that, the PT master sent some of his favourites to haul us out, and we were taken to the headmaster and caned. There was no understanding. If you looked at my school reports, you'd see what I mean. I was just thrust into it and expected to perform like anyone else. It's not even as if they didn't know what I'd been through, by that time; they didn't even have that excuse any more. They called me 'Jew-boy' and 'filthy foreigner'. 'Where're your clogs?' they'd ask. Of course in the Forties no one had travelled like they have today, and foreigners really were foreign. I realize that now, and that those English kids had probably had a hard time too, with their fathers away in the war. I remember we did do a class project on the Nuremberg Trials, though I didn't relate to it much myself. What concerned me most was that I was unable to defend myself. I had no one to talk to, no uncles or aunts. They were all gone. My parents didn't stand up for me – but I was afraid to take them into my confidence in any case, for fear that I had actually done something wrong. They didn't take into account what I had and had not experienced – they still don't. All they wanted to do was forget that any of it ever happened. Even today, even while I've been going to Professor Bastiaans, whenever I try to talk to them about it, they'll change the subject: 'Oh, aren't the plants in the garden nice today – have you seen that one?' But it's not even as if they do it deliberately; the conversation just drifts away from what I want to talk about. Of course I understand that they had to rebuild their own lives after the war, spiritually and materially; but they had no time for me. Nowadays our relationship is distant. I do things for them now and then. I visit them regularly. It's superficial . . . I remember that in Amersfoort some people started to organize things for the children – to teach us Hebrew songs and dances. When my father saw me doing that he hauled me out: 'I don't want these Zionists ramming things down your throat.' I am bitter about that. He didn't want me converted to Zionism.

My parents couldn't adapt to life in England and they continued to treat me very much as a child would have been treated in the Netherlands. When everyone else was in long trousers I was still in shorts. I had less pocket-money than other boys. It embarrassed me to bring other children to my home; it was so foreign, so Dutch.

During my whole growing-up I had no one to talk to, no adult to explain things to me. I lived from day to day, and felt miserable without knowing why, and very lonely. But I used to enjoy swimming a lot, and there was a youth centre off the Finchley Road. I met my first wife there.

We got married in July 1955. Shortly after that, we went to live in Rhodesia, where I'd fixed myself up with a job. We stayed until March 1958 – but the marriage didn't go too well; I was trying to go into business for myself, and she was going through a difficult period; her mother had died of cancer when she was 13, and she hadn't got over it. We were away from England, her home, and we weren't rich enough to make it in white society, who were a bunch of crooks in Salisbury anyway. We were isolated, and I was too busy at work to put enough into the marriage. We returned to the UK, after which I went off to Switzerland and we became estranged. It died a natural death.

I'd gone to Switzerland with the idea of putting my languages to some use. I spoke Dutch and English, French and German, though I was hopelessly unqualified in terms of degrees and diplomas. But it was a nice trip and at least it taught me that I'd better do something about my neglected education. I came back to England at the end of 1958 and enlisted at Westminster College, a college of further education which at the time was full of people like me who for one reason or another had missed an important chunk of their education.

I studied there and collected some 'O' and 'A' levels. I did them very fast, in two and a half years, in fact. Then I went on to London University and read Dutch with French subs from 1961 to 1964. Meanwhile I'd met my present wife, whom I married in 1961. She's Italian. She was working as an au pair. We lived at my parents' house and my first son was born there in 1962. The atmosphere wasn't easy.

After university I joined IBM Sales and I've been with them ever since.[5] But lately I haven't been able to work properly. I'm there and I go through the motions, but the work no longer interests me. One of the great drawbacks of my life, which may also have some bearing on the breakdown of my first marriage, is that I've had no time in which to play, in which to relax. I've never felt relaxed. I've never felt easy even trying to relax. I cannot enjoy personal pleasure: maybe tinkering around with a car, but that's not really enjoyment. The only way I can escape is by doing things, all the time. But I think it also has to do with the fact that I wasn't allowed to enjoy my childhood. I can't even sit and listen to music – a short piece is fine; but I do find it extremely difficult to concentrate.

I think what triggered off my going to see Bastiaans was this: I have two sons, one born in 1962 and the second in 1965. When they were the same age as I was when I was in the camps, I suddenly saw what kind of childhood and youth I might have had. It made me very depressed. Neither of them have wanted me to tell them about my experiences: they have made that very plain to me, and that hurts, considering that they are intelligent individuals. And it's also sad because, apart from the war, we have an interesting family history which goes back to the end of the sixteenth century, when the family moved from Portugal to the Netherlands.

It was probably about 1972 that I went to see my doctor and told her about my problems for the first time. She said, 'Oh, I didn't realize,' and gave me some Valium. That was the answer for quite a few years: Valium will resolve everything. Then early in 1978 I just felt so exhausted, so depressed, so tense. I knew a little bit about the concentration camp syndrome, and I tried to find out if there was anybody in this country who might be able to help me, and so I contacted the Royal College of Psychiatrists. It was they who put me on to Professor Bastiaans. I went to see him in April, and we set up sessions for June and August. What I told him was nothing new. He hears this kind of thing all the time. Since then I have had 13 sessions. Each time you stay for a few days, in the lodge, which is just like a big house – a sort of private hotel. It doesn't feel like a hospital; it's very informal, no one wears a uniform, or even a white coat; and it's peaceful. Most of the people under treatment there are suffering from depression and grief. You can be by yourself, or talk to each other. I find some of the other patients have a rather morbid pleasure in talking about their LSD therapy – deliberately trying to scare you: actually it's they who are scared. I may be scared too – but I am aware of memories which are buried too deep within me to come out any other way – and I am aware that until they do they will fret me from within.

I approached the whole thing with trepidation, but I didn't hesitate. The second session was harder than the first, because I knew by then how horrible those sessions can be. But probably the worst thing was a kind of fear of making a fool of oneself; it reminded me of the anxiety I always had in the camps – of whether I would make it to the privies in time: it was a common occurrence that people didn't.

The individual sessions are intermingled in my mind. They make tapes of them and Bastiaans encourages patients to take a cassette home and listen to it to help self-therapy, to see what's come up.

Questions tend to follow the patient, not lead him, but to keep him to one line of thought as far as possible. I do listen to them, but I find them rather boring. I think that's a good sign. I get tired of the sound of my own voice. I'm aware of how depressed it sounds, how I seem to whine. I think that what is good is being close to a man like Bastiaans, who has spent so long with people like me that he really knows what we have suffered.

Sessions are nearly always done in the evening. The room is usually dimly lit – it's a large room, furnished like a sitting room. You loosen your tie, take your watch off, your shoes off, so that you're comfortable. And you are given the injection of LSD, and after a short while it begins to take effect, and then very gently Bastiaans will start to talk to you. 'What do you see over there? What colours do you see? What do they remind you of?' There were even long periods of absolute silence during the first sessions, which I think reflected my real inability as a little child to put into words what I had experienced. The periods of silence made me worry that I was wasting his time. Nothing was surfacing, and during a number of the sessions I felt nauseous, and I was in fact slightly sick; you're not allowed to eat before a session, so the vomit was just watery fluid. But Bastiaans told me not to worry about it – 'It's just the anger coming out, nothing to do with the LSD' – and I believe that, but I was embarrassed nevertheless by the mess I made.

Once I felt cold and I wanted to hide, and I wanted a blanket, and they gave me one and I wanted it right over me, over my head, as if I were in a tent or a bivouac. I wasn't reliving a real experience, though: my parents were too poor to pay someone to hide me. But I remember the cold in the camps; and it's cold in the therapy room in winter, because Bastiaans smokes heavily, and he has the windows open to prevent a fug. I remember that at one session I started to feel terribly cold, and he asked me, 'Was it as cold as that in the camp? Tell me a bit about it,' – all in a very pleasant, fatherly fashion.

I live in Wembley in north London, which is in the flight-path to Heathrow Airport sometimes, and I used to be very affected by the sound of aircraft. The train they took us on from Belsen was attacked by Allied planes, and at those times they let us get off and hide in the ditches by the side of the tracks. It was a frightening experience, and the association with planes later was obvious once it was identified; after that, I felt no more uneasiness at the sound of aeroplanes. Near Leyden,[6] at Utrecht, there's a military airfield, and during my second session with Bastiaans one of the Air Force planes came overhead, and that triggered exactly the emotions I'd felt in the war. But pleasant memories could be triggered, too. The lodge is in grounds full of trees, and there are many birds. During one session I suddenly became aware of their song, and that immediately made me remember going to the zoo with my grandfather when I was two or three.

There are other things that remind me. I don't feel happy in theatres or cinemas because I feel trapped in them; but I don't mind being mobile in a large crowd – in Selfridge's during the sales for example. It's being captive and inactive in a crowd that I can't stand. I won't do it, I can't! I can't concentrate and I can't sit still for long periods. And no one is ever going to dictate to me again what I must or must not do!

The Holocaust is becoming a part of history. There have been other terrible events in the world since, in Biafra, Kampuchea, Vietnam; and there will be others; but my hope would be that learning from such a catastrophe would encourage the world in future to put some meaning behind its words, when it talks of peace. As for Germans, I've nothing against them. My car is German, and I have German products in my house – even my parents have lifted their ban on German things. Speaking German doesn't bother me either. But I do remember one occasion when I was on my way back from a holiday. I was driving through Germany, and I decided to break the journey at a motel. I drove up the drive, and there, in the gardens, was a group of older Germans having a party. You know how loud they are. I just turned the car round and drove off. Older Germans – I could tread on them. They are all responsible and you cannot trust them. But young Germans are all right; it's not their fault, and I think that some of them feel a guilt which really they needn't feel.

It's very odd that although I've lived there so little of my life, the Netherlands is still the only place where I really feel at home. I still feel homesick for it, and when I hear Dutch radio come on in the car as I approach the frontier, I get tears in my eyes. As for staying in the UK, the way things are going here I do not think I would feel secure in my old age in this country, because no one knows or cares about my illness here. I think I might go back to Holland when I retire. Nobody can call me a stranger or an outsider there: my family lived there for 500 years.

LSD-assisted psychotherapy is not common, and not viewed with enthusiasm by all psychiatrists and psychotherapists. The arguments in its favour are that it can speed up therapy and also break down barriers more effectively, enabling patients to express themselves about fears for which they have not been able to find the words before. LSD has been looked at askance because of the bad reputation it acquired when used as a hallucinogenic drug outside a medical context in the Sixties, which in turn devalued it as a medicine. In therapy, dosage is very strictly controlled. Sessions are very long, about five hours, though after 90 minutes of therapy, doses of Librium will be administered to abreact the patient. The whole session is followed by one or two days of rest. The experience can be exhausting, both for the patient and for observers.

SEPTEMBER, LEYDEN

This particular LSD-assisted therapy session was to be the 14th in a course which had covered a period of eight years. The first 12 sessions had been completed by 1982, but a regression made another necessary in 1985. Bastiaans is the only man in the Netherlands currently licensed to practise this kind of therapy; he is aware of hostility to the treatment within the Dutch Health Authority, which believes it to be too experimental.

The session started in the middle of the afternoon on a Saturday in late September. The light was just beginning to fade, staining the leaves of the beech trees in the grounds of the Institute golden. The patient had already arrived and was walking in the grounds alone – he is a small man and the size of the trees emphasized this, and his isolation.

In his office Bastiaans runs through a little of the case history.[7] The patient's trouble stems very much from his need for a father figure; his disillusionment with the world is that of a little-boy-lost. Two other psychiatrists are to be present at the session, and a nurse. I am the other observer. Bastiaans explains that at some sessions he uses noises on tape (such as the sound of leaves in the wind) and smells to evince certain reactions, though this will probably not be the case today.

The room in which the session is to take place is nearby. It is very large. It might be the sparsely furnished sitting room of a small hotel, apart from the large wash-basin against one wall and the low hospital bed near the windows. The patient, who has been given a dose of 200 milligrammes of LSD-25 by injection (the low dosage leaves the subject liberated, but still in intellectual control), sits in a small armchair and we join him, sitting on low chairs in a rough circle. Although Bastiaans presides, the rest of us may later ask questions at his invitation, and talk to the patient. In the course of the session, the patient will ask for his hand to be held, and each person (myself excepted) takes turns to do this. Bastiaans mentions that although this demonstrates a basic need, once or twice in earlier sessions the patient has taken a participant's hand and experienced a violently antipathetic reaction.

The curtains are drawn, the door closed. The patient looks terribly strained, and has a hunted expression. Bastiaans puts a reassuring hand on his and asks him what is the matter. At first he expresses trepidation that he will make a fool of himself under the inhibition-breaking influence of the drug, which is a common sensation. Then he speaks more personally.

'I feel the world is against me. And I have this incredible anger in me. I don't know what to do with it. But look, I'm not the only one. Lots of people like me started to crack up in the Seventies. You can only keep it up for so long. Then you can't contain the anger and the grief any more.'

He doesn't stay on that subject, but turns, prompted gently, to times when he felt happy – to very early childhood. Stamp collections . . . visits to the zoo with his grandfather. He seems to have been spoiled by this grandfather, though the grandmother is remembered as strict and old-fashioned. 'But my grandfather was nice to me. We went to the museums together, and the Tropical Institute. I liked the parrots in the zoo.' We are still in the introductory phase of the session, and the conversation is not yet focused. Life has been manageable but increasingly difficult. The last two years have been the worst, with an increasing feeling of isolation worsened by his sons both having reached an age to leave home. He recounts a conversation he had with me the previous night at the hotel (I arrived to find him waiting for me) about his anger at the British government for not offering more care for people like him. Then:

'I feel a terrible tension going down my arms.'

'Do you see any colours?'

'I thought I saw a little orange.'[8] He goes to lie down on the bed. 'Hold my hand.'

'When you close your eyes, what do you see?'

'Different coloured balloons. They may be from inside my stomach.'

There is no dramatic transition, but the patient is talking quite freely now; there is none of the former inhibition. His voice is firmer too – no longer whining or complaining, its tone hits a plateau of the bleakest isolation. And isolation is his theme: neither at home, at work, nor in society generally does he find the sympathy he desires: 'I've had to do everything in my life alone. There were some colleagues at IBM who were friends, who understood; but they've gone now. Now there's only Alan . . . he's got a heart of gold. He's been very patient with me; but I don't see him so much, now that he's moved.[9] If only there was somebody I could talk to regularly, then I wouldn't have to keep coming to Holland all the time . . . I've had no help at all . . . except occasionally a little bit from people like you . . . Nobody ever told me anything, or did anything for me.'

Bastiaans takes him back to his childhood in Amsterdam before 1941. A picture emerges of a street urchin who was left to his own devices, whose parents were too preoccupied to bother with him. Traces of a Dutch childhood song are remembered and sung. Neither Bastiaans nor the patient can remember the words — 'That song always comes into my mind when I know I'm coming to Holland.' Bastiaans encourages him, and mentions a song about Santa Claus, which the patient sings.[10] Once the song is over, the spectre returns.

'I antagonize people because of my suffering. I don't look nice. My facial muscles are taut . . . I don't smile easily, and people mistake my expression for an angry one; but it's that I am in pain all the time.'

'What can we do for you, then?'

'You are doing all you can. Hold my hand.'

'Why do you want your hand held all the time?'

'It's warm.'

If Bastiaans forgets this contact for a moment, the patient becomes querulous, fretful to have the hand back; and he complains of cold. The response is the same if Bastiaans, in explaining what is going on to the rest of us, neglects him for too long.

'What are you thinking?'

'That I seem less and less able to communicate with people. I like language, i am sensitive to it, and yet it's becoming a barrier. I used to get so much pleasure from trying to speak other languages, but now even when I go to France I can't make the effort to speak French. I force people to speak English. It's almost as if I were saying to the world, "I'm tired. I've struggled enough to communicate with you; now you make the effort to communicate with me." . . . My parents were too demanding. My father could only have any regard for me in relation to what I'd achieved. And in the camp, I'd be left all to myself, dirty and cold and lonely, and itching with fleas and lice running all over me.'

Speaking of Belsen, he reverts to Dutch. The camp, too, is associated with the all-pervading loneliness of his life, and now he sees the different languages spoken by the various children there as barriers. He remembers being put into bed with a little girl, a fellow prisoner in the KZ, for warmth. He wanted to talk to her but he couldn't because she wasn't Dutch. Even then he felt his isolation, and says that the German Jewish children excluded him from their company, which he felt keenly. Bastiaans asks the nurse to take over holding the patient's hand.

'How does that feel?'

'Friendly.'

The search for a bond is continued as he describes how bitterly rejected he felt when Hannah Lévy-Hass had been unable to see him. 'She is a Yugoslavian who looked after the children in Bergen-Belsen. I didn't know her there personally, but I read her book later, and I was so deeply moved by it that I wrote to her through her publishers. She replied. But I wanted to say thank you to her on behalf of all the children in the camp . . .' And he starts to cry. 'Even though I didn't meet her I know she was an unselfish woman, a true heroine, helping those little children, abandoned to all the muck, all the filth.' He is not able to accept that she did not see him simply because it was not possible, not because she didn't want to. Reflecting again on his own childhood, the bitter self-pity intensifies, and images of deprivation then, in the time before the camps, fuses with his sense of being emotionally 'winged'[11] as a survivor. 'I had no ball to play with. I never went swimming in the sea. And I'm not asking that other people should have suffered as we did; but why do they have to put more obstacles in our way?' He is very upset, and is wailing. 'Why do we have to be witnesses, why do we have to keep reminding people, why do we need to? Why do we have to keep screaming it out all the time? Why can't we be left in peace?'

'You expect rejection. Isolation is a defence for you.'

'I don't know what to cry out. I just want to be accepted . . . When I walk around I feel physical pain in my shoulders. And it shows in my face, and people turn from me. You see, I've got no past to share with anybody. If you and I had played together as children we could reminisce about it now; but I've got no one I can do that with. I've got no contact with anybody.'

His longing to be accepted is constantly interrupted by his railing against the unkindness of fate. All the time the nurse is holding his hand. He speaks to her in Dutch, he tells her she is holding his hand as if it were an instrument – she feels like a technician. At the same time he is afraid of hurting her by squeezing her hand too tightly. He repeats the story of his first caning, and how he was used as a scapegoat at school. The nurse relinquishes his hand to Chaim, one of the other psychiatrists, a Syrian Jew. He tries to approach his sense of loneliness from another direction. His need for affection was neglected by his parents, and his father suffered in the same way at the hands of his own parents. Is it the frustration of his own 'rejected' affection that continues to plague him? He should be angry with his parents, but the anger is redirected against the world, which also becomes harsh and rejecting. For he is too good a son to be angry with his parents. 'I'm angry but where do I get the opportunity to express it? Where do I direct it?'

'Is there anybody you hate?'

'I hate hypocrites.'

'Well, what would you say to them?'

The patient hesitates, then speaks as if he's being greatly daring: 'Go and stuff yourselves.'

'Say it again.'

'GO AND STUFF yourselves!' Which starts as a shout, and ends on a down beat, apologetically, with an awkward half-laugh. The anger continues against the remembered torturers, the schoolteachers of his childhood in London after the war: 'I can express my feelings, my experiences, to you in words now; but I was a child then – I couldn't! Now I've got to try to find the words . . . I need to hold hands, to feel I'm not alone in the world, that there's someone standing by me. If I could get hold of that rotten old headmaster, I would drag him before the courts! It was scandalous what he did! I'd like to knock their heads together! Fancy caning a child who hadn't been out of the camps 12 months! I feel like spitting on those people, trampling them in the gutter! Little sadists, taking advantage of poor little children!'

Bastiaans intervenes and soothes him. 'What do you see?'

'I see dancing lines and lights that are pleasant shapes, cushions and balloons.'

'Do you hurt?'

'I feel tense, in my arms and shoulders.'

The anger is not far away, and soon surfaces with even more vigour. Its object now is the English Jewish community. The complaints are the same as he made against it to me in London, but now he screams with rage, choking on his fury. 'They stink! They are so foul! I detest them as much as I detest the Germans who put us through the Holocaust! Fancy not helping people who went through that!' He collapses into a chaotic fury in which all the spectres of his past jumble together. Objects of rage range from the coolness of the British in general, to the Spanish persecution of the Jews in the fifteenth century. Bastiaans interjects, as the patient subsides, to say that it would have been better if his parents had explained things to him, taken him into their confidence. Bastiaans tries to reassure him, speaking in Dutch, telling him that he's done well in life.

'I know I've done well.'

'But why won't you let me tell you, too?'

'I did what I was capable of doing.' Aggressively.

The time has come for the first dose of Librium to be administered. Four tablets are given at each dose, and doses are at 20-minute intervals. As the patient returns to normal, which takes about an hour, he is kept talking. Nobody leaves. The patient feels warmer, smiles. The face is more relaxed but the eyes are still watchful, and he is still jumpy. One is aware that some kind of exorcism has taken place, but wonders if in this case there will ever be a complete cure, but only a temporary relief due to the ventilation of the feelings.

But he says, 'This has been the most successful session of all. It's been a hard journey but –'

'– Doors are opening?'

Certainly for the rest of us there is a sense of human intimacy, of euphoria even, for we have all been mildly affected by the drug. The patient is very thirsty, and begins to get sleepy.

Before sleeping, the patient mentioned again what he said to me in London some months earlier, that when the windows of the room were opened, the sounds and smells of the outside world were let in, and became woven into the mind under therapy, with associations with the patient's past. It has been mentioned already that noises and smells are used deliberately to try to trigger responses in patients, and some have proved to be quite consistent. The smell of urine, for example, brings an association with the camps into the minds of most survivors. The range of stimuli which can be supplied in this context is wide. Photographs and even simple plain colours have been used to effect, as well as music. Bastiaans remembered that in a previous session the present patient had responded with screams of rage to hearing Vera Lynn singing 'Land of Hope and Glory'. Bastiaans had to remind him gently that soldiers needed their morale boosting, too; and that there was nothing wrong with the song, even if he found its imagery offensive.

All possible channels are used to try to open doors, and the effect in one session can be dramatic because each one, from the emotional point of view, is ten times as strong as a conventional therapy consultation. The important thing is to get patients to ventilate their feelings emotionally. Severely traumatized people need to talk and talk. Their families might listen sympathetically for a week or a month, but then they will have had enough. The survivor, however, has not had enough: a sympathetic ear must be lent for years in most cases, or the feeling of isolation gets the upper hand and the subject cannot progress. The healing process is further inhibited, as has already been indicated, by any disruption of the normal mourning process. One can point to the expression of formalized grief in some tribes and societies as a good way of externalizing grief and ridding oneself of it – in a way recognized and sympathized with by all other members of that particular group. But when the mourning process is suppressed, no healing can take place. Another factor is the inability to put into words the emotions which are felt after the experience, or to find words adequate to describe the KZ experience itself. In ordinary life, it is sometimes hard to find words to describe the emotions felt on hearing a beautiful piece of music, or after attending a particularly moving play or film. That difficulty stretched to the limit is one which confronts many survivors and similarly traumatized people, and again impedes the healing process. This inability to express feelings is known as alexythymia. In a paper presented at Heidelberg in 1976,[12] Bastiaans stated: 'Sometimes, even only a quarter of an hour after the beginning of an LSD session, a so-called alexythymic patient may change into a personality who is well able to verbalize strong repressed emotions.' If one hears the expression from survivors that 'I cannot tell you what I went through because you were not there yourself', however, it seems to me that there is a possibility that they will be very pleased to try if they are assured that yours is a genuinely sympathetic ear. By saying that, I do not mean to oversimplify the complex problem confronting those who treat people in need of psychiatric help: for many KZ-survivors, it is only with such help that they will ever be able to express themselves.

In the process of trying to come to terms, or of failing to come to terms, the survivor's family can suffer considerably. Bastiaans says that he feels sorry for the family of the present patient, because they can neither understand nor reach him. He adds that in this case the process of healing could have been greatly facilitated if the patient had still lived in the Netherlands, or had been able to have sessions every three weeks or so;[13] then there might be a real chance of curing him, instead of just making things better for a while. However, as long as the profession in general remains sceptical about the value of this kind of therapy, it will in any case be available to only a very few. Dutch government reparation payments have made it possible for the patient described here to continue his course of treatment which, it goes without saying, is expensive. There is also the question of a patient's own reaction to the therapy. Discovery of a way towards a cure can lead to the expression of great anger. The anger is born of a feeling of having lowered one's guard too much to a stranger. In one case Bastiaans was able to help a British former officer who had been a prisoner-of-war of the Japanese and who had kept the emotions he had felt at the time suppressed for 30 years. When Bastiaans brought them out, the former soldier was furious because he felt that he'd behaved in a 'weak' manner by admitting his feelings.

Bastiaans himself has been working for 40 years, and in the course of his use of LSD-assisted therapy he has treated 300 patients. He was a student at the University of Amsterdam, but was thrown out after the invasion of the Netherlands, when he became involved with the resistance. He might have been deported to the camps himself, but during treatment for pneumonia he was given a wrong injection, which temporarily paralysed him, and has left him permanently lame in the right leg. 'I wasn't deported, because nobody expected me to give any trouble as a semi-invalid.' Many of his friends died in the war, however, and the experience of that loss stimulated him to help those who survived. The lameness was also to contribute to his choice of career, since he had been studying surgery, but had to give it up since he could no longer stand for prolonged periods. He made psychosomatic medicine his special area of research. In 1954, aged 37, he was appointed Director of the National Psychoanalytical Institute in Amsterdam.

Research into traumatic situations was stimulated in the Netherlands by a rash of hostage-taking and terrorist incidents that occurred in the Seventies. It is difficult to make comparisons between the victims of these incidents and KZ-survivors, not least because the longest period of captivity for any Dutch victim was three weeks. However, Bastiaans was an adviser to the United States on the question of the Iranian hostages; they had been held captive for a considerable length of time, and received comparatively little help after they had returned home. In a follow-up study conducted nine months after their release, Bastiaans found that many of the former hostages were ill, suffering from a sense of insecurity, anxiety and depression. 'One man was driving his wife crazy because he had started compulsively to buy trousers; the reason being that he had had only one pair for the entire period of his captivity.'

Despite the facilities available, it has been Bastiaans' experience that survivors are reluctant to seek psychiatric help for fear of being stigmatized as 'mental'. Patients, too, seldom come to him via recommendation by their own doctors, but through friends of family members who are aware of his work. 'And I have friends and colleagues abroad who make recommendations to patients who have already come to them as specialists. Usually they are used to general psychiatric procedure because they come to me after the failure of conventional therapy. But of course we explain to them what will happen. It can be more dramatic than what you have seen. Recently we had here a Portuguese who had been active in politics some time ago, and had been a political prisoner for a year, during which he was tortured by daily electric shocks on the genitals. During his sessions here he would jump as if he were reliving that treatment. But through reliving it and then immediately talking about it, he was able to come to terms with it . . . You don't have psychodrama in a conventional session, because the patient is conscious . . . but I believe that, as you saw a little bit yourself, the encouragement to shout, to cry out, has therapeutic value. All the time one is encouraging the patient towards solving for himself, or identifying for himself, the source of his woe, bringing it out, and dealing with it.'[14] The psychodrama can be very full indeed, involving movement, the use of 'props', and the participation of all those involved in the session.

Reactions to the proposal of such therapy vary. At first some people are afraid of losing full consciousness, but after one or two sessions they become used to it, and know it doesn't harm them. It is of paramount importance for a trusting relationship to be built up between therapist and patient before treatment begins; though the first session is the most difficult for the majority of patients, since they feel the same sort of nervousness they might feel before an actual operation. Once it is passed successfully, trust is established. The dosage and the entire session are both minutely monitored. 'I have conducted over 4,000 sessions without any bad consequences . . . We give them cassettes of the sessions not only so that they can use them to help themselves, but also so that they indeed believe all that they have said during the therapy.' Bastiaans is annoyed that the bad reputation LSD acquired in the Sixties still affects official thinking on its use in medicine, particularly as so many anti-depressant drugs have come on to the market since, and are prescribed by general practitioners who find it easier to do this than to refer their patients for psychiatric treatment which is designed to rid them of any need for such drugs. Another stumbling block has been that so many people who could have benefited from treatment have been reluctant to make too many demands on their overworked family doctors. It is a feature of a generation brought up to believe that it is 'unmanly' to complain about, or try to improve, whatever ills befall one. The attitude is one of 'we will not capitulate', and surrendering yourself to a doctor comes under the heading of capitulation.

'I started using this form of therapy in 1961. Some colleagues had already experimented with it, since we were not entirely satisfied with narcoanalysis.[15] The problem we had to tackle was that of mental rigidity, which has to be overcome if the patient is going to make progress.' Quite often only six or seven sessions, interspersed with conventional therapy, are enough to set the patient well on the road to mental recovery; and the progression is measurable. More and more emerges with each session, and, as it does, so do the patient's sleep-patterns improve, and they are better able to express themselves under normal conditions. 'They suddenly have the feeling, we can cope with the situation much better.'[16] The treatment is considerably faster than conventional treatment, too: 'The average number of hours spent in sessions and interviews by the therapist is 50, far lower than the number needed for regular psychoanalytic treatment [in Holland usually 600–800 hours].'[17]

Patients go over their tapes with a therapist before they return home, but the more intelligent patients are very soon able to work through them without assistance. Questions arising from them, and goals reached, are objects for discussion at the next session. Patients are also able to help one another, and it is possible to investigate a common problem within a group. 'If you take a number of patients suffering from hypertension, you are confronted by the fact that they have a character profile in common, and we call them "tigers in cages". They want to spring on their prey but they can't. Usually it occurs in long-term depressed patients, well adapted on the surface but embittered beneath; and they want to kill their enemies but they don't do it. Now, a tiger is hypertense before his attack; but the action of springing releases the tension. These people, because they cannot spring, remain hypertense: on the point of doing so.' Elements of this type are visible in the survivor whose therapy has been discussed. It was interesting that even in the midst of the most unbounded fury, he never used obscene epithets in connection with the objects of his anger: they were 'rotten' at worst, and the most unpleasant thing he wants to say to any group of enemies is 'go and stuff yourselves'; and even this mild curse causes him some embarrassment. 'In the midst of it all he still has to remain a well-adapted, polite boy . . . Patients of his type want peace, not conflict, and they repress their traumatic experiences to keep life quiet, and knuckle under to more dominant personalities. He is a rather rigid man, with regard to the intensity of resistances and character traits, and I cannot say that this 14th session will be sufficient to bring him to terms with this world.'[18]

II

Before moving on, an attempt must be made to define the concentration camp, or KZ, syndrome.[19] Eitinger and Askevold write that 'There is no full agreement as to the exact extent of this syndrome. Most authors accept chronic fatigue and disorders of memory as being the most influential signs. Herman and Thygesen (1954) were the first to point out the consistency of these symptoms. They say: "The symptoms' almost photographic similarity from patient to patient compels us to suppose a pathological reaction based on one or the same causes. The consistency and regularity of the constellations of the symptoms justify the name of syndrome."'[20] Eitinger and Askevold give the following symptomatology:

1: failing memory and difficulty in concentration
2: nervousness, irritability, restlessness
3: fatigue
4: sleep disturbances
5: headaches
6: emotional instability
7: dysphoric moodiness
8: vertigo
9: loss of initiative
10: vegetative lability
11: feelings of insufficiency

In connection with this, a study[21] of the frequency of nervous symptoms in a group of repatriated members of the Danish resistance movement conducted shortly after the war produced the following results: the bracketed figures represent the percentage of the total number of men examined (the number of women involved was so small that the construction of a representative group was not possible):

restlessness	(63%)
excessive fatigue	(58%)
increased smoking	(58%)
irritability	(47%)
emotional instability	(46%)
headache	(40%)
insomnia	(40%)
increased sleep requirement	(40%)
defective memory	(39%)
depression	(36%)
sweating and hot flushes	(27%)
intermittent diarrhoea	(25%)
palpitations	(21%)
increased consumption of alcoholic drinks	(20%)
sexual difficulties	(19%)
palpitations and dyspnoea	(17%)
dyspepsia	(11%)

These are included here as a guide only, since they were symptoms that manifested themselves almost immediately. In some individual cases, such symptoms disappeared with time; in others, they persisted. In further cases, symptoms of any kind did not appear until long after the events which triggered them. However, the most common and persistent symptoms seem to be restlessness, nervousness (especially in reaction to unexpected noises or sudden movements), proneness to hot flushes and outbreaks of excessive sweating, an inability to concentrate, tiring, headache, and sleeplessness. Feelings of guilt at having survived, and depression, are also strongly present. A reduced life-expectancy and an older physical appearance than the actual age of the survivor would suggest are also factors. The latter case I have not found to be true, rather the opposite in many cases, but this will be returned to later.[22] To sum up, the syndrome manifests itself as 'a state of chronic, and often disabling, bodily and mental weakness which is manifest in the same way in those who have never completely recovered from their time in the KZ . . . The symptomatology of the KZ-syndrome is non-specific, and it is naturally non-static. The syndrome was seen in its "purest" form 5–10 years after liberation.'[23]

The bulk of what follows stems from a discussion I had with Leo Eitinger in Oslo. Born in Czechoslovakia in 1914, Professor Eitinger is one of the most eminent psychiatrists involved in work with concentration camp survivors. Already working as a young doctor in his homeland, and having just started to work in the field of psychiatry, he went to Norway as a refugee when the Germans entered the Sudetenland, and continued to practise as a doctor there. When the Germans invaded Norway, he was one of the 762 Jews of Norway's community of 1,000 to be arrested and deported.[24] He was in Auschwitz and, later, in Buchenwald, the camp from which he was liberated. He returned to Norway, one of the twelve survivors of the original 762, and worked as a psychiatrist with the Norwegian armed forces. In 1957, he became a founder-member of a 'medical-psychiatric-psychological team of university teachers, whose task it was to investigate ex-prisoners [of the concentration camps] thoroughly'.[25] How this team came to be founded he describes thus:

On 8 May 1945 . . . the concentration camps were opened. Some of the inmates were not able to resume their activities. However, most of them recovered quickly, inspired by an enthusiasm due to a feeling of having escaped the realm of the dead. This – perhaps unrealistic – optimism which characterized the former prisoners was also present among the doctors whose purpose was to evaluate their health and working capacity. By the end of 1946 only a few registered war casualties needed a disability pension. This idyllic state did not last. More and more reports appeared describing symptoms and signs of a rather diffuse character among previous concentration camp prisoners. Both presumptive experts and, not least, the administrative personnel of war indemnity offices took a sceptical attitude to these somewhat vague complaints. The opinion prevailed that since the ex-prisoners had recovered and had been at work without symptoms for months or years, the later appearance of an illness could not be referred to events during the war. The war veterans held another view . . . Without precise knowledge of the reactive patterns and possible symptoms and signs of war damage, they realized that a thorough investigation was essential for an objective and fair judgment. They also had an open mind over the possibility that the system of laws and regulations was defective and that the knowledge among doctors might also be inadequate. The meeting resulted in the establishment of the 'Board of Norwegian Doctors of 1957'.[26]

The board was able to conduct extremely detailed enquiries at every level into the mental and physical disabilities brought about by the effect of the concentration camp experience.

One of the aspects of the concentration camp experience that has been mentioned is that in many cases it was several years before it manifested itself. It is also true in many cases that only in recent years have survivors decided to 'break the silence' – to talk about what they went through. Why does this latency period exist? Eitinger's hypothesis, based on his own experience with patients, is as follows: to start with, there is one general reason, and it is especially noticeable among the Norwegian former KZ-inmates whom he examined. They were so happy, even euphoric, at having escaped from the realm of death that everything else – and any bad side-effects – just didn't present themselves. But in addition to this there were several psychologically more complicated reasons. The experiences they had been through were of such character that it was simply impossible for a normal person to accept them. What one had to do therefore was negate them, and give oneself the impression that they were not true. This kind of blocking-off of the experience is a common reaction, especially in connection with intimates who have not shared the experience: it is a form of self-protection, because normally one would expect an intimate to sympathize, if not empathize with you. However, the KZ experience was simply beyond the imagination, let alone the experience, of others. There could be no common ground for sympathy to be born. By saying nothing, the former inmate avoided the possibility of being disappointed in his search for sympathy. With time it has become possible to view the experience with some detachment, and also public awareness of it and sympathy towards those who went through it have both increased with knowledge. The atmosphere is now a much more congenial one for the survivor to unburden himself.

Immediately after the war, however, people frequently did not have the time or the inclination to reflect on their experiences in the camps. They were too busy rebuilding their lives, and this was especially noticeable in Israel. People going there to live in 1948 after Independence were told: you are coming here to build a new country, and you must think of that, not of the past; your past is of no interest to us. We all have to start a new life here. Thus it was to all intents and purposes impossible to talk about the KZ in Israel. The first time the subject was discussed openly in Israel was at the time of the Eichmann trial.

As for the survivors themselves, they entered into the spirit of that 'new start' attitude. Many of them wanted to forget. But it isn't easy to forget. There was a tendency to deny that what happened in the KZ was of really cosmic importance, both while it was going on and afterwards; but denial cannot keep out the truth for ever. Sooner or later the truth has to be faced. Denial has many facets. In some people it may have served the purpose of blocking out feelings of guilt and shame; but for most people, they had simply seen and experienced things which they would prefer to forget. In fact, the majority behaved decently. If they were forced to do something in conflict with their basic values, this would have been as the result of being in an extreme situation.

The important thing is that the experience is so overwhelming. 'Personally, when I was in Auschwitz, I met all sorts of young people, not only Jews, and as a psychiatrist I was able to ask myself how they would be affected by this milieu. There was the whole question of the effect of the milieu on the individual, in a long-lasting extreme situation such as that. What would become of these people later in life, after it was all over? But I was not able to take up these questions immediately after the war in my scientific work ... After the war I assumed military duties in that I was psychiatric consultant in the Norwegian armed forces. There I was able to investigate how military life influenced the psychological drive of young Norwegian men ... And then I investigated the refugees who came to Norway. And many of them were KZ survivors, and so it was that I came to my life's work, concerning KZ survivors in the years following their liberation.'[27]

I wondered if it had helped him in the camps to be able to observe the milieu as a scientist.

Two things helped me. One was that I knew German, and the other was that I had a certain understanding of the psyche of the SS-man. I don't want to exaggerate, but to a certain degree I knew how to handle them. I knew how they would react, so I was able to man-oeuvre to a certain degree. Of course it was limited, but it was a practical application of my training. Survival is a job of work: to an extent the practical application of your own knowledge and instincts, whatever they are. I don't think that the SS were fully aware of what they were doing, in the sense that it was worked out intellectually; they just understood that when you took everything away from a person you could erode his personality. When you take away a person's ability to defend himself, you take his very name away.

Allied to the question of communication must be the question of survivor-guilt. I was struck that not all those survivors I met felt it, but those who did so felt it keenly, and could not get over it, or even imagine that there were survivors who did not feel it. The great majority of those who did were Jewish survivors who had lost most or all of their close family. Eitinger points out that there are two kinds of guilt feeling: one that is based on not having lived up to one's own social norms; and one which is the general feeling of guilt which all survivors of all catastrophes have: 'if you're the only survivor of a car crash, you will think, "Why me and not the others?" Norway is the extreme example from the KZ – so very few of us returned to the Jewish community. Naturally we thought, why us? What did we do?' He adds that in the first writings on the subject after the war guilt feelings were seen as of central importance; but it could be that the psychiatrists said to themselves, 'There must be guilt feelings,' and then set out to prove that there were, by hook or by crook. He himself suggested that they were projecting their own guilt feelings for not having done anything on behalf of the survivors, for which he was much maligned.

In terms of bystander-guilt, and the indifference of some of those receiving survivors, especially within such groups as the local Jewish communities whose attitude has given rise to such anger among many of the survivors I met, there are two basic arguments. One could say that such people didn't want to hear about the camps for the same reasons that one is reluctant to hear of the brutal misfortunes (such as robbery with violence, or rape) that happen to a loved one, because there's nothing you can do about it, and you become angry, perhaps even disliking the loved person because of what they have 'allowed' to happen to them. In the case of the attitude to KZ survivors, however, there is a more convincing argument, which suggests that they make one feel guilty because deep inside one feels that one might have been able to do something at the time to alleviate or even terminate their sufferings, and now one blames oneself for that neglect.

The degree of weight-loss experienced in the camps played a central role in the aetiological determinations that followed after the war. This was because weight-loss is one of the contributory factors to the KZ syndrome which can be measured. If, as a prisoner in the camps, you managed to get a job as a *Revier* assistant, or if you were very fortunate and had a job as a clerk, your need for food was less than it would be if you had to work at heavy outdoor labour, in a ditch, say, so your loss of weight was not so great, since everybody was given the same basic food. By the same token, the fitter, tougher prisoners condemned to heavy labour were better off than the weaker ones, since the same amount of work was expected of each prisoner irrespective of sex, age or strength. For those prisoners with higher-status jobs, there were not only greater and better opportunities for 'organizing', they were also treated in a different way, more nearly as a human being, by the camp staff. They were also less likely to come in for extreme physical punishment. All these effects are interrelated. The better-off prisoners had more self-respect, and one positive thing built on another. But if on the other hand you lost 50 per cent of your body-weight through too little food or ill-treatment, that was an indication that your status was very bad. There is an upward spiral in one case, and a downward spiral in the other. The worst affected afterwards, and those who have had the hardest struggle to come back, are those who suffered most – those who reached Mussulman status. 'There is an obvious analogy in our researches here at the Institute of Disaster Psychiatry: if there's an explosion in a factory, those nearest are more traumatized that those 50 metres away, who are more traumatized than those at the factory gates, waiting to come on shift; but in the KZ it isn't even a question of clinical shock, it's a question of coming back from the dead, and of coming back from a sustained period in hell.' Eitinger has referred to 'winged' individuals in Israel.[28] These people are not able to enjoy life adequately. In some cases they merely perform the functions required of them by life, existing rather than living. The joy of life, the vital spark, is gone. They feel they are not the same as they were before the war. This is true of nearly all KZ survivors who endured extreme suffering; but in the case of 'winged' individuals, the post-war person is unable to take up the threads of life.

Eitinger also draws a very significant distinction between Jewish and non-Jewish survivors. The point is, broadly speaking, that only psychiatrists were able to find any 'bad results' in Jewish survivors. 'The reason for this, of course, is not that the Jewish survivors had fewer somatic after-effects than, or were not as maltreated as, for instance, the Dutch or Norwegian ones. On the contrary. The reason is that the Jewish prisoners had only an infinitesimally small chance of survival, and thus of being considered eligible for compensation today. They are an extremely select group of people and cannot be considered representative of the Jewish concentration camp prisoners in the same way as, for example, the Dutch or Norwegian (political and resistance) survivors can be considered representative of their groups. Any discussions that do not take these factors into consideration must necessarily come to incorrect conclusions.'[29]

To bear this out, it is worth citing an example from another of Eitinger's papers,[30] where he is discussing the case of a Norwegian (Gentile) schizophrenic, born in 1915, who 'was arrested *because* of his psychosis. As a long-term in-patient he was on brief leave. He was walking in the street, hallucinating, talking loudly to himself, when a German soldier conceived this as directed against him. The patient was arrested and sent to the Sachsenhausen camp, but there it was discovered that he was severely psychotic and he was sent back after a relatively short period of time . . .' Another similarly mentally ill man was 'taken care of by fellow prisoners, kept in the sick bay [again of Sachsenhausen] and thus survived'. Several others in a similar condition managed to survive under similar circumstances. Eitinger comments, 'It is noteworthy that these marginal patients managed to survive in the camp. This can be explained by the Germans' lenient attitude to prisoners with "German backgrounds" and by the Norwegian fellow prisoners' effective mutual self-help during imprisonment.' This kind of behaviour on the part of the Germans may be compared with the nightmarish description of the reception of a transport of Jewish lunatics at Auschwitz which is given by Rudolf Vrba.[31]

While the Scandinavian Gentile inmates of the camps were treated better on account of their common Nordic heritage with the Germans, it would be wrong to give the impression that they were not scarred by the KZ experience. By the time Leo Eitinger arrived at Buchenwald, the red triangles had taken over prisoner control of the camp from the greens, and conditions there had become relatively much better than they had been before. However, the 'reds' also tended to look after their own at the expense of other groups, and this was especially true of the Communists. No 'red' was normally ever as cruel as a 'green', but when it was a question of making up transports which were bound for *Aussenkommandos* (work details on sites away from the main camp) which were known to be bad ones, they would make sure that their friends were removed from the list and replaced by 'neutrals'. Professor Eitinger remembers that one Norwegian friend of his, also a former inmate of the KZ, subsequently suffered deep depressions as a result of the guilt feelings he had about doing precisely that: sending others on transports and thereby saving friends.

In the camp itself there was no time for reflection, or philosophy:

Not in the sense that you would think about the relative morality of someone being sent on transport instead of you; and it was rarely that one had time for reflection on the general situation. Cases of altruism, such as that of Father Kolbe,[32] were very rare indeed. There were some people who voluntarily joined the old people and the women with children on arrival at Auschwitz – but of course they didn't know at that time that they were destined immediately for the gas chambers. After that, it was a question of chance at a selection – right or left – you never knew if you were making the right decision. When you had the choice. But it remains true that those people who survived by chance had a much more neurotic aftermath than those who thought they had done so because they had worked for survival.

How much is the personality affected? The personality you are born with can help you through but only to a certain degree, because the personality can be permanently changed by long-lasting traumatization, or deep-going trauma.

I had a [Jewish] patient who is now dead who was at Kiev at the time of Babi Yar. She was 16, blonde, and had only Ukrainian [Gentile] friends. She spoke fluent Ukrainian.[33] Now, when they came to round up the Jews for the slaughter she was alone at home with her mother, since her father happened to be away. Her mother, thinking that they were going to be taken to a camp, collected her jewellery, which she had hidden in the house. And her mother said to one of the Ukrainian guards, 'Look, you shouldn't arrest this girl. She isn't family, she isn't even Jewish. She was just visiting.' And she didn't look Jewish, the daughter. So the guard asked her to recite the Lord's Prayer, which she was able to do; and he accepted the jewels which the mother offered him, and then told the girl to run, to disappear; not to look back. And she did. And she spent the war running, hiding, arrested for not having papers once or twice but never being questioned about whether she was Ukrainian or a Jew. Later she worked for a German family as a maid, and they were kind to her. But after the war she couldn't stop running. She had to keep moving; and in the end she became psychotic. This reactive psychosis changed her personality permanently through one terrible experience.[34]

In the post-traumatic stress syndrome, the brain does not necessarily have to have sustained physical damage. The syndrome represents the permanent psychological effect on the brain of a major trauma. The name it goes by is more all-embracing than 'KZ-syndrome'. What is important is that although the KZ experience was unique, the kind of stress it caused isn't. There are parallels to be drawn, as will be seen later, between the experiences of sailors on merchantmen in wartime and the KZ-survivors, although the sailors had ample food and warmth. In the camps, the lack of food may be seen as lying at the core of survival, since it has been argued that 'with unaltered diet and unchanged labour conditions the prisoners in the German concentration camps during the last years of the war would have died even had there been no terror system, merely because of their negative nitrogen balance';[35] but there remains the elusive factor of the spirit: those who survived the concentration camps taught us that human beings in an extreme situation can survive on far, far less, and tolerate far, far more than had hitherto been thought remotely possible, if they are given the fraction of a chance.

A sense of community helped in the battle to survive: in his studies of Norwegian ex-concentration camp prisoners Professor Eitinger asked them why they had managed to survive, 'and virtually all of them said that it was because we were together with other Norwegians'. As Kogon[36] has observed, loners died. But for the Norwegians, coming as they did from a small, homogeneous country – small enough indeed for everybody to know, or at least know about, everybody else – each other's company provided a sense of humanity and continuity, a sense of things being as they were before the war. However, Norwegians in the hands of the Gestapo had no easier a time than any other victims.[37]

*   *   *

Ways in which the KZ past is confronted or avoided have been described. Survivors frequently describe their liberation as 'being reborn', but no one can really be reborn, in the sense that they start again with no memories of what went before. It has been attempted. At least one survivor I know of, who is now a happily married man with two children, has never once mentioned to either his family or anyone else one word about his entire life before 1945. That the existence of his 'secret' is known at all is only due to the fact that one of the children, when grown, asked a family friend what she knew of her father's family history.

Two reactions former KZ-inmates have in common with ex-resistance fighters are these: first, that they will prefer when in a public place to sit in a chair with its back to a wall. Since smoking cigarettes was punishable by death in the camps, another common feature is that a former inmate will always look around before lighting one. I have noticed too that, while talking to them, survivors will be instantly aware of the slightest drifting of one's attention: if something catches your eye and takes it away from them during a conversation, they are aware of it, and will even ask what it is; though I think that their own hyper-awareness may also be due to the tension created by the subject of conversation. Although I have met one or two former political prisoners who have appeared to enjoy reliving their time in the camps, like old soldiers fighting their former battles, I have not been aware of this reaction in the majority of survivors I talked to. For most, however necessary it is for them to talk about it, it is always extremely painful, as it involves reliving the experience. It does seem, however – and this is not surprising – that those survivors who have had the most fulfilled and busiest lives since liberation are those who are best able to talk about the KZ without being haunted by it. Hand in hand with this goes their ability to express themselves and their feelings, either in words, music, painting, scientific enquiry – any articulate talent, and not necessarily associated with the KZ. It does seem significant, too, that so many survivors have gone into work like building, health care, and baking.

Among the Norwegian survivors examined by Eitinger and his colleagues, many wanted to have nothing to do with compensation at first. Finally, however, their own inability to look after themselves became apparent and they or they families then applied. There still remain a few who will not apply because they see admitting to the need for compensation as an admission of weakness, an admission that there is something wrong with them. As has been seen, the mechanics of applying for compensation could be off-putting, too. Professor Eitinger was very much involved with the commission for determining degrees of compensation to be awarded to returning Norwegian former

KZ-inmates, but he also interviewed a number of Jews who came to Norway as refugees and who were therefore not entitled to compensation from Norway, only from Germany. He was generous in their favour in his assessment of their disabilities. As has been seen, the situation in Germany was very complicated because every case was a private one brought against the German state by the victimized person. Eitinger found the concept of a court hearing in such cases completely nonsensical. 'In Norway we caused the law to be changed so that reparation was automatic unless the Institute of Insurance chose to prove that your disability was not caused by your stay in the camps. And later, to simplify things, the Germans agreed to settle out of court, as it were, for much lower considerations than were being contested, but paying up there and then. And most victims accepted those terms, to be free of the bother, even if that meant getting 50 per cent less than their potential entitlement.' In Norway, compensation was initially related to earning capacity: if you are capable of earning 100 per cent *pro rata* of what you earned before the war, you got no compensation. Discrepancies of −8 per cent upwards were compensated with the difference. A student at the time of incarceration would have had his compensation based on the average earning of the profession for which he was studying. In very many cases throughout the world, survivors found that their intellectual capacity was impaired and had to settle for far less demanding or stimulating jobs than might have been their right. Similarly, for those starting life afresh in a new country, the chances of a job of similar standing to the one enjoyed in the homeland could be slight; though equally many survivors, by dint of having to struggle harder, actually became higher achievers than was the average in their new homeland.

Another psychological factor in the determination of compensation is that, already briefly referred to, of 'bridge symptoms'. These are normally the symptoms that set in immediately after an accident or trauma occurs but which don't actually surface until the need is felt to go to the doctor. They are hard to detect in the case of the former KZ-inmate because of his post-liberation euphoria. He doesn't know that he is not perfectly all right; that only comes out much later – years later. 'After they were set free, people wanted to be themselves again, that was the most important thing.' The sense of happiness at release was obviously more evident in those former inmates who could return more or less immediately to their own homes and families.

This is especially clearly demonstrated in the Scandinavian ex-prisoners who were picked up in Germany by the Swedish Red Cross. They were shown the greatest solicitude and care, brought to Sweden even before the end of the war, and home to Norway immediately after liberation. Here they were received with open arms by the population as the war victims and heroes they indeed were. They were thanked for their sacrifices, given the immediate medical help they needed, and then – people returned to their everyday lives, started to rebuild their ruined country, and tried to forget that there had ever been a war, concentration camps or concentration camp prisoners. After a comparatively short recuperation period, the majority of the ex-prisoners also tried to resume their work. Nearly 90 per cent of a representative sample were fully occupied one year after the repatriation.

The immediate impression shared by doctors and concentration camp survivors was that the primary results of the stay in a concentration camp were not too horrifying. It was not before diseases and defective conditions developed in some survivors that the investigation started and that probable causal connections between the sufferings in the camps and the actual diseases were described. It is important to draw attention to the fact that the symptoms became manifest after long, sometimes very long, symptom-free periods of time. The notion of the so-called 'bridge-symptoms' between trauma and reactions being a necessary precondition for causality could not be substantiated.[38]

A further contributory factor to the post-war tribulation of the former concentration camp prisoner is, fortunately, less prevalent now than it was in the Fifties and Sixties, because today the degree of their suffering is more widely recognized and acknowledged. In the camps, people tended to think of the outside world in idealized terms – and indeed anywhere would have been better than where they were. They were liberated into a world which they believed would have to change for the better; and the world disappointed them. In a speech[39] given in 1961, Eitinger said:

The ex-prisoner who takes stock of the situation today, and looks upon the goals he fought for, and gave his freedom and health for, must admit, regarding the position from a world-wide point of view, that he has hardly gained any of the objectives which during the war seemed so much a matter of course. Increasing doubt enters his mind, and he wonders whether all the sacrifices made at that time were in vain, and whether, after all, it would have been better to let someone else pull the chestnuts out of the fire while he himself sat and watched. His unconscious and strongest motivation has thus been undermined, and the ex-prisoner starts to think and to compare himself with others in the country who were 'lucky' or 'careful', as it is so nicely put, and who remained at home, continued in their jobs, and increased their earnings and improved their standing during the war, as though the world had not been on fire. He himself is now subject to the same ideas which, immediately after the war, he so bitterly attacked and exposed.

When I asked him about that 25 years later, he told me:

I used that description because I was trying to make the problem familiar to a wide audience – I made that speech soon after we started our investigations, when survivors were coming to us and saying things like, 'Was it worth while? Nobody cares any more.' I think the historical situation has changed since then. The public does care, and in Norway at any rate the survivors have got their rights, their pensions; and the law was changed in their favour. They are acknowl-edged, and I think today their attitude is much more positive towards what they did . . . Survivors in my experience are no longer frustrated that other people who haven't had the KZ experience can't see the world through their eyes. I think there is a certain balance now, that comes with time. There's an understanding that we and you are different, but that our experience doesn't make us better or superior people. I think with time there is mellowing, though that's an impression only – I have no data on it. But the strong reaction mentioned in that speech doesn't exist any more.

And in fact even at that time, he noted how quickly changes could be brought about in the individual bitter and introvert survivor who, at last and often for the first time, could discuss his problems 'with a team of doctors who had some familiarity with the conditions in the concentration camps and whose only task was to help victims'. Eitinger's own personal experience of the KZ made him – and other doctors who, like him, had been through it – ideal counsellors to KZ-victims, because they knew *exactly* what the survivor was talking about.

About the inability some survivors have expressed to feel sympathy with others, he says:

An emotional blunting was necessary in the camp, and some con-tinued with it – but in others the opposite happened, and they are now more sensitive to the suffering of others. I remember a Jewish survivor, a doctor, who came back from Auschwitz to Copenhagen after the war, and he was doing the round of the wards in the hospital where he worked for the first time, and he said to the doctor who was accompanying him, 'I notice you've got a lot of older people here, people over 40. What are you keeping them for?' And then he suddenly realized what he'd said, and why: he had become so used to anyone over 40 being classified as 'old', and therefore being sent to the gas. He told me later, 'I suddenly remembered that I was a doctor and that these people had the right to be treated.' And there was another one who returned, and fairly soon afterwards had to attend the funeral of an aunt who had been very close to him; but it meant nothing to him at all, until during the service he looked at the other mourners and realized that death could be a significant thing: he had come to regard it, as we all had, as an absolute normality: a corpse in the camp meant no more to us than litter on a city street means to a pedestrian. But suddenly this man began to feel like a human being again, and that was a splendid feeling – just to be able to feel, to shed that necessary blunting of emotion. It's accompanied by a tremendous sense of relief and release – and thankfulness. Very similarly, there was a Jewish girl who told me that she couldn't understand why people cry at funerals, where only one person had died – why cry, when there were no tears for the thousands who died every day in each concentration camp?

It has been established by a number of observers that neurotic symptoms in the usual sense did not develop in the concentration camp, and that such illnesses as nervous headaches, hay-fever, certain ulcers and asthma ceased to present themselves in the KZ. Elie Cohen says that 'probably all prisoners – including the neurotics – soon came to realize the relative insignificance of what once they had thought to be important'. Minor phobias and psychosomatic illnesses didn't appear any more. The interesting question seems to be: do they reappear after the stress has been removed and, if so, when? The answer is that they do reappear, immediately. Dr V. A. Kral has identified this. He had worked as a prisoner-doctor in Theresienstadt and was able to compare the state of health of people there with their state of health after the war when they were living in Israel. Even during the imprisonment in Auschwitz, Eitinger made one very persuasive observation.

We were detailed to a new sub-camp where the SS hadn't yet arrived, and our kapos didn't know what to do with us or what work we were supposed to be set to, and so we lived for a few days in this camp without real maltreatment or suffering. We were just sitting around and waiting, and during those days I had I don't know how many inmates coming to me with all sorts of psychosomatic complaints. They had simply had the breathing space to develop them, to think about them. And that happened in a very short time of respite, and despite the fact of physical exhaustion through lack of food. There is, however, no mystery here. If your life is on an even keel and relatively pleasant, you don't need psychosomatic illnesses. If you have small difficulties, they are useful; but if the difficulties are so overwhelming that they will not be useful any more, you throw them overboard. And however much one may be consciously aware of this mechanism, it's not easy to talk oneself out of being prey – or host – to these complaints.

The destruction of the libido, the cessation of menstruation in women and penile erection in men, was naturally not only due to the lack of food. The impact of the change in environment, and the nature of the change, was so great that it was impossible to leave room for sexual desire in the average prisoner. Dirty talk was not heard in the camps, and fantasies centred on food, a much more important deprivation. In general terms, the best-off psychologically were those prisoners who took part in some positive function, whose work had some meaning. It might be thought that, of these, the prisoner-doctors were the most fortunate; but, as will be seen, prisoner-doctors could find themselves tragically compromised by the SS tormentors. Nobody, however, could escape the emotional levelling of the initial stage in the camp, when 'contact with others is lost in an affective anaesthesia, together with the intimacy of life, cordiality, morality, respect for death and the dead'.[40] Such an apparently basic thing as hanging on to ordinary social manners, saying 'please' and 'thank you', as a bulwark against mental crumbling and the total loss of self-respect, could mean the difference between life and death.

After the liberation, the recovery of the sexual process depended on the individual, but here the somatic rather than the psychological status of the prisoner was the most important. If people were severely undernourished, there was no libido at all; but as soon as people were able to eat and drink and gain strength, it returned quickly. In some cases, not unnaturally, it returned very strongly. I would like to mention the marvellous feeling women former prisoners told me they experienced when they began to menstruate again. Rabbi Isaac Levy, a chaplain with the British forces that liberated Belsen, tried soon after to provide women prisoners with whatever cloth, needles and thread he could find so that they could make themselves dresses and so be able to get rid of their demeaning KZ clothes. This gesture is remembered with gratitude, but it is very hard to convey the warmth that comes into the voice when a woman survivor speaks of, as one of them put it, 'my returning womanhood'.

Within the camps, 'the radical devaluation of all conditions which did not serve the purposes of self-preservation led to "criminal" habits. Every day numbers were subjected to corporal punishment for theft, usually of mangels or potatoes. Some were hanged for this, and their fellow-prisoners compelled to watch the executions on the parade ground. In the majority the reaction to this was blunted, depending on the "stage" which the prisoner had reached. Primitivization, or "regression" could lead to animalistic fights during the distribution of food and led to prisoners licking the earth for the contents of a spilled bucket of mangel soup. Cannibalism was not unknown.'[41] Eitinger thinks incidents of cannibalism were rare, and I have heard only three instances of it; in any case it was unusual for the very simple reason that there was virtually no flesh on the bones of those who died, and no means of cutting or tearing off what there was. In terms of such behaviour ever having a bearing on a survivor's life after liberation, it is most likely that the majority of them adequately suppress memories of actions taken in the camp of which they are ashamed. 'It is like the aphorism of Nietzsche: "I have done this, says my memory. I can't have done this, says my self-respect. Slowly but surely my memory gives in." This applies to a whole range of people, from survivors to politicians. It is a form of unconscious self-help.'

On liberation, however, there was a more-or-less immediate return to normal ethics and morals; more, in fact, than one might have expected. Immediately after liberation, survivors could do whatever they wanted to in Germany. The Germans were scared, and certainly in Professor Eitinger's experience of the liberation of Buchenwald the US military authorities were not too concerned about the odd killing of a German. 'There were a few youngsters – especially Russians, who liked wristwatches because they had never seen them before – who went into the villages and stole things like that. Some of them would come back with five or six watches on their arm. But this was exceptional. I do remember that they caught one SS-man and brought him back. Some wanted him killed; others wanted to make him do "punishment exercises"[42] on the roll-call square at Buchenwald; but a third group said simply, "No, we don't want to be like them – he is a prisoner, and that's enough." The third group was the majority.'

Revenge is not a natural reaction in such circumstances as these; it was in fact very rarely that individual KZ-inmates took revenge on SS-men, though fantasies about revenge were one source of mental sustenance through the time in the camps. Several survivors have explained to me that when the longed-for moment of revenge arrived, the desire to take it fizzled out. Either the SS-man or -woman at their mercy had become so craven that they didn't excite aggressive feelings, or they were not SS known personally to the survivor and so there was no specific motivation for killing them. This is not to say that people did not take revenge, nor that it didn't afford satisfaction. I have met two survivors who killed or maimed SS-personnel and who remember their action with approval and satisfaction, but this is very exceptional. In the course of many years' work, Eitinger has interviewed in depth 2,000 survivors, in Europe, Israel, the USA and Australia: of all of them, only two or three mentioned revenge with approval.

And in the long run revenge has a damaging effect upon the person's psyche. These two or three couldn't forgive themselves, either. There was one who really was an extreme psychopath – or at any rate, he became one. He was a young boy, he had lived in the ghetto and remained in it after it was liquidated, in hiding. He lived exactly like a rat; and in the end they caught him and took him to Auschwitz. There, in Birkenau, he was detailed to the terrible Sonderkommando.[43] He survived somehow, and I met him in Israel. He'd been a very daring soldier there because he'd wanted to avenge himself, to kill as many Arabs as possible; but after 1948 he continued. His view was, 'The whole world is a camp; you have to fight everybody to stay alive.' To be locked into such an extreme antisocial personality is very rare indeed. He was only ten in 1940, in the ghetto. He was thus 18 when fighting in the independence wars in Israel, and he had nobody at all. But you can't make the hypothesis that the seeds of that psychopathy were in him in any case; they were sown by his experience and grew because of it. He had no parents, no one to set him any kind of example. And he'd lived for several months in the ghetto, really like a rat, hiding himself in the sewers during the day and coming out at night to run around in search of food to steal or forage . . . in his teens. His most formative years. So what can you expect? In Auschwitz he lived his life in the same way, and he came to Israel via the British internment camps in Cyprus, illegally.

I met another who admitted that he wanted to revenge himself. He was 18 or so, and had lost his whole family, killed by the Germans; and so he wanted to kill Germans in return, which he did. But luckily for him, he realized that it wasn't helping him, so he stopped. He knew that he could kill the whole German nation and it wouldn't relieve the feelings he thought revenge would relieve.

Despite the fact that arms were readily to hand in liberated Buchenwald, very few prisoners even wanted to experiment with revenge. The Germans had failed to brutalize the prisoners as thoroughly as they had wished, and that saved them. Lest it be thought that this was so only because of the discipline the 'red triangles' had managed to impose on Buchenwald in the last days when the camp was virtually under their sole control, it should be added that even on Eitinger's transport out of Auschwitz nobody thought of smashing down the buildings they were leaving – although the SS guards had left them unsupervised and were waiting at the gates – 'not even that was considered a worthy outlet for the feelings of aggression that had been suppressed for so long. We desisted not because we were too exhausted to do it; it was simply that we were too decent; enough of our upbringing had remained, despite all the Germans had tried to do; one simply doesn't do things like that.'

As can be imagined in view of the development of the KZ-syndrome already discussed, the incidence of suicide was low immediately after liberation, but rose in the Sixties and Seventies. There is evidence to suggest too that many survivors caused their own deaths through abuse of alcohol and tobacco, itself a consequence of nervous stress, or through simply not caring about themselves or what they did, from neglecting their health to killing themselves through careless driving – indirect suicide. Eitinger believes that there were far more suicides in the camps than is usually admitted, though many would disagree with this. As time passed after the end of the war, disillusionment with the world, an increasing impairment of mental and physical function, and sheer tiredness caught up with many survivors.

In the same way you will find survivors who refer to the world with indifference if not with actual dislike, since the world did not live up to our expectations. Here in Norway were admitted so-called hard-core refugees from the DP camps. These were refugees, mainly Jewish, who were not admitted to any other country, because they had TB, or were disabled. Norway admitted a certain number of them. The TB patients were cured when it became possible to do so in the Fifties. They adapted relatively well, with the help of social workers, and despite all their handicaps, and they started to work again. And then came the war crimes trials in West Germany, where former Nazis were given sentences like three years for killing 150 people – ridiculously lenient, notional sentences. Awareness of these trials brought tension, and the fact that these criminals were clearly not being considered as all that 'guilty' after all came as a terrible blow for these survivors. But the situation in Israel had a still greater impact, especially the Yom Kippur War, and the attitude of the world after the Six Day War. It seemed as if the world had turned against Israel. Only in Denmark was there no overt anti-Semitism at those times. The former DPs here were frightened, incapacitated. It looked to them as if the Holocaust could happen again, especially after the Yom Kippur War, and that affected their fragile sense of security. Where would they run to next if the need arose; and if Israel were swept away, what final refuge would there be for Jews in the world? Not only survivors felt like this, of course. All Jews did; but these former hard-core DPs were test-cases. They had fought hard to re-establish themselves, but the slightest disruption or threat would be enough to bring them out of their very labile stability; the stability they have attained remains fragile, however long they maintain it, and its maintenance costs continuous effort.

These survivors are also people who have to cope with particularly severe disabilities, such as blindness and paraplegia.

Survivors' memory-loss is not selective. It was thought at the beginning of research that it was caused by organic brain damage, but today that seems less certain, because it has been found that there is memory-loss even in people in modern instances who have been taken hostage for a relatively short time, and that memory-loss is serious and long-lasting. Thinking nowadays inclines to the view that it has more to do with an inability to concentrate properly than with the loss of memory *per se* – and in technical terms this amounts to the same thing. The effects are the same, and the aetiology has not so much to do with organic brain disease. Additionally, 'those people who had severe organic brain disease immediately after the war do not have it any more', while their memory may continue to be impaired. Brain damage sustained in the camps was due to beatings, encephalitis, typhus, and long-lasting inanition.

A survivor's memory of the camp can however be photographic. 'I think that the experience was so extreme that every detail was etched on the brain and charged with significance.' If people remember where a red tin bowl was on a table, or how many potato peelings there were in the soup, then those details are important for them. Each of us remembers the traumas of everyday life vividly, after all.

Three main forms of reactive psychotic neuroses occur: paranoia, depression, and persecution-mania. No one of them is noticeably greater in incidence than any other. Those non-Jewish refugees who came to Norway after the war had a much higher incidence overall of such neuroses than the average population, and even than the survivor population, especially paranoid psychoses; but this is nothing new. Refugees do have more paranoid reactions because they are strangers in a strange land. This reaction is made worse if they are political refugees who may be right in their assumption that they are being shadowed – be it by the local police or by agents from their homeland. Eitinger knows of many hundreds of survivors and political refugees who are automatically frightened of policemen. The uniform produces a gut-reaction, but with policemen the association is also with unwelcome and unpredictable authority, and with the police's political role in undemocratic countries. A dislike of uniforms of all kinds is common among survivors. One told me that even hotel commissionaires' uniforms made him uncomfortable.

In terms of the spread of these psychoses, reference can be made to findings among patients hospitalized in Norway between 1960 and 1975,[44] which Eitinger says is 'more typical for the survivors [today]. Also the diagnoses might by now be more correct because the doctors have learnt more about what they are dealing with.' The findings show that in the group of 79 ex-prisoner patients investigated, 34 had reactive psychoses, of whom 9 were paranoid, and the others mainly depressive; 21 had an organic psycho-syndrome; 13 were suffering from alcoholism; 10 from senile or presenile dementia, and one from a manic-melancholic psychosis.

The investigation carried out in Norway was a very thorough one, better perhaps than any other and closely linked to the university hospital in Oslo and to all the relevant university departments. They started without any knowledge of what they were going to find, or of what they were supposed to find. They were dealing with people who had been in the camps and who couldn't work any more, and that was all they knew. The patients were admitted to the Department of Neurology because there were beds available there, and they were investigated by all the specialists working at the hospital and in the various university departments. The reaction of the patients is typified by the fact that when volunteers were asked for to undergo pneumo-encephalography (a painful process in the investigation of the brain whereby air is pumped into the brain, now superseded by computer photography), all but a small percentage volunteered. 'There was a strong sense of wanting to help not only oneself but the rest of the group, by participating as actively as possible.' It is significant that many survivors want and need to help other people. It is not fanciful or sentimental to state that this is a healthy, normal reaction to cruelty. The pendulum swings away from what was experienced and the direction away from cruelty is towards kindness.

In therapy, self-understanding is of major importance and has played a large role in the work in this field conducted in Norway.

Simply to understand that the KZ experience is part of your life, and has changed you, and that change is understandable and a normal reaction to an abnormal situation: this is important. It is a great help to be able to say to yourself, 'I'm not crazy to be thinking or behaving as I am. Anyone in my position would be the same.' And it helped survivors, obviously, that I was a survivor myself and a refugee to this country. On a practical level I spoke the language of the camps – I knew what a word conveyed – the special camp sense of a word.

If you have a doctor and you have to explain to him what it means to stand on the *Appellplatz*, what can you expect of him?

Certainly therapists dealing with survivors today are much better informed, generally, of the KZ milieu and its terminology than they were when the Norwegians were making their initial investigations. One of the problems, and one which anyone involved in any way with the concentration camps must face, is how to find a way at least approximately to know the feelings of survivors oneself. It is a complicated matter for survivors themselves, at a distance in time from the experience.

We had a friend, a lady who was in Ravensbrück, and she wrote a book about her experiences which I couldn't bring myself to read at the time, and then it was out of print; but a few years ago it was reprinted and this time I did read it, and my first reaction was, 'That can't be true,' and I caught myself thinking that, and I said to myself, 'But you were there yourself!' So, you see, don't worry about your inability to project yourself imaginatively in the fullest sense of the word into the camps: if I can react by thinking, this is so horrible it can't be true, having actually lived through it! And that is a kind of safety-measure in my mind too . . . But the phenomenon continues: we know that the most appalling things are happening to people in prisons in various South American and African countries, and in Russia, and elsewhere, too, but do our minds accept it? Our immediate reaction is, it can't be true; and I think that that is a decent reaction. At bottom, we humans want to believe that we are good. We want to be able to be optimistic about ourselves, and to be proud of the creature we are.[45]

I mention that the group of people I have been talking to not only look younger than they are, but also have extreme vitality and interest in life.

'I would guess that you are talking to a very selected group of people, who are ready to talk to you. That they have volunteered to do so suggests that they have got things much more into perspective than the majority. It may be that some people's characters have been strengthened by the KZ experience, but the last impression that should be given is that *concentration camp is good for you.*' There may, however, be a parallel to be drawn with stress theory: that if you are exposed to a certain amount, your power of resistance grows; if you aren't exposed to any, your resistance slows down. But if the stress is extreme, there is a maximum of positive effect, after which no further good is done, and indeed resistance can start to break down. As survivors grow older, so the surviving group becomes more highly selected. Hypermortality is highest in the younger survivors. In other words, the older a survivor grows, the more likely he is to live out his natural span. They may remain sensitive to triggers which will set off acute memories of the camps, however.

> In 1968, university friends of mine, who were well able to defend and justify themselves in argument normally, collapsed when they were verbally attacked by the students during the revolutionary uproar of that year. What caused the collapse was that they picked up the aggressive attitude of the students and associated it with the aggression of the SS, which association automatically triggered the same reaction they had had when the SS were bawling at them. These things can be buried, laid to rest, but never erased. They will always be present and there is always the possibility that something will bring them out.

Professor Eitinger did not wish to talk about his own experiences in the camps,[46] but he did talk briefly about his own liberation. The tension of the last days in Buchenwald, as the SS made final desperate attempts to transport the inmates away, and the inmates, with even greater desperation, resisted them, was intolerable, broken only when the SS actually abandoned the camp. The American troops arrived on 11 April, which meant that Eitinger could work as a doctor again. The fact that food was available, and enough medical supplies at least to begin to stem the flow of disease, meant more to him at first than the realization that he was free. He was the oldest of five Norwegian Jews in the camp, and at the time they thought they were the only survivors of Norwegian Jewry. The fact of liberation didn't hit him until a few days later. He had a Sunday off hospital duties and decided to walk down the hill from the camp to the town of Weimar.

> And suddenly I realized that I could stop walking when I wanted to, and look around at the landscape; and that there would be no one behind me to hit me, or any such thing. This was when the euphoria came to me. Of course from the moment I saw the SS fleeing the camp there had been a superficial feeling of joy, but the introspective feeling that came then – in Weimar – that I could stop and look around – just that – and was free to do so – marked the moment of liberation for me.

PART TWO

PART TWO

7

In Denmark.
Healers and Fighters

I

Paul Thygesen has already been mentioned. He has recently twice undergone major surgery, as the illnesses he succumbed to in the camps catch up with him, and he writes to me with typical humour that he finds himself 'rather handicapped from the collar-stud and upstairs and from the waist and downstairs'. He was born in 1913 and became a doctor in 1942; he is credited with being among the very first to identify the KZ-syndrome. Like Professor Eitinger, he has spent his life helping the victims of the camps. He is a major contributor to many publications, of which the two cited and used here[1] are of primary importance. It was in Scandinavia, and especially in Denmark and Norway, that the most important pioneering work into the post-war problems of KZ survivors was done, and Thygesen, though a neurologist by training, is also Denmark's pioneer clinical psychologist. The work undertaken had no precedents to build on; no one had ever experienced anything like the concentration camps before. Diseases like spotted typhus had not been seen in Europe since the Middle Ages, but in the camps it was rife. Some recent experience of the treatment of semi-starvation had been had in dealing with the victims of famine in Bengal. What is as important in the work of the Scandinavian doctors as the help they gave to KZ survivors is the application of what they learned to similar cases occurring in the post-war years.

It is hard to draw absolute divisions between the physical and mental after-effects of the KZ because often one informs and influences the other. What follows, unless otherwise indicated, stems from correspondence with Professor Thygesen. I have included the personal references he makes because I find them striking. One more prefatory remark should be made: that research here was based on returning Danish resistance fighters, interned policemen and members of the gendarmerie. The resistance fighters were sent to 'harsh' camps, for obvious reasons, but the distinction drawn between the police and the gendarmerie deserves a brief comment. For some reason, the Germans decided that the gendarmes should be classified as political prisoners. They were therefore deported to two 'harsh' camps, *Aussenkommandos* of Neuengamme: Alt Garge and Schandelach. The Germans also interned 1,981 policemen, a quarter of the national force, on 19 September 1944 and deported them to Germany, first to Buchenwald and then to a variety of camps. The reason for this move was to pre-empt any possible organized uprising by the police, who were giving increasing help to the resistance. The policemen, however, were treated more or less as regular POWs, allowed to keep their own warm uniforms and to receive food parcels. This, and the fact that their average age was much younger than that of the gendarmes, meant that their mortality rate in the camps was much lower.

The question of how much a survivor's age at the time of his imprisonment affected his subsequent life is an important one. There is no simple answer in Thygesen's researches. Disablement showed a progressive course, and 'up to 1980, 51 per cent of the political prisoners were known to be at least 51 per cent disabled. This was not, as might have been expected, primarily due to the ageing of the group, since those who were youngest at the time of the deportation were most frequently disabled. Approximately three-quarters of those more than 50 per cent disabled were less than 60 years of age.' In other words, the older you get without a marked increase in disability, the better off you are, relatively speaking.

The age of a prisoner at the time of his detention can affect his or her marital status, or dependency upon relatives. My own observation is that those who were still children (pre-adolescent or early adolescent) and survived had quite some difficulty in readapting – partly because they were still dependent upon their parents. Of course very few young children survived the camps, as those imprisoned as children were virtually all Jews or Gypsies (Kogon writes that 'During the final phase there were 877 minors at Buchenwald, the youngest a 3½-year-old Polish child whose file-card actually listed him as a "partisan".'[2] Those in their early twenties and above, who had married and had dependent children equally had greater problems after liberation, very obviously because the young husbands frequently lost their wives and young children, who were taken off to be gassed as soon as the transports arrived at Birkenau. However, in a significant number of cases a unit of mother and daughter or father and son (where, say, the parents were in their mid- to late thirties and the children in their early to mid-teens), a very strong relationship developed which helped both partners through. It was not just a question of having someone to look after you which helped psychologically: it was rather a matter of having someone to look after. There is no doubt at all that membership of some kind of mutually trusting small group was vital.

In general, though, people who were independent of family ties just before the war seem to have survived best in the camps and to have adapted most successfully after liberation. To be independent in this way meant that you were in your mid-teens to early twenties, no longer dependent upon your parents and having not yet formed secondary dependencies. A second group who seem, at least in a number of cases, to have adapted well after the war were considerably older – their parents were perhaps already dead and their children had grown up and were independent of them. It is hard to find survivors in this second group today. Mortality in the KZ was highest among the oldest prisoners, and few of those who survived are still alive today. I have only met three survivors who were born at about the turn of the century. The majority of those I met were born in the Twenties, and were therefore in their teens and early twenties when they were in the camps.

In coming to terms, as has been pointed out, a good education was an advantage. Thygesen says: 'it is generally true that educationally superior persons adjusted better afterwards – at any rate socially. And this is not specific for KZ survivors. The same trend or pattern is obvious in all group investigations of disability, regardless of its "medical" cause.' However, in the light of his researches, '"superior" prisoners in no way adjust better to private life and family life', and as a complicated rider to the education–recovery relationship, he points out that the 'early resistance movement in Denmark, especially the hard and dangerous work, was often accomplished or directed by politically conscious manual workers, respected in their circles, many of them with official posts within trades unions and so on.[3] Many of them were not, however, able to resume their special jobs after the war.' Coming to terms also involves a recognition of reduced capacity, and compensating for it by so tailoring your life that you can work at full capacity for some of the time; but it takes intellectual awareness and outside support to be able to do this.

Thygesen's original paper, *KZ-syndromet*, was published with Knud Hermann in 1954. A follow-up study appeared in 1970, and further findings by Nielsen and Sørensen appeared in 1984 and 1986.[4] There are far too many facets of the syndrome and individual social responses of survivors after liberation to be included here, but one further aspect which should be mentioned in conclusion is that of being alone. There was absolutely no privacy in the concentration camps. This, coupled with the association of crowded conditions with the transports and the *Blocks*, led in post-war years to two linked responses – a desire, amounting to an actual need, to be alone for periods of time, and a dislike of crowds.[5]

II

Jørgen Kieler was born in 1919 and was one of the younger contributors to the *Acta Medica Scandinavica* supplement of 1952 to which reference has been made. He is now director of the Fibiger Institute for cancer research in Copenhagen. He is also President of the Frihedsfonden (Ex-Resistance Fighters' Organization). When war broke out he was a medical student; as the Danish government's attempts to maintain its rule of a notionally neutral country under the shadow of what was German occupation in all but name faltered, he joined the resistance, initially working for the underground newspaper, *Frit Danmark*, later being involved in the publication of a variety of anti-German literature and the circulation of banned books. However, 'when capital punishment for sabotage was introduced it was obvious to me that the distinction drawn between workers in the resistance and students in the resistance, that the former should be involved in sabotage and the latter in illegal publications, no longer held good'. Through a friend in his home town of Horsens he got hold of some explosives and embarked on his first mission: to blow up a railway bridge. The attempt was a failure, but as the resistance became more and more organized, proper sabotage training was set up both within Denmark and through the British Special Operations Executive. In 1943, Kieler was heavily involved in the successful operation to get the Danish Jews out to Sweden. His 'cell' operated two routes, through which 1,500 Jews escaped, with only one casualty, a member of the cell called Cato Bakmann. When the operation to save the Jews was successfully concluded, Kieler's student group was reinforced by a number of naval cadets who had been released from internment (the rivalry between the Nazi High Commissioner to Denmark, Werner Best, and the head of the German armed forces there, General von Haneken, meant that the Germans never ran Denmark with the efficiency necessary to an occupying power). They made contact with the two remaining members of a successful resistance sabotage group called Holger Dansk (after a legendary Danish giant-hero), and with these two experienced underground fighters formed Holger Dansk 2. or HD2. The two men were called Finn (Jens Lillelund) and John (Svend Otto Nielsen) – who had been a maths teacher in civilian life. Under their guidance, HD2 became one of the most successful resistance groups during the winter months of 1943–4, their greatest coup being the successful destruction of the giant Burmeister &

Wain shipyard, which the RAF had failed to destroy in January 1943. They also immobilized a big steel-mill in Jutland. 'Our successful actions reduced the risk of innocent lives being lost and other property damaged – both would have happened in air-raids. As it was, the success of the resistance movement obviated the need for air-raids and Denmark was intact at the end of the war.'

However, the group suffered severe losses and John was arrested by the Gestapo after only two months, in December 1943. In trying to escape, he was hit by seven bullets, 'one of which broke his right thigh. During the following interrogation the Gestapo agents kicked the fractured leg and bent the lower part of the leg outwards to form a right angle with the upper part. He fainted several times, but didn't talk.'[6] John had been betrayed by a woman, a Norwegian. 'Now, she could not be excused. She had got into economic difficulties with her fashion shop, and in order to get some money she sold John to the Gestapo. She betrayed him with a kiss – that was her signal to the Gestapo. We tried to liquidate her but she escaped to Norway. However, six months later she was foolish enough to return. I was in prison by then, along with most of our group, but "Flammen" (Bent Faurschou-Hviid) was still at liberty, and he killed her. The executioner was always a disinterested person, so there could never be personal motives for the killing, but "Flammen" avenged many.'

Kieler had been arrested five times already, so he knew something about interrogation and how to handle it. Three times the Danish police had arrested him but let him go; once the harbour police got hold of him and four companions, but they managed to persuade them that they were not planning sabotage but were trying to escape to Sweden. 'We were handed over to the Danish courts and were sentenced to serve 80 days at the end of the war. I still haven't served that sentence!' On another occasion, when two different Gestapo departments were after him, one couldn't find him because he was already in the custody of the other, and before the two sections could liaise, he had been released again. But on 5 February 1944 in South Jutland his group got into a gun battle with the Germans and he was shot through the neck. 'I had a fracture of the cervical spine, but with no paralysis, so I was lucky; but then I was hit over the head with a rifle-butt so I was in pretty poor shape when I was brought to the German prison in Copenhagen, and in even poorer shape when I learnt that they'd also arrested my father, my younger brother and two of my sisters. Only my mother and my youngest sister, Lida, were still free. All my family were to survive, however. The Gestapo concentrated on me because I'd spent about six months studying in Germany just before the war and could speak fluent German at that time. They were flattered to be involved in an actual conversation about, say, conditions in Germany, and we would also discuss art – the qualities of a Holbein, for example. I'd studied the history of art earlier in my student career, and I knew Germany very well. So they would talk to me, and I strung them along by confessing – one at a time – to a whole series of acts of sabotage – after all, they had caught me red-handed, but they could only kill me once, so I thought I might as well take the blame for as many "crimes" as possible. But I was playing for time, too, because I was hoping to keep them from actually sentencing me – we believed that if we could hold out long enough, we would be saved by the Allied invasion.

'Shortly after I arrived at the prison I saw John again. He was lying on his bed in his cell, unable to move because of his broken leg. He had not received any medical attention and for almost three months nobody had been allowed to carry him to the lavatory or to wash him. Before I was allowed to see him, the guards cleaned him up and shaved him. Subsequently I was allowed to visit him several times. We were alone, but we knew of course that the Gestapo were listening. I was allowed to carry him to the lavatory and even out into the prison yard, where he enjoyed feeling the sun on his face. As any hope of an early invasion faded, I could see that John was giving up hope. "You have a chance still," he said. "But I am lost."'

John was killed in April 1944. In the letters he left behind he wrote, 'How are they going to shoot me? I cannot stand.' His body was found after the war at what is now the Memorial Park at Ryvangen in North Copenhagen – at the time used by the Germans as an execution site.

Kieler was never tortured, and at the last minute his execution was deferred on a technicality – he believes his interrogator may actually have interceded for him – and with his younger brother Flemming he was sent to the concentration camp of Porta Westphalica where the prisoners were set to excavating underground factories meant to house the Philips plant moved from the Netherlands. The rock they were working on was granite. Nevertheless a tunnel was constructed, 22 kilometres long and broad enough to take two railway tracks. The majority of the prisoners were Russians, and the conditions were so hard that within six months 45 per cent of the original Danish prisoner population was dead. The total prisoner population was maintained at 1,500, with fresh transports from Neuengamme brought in to replace the dead. 'The first wave of Danish prisoners were resistance fighters and knew why they were there; but later the Germans brought in criminal elements they had arrested in Denmark – they simply arrested everyone with a criminal record in order to keep crime down after they'd deported 25 per cent of our police – and these people succumbed very quickly. They had no solidarity, and they did not know why they were there. I think too that those people who were able to persuade themselves that the war would soon be over had a better chance than the pessimists, or the realists, however they saw themselves. To hope was better than to rationalize, despite the fact that sometimes one's hope was disappointed.

'I don't know how much one's professional or intellectual or educational standing was a factor. There is a story in this connection. There was a man who was the youngest son of a farmer in West Jutland. He became a bus-driver and later he acquired a state-supported farm just big enough for one family to manage. They were very poor, and they had five children to feed. His great ambition was to own a tractor; but he became enormously strong because he had to do all the work on the farm manually. During the war he allowed the resistance to store arms there. The Gestapo found out, and he was arrested and taken to Porta. I come from Jutland myself, so I could understand him, but he spoke Danish with such a pure Jutland accent that many Copenhageners couldn't understand him. He was adored in the mines – he'd help anyone too weak to manage alone, regardless of their nationality, and he'd share his food. But being big and strong, he was also exposed to starvation to a higher degree than other people. Now it happened around Christmas time that the Danish Red Cross managed to send food parcels to Danish and Norwegian prisoners – by then we were down to 800 calories a day, where 3,000 would have been needed in view of the work we were doing, so we were all starving. The SS and the kapos took their share of the Red Cross parcels and then they arranged something which was very evil, because of course they knew we were all starving. They lined up the Danes and the Norwegians on one side of the yard and distributed the extra food to them, but not to the other prisoners. This bred envy and hatred. The Russian prisoners moved against us, and the SS and the kapos stood back to watch the fun. Then the farmer, whose name was Nicolaj Nicolajsen, went towards the 500 or so Russians and stretched out his arm and shouted "STOP!" I saw this. There was maybe a minute of enormous tension, but then he had those starving Russians under his control. They didn't move another step. Then he turned to us, and said, "We will share our parcels with them."

'Not long afterwards, early in 1945, he died of starvation in the *Lazarett*. I was working there and I was with him. A Russian passing me near the body saw that I was crying and asked, "Was he your father?" And I said yes, because he was my father: he was a father to all of us. And the SS came and threw his body naked on to a heap to await burial, but while it was lying there prisoners came from all over the camp – prisoners from Russia, Siberia, Yugoslavia, Holland, Denmark ... and stood to attention by that naked body. I have his photograph on the wall at home, together with that of John – they died, but they inspired us to believe that the human spirit could be decent, and therefore to live for its sake, for their sake. I think so, anyway.

'In the camps I met many people with little or no education, like Nicolaj, who proved to be of the most enormous quality, and whom I admired very much indeed; but I think that for those who did not have such quality naturally, and that means most of us, education could play a role in how well we coped. Generally speaking in Porta the "politicals" had a higher standard of education than the rest. The French particularly had high morale and good discipline. After roll-call and food, most of us would fight for a bunk and sleep; but the French always gathered into small groups for conversation. It might be about food, literature, or politics, but it would at any rate be social intercourse, and that civilizing influence helped; practically speaking, it was very good to keep the brain stimulated and alive, to give it a sense of a world other than that of the camp. I shared a bunk with a French doctor when I was working in the *Lazarett*, and thus got into contact with the French prisoners, and this conversation they had was as important to them as the beets and dry bread we had for supper. Ever since, I have had a certain respect for the almost stubborn French desire for intellectual stimulation – it reminds me of the British love of sport and sense of fair play. Something a nation won't compromise on. I wasn't aware of such a strong *esprit de nation* among the Danes.'

Many people may have looked for support in their religious belief, Kieler thinks, though he knows of only one person who was actually converted to religious sentiments by his stay in the camps: that person was his younger brother, who became a Catholic after the war. 'But not down there. In the KZ those who were convinced Christians remained so, and those who were not didn't change. Hope was a different matter. I know of only one case of suicide in the camps. It was different after the war. There were many suicides then.' In the camps it was simpler: hope could be focused on liberation – what lay beyond it didn't come into consideration; nor did prisoners themselves know what the long-term effects on them of their imprisonment would be.

For Kieler personally, the fact that he was a doctor helped, to the extent that he understood what the hunger syndrome was, and therefore forced the food down, however atrocious it was. He also understood that it was sensible to work as little as possible, partly to give the least possible help to the Germans, but mainly to conserve energy. He was also able to instruct and help his fellow-prisoners, sometimes forcing them to eat when they began to deteriorate, and in that way helping some at least to survive. 'There was one terrible situation, though, that affected me as a doctor. The most senior of the Danish prisoners was a captain in the army. He contracted a throat infection – a swelling –

and he died in my arms. He was the first Dane to die. He was choking to death and I knew that what was needed to save him was an incision in his throat; but I had no knife, and anyway I was still a student; I hadn't finished my studies and I'd had no surgical training. Even if I'd been able to get a knife, I don't know if I'd have had the courage to perform the operation, simple as it was, or if I'd have done it properly. The fact is that I did nothing, and I still feel a kind of guilt about that. He died in my arms and there was nothing I could do.

'As a result of that I made a vow that after the war I would study to become a very good surgeon indeed.' Ironically, it was the KZ that put paid to that ambition. Kieler contracted TB and had to switch from surgery to research work. 'It was a disappointment because I had studied rather fully, before the career change was forced on me, in Munich and Paris, for a year in New York after the war, and for nine months in Cambridge, which were perhaps the happiest months of my life. I feel my career has been of value, but I have always missed working directly with patients.'

Kieler's younger brother had also contracted TB and would have died without his care. They both suffered from the universal camp illnesses of hunger diarrhoea and oedema. They did not give up hope, but one day, helping Flemming back from the mines, Kieler came close to despair as he sensed the onset of the apathy that heralded the end. 'I was trying to cheer myself up with thoughts of returning home after the defeat of Hitler. But suddenly I couldn't dream of that any more, or see the faces of my parents, or my sisters or my friends. I was dreamless, and I felt this mental deterioration, coming so suddenly, as the last warning. I had no energy to heed the warning, and only just enough to register it. I was on the verge of becoming a Mussulman, one of the walking dead. I would not be here now if it hadn't been that at that moment fresh orders came through and we were transported back to Neuengamme. I was saved in the nick of time, though alas I contracted TB the day before I was repatriated.'⁷ Of the five HD2 members in Porta, four survived; rescue came too late for Klaus Røn-holt, who had played a central role in the rescue of the Jews.

Kieler arrived home in Denmark on 20 April 1945, on one of the last of the white buses. It was Hitler's birthday, but it was also Kieler's mother's birthday. The buses deposited the returning prisoners at Frøslev; this had been a concentration camp, but was now a Red Cross transit camp. 'I had no idea how many – if any – of my family had survived. Then I overheard two women speaking Danish – the first Danish spoken at home that I'd heard – and one said to the other, "Mrs Kieler's over there, looking for her sons. Poor thing, she doesn't know yet that they are both dead." And I saw my mother, and went over to her and said, "Happy birthday", and told her that Flemming was alive too. It was very moving. She recognized me of course, but only just, and I have to say that I had difficulty recognizing her too, for she'd had typhus, which had spread from a KZ they'd set up at Hørserod near our town, and she looked more like a Mussulman than I did. But somehow she'd made the very difficult journey – in those times – of 150 miles from Horsens down to the frontier.

'We were all reunited and it was a wonderful feeling after unspeakable anxiety to see that we were all alive – but we were equally all in a very bad state. I would say that the one who was least hurt was possibly myself. I was able to recommence my studies fairly soon and I finished them in due time; I hadn't missed too much either because I'd completed the first part of them before joining the resistance. Now, I wanted to knock my studies on the head as soon as possible, because after what I'd been through I felt too old to go on being a student. I had no doubts about my career choice. I wanted to be a surgeon, and my dream was to go to Africa or China, or somewhere else where my medical expertise would be badly needed. Of course I didn't know at the time that TB would put paid to that ambition. But what I wanted very strongly was for my life to be meaningful; to have an aim.

'It is possible that those who collapsed after the war tended to be those who had no strong sense of aim. In my own family, two sisters and my brother converted to Catholicism, but I think only my brother's conversion was directly due to his experiences in the KZ and as a result of his illness. He faced a very uncertain future, and his own ambitions to become a doctor had been sunk. By and large I think that people with definite goals who were able to fulfil them, at the very least in part, did make a better and fuller recovery afterwards. All kinds of people joined the resistance, and all classes, even the criminal classes. The one thing they had in common was that they were active people, people who would take the initiative. So it's not so odd that people from the resistance returned from the KZ and became high-achievers – not house-painters but proper decorators; not carpenters but cabinet-makers. And they were their own men. Of course they might have been like that anyway, given their basic character; but in one way the experience of the KZ made the strong stronger, if they survived it with their minds whole. In Denmark, too, it took quite a lot of independence of mind to join the resistance in the first place, especially in the early stages, because the Danes are a law-abiding nation, and because we were officially a neutral country until the government fell, the resistance and the Freedom Council were revolutionary, illegal organizations. People who had been through all that would not happily accept an ordinary life or a subordinate role afterwards, and that of course brought its own problems with it. However, the ability to get into a leading or an independent position after the war could also be a great advantage for survivors, because it meant that they could either delegate responsibilities or simply organize their time to suit themselves and their own capacities.

'Of course, there are attendant tensions too in being independent or running your own concern, but they do not contribute to a decline until several years after the event. Take me. I am 67 and I may retire now if I wish – 67 is the retirement age here – but I may continue until I am 70. Now, there are colleagues who advise me to retire because it is hard to keep up with the progress of medical science and so on. If I retired I'd get a slightly lower pension – but that would be more than made up for by my war pension. I've thought about it, and I've decided to carry on until I am 70 because the Institute is beset with political problems at the moment and I think that the only person who will really fight for this place is me, because I actually fear nothing. All they can do is fire me, and so what? Nobody else dares criticize our sponsors when they come along with foolish proposals that will dismantle this Institute. So, to the relief of my collaborators I have announced that I will continue until I am 70 – or until they throw me out! You see, one thing that really is a help is that if you go through the KZ, nothing else that comes along can really bother you too much again, just in terms of confrontations. For me, there are many negative conclusions to be drawn from the KZ experience, but the few positive ones are like rocks: the example set by John and Nicolaj, and my own lack of fear.'

One of the great disappointments that Kieler felt, along with many other members of the resistance movement, was that the old politicians were returned after the war, and it may be that this sense of disappointment was sharpened by the fact that the Freedom Council could have taken over control of the country. It didn't because the Allies were terrified of the possibility of any remotely socialist party taking over in a country so important to the Western Bloc. Even the former wartime prime minister, Vilhelm Buhl, who had actually encouraged Danes to inform on saboteurs to the Germans, was reinstated. This seemed a betrayal of all that the resistance had fought for; and it was equally disheartening to see the various political parties, which had buried their differences and fought shoulder to shoulder against the enemy, now fall again to petty bickering. 'Of course one knew that such a close system of mutual aid couldn't continue into peacetime, and we had seen that where Social Democrats and Communists went into government hand in hand, the Communists would take over in the end. In that sense I can see how the resistance movement which depended upon a coalition which was itself dependent upon an outside force to keep it together couldn't have formed a government; but I was disappointed to the extent that the old parties didn't at least choose new leaders.'

Kieler's sense of isolation contributes to one of his fundamental motives for wanting to have his own book of war memoirs published. All of us need to share our bad experiences, and for former KZ-inmates this need is only partially met, because however loving other people are they can often only partially recognize the size of the need. 'I am married and I have three children, and I have a good family life. On Christmas Eve at 4pm my children and now also my first grandchild join me at the Memorial Park of Ryvangen and there is a ceremony lasting half an hour and we do that rather than going to church. My children have always insisted on accompanying me on that occasion and, generally speaking, they have been interested in what happened to me, and they have read my book very keenly, but they have not asked many questions. Perhaps they have been reluctant to do so; perhaps they have wanted to protect me – but I also think that the whole revolution that youth has been through since the Sixties has found no inspiration in our resistance movement, and that their revolution has nothing to do with ours, no connection with what we did. Thus it is that it is the *next* generation, born in the Sixties, that has become interested in the history of the Second World War; so that I have felt that I have lived in some isolation from my family and, to a greater extent still, from my colleagues here. I feel ashamed to tell them about my experiences because I feel that I am imposing upon them. I remember once that I was going to Paris with my wife. Our route lay past my old camp of Porta, and I asked her if she would like me to show her the site. She said no. That hurt. I feel strongly that she thinks it's bad for me to go back there, but I feel even more that my wife, my children, sense that I've had a second life which they've had no part in, and you could say that they are jealous of that. They do not want to hear what they feel they cannot share, and they cannot see that I would desperately like to feel that they wanted me to share it with them. I have been tremendously moved when young people of my children's age – people in their late thirties – have said to me, "Why don't you take me out to Ryvangen and tell me something about your friend John?" This has happened to me two or three times and has been an enormous stimulation to me, which is why I am so disappointed at being blocked over the book as I am by some former members of the Resistance – I so want to share the experience.

'In the sense of helping me to come to terms with the KZ experience, I think the people who were most helpful to me were my parents, especially my mother who went through such a horrible time herself. She was very courageous and I think she was probably the person who has been closest to me as far as all this is concerned. But I don't want to give the impression that I want to pore over the past all the time. I can't bear the annual reunions, when people get together and repeat the same old stories, year in, year out. If I go, I do so only for an hour or so, to see if there is anybody who needs my help. For me, it's important to relate the past experience to the present: can it be used for something that is relevant now? As President of the Frihedsfonden I have responsibility for nine student hostels, called the *4th May Colleges*, in nine different towns here. They were originally for kids whose fathers were killed in the war, and they still fulfil certain obligations, one of which is to commemorate the day of liberation. The colleges are a memorial to those who died, and serve to remind future generations of the collaboration across all social and political barriers that went into freeing Denmark. To respect the individual and to fight for freedom, those are the tenets we want young people to recognize. I give lectures about my own experiences fairly frequently, and I am pleased to say that they usually meet with success. The other day I was talking to a group of 15-year-olds and they wouldn't let me go afterwards with their questions. When I am asked to give such lectures I always say yes. The recollection does not give me personal pain, though it took me a long time to make peace with Germany within myself. It was only when I became President of the European Association for Cancer Research that I had to communicate with Germans again. When I became President, I got in touch with the Cancer Research Centre people in Heidelberg, and of course I met a lot of very nice people, and none of them could be held responsible – most of them were born after 1945, anyway. I've been back to Heidelberg three or four times, and now I can even bring myself to speak the language again. I disliked them so utterly before that I couldn't even bear their tongue. It wasn't just because of the KZ and the SS; it was because of the civilian population too. At Porta, marching back from the mines, carrying our dead, the German civilians would spit at us; and afterwards they said, "Oh, we didn't know."'

What about later responses to the cruelties of the KZ?

'Some of the people who come to the Frihedsfonden for help complain of nightmares. I have never had nightmares myself, but I can well imagine that if, for example, I had been reduced to cannibalism, it would be a terrible thing to live with now. I think my brother and my friends and I succeeded in keeping a distance between ourselves and the reality surrounding us. We did not at any time identify ourselves with the KZ and its inmates. We faced it as The Evil, The Enemy, and we felt that the maintenance of moral standards was our continuation of the fight against Hitler. When self-discipline broke down, and when you were no longer master of your thoughts, that was the beginning of the Mussulman stage. Cerebral degeneration could be brought about equally by starvation and blows to the head. One did one's best to avoid both. What I have been left with is impaired hearing, and I depend to a very great extent upon lip-reading. Thus it is that I hate the radio and

I hate the telephone. That is why I have a secretary to speak on the phone for me. I can't understand what people are saying, but I can't use a deaf-aid because my deafness is caused by actual nerve decay: they're not weakened, they're gone. But the nerves that are intact are perfectly all right, so that increased noise on them is very painful. My ability to understand also depends on the voice level of the person who is talking to me. I can easily understand you, but I have difficulty understanding my wife. I hear only about a third of what she says to me. It depends on the wavelength. I am nervous about dinner parties. I can entertain the lady on my left, but not the one opposite me; and if they are talking about something else across the table, I am lost both for that conversation and the one on my side. When my children come home and there is a family gathering, very often I am left alone, left out, because I cannot hear. It is another form of isolation, there in the very middle of my family. And it is increasing. This is a traumatic disease due to exposure to very loud noise levels, like explosions, during the war. It is getting worse and worse. That is one of the drawbacks of being a doctor – you can see what's happening to you; and professionally I can see how useless I'm getting at my work when it comes to international conferences, especially when people speak in bad English. And I have no objection to giving talks in English; but if the accent in which questions are asked afterwards is too strong, I can't make them out; and that makes me nervous. Here at the Institute we have a seminar every Thursday in the library. As director, I have to be there, but I can't follow it – I can't hear what they're saying. And that is enormously tiring. It's an organized waste of time for me. So I can understand when people complain of failing memory and an inability to concentrate: these same things cause professional problems for me. To compensate requires a greater input of intellectual effort, which in turn exhausts me more. I am not bitter, because I feel that my life has had some meaning; but I am a little intolerant. This is a research institute and I allow my collaborators a pretty free hand, but I do insist that they clearly justify any programme to me by explaining of what benefit it can be to a cancer patient. If the research seems purely academic, to have no connection, I veto it. Work must have an immediate meaning.

'I spend most of my free time working with the Frihedsfonden and the colleges. I also help Amnesty International, and I am an adviser to the Medical Centre for the Treatment of Victims of Torture which has been established in Copenhagen. I feel these are natural things for me to do – and there are many more jobs that I would like to take on, but I don't have time. I only contribute money, for example, to the SOS organization for orphans' villages internationally. Anything related to the youngest generation has my interest, because I still feel hope for the future despite my experiences and all that has happened since in the world. But there's more to it than that. It harks back to the question of isolation. I think I am finding a solution to it through the very intimate relationship I have with small children – I'd never thought of that before, but now that I do, I see how true it is. I deeply regret that I have only one grandchild, a wonderful little girl of nine whom I love dearly. And there is a group of maybe half a dozen small children who come and use my swimming pool, and they are my friends, and I take them to the circus or to the Tivoli. Their confidence and their affection; their response when I am telling them fairy-tales, or making up stories for them – these things bring me out of my emotional isolation. I like children of all ages but of course when they reach puberty they want to have friends of their own age more and the close contact is broken. I would say that I have the best contact with children aged between 3 and 12. They have straightforward loyalties, and their loyalties are without limits. If they declare friendship, then it's friendship. They will never talk evil of you, or believe anyone who does. And I think it is the quality of their straightforward affection that brings me out of my shell: you cannot turn away from it, and you cannot *not* respond to it. One is tempted to say that human beings are at their best up to the age of 12 years!

'And I will take these little ones at least once to Ryvangen and will tell them about my friends who lie buried there, and they will listen with great interest. I go to Ryvangen myself not only on official occasions, but quite frequently alone. And if I ever have a problem, or if I have to make an important decision, then I always go there to deliberate. There are three graves I go to particularly, and I ask myself what the reactions of my dead friends would be concerning a particular problem. There is no feeling of despair or bitterness, but sometimes I have a longing to join them, especially sometimes in moments of defeat, when I find that the friends I'd like to turn to are in fact only friends as long as I am strong. It's to do with the feelings of isolation and disappointment too, and the feeling that the only people you can really talk to are those who have been through the same experience as you. I think that this feeling accounts for the high rate of suicides after the war. I am not inclined to suicide myself though – it is just in those moments of weakness that I need the support of those friends who sacrificed everything; and in moments like that I can very well understand that the step from here to death does not seem so very great. My memory is also still stimulated by my involvement with the Frihedsfonden, but you will frequently find that if you ask people what the happiest time of their life was, they will say the Occupation . . . the memory of the deep friendships and fundamental emotions – and maybe, too, of the excitement. (Living, perhaps, as we are designed to live?) One important corollary to this is that friendship for us denotes something much deeper than it does for other people, so that we are sometimes disappointed. Friendship for us means more than knowing someone who is merely nice to know.'

It was not, however, the sense of isolation that led to the suicides of former KZ-inmates after liberation. There were in fact relatively few suicides immediately after the war, followed by a long period of quiescence, 20 years and more, which was followed again by a spate of deaths. 'People got tired, and they were surprised and overtaken by the late effects of the KZ-syndrome. It was naturally acceptable that you felt weak immediately after the war, but you fought your way back to normal health and, as far as possible, to a normal life. That state of affairs could then last a quarter of a century and more. But then, like a boomerang, your past comes back to you and hits you once more; but there isn't a second chance now, because you are that much older – all you can hope for is a pension and nothing more. I think it hits people at that precise time because they arrive at a turning-point. Normally one is at one's most efficient at around 40. The triumph of your life should be at around 50–55, and your decline starts at about 60, though the beginning of that phase still has the impetus of former years. But in the case of the former KZ-inmates, who age prematurely, this phase may start ten years earlier than it does for their colleagues. They were strong enough to get through the KZ, but they cannot be strong enough to withstand the depredations of biology. A sort of exhaustion catches up with you and has to be expressed in the body. There is a certain amount of strength in any person which comes to an end sooner or later.'

III

Frode Toft, who died in December 1986, worked in the Ministry of Social Affairs before the war and returned to his job after liberation. He was invited to join the Frihedsfonden in 1976, but at that time was too ill to accept the invitation. He finally joined in 1981, though he had already been closely engaged with the ex-resistance organizations in Denmark through his civil service work.[8]

'For the returning KZ-inmate who was, for example, an unskilled labourer, it was relatively easy to adapt back to normal life at first, but he succumbed earlier to the after-effects because of the toll his physical work took on him. Skilled workers ultimately did a little better, and people educated to university level seemed better adapted anyway to organize their lives, but all of us were together in being victims of the late effects. I saw an example last month: a man who as a student had been a member of a sabotage gang and was arrested but had his death-sentence commuted on account of his youth to life imprisonment with hard labour. Well, he was liberated in 1945, finished his studies and went on to become Director of Social Affairs in Odense, which is our third biggest city. Now he is 62, and suddenly he is tired; his memory has degenerated so fast that he cannot do his job any more. And yesterday there was another report, of a man who was Finance Director of a little municipality in Jutland – at 63, he simply can't manage any more. His doctors have told him he is unequal to the responsibility of his work. Most people to whom this happens react with resignation rather than depression. They will, after all, be financially secure. Their jobs carry government pensions and they will get additional help through the Frihedsfonden, which they will now apply for. The channels to apply for such help will remain open until there is no one left to need them.

'There was no decision for me to make about joining the resistance. Before the war I was already among the leadership of the Young Communist League, and I was arrested as early as 1941 by Danish police acting on German orders. I was in prison here and also in a camp, but under Danish administration, until the Germans took over in 1943. Until then it wasn't too bad, though it was rather strange for the Danish prison administration to have to deal with people who weren't criminals, I think. It was their first experience of having to deal with political prisoners. But we were not set to work, and the camp in North Copenhagen was like a high school, because the place was full of academics and lawyers. However, most of us were very bitter about the Danish authorities who, by interning us, had prevented us from joining the resistance. Worst of all was that they broke their promise to us when they handed us over to the Germans.

'In October 1943 we were transported by boat and cattle-waggon to Stutthof. We were very frightened, but we were lucky in so far as there were 150 of us altogether, and we knew each other, so there was great solidarity. We knew each other's strengths and weaknesses: this one is ill, we must help him; that one speaks good German, he can be our interpreter. When we got to Stutthof, they put us all in the same *Block* together, and we were also lucky in that we were the first prisoners from Western Europe, and that flummoxed some of the SS, for we were fellow-Nordics, not Russian *"Untermenschen"*! They couldn't understand why we were there, and their attitude was relatively lenient at first. They interrogated us, of course; a lot of pro-forma about things like one's mother's maiden name, but the last question was: "Why are you here?" When we told them we were Communists, they were confused. They didn't know what to do with us.

'Most of us were skilled workers, builders and engineers, and they needed such people. As a civil servant I was less lucky – for I was, in a manner of speaking, unskilled. In the first week a journalist and I worked as hod-carriers for the building works, but one day while we were at that job one of the SS officers in charge came over and talked to me. He asked me what my real job was and I told him. "Then you are an official," he said. "We must get you a proper job." He was very German! The next week he took me to a nearby village where there was a factory doing work for the Germans, and I was given an office job there: prisoner I may have been, but my old civilian status had to be observed.

'Among my group was a Danish count. Our SS overseer wanted a liaison officer between himself and us from among our ranks, and predictably he chose the count, especially as he went by "the fine German name" of Moltke! The count, however, who was also a Communist, declined the honour. This didn't prevent yet another SS officer seeking him out for conversation, on the grounds that the SS-man was also a count, and wanted to greet his social equal. He was unable to provide our count with the food and cigarettes that he asked for, but at least he found us some matches, which were in very short supply at Stutthof. He was embarrassed that he couldn't do more – in the midst of all that misery. The German mind is a strange thing.

'I was in Stutthof from October 1943 until May 1945. I had my office job for six months, but I wasn't allowed to stay longer because the SS didn't want their prisoners to develop close relationships with the civilian staff. Later I had to do heavy labour humping sacks of cement. It was dreadful work because the sacks were made of cheap paper and if one broke it was deemed to be sabotage and you were punished. The punishment depended on the kapo or the SS-man who caught you. The German criminal kapos would whip you. Luckily I was recalled to the factory. They really needed people like me because all the German manpower had been sent to the front and most of the workers were little girls – 15- or 16-year-olds. Working for the German war effort was difficult, but one did as little as possible. In my experience no prisoners ever became so interested in the work they were doing that they did a good job in spite of themselves. The first thing you learnt – from the Russians – was to keep a lookout for the SS doing their rounds. The rest of the time they kept telling us, "You're still working too quick!"

'This "soft" work helped me to survive, for the food was very bad; but after three months we were given access to Red Cross parcels, which thereafter appeared monthly, and contained bread, butter, sausage, sugar and vitamin tablets. This was the first time they tried to get supplies from Denmark to a concentration camp, because we were the first group of Danes to be sent to one. One day our *Block* – number 13 – was called out and we were terrified, because we were taken to what we knew to be an empty *Block* near the guardhouse. But inside were all the Red Cross parcels. We had to form a queue and each man signed for his parcel. Later on, the minor SS and the kapos pilfered the parcels before we got them, but three months later a Danish SS-man arrived at Stutthof. His job was to keep us and the Norwegian prisoners who subsequently arrived under control, and to censor our letters; but in fact he helped us as much as he could, for this was after Stalingrad, and he knew which way the wind was blowing. He made sure we got the Red Cross parcels intact; only he kept for himself those designated for comrades who had died. But those packages were of great help, not least psychologically: they showed that someone outside the world of the camp thought of us, cared about us. We knew how well off we were, but it was brought home to us when a transport of Jews arrived after the liquidation of the Riga ghetto in the face of the Russian advance. Some of them were barracked with us, but we were not allowed to help them or give them medical attention. Some of them were badly beaten up or wounded, and we organized whatever help we could for them. I remember talking to an old man who was dying. He'd been severely beaten and his teeth were smashed. He told me that some of the young Baltic Jews had got away and fled to the Russians. "Why didn't you go too?" I asked him. "Because I am a German," he replied. He was from Hamburg. At least we knew why we were there; in a sense it was a matter of choice. A Jew could do nothing about his situation; they were not organized as we were, and the fact that they were all Jews didn't mean that they were a coherent group at all – rather the opposite in many ways.

'The SS encouraged division amongst the prisoners. We were introduced to a group of ultra-right Polish nationalists as dyed-in-the-wool Bolsheviks; but we were all politics in the end. There were some power-struggles between the greens and the reds, but we Danes wouldn't join in: we didn't want to be placed in the position of having to become kapos or *Blockälteste*[9] – we didn't know what that might do to us.

'Most of the Scandinavian prisoners were finally liberated by the Swedish Red Cross with the white buses in April 1945. The white buses also collected the 600 or so Danish Jews who had been sent to Theresienstadt. Fortunately, Denmark had kept up such pressure on the Germans about these nationals that none were sent to the gas chambers, and the 50 who died in the camp did so from natural causes. But these buses didn't get to Stutthof, because the Russians were so close to us by then. On 20 January the Germans evacuated the camp, and the prisoners were forced to march westwards through the snow. Many died. I was left behind with a mixed bag of 30 other prisoners who were needed to continue work in the factory, so I was spared the death-march. Of those of us who remained behind, the Russians were treated best, because the factory overseer knew perfectly well that the Red Army was practically at his gates; but orders were orders and he kept the place going long after there was any point. Finally, on 3 May, there came an order that the factory files should be cleared out, and three Poles and I were delegated to take them in big boxes to the nearest harbour. By now the Russians were in Danzig [Gdansk], which was only about 30 miles away. We could hear shooting and even see a battle raging on the other side of a little river nearby. Thousands of German troops had been shipped in to fight a last-ditch stand. We sheltered for two days outside a bombed-out little town called Hel, then on 5 May we were loaded on to a Baltic passenger cruiser, built by the Germans under their *Kraft durch Freude* enterprise, which had been converted into a troop-carrier. Some 7,000 prisoners, wounded soldiers, German officers and civilian refugees were loaded on to that ship. We passed Copenhagen on 7 May – of course we didn't know that it had been liberated. We hoped that we might land there, but the next day we turned south because the war had officially ended, and we put into a little harbour near Lübeck called Neustadt. We were liberated there by British troops on 9 May. I was the only Dane to be liberated in this way.

'Getting back to Copenhagen was difficult. Neustadt was quarantined because prisoners leaving Neuengamme had brought typhus with them to the town. However, after a week I was allowed to leave, and I was able to make my way to Kiel, and thence to Flensburg, and thence to Denmark, where I arrived on 29 May.

'I think it is very important to be able to return to an intact home town, to your own family, friends and even job. For the Jews and those from the Eastern Bloc it was much harder. We were so lucky that the war stopped exactly at the Danish frontier.

'In Copenhagen my father was waiting to greet me. I had as yet no wife, and I found that my mother had died during the war. I was happy, but I was also very tired – and ill, for I had contracted jaundice. I was put on a special diet – very plain food, fruit and fish. No *aquavit*! Just water, a little thin milk, and weak beer. And I got better . . . The next job was to get back in touch with those of my comrades from Stutthof who had survived. Each set of prisoners from the different camps formed their own little club, and there is also a big club for all of us. The Stutthof club was founded by three of us – me, mainly! There were many problems to solve for our comrades: problems of finance, health, housing, and social problems. This was achieved mainly through the Directorate of Accident Insurance (*Sikringsstyrelsen*) which was an old government directorate already in existence. I returned to my old job, which was in the accounts auditing department to do with social welfare payments; but it was very difficult to go back to such a life after four years. It didn't seem to have much to do with real life, somehow. I took a two-year sabbatical and became cultural organizer to the Young Communist League. When I later returned to my Ministry I felt much better adjusted to the work I had to do there.

'I married just after that time, and I am still married! I am lucky, though. Many of my comrades couldn't settle down to domesticity; they had changed, and if their spouses had no inkling of what they had been through, they were unable to relate to the changed personality of their partner. They didn't speak the same language any more, and many relationships broke down. I think I was lucky to meet my wife after it was all over, and although I thought a lot to myself about my experiences, at first I didn't speak to my wife about them. She doesn't like to hear about it, but I understand that so it doesn't bother me. My son is interested, and has been since he started school. He attends the Bernadotte School, which is a private place where there is a very wide international mix of pupils, and they are taught in Danish and English. I think it is important that he gets to know as many different peoples and cultures as possible, as early as possible. But I've never felt isolated, as I know Jørgen Kieler does. Also, my work has kept me very closely in touch with former comrades.

'Later I was asked to give lectures. At first I said no, but then I came to see it as a duty. The first time was very difficult, but it became easier. Young people were very interested here in the Forties and Fifties, and then there was a lull – the KZ was consigned to history. But then there was a TV soap-opera about the Holocaust which brought a new interest in the real thing. Young Jews here seem especially to be exercised by the problem of why their grandparents didn't resist: one has to explain how hard it was for them. I have been back to Stutthof, and for me it didn't hurt too badly. But when I went to Auschwitz in 1961 I was very moved, though I was not in that camp myself. It is so big. I thought of the number of people. But I have been back to Stutthof several times because I have Polish friends who live in Gdansk and Gdinia, who were fellow-prisoners. Again, I am fortunate. On our first return-visit to Stutthof, a friend accompanied us. He had fought in the Spanish Civil War and then returned to Denmark after a time in Canada. He ended up in the KZ with us, but after the war he seemed to have made a complete recovery, and had started a successful career as a restaurateur. The visit to Stutthof took place in 1949. The day after we got back to Denmark, our friend killed himself. Too many bad memories had been awakened.

'The Danish government was very helpful – it had to be! Every man who had been in a KZ was automatically entitled to DK50 for every week he had spent in the KZ abroad, and DK25 for every week in prison in Denmark. This was paid as a lump-sum and was independent of other claims. We have been quite fortunate in Denmark, and I think I have not had too many bad effects since liberation. All of us have stomach problems. The doctors put mine down to nerves, and I think that is common, too. For two years after the war I couldn't bear the sound of aeroplanes. There had been Russian bombing raids during the last few days at Stutthof, and every time I heard a plane I would automatically look for cover, but that was really nothing. I had bad dreams, and they have lasted right up to now – all my life. Usually I have them after a discussion about the camps, or after I have seen a film about them. The dreams are always about our persecution, and about the executions we were forced to witness. One Christmas they hanged two prisoners five metres from the Christmas tree they had forced us to erect. We had to stand and watch all day. It's very hard to understand the Germans. The technical director of the factory said to me one day, "Conditions in the camp aren't so bad, are they?" And I said, "Didn't what happened the other day give you some indication?" – a prisoner had arrived late for roll-call and had been whipped unconscious. "Well, that was only a Pole," the technical director said. And do you know, he wasn't a bad man; he just wasn't able to think.

'Today I have no difficulties in relating to Germans, though for many years I didn't like to go to Germany, and still now I prefer my trips to be short. Some Germans can provoke my dislike by their aggressive nationalism. Not long ago I was on holiday in Norway and there was a big German group in one place, and where many Germans are together they can be very noisy and domineering. That I don't like; but of course by no means all of them are like that. I think we in Denmark can forgive, but not forget – forgetting is the problem: it is a taint. The resolution is somehow to learn to live with the memory. I think one must forgive – for no revenge is possible for what they did to us. Those were almost the last words my friend the restaurateur said to me.'

8

A Home in England

I

Fela Drybus was born in Lodz in 1927. She went through the Lodz ghetto, and was in Auschwitz-Birkenau, Ravensbrück and Bergen-Belsen. She is now called Phyllis Bernstein, and lives in London.

'There was some anti-Semitism in Lodz when I was a child, but I didn't notice it. Occasionally you might hear someone shout out – "Why don't you Jews go to Palestine!" – but we were children, we didn't pay it much attention. We lived quite peacefully with the Christian people in Poland. My father was a shoemaker, he was born in a little place outside Lodz and he had a lot of Christian pals because he was born in the country. It was a different life there: no TV, no radio – it was an enclosed community, and he was the third generation in his village. But he came into Lodz to learn his trade and he met my mother – she was a city girl – and stayed. He fought in the First World War and was taken prisoner in Russia – he had some terrible experiences there, but he came through – he was an adaptable man, and he could pull himself out of any bad situation. He was 18 when he married my mother. Eighteen. Then he was called up.

'He died in the Lodz ghetto in 1941. He died of TB, malnutrition, starvation. He neglected himself. He couldn't understand why he was so ill. He was ill for a year, but he only took to his bed for the last three weeks. We knew he was going to die when he gave up smoking, because my father was a chain-smoker.

'I have been back. The Christian people have got everything that the Jews had before. But there is an old chemist's shop that I remember, and the building is still there that was used as a store for old rags for the weaving factory in the ghetto. There was a big *selection* in the winter of 1941–2. We hid in the rags. My older sister and my younger brother. We were in the ghetto for four and a half years, so going back was a kind of pilgrimage, to celebrate 40 years since the liberation. I took my daughter for company, but we had quite an easy time, no troubles, no obstacles. We stayed in Lodz for about a week and travelled a little bit. I took my daughter to Auschwitz and we photographed ... the places. A week wasn't enough time. But in Lodz we found my mother's birth certificate, and the young lady there typed me out a copy. My mother was born in 1899, and that part of Poland was under Russian rule then, so her card was all in Russian but the girl typed it out in Polish. They only charged about ten bob [50p] for it. I couldn't find my own birth certificate, but in Warsaw there are still records that go back to 1820, when they started registering the Jews in Poland, and the Germans didn't destroy them. I'd like to go back to Poland with my sister, but it would be difficult as she is an Israeli citizen now, and Poland and Israel haven't had diplomatic relations since 1967. The Poles didn't mind about letting me in, though. Nobody minded – all they were interested in was the money – the dollars – I could have bought half Poland for dollars! But everybody was very polite and kind, and when they heard that I hadn't been back in central Lodz – outside the ghetto – for 45 years, they were tremendously interested, and they complimented me on my Polish, which isn't very university-educated, because when the Germans came, all education for the Jews stopped. I saw my school, my old school. I could have wept. It's an old people's home now.

'There was so little food in the ghetto. My mother had to lock up the food we had with a padlock so that no one would take more than their share, and every month when we got the rations from the cooperative, my mother would sit with scales and weigh everything, measure everything out, everyone's portion. I remember once when there was soup on to boil, one of the neighbours actually weighed it when she had to go to the loo so that when she came back she could check that none had been taken. I can't imagine that we actually managed to live like that for years.

'When they set up industries, I went into the straw factory. We'd plait the straw into two-inch plaits and make overshoes for the soldiers guarding the ghetto, and wherever else they were guarding, to wear in the winter. I saw some of the shoes in a little ghetto museum in Bydgoszcz when I was there with my daughter: "Look, Esther," I said to her, "that's what your mother worked on when she was in the Lodz ghetto." My sister plaited; I sewed the plaits into boots. Nowadays they've got lovely blocks of new flats where the old factories used to be. It was very emotional going back to Lodz. No one's gone back there to live. Only one woman, a bit over 60, my sister's age – she told me she'd been waiting so long for someone to come back, but no one had. No one from our whole block of flats – 90 families.

'Our family was sent to Auschwitz when they closed down the ghetto in 1944. My sister and I were sent to one side; my mother and my little brother to the other – it all happened so fast that when I looked round for them, they were already gone. To Birkenau. To the part where the gas chambers were. My little brother was 15, but he was small, undernourished. One winter in the ghetto we had spent practically all the time in bed – it was the only way to keep warm.

'My sister and I were together the whole time. We were lucky. We were only a short time in Auschwitz. After the baths, after we'd been shaved, we couldn't recognize each other with bald heads – but we found each other and then we were *selected* again – naked – and we were thrown rags to wear. To them, we were worse than vermin, worse than lice. But it never occurred to me to give in. I was growing. I was 17, in my bloom. And my breasts were hurting. They were growing.

'They selected us at night. They always seemed to select at night. We were confused, and they shepherded us on to a train. After the war, I couldn't travel anywhere in the night. And even after I'd been some time in England, I might be walking down the street, and I'd suddenly get into a panic and think, where's my star – the Star of David, I mean – you had to wear it front and back in the ghetto. And I'd have to calm myself down, tell myself that I was safe now.

'The transfer from Auschwitz was to Ravensbrück first, but there was little more than a stopover there. It was a nasty place. They stuck us in a *Block* with Gypsies who ganged up against us. We had to take punishment for their misdemeanours, and they'd steal anything we put down, or took off.

'It was late 1944 by now and by that time the Germans needed workers. They needed workers in Lower Saxony. All the Germans were being called up, all those who were left. So there was another selection: they wanted 500 girls. It took all day on the Appellplatz, naked as God created you, and it was cold. I remember the SS doctor came and looked in my mouth at my teeth, and my teeth were perfect, and he said, "Never in my life have I seen such a perfect set of teeth." I still remember that. And we were selected, and once again in the dark night – they did things by night by then simply because they were frightened of the Allied bombers – they sluiced us down with water and marched us to the train. It was freezing. I remember the sensation of thirst so well on those train journeys that I only have to see a movie with people in a desert, without water – there was an old John Wayne one on the telly the other night – and I sense it again.

'There must have been some kind of mix-up because they took us to Dachau. The train stopped outside Dachau and we could hear the commandant shouting, "I've got no room for women." The SS quarrelled for a while but our lot gave in and they took us on to a town called Mühlhausen[1] where there was a munitions factory. They weren't ready for us, so we camped out over Christmas in the civilian workers' canteen. But by early 1945 they had our *Blocks* ready. They never gave us a striped uniform, never once – we were always given a motley of steam-cleaned rags filched from the dead.

'It was a great comfort to be with my sister. We never let each other go. I think they allowed sisters and cousins, even a young mother and her daughter – for there were no old mothers – to stay together, if they were both fit for work. We talked of food, and survival, and revenge. Revenge kept you going. We made some friendships at Mühlhausen, where the atmosphere was more relaxed. The factories were camouflaged in forests; they had things growing on the roof, even. They were half an hour's walk from our *Blocks*. I remember that Mühlhausen was a beautiful little town – little houses with red roofs. We worked shifts, 12 hours day or night, alternate weeks. It was a huge complex. I used to keep out of the way of the guards – I had a non-involvement policy: the best way to survive was to keep your head down. I tried to put myself outside of all of it: it wasn't taking place. It was like watching something going on and standing in the shadows, on the sidelines. And that was Mühlhausen.

'Then they took us to Belsen. About 500 of us arrived from Mühlhausen and we had to stand in a field nearby just waiting until they could fit us in. While we were waiting another transport arrived and the girls in that one were lined up opposite us, and in all that bunch when I looked across I saw a childhood friend. She went to live in Argentina in 1946, and I have not seen her again. The camp was overflowing when we arrived, and we got on to a good *Block* by pure chance, it was just where we could be fitted in, but it meant we got the office, kitchen and laundry *Kommandos*, and even then we had no work unless we could be specially detailed to one of the three. It was good there apart from the kapos – bloody whores, bloody, bloody whores. One of them gave me a black eye for getting out of step once. The thing to do was keep out of it, keep away from them, not connect with them. I used to hide in the latrines when I wanted to avoid work – the SS-women and the kapos didn't dare go near them in case of infection. But there was always danger. The Ukrainian girls among the prisoners used to point out which of us were Jewesses to the SS. A friend of mine had her face whipped open by a 17-year-old SS-man because of those Ukrainian girls. When I saw that, and I knew what was going to happen before it did, I thought, that's not going to happen to me – this little bird's going to get cute.

'I'm not much in contact with Germans today. If I hear the language it bothers me. As a matter of fact I'm going to the Embassy tomorrow – it's an annual visit – to get my reparation. I applied for it as soon as I could – we were advised how to do it by the United Restitution Office[2] and it came through quite soon. I got one little bit in 1957 –

about £800 as a lump-sum; and then I was entitled to a pension. I asked my sister about that when I visited her in 1958 – she'd already applied and was waiting for it to come through. I asked at Bloomsbury House[3] when I got back and applied myself. It came through in 1965. And once a year I go to their Embassy – they send me a form: name, date of birth, place of birth, nationality, passport number, maiden name – and I sign it and date it, and that's it. Every October.

'I think it's a good thing that Germany is split in two. If they were united, they would try again. I'm not sure why they are like it – something in their character? They are a clever race, very cultured, very intellectual. I have a German girlfriend: what possessed your people, I asked her. But how can she answer? She's only 45 or so, and yet she feels guilty about it. They must have suffered temporary insanity. The atrocities they committed, and the pleasure they took in torturing people made me at least opposed to all kinds of violence. I've never hit my kids even, not once. And I am certainly a pacifist. The saddest thing is that we have learnt nothing from the KZ. We go on persecuting people. It is something to do with greed. When I was 14 I was fighting for my life, for a piece of bread, for a piece of peel in the gutter. And there is so much today, and it is such a beautiful world. But people will eventually destroy it. I can't be religious, not after what happened to me, though I was too young to bother about thinking about religion at the time. I had other things to think about, too: how to survive, what to eat. But I do believe that God put enough on this planet for us all to share, if only we wouldn't grab. I do belong to a synagogue but that's about it – just to keep my burial society payments up.

'We were liberated from Belsen. You can imagine the faces of the soldiers when they saw us. They were aghast. And we were stunned too. We could hardly believe it. I remember that soon after, they came and asked us who wanted to go to Sweden. The Swedes were taking 200 girls. My sister asked me if I wanted to go, and I said, no. I didn't want to go anywhere. I didn't want to travel any more.

'My sister had had typhus. After liberation they took her to the upper camp, when they burnt down the lower one. When we were reunited I thought she looked 80. But she was 21. The press came to photograph us. Even after I got to England, people came to look at us. They called us "miracle people"; and that's how I still describe myself. "I am a miracle person, because I went to hell and came back."

'My sister Miriam emigrated to Israel – not because she was a Zionist, but because she had married a Russian Jew in the DP camp at Belsen and started a family there. There was nowhere else for them to go. It's one of the reasons we've both kept up our Polish, because I don't speak Hebrew and she doesn't speak English, and at home we never spoke

Yiddish. My sister's had a hard time. The British interned her and her husband in Cyprus because they were caught trying to make the *Aliyah* illegally. She hated Israel at first – all that heat and the flies, she used to say. And now she's alone. Her husband was killed in a car accident in 1978. She won't talk about the camps; she had a worse time than I did. It was a shame that she caught typhus after liberation, after holding out for so long.

'I came to England because the Pole in charge of our barrack at the DP camp came in one day and asked which of us was under 16. I was more, but I looked 12, I was so starved. The British were going to take 35 boys and 15 girls. I was the first to put my name down. I came because there was family here – all I had left. They were first cousins on my father's side but I have never been able to find them because I never knew their married names. We arrived in Southampton on 31 October – ten days after my 18th birthday – 250 kids from all over Europe. I lived in hostels near Cambridge at first, and then in the East End of London, near Aldgate. There was still a big group of us concentration camp children together, so it wasn't too bad, and we were looked after by Bloomsbury House. I didn't feel any sadness. There was too much to do. We all had to learn English, and I managed that fast, by ear and by copying people. Apart from one or two sessions in the hostels, I've never had a formal English lesson. As for feeling homesick, how could I? I just felt lucky to be able to come to England. It was as if I were drawing a line across my life, and saying: now all that is behind me. For many years I never talked about it, because I couldn't see how anyone would understand what I had been through. I locked it all up inside me. I am as hard as wood. I don't think I cried until I was giving birth to my daughter in 1956, and then I cried for my mama – but what could tears change then? What can I do about anything, I think. It's not up to me. Whatever happens, I accept, I tolerate, and I adapt. All the time I adapt. And as far as possible I try to keep out of things. I don't want to get involved. I always consider myself on the outside of things; on the outside, looking in. But I am very strong, and I don't let the memory get to me. When I see a film about concentration camps today I can't believe that I went through it myself, that I lived in such an environment for so long. It was like a hard school for me – a horrific school. But I think I have come out the other side, and I am grateful. Funnily enough, I did go to therapy for two years after my son was born in 1961, but I packed it in just before my sister came over for a visit because I was afraid of what she'd think of me. Then I discovered that she had also been recommended for it in Israel. She went only once and didn't go back. She was frightened of what might come out. But after her husband was killed, she started to go to therapy – because he was killed before her eyes.

'When I'd got myself settled in London I got a job as a nurse at the London Jewish Hospital. It was too hard and I had to give it up after six months. All those dead bodies of old people, I'd had enough of that, although I didn't realize at the time that that was why I couldn't go on with it. Even in the hospital, though, death was different from what it had been in the KZ. There, death was part of the everyday. There was no individuality to it. After nursing I worked as a dressmaker for Alfred Young in Poland Street in the West End of London for eight years. And when my daughter was born I gave it up, and I've just been a housewife ever since.

'To begin with I lived with some kind people in Hampstead who sort of unofficially adopted me. I met my husband in 1952 and we married two years later. We met at a dance. He was a cutter and glazier then; he drives a minicab today.'

Her husband had arrived unexpectedly during our conversation which she'd had to break off.

'I can't talk in front of him. He doesn't understand it. I never talk with him much. He's never asked me and I find that sad, but I've never asked him why. Maybe it's because he loves me, I don't know. But I prefer to leave it dormant, to let it die a natural death. My experiences have had no effect on my family, for I have always tried to hide my griefs, my depressions, my illnesses from them. Why should they be affected by what I suffered? Of course they are aware of it. I have troubles with my stomach – I don't sleep through one night even now without having to get up and come downstairs and eat something. I don't need it; I don't particularly want it, but I can't sleep without reassuring myself that it is there. And I make sure that I never run out of bread; as long as there's bread in the bin, I'm OK. Bread is fundamental. It's got to be there. I was down last night, at half-past two, having a sandwich and a drop of milk, to calm my stomach. I crave food. Without it I get nervous. Don't think I'm crazy. I'm not crazy.

'Despite everything, I am an optimist. I give people the benefit of the doubt, and I do confer trust – life wouldn't be worth living if I couldn't do that. But I don't have a large crowd of friends, because most people only want you for what they can get out of you. And I like to keep quiet.

'I'm happy with what I've got. Anyway, three-quarters of my life has gone, so what do I need more than I have now? I never save – I don't believe in it – money's for spending, and after all, I've seen people's fortunes turn to ashes in moments – all that they had accumulated, all that they'd built – as soon as those bastards marched in.'

II

Because Miklos Horthy managed to maintain a kind of *entente* with Hitler, the Jews of Hungary were relatively safe from persecution until 1944, when the Germans invaded their country and replaced Horthy with a fanatical Fascist, Ferenc Szalasi.[4] However, although Horthy had been able to hold the worst excesses of the Hungarian Arrow Cross and the extremist *Nyilas* in check to some extent, many Hungarian Jews found themselves in labour camps before then.

'AB' was born into the Jewish community in the little town of Mosonmagyarovar, not far from the Austrian frontier, on 15 May 1909. He came from a working-class family, and his father was amiable but lazy: nevertheless he made all his seven sons and daughters work hard, though they were also given as much education as he could afford, and all the daughters married well and had families before the war. AB himself did his three years' national service between 1930 and 1933, having served an apprenticeship to a grocer before that. He married Sylvia, a woman of his own age, in 1935; in the course of time they had two daughters: Boruska, born in 1937, and Marta, in 1939. Life was settled, and the family circle was wide, but close-knit.

Their happy existence was interrupted by events following 1938, when many Jewish men were pressed into working at labour camps in Russia and Czechoslovakia, as well as at home. AB saw none of his brothers or brothers-in-law again after that time. After a brief period in the Czech work-camp of Szerdahely, he was transferred to kitchen duties at the Hungarian camp of Komaron Oreg Var. However, he was subsequently allowed to return home to his wife and parents, through the intervention of a friendly army captain. The reunion was not to last long. After the Germans had annexed Hungary, the Gestapo went to work very quickly, and one evening towards the end of April 1944 the SS arrived in Mosonmagyarovar with a Hungarian *Volksdeutsche*, a hatter called Schwarz, whose job it was to identify the Jews for them. Some 160 people were rounded up and sent that same evening in 12 lorries to Győr, where they were deposited in the prison. AB was separated from his family for just over two months, but was later reunited with them at the camp which had been set up at Győr. Not only his parents, his wife and his daughters were there, but also his sisters and a handful of older relations, mainly women. By the time of the reunion, there were 10,000 Jews in the camp.

The reunion took place on a Friday. On the following Tuesday, a call for volunteers for labour was made over the camp loudspeaker system. AB responded to this call, thinking that any work would be good for him and his family, if it meant that they could stay together. They were assembled with the other volunteers and marched for half an hour to the railway station, where a goods train was drawn up. On the outside of the waggons was written: '6 horses or 40 men'; but 70 people were crammed into each one. The window-slits were covered with barbed wire and they were locked in. It was pitch-dark in the waggons once the doors were closed, and they travelled for what seemed like a day. At least the family had managed to keep together, though one of AB's cousins had bled to death in the waggon, since she had been forcibly taken from the camp hospital and loaded on to the transport. They knew by then that a hard fate awaited them, and that the talk about 'voluntary' labour had been a ploy; but they were totally unprepared for what awaited them. When the doors were opened, they were at the ramp at Birkenau.

His parents, his wife and his two little daughters, then aged seven and five, were immediately taken off to the right.[5] He didn't know what their fate would be at that moment, though he learned it soon enough afterwards. He only knew that if he was going to survive, he could not allow himself to think about them. He turned his face, and his mind, away from them.

He was not long in Auschwitz, but was sent, via Dachau and then Mauthausen, to the concentration camp at Melk.[6] In the shadow of the famous baroque monastery on the banks of the Danube, the KZ-inmates lived in sheds next to military barracks, separated from them by barbed wire. AB had arrived in a transport of 1,500 men. At first he was sent to a mining detail, but later transferred to carrying bricks from the railway track to the site of the new crematorium which the prisoners were building for the SS. He spent ten months at Melk, and says that they were fed well, because the Germans pillaged the livestock of the Hungarian *Volksdeutsch* heading west in the face of the Russian advance. They were fed on meat and macaroni – an unheard-of diet for a concentration camp. However, the Russians pressed ever closer, and in March 1945 a transport of prisoners was sent to Ebensee,[7] where conditions were appalling. By that stage of the war there was no food for anybody, though the construction of underground factories went doggedly on as the Germans struggled to produce aeroplanes and new rockets in a last attempt to turn the tide of the war. AB remembers that conditions were so desperate that prisoners who reached Mussulman status were simply stripped naked and left to wander. He managed to survive for six weeks at Ebensee before it was liberated by the Americans; by then, he was suffering from kidney trouble leading to polyuria.

He doesn't know what gave him the strength to survive after he knew for sure that his family had been killed, but he says that it was almost an advantage that the SS never gave you time to think. He was also accompanied by some of his surviving male relations. 'None of us ever spoke of our losses; we kept our hurt inside. There was in any case nothing to do but just carry on – the shouting and the beating were so heavy that it was all you could do to keep going – and no sooner had you finished work and gone to your bunk to snatch a few hours' sleep than they were shouting, "*Aufstehen*," and you had to get up again. There was no time for reflection, for thinking. I was lucky. I was healthy, so I came back.' He has always believed in hard work and he has no time for people who do not. 'My first words on arriving here in the UK were, "I want to work!" If I want to survive, I need to work. That is my nature.' He remembers one of the civilian German miners, who were drafted from the Saar to teach the prisoners how to excavate, saying to him in astonishment one day, 'I can't understand it – you work hard, you behave well, you're clean – how can you possibly be Jewish?' – 'Of course, the man had never met a Jew before and all he had to go on was what the Nazi propaganda told him Jews were like.'

The US army office set up at Ebensee issued the former KZ-inmates with papers to certify that they were liberated prisoners, provided them with excellent food and hospital facilities, and transport to Vienna. The Americans were not able to help AB and the small group of comrades who also came from Hungary to get home. They made their way east from Vienna, following the Danube, until they reached a large town. 'We asked a man with a milk cart where we were and he told us, Pressburg [Bratislava], so we knew that all we had to do was cross the river and we'd be home.'

Home, with his family gone, was a mixed blessing, and there was time now to reflect on his dead loved ones. 'But I am not a soft man. I am tough. I was not ill from sadness. You just carry on.' There is, however, a good deal of sadness in his voice as he speaks. He resumed work, his universal panacea. Before 1938 he had owned a small farm but, since Jews had been forbidden to own property, he had handed it over to a Christian friend who was still there when AB got back. Although they were both penniless, they formed a partnership – the friend seems to have been one of those rare Christians who rewarded the trust reposed in them by Jewish neighbours returning from the KZ – and managed, with the help of other friends, to obtain two horses. By the beginning of 1946 they had started to breed horses on the farm, and they were able to barter home-made vodka on the black market with the Russian troops still in occupation in exchange for farm machinery confiscated from the Austrians.

AB was not in sympathy with the new Communist regime in Hungary, however, and soon he was experiencing a new kind of persecution. Because of the decline in value of the Hungarian currency, all nationals in possession of foreign currency were ordered to register it at a bank. AB, because of his black-market dealings, had quite a supply, including US dollars which were highly sought after. Acting on a tip-off, the local secret police raided his house, impounded the money and sent him for trial in Budapest, where he spent six months in custody before being released. The money stayed confiscated by the police, and he never saw it again. He was, however, a man whose great ability was to bounce back. By 1949 he had married a girl called Ilona, who had also suffered under the Nazis – working in I. G. Farben factories near Berlin – and with four remaining horses was running a small delivery company. It met with success, but in 1951 it was compulsorily nationalized.

AB was made manager, but disillusionment was beginning to creep in. Then, a couple of years later, a friend who had already managed to get most of his money and movable goods out to England asked him for help in getting across the nearby frontier into Austria. He agreed, but the plan was betrayed, and for his part in it AB was sentenced to three years' hard labour in the coal-mines near Oroszlany.

He was released in 1956, and was now determined to leave. Taking advantage of the fact that the Hungarian revolution of that autumn left the frontiers with Austria unsupervised for a few crucial days, he bribed a friend who had a lorry to take him, his wife, and his eight-year-old son across. They arrived in Vienna on 5 November. He had a sister in England who had managed to get out in 1938, though he had completely lost contact with her. Nevertheless he went to the British Embassy and managed to arrange permission to go to the United Kingdom. Everything was organized with exemplary speed, and on Saturday, 17 November 1956, they landed at Blackbushe Airport in Hampshire. They had nothing: no money and no passports – just a few blankets and some spare underclothes for little Gyorjy. By a miracle, their arrival was covered by a television news crew; his sister, who was then living in Kent, saw it broadcast. The following day she came to see him, having traced him to the LCC hostel where the refugee families were being put up.

AB was a good mechanic, and that was lucky for, despite his total lack of English, with his sister's help he was able to get a job straightaway at a garage near where she lived, two days after his arrival in England. 'On the Tuesday I started work, and on the Wednesday I took my son to the primary school. I had a dictionary which the local paper had given me to help me get by.'

The fact that he had a warm welcome in England and encountered no problems gave him tremendous encouragement and inspired him with the energy to get started again on his own. That energy, at the age of 47, when few people welcome an enforced new start, must have been enormous. He started work at the garage on £7 a week, but six months later he was earning double that. 'I worked all the hours God sent because I needed the money, and I was learning English at the same time. But I had the luck to be befriended by two Englishmen who were very like me, and we were able to find lodgings with a young English couple.' He saved hard until he had £250 – just enough to put down a deposit on a house, which he did with the help of the Anglo-Hungarian Refugee Society; but he was also aided by an Englishwoman who befriended the family and lent them money at a very low rate of interest. The hotel which he now owns is named after her.

It was not to be long, however, before the grim legacy of the KZ started to make itself felt. Ilona, who had a bad heart as a result of her treatment in the Farben factories, was also suffering from deteriorating eyesight. Her eyes had been damaged by the aluminium dust in the factory. In 1959 she began to get homesick for Hungary. AB knew that it would be impossible to return, but he also realized that he could no longer leave her at home alone. He had to find a way of earning a living that would enable him to stay at home with her. 'I borrowed money, bought a bigger house, and on 11 January 1960 I opened my first bed-and-breakfast hotel. That was how I got into catering. Out of a need to look after my wife.' The business prospered, and he bought up adjoining houses in the terrace in order to expand. 'I call myself a lucky man because I have lots of drive, and I can turn my hand to anything. I have done everything in the hotels I've run, from cooking to carpeting. As for washing and ironing – at one time I ironed 150 shirts a week!' In 1965 he bought three large terraced houses and converted them into his present hotel, where he manages a staff of 60, though he has turned over the reins to his son now. But there was nothing he could do to save his wife's sight, and Ilona died of a heart attack in 1970.

After her death, he returned to Hungary for the first time in 25 years. It was also his first holiday. He has been back since, but he does not appear to be affected by nostalgia. He says he is a healthy and a happy man. 'I am lucky because I have courage. With courage, you pick up luck,' he says. He also seems to be more naturally able than most to live in the present and for the future; and he has barely allowed himself to draw breath since the end of the war.

III

Not much more than 30 kilometres south of Auschwitz is the town of Bielsko-Biala, where Kitty Hart was born. She had a marvellous childhood, secure and happy. Her father was a lawyer-turned-businessman who had inherited an agricultural-produce business. They belonged to the prosperous middle class. Her parents took her on wonderful holidays, there was a lot of travel, and she went to the best schools – though her education was brought to an abrupt halt when she was 12. Nevertheless she learnt English from her mother, who herself taught English-teachers, and at school she had done French and Latin. In that cosmopolitan part of south-western Poland, the family spoke German at home, and she picked up Czech in the town. She also played the piano, but her great enthusiasm was sport. She skied, climbed and skated, and had won a bronze medal for swimming for Poland in junior events. 'I had a solid basis, a past to fall back on.' Her older brother, Robert, had even gained a place at Nottingham University in 1938, but the Poles wouldn't let him go, because he was 17 and almost ready for call-up. He fled to eastern Poland and later joined the Russian army. He died at Stalingrad.

Kitty has described her journey through the Lublin ghetto to Auschwitz, and then on to Porta Westphalica, in her own book,[8] and she has also made a film about a return visit she made to Auschwitz with her older son;[9] her interest in that period of her life remains very strong.

Kitty has had her own tattoo removed, and she had her mother's removed too after her death – 'She would never have agreed to it in life, and I had to get special permission to have it done.' Both pieces of skin are preserved – little slips of parchment, 39933 and 39934 – in formaldehyde in a small plastic container on the chimney-piece in her study. She picks it up and shakes it. The formaldehyde is getting a little cloudy, which is worrying. 'The most important thing was that the number on your uniform tallied with your tattoo. You might have got a tunic with a different triangle on from the one you should have, but nobody much knew about that or cared – so long as the numbers tallied.'

It was important to have a unit of friends who helped and supported you if you were to survive in the camps, and Kitty's closely cooperative relationship with her mother was one of many examples of such cases helping both parties through. Kitty's voice is warm when she speaks reminiscently of her self-help group at Birkenau, and one can understand that for her, as for Jørgen Kieler, the word 'friendship' carries a much deeper sense than it does for most of us. 'Within your own unit there was complete honour,'[10] says Kitty. 'Friendships were dictated by what was practical. You formed a small interdependent group; each member worked in a different area and could therefore bring something different into the "community": one worked in the kitchens, say, one sorting clothes; someone might have access to water, another to medicine. They were little economic communities.' Later, Kitty found herself isolated in *Kanada*, but then everything was available there. 'You only needed each other for moral support; but oddly the relationships were not so strong, because they were not so essential.'

Kitty feels that the friendships built up between women in the camps were stronger than those between men.

Concerning her relationship with her mother in the camps: she is certain that neither of them would have survived without the support of the other, although they were not together all the time. The important thing was that each knew that the other was there, and that sustained morale. 'In the camp, there was never a day when I didn't think that I was going to die; but there was never a day when I didn't tell myself that I was going to live. If you stopped caring, you stopped fighting. As soon as you said, "I don't think I can go on," that was the first step to becoming a Mussulman, because if you didn't care you wouldn't fight; if you didn't fight, you wouldn't get any food. If you didn't get any food, then you became ill, and so it would go on. It was vital to get hold of people as soon as they said, "I can't go on," and face them spiritually, give them moral strength. You had to resist the rape of the senses, or they would be able to make you lie down and die like a dog.' One of the things she remembers most vividly was what des Près[11] has accurately described as excremental assault. 'You go there now and you see grass, flowers. Then there was mud. Only the *Lagerstrasse*, the main street at Birkenau, was paved. And prisoners were not allowed on it. Everything has to go – all you ever learnt about toilet training. You have to learn a whole new set of rules and terms and live by them. The whole essence of survival is adjustment, and immediate adjustment, and if you couldn't do that you were lost. Older people found it harder. You never thought about the future. You only thought about today. "Today I live and I've got to find something to eat." Just like an animal.'

Kitty says that she pictured herself as an animal. 'In a sort of child's fantasy way, for I was basically still a child, not really developed. I saw myself as a fox, avoiding the hunters. If you're afraid you must creep away, you mustn't fight; and that in my own little way was my route to survival. Thinking was out. If you started to think, you were finished, unless you had a good job. My mother made sure I was never in a job with too close contact with the SS, though one other ingredient of survival was an ability to understand how the Germans thought, and to be able to anticipate and sense their plans and their moods. Luck was important, very important; but it was helped by staying one jump ahead of the Germans all the time.'

There were other ways to survive; but of all the people in the camps, the ones Kitty cannot forgive are the collaborators. She hated them then and still does. Although she refused the opportunity after liberation to kill a group of German civilians in revenge, she isn't sure if her reaction would have been the same if she had known them to be collaborators. Her own friend Henia, who because of her good looks caught the attention of the commandant of the Sosnowiec ghetto, enjoyed a privileged position in Auschwitz. 'She will talk about the rest of the war today, but she won't talk about the camp because she survived the wrong way there, and for years afterwards she lived in mortal fear of reprisals against her, even though she was relatively innocent. She couldn't face coming back to Auschwitz with me for the film I made, though I asked her to.'

Kitty and her mother were liberated by the Americans in mid-April 1945. With her friend Henia and her mother, she worked as an interpreter for the Americans. They were moved to a Quaker-run DP camp at Broitzem, a suburb of Brunswick. 'My immediate response to liberation is hard to define. I wasn't thinking of the future, I just took life as it came. I had a fantastic life in the DP camp, and enjoyed every minute of it. There were so many interesting people there, and so much freedom, and I fell in love.' The man was a young Quaker working in the camp. He was one of the reasons why Kitty and her mother came to England to live, although there were also relatives living in Birmingham upon whom her mother depended. The love-affair did not work out, but in the DP camp, a place where many survivors were at a low ebb, everything came into flower for Kitty. 'It was marvellous, one of the happiest times of my life. I had a glorious 18 months. I was fed, clothed, looked after, and I didn't have to learn anything. I travelled all over Germany, hitch-hiking or on trains, and I didn't have any money, but I just showed my KZ number and they let us on. We travelled from DP camp to DP camp – we were always fed – and we led a charmed life. Although we were young girls and beginning to look attractive again, we never encountered any unpleasantness from men. As for the Germans in general, they didn't want to know; they wouldn't even talk about it. It was as if they wanted to block it out.'

Germans today hold no terrors for her. She is mistrustful of those of her own generation, but 'anyone else is OK. When I'm in Germany or Austria, skiing for example, and people ask me how it is that I speak such good German, I simply tell them that my mother was Austrian – which is true – and it stops there. It's only when people start asking further questions that I start to weigh things up. Then I decide if I want to go on with the conversation.'

Kitty's instinct was to visit Germany after the war and visit it often. 'It was a bit like forcing yourself to stroke the Alsatian that's just bitten you in order not to get traumatized for life, but there were perfectly human, selfish reasons too. I wanted to go back and show them I was still around: Look, you tried to get rid of us, but here we are, alive and well fed and with children. That was very satisfying.' She also felt that it was very important for her two sons to mix with Germans, though they have grown up not caring to. 'To be honest, basically I don't like to much either. You do see something in the German character which is arrogant; you can't get away from that. I see it on holiday – always on holiday. The German tourists have always got to be first, and they simply push you out of the way – it doesn't matter who you are.' She remembers being at the railway station at Zermatt one year. A crowd of Germans were pushing and shoving to get on to a train, with the result that a small German child was getting crushed. 'I managed to rescue it but I really lost my temper with those people. I shouted at them, "How typically bloody German!" I think it gave them a bit of a shock, hearing that in their own language.'

She and her mother came to England in September 1946. She found it a shattering experience. 'At least the UNRRA people knew a bit about what was wrong with us, and the Quakers who'd helped us had been among the first at Belsen.' England was cold and unfriendly. The uncle whom they had come to stay with in Birmingham forbade any mention of the camps. Birmingham itself came as a shock. 'I'd never seen a city: all that noise, and the traffic. And I couldn't understand traffic-lights, but when I asked my uncle about them he looked at me as if I were quite mad. My cousins, who were about the same age as me, just thought I was weird, and they didn't help me either.'

There was no question of her being able to stay in her uncle's house for long. With the help of a doctor at the Royal Orthopaedic Hospital in Birmingham, she trained as a radiographer, something which she could qualify for relatively quickly and start working and earning; the most pressing need was to be independent. The practical reason for choosing such a career was that she could live in at a hospital hostel while she was training. Looking back, she feels that she would have been happier training as a physiotherapist; but the training would have taken too long, she didn't have the money to pay for it, and she couldn't have lived in . . . 'and there was this doctor who was willing to give me a helping hand, so I took it; I had to take it. And you sort of grow into it like any other job,' she adds, a little sadly.

She met her husband at the Birmingham International Centre. He was born in Königsberg (Kaliningrad), but managed to get to England just before the war. They married in March 1949, and set up home in a tiny flat at the top of a house in a run-down corner of the city. Kitty felt a great need to produce a family, to bring Jewish children into the world to make up for those who had been killed. Her sons were born in 1951 and 1953. The first 15 years in England were very hard indeed. She had to support her mother, and as her husband was getting his upholstery business on to its feet there was very little money. Although the flat was bleak and water came in when it rained, she remembers it with pleasure, because it was home; but frequently there was not enough to eat and, apart from the material considerations, there were the spiritual ones. Kitty felt isolated. 'People didn't understand. In some ways the suffering I endured in the early post-war years was worse than it had been in the KZ. Personally, I certainly found that time more traumatic. To begin with, I couldn't adapt to what was normal, or accept normal things, normal concerns, normal behaviour. I think my own reactions were probably due to people expecting me to behave in a certain way. I was a bit strange to them but they didn't quite know how – and they didn't want to know.' No one encouraged her to open up and talk about her experiences in the camps, though that did not deter her from trying.

This part of her life is remembered with great depth of feeling. 'While I was training at the hospital, and later when I was working there, I could feel the antipathy. The other people in the department didn't think I fitted in. I tried very hard to be friendly but I found that people shied away. They didn't want to know. They knew there was something there but they didn't want to ask what – and I really didn't have anything in common with my contemporaries. Although I was only 20, I lived on a different planet – conversations about clothes and boyfriends meant nothing to me. And in the hostel where I was staying during my training, I couldn't bear being shut in at ten o'clock at night, but they didn't understand why. It wasn't that I wanted to stay out all night. I just didn't want to be shut in.' On the other hand, she wouldn't accept being locked out either. She would deliberately arrive back too late to be able to get in by the front door, and then climb a drainpipe and get into the hospital through another girl's window – just to show that she wouldn't accept their rules. In fact, she felt compelled to break them. 'I broke the German system, and I was going to break this system, too. They wouldn't accept or understand why I was doing it; they just thought I was sleeping with a boyfriend. It would have been impossible to explain to them in any case – and not worth trying, because they didn't want to know. So I wasn't popular with the authorities, and since everything depended on success for me, I worked harder and better than most of the others – so I wasn't popular with the other trainees either.'

All this time was tainted by the most aching loneliness, and as loneliness was something she had never experienced in the KZ, it came as a shock to her. She had learnt English from her mother, but in the late Forties she found herself in a cold and unfriendly country, in an unattractive town, facing career prospects which must have fallen far short of those she had promised herself barely six years earlier. She has a strong, intense personality, and it is not hard to see what its effect might have been on provincial English people unused to foreigners in the years immediately after the war. But there was also a sense of isolation within the family. 'No one invited me out. I missed the presence of other KZ people, and I missed the group of four friends who'd battled it out with me in Birkenau.' With that precious feeling of interdependence gone, it was not surprising that in one sense there existed a nostalgia, not for the camps but for the solidarity they called up.

She was a child when she went into the KZ system, and a young adult when she came out. One of her principal difficulties was simply that people assumed that her development in those crucial transitional years had been a normal one, and that she'd know how to behave socially and in a modern bureaucracy. 'But what I am most bitter about is the loss of my education. Those are years you can never get back again. I am still trying to catch up with them, but I never will. You can recapture any years of your life, perhaps, except for those years between 13 and 18. There were no provisions whatsoever for people like me when I came over to this country. There was no way I could get a grant or any help in rehabilitation. I wanted to go back to school, and if there had been a chance I would have made up for what I had lost. I had to do it in physics in any case to become a radiographer. What I find it particularly hard to forgive is that there was no programme even within the Jewish community. In fact, I cannot mix properly with the Jewish community here because I cannot forgive this. They did not want to know what had happened to us survivors of the Holocaust. Maybe they were a little afraid for themselves; being Jews, maybe they thought they'd have to be more English than the English. Once or twice the local rabbi asked me to dinner, but even then the subject was not discussed.'

The experience of the KZ never leaves her. 'I always think about it, it's always somewhere in my mind. I hate it when I'm jammed in with a lot of people somewhere – in a bus in the rush-hour, for example. That always makes me think of the camp. And the behaviour of people who are crushed together is the same – it brings it back to you. I don't like smoke, even bonfires, either, but it's crowds that really get me.' There is something else, which she shares with many survivors: that whenever she meets somebody new, she automatically assesses how they would have been in the KZ.

Not long ago she was asked to be technical assistant for the Auschwitz scenes for the film called *Sophie's Choice*, based on the novel by William Styron. She remembers the work with great enthusiasm. 'They were re-creating the camp in Yugoslavia. When I got there they had already built the Birkenau set and everything was wrong – to such an extent that the watchtowers were inside the wire; and there was a crematorium that was much too close to the *Blocks*. And it wasn't muddy, so we had to make mud, but there was no water, so that had to be brought up in tankers. The action was unbelievable. The director wanted to show women working and he had a few extras trotting about carrying a few bricks. So I said, this really isn't right, leave it to me. I organized some extras who really looked like prisoners – the girls he'd got just didn't look right; we negotiated with a nearby institution for mentally handicapped young people. They were cross-eyed and walking anyhow, and they were just right. I told the film-makers that we would reproduce *Block* 25.[12] And we shaved the heads of the mentally handicapped youths and trained them to stick their hands out of the barred windows and call out for food, and they thought it was a huge joke, but it was most effective; and then I had a couple of girls walking by carrying buckets of shit – a job I did myself on the *Scheisskommando* at Birkenau. Some of the cast were crying, they were so upset by it. I think I was the only person who was not upset. I'd seen it all before; but it was very real when we had finished. For the mentally handicapped extras it was a nice day out; nothing hurt them, and they made perfect Mussulmen because they had the same utterly vacant expressions. And we didn't show any horror – a flogging, or a kapo strangling someone with the heel of his boot, or dogs set on to children. You don't need to show the horror to shock people – just the everyday life of the camp.'

She is still a rebel. 'When it comes down to it, things more or less run themselves, don't they? What the authorities want to do is run *you*.' She thinks those survivors who went to live in Israel may have had it easier, because it was a new country and everyone was starting out together. But she was never tempted to go there herself, because she wanted 'to get away from all the Jews, in a way. If it had been a multi-racial society I would have gone, but all Judaism has ever done for me is destroy my life.'

Two Friends

Hugo Gryn and Ben Helfgott both came to England as teenagers, and became friends there.

I

Hugo Gryn was born in Berehovo, Ruthenia, Czechoslovakia (now Beregovo, in the USSR). He now lives in London.

His father was a successful businessman, working in forest development on an international level; and his mother trained as a doctor, though she never practised. Their home was in the Carpathians, but they had a second house in Carlsbad (Karlovy Vary). His brother Gabi was three years younger than he, and was one of twins, the other of whom died at birth. They grew up in a comfortable, happy environment; then came 1938, when Ruthenia ceased to exist. Carlsbad was in the Sudetenland, and had already been annexed when Ruthenia was 'liberated' by the Hungarians, who proceeded to conduct a campaign of terror which provided Hugo Gryn with his first taste of what was to come. His paternal grandparents lived in a village in a farming community on the River Tissa which formed the frontier between Hungary and Czechoslovakia at the time. One day in October 1938 his father received a distress call from them, and Hugo went with him to see them. The night before, Hungarian terrorists had crossed the Tissa and killed the cattle belonging to the Jewish homes; his grandparents' cows had had their stomachs ripped open. That was the start of the war for him; he was so stunned he couldn't speak – he couldn't even cry.

'Liberation' for Berehovo soon followed. Their town was renamed Beregszasz, and there followed a mass of new legislation discriminating against the Jews. The population of the town was about 25,000 of whom 15,000 were Jews, and the Hungarian Fascists fleeced them. The Jewish schools were closed, and the *Gymnasium*[1] had to have a *numerus clausus*, by which in a predominantly Jewish town only three per cent of the entrants could be Jewish. Hugo Gryn got a place, but he went into a deep depression at the thought of going to the school. He was fortunate, however, because his father showed great compassion and managed to locate a Jewish boarding school in Debrecen which took him as a boarder.

At that time the Jews in Hungary were subject to certain restrictions but still relatively free. He started at the school in 1939 and stayed for three years, returning home for the holidays. The shadow of the concentration camps had yet to fall across Hungary, and the Jews of Berehovo formed a 600-year-old community, entitled to claim Hungarian citizenship and the protection that afforded. There had been, however, an influx of Jews from Galicia. These people had fled Polish persecution only 20 years earlier, and they were now deported. Hugo Gryn remembers that on Sunday mornings there were film-shows at school. 'On one particular morning the newsreel we got along with the feature showed the usual scenes of the victorious Hungarian army beating the Russians rotten, when all of a sudden I saw a shot of our former neighbours being marched along a road, looking dreadful.' He wrote to his parents immediately to find out what was going on. He and his fellow-Jews at the school began to experience a sense of unease. 'Our school was still all right, and we had brilliant teachers, who were in fact Jewish academics who had been sacked from their university posts. But there was a Calvinist school in the town too, and their sixth-formers used to beat up our first-formers. Unfair and unpleasant street-battles ensued which the police did nothing to stop. Our own gym teacher had been the Olympic wrestling champion in 1932 and 1936 – his name was Karpov – and he taught us self-defence instead of callisthenics. Thus at the age of about 11 we were being taught street-fighting. We grew up in a funny way, but fast.'

There was another aspect of discrimination which the school could not shut out. All the other schoolboys in Debrecen had to do some form of military training, but every Wednesday afternoon the Jews were sent to a gasworks where they were set to shovelling cinders from one huge pile to another. The following week, they had to shovel the new pile back to where it had been before. It was pointless, tiring and humiliating work. Adult Jews in 'non-essential' jobs, such as the male members of AB's family, mentioned in the previous chapter, were put into so-called labour camps, where the work involved ditch-digging for the German Front. It was not long before the blow fell upon all Jews.

'I was delegated to collect ration coupons from the central offices for the school. By the age of 12 I was being treated as an adult. And that is how it was until one day I went home for the holidays and the Gestapo were heading for Berehovo on the same train. They came with good intelligence, for they had done their homework about our community, and I was home in time to experience its destruction.' The pattern was not unfamiliar: they took about 13 men hostage, carefully chosen either as leaders of the community or as the fathers of large families, popular men. The hostages were then simply held for ransom. The Jews of the town were asked for one million *pengoes* in return for their lives, or the men would be shot at midnight. The community desperately tried to raise the cash but it was an impossibly large sum; whereupon the Germans said that they would extend the deadline and additionally would accept certain kinds of bank-book. Hugo Gryn was one of the children sent round with collecting-boxes from house to house. Still there wasn't enough. 'So the Gestapo said graciously that they would accept at their own valuation jewellery and watches.' Finally the men were released, but the community had been reduced to poverty, and the poverty was a trap. Without money there was no mobility – even if mobility had been remotely possible. 'And in view of what was going to happen to us soon, the Germans had stripped us of all we owned without complication, with minimum effort and maximum security. But they had kept their word about letting the hostages go once the ransom had been paid. And people always want to believe that everything will be all right: pathetically, we always want to think the best of those with power over us. So one entered into this bizarre game – into a kind of collusion, as I can call it with over 40 years' hindsight. But what choice did the community have?'

A ghetto was formed at Berehovo, in one area where there were brick factories with huge storage sheds, and sawmills. The story the Jews were fed was that they were to be held there prior to deportation to the East to help the German war-effort in forced agricultural work. But the true destination was Auschwitz.

Hugo Gryn was deported with his family. 'It was all very carefully done. The train would come into the railway siding by the ghetto. I was a nosy kid, and I found a slip of paper in one of the waggons and pulled it out. Someone had written the route out on it: Berehovo – Presov – Cracow – Auschwitz. We didn't know what Auschwitz was . . . Day after day people left on transports. We were on the last. As far as I know I am the youngest survivor of Berehovo. We were taken to Birkenau.[2]

'That's where I grew up. My life was saved on arrival by one of the prisoners already there who were waiting at the ramp to deal with the luggage we'd brought. These prisoners muttered over and over in Yiddish, so that only we could hear, *"Ihr seit achzen johr alt und ihr hott a fach"* – "You're 18 years old and you've got a trade." My father understood what was meant, so that by the time my turn came in the queue up to the SS-man who was making the selection, I was coached to say, in good German, that I was 19 – I went one better – and that I was a carpenter and joiner. My brother was too little – he was 11. He tried to say that he was 18, but they just laughed and sent him the other way. My mother ran after him, but they pulled her back. "Don't worry, you'll see him later," they said. The men and the women were separated, and the old and the very young were in a third group. But from then on I was 19, and I had a trade.

'I don't think any of us had an inkling of what was going to happen. I followed my father, and we went through the process of being shaved and disinfected, and so on. We were issued with uniforms and detailed to a *Block*. I wondered what had happened to the rest of my family – my grandparents had been on the same transport – and I asked a man who was already a prisoner there, "What goes on here, when will we see the rest of our family again?" And he answered, "You'll never see them again, they are already dead."[3] And I said, "Look, I'm really scared, and it's so frightening here – why do you have to make such stupid jokes?" And he said, "OK, if you think it's a stupid joke, it's a stupid joke." It was at least another day before I either realized, or allowed myself to realize, what was truly going on.'

He says that it is very hard to answer the question of whether there was a precise moment when he decided to try to survive. Because both his father and he had said they were skilled at a trade, they were kept at Auschwitz for only six weeks before being selected for transport to the 'work-camp' of Lieberose, one of the sub-camps of Sachsenhausen. 'Once you were away from Birkenau you breathed a bit easier – at least you weren't that close to a gas chamber any more; and I had one big thing going for me: I was with my father the whole time. It was more than just a moral help; he saved my life. He saved it by practical advice, like telling me to save some of my evening bread ration for the next morning; but I also learnt to work things out for myself.' He was quick to see that no one could possibly do the heavy work expected of them on the number of calories they were given and that, to survive, he would have to balance the energy he was getting from the food against the amount he could afford to expend in work. This calculation became a mathematical problem for him which had to be solved daily. He had to do whatever he could to preserve strength and energy, and he spent a lot of time inventing ways to do this. It was fortunate that his pretended skills were never put too greatly to the test, but the demands of the general building duties he was assigned to were cruel, and it demanded ingenuity to avoid them without appearing to do so. 'On one occasion, when we were on a detail where you had to fill cement bags and then carry them two at a time, I managed to fill four with insulating material, which weighed next to nothing, and I used them to ease my labour. And sometimes you could find a bolt-hole and rest up for a couple of hours in the middle of the day. It wasn't always easy, or possible, but you became an experienced prisoner and you learned the ropes. The only attitude I developed, which I knew was there at the time but which I can only describe now, was my complete conviction that I was not guilty. I knew that I was innocent and that, contrary to appearances, it was our gaolers who were the guilty ones. I had no illusions about our captors. I never even wanted to think that they were better than they were. To think that way could be a trap. People tried to curry favour with the guards sometimes to try to survive better, but that was a very dangerous game, because the guards' moods were not consistent. I tried to have as little as possible to do with them. As far as possible you kept your head low, though it was inevitable that from time to time you would attract their attention. If that happened, you could always fall back on the fact that you weren't a person, just a number. But they weren't people, either.'

With the Allied advance the Germans withdrew, taking their prisoners with them – Hugo Gryn and his father were taken first to Mauthausen in Austria, and thence to Günskirchen, 'A nothing place we were marched to from Mauthausen in April 1945 – it was just a place where they were going to finish us off.' Before the SS could do this, the camp was liberated, by the Americans, on 5 May. 'I was barely able to react to liberation. Everyone was very ill – nearly all of us had typhoid. We were taken to a temporary hospital the Americans had set up in a place called Hersching, near Linz. There were two people to a bed. I shared a bed with my father. And he died there. Of typhoid, of starvation. And I lost consciousness, so that there is a period about which I remember nothing, and I have not been able to find anybody who is able to tell me about that time. I'm not sure how long it lasted, either. I was told that as they carried my father out – they were using German orderlies for the work of carrying out the dead – I went for one of them, wanted to kill him. I don't know whether they gave me an injection or if I collapsed then, but I did not see my father's body again, and I don't know where they took him, where he is buried. They must have put him into a mass grave. It is a very bitter thing to know that he survived all through the KZ only to die within days of liberation, and that was a moment when effectively I gave up. I have no memory of dates or sequences of events, only that it was some time in May. I've tried to reconstruct it, what must have happened, and I can't. I have wanted to write it down for my own sake, but there is no precision, so it is very difficult. And I can't say prayers on the anniversary of his death because I don't know exactly when it was. One older ex-prisoner told me later that my father's *jahrzeit* was on such-and-such a date, but it doesn't figure: I think it's too late, and my guess is that he just told me so that at least I'd have a day. I don't know. Maybe I wasn't even told it, but a date stuck, even though all it may be is an indication of the chaotic state of my mind at the time . . . But in the end, life took over, and I got better. My hair grew again, my teeth became firm in my gums again, and I wanted to go home, to see if anybody else had survived. If they had, I assumed that they would go home.'

Home was now in the Russian zone of occupation. He left Hersching and got on a boat on the Danube, which took him as far as Wiener Neustadt; this was as far as the boats would go, because beyond that the river was still mined. He joined forces with a handful of fellow refugees there, but he had developed a severe phlegmon on his chest and, on his birthday, 25 June, made his way to a Russian army camp, where the medical staff agreed to lance it for him. 'They were very nice – there was no anaesthetic, and they had to find a way to take my mind off the pain when the doctor lanced this massive boil – my chest was double its normal size. So the nurses unzipped their blouses and let me feel their breasts, which certainly did the trick. The relief once the thing had been lanced was enormous – it was almost symbolic – the ugly pus which came out was like all the badness I had been through leaving me. I know that I saw it as symbolic even then. It was a turning point for me.'

The following day he felt well enough to travel, and he teamed up with two or three others and stole a horse and buggy, which they drove to Pressburg (Bratislava). There they abandoned their transport and he went to a transit camp for Jewish DPs to beg a shower. While he was taking it, however, someone was stealing all his things; when he came out, everything had gone except for the liberation certificate which mercifully he had left with the camp management. Everyone was sorry for him, but there was nothing much they could do. However, by means of a whip-round they organized some replacement clothes for him: an old army jacket, some shorts and some leather clogs. 'I must have looked bizarre, but I had to press on. I caught a night-train to Budapest. I remember that there were hundreds of people waiting for this train – the only train there was – but I managed to find out what siding it was on and climbed aboard before it was rolled to the platform. I got into one of the better carriages – one with windows, for the trains were very beaten-up just after the war. That night was very memorable. When the train pulled into the platform no one got into my carriage although the train was packed. Then I saw why: it was reserved for Russian soldiers. But when they arrived they didn't throw me out. They were friendly, and we started to chat, as my Russian wasn't too bad.

'In the middle of the night they got up and started to rob the train. Most of the passengers were peasants going to sell their produce – chickens and so forth – on the black market in Budapest. These soldiers fleeced the passengers: watches, money, the lot. They were kids, not much older than I was, and I think they reckoned the Hungarians owed them something; but when they returned to our compartment, they cut me in for some of their loot, with the result that I arrived in Budapest in the morning wearing a Russian uniform. And I had a spare uniform, and seven watches, and three full wallets, and two or three pairs of shoes, and a loaded gun with some spare ammunition that I later discovered didn't fit. I was set up.'

He went to see some relatives in Budapest, whose address he remembered and who he thought might have been spared. 'It was an unpleasant experience. I arrived at their house still early in the morning, and they opened the door to me, but they wouldn't let me in; they just didn't want to know. Of course I was wearing a Russian uniform, which wasn't too popular in Budapest at the time, but they knew who I was. It was awful. Like a hammer-blow. And I went away and I cried.'

As soon as it was possible, he caught a train to Berehovo. Two stops before his home station, a man he knew got on and told him that his mother was home, but that she was expecting not only Hugo, but his father as well. There were people who had also come back who had told her that they had seen both of them on the road home. He told the man that his father was dead, and when the train arrived at Berehovo, he didn't want to get off. He didn't see how he could face his mother, and even asked the man to go and break the news to her himself. They held the train up at Berehovo until they managed to persuade him to get off.

'It was a sad reunion with my mother. She knew without my having to say a word. She just instinctively did what Jews do. She pulled out a little low stool and sat for an hour *shevah*. You're supposed to sit for seven days – that's what *shevah* means – but if you hear news of the death later you just sit a symbolic hour. We mourned together, taking comfort in the ritual. After Birkenau, they had taken my mother to Stutthof, where she stayed until the camp was evacuated. One night on the death-march west she managed to organize things so that a group of women were able to stay hidden in a barn they had been using for overnight shelter, when the others moved on in the morning. They stayed in the barn for three days until the Russians liberated them. My mother was decorated by the Czech government later for helping save so many lives.'

At the time, his mother was living in an uncle's house. She told him that their own family house now had other people living in it – some Hungarian Gentiles. Later that afternoon, he took a walk down the long garden that connected his uncle's house with their old one. He wanted to go back because he had hidden a few things there, such as the camera he had been given for his bar-mitzvah. 'And a man came out and spoke to me quite roughly: "Who are you, and what do you want?" "This is my house," I said. "Not any more," said the man. "It's ours now – so get lost!" I don't know whether it was the tone of his voice or what, but I decided to act exactly like the hero of a cowboy film. I said, "Look, I'm coming back tomorrow and you'd better not be here!" I was very, very angry. And the next day I went back, with my gun. They were still there of course, so I shouted and yelled, and fired the gun. To tell the truth, I knew that I probably wouldn't get into too much trouble, because a cousin of mine had been promoted to post-war chief of police of the town. But the Hungarians were scared: here was a mad kid firing real bullets. I fired off the six or seven rounds in the pistol, and they ran. Then I wanted to reload, and that's when I discovered that the spare bullets wouldn't fit!'

He was able to reclaim possession of his family house, but his mother wouldn't move back into it because of the memories it held, and so they decided to put it at the disposal of any Jews coming back from the camps and finding themselves homeless. 'At about the same time there occurred something which has coloured my life since. There is a Jewish law – a very difficult and complex law – by which a woman who is married to a man who has disappeared is, so to speak, chained. She cannot divorce, since the man's whereabouts are not known, and she cannot assume that he is dead, and thus free herself to remarry. She is said to be an *agunah*. This is one of two or three tenets in Jewish law which are intractable: there is no remedy for it. In view of this, I was approached by some other men who had returned from the KZ and asked to meet with them and try to recall which of the other men from our community had certainly died, so that in the event of any of their wives returning, they would not be placed in the position of being chained. And I sat with them for hours, and they questioned me with the understanding that only people who have shared the experience of the concentration camps can have, and I was amazed at how much I could remember; but I was also profoundly impressed by this continuing respect for Jewish law, and by the foresight of these men. Immediately, they had started to think about how lives were going to be rebuilt.'

At the time we had this conversation, we were driving north from the West End of London to Hampstead. It was late afternoon on a November day. 'This kind of weather reminds me of the camps. Cold and grey. It always seemed to be like this. I know that there were hot days too, in summer; but this is the weather that lingers in the mind – the characteristic, unbearable weather. The most unpleasant things always seemed to happen in this kind of weather, and during roll-call in winter.'

There was no future for him in Berehovo. The town had effectively been destroyed. Of the 15,000 Jews who had lived there in 1938, a scant

800 remained in 1945 and, of that number, the majority were men who had survived the work-camps, rather than survivors of the KZ. He felt that living in the town was like living in a cemetery. A dozen friends of about the same age had managed to survive, and used to meet, but there seemed to be a huge pointlessness about everything. That same summer of 1945, he got a job with an UNRRA team which was passing through Berehovo, and travelled with them into Russia as an interpreter. 'I'd learnt quite a bit of Russian in the camps, and the leader of the UNRRA team was French, so, as I could speak some French as well as good German, I was all right. What I couldn't speak a word of at the time was English!' The job entailed the location and repatriation of refugees. It was a kind of deliverance for Hugo Gryn, who was unhappy to stay where he was, and ready for anything. He travelled long distances, deep into Russia, with the UNRRA team, and when at the end of his tour of duty he returned to Berehovo, there was a new decision to confront. 'The cousin who'd become chief of police had got the job as a kind of reward for loyalty. He'd fought first in the Czech and later in the Russian army. And he had pulled strings on my behalf to arrange for me to continue my education in Moscow, now that our town was to be a part of the USSR. I was placed at a crossroads. It was lucky that I had had such recent experience of Russia with the UNRRA job – because I now knew enough to know that I did not want to make my home there. This had nothing to do with politics, it was a purely personal reaction.' So instead of accepting his cousin's offer, he headed westwards – to Prague. This was possible because technically he was still a Czech citizen '– or so I thought! Anyway at that point in history everything was in such confusion that nobody really gave a hang about what nationality you were. And I had my liberation certificate from the Americans.'

In Prague, within a relatively short time he was able to get on to a university course, because he had what was called a war record, and in those days the authorities were careful not to make a distinction between military service and time spent in Nazi prisons. It was possible to sit a special examination in lieu of having matriculation certificates. He was accepted on to a course to read law – he took it more for the sake of something to study than from a special interest in reading that particular subject. 'In fact, I spent most of my time in Prague working with the Jewish community.' By this time, something had happened which would have been difficult to foresee. Jews, especially those who went back to Poland, experienced a new wave of anti-Semitism. 'When my friend Ben went back to Poland, he was nearly killed in Czestochowa, and other people had similar experiences which, if not as bad, were certainly a strong indication that Jews were not welcome back. So there was a tide of refugees flowing westwards, and many of these were Jewish Poles passing through Prague.' Much of his work, which was voluntary, involved meeting these people off trains and helping them with their further arrangements, as well as escorting them to railway stations and putting them on the right trains for their onward journey, or taking them to the border, and even as far as the US zone. 'I remember accompanying a group once together with Joe Schwarz, who was an American representative of the JOINT in Prague. At the frontier an American soldier told him that the group couldn't go any farther. "In that case," said Joe, "you'd better shoot them, because they're not going back to Poland to be shot by Poles. They might as well be shot here by Americans."' He also worked with children's groups that were organized for onward journeys in Prague, and as a reward for that work he was allowed to escort them on flights to England. 'The Central British Fund had had long negotiations with the British government to allow 1,000 Jewish children to come to Britain, whose surety the CBF would provide. At the time everything was in a mess. There were few places for refugees to go. The United States quota system was rigorous, and emigration to Palestine was next to impossible. The Central British Fund's goal was to secure shelter at least for these thousand Jewish orphans under 16 years old.' In the event, no more than about 725 such children could be found. Gryn escorted two or three groups of these children. The planes flew in to Croydon airport. On one occasion at the very end of 1945, while he was waiting for the plane to refuel so that he could return with it to Prague, the Central British Fund's man in London, Leonard G. Montefiore, stayed with him to keep him company. 'He was just being nice, speaking to me in terrible German about my plans, my ambitions. I told him I had none. "Well, why don't you come to London?" "I have no papers." "We should be able to arrange something." It was very cold on the flight back to Czechoslovakia, and all the way I sat there among the empty seats thinking over what he'd been trying to say to me, and I decided that what lay behind his words was: Get the hell out of there.'

Everyone in Europe seemed to be on the move, and that was infectious. The position of the new Czech regime under Benes did not seem all that secure. When he consulted his mother about his possible plans to leave, she was encouraging. The last transport of children out to England was in February 1946. 'By an administrative error the accompanying docket said 26 children, instead of 25 children plus one escort. I managed to pass myself off as the 26th child. The plane was loaded with friends of mine – I'd promised them all the bright lights of London. In the event, we were all sent off to a farm in Scotland.' He'd decided almost on impulse to get out on that last transport: the unexpectedly available extra space had seemed like fate – and his instinctive feeling was that he should get as far away from Central

Europe as possible. The farthest away he could think of at the time was London. 'But I found myself in Scotland, milking six cows a day.'

There was little time to reflect upon the experiences of the concentration camps, and at that time nobody wanted to, either. 'I wanted to put it behind me geographically, certainly; but I was still a teenager; I wasn't very reflective. The biggest problem was my mother – I got her out of Russia – to Carlsbad – but when I tried to persuade her to join me in England later, she wouldn't.' His mother had had enough of upheaval, and the thought of a new language concerned her. She remarried after some time, but died of cancer in 1964. He managed to see her again in 1947 when he returned briefly to Czechoslovakia on a visit, but after the Communist takeover there in 1948 he was not able to return until the thaw of 1966.

He went to Israel as a volunteer in 1948, and went to some lengths to conceal this from her to spare her worry. With a group of largely English-Jewish young men, who felt that they'd had a relatively easy wartime, he was attached to a fighting unit and saw plenty of action. Too much, he says dryly. 'But I got a lucky break – I was made a corporal. It came about this way: our unit was down in the south, near Beersheba. We weren't exactly veterans, and we had nothing but a few old rifles. And then one day we received a brand-new machine-gun, beautifully crated – from Czechoslovakia! I was the only one who knew how to read the instructions that came with it. I didn't know how to put it together, but I did know how to read the instructions! So I was put in charge, and promoted to corporal, and given two assistants – one of whom I thought might have seen a machine-gun before. And we worked out how to fire it and how to clean it. But then unfortunately for me I got jaundice, and was invalided out, and ended up getting over it in Marseilles, en route for England. I didn't want to settle in Israel. I was still very young, and I knew that my education was still very incomplete. That is what I wanted to pursue.'

The pursuit led him to a serious study of mathematics, and it was his original ambition to become a mathematician; but hand in hand with that interest was another, that went just as deep, in Jewish law and its history. 'I went to a lecture by Leo Baeck[4] in London at the Stern Hall before I went to Israel. I guessed this must be the same Leo Baeck who had been in Theresienstadt and I quite wanted to hear him, so I decided to go. That really marked the beginning of our friendship. Much later on, he gave me private tuition in premedieval homiletics: at that time it seemed to me that there were only two people in the world seriously interested in Jewish studies – him and me – and I wasn't too sure about him! Well, he took this for a long time, and finally one day he said to me, "Look, if you're really so serious about all this, why don't you do something about it?" At the time I wasn't planning to be a rabbi at all.'

The decision led to a prolonged period of study in the USA. He had no fixed plan to settle there, but there was nowhere else to go to study. In London, there was only the Orthodox Jews' College. The Leo Baeck College that is there now didn't exist. All the German institutions had been destroyed. The Rabbinic school in Cincinnati was virtually the only place where one could study to be a Reform Rabbi. The choice was further influenced by the fact that Leo Baeck taught for one term a year at the Hebrew College in Cincinnati. There was a strong bond between the two men, perhaps partly because of the shared experience of the camps.

Gryn took United States citizenship in 1956, but until then had had a stateless passport. 'That is the most inconvenient kind of passport to travel under. The moment border authorities see one, their eyes light up: "This one we can take apart," they say to themselves. "Who can he protest to – the High Commissioner for refugees?" I remember once taking a train across Europe. After the first frontier, I didn't bother to repack – I just left everything hanging up in the compartment.'

He was in America from 1950 until 1957. He left to go directly to Bombay to become the first rabbi ever to the Jewish community there. He jokes about it: 'People ask me why I went there, and I say because I thought when I was offered it they meant Bombay, Indiana!' In fact, he took the post because one of the unofficial conditions of his scholarship had been that he should work for at least a time outside the USA, and his own feelings were that as he had been helped so much by Jews who did not know him, so he wanted to give something back by trying to help Jews whom he didn't know. He returns to India still from time to time to visit the now minute community: many have emigrated to Israel in the time since he was their rabbi.

The nightmare of the camps remains, not as bad dreams and unhappy memories; these things he has been able to confront. 'But I have not got over my guilt that I am alive, and I think many of us have that problem.[5] Rationally, I know that it is not my fault that I survived, but guilt is not always a rational thing. My brother was a much nicer person than me. That is an objective judgment; he really was brighter, altogether nicer – so why isn't he alive, and why am I? And my father was a wonderful man. It is a difficult thing to live with. I can't explain my guilt, but I am always conscious of it. I have tried to expiate it in my work, but I don't succeed.

'The other thing that marks me is an implacable hatred of racism in all its forms. If I see a National Front poster I tear it down. Not the kind of thing respectable middle-aged rabbis should do. I also have problems within the Jewish world, where we are now polarizing. I have been very upset by the stand taken by Meir Kahane in Israel, and feel that he is an obscenity. I once nearly came to blows with him. It was at the World Gathering in Jerusalem,[6] itself a remarkable experience, and Kahane was going to take over a symposium that was in progress. He'd timed his entrance for maximum effect, and he had an American TV crew in tow, whom he'd obviously primed. And he started to march down the aisle to the rostrum, shouting out that he had something to say to the meeting, and I confronted him – I was backed up by my buddy Ben, who as you know is a former Olympic weightlifter, so I felt a little braver, and I blocked the gangway and said, "Meir, you are not going past me." "I am going there!" he said. And I said, "This is not your meeting. This is not your story. It has nothing to do with you. You are here to disrupt; you are here to preach hate. There is only one way you are going to get to the rostrum – you're going to have to knock me down – and I am just man enough to knock you down first. And if you want that televised, have it televised." And he walked out. He started to fume outside, but that was the end of him for that evening. On the other hand, he is so obvious. It's easy to distance oneself from him. But there are all sorts of tensions among well-meaning Jews. My notions of being Jewish are all-embracing, non-exclusive; and I think my attitude is coloured by my experience. But I can also see that experience bringing people down on the other side: their argument is that the Jews should close ranks against the rest of the world. But I think that fundamentalism breeds hatred, and that liberalism breeds love.

'But I will not go to Germany, so I'm not personally free of hate. It's quite irrational. You see, I won't even go to Spain, because of Torquemada, back in 1492. That's really dotty – because of Ferdinand and Isabella and all that crew. And if it is on principle, as you generously suggest, then it's not very rational.'[7]

II

Ben Helfgott was a schoolboy in Piotrkow when the war broke out. His father was in the flour business, as were most of the family, on both sides. They bought grain from the peasant farmers, and his father and uncle ran flour-mills in the town. In terms of the general standard of living in Poland at the time, the circumstances of the family were comfortable.

The Germans reached Piotrkow on 5 September 1939, and within a month a ghetto had been established. All the Jews of the town and its environs had been moved inside it by the beginning of November. The area they had to live in was small. Of Piotrkow's pre-war population of 55,000, 15,000 were Jewish. They now had to move into a quarter of town previously inhabited by only 5,000 people; furthermore, their ranks were swollen by other Jews who had been driven away from their own homes by the invasion – for example, the ancient community of Gniezno – a town which had been the first capital of Poland. 'These were Germanized Jews, and they were more German than the Germans – they even spoke Polish with a German accent.' By the influx of these and others the ghetto swiftly expanded. Into that small space, 28,000 people were eventually crowded.

'I never wore the armband with the Star of David. In a sense it was an act of defiance; but when it was expedient I pretended that I was a Pole. On my own, I could pass for a Pole. The Piotrkow ghetto was an open one to begin with – there were no walls, not even barbed wire – there was just the rule that any Jew found outside it would be shot.

'I was never hungry. With a full belly there was room in my mind for other pursuits. I'd read in the evenings, I'd exercise, I'd think. My father provided great moral as well as practical support. In return I made myself useful. I would smuggle newspapers back into the ghetto, for example; and I read them, too, which made me politically quite aware at an age when one wouldn't normally be. I knew who all the central players on the wartime European stage were. But even before the war I'd been interested in newspapers, and I suppose that this helped to make up for the formal education I was missing. And I was growing up very fast, both mentally and physically . . .'

Later, in 1941, after Germany had moved against Russia, his father managed to get a pass allowing him to come and go from the ghetto. This was because the Germans needed people to go round the villages to buy up rabbit-skins from the peasants to make fur coats and boot linings for the soldiers on the front line. His father used this activity as a cover for his own activities – he'd got the pass in the first place by bribing local officials. 'He wouldn't take lying down the kind of treatment we were getting from the Germans. It used to shred my mother's nerves, though. He'd be away for days sometimes. But he was always a doer, restless – he needed to be active.'

When the time inevitably came for the transports, rumours flew around that the only people who would be allowed to stay in the Piotrkow ghetto would be the *Judenrat*, the Jewish Police (*Ordnungsdienst*[8]), the sanitary police (for by that time typhoid had broken out in the crowded, unhygienic conditions – among other diseases), and those employed by German or German-allied concerns. Ben Helfgott's father made arrangements for the family – Ben's mother and two younger sisters – to go into hiding, because by the summer of 1942 it was virtually impossible to get any 'legitimate' work. Fortunately, one of Ben's father's Gentile friends from before the war was the director of the local glass factory. Ben boasted to his friends that, despite everything, his father could still organize a job for him there. Since his boast met with cynical disbelief, he went to his father and insisted that he prove his point. His father, however, demurred – he had already made arrangements for the family to shelter with Polish families, and his two sisters were already catered for, outside the ghetto. Ben, who was curious about the factory anyway, begged his father just to make it possible for him to go to the factory for a short time – after that, he'd do anything he asked.

'I was better off than most and was quite self-assured. Although I was set to work on the night shift I refused to go to sleep the day before. I was put on a team which I later learned was run by a real Jew-hater.

'The heat in the factory, especially near the furnaces, was intense. I was given a job which seemed simple. I had to keep a supply of cooled wooden moulds available for the glass-blowers. I sat on a low concrete block and cooled the moulds in a bucket, while the glass-blowers worked on a platform a little above me.

'After a time they started to mock me and hit me on the head, which confused me, as I was getting tired and had to keep track of the flow of cooled moulds. This was also my first taste of bad language: every second word was "f—ing" – to each other as well as to me. After what seemed hours, one of them told me to go and look at the clock to find out what time it was. I went gratefully, taking my time, imagining that half the night must surely be over by now. But when I reached the clock I found that only three-quarters of an hour had elapsed. My heart had never been heavier. I felt very sorry for myself, and slowly returned to my workplace. They swore at me for taking so long, and guffawed a lot. Then they told me to sit down – which I did, but sprang up again immediately, for they had made my concrete block red-hot with molten glass in my absence. As soon as I stood up they hit me on the head and cried, "Sit down, you f—ing Jew!" This must have gone on for a couple of minutes.

'How I ever survived that night I really will never understand. It was a shattering experience. I was quite an innocent, and this was the first real job of my life; and I was 12 years old.

'When I returned home I was determined not to tell my parents, but of course it was impossible to disguise what had happened from them. My father said that I needn't go back, but I told him I would. I slept like a log all that day, and in the evening I joined the other Jewish workers from the ghetto for the march to the factory. That night the bullying was less, and a little later our deputy shift leader was introduced to my father, who arranged to pay him some money from then on at regular intervals. As a result, my life became more bearable. I was put on relief duty, which meant that I only had to work if there was a gap to be filled; and although the deputy shift leader was anti-Semitic, he had his favourite Jews, and he had great respect for my father.'

Deportations to the camps continued and were stepped up. One evening in 1942 Ben went on night shift as usual, leaving his mother at home with her younger sister – his father was outside the ghetto. The next morning, the Jewish factory workers prepared to return to the ghetto but were prevented from doing so; it had been sealed off, and people were being rounded up for transport. Over the next few days, the SS went through the ghetto, street by street; those without work-passes were taken to the trains. The factory workers were kept there, billeted in stables; but they had no news of their families. All Ben managed to find out was that neither of his parents had been seen at the assembly point for the transports. Some 22,000 people were taken over seven days to Treblinka. Of his entire school class, only one other person survives.

After that round-up there were only 2,400 Jews left in the ghetto, which was accordingly reduced in size. Ben returned and lived with a friend who was still 'legitimately' there, as were his uncles. Within a few days he heard that his parents and his aunt had managed to find hiding places outside the town. The only member of his family to have been deported was his grandfather. He made contact with his parents, and his father returned with him to the ghetto – smuggled in among a returning detail of Jewish workers. They went to the single room where Ben's uncle was staying. The uncle, who hadn't known of Ben's plans, was furious. In the time that he had been gone, the SS had returned and they had been shooting people in the streets, regardless of whether they had work-permits or not. Ben and his father had walked into a death-trap. 'But I didn't care. I was happy to be standing next to my father.'

With the help of relatives, they managed to 'legitimize' his father's position in the ghetto. They even found a place to stay. But within days there were fresh problems. His mother and her sister had to rejoin them because the wife of the man who was hiding them had made increasing demands for money.

A few days later, Ben's youngest sister had to come back out of hiding, and in time his other sister had to come out of hiding too; but the Germans announced that the small ghetto would be left as it was from now on. There would be no more deportations or killings, and an amnesty was declared for all those not 'legitimately' in the ghetto. Those people accordingly came out of hiding. On 20 December 1942 the Germans rounded 520 of them up, took them to the Rakow Forest just outside town, and shot them. Among them were Ben's mother, Sara, who was 37, and his sister Lusia, who was eight. 'There were four of us now: my father, my sister Mala, a five-year-old cousin, and me.'

In August 1943 the Germans decided to liquidate the ghetto. Only

1,000 Jews needed for labour at the local woodworking factory, and 800, including Ben, with jobs at the glass factory, were to be left. 'My father, sister and cousin were already on the lorry, waiting to be transported; but then my sister jumped down and ran to the captain of the gendarmerie in charge of the round-up, and said, "Excuse me, my brother is still in the ghetto. May I stay with him?" The captain must have been very taken aback, but he said yes. And then my sister asked if my father and her cousin (whom she called her sister) could stay too; and the captain agreed. So they climbed down from the lorry, and later they were allocated jobs in the wood factory, where my father arranged for me to join them. Fate kept playing such extraordinary tricks. When the ghetto was liquidated, the remaining Jewish workers were billeted in the factories. The captain took quite a paternal interest in my sister, and came to see that she was all right, when he visited the camp.'

They remained in the woodwork factory until November 1944. Ben's father was able to continue 'organizing' food, and so the little group did not starve. 'Wherever my father was, it never took him long to find a means of getting food. He was a natural wheeler-dealer: put him down anywhere, stack heavy odds against him, and he'd fight through and prosper.' But already by August 1944 the Russian army had pushed the Germans back to the River Vistula (Wisla), and there was a Communist government established in Lublin. Early in August came the Warsaw Uprising. 'About this time, suddenly, all the Germans in Piotrkow disappeared. No one was guarding us, and a rumour went round that the Russians would liberate us in a day or two. The countryside was flat, indefensible. But the Warsaw Uprising was led by the *AK* – the *Armia Krajowa*[9] – which was anti-Communist, and supported the government-in-exile in London. Some elements of the Polish resistance were also anti-Semitic. In some cases Jews who escaped from the camps and tried to join the partisans were shot when they made contact.' The Jews formed their own groups in the woods, where life could be as hard as in the camps, for these people were not equipped or trained to live rough, and they had women and children with them. Food was almost impossible to find, and many died of starvation and exposure.

Piotrkow was not liberated. Stalin did not want the *AK* to win, so he chose not to support them. He ordered his armies to regroup, deliberately giving the Germans breathing space. The Warsaw Uprising was crushed. The Germans also returned to Piotrkow. 'About 300 Jewish men were sent directly to Buchenwald . . . 300 men and 100 women, including my sister, were sent to the camps at Ravensbrück. The others were sent to Czestochowa.

'With my father, I was on the relatively lucky transport to Buchenwald. Unfortunately, the doctors had diagnosed a severe stomach ailment which I had at the time as appendicitis, but there was no time for them to operate before we were sent to the train. "Only a miracle can save you," I was told. "All we can suggest is that you do not eat anything." We were loaded on to cattle-waggons, 100 to a truck, so tightly packed that we had to stand, and the journey lasted seven days. There was nothing to eat, just a little water.

'When we arrived at Buchenwald we were sent to the showers, and by that time news of the gas chambers had filtered out, so we thought that we were being sent to our deaths. I can still picture the scene now: a vision of Bedlam, naked men, some weeping, some praying, some even joking. All I could think of was the pain in my stomach. It is odd how pain can take your mind off anything else: there was no room there for me to feel fear . . . But of course the showers were real, and we were shaved afterwards, and given our uniforms – they just handed them out, irrespective of size; and we looked like a collection of clowns. People actually laughed. We exchanged our uniforms with each other until we had clothes that more or less fitted. They weren't striped KZ uniforms, it was too late in the war for that, just a motley collection of old clothes. As we were marched to our *Block* my father disappeared. It wasn't unusual for him to dive off like that, he was always doing it; but I was concerned when he didn't answer his name when we arrived at the *Block*. Half an hour later he turned up, produced two loaves, and said, "Quick, hide these." Of course he got a good beating for being late, but he had got that bread.

'After the first night in the camp, the pain in my stomach miraculously disappeared, and a few days later we were set to work in a quarry, where we had to carry away stones. But a few days later still, we were given new work-details. All this time I had felt fine, despite my illness and my seven days' fast. But now my father was not selected for the same work-detail as I and, as I got on to the train to go to the sub-camp, I had a terrible premonition. All I can remember of that two-day train journey was that I cried and cried and cried. I knew I had seen my father for the last time.'

The sub-camp was a munitions factory at a place called Schlieben. 'They gave us stinking soup – it really smelt like sewage; and there was no salt; although we were very hungry, we simply couldn't eat this soup. But the prisoners who were already there got wind of this, and they came over to us. They were skeletons, teeming with lice – the very sub-humans the Germans maintained that we Jews were. And they fought each other for the soup. One of the cauldrons was overturned and they fell on the ground, licking the liquid from the dirty floor.

'We were appalled at these people, but I tell you that within two days we were eating that soup with them, and the only thing we thought was how foolish we had been to let our first ration go.'

Their regime in Schlieben was that they were awakened at 4.30am and given a cold drink of unspeakable flavour which went by the name of coffee for breakfast. From 6am until 12 noon they worked, when they were given the soup described for lunch. They then worked again from 1pm until 6pm. At 7, back in the *Block*, they were given a morsel of soggy bread, a spoonful of 'jam', and a smear of 'margarine'. Supper, Ben remembers, took about one second to eat.

There were 250 people on his transport into Schlieben, and within a fortnight they started to die. 'My own greatest desire was to have a loaf of bread. I swore to myself that if ever I got out alive I would sit down every Friday for the rest of my life and eat a whole loaf in memory of my hunger.' The factory made *Panzerfäuste* (anti-tank weapons) – shoulder-launched rockets that were accurate to 150 metres. Ben was lucky; he got a job indoors where it was warm. He was part of a juvenile group, working with German women, who also had to see that the young prisoners were doing their work properly. One great advantage of working with the women was that they insisted that the boys were kept clean, with the result that they had hot showers twice a week. They still had the same uniforms that they'd been issued with at Buchenwald, however, and these were not cleaned. Sometimes one of the German women might slip Ben a piece of bread. 'And I made friends with a group of French women prisoners who also gave us a little bit extra when they could, and that was a tremendous help. I will never forget, though, the sight of women with shaven heads.

'To keep my spirits up, I set myself targets, challenges. There were a couple of girls, sisters, who'd been evacuated from Aachen and who were pretty fed up with the war. One of them let me try her bicycle, to see if I could still ride. I could, but I was stopped by a *Hitlerjugend* type, who was making up to the younger sister. I told him I'd been given permission, and when he went back to check, the girl told him to mind his own business. But he got back at me when it was time for the midday meal by pouring the soup all over my face, instead of into the rusty tin plate I had to eat from. "You want soup? Lick it off the floor," he said.'

Never at any time did it enter Ben's head that the KZ might kill him, though people were dying around him all the time. He kept setting himself challenges. 'There was a "green" kapo in the camp. He had two *Stubendienste*[10] in our *Block*, whom he gave extra food to. I challenged them to wrestle. They were older and better fed than I, but I got them both down. That was satisfying. But one got unpleasant shocks too. One night I couldn't sleep. My bones hurt, and it was as if I were sleeping on a stone. So I put my hand round to my backside where the pain was, and I felt the bare boards of the bunk, and I felt for my backside, and simply touched bone: my backside had gone;

there was no flesh left. I hadn't realized that that had happened, because I hadn't seen myself for so long. I had no idea what I looked like, but I couldn't imagine that I looked like the skeletons around me. I couldn't sleep for the rest of the night.'

Not long after that experience, Ben earned some unexpected extra food. 'A *Wehrmacht* officer came to our *Block* and ordered a few of us out. There were boxes of *Panzerfäuste* to be loaded on to his lorry and he was in a great hurry. I stood on the back of the lorry and the others handed the boxes up, which I then swung on board. The officer was so impatient to get the job done quickly that he climbed up and worked with me. Suddenly he became aware of the job I was doing. "How can you do this in your state?" he said. "It's impossible." When he'd dismissed the others, he took me to the German staff kitchens and ordered them to give me as much food as I could eat. But you see, I had enjoyed the work, I enjoyed being physically active, even then. And I sat in the kitchen and feasted; thick soup, tasty, unbelievable. I took my time, enjoying the food, and then I went and asked for some more, which they gave me, though the officer had left by then. I'd have gone back for a third helping, but I just didn't have the courage: I thought I'd better not push my luck. But on the way back to the factory, I worked out the value of the food I'd just eaten: it came to 20 days' normal rations.

'I always worked out the value of my food every day. If I got a bit extra one day, I felt that much better. But after that particular meal, I thought: the only thing that will kill me now is if they actually come and shoot me.'

They stayed at Schlieben until 14 April, then they were loaded on to trains and shunted this way and that as the Allies closed in to finish off the Third Reich. Their journey ended at Theresienstadt. Their clothes were in rags, and their bodies were completely torn from the bites of bed-bugs and lice. 'Nevertheless, here is an example of the indomitable naïveté of a 15-year-old. We were the first Polish Jews to arrive in Theresienstadt. We looked pretty wild. Someone came up to us and said in German, "Be patient, here, you'll get all you need." As soon as I heard that I asked him if they had a table-tennis table. Of course, the man thought I had gone insane, but I meant it; I wanted to play table-tennis. It has to be said though that, once we had arrived at Theresienstadt, the ordeal, for me at least, was over. The danger was still there, but I felt that a corner had been turned, and that I was on the road back to normality. Two things indicated this: firstly, they cleaned us up; and secondly, we didn't go out to work any more. The first few days I slept and slept and slept. I only got up to get my rations, which weren't huge, but which were much better than what we'd had at Schlieben. But rest was more important than food. Not to have to get up at 4 in the morning was bliss. And we started to talk about what was going to happen next. All kinds of transports were arriving – some, like us, by train, but others, in far worse condition, on foot. I saw people arriving from the death marches whom I knew, whom I'd last seen being taken off to Czestochowa, who I imagined would long since have been liberated.

'There was news of my father. A man had been on the death march with him: he had been one of a group who had run away, but they had all been rounded up and shot. The man told me kindly, but he told me straight; he didn't want me to have any illusions which might cause more hurt later. And I knew from this that there was no chance that my father might have survived.

'I was liberated on the morning of 9 May by the Russians. They gave us a free day to do what we wanted. By that stage I was very much recovered, physically healed. About a mile away was a little town which was Sudeten German, and of course the Czechs were chasing the Germans out as fast as they could. Now it was the Germans who were being forced out on to the road. And I saw two young Hungarian women beating up a German woman, who had a little boy, and a child in a pram with her. The little boy was crying, seeing his mother being beaten up. I went up to these two women and I said, "What do you think you are doing?" "Paying them back," said the women. "By beating up a mother and making her child cry?" I looked at the little boy and he somehow reminded me of my little sister, and I felt a pang of pity for him. The women said, "This is our free day given to us by the Russians to take revenge." And they wouldn't stop, so I threw them into the ditch by the side of the road. The German woman started to thank me, but I said: "No, don't thank me, I can't stand it: just go." I got to the little town, and there was another Bedlam, this time a Bedlam of looting. I got to a shop and helped myself to a big sackful of rice and one of sugar, maybe 30 kilogrammes, which I took back to Theresienstadt and used for barter. I was in business. That was my first day of liberation.'

A few days later he made his way the 40-odd kilometres south to Prague, which was a real melting-pot of refugees in those days. There were many soup-kitchens and, as a former KZ-inmate, he was given clothes and some money. He had a liberation certificate from the Russians. He also had some money from the sugar and rice he'd traded, and he had collected some clothing to sell, so he wasn't short of anything. 'Necessity is the mother of invention, and I had the great advantage of recovering quickly.' He met a friend by chance not far from Vaclavske Nameste, and he fell in love with Prague. 'Everything was a treat, even going on the trams. It was an absolutely gorgeous city. I would get up in the morning and hire a boat, and go rowing for an hour on the Vltava, breathing the fresh air, looking at the Hradcany Palace. I took to Czechoslovakia like a duck to water. I learned basic Czech immediately, from newspapers – it's not too different from Polish, but in any case it was as if my mind had been released; it was revelling in being able to learn again, and I have always been a great newspaper-reader; even today, the very first thing I do every day is read the paper ... At lunchtime I would eat, and I would go from one soup-kitchen to another from 12 to 4, sampling the fare. My capacity for food in those days was unreal. After lunch I would go to the cinema, and again I'd go from one to another. There were a good many Russian films about the war, with Stalin as the Great Hero. It was all very inspiring to a youngster like me. We all thought the Russians were gods; they were our liberators, and everything we heard about communism was, of course, better than good.'

After three weeks in Prague, he decided that he should return to Piotrkow to see if anyone had come back. He made the difficult rail-journey and arrived in June. He found two aunts alive, one of whom was the younger sister of his mother who had been in hiding with her. Having established that there was someone at home, he decided to return to Theresienstadt to collect a younger cousin whom he had left there in the camp hospital. The cousin had also come to Theresienstadt on a transport from the Buchenwald camp complex, but they had been shunted around for a whole month, and most of them were dead on arrival. The cousin's name was Gienek Klein and he was 12 years old, though illness and malnutrition made him look much younger.[11]

'He was recovering but he was still very emaciated. As we were going back to Poland, I collected two large suitcases of clothing, which was very scarce at home then. Gienek looked like a ghost; the Czechs were always offering him food. We crossed the Polish frontier and had to change trains at Czestochowa. There were lots and lots of people milling around the station. Two Polish officers approached us and asked, "Where do you come from?" I said, "Look at us, look at my cousin – where do you think we have come from?" "Yes, we know, but have you got identification?" I showed them our papers, but they said they would have to take us to the police station to double-check. I was so naïve, I didn't suspect a thing. So we followed them, with me carrying the two suitcases. We walked out of the station, and we went on walking, on and on, and the cases were getting heavy, so I asked if we'd be getting to the police station soon. And the reply came back: "Shut your f—ing mouth, you bastard, you Jew bastard." I knew then of course that we were in trouble, but the streets were empty – if there had been a Russian soldier about I could have appealed to him for help, but there was none. It was dark, and there were no street-lights.

Eventually we got to a house and a young woman opened the door to them. They pushed us into a room and told us to open the cases. They stole everything, just leaving behind a few bits and pieces, and then they said, "Right, now we're taking you to the police station." I didn't believe that: did they think I'd tell the police that they had been nice to me? But I had no choice, and we left the house and walked again, on and on, until we came to a completely deserted place. And they took out their revolvers and said, "Get to the wall." I didn't move. I said, "What do you want to do? Finish us off? Do the job the Germans couldn't manage? And why are you doing it? Am I not a Pole like you? Didn't I suffer? You call me a Jew, but what is the difference? I have come back here to build a new world, a new future after what we have been through – and this is what you try to do to us? Look at us . . ." And I kept on talking, talking. And they shouted, "Get to the wall!" but I went on talking, saying God knows what . . . and finally one of them said to the other, "Come on, let's leave them; they're only boys." And the other said to us, "OK, we'll let you live – you're the first ones that we've let live. We don't want your kind here." And off they went. But we were lost. The first people we blundered into were a couple of Russian soldiers. We were disobeying the law because we were walking the streets after curfew; but luckily they were drunk and had a couple of girls with them. I tried to explain what had happened, but they were not remotely interested. One of the girls directed us to the railway station, which wasn't far, as it turned out, and we caught our train the next morning. There was a Polish headmaster in our carriage who asked us about ourselves. I told him what had happened to us the night before, and there were tears in his eyes. "The war corrupted many people," he said. "You must try to help rebuild and repair the damage."'

When they got back to Piotrkow, Ben heard that his middle sister, Mala, was still alive, and that she was at Belsen with his little cousin who had gone with her on the original transport to Ravensbrück. Ben's next job, as he saw it, was to go and collect them. He started out by the route he knew, via Prague and Theresienstadt, and he travelled with Gienek's cousin Bronia for company. However, when he arrived at Theresienstadt again, the friends who were still there told him that they were going to England. If he wanted to join them, he would have to hurry if he was to collect his sister and cousin first, as they were leaving soon.

He got as far as Pilsen (Plzen) but the American authorities there told him that the journey to Belsen was virtually impossible at the time. Meanwhile, his thoughts were full of England, 'which was the country of my dreams as a child. We were very influenced by films – all the ones we saw were British. I remember we had cutlery at home with MADE IN SHEFFIELD written on it, and that whenever I looked at a world map, I was impressed that so much of it was pink! My father had his suits made of English cloth, and when we played a game that involved each of us taking the name of a country, I was always *Wielka Britannia* . . . And now out of the blue there was an opportunity to go there.' Bronia told Ben that she would go back to Piotrkow, collect Gienek, and meet him with her brother at Theresienstadt. They could all go to England together. The plan was not to come to fruition. Ben made his way back to Theresienstadt and put his name down to go, but he waited for Bronia in vain. As he found out later, when she got back to Poland she found that Gienek's father had returned from the KZ. He refused to let his son leave. Ben came to England alone.

The journey was organized by the Central British Fund, which was set up before the war to help Austrian and German Jewish refugees. However, they had realized that when the war ended there would be others in need, and it was for this reason that they had set up the Committee for the Care of Children from the Concentration Camps (CCCC), whose moving spirit was Leonard Montefiore. Ben's decision to come to England and try to contact his sister once there was a wise one, as it turned out, for she had already been taken from the DP camp to Sweden with a children's group. He managed to get in touch with her there, and in 1947 the CCCC helped him arrange for her to join him in London, where they both still live.

Ben came over with a group of 300 – 250 teenaged boys, 30 girls of the same age, and 20 little children. They arrived in England on VJ Day and were first lodged at Windermere in the Lake District. Subsequently the group was split up and 30 of them were sent to a hostel in Loughton, Essex, where they were to live for the next ten months, though all the members of the original group stayed firmly in touch. Ben later moved to another hostel in Belsize Park, London, where he and some others helped set up a youth club for people like them, called the Primrose Club after the local telephone exchange. The club was established downstairs in the hostel, and they lived above it. Ben, who by that time was at Plaistow Grammar on the other side of London, kept abreast of events by reading the *News Chronicle* on his journey to and from school.

One of the great joys of his life at that time was being able to participate in sports again – 'Gymnastics was my *forte*. I almost flew over the vaulting horses, and I played football, basketball, and table tennis.' He also revelled in the renewed opportunity to learn, after missing five years' education. He got on well with his teachers, who appear to have been sympathetic. 'I was lonely in so far as I had no parents to talk to, and had no shoulder to cry on, but I think I was beyond tears by that time. I had been hardened by calamity; and I was not lonely in the sense that I lived at the hostel, first in Loughton and then at Belsize Park, where there were boys of similar background. We helped each other, nurtured each other. It would have been more difficult if I had been living in digs on my own. If I had been physically alone I would have felt a great void – a great lack of warmth, of someone to take care of me. But as matters stood I got those things from the other boys in the hostel. We had a common past and an understanding of that past which no one else, however sympathetic, could possibly share.'

He had been introduced to weight-lifting before going up to university. 'During the summer holidays around 1948 we used to go swimming on Hampstead Heath, and we saw some people doing weights there, and I watched them and asked if I could try; but the man I'd asked said it would be too heavy for me. That made me only more insistent. So I went up to the weight, cleared it to my shoulders and pressed it straight up as if I'd been doing it all my life. And the man looked at me open-mouthed – he couldn't believe I'd never done it before in my life. That first time I touched 180 pounds, and at the time the British record was 210 pounds. I just took to it naturally.'

Weight-lifting was started at the Primrose Club, but Ben was unable to benefit from it since he was about to go to Southampton University, and at Southampton there were no facilities. However, the club's manager suggested that Ben train for the 1950 Maccabinh Games in Israel. They sent him some weights from London, and he won the trials for the games, the first competition that he'd entered. He went on to win the Home Counties Championships, and in due course went on to win a gold medal at the Maccabinh Games. After that, he took up training at the Maccabi Club in London, and went on to be British Champion. He took the title four times between 1954 and 1960, but in all those seven years he was number one on overall points. In 1956 and 1960 he was in the British Olympic team – but that he continued at all after 1957 is miraculous, because in February of that year he had a terrible accident. 'I was climbing a drainpipe to a first-floor window, having locked myself out, and my hand slipped on the window-ledge and I fell on to the railings below and split my rectum. But by July I was competing in Moscow. You see, I have always been a fighter, and I think the KZ made me even more of one.'

He wanted to become a teacher – 'to put something back into the system' – but doubts about such a career started to creep into his mind before he had completed his degree course. There was an additional influence. He was 21 by now, and beginning to feel that he should be financially independent. A friend from Plaistow Grammar School was already working at the paper company, Bunzl, in the City of London, and urging Ben to join him.

He stayed at Bunzl's for two years, but he was in the shipping department and he became bored. It took him two hours to do his day's work, so he took French classes in his lunch-hour; but still the days were too long, so he left, and joined Great Universal Stores as a trainee manager. 'And they put me into their credit division. It was tough, but I found it valuable, because it gave me a whole new insight into the attitudes of English people, and their way of life. I was dealing with people who could only afford to buy on credit. Initially my job was collecting the money, and at the same time trying to sell them more. At first I really couldn't stand it, but then I said to myself, get through the training and then chuck it if you don't like it. Once I'd made up my mind to finish the training I did the work well.'

He did well with the company, going on to become an area sales manager and a store manager. But in the late Fifties, on a visit to Israel, he met one of his surviving uncles who had gone there to live after the war.

'He asked me how I was doing and I told him, thinking he'd be pleased, but he wasn't. "The future is in your hands. Security is in your hands. Did your father ever work for anyone? Did your grandfather? Did I? Did any of our family? We were all independent people. And are you going to be the one to let the side down?"' Ben returned to England and to his job at Great Universal, but the seeds had been sown. He knew he would have to try on his own. Ultimately he went into partnership with a friend who ran a dress business. 'I didn't know anything about the garment industry, and I never notice what people wear – not even what women wear: it's the person I notice. I think I didn't notice clothes so much because I am not materialistic: that stems from the camps too, I'm sure. I think that the more you've got, the more you have to worry about.' But once he had taken the bit between his teeth he enjoyed his new occupation and learned quickly. 'I found it exciting, because it's a creative business.'

The memory of the concentration camps has never left him: 'I remember things – all kinds of things – in great detail. That is partly because I try to take a historical view of past events, even personal ones, and to relate one experience to another.' It certainly seems that the concentration camp experience is something which Ben has been able to take on board without its affecting him remotely in a corrosive way. He makes the point, however, that his KZ memories are there in his mind, in 'drawers' which he can open and close at will, but which he cannot empty. He says that the past continues to live alongside his outer, present life, and that it is never absent. 'For a long time, and still occasionally now, I have dreams where I shout "Help!" I don't know what triggers them. I know somehow that the dreams are to do with the camps, but also to do with the present day. I am here but I am also there. I am in a room somewhere, it could be here in England, and someone knocks on the door; and I hide myself, but they come in. That is when I shout "Help!" The feeling is one of helplessness, impotence to do anything to protect myself. But the dreams are getting rarer. But as far as the memory of the camps is concerned, that does not fade for me – it is a part of me; and I don't want to escape from it because I would be an incomplete person without it. It is built into me as are my hands, my legs. I would be denying myself if I ever tried to get away from it. I feel easier when I face up to it, and it has never made me feel afraid or ashamed, because I've got nothing to be ashamed or afraid of.'

He met his wife in 1966 and they were married within six months. 'I think that marrying and starting a family helped; but I think marriage is a fulfilment anyway, for anyone. The act of marriage is an act of giving away some of one's selfishness, and having children makes one give away more. My wife always gives me a receptive ear when I want to talk about the KZ – if the question of it arises out of some news event, or reading, or whatever. And she listens, and asks questions. In this way she can be a sounding-board to me, and I know that I am very fortunate in that respect. I haven't talked to my sons specifically, except for occasional stories; but when I went to Poland in 1985 I took them with me, and I think for the first time everything fell into perspective for them. They knew something of it before, because if ever they asked me questions, I would answer them. I would never keep anything to do with the concentration camps buttoned up, because I think it is important to talk about that time, and it is the least I can do for those who died – to carry the memory on.'

Ben never wanted to become a professional sportsman, because he prefers to do the things he enjoys for pleasure, not money. 'I like to give of myself, and to put back into the community some of the benefits I derived from it. Also, I am a purist about this, I would say, to the point of stupidity. In 1955 I was one of the first people of Polish origin who was invited to go to Poland to take part in the World Festival of Youth. Stalinism was still very much in the air and there was still a year to go before Khrushchev's famous speech to the 20th Congress. To go back to Poland at that time meant taking a considerable risk, in the eyes of everyone – my friends thought I might be arrested and held there, despite the fact that by then I was a British passport holder. So I wrote a letter to the Chairman of the British Weight-Lifters' Association for him to open in the event of my being detained over there, explaining that in that case it should be understood that it was against my will. I went, and returned unscathed. I was asked to do an interview for the BBC World Service. In the course of it I recounted my impressions – broadly, that poor people now had shoes on their feet, but that they were afraid to open their mouths. They offered me a £10 fee for the interview, a lot of money in those days, but I refused it because they were interviewing me as a sportsman, and I did not want to earn money by any means in that capacity.

'I think I had a kind of over-fastidious reaction to the suggestion of corruption because of my experiences in the camps and also in Poland after the war. I was very lucky that I was able to survive without its being at the expense of others. I cannot make any judgment of collaborators, because I do not know how I would have reacted if they'd said to me, give us such-and-such names and we'll see you better fed. I was lucky to be spared that temptation. Collaborators were wrong, but if it had truly been a question of survival, would I have been strong enough to resist? How far were Czerniakow, Rumkowski or Gens[12] collaborators, in the strictest sense of the word? Where do the border-lines blur? And it is even worse when it's a question of sacrificing one set of people to save others. I remember a man whose wife and son were at the mercy of the Gestapo, and they told him that if he didn't tell them where his parents were in hiding, they would kill his young family. He went to his parents and asked them what he should do, and they said, "You must give us up"; so he did. And he survived the war, as did his wife and child. I have seen him a few times – he lives in New York now – but I can never meet him without thinking of the permanent agony those sadists condemned him to because of what they made him do. There are many survivors who have such things on their minds. I would even say that the majority have some skeleton in the cupboard, but they will not talk about it, and many will have buried it, or created a lie that they themselves now believe, to conceal it. No book will ever be written about that aspect of survival, because of the silence; but under the circumstances of the time, half of them didn't know what they were doing; they'd been forced to go without sleep, they'd been beaten to a pulp, they had no time to think. In such circumstances, you will do anything to stop the pain, and you betray others just to gain a moment's respite for yourself. But then for the rest of your life you have somehow to cope with the memory of that second or two when you told them the name, or the place. Similarly, the story of the habitual collaborators, such as the members of the *Ordnungsdienst*, or those who let their families go on transports but themselves stayed behind because they had work-permits, will never be told.

'As for the average SS – German, Latvian or Ukrainian – I don't think they gave it a second thought. They relished their power; they were for the most part peasants of the lowest intelligence, suddenly given smart clothes and a gun, and power beyond their dreams. However, I will not now discriminate between nations. I take people as individuals, so I could never condemn a nation. I treat Germans today no differently from any other people. I think it is wrong to think in terms of nations, and to label people. I can say that I never felt the slightest hatred for Germans from the moment I was liberated. The minute you hate, you diminish yourself. But it's easier said than done, and I can't claim any moral strength – it's just the way I am made. Perhaps paradoxically, I am quite aggressive – very much so, if I feel threatened; but it is momentary. Once the danger is past, it's past. At the time I wouldn't have turned the other cheek to any German who maltreated me, if I'd been able to hit back; and in the past, in the Sixties, say, whenever I saw a German I would wonder what he'd been up to in the war, whether he had been a concentration camp guard. I feel less like that now, because that generation is old, and past it; but the other thing about hate is that if you start, where do you stop? If I were to hate the Germans, I would also have to hate the Russians and all the Western Allies as well; because the Russians delayed for political reasons in 1944 when they could have pressed forward, and the Allies would not respond to the news that was constantly coming out of the KZ and would not bomb them or the railway-lines to them, not to mention the attitudes of the Allies before the war and at the conferences of Evian and Bermuda. No wonder the Jews felt abandoned by the whole world.

'One of the by-products of my experience is that I don't expect anything from anyone – I rather expect the worst from them; but because of that I often find myself pleasantly surprised, and that encourages me to see goodness in people. However, I do keep my guard up as an instinctive self-protection, and I find that when I meet someone for the first time I size him up. I will be prepared to trust someone, but built into that is a mental safety-net, should that trust turn out to have been ill-founded. I am always on my toes, always ready to protect myself if necessary; so that I think the KZ experience has created a barrier in me; but more, it taught me about love, and understanding my fellow human beings. I would never give up faith in humanity.'

As with many survivors – the majority of those I met, Jewish or Christian – the degree of his religious faith was not affected by the concentration camp experience. Ben was influenced early in life by deep religious feelings but, even before adolescence, doubt had entered his mind, and since then belief has not played a great role in his life. Those who did believe before the camps in general continued to; those who were mildly or conventionally religious quite frequently lost their faith; those who had no faith did not gain it through the camps. The effect of the camps seems rather to have been on a person's relation to humanism and realism and, in the case of Jews, to increase their awareness of their race. There remains the question of guilt: 'I regard my life as a gift, and this is why I believe in serenity, and avoid wasting time in quarrels. And I live from day to day, never counting on the fact that I will be here tomorrow. I do not believe in an after-life. Because I was denied freedom and equality, I cherish them, but I can't just enjoy life. Better people than me died, and so I must try to make something good of myself, for the only way to triumph over evil is to make sure that some good comes out of it.

'I think one is born with a set of qualities, which are then shaped by experience. My survival instincts have obviously been emphasized, sharpened. I don't think it is sad that the KZ experience has made me look at people with a slightly more cautious eye, because I haven't lost my warmth, or my ability or even desire to trust, and make friends. And if I'm let down, as likely as not I'll shrug my shoulders and put it down to human nature. I am even willing to find excuses for a person's bad behaviour, and I will only very reluctantly stand in judgment. Of course, if a person keeps on letting me down, I'll cool off. But look at what happens when people who do like each other fall out over something and break off relations. Usually that is a foolish thing to do, because they throw away all the good things that they have enjoyed together, as well as their fondness for each other. People quarrel over nothing because either their vanity or their ego is hurt, and how much pleasanter life is when you can rise above your ego. Life is far too short for sustained quarrels – indeed, for any quarrels. Why waste life over such nonsense: *you are wrong and I am right*. It's better just to say, "OK, you want to be right, you're right," and then the argument is finished. You might even get them to question more whether they are right that way.

'When I think about Poland, I think about my childhood, about my parents, my uncles and aunts, my sisters, my cousins, my friends – all the people who lived there, and who stopped living in 1942 and 1943. I like thinking about them, because as long as I live, they will live, in my mind; and thinking about them gives me a tremendous drive for life. I don't think about them consciously; they just come to me, and in a way I am living my life for them too. Look at all those opportunities missed, all those talents and ambitions, loves and plans – gone. You could go to the sites of any of the camps, and let your imagination play over the stories of the people's lives that were ended there, and become possessed by it: the mind can still barely accept what was done.'

Ben Helfgott is chairman of the Yad Vashem Committee in the United Kingdom. Its work is mainly concerned with bringing about a greater awareness of the Holocaust in this country through education. Secondarily, there is a link with Yad Vashem in Jerusalem, and they keep an eye open for articles, books and plays which they feel may misrepresent the Holocaust. The main job of the Committee is to provide information on the Holocaust to schools and universities, and to advise on how to teach the subject as history. 'The main thrust is objective; we don't want to impose our ideas on young people, that is not our job; but the Holocaust is being exploited – by the Left, by the Right, the Revisionists, even by artists, for their own ends.'

Teaching materials and survivor-lecturers are made available through the 45 Aid Society, of which Ben is also chairman, but whose function is not primarily educational. It is made up of all those who came to Britain under the auspices of the CCCC as children and teenagers in 1945–6. 'After the hostels we lived in first were closed and we moved out into our own homes, we all felt we wanted to maintain contact with each other, for we had no other family. Our rehabilitation was successful because of the way we helped each other within the group: we had little help from the outside world beyond that they gave us things: toys for the little ones, for example. Sops to people's consciences. The real help, the heart-help, came from within the group.

'Once we were spread out all over London (and later across the country), we had our first base at the Primrose Club. Out of that grew a mutual-support society, and the reason the club excelled at sports and won so many trophies was that we were so close-knit: we were a family. It is quite an indescribable thing to be part of such a group. The doors of the original club were thrown open to local young people, however, and this was another important step in our reintegration into society – many of our members met and married local boys and girls.

'As the years went by, we got involved with our own work, and our own families, and so by 1953 many of us felt that we should set up some kind of formal framework to keep us linked, and especially to help those of us who were on their own, or less well able to get over the experience of the camps. We gave what spiritual and material help we could. One of our members, for example, has been in a mental home for 20 years, and we have a visiting rota: every Sunday he gets visitors, and he receives a monthly pension from the Society. Some of us moved away from Britain – to the USA and Israel, mainly – and so our network has become international. We have had reunions in Israel, where we support an institute where deaf children are taught to speak.

'We keep in touch via an occasional newsletter, but mainly informally. It is unbelievable how the closeness has remained between us, but we really are a family, and some of our members have no one else from their past, as they are the sole survivors of their families. Indeed, one of our members is not only the sole survivor of his family, but of his entire community, so that all of his past exists only in his mind; he has no one to share it with at all. When you have a family, you take it for granted; it's only when they are gone that you begin to wish that you'd asked them more about themselves and their lives and experiences. So often in a family, all the conversation is mundane. But at least I can recollect with other survivors of Piotrkow – and together we remember not only people who no longer exist, but people who have no relatives left to remember them. They only exist in the minds of survivors like us, as shadows, because all their people were wiped out – entire extended families of 100 people and more. That is why I consider it such a compelling duty to keep them in my thoughts, and to cherish their memories. It is hard to explain. How many people do you remember from your school class, 20 or 30 years on? And does it bother you that you don't remember a lot of them, not their names and barely their faces? In my case that plays on my mind because, out of my class of 32, only one other person survived. She lives in Israel, and when I see her, we often talk about our schoolfriends; we're talking about kids of eight or nine, but we speak of them as if they were older people – because they have no one else to remember them. And oddly we revel in such conversation. I know that must sound crazy. But they were robbed of their lives aged 12 in 1942. So long ago. I wonder, if they were alive, what they would be doing today?'

Jews of 'Greater Germany'

I

K was born in Vienna in 1921. Today, he looks ten years younger than he is; is aware of this, and proud of it. His home is opulent; his manner generous, kind and gentle to a degree. He is the youngest of three brothers who grew up together in Vienna, where his father was accountant to a wholesale clothing concern. They were not rich, but comfortably off – a decent bourgeois Jewish family, who took their holidays in the Austrian countryside.

As the clouds gathered, his first instinct was to try to get hold of an exit visa. This was more difficult for him than for his brothers, who both had qualifications. He tried Chile without success, and Shanghai (at that time China was allocating a small number of visas). Anywhere, he says, would have done. The embassies were not insisting upon qualifications, but each might have only ten or a dozen permits to give out each week, and there were thousands of people after them. Some first cousins decided to go to Belgium illegally, and K's parents suggested that he go with them. He begged them to go with him, but they said that as they were older they would certainly be left in peace. Reluctantly, he made his way to Belgium and Antwerp, where some friends of the family, whom he'd never met, lived. The Jewish community there welcomed him and took care of him. In 1939 he was sent to live in a refugee camp run by the Jewish community at Mercxplas, where he stayed until the German invasion of Belgium in 1940.

They fled westwards to the French border. There, despite the fact that his Austrian passport was stamped with a 'J' (for 'Jew'), he was arrested as an enemy agent and taken to Orléans, where he was interrogated and beaten up by the French security forces, after which he was transported to an internment camp at St-Cyprien, where he remained until 1941. When cholera broke out there, he became frightened and made his escape. The camp was neither efficiently guarded nor well fenced, and he just walked out one day, making his way to Avignon. He was tired and hungry on the road, but he didn't feel unhopeful of getting by. He had learnt French at school, and his years in France and Belgium had perfected it. He fell into company with a boy scout; as he had himself been a keen scout before the war, he decided to take his new friend into his confidence. His trust was well founded. The scout took him home, where he was fed and made welcome. He did not, however, want to stay in that region of France and, after he had fed and rested, the family gave him the address of some friends who lived in Limoges, near the demarcation line between Free and Occupied France. He found a safe refuge there – 'But after a while I became bored, and I decided that I would like to visit Paris. I know that sounds perfectly crazy, but when you are young you don't have any concept of fear. In any case I didn't know what lay ahead for me, and I'd never seen Paris. I knew it was occupied, of course . . .' He got there without difficulty and, when he had arrived, made his way by chance to what was then one of the riskiest parts of town imaginable: the area around the Place Pigalle. 'I met a man who told me that he earned his living as a guide to the night-clubs and brothels for the German soldiers. "You could do the same," he said to me. "Your German is better than mine." So that's what I did. The clubs gave me a commission for bringing the customers, and I did very well – made a lot of money, in fact. I took a room in a small hotel where the girls rented rooms by the hour.' Once established, he was accepted by the local underworld, who arranged false papers for him – which was just as well, because at one point he was arrested by the Gestapo for living on immoral earnings. They let him go, but things were getting a little too hot for him, and in any case he had decided that the time had come to do something against the Germans. He started to cast around for ways to join the resistance. This was never easy, for the resistance was very aware of the danger of German infiltrators or collaborators; but he finally managed to get himself accepted by them early in 1942 and moved to Macon, where he did liaison work between Macon and Paris. He is modest about the courage it must have taken to do this: 'I was happy-go-lucky, not a great worrier.'

Perhaps it was as a result of that attitude that he remained free for so long, but his luck ran out in 1943. He suspects that he was betrayed by a girlfriend. After his arrest he was taken to the prison at Fresnes (the start of the journey to the KZ for many arrested in France), and interrogated by the Vichy authorities. 'I was unsure of whether I'd be able to hold out under torture and so, rather than run the risk of betraying my friends, I decided to admit straight away that I was a Jew. Of course I knew nothing then of the death camps. I knew that if I confessed to being Jewish, they would probably think that I had just

been hiding out, rather than that I'd been anyone of particular importance in the resistance.'

The ploy worked. They took him to the camp at Drancy, where he
remained for only a few weeks before being taken directly by train to
Auschwitz, where he arrived in the spring of 1944. Being relatively fit
and well fed, he was immediately selected for work at the I. G. Farben
ersatz-rubber works at Buna-Monowitz, or Auschwitz-III (Monowice),
and taken there directly from the station. His train did not go up the
spur of track to the ramp at Birkenau.

'All my life I've had an innate belief in my ability to pull through. I
felt like that before the war, too. During my imprisonment, I didn't
analyse things. I took them as they came, and if it was something bad,
I tried to say to myself, well, don't worry, this can't last for ever. You
had to live from day to day – the things to avoid were brooding, and
letting yourself go. It was very important to hang on to your self-respect;
and to remain convinced that you were not a criminal. They did
everything in their power to make you into a creature lower than an
animal: that justified them in killing you; you had to become what
they believed you to be: sub-human. But you could never show defiance
openly, either. That had to exist in your inner life, and it had to be
somehow positive, not despairing. The first assault was the shock of
arrival. I saw a child killed straight away in front of its mother. That
said more clearly than anything what they wanted to say to us: you
are nothing; we will kill you as carelessly as we would crush an ant. If
you could withstand the shock of arrival, you were over the first hurdle.
Many didn't get that far, even if they weren't selected immediately for
the gas.'

Conditioning through the various prisons and internment camps also
helped K to get into grim training for Auschwitz; but luck, he believes,
also played a very prominent part, and he acknowledges that he had
the greatest luck in being selected for Monowice – away from the gas
chambers – rather than Birkenau. However, his life before the war had
not prepared him at all for what lay in store. 'I was born into a sheltered
family, and then suddenly in 1938 I was thrown headlong into life – I
had to grow up, harden up and adapt very fast indeed.'

In January 1945, when Auschwitz was evacuated, K was sent on the
death-march westward through that bitter winter, and ended at Dora,
the appalling camp in the Harz mountains where V-1 and V-2 rockets
were manufactured in underground factories. He worked here under
the hellish conditions that have been described elsewhere[1] until early
April when, under pressure from the approaching US forces, the
Germans moved their victims again, this time to Belsen, where K was
liberated on 15 April by the British – two days after his 24th birthday.

'The first thing I wanted was revenge, but circumstances didn't allow the possibility of taking it, which was probably just as well.' For a long time after he was freed, he was unable or unwilling to talk about his experiences, but with time that feeling ceased, and now he not only finds it easy to talk, but thinks that it is a help to be able to do so. Like so many survivors, however, he feels a sense of isolation – of being cut off from other people by the experience. His wife, again not alone among survivors' spouses, feels it too, in that she is excluded by it – cut off from the inner circle because she did not go through the KZ herself. The impression is that she wishes he could forget all about it.

He was repatriated to France because he was a former resistance fighter, and there he was taken care of by the French authorities, France being among the first and one of the most generous countries in terms of post-war care of former KZ-inmates. He recuperated in Nice, where the bitter news of his parents' death reached him. But there by chance he also met a cousin who had survived the war by concealing the fact that he was Jewish and working in forced labour in Germany during the war.[2] This cousin had settled in Limoges with his family, and K joined them there. Meanwhile one of his two brothers, a doctor who had settled in America, having got out before the war, was able to provide an affidavit for K to join him there.

The first year was spent in New York, working in a dull job as an import/export clerk, and learning English, which he managed quickly – he attributes this to the fact that he is a keen (and very good) amateur cellist. 'Being a musician, I have a very good ear.' As for his feelings, outside being bored by his job, 'Everything was rosy. It was heaven: wine, women and song. I had survived. Nothing was a big problem.' At the end of the first year he moved to Baltimore at the behest of a friend who had emigrated to America with him, and took a job there as a packer for a textile wholesaler – his English was not yet good enough for him to take a salesman's job. He persevered with his English classes, and gradually worked his way up the promotion ladder at work. Meanwhile, he had met his wife, an English girl who was working for one of the disc-jockeys at the local radio station. It was because she was homesick for England that, after two years, he agreed to go and live there. He had never been to England before, but had nothing special to tie him to Baltimore, and no ambitions. His academic career had been interrupted by the war, and now he was adrift, with no special urge to resume his studies, though he did nurse vague hopes in the direction of music. He still plays the cello, and one of his daughters plays the piano seriously enough for there to be a large one in their house. There was no temptation to return to Austria.

Once in London, he took up the offer of a friend in New York to run the European end of his finance business: loans to soldiers based in Europe to enable them to buy cars. Two daughters were born, in 1953 and 1956, and in 1967 his wife, following her own family's business, opened a rainwear shop. By that time the dollar market was open and K's finance company closed in the face of too much competition, but he was good enough at his job to be head-hunted by another firm.

He still suffers from dreams about the camps, about getting 25 lashes, but he says that the nightmares don't occur now more than once a year or so, and that their effect is no worse than any other nightmare. 'I don't think I'm different from anybody else, and I don't think my dreams generally are influenced by memories of the camps. On the other hand, that's like saying: the only people who swear they are completely sane are the nutters!' He laughs; but his wife disagrees, and says that she thinks he is much influenced still by the camps. He didn't start to talk about the KZ until 1980. Before that, he had given his wife only a brief outline of what he had been through, and to his daughters he gave just the facts, but never details. He never dwelt on what happened. 'Until recently, I have never had the desire to talk about it, but I have always taken an interest in films and books on the subject – maybe they give me a kind of relief, I don't know.'[3] Certain things affect him more than others: when he sees a film about the KZ, it is the trains: 'Whenever they show train journeys – they affect me terribly. Whenever I see those people on the trains I see myself, and that affects me terribly.'

The impression is that his wife dislikes and even envies the camaraderie of former KZ-inmates, but K says he really thinks he has got something in common with other KZlers that he doesn't have with anyone else – a closeness that he cannot share even with his wife. He wanted to seek out the company of former inmates now in England. 'I managed to get to a reunion of the 45 Aid Society, and I wanted to join them. I wasn't one of the original group, of course, but it seems that they are the only survivors' group in England. I was working on joining them, and they were not terribly excited about getting new people in . . . but I wanted to be one of them. Maybe that's an obsession too. I can see what my wife means . . .'

His wife points out to him that he watches any film or programme about the KZ, and reads many, many books about it. 'I don't do that out of historical interest, but it does provide a kind of release. Also, I don't find it unhealthy to remember. In fact, you may think I'm crazy, but whenever things get tough now – bad business, or upset in the home – I think back to those times and I tell myself, you're crazy to worry about what's happening now – look at what you lived through then, and you survived it. Whatever you have now will be a bonus – everything you've had since 1945 has been a bonus. And I talk myself into a kind of serenity that way. I am healthy; I believe I am normal. You know, I think I can talk myself into happiness by reminding myself

– by looking at TV, by reading books – and I say, look at that, it's marvellous – you are terrific – you are alive! . . . No, I don't feel guilty – how can I answer that question? I feel proud. Do you know that I feel proud to be a survivor? I have achieved something that not many people have achieved. We are a kind of elite. I think it is true to say that I feel I belong to an exclusive club – that's a crude way of putting it, but maybe you can't help it.'

K has never been consciously aware of creating a mental safety net for himself, either during or after the camps, but says that the proposition makes sense. He adds that self-pity has never played any part in his make-up. Neither he nor his wife think that their daughters have been adversely affected by his experience of the camps, though they say this with slight reservation; one caused them great concern in her childhood because she suffered for some time from terrible nightmares. It does not seem that this can have had anything to do with the KZ, since at that time K never mentioned it and presented a completely normal front to the world. My feeling from the children of survivors whom I have spoken to is that they are affected to a degree which is in proportion to how successfully their survivor parent or parents have readapted, and the way in which they have either found out about, or been told about, the camps.

He finds an outlet for talking about the camps well provided by the 45 Aid Society. 'In many ways that may be of profound help, for the KZ experience does not affect me at all in my work.' He adds, however, that he finds he must always keep himself busy. He works right through weekends and, if he is not working, he gets annoyed with himself – he cannot easily sit still and watch television, say, if there is no reason for the activity other than relaxation. In addition to work, he has an engrossing hobby – philately – and every Tuesday goes to play the cello in an amateur orchestra he belongs to. 'I do not say that I keep myself busy in order to avoid brooding – but how can I tell? Consciously, I wouldn't have thought so, but I cannot deny the possibility. But also I think I am by nature a very fidgety person, and apparently I am not even a calm sleeper, but always toss and turn.' He does not like being alone.

He is not sure how much the experience of the camps may have changed him. 'I used to regard myself as a sensitive person, but once you're in a camp you can't afford to be – no way – so I had consciously to try to suppress that facet of my nature – sensitive people didn't survive. And that "trick" of suppression has stayed with me – I am aware of it, even though today I perform it without thinking. It switches itself on when it is needed – if I have to be tough in business, for example, either with someone else or even with myself. But that instinct was certainly born in the KZ. All survival is based on instinct.

It may start with a conscious decision: I must wash; I must resist the Germans' effort to degrade me. And you must look at it all as if you were an onlooker. From that starting point, instinct takes over.

'You could not live without hope. If I'd felt there was no hope, I wouldn't have survived. It was a tool of survival, not a delusion. I knew that the KZ couldn't go on for ever, couldn't continue for my whole life – though I admit that I didn't take that thought to its logical conclusion and consider how long my life would be – that in fact the KZ could very easily last for the whole of the rest of my life, and that needn't be very long; no, I considered my life as stretching out ahead of me for its normal span.

'Hope filled our conversation, and our fantasies were filled with food. Sex didn't come into it, we were always too tired, too frightened; but interest in food increased with the lack of it. I tended to be with the French inmates, and there was one funny thing that happened. We were digging roads, and talking to each other a bit, and the French of course talked food. Everybody was telling each other what the first meal they'd have on liberation would be. Some were describing really intricate recipes – lobster thermidor, things like that – but when it came to my turn to tell, all I could think of was to have a saucepanful of hot chocolate, and I'd be lying on a couch – I imagined the old couch we had at home in Vienna – listening to music on the radio and eating biscuits, and drinking my hot chocolate. And when I'd finished telling them they were quite indignant. "You're crazy," they said. "Don't you have any better fantasies than that? You could have anything in the world you liked, and that is what you choose!"'

He thinks that being doublecrossed in business since the war, which inevitably has happened a few times, has done more to undermine his faith in human nature than anything that happened in the camps, because the camp guardians – the SS and the kapos – didn't seem part of the world of ordinary humanity, and so people in the post-war world couldn't be judged by the yardstick of their behaviour. 'I've always had an optimistic nature, and I think that goes hand in hand with a trusting nature. At the beginning of my business career, I was very trusting. I wanted to think the best of everyone – is that unusual, in other survivors? The only people I wouldn't trust, of course, were the Germans. As far as they are concerned, obviously I remember best the kapos and the SS who beat me, and I remember them with hatred – but sometimes I wonder, if I had had the opportunity to survive by becoming a *Prominent*, would I have taken it? Because in my mind only one thing was paramount; and that was survival. I remember a Mussulman in my bunk died in the night, and as soon as I was aware of it I looked for his bread. I wasn't aware of having any standards of decency shaping my method of survival and, to be honest I haven't thought about it before, but I was never in a position where my survival depended upon doing another person down. That is fortunate.'

Of the Germans today, he recalls the adage, to understand all is to forgive all, and says that as he cannot understand why they did it, he cannot forgive. Nor can he forget. But he repeats: 'I cannot forgive;' and adds, laughing, 'It's the only thing that keeps me sane. It goes beyond my thought that anyone could consider forgiving them – anyone who has been through it. Perhaps I have to live with . . . what can I call it? Hate? I don't hate Germans now, in general; but I hate what they caused to happen, and I hate Germans of that generation, and when there is a trial I hope that they will die. The sentences handed down by the West German courts are ridiculous. I don't think I am a particularly aggressive man by nature, but I would like to see everyone who was involved in running the camps exterminated. They didn't need to follow those orders. There used to be a saying about the Austrians, "They are very bad Nazis but very good anti-Semites." With the Germans, it was the other way round; but between them they almost finished the job.'

He takes the threat of neo-Nazism seriously, and had made a collection of press-cuttings concerning their activities, which he got rid of only recently. Deep memories are stirred when he sees photographs in newspapers today of desecrated Jewish graves. 'I worry about it, and I worry about the revisionist historians, and those who seek to prove that the Holocaust was a hoax – that it didn't happen. There's a book, *Did Six Million Really Die?* – I am fascinated by the horror of these things, but it surprises me too that they can raise their heads so soon after the end of the war. There are young Germans too who are still fascinated by it – seduced by it. How can they be, of all people? If it is just an adolescent, romantic attraction, it's no less dangerous for that. So many of the top Nazis were only in their twenties and thirties. People forget that. It seems to me, though, that we should all worry more about the threat of the other great holocaust – the nuclear holocaust – under whose shadow we all live today.'

There was no problem for him in terms of his welcome by the Jewish community in London – he was not arriving alone, or straight from the camps, both of which are important factors; also he had married an English wife. Equally, he did not wish to talk until recently; but 'when I did want to, people looked at me and said in tones of polite awe: "Oh really? You were in the camps? How terrible" – and that was it. End of conversation. They didn't want to hear any more about it, or discuss it.' His wife suggests that perhaps this was because they didn't want to upset him. He is not convinced, though politely he acknowledges the possibility. I wonder why it took him so long to get to the point of wanting to talk about it. 'I don't know. Maybe *I* didn't want to upset anybody. I mean, who do you talk to? You talk to your family, you talk to your wife . . . Maybe I didn't want to upset them . . . And my wife never asked me any questions about it . . . I felt that she couldn't understand why I was reading about it, why I wanted to watch programmes on television about it. But there was no other outlet; the 45 Aid Society has only come into the picture very recently . . . I had no outlet with anybody. Possibly I managed to live with it just by keeping busy, and reading about it.'

II

On 6 October 1938 the Polish government passed a decree revoking the passports of all nationals whose bearers had lived abroad for five years or more. The order was to come into force on 31 October, and those who would principally be affected by it were the 15,000 Polish Jews then living in Germany. For their part, the Germans did not want to be encumbered with 15,000 stateless Jews, especially as the Evian Conference earlier that year had made it clear that almost no other country would be prepared to accept them. On 27 October, they rounded up the expatriate Polish Jews and forcibly transported them to the Polish border, where they were left, principally at the frontier town of Zbonszyn. Eventually the Poles relented and allowed them back into Poland. Among those who suffered in this way were the family of Herszel Grynszpan, who was himself living illegally in Paris at the time. When he heard of their plight, his reaction was to take a pistol and go to the German Embassy, where he shot and mortally wounded the Third Secretary, Ernst vom Rath, whose death triggered the infamous *Kristallnacht*, as the Germans called it.[4]

Henry Wermeuth and his family were also among those forcibly repatriated. He was 16, and had been born in Frankfurt-am-Main in 1922; but he was on his Polish mother's passport. His father had been born in Poland, but came to Germany with his parents when he was nine months old. The deportation to Poland – an alien land to Wermeuth – was the initial shock to the senses: the uprooting, the lost home, the grim railway journey, the infectious panic of his fellow-travellers, were all a foretaste of what was to come. Wermeuth maintains that for him the worst thing of all in the war was not the camps, but the train journeys between them.

They found refuge with relatives in Cracow, and for a while they were safe; but inevitably the arrests and the round-ups started, following the German invasion. The family was sent to the ghetto at Bochnia; later, Wermeuth and his father were taken to the concentration camp at

Plaszow, which at the time was under the command of the infamous Amon Goeth. After Plaszow, he and his father were sent with a transport to hard labour at Kielce, but here there was a respite of sorts because they worked under civilian administration; there was no killing and there was plenty of food. The respite was not to last. On 1 August 1944, in the face of the Russian advance, they were shipped to Auschwitz with 600 other men. There, because they were strong and well-fed, they were selected for Buna-Monowice. 'None of us was killed, although our first reaction to Auschwitz was, well, this is it. I am trying to write a book myself about my experiences, and I want to call it *Breathe Deeply, My Son*, because that was my father's advice to me when we were sent to the showers at Auschwitz, and he thought they were the disguised gas chambers – by that stage in the war we knew a little of what to expect at Auschwitz. However, from my own experience, life there was not as bad as it had been at Plaszow. In Auschwitz you knew to a certain extent where you stood – at least I did, and I know very well how fortunate I was not to be sent to Birkenau. From time to time there would be selections, but, if you kept strong and had some luck, you might get through. In Plaszow it was different. You never knew from day to day whether or not the whim of that monster Goeth would bring about your death. Death would come by pure chance. It was like being in a pen from which the farmer selects beasts for the slaughter willy-nilly. Plaszow was the worst time for me, because of the tension. It was even worse than the very last few months of the war, when they evacuated us from Auschwitz, eventually to Mauthausen.'

Wermeuth believes that one needs a certain kind of personality to survive. He describes himself as a schemer and a go-getter, 'a so-and-so'; but adds that he was made that way by what he had to endure in the KZ, and what he had to become to survive. 'I was a child and I became a man – the process took hardly any time at all. Normally it takes years, but I missed adolescence completely.' He thinks too that anyone who did survive the camps was born with an instinct to do so – only a very few survived by pure chance – but added to the instinct is the element of learning the tricks of survival, without which the instinct would not be enough. 'In summer, 1942, we were in the ghetto in Bochnia – there were my father, my mother, my sister – living in one room. My mother said, "Two million Jews have already been killed"; she was quoting something Goebbels had said, and one of us asked, "What is going to happen to us?" She replied: "What is going to happen to all the Jews is going to happen to us;" but there was a voice inside me saying – even if all the other Jews die, this one will survive; and I meant it, but I was equally aware that most of us would believe the same thing: they will get everyone else, but somehow they won't get me. It would take a book just to describe who I was and what I became

– how every part of me became dedicated to survival, which, once learnt, in turn became instinctive.'

His father was with him throughout the camps, but was not to see liberation. 'We spent the last few weeks of the war being shunted here and there by train. There was no food – nothing. My father had done something to annoy one of the guards and he received a terrible blow on the head. They transferred him to the next waggon to mine – the so-called *Krankenwagen* – and he died there, on the way to Mauthausen. It was a week before liberation. I found out when we arrived at Mauthausen. I remember that I shed one single tear. I did not have the strength to shed more; there was a new camp to face up to. It was overflowing with prisoners who had been evacuated from other camps nearer the Allied fronts, but there was no more gassing there. Not that it was necessary; people were dying of starvation and disease just as fast. A lot of skeletons walking about, many of them naked – the majority, perhaps.' They slept five to a bunk, lying alternately head to feet in order to fit in. One of those sharing Wermeuth's bunk was too ill to get up any more. There was a table in the *Block* near their bunks, and Wermeuth offered to sleep on it, to give the others more room, in exchange for the single blanket they shared. The others agreed, and so he moved to the table, sleeping by resting his body on his knees and elbows – 'the only places that could take the weight of my body, for the rest of me was all bone.' His weight had dropped from 75 to 35 kilogrammes while he was in the camps. 'But I still clung to life – I managed to steal some soup. And the way that I did it was by adapting a conjuring trick my father had taught me as a child – really it was just sleight-of-hand: there was a large cauldron of watery soup they gave us outside, ready for the midday dole out. Wrapped in my blanket I strolled past it, and past the 600 or so people already gathering near it. I had my mess-bowl hidden under my blanket, and as I passed the cauldron I managed, under cover of the blanket, to lift its lid and scoop out a bowlful of soup. I went back to my barrack where I tried to hide under my blanket to eat all the soup by myself, but of course I hadn't been all that clever – some people had seen me and I was immediately surrounded by several poor hungry vultures. So of course I had to share what I could of it; but even then I had a few extra mouthfuls – and they could be enough to make the difference between life and death. Another little trick of mine – and I was the only one among our *Block* of 600, just to show that maybe only one in 600 had ideas – was to get double rations of soup. This I did in the following way: the *Block* was divided by a corridor down the middle, between the bunks. It happened that on occasion we were called out for soup one side at a time. Once my side had had its share and we'd returned, I slipped across the corridor and joined a bunk which was one man short. I knew that the SS wouldn't recognize me, nor would anyone else, come to that, for we all looked alike. Starvation does that to people. Naturally the people on the other side didn't want me to join them, but they agreed when I promised them some of the extra soup that I'd get. It was the soup that kept me alive. If someone could live on two spoons, I would try to get three. Every spoonful, let alone bowlful, counted – and yet it was no more than warm water and potato peel.

'Then came the day of liberation. How does one describe the major event of one's life in a concise way? I was lying wrapped in my blanket in the *Block*. Someone else was looking out of the window, and I heard him say in Yiddish, "An American soldier." I didn't get up. I didn't move. I lay there. The feeling cannot be described; you would have to make up a new word. "I've done it. I've made it." But then I thought: who has survived? I. I alone. My father had just died. My sister and my mother were gone. I covered my head and wept. That was the moment of my liberation.'

Soldiers liberating the camps have said that one of the most shocking things was – not only could they not distinguish individual characteristics among the survivors because of the way they had been starved and maltreated – they could not even distinguish between the sexes. Wermeuth could no longer walk; he had to crawl; nor could he speak properly: his voice was slurred. Nor were the dangers over yet; the Americans gave the prisoners food, a kindly, spontaneous, but deadly act of humanitarianism performed before doctors could arrive and determine what special diets the starving needed. 'We could not cope with the food they gave us. Thousands who had survived years of German inhumanity died of American kindness. People ate, and died as they ate.' Despite the abundance of food, camp habits died hard. Wermeuth remembers seeing another ex-prisoner hunched up over a pan in which he was boiling potatoes. 'I slunk up behind him on all fours – I really was an animal – seized a potato and scuttled off as he threw boiling water at me.'

Some sixth sense had warned him, and many others, not to gorge themselves – many, possibly lucky ones, were in any case incapable of ingesting food. Soon they took him to the temporary hospital they had set up, where he lay, trying to recuperate. 'People were dying all round me – I remember a boy of about 14 in the next bed. What struck me as most odd there was that whereas days before I'd been fighting for an extra spoonful of soup, I now had more than I could manage and was throwing it away.'

It was three months before he would walk. He remembers going to look for his father among the great conical piles of corpses, but there were too many of them for his search to be possible. He remembers sitting outside on an upturned bucket eating soup, wrapped in his old blanket. An American soldier passing by stopped and took his photograph. 'I wonder where that picture is now. I would like to have it for the cover of my book.'

One day he went towards a *Block*. It was dark inside but there were some panes of glass in its windows. As he looked through the window he saw a skeleton staring back at him. He was not shocked by it but, as he moved back, so did the skeleton. It was a sunny day. It was the first time he had seen his reflection in years.

As he grew stronger, he became aware that people were signing up to go to Palestine, and that appealed to him because he had relatives there, and already the adventurer in him was beginning to stir again. Nevertheless he hesitated, wondering whether he should not return to Frankfurt first. There was a faint chance, he argued, that his mother and sister might have got through. They had been taken from Bochnia to Belzec on 24 July 1942, but at the time he naturally had no idea how efficient the Belzec programme had been. Still he vacillated, and then, arguing finally that if they had managed to get home, he would be able to trace them from Palestine ('I prefer to say *"Palestina"* because that is the way we pronounce it'), he went to register for emigration, only minutes before the office closed.

'It must have been six or eight weeks after liberation that I found myself on a convoy of lorries heading for the Italian border. The Jewish Brigade were looking after us. For some reason, when we got there we were told to sit quietly, not to make a sound – there must have been something political in it. But we got through the border, and the next day the sun was shining, and Henry Wermeuth was alive, looking out of the truck and seeing palm trees: something you dream of when you are a child, going to a country where there are palms. It was a world unreal. In the whole convoy of 35 lorries, one man climbed on to the top of his truck to look round – me.

'Our first stop was Modena. People stopped to stare at us, and no one could blame them. I don't know where I had got my clothes from: some old boots, no socks, a pair of gaudy boxer-shorts with the fly sewn up for trousers, a grey short-sleeved shirt and a green straw hat.'

His gentle wife is sitting with us. She is also a German Jew, and spent the war in hiding, protected by German Catholics. 'You were a kind of hippie,' she says.

'No,' he says. 'A kind of scarecrow.

'I was still very thin, a walking scarecrow. A few years earlier, I would have felt ashamed, but now I felt great. I thought: "I am alive! What have *you* done?" The world is mine! Later, I travelled about Italy in trains, and when the guard asked for a ticket I would look at him in genuine amazement: "But I'm a KZ survivor!" – and the guard would go away. I really felt that the world was mine. "You want a ticket from me?!" The world was mine – it belonged to me. For a long time I felt

like that. What can happen to me? What on earth can happen to me?'
He becomes very excited. His wife calms him.

In Modena, he began to have second thoughts about Palestine, as the attractions of Italy presented themselves to him. He went to Rome with a friend made in the camps, and with him started trading old clothes in a market, where he learned about business. 'I must tell you this story, because I did become a businessman, for better or worse, and I am not a good one. I had an overcoat that my partner wanted me to sell for 4,000 lire. The first customer I told the price to offered me 2,000, so when the next customer came along I asked 5,000, and he offered three. I thought, next time I will ask 6,000 lire, and get my four. Which I did, and the man looked at the coat, and looked at me, and offered me one lira!'

The black market was in full flood, and Wermeuth got into it – owing to circumstances, rather than because he wanted to be a war profiteer. He was quick to pick up Italian and spent six months in Rome before becoming involved in smuggling cigarette-papers into Italy from Austria, where they could be bought at a quarter of the Italian price. This he did with some success, despite the occasional brush with the border patrols, crossing to Innsbruck to buy the papers and then selling them in Bolzano; but inevitably things finally got too hot for his gang and they decided that they had better make for Germany. Much to their surprise, they succeeded in crossing both frontiers from Italy without incident, early in 1946. Wermeuth returned to Frankfurt. He would remain in Germany for five years.

'In the camps I had two dreams. One was of food, and the other was to get hold of a machine-gun and shoot every German in sight; but the odd thing was that the first "enemy" people I saw after the war were a group of little girls – and I thought of my sister: she was a little girl, she was innocent, and she died; how would it be if I took revenge against these kids? What would it solve? Or relieve? And wouldn't it reduce me to the level of an SS-man? My intention in going to Germany was to see how the people were after the war, what they were like, if they had changed. I also wanted to go to Frankfurt again. It was, after all, my home town. I wanted to see who else had managed to get back alive, and I wanted to show the people there that I was still alive. They couldn't get rid of me that easily! At the back of my mind too was the idea that I might be able to unearth some Nazis, but I didn't have a coherent plan. I was drifting at that time; I was a man free of everything: nobody could tell me what to do. I was 23 years old, I'd tried to get rich quick. What happened to me next was that I discovered girls, for the first time in my life, and that, I am afraid, distracted me from any systematic quest for Nazis.'

He does not blame the Germans any more, but feels rather that they were victims of their own gullibility. Both he and his wife can even find extenuating circumstances: Hitler reduced unemployment, and with his programme of *Winterhilfe* he was like a saviour to the poor people: because of him, they had a good Christmas, and no one thought of the consequences, or where the food and clothing furnished by *Winterhilfe* were coming from. 'I had an aunt in England who was the only survivor of my mother's family, and I exchanged letters with her when I was still in Germany. I must have written letters to her which she didn't expect. The Germans had tried to crush the Jews, and here I was, in Germany again, writing her letters full of excuses for them. Finally she wrote to me in words I will never forget: "I suppose in your next letter you will write and tell me that the six million killed themselves." I realized that I was losing myself in a Germany that I was peopling with innocent Germans because that is what I wanted to believe. Now my aunt's letter brought me to a crossroads. I couldn't go to America because I had had TB, but in 1950 I was able to accept an invitation from my aunt to visit her in England. It was like making a pilgrimage. I was to stay for six weeks, and in the course of that time I felt myself pulled two ways: back to Germany and towards staying in the United Kingdom.

'As time passed and I realized that I didn't want to go back to Germany, there was one way I could stay here – by enrolling to do a course at an English college of further education, which was good for two years. But at the end of that time I was still determined to stay. I wrote a letter of supplication to the Queen – that is, to King George VI's consort; and I got an answer back, "commanded by Her Gracious Majesty", which informed me that I could stay if I could find work. A suitable job was hard to find. There were few jobs available, and people were disinclined to employ a foreigner, still less one with a German accent. Finally I was taken on as a kind of valet to an elderly gentleman. It was fortunate for me, because shortly afterwards I fell ill again with TB, and was not free of it for another four years. Now, however broken my health is in other respects, TB at least is a thing of the past, thanks to the treatment I received in this country.'

The ill-health shows, though he will not allow it to dominate him. The wry but slightly desperate humour he uses to cope with it is also effective against the intrusive memory of the KZ. He is seldom disturbed by war films, even films of the camps, though he found Lord Bernstein's film about the liberation of Belsen – *A Painful Reminder* – very disturbing – 'It showed me more than I actually saw myself, and triggered a bad night' – and was deeply affected by reading *Schindler's Ark*.[5] He does dream, though not regularly; nightmares can occur twice in one month, and then not again for a year. 'Mostly I am back in the camp – but as a hero – doing all the things I didn't do. I am young. I feel strong. I adventure. I steal cars. I shoot. I stalk through closed gates. I outwit Nazis. But there is always the feeling that I am not winning. And I'm glad to wake up.'

III

Edith Kramer-Freund was born in Königsberg, East Prussia (now Kaliningrad, Lithuanian SSR), in 1899. She studied in Munich and Jena and finally took her doctorate in medicine in Berlin, where she subsequently worked in the dermatology department of the university medical faculty. Her first husband, also a doctor, died of leukaemia in 1937. After the introduction of the Nuremberg Laws, Edith Kramer-Freund worked as a medical practitioner for Jews[6] in Berlin.

Possibly as a result of having helped the Jewish girlfriend of a senior SS-officer at his request by signing a medical certificate stating that the girlfriend was unfit to be transported to the East, Dr Freund was spared the immediate attentions of the Gestapo. A month after she had performed this service, at the end of April 1942, she was sent a letter ordering her to report to the District Health Authority in Posen (Poznan) within three days. This seemed either to be too good to be true or a trap. She went to Police Headquarters in Berlin, which had issued the letter, and asked for details. She was told quite politely that she was to help look after a section of the civilian population of Posen for a few months, after which she could return to her Berlin practice. A salary would be paid directly into her bank account, from which she could draw at will, and she would be allowed to keep her Berlin apartment.

'My friends congratulated me; they thought I was lucky to be relieved of the fear of deportation to the East, the nightmare of all the Jews.' She was given a train ticket but left to choose her own departure time. Amidst her hurried preparations, she found time to have an inoculation against typhus. Such inoculations were forbidden to Jews at the time, but a colleague did it for her 'illegally'. She packed a small suitcase with some light clothes, since she expected to be away only for the summer ('How wrong I was'), and caught an ordinary passenger train to Posen. Although she was wearing the Star of David, her fellow-passengers were polite to her, and even offered her a seat.

When she arrived, she learnt that the German population was to be protected against a typhoid epidemic which was spreading from the Polish labour camps nearby. Her work would start at a quarantine camp for women established at Fort Radziwill, which had been sealed off from the outside world. The conditions in this camp were dreadful, and lack of food and medicine increased the already high mortality rate. Six weeks later, the camp was closed and its inhabitants transferred to a labour camp established at Antoninek, formerly the mansion of an aristocratic Polish family. The mansion was not big enough to accommodate the 300 girls from Radziwill, who had to build huts, even making the bricks for them themselves.

Dr Freund was also given charge of the medical welfare of a nearby men's camp, and given a bicycle in order to commute between the two. 'I must have looked very strange, wearing the Star of David and riding a bicycle decorated with swastikas.' She used the journey and her bank account in order to stop off and buy additional medicaments. Additionally, and with the consent of her chief, a surgeon who had been in the National Party and was therefore no Nazi, she declined to write 'heart-attack' or 'TB' as the 'official' cause of death of her charges on their death certificates, but wrote the truth: 'malnutrition', 'starvation' – and put in an application to WVHA for better rations. 'The girls were used for road-building, which was very strenuous work. At that time we didn't yet realize that the "Final Solution" was to be carried out. We still thought the Jews were being used for forced labour, and it seemed reasonable to expect them to be adequately fed.' By one of the many quirks of the Nazi administration, her application was granted, and conditions at Antoninek improved considerably.

By the same utterly unpredictable nature of Nazi thinking, however, but perhaps also inevitably, she was finally arrested by the Gestapo, for 'sabotage' – that is, for writing the true cause of death on the death certificates. In the summer of 1943 she was taken to the Gestapo prison in Posen. The girls she had helped so much now helped her to hide some money in her little suitcase. It was a sad leave-taking, and Dr Freund never saw any of the girls again. Shortly after her departure, Antoninek was closed down, and its entire population was transported to Birkenau and gassed. Of that small camp she is the only survivor.

She remained in prison in Posen for six weeks. Then she was transferred to Berlin, to the Gestapo women's prison in Bessemer Strasse. 'Here, there were not only political prisoners but also ordinary criminals and inmates of other concentration camps who were to be sent on to other camps because of overcrowding. I had to wait several weeks for my interrogation. One Sunday, I was called by the supervisor of the prison. A co-prisoner, a Ukrainian girl, was in labour and the doctor in charge was not available. The supervisor had done a course in midwifery but she was not willing to take the responsibility. I asked for clean linen, and scissors, needle and twine to cut the umbilical cord. It was an easy delivery and I got half a loaf of bread as my "fee". I shared it with my cell-mates. They wished for more deliveries of that kind.'

One after another the women in her cell were called for interrogation, and few returned. Finally she was summoned; but there was no record of her case: the files appeared to have been lost. The interrogator asked her what she had done. She told him, and he dismissed her, but not to her cell. 'We're going to let you join your girls,' he said with a malicious smile, the sense of which escaped her at the time, but which was enough to worry her.

They took her to a collection centre for transports in a school on the Grosse Hamburger Strasse. The school was on three floors: on the top floor those destined for Auschwitz were collected; and on the second, those for Theresienstadt. Dr Freund, having been cut off from the outside world for so long, had no idea what those two names meant. By an enormous stroke of good luck she encountered two former patients of hers who said they had managed to bribe an SS-official to organize Swedish exit permits for them. They expected to leave that day. In the exchange of news she told them that she was to be transported to a camp. They asked which one, and she told them, 'Auschwitz.' They were horrified and asked her if she had any money available, or if she could get help from outside. Time was very tight indeed, as the transport for Theresienstadt was due to leave the following morning at four, and the one for Auschwitz at six. Her friends said that when they left they would immediately contact a Jewish lawyer who had good connections within the Gestapo, and ask him to help her. She also gave them a letter for her sister, who was safe for the moment at least because she was married to an Aryan.

Her friends' arrangement with the SS was not betrayed and they left later that morning. Dr Freund's luggage had already been collected for the transport to Auschwitz. 'Among other things it contained the diary I had kept at Posen. Even today I miss those notes, which listed the names of all the girls, and the songs we used to sing.' She spent the whole afternoon waiting, and the lawyer did not appear. During that afternoon, she learnt the real difference between Auschwitz and Theresienstadt – many of those destined for Auschwitz jumped from the third-floor windows or, if they had it, took poison. Dr Freund herself had a cyanide capsule, for use *in extremis*.

She had all but given up hope when the lawyer appeared, late in the evening, and only a matter of five hours before the Theresienstadt transport was due to leave. He didn't waste any time, but ushered her along to see a Gestapo official who appeared to be expecting them – pushing their way through the corridors crowded with nervously waiting people, their faces drained of colour by fear and the cold electric light.

The Gestapo man looked at her. 'Are you married? Do you have children?' he asked.

The lawyer answered for her: 'She is a widow. There are no children.' He added for good measure that Dr Freund's first husband had been decorated with the Iron Cross, First and Second Class, for his service in the First World War, which was true, and that he had died of wounds received in combat then, which wasn't.

'How many are due to go on the next transport to Theresienstadt?' asked the official.

'Fifty-nine.'

'All right, then; we'll make it a round 60.'

She was able to move down a floor.

The transport to Theresienstadt consisted mainly of doctors and nurses from the Jewish Hospital in Berlin, which had been closed down. They travelled in ordinary third-class passenger waggons.

Every newcomer – whatever his or her previous occupation – had to join a so-called *Hundertschaft*, a group of 100 people. They were made to work ten hours a day, seven days a week. Dr Freund's team was set to digging potatoes, and later to stacking timber. Both these details were outside the town. They had their advantages, for one could steal a potato occasionally, or a few bits of wood for a fire or for barter. The risk was great, for such acts of theft were considered by the SS to be sabotage, and resulted in the culprits being sent to the *Kleine Festung* – the 'Little Fortress' – the prison, or *Bunker*, of Theresienstadt. Almost no one came back from there.

During this period she was lodged in a long attic with broken windows – a mass quarters for women. It was cold at night and Dr Freund, having lost her luggage, had only the light clothes she'd been wearing in the Bessemer Strasse prison: a blouse and a threadbare pair of slacks. 'It was imperative for me to "buy" a blanket in exchange for half a loaf of bread. What that means nobody can realize who has never been in such a position . . . There was a chance to get some clothing from the so-called *Kleiderkammer*, where former belongings of those who had died or been sent on transports were stored, but it was by no means easy. The distribution of clothes was an eagerly sought-after job, and therefore reserved for the Czechs. Everything depended upon whether the applicant made a good impression on the issuer or not. Being German, I was advised to "prettify" myself. I should put on lipstick, which in turn had to be bought by barter, but the investment was worth it.'

Life in the attic was not harmonious: there was no space, no privacy, inadequate privies and washrooms, and a babel of different tongues. Nevertheless, there was also humour. 'I remember one occasion when, above all the noise and the cursing and the bickering, a girl started to sing, *In diesen heil'gen Hallen / Kennt man die Rache nicht!*'[7]

She spent three months working with the *Hundertschaft*, after which she was detailed to do medical work. She was allocated a room, which she had to share with the five Czech doctors already in residence. Most of the floor-space was taken up by five beds, and the Czech women ordered her to sleep on the floor. They could speak German but would speak only Czech, and made their hostility to their new room-mate felt, simply because she was German, never mind that she was also Jewish. One of them, however, Dr Anna Krasa, befriended her. Dr Krasa and she 'had many interests in common. She was very musical, and I still remember to what lengths she would go to get the use of a piano for practising. There were a few pianos in the ghetto, but they were in demand, so Anna had to practise between five and six in the morning. To maximize her playing time, she would take the music to bed the night before and hum the tunes to herself. She was deported to Auschwitz on 28 October 1944, on the last transport to be sent there, and I later learnt that she was among the last 4,000 to be gassed. Before she left, she gave me the address of her friend Ninon, who was married to the writer Hermann Hesse and lived in Switzerland. They were to be of great help to me after my liberation.'

Working in the *Geniekaserne*, a building used as a hospital for the old women of the camp, was disheartening. Little could be done for the poor patients among whom TB was rife. Dr Freund tried to separate the healthy from the infected, but there was little else she could do. In the hospital was a laboratory where the sputum could be examined, and here among others worked Dr Adler, the wife of Hans Günther Adler, who was later to write the definitive history of Theresienstadt.[8] Both the Adlers were deported to Auschwitz. Only he survived. In the hospital, hardly any medicine was available, and the food ration was even smaller for the bedridden than it was for the working population. They used to delay registering deaths for a day or two, so that those who lived on could benefit from the few extra rations thus provided.

Deaths occurred daily. 'One of my patients was the sister of Rabbi Leo Baeck, but she died very soon after I had started work in the hospital. Her daughter, Nelly Stern, was also a doctor, and worked with me. We became good friends, and she introduced me to the discussion evenings led by her uncle. These meetings were held from time to time and usually six to eight people were invited. Each of them could choose a subject to lecture on, and Rabbi Baeck conducted the discussion which followed. One could prepare oneself with the help of the ghetto library, which was quite good. Rabbi Baeck would offer his own comments at the end of the discussion. This used to be the highlight of the evening, because he was so well versed in all areas of science, art and politics. Those discussion evenings were one of the few bright spots in life in Theresienstadt, though many talented people were held prisoner there, and we organized concerts, operas and cabarets. There was an unforgettable performance of Verdi's *Requiem*, which Eichmann attended, the performers of which were sent to Auschwitz soon afterwards to be gassed.[9] One of my deepest impressions was of the children

who gave a concert of songs from *Carmen*. The day after the performance, the children were deported to Auschwitz. They were looking
forward to the railway trip and sang a chorus while they marched to
the station, not knowing that it was their last song.'

Her activities were not restricted to medical matters. Every few
weeks she and some of the other women doctors were ordered to clean
up Eichmann's office and quarters, which he used on his occasional
visits to the 'model' camp, and which had to be kept spotless – so great
was the emphasis on hygiene for the great administrator of death that
ordinary cleaning women wouldn't do – they had to be doctors. 'I did
not see Eichmann on these occasions, but I did meet him once at the
railway ramp when a transport from Hungary arrived. It was my duty
to find out how many had died in the cattle-waggons, and, alas, it was
a considerable number. Eichmann said to me: "How many?" I told him
and he said: "Good." Fortunately this was the only time he spoke to
me. It was hard enough supervising the transports in and out. The
worst were those involving the crippled and the mentally ill.'

She was liberated unexpectedly at the beginning of February 1945.
News had spread through the camp that a transport was being arranged
to take people to Switzerland, and volunteers were being sought to join
it. By this stage of the war, the KZ-inmates knew well enough about
the wicked ruses of the SS, and the very word 'transport' carried a
connotation of dread. By then, too, they knew what the destination of
those transported from Theresienstadt during 1944 had been: being
assigned to this 'model' camp was no guarantee of escape from the gas
chambers of Birkenau. Switzerland, too, had been used as a blind before.
Some 18 months earlier, 1,000 orphans of the Bialystok ghetto, children
who had seen their parents murdered before their eyes, were lodged in
special quarters, treated with especial care by the SS and, for some
unholy and unfathomable reason, duped into thinking they would be
sent to Switzerland and safety, whereas of course they were sent to be
gassed at Auschwitz like all the rest.[10] It was small wonder that there
was no queue of volunteers for this new transport to Switzerland.

There were, however, some grounds for optimism. From the secret
radio receivers the inmates of Theresienstadt had built into their
bedsteads they knew that the war was nearing its end. Life in the
camp-town had also become more bearable after the last transports to
the East in the autumn of 1944, in which 19,000 people had been taken
away, reducing the population of the KZ to 11,000 – a change indeed
from the 50,000 its maximum population had been. Sad as it was, more
food was available, and there was more food and fuel to go round. The
prisoners received food parcels. There was an argument that said that
it would be better to see the war out in Theresienstadt, rather than
risk the unknown. On the other hand, to stay might be to invite

extermination by the SS at the last minute. Already there had been plenty of signs of their attempts to cover up their crimes – 'One of these was the removal of 20,000 so-called "urns" in November 1944. These urns were in fact miserable paper bags of ashes on which the names of the deceased had been scrawled. They were loaded on to trucks by the SS and, as we guessed, dumped in the River Eger.' Documents and card-indexes were burnt. Memories were awakened of the 'census' of 1943 when, on a cold November day, the prisoners were suddenly all chased into a valley outside the town. Soldiers stood around the edges of the valley. What had that been, if not a rehearsal for slaughter?

Dr Freund decided to volunteer for the transport. She still had her cyanide capsule to take if things went wrong, and she was encouraged in her decision to go by Rabbi Baeck, though he would not go himself, as his duty was to stay with those who remained behind. Nelly Stern would stay with him. Those prisoners of Austrian, Czech, Dutch and German nationality were ordered to assemble in the *Sokolowna*, the official headquarters, at three in the morning to register their choice: to go or to remain. The Danish Jews were explicitly excluded from joining the transport – but with hindsight Dr Freund guesses that this was because they were already enjoying special protection and treatment; it was probable that the Germans already knew that the white buses would be sent to collect them. The *Sokolowna* was brilliantly illuminated, despite the usual blackout regulations, and volunteers to go had to register by placing their fingerprint on a card. People dithered, changed their minds, were worried by the mere fact that for the first time in years they had to make a decision for themselves. There was chaos, and it was not helped by the camp commandant, Rahm, who would overrule or reverse decisions already made as he saw fit. The waiting prisoners who had volunteered had to stand in the icy cold for hours, awaiting a final decision, but that was nothing new to them.

'Finally my turn came. In the long hall which I had never entered before, two men sat at a long table: Rahm and Brunner. Eichmann stood behind them, the race researcher Günther and his brother from Prague were also there, with other prominent persons. Their manner was amiable, and there was nothing to remind us of their usual savagery. They looked at us with faint irony. A supervisor called my name and I was led up to the table. "Married?" asked Rahm. "Widowed." "Did your husband die in a concentration camp?" "No, of illness before the war." For some reason that reply seemed to please him. "Children?" "None." "Have your relatives been deported to the East?" "No." Rahm stamped my papers and I knew that I had been accepted for the transport.'

There was not much time left for saying goodbye to friends. Many of them pressed addresses of relatives already in freedom upon her. Rabbi Baeck asked her to get in touch with his children in London. Then it was time to pack. The SS had allocated to the departing volunteers the smartest suitcases they could find from the camp stores. 'But I jibbed at that. I loved hiking and skiing, and I had often been to Switzerland before, but never with a suitcase – always with a rucksack. Now, for some mysterious reason, rucksacks were forbidden on the transport, but I was determined to use the old one I had managed to keep with me through the sad years. It used to accompany me on trips in happier days, and in prison it had been my pillow. I restitched it where it was split, shoved my few things into it, and managed to smuggle it on to the train.

'To our surprise, the train was not made up with Red Cross waggons, but with ordinary passenger cars. Before we boarded, each of us was given a large serving of hot goulash with bread, and we were given packages of tinned food and vitamins for the journey. From the labels we could see that they had been taken from Swiss food-parcels sent to us some time ago, but withheld. Obviously the Germans now wanted to show the Swiss that their parcels had arrived and got to the right recipients. As always, SS organization was perfect; formerly they had all been geared to destroy us. Now, they were friendly, smiling at us, waving, helping the elderly up the steps to the train, handing in luggage. Rahm was there, and he had a few words for us: "You'll be well taken care of where you're going, but don't forget that things weren't too bad here either. They'll give you postcards in Switzerland and everyone should write to his friends here and confirm that he's arrived safely. We'll be sending another transport in a few weeks and we don't want any misunderstandings."

'At the last minute Dr Baeck and Nelly came to say goodbye. Dr Baeck visited me after the war in Zürich but I never saw Nelly again. She lived to see the liberation, but was run over by a car on the way to a refugee camp. She was attending a patient who had had an accident by the side of the road, and both she and the patient were killed instantly.'

Some SS accompanied the train, and sealed it. Once it was moving, she looked around at her fellow-passengers. They were mainly elderly, 60 or more, and most of them were women; there were also about 40 children, some of whom had a card hung round their necks with the word 'orphan' written on it. Everyone was haggard and pale, most had swollen legs as a result of malnutrition. But they were hopeful. The goulash warmed them and lifted their spirits, though at the same time hurt them because of the difficulty they had in digesting it. Despite that, some people opened their tin cans and started to gorge. No one yet knew for sure where the transport would end; but for the moment it was pleasant just to sit and travel. She kept her rucksack on her knees. In one of the outer pockets was a notebook – a parting gift from Nelly – in which she had written the addresses her friends had given her. To the outside of the rucksack her one-pint tin mess-bowl was attached: 'I'd bought it for half a loaf of bread some months earlier. It was very useful, though my rations never more than covered the bottom. Except for the goulash. That was the last meal I had from it.'

They were forbidden to look out of the windows or to lean against them – probably because the SS did not want their yellow stars to be seen. Nevertheless, they tried to get some sense of where they were going. As they sped through one station, a woman who knew the region caught its name: Leitmeritz. They breathed a sigh of relief; they were not heading east. They had no watches, and could only guess the time. When night fell, the train stopped. Many of them slept exhaustedly through the night, despite the noise of distant bombing and air-raid sirens; but Dr Freund stayed awake, thinking back.

The next day the train raced on westwards, now through the ravaged countryside of southern Germany. There were Bavarians among them who recognized places, names: wasn't this town Bayreuth? They were getting thirsty. The SS had provided plenty of food but nothing to drink. At Augsburg the train stopped. The SS opened the doors and ordered everybody out, separating the men from the women. They were shouting again. People were thrown into panic. The women had been left on the train, the men and the SS had vanished. A crowd of civilians, noticing their yellow stars, stared at them angrily. Then the SS reappeared to fetch them. But it was only to change trains. The men had been required to shift the luggage.

The new train was as luxurious as the one from Theresienstadt, and had heated carriages. By nightfall they had stopped near Lake Constance; Switzerland was on the other side of the lake. 'On the morning of 7 February we had a big surprise: the SS-men told us to take off our yellow stars and they gave the women lipsticks to "beautify ourselves". They smiled ironically. I suppose they were following orders, as usual. What sense did it make anyhow? Lipstick to cover up the ravages committed on elderly, emaciated women. But what sense had any of it made? Above all, it was a relief to take off the stars. Those who have not lived through the time of the Thousand Year Reich cannot imagine what a relief it was to get rid of this degrading sign; only the day before in Augsburg we had been reviled because of it. Now, we really began to believe that we might be saved. We embraced. We wept.'

But there was a delay. All afternoon the train stood motionless on a stretch of track in the open country, but ominously near a barn. Would the SS take them into the barn and shoot them? Surely, after all this . . .

'Fortunately, our fears proved unnecessary. The following morning the train moved forward again, before coming to a halt on a branch line. We saw "our" SS-men get down and go over to meet a group of civilians standing with some others in Swiss uniforms. A few carriages were opened and the Swiss checked inside; then documents were exchanged and signed for just as if we had been some kind of merchandise. Then the SS ordered us to disembark and join another train further up the track – a Swiss train! I noticed a name on a sign-board: Kreuzlingen.

'In the new train a man in Swiss uniform awaited us. In my exaltation I embraced him, but first I took off his cap and looked hard at the Swiss emblem to make sure it was real. Then I gave him a kiss, which made him blush. The SS-men had seen us on to the train, but now they jumped down, and to our great surprise they wished us "All the best"; then they were gone. A tremendous emotion swept through all of us. The feeling of being free was indescribable, and few could hold back their tears. Only the handful of younger people were less sentimental. One girl sang, *Sag' zum Abschied leise "Servus"*, and *Wer wird denn weinen, wenn man auseinandergeht?*'[11]

For the rest of their journey, rows of people stood along the streets adjoining the tracks and on the platforms of the stations they passed through, cheering and waving and throwing chocolates, sweets and apples into the train. The warmth of this welcome already started to rekindle some kind of faith in humanity. Their final destination was St Fiden, near St Gallen, where they were welcomed by Saly Meyer, the JOINT's European bureau chief.[12] They were reorganized into smaller groups and dispersed for convalescence. Liberation was to be a mixed blessing for many who were to discover now that their loved ones were all dead. Dr Freund was sent to recuperate at a hotel at Les Avants, above Montreux. 'While travelling there we were deeply impressed by the sight of lighted windows and people sitting at dining tables behind curtains. We had not seen such peaceful scenes for a long time.'

As refugees in Switzerland, they tried to prepare themselves for resuming a normal life, and suddenly realized how difficult it would be. They had waited years for their liberation and now they saw that they would have to draw afresh from their depleted store of energy to begin a new struggle. 'This was quite unexpected for most of us, and came as a terrible shock for those who expected that from now on they would receive preferential treatment.' Many could not cope with yet another battle. Of her three room-mates at Les Avants, two committed suicide. For Dr Freund, the greatest boon she could have wished for was the address of Ninon and Hermann Hesse.

'I wrote to Ninon at once, sending Anna Krasa's love and explaining my position. I remember apologizing that I had no stamp to put on the letter. She replied immediately, very kindly, asking after Anna, because she was so worried about her fate, sending greetings from her husband, and expressing the hope that we should meet soon. She enclosed a whole sheet of postage stamps. We started a correspondence that lifted my spirits tremendously, as I had no one to turn to in Switzerland. Through Ninon I gathered new hope, and regained faith in the goodness of mankind. A few months later I was well enough to work again, and became doctor in charge of a home for refugees in Brissago. Lugano was not far away, and soon I received an invitation from the Hesses to visit them at Montagnola. I took two days off and walked on foot over the mountains, partly because I lacked money, and partly because I like hiking.

'They greeted me at the garden gate. From the beginning they were kind and warm-hearted. Hesse was dressed like a gardener, I remember, and wore a big hat that protected him from the sun. He had a cat called Schneeweisschen that never left his side. He was 68 years old then, and suffering from leukaemia. Ninon was 18 years younger than he and had beautiful, lively features. The large house with its big garden belonged to the Bodmer family and had been lent to the Hesses for life. It was cosy, and simply furnished. On the ground floor was a huge room with rows of books. Upstairs, the bedrooms, and a room to house their small art collection, and Ninon's study, full of archaeological artefacts.

'The first thing they did after they had made me welcome was to ask me about Theresienstadt, and of course they wanted to know what had happened to Anna. They encouraged me to describe every detail. Hesse stressed that what I had witnessed was extraordinary, and he insisted that I describe everything in as much detail as I could, even things that seemed unimportant. While I spoke, he listened with closed eyes, and I worried that I was tiring him, but later I gathered from his questions that he had not missed a word. He was interested in everything I did. He even produced a hiking map of the district and made me point out which way I had crossed the mountains from Brissago, a feat which he considered remarkable. They both also talked to me about my work at the refugees' home. They understood at once that I was worried about my profession. I had been out of touch with medical science for years and needed to brush up my knowledge. They advised me to work in a children's hospital as a volunteer. I followed their suggestion and found work in a paediatric unit in Zürich. The Hesses visited me frequently, helped me to find lodgings, invited me to concerts, theatre performances, and to visit friends.

'At about that time Hesse was awarded the Nobel Prize. He was not well enough to go to Stockholm, and so a celebration was arranged in Bern. He told me that a friend had marked the occasion by donating a sum of money to be used for a refugee who wanted to continue his or her studies in Switzerland, and that he had recommended me. I suspect that the anonymous donor was in fact Hesse himself, for I was never allowed to find out who it was, or even write a letter of thanks.

'A year later I was working in a hospital in Davos for orphan boys from the concentration camps who were heavily infected with TB. Most of them were completely alone in the world; through this work, at the beginning of 1948 I was asked by the *Organisation Secours Enfants* in Geneva to take charge of another group of orphan boys – children from East European Jewish families, whose parents had perished in the Holocaust – and accompany them to Australia, where new homes had been found for them. I was tempted, but first sought the advice of the Hesses, who unreservedly told me that I should go. Hesse sent me the poem he wrote called *Stufen*:[13]

> *Es muss das Herz bei jedem Lebensrufe*
> *Bereit zum Abschied sein und Neubeginne,*
>
> *Um sich in Tapferkeit und ohne Trauern*
> *In and're, neue Bindungen zu geben.*
>
> *Und jedem Anfang wohnt ein Zauber inne,*
> *Der uns beschützt und der uns hilft, zu leben,*
>
> *Wir wollen heiter Raum und Raum durchschreiten,*
> *An keinem wie an einer Heimat hängen,*
>
> *Der Weltgeist will nicht fesseln uns und engen,*
> *Er will uns Stuf' um Stufe heben, weiten . . .*

'And I went to Australia with those 18 orphan boys and, like them, I found a new home there.'

The voyage was a nightmare. It was made on a converted Egyptian cruiser, the *Al Sudan*, which set out from Marseilles – after a three-week delay due to unseaworthiness – at the end of January. The boys had to sleep on hard bunks in cabins that were not properly ventilated, along with several hundred other emigrants – mainly Jewish. They were all in the care of the ship's doctor, who was rarely visible and, when he was, never sober. The staple diet was salted fat mutton and sour bread, and there were no fruit or vegetables. Despite her offers of help, the ship's doctor refused to hand over the key of the medicine chest to Dr Freund. Many of the passengers fell ill owing to the lack of vitamins. They finally docked at Melbourne, more or less in one piece, on 29 February, and Dr Freund was able to hand over her charges to the Jewish Welfare Society.

Her job done, she could have returned to Switzerland, for she had a re-entry visa and a return ticket; however, she had already been in correspondence with Fred Kramer, a Viennese violinist a couple of years her junior whom she had met briefly before the war but who had emigrated to Australia before the Nazis came to power. He had heard through the Jewish community in Melbourne that she was alive and in Switzerland, and got in touch with her there through the Swiss community.[14] It seems likely that getting to know him influenced her decision to stay in Australia, since they were married in 1951. She loved the country too, so, the decision to stay once made, her first task was to find out how she might start working as a doctor again. Regulations for foreign doctors were stringent, as they were everywhere, and the information office at the University of Melbourne told her that she would have to re-do the whole six-year medical course to qualify. However, she found out through friends that in New South Wales the regulations were less severe, and that there she need only re-do the 'clinical' studies – a three-year course. This seemed infinitely preferable and, with the help of the Jewish Welfare Society, which also paid her fees, she enrolled at Sydney University. Apart from the difficulty of being a woman of nearly 50 among young students, which did not bother her too much, there was the problem of understanding English. Her English was not yet good, and the Australian accent made compre-hension hard. Fortunately her fellow-students lent her their lecture notes, and with their help she managed to keep her head above water. 'Of course, I made mistakes in the written papers; for example, I wrote "fleas" instead of "flies" when I was describing the carriers of poliomyelitis. The examiner – a woman – sent for me and asked what I meant. After I'd drawn a sketch of a flea, and then one of a fly, the matter was resolved. She smiled, asked me how many months I had been in the country, and awarded me a pass; but she told me that I had a long way to go with my English.'

Meanwhile the friendship with Fred blossomed and they were mar-ried on 2 January 1951, during her final year. 'Since the new academic term started that day, I was reprimanded for my absence, but the reprimand passed me by!' Fred was still living in Melbourne, pending his acceptance as a violinist by the Sydney Symphony Orchestra, but within a relatively short time his appointment was confirmed and they could be together. After Dr Freund had requalified, they found a ramshackle cottage in Lane Cove, which was nevertheless charming, which they could afford, and which was repairable. As she had no money to buy a practice from a retiring doctor, she asked a local chemist for advice about the prospects of setting up a practice there, and received a positive answer. They bought the cottage and some second-hand furniture, 'and then I had to "squat" and wait for patients. It took a long time, six months or more, and I began to think that I had made a mistake; my colleagues who had stayed in the fashionable eastern suburbs already had flourishing practices and fellow-migrants as patients ... But one day, when I really had given up hope, I had an urgent call from a very sick man, a grocer, who lived not far from my surgery; it was a long weekend and his own doctor was away. I was able to cure him quite quickly, and he was so grateful that he recommended me to all his customers. From then on, I was kept busy, and my waiting-room was always full.'

And so the years passed. In the mid-Sixties they retired to a cottage they had built for themselves in Terrigal, bought a Dormobile and toured Australia and New Zealand; but after only three or four years of this they decided to return to Europe. They moved back to Fred's home town, Vienna.

'For one thing, we had friends and relatives here; we had no family in Australia. And we are interested in European culture. When we first came back we had a car, and we spent years touring Europe and enjoying its galleries, and going to concerts, plays and operas. I had never been to Vienna before in my life. We considered London, or Berlin, or somewhere in Switzerland. Berlin was out because it is so sad now; and London was a bit too large for us; but Vienna was just right, central for touring Europe, and it is such a musical town. But we have many friends who fell out with us because we came to Austria, and in Vienna I think there is more anti-Semitism than anywhere else in Europe, even today. The Jewish community is very small here now. It did bother us, but one has to live somewhere. We knew a professor of law at the university here, Professor Merckel; he'd been in trouble with the Gestapo during the war but survived; and he and other friends said that Vienna would be quite safe to come back to. Even so, I was a little uncomfortable at first, coming here; even today, I won't say that I feel at home – that would be an exaggeration; but it's not unpleasant. I think the worst thing for me was that there were a number of Austrian guards at Theresienstadt – the worst kind of Austrians – and I couldn't stand the way they spoke German. The accent here reminded me of them. Going as far away as Australia was a great help in the rehabilitation process, because it meant a completely new start in a country that was far from the centre of events. Even so, for 20 years I cried in my sleep. Though that has happened less and less often since then, still I am not free of it, and every few weeks I dream. The dreams centre on persecution, on the feeling that I am being chased, that someone wants to arrest me, take my liberty away. The "stories" of the dreams aren't precise; but the feelings they engender are. I am, however, fortunate in having a husband who is very patient, with whom I can talk about it. He knows the why and how of my being upset.[15] And although from time to time, if I started to talk about the KZ, afterwards people might advise me to forget all about it, I never found people unwilling to listen, as it were for their own sakes. I remember how I felt when I was liberated – it was like a dream, and it took months to accept that it was true; but as soon as I started to work again I forgot about it, and concentrated on the challenge of becoming a doctor again. I think it's important to live in the present and for the future. However, in 1957 I visited my brother in South Africa, who'd been living there for years, and when I saw park benches with "Whites Only" written on them, that brought back a flood of memories of what had been forbidden to the Jews before the war, and I started to cry. If I hadn't been staying with my brother, I would have left the same day. He was used to it, of course, but he'd been there for years and had never had a scent of what it was like in Europe under Hitler, let alone of a KZ. He told me things weren't as bad as all that in South Africa. He wouldn't listen to my wartime experiences either – he just wasn't interested. Have you found that with other survivors and their relatives?

'I was most fortunate in meeting Hermann Hesse; he not only listened and questioned sympathetically, but encouraged me to write my experiences down. He was a very kind man. Ninon was Jewish, and we discussed Judaism, and even whether I should get baptized as a safeguard; but Hesse thought it would be a bad idea; Judaism was a good religion, and there was no need to change one's faith. Many people converted; their argument was, why should we suffer all the time as Jews? We want to be like other people. I am a Jewess, though I am not especially observant; and the KZ didn't change that either way: what it did do was confirm my pride in being Jewish. I don't think I would have collapsed even if I hadn't had the Hesses' help; suicide is not in my nature, and I had no dependants. Of course the Hesses were very well known, and through them I had an entrée into Swiss society, which was very good, very interesting; but above all when you have to work hard you cannot think about the past too much, and I had to work hard, and I had a future. That is a very important element in recovery. The other thing to take into consideration was that I was basically a healthy person. It took me a full year to get back into shape, but I was able to ski again, modestly, maybe eight weeks after liberation. But I was extremely lucky; I was the only one of the group I was liberated with who could do that.

'As for *deciding* to survive, that is a difficult question to answer. I had my cyanide capsule, but I always seemed to think, no, this isn't the moment; things are not yet desperate enough for me to kill myself. I can wait a little bit. In an odd kind of way, having that sure means of escape encouraged me to go on living: the capsule gave me a kind of power – at least over one decision. However, it was also important that

I was working as a doctor; it's a useful profession, because you can do it anywhere, and helping people helps you, especially in adverse circumstances. But quite a few people before the deportations kept their spirits up somehow until the last moment, and then killed themselves on the eve of the transports. Many others killed themselves after the war. I mentioned my room-mates at Les Avants. Both were women in their mid-forties, the same age as I was. One of them had a son whom she'd got out to Sweden before the war when he was six. When she went there after the war to see him he was adolescent. He had forgotten how to speak German, and could only speak Swedish, so they couldn't talk to each other. Then her nursing qualifications weren't good enough for Sweden, so she had to find work as a charwoman. She couldn't take it and came back to Switzerland, but the separation from her son was too much for her and she killed herself. In general, though, we were emotionally exhausted when we got out, and I think we expected to be treated like martyrs, or heroes, or whatever; but of course people had their own lives to get on with and they expected us to look after ourselves. It was easier for me because I could earn my living as a doctor up to a point. The other woman who committed suicide was also a nurse, and she had an affidavit to go to the States, but her relatives there advised her to try to qualify for work in pathology, as there were no jobs for non-specialist nurses. She trained, and took the exam; but she failed it and in her depression she killed herself.'

They are both aware of a sense of guilt at having survived, Fred because he was able to avoid the suffering in Europe altogether, even though he left before Hitler became Chancellor. His wife questions her right to be alive when people like Anna Krasa and Nelly Stern are not. But she adds that she has less and less sense of it with the passing of time – there is only a great sadness at the thought of those who did not make it. It all seemed such a hopeless, meaningless mess. 'I mentioned that the SS wished us "All the best" as they left the train at the Swiss frontier. I think they did that because they were off-duty. There was no personal animosity for us: killing us was just a relatively unpleasant job for them. But there was method in their madness too, like giving us so much food for the journey. They knew that the end was coming and they wanted to make a good impression on the Swiss, and leave us with a good impression of them, to mitigate any eventual punishment. I think that some of those SS would have loved to stay in Switzerland with us; but they had to go home.

'I remember I had several letters immediately after the war from former SS – we called them "Persil" letters, after the soap powder, because they contained requests for statements from me saying that they had always been friendly and humane towards the Jews. These letters even came from SS I hadn't known, or had only been briefly acquainted with. Sometimes I complied, and sometimes I refused. When I complied, it was in cases where I knew that those people had been pressed into KZ duties, or were among the very few who, realizing what was happening too late to do anything more about it, genuinely tried to alleviate our situation, as far as they could.

'I think it could certainly happen again, anywhere, and what I really cannot understand is why people never learn from the past. I can understand why people conformed at the time, not why people don't learn now. At least in Germany now no attempt is made to sweep the Third Reich under the carpet, or apologize for it; whereas here in Austria . . . Well, I don't have a high opinion of humanity, to tell you the truth; I have too often seen it at its worst – in Jews and Gentiles. We are all very weak people, me included. You don't have to be in a KZ to lose faith in humanity.'

IV

The circumstances of Simon Wiesenthal's life and work are well known, from his own books and from the many articles written about him.[16] He was born on 31 December 1908 in the predominantly Jewish town of Buczacz, Galicia, then in the Austro-Hungarian Empire, and now part of Poland, where his father was a commodity dealer. His father was killed in action in 1915. As a boy, Wiesenthal experienced persecution by precursors of the Nazis in the shape of Bolshevik and Ukrainian cavalry raids on his town. Later, he spent four years studying at the Technical University in Prague, since it was impossible for him to get into the university at Lemberg (Lvov) because of the *numerus clausus*. In 1936 he married Cyla Muller, and opened his own architectural office in Lemberg, specializing in private houses. For a short time things went well; but when Lemberg was annexed by the USSR, Jews became second-class citizens, and he had to take a job as a mechanic in a bedspring manufacturing plant. On 30 June 1941 the Russians withdrew from Lemberg in the face of the German advance. When they arrived, the predominantly Ukrainian units slaughtered 6,000 of the town's Jews.

Wiesenthal himself was arrested on 6 July, and narrowly escaped summary execution by the Ukrainians in the Brigidki prison. An auxiliary policeman who knew him helped get him out of the prison and he was able to join his wife in the ghetto; but only for a few months. Then he and his wife were rounded up for forced labour on the railways, and sent to the camp at Janowska. At that time the *Ostbahn* works were run 'correctly' by German civilian officials. As security was not tight, Wiesenthal managed to ensure his wife's escape from the camp with the help of the local Polish resistance. He spent the winter of 1942–3 alone, not knowing whether or not Cyla had managed to get to safety (in fact she reached Warsaw, where she lived as a Gentile and survived the war). Once again he narrowly escaped death when there was a summary execution of intellectuals at Janowska to 'celebrate' Hitler's 54th birthday on 20 April 1943. He was saved by a civilian *Ostbahn* official literally at the last minute, when he had already been stripped naked and was standing in the sandpit with the other victims – the SS had already started shooting. The official, Adolf Kohlrantz, was one of two honourable Germans who ran the repair works. He died shortly after the war; but Wiesenthal invited the other, Heinrich Günthert, to his daughter's wedding in 1965.

In late September 1943, he was helped to escape from Janowska by friendly Poles; but after nearly a year of hiding he was rearrested in June 1944. Faced with interrogation and torture, he cut his wrists in prison, but was discovered in time for them to save him – they told him that he would die when they decided that the time was right. He made a second suicide attempt, which was thwarted, but when he was healed he was again sentenced to death. For a third time he avoided execution, this time because an air-raid provided the distraction which enabled him to switch from a group of condemned prisoners to another group destined for return to Janowska. There, the commandant, who recognized him, spared him on a whim, though the rest of the group were summarily shot. From Janowska he was transported to Przemysl to work for the *Organisation Todt*,[17] but almost immediately the retreat westwards began, first to Plaszow, then Gross-Rosen; then briefly to Buchenwald, and finally to Mauthausen, where he arrived on 7 February 1945. By that time both he and his wife had received news that the other was dead.

After the war, they found each other again only by the merest chance: 'I discovered that my mother, whom I had had to leave behind in the Lemberg ghetto, had been taken to Belzec. There was no word of my wife, and I was later to find out that she had been liberated by the British at Gelsenkirchen, where she'd been working with Polish forced labour at a machine-gun factory after she had escaped the destruction of Warsaw. After the liberation she decided to try to get back to Lemberg but on the way she got in touch with an old friend from Buczacz who was now living in Cracow. Fortunately he had already heard from me – I was in Linz by that time – and he was able to bring us together. But the fact that she met my friend at all was the result of a decision made on impulse. Changing trains at Cracow, her suitcase was stolen, and so her journey was delayed. She met another acquaintance from Lemberg in the town, and he suggested she look up my friend Biener – she had no idea he was even in Cracow. If her suitcase hadn't been stolen, if she hadn't met Biener, she would have gone on to Lemberg, which of course by then was in the USSR, and we might never have been reunited. I was sure she was dead: in fact, I was trying to trace her grave when I first contacted Biener.'

Immediately upon liberation, he had contacted the American authorities with a view to seeking out SS war criminals, and had been assigned to a former Russian aristocrat who had emigrated to the USA in 1918 and was now Captain Tarracusio. They moved to Linz when Mauthausen fell into the Russian zone of occupation, and Wiesenthal was employed by the US Office of Strategic Services and the Counter-Intelligence Corps. Subsequently, in 1947, with meagre help, he set up the first Documentation Centre in Linz, to help trace missing relatives of fellow Jews and to seek out former Nazis. In 1954 that Centre closed down, and Wiesenthal moved to refugee work; but with the capture of Eichmann, the Documentation Centre reopened in Vienna. It was financed initially by the Board of Jewish Communities in Austria, and later from private contributions. Its offices are still in central Vienna, in an anonymous modern grey building not far from the Danube Canal. The office is large and light, and astonishingly cluttered. The door wall is solid with books on the Second World War and the Holocaust. The wall adjacent to it, opposite the large desk at the other end of the room, is covered by a vast map of Second World War Europe, which shows the locations of all the concentration camps and marks the number of people who died in each one. Behind the desk on the wall hang a number of pictures and one or two diplomas. Not all the pictures have to do with the KZ. Two old red armchairs stand near the window wall, and between them is a small table covered with periodicals and letters.

'Many people just wanted to survive; all their energy went into achieving that and, having done so, they became apathetic; they couldn't build up a new life. In many others I've observed a pressure to catch up with, or make up for, the lost time somehow. That operated on the sexual level too – I've known people after liberation taking three or four women a day, whenever it was possible; but they were chasing a will-o'-the-wisp, because it is impossible to pick up the threads of your life after such an interruption, as if nothing had happened. They tried, though; many suppressed the memories, and I'm talking about survivors as well as Nazis. The problems arise later: they start with nothing after the war, they work hard and win for themselves a position in the business community; but then at the end, when they retire, they have nothing but an empty life to look back on. There is another element. One thing that I believe all survivors have, and I certainly have it, is a feeling of guilt at having survived at all. That feeling cannot be suppressed, no matter how hard you try, no matter how deeply you bury the KZ experience under a materially successful subsequent life;

and it is a feeling that persists even though one knows one has not survived at anyone else's cost. Survival in my case, and that of many whom I know, was a matter of pure chance – a religious person might describe it as the will of God. But the fact remains that in the competition between life and death in the camps the balance was heavily weighted in favour of death. There was a saying, "Freedom is half an hour away; but death is fifteen minutes away." Against that, and I speak only from my own experience, especially in the last months, it became marginally easier to cheat death, and by taking advantage of that some survived who might otherwise not have done. But all the time you had only two possibilities: to survive or to die. And the anxiety you were under was a relative thing. People who survived by living free but with false papers could suffer as great or worse anxiety as those in the camp. In the camp you were not alone. You knew it was a question of time: whether in 15 days or two months, sooner or later you would die; we had all been sentenced to death; only outside intervention would save us. But we were free of the terrible fear of being discovered or denounced. My wife was in Warsaw. She didn't look remotely Jewish, but there was always the chance of being denounced, and although she lived in apparent security and apparent freedom, the emotional stress was enormous and unremitting.

'There were so many battles to be fought after liberation as well, and I was among the perhaps one per cent of very lucky ones because I was reunited with my wife. Even so, it took us a long time to be comfortable together again because we had to approach each other across the differences between our experiences. Nevertheless, the KZ was clearly not a taboo subject in our household. I have noticed that the children of survivors – I've noticed this particularly when lecturing for example to Yiddish communities in America – know far less about what went on in the Second World War than the children of people who were not involved in the KZ. I think this can be related to the difficulties my wife and I had, even though we had both survived the same general fate: there is a communication gulf between the survivor and those who were not involved. My feeling is that that gulf can be especially wide when the survivor is a parent and the other his child. However, there are many reasons why the children of survivors do not know much about what happened. There is the typical survivor response: "I have suffered enough and now I just want to draw a veil over the whole thing." Others say that the past is the past and has nothing to do with the life they're leading now; but I have noticed that many of these people are actually scared of the questions their children might ask. A friend of mine was like this. He had a very bright young son, but the boy didn't know a thing about the camps. When I asked my friend why this was so, he replied: "The boy asks questions, but what can I say, what's the point of going over all that?'' And I said, well, he's going to ask you what happened to the rest of the family sooner or later, and you'll have to tell him that they were killed by the SS; and then he's going to ask you what you did about it after the war; did you do anything to try to track down the murderers of your family? And you will be naked in front of him, because the answer to the question: "What did you do?" is: I made money. This friend was not the only person I've talked to like that, and their reaction is always the same: they begin to cry. For me that is clear proof that guilt feelings are less to do with having survived than with having done nothing at all with that survival to right the wrong that was done to us all. I know that through my work I am not only a "bad conscience" for the Nazis; I am also a "bad conscience" for the Jews – because what I do could have been done by 10,000 others as well. But as well as being a "bad conscience", I am probably also its cure – because people say to themselves, "OK, I'll send Wiesenthal ten dollars and *he'll* do something . . .!"

'There are the ones who saw security in money, curiously enough, after liberation, and felt pressured to make more and more of it to increase their sense of security. Or those who wanted to get away from Europe, because they felt that no good could ever come to them here again. But of course the USA and Australia simply aren't far enough away to escape from what you carry with you.

'Then there are the ones who believe in a life after death, and they worry about what they'll say to the dead when they meet them again and have to face the question: "What did you do to find justice for us?" The blow comes for survivors when they retire, when they have time to think, to reflect, and when they want to come to terms with themselves. It is very hard, being a survivor of the KZ.

'I was an architect in Lemberg, and when I was in practice there there were 149,000 Jews in the town. When I prepared the Lemberg Trials after the war, I wanted witnesses to testify against the accused, more than half of whom I'd had arrested myself. Do you know, we couldn't find 500 Lemberg Jews who'd survived? And I thought of all those who had died – of all the talented people, the doctors and the artists, the humane people, the philanthropists – and the engineers – everyone. It is a burden to know that they died and you survived. Why you? When there were so many who would have been so much more useful to society? In me that thought developed into what I'd called a Representative Complex. I would have to represent those people somehow: to do the job that better people than I would have done, had they lived. I know that I am an exception, but my work has not liberated me from the fact that I am a survivor. No one I know who has been through the camps, and this struck me watching the people at a Lemberg

Remembrance Day in Israel, can feel pure joy in the way that someone who has not had the experience of the concentration camps can. The reason for this is that we observe life as if it were a film – or, better, as if there were a silk screen between us and life – something holds us back, something that casts a shadow on the sun. For our souls are so deeply wounded that they will never heal. That is how I see the situation, and although it may depress me terribly that I have not been able to go back to my profession, which I enjoyed, I know that the war will not end for me until every last one of the criminals who brought us to this pass has been punished, or I am dead. That is how I have been deformed, if you will, by the KZ.'

He shows me a copy of a long letter with a list of names, neatly laid out and in precise, architect's sloping handwriting.

'Let me tell you a story about this. I'd forgotten all about it, but the Americans wanted to make a TV film about my life story and they were looking for material. In the National Archives in Washington under the Twelfth Army Group they found a letter that I wrote while I was still in camp, in May 1945, to the commander of the US forces. I'd heard that they were rounding up war criminals. This letter contains a list of 91 of the Nazi criminals, their crimes, their ranks, where they worked, and even where they came from – all that I did from memory: people and actions memorized during my years in captivity. I was still lying in hospital at the time. One of my friends was working as a doctor there; in fact we met again recently in America after 40 years, and he told me that he knew what I'd do with my life, even then. When I was liberated I weighed 44 kilogrammes. I lay in bed and wondered what to do now. Go back to being an architect? I need a house, other people will need houses . . . No! First some kind of justice must be established. And as I'd learnt that there was a war crimes unit with the division that had freed us, I decided to write them this letter. Is it in German or Polish? Apparently it is unique, in that it was the only one to be written immediately, while the writer was still in camp. I did have an advantage: my memory. It is one of my great strengths.'

I ask why he has chosen to stay in Vienna. 'I am Austrian by birth. My father fell as an Austrian soldier. I was liberated in Austria. But there is another reason: although Austria represented only 8.5 per cent of the Third Reich, she provided 50 per cent of the SS criminals. 80 per cent of Eichmann's staff were Austrian, as he was, effectively, and as were 75 per cent of the staff of the extermination camps. But also, 75 per cent of all the Austrians in the SS had Slavic names – their Germanic roots were not deep: certainly their grandparents wouldn't have been German-speaking. Vienna is at the centre of my sphere of operation.

'There are thousands of SS criminals still at liberty. We lost eleven million witnesses – the six million Jews and at least five million others.

My view is that no punishment can fit the crime, but to bring them to justice is symbolically necessary. My motto is, whoever was involved in operating the Holocaust has no right to die in peace. That is the part of the punishment that means something, and my job is to issue a warning to the murderers of today and of tomorrow – they must know that they will never be allowed to live in peace if they commit crimes on the scale of the Nazis. Late in November 1985 we arrested a man in Buenos Aires, 44 years after his crime, and 10,000 miles away from where it happened; and he was just a 74-year-old company director who had a quiet life and wanted nothing more than to coast home quietly and die in peace. But he had no right to a quiet death. We had been working on his dossier since 1975, and we are relentless; but this has less to do with revenge than with a lesson for the future. If would-be Nazis of the future saw that the Nazis of today were not allowed to die in peace, even if it took 50 years to hunt them down, they might think twice about becoming Nazis; and perhaps by example when the need arises for someone like me again in the future, there won't be just one of me, but several – maybe 20, maybe 50, maybe just five – but at any rate people who won't accept that you can put a time limit on justice. And I go on despite the fact that some of the sentences handed down are a slap in the face to me; we've just dealt with the case of a man who we could prove to be an accessory to murder in 900 cases – and today we've heard that he's been given a two-year sentence; but we have judgments on record that work out at about two minutes' jail per murder. Our laws are inadequate to deal with the crimes; the laws are a century old, and in those days there was no concept of a bureaucracy of murder. Hitherto, mass-murderers had been mentally ill; but these killers were politically convinced: doing it as a job, without any special hatred, but certain of their rectitude. They gassed us with as little feeling as a New York exterminator gets rid of cockroaches.

'The difficulty of bringing them to justice is that so many of them have no documentation. A survivor might remember a name, a rank – but the name might be written down phonetically, and a lot of mistakes can be made that way, especially with Polish or Slav names; or the name might have been a first name. But the main problem is that there aren't enough Wiesenthals. Why not? Because people forget too quickly, they go to sleep. In 1969 the mother of Raoul Wallenberg wrote to me in despair that the Wallenberg Committee was folding up. I revived interest in the case, in finding out what had happened to him, and I stirred up journalists, who'd never even heard of him before, and now thank God there are maybe 50 Wallenberg committees worldwide.

'There was a time, too, when I could have done far more than I was actually able to do, but I lacked funds. I started up for the first three years with fellow-survivors; in fact the first year was spent in close cooperation with the Americans. Since then we have carried on, but money has been a problem frequently. The first time I went to America I had no money. We used our last resources to nail Stangl.[18] Today, of course, I can get as much money as I want, but I've lost a lot of time, and a lot of people have slipped through my fingers who wouldn't have done if I'd had the money earlier. For example, in 1977 I received information that Mengele's son was flying to South America; and I knew where and when, and what flight he was going on, and I had a pretty shrewd idea why. I had two people to send on the same flight. But I had no money to finance the operation. I needed $8,000. I went to a big Dutch newspaper offering them exclusive rights on the story in return for the money if we got Mengele; but naturally there was no guarantee, and they turned me down, and I was helpless. Now of course the story of Mengele's death has broken, and his son says that he did go and see him in 1977 . . .

'I am bad with money, to be honest – I have to spend it, but I'm bad at collecting it. Still, now that there's a renewed interest in the Holocaust, we have an office in America, and I can ask for money any time I want it. Even so, it's rather like getting your Christmas tree on 27 December.'

V

A close contemporary of Simon Wiesenthal is Ivan Hacker, President of the Jewish Community of Vienna.[19] He was also born in the Austro-Hungarian Empire, on 4 May 1908 in Steinamanger in the Burgenland (now Szombathely, Hungary). From the ghetto there he was taken to Auschwitz on 4 July 1944, but was selected for work, given the number 78557 and transported to Kaufering III, a sub-camp of Dachau. He was liberated at Allach on 30 April 1945.

'I was detailed to that transport to Kaufering just to make up numbers, so that in a sense I was just in the right place at the right time, or I would have been swept away in the great slaughter of Hungarian Jews. So much depended upon luck – there wasn't much you could do to determine the course of your fate in the KZ. But I certainly determined to survive if I could from the moment I was deported to Auschwitz. I'm not a particularly religious man, but I do have belief, and there's a difference: you can have one without the other. And – I get this from my father – I have always had a very positive outlook. I said to myself, somehow I'll pull through. In the paper tents we had to live in, at least 15 died every night, of cold or exhaustion, but I never thought for a moment that I'd be one of them.'

The camp Kaufering III was non-existent when they arrived, just a site with a couple of *Blocks* enclosed by barbed wire a few hundred metres from Kaufering railway station. The new arrivals, who had endured the usual cattle-waggon transports employed by the SS for deploying KZ prisoners and slave labour, were lodged in 60 or 70 round tents, made of a papery material, sleeping in trenches which they dug themselves, which were covered with corrugated cardboard for protection against the elements. The kapos had a wooden *Block*, and there was a kitchen of sorts and a medical facility which provided a white powder, based on coal, against diarrhoea (the most common ailment), and iodine as a panacea. However, as in most camps, very few people who dared to complain of illness were given any treatment other than blows over the head. Prisoners were called at 4am and lined up in the usual fives[20] for roll-call. Meals were if anything worse than in the main camps as, apart from the usual thin ersatz coffee and soup, their daily bread ration was only 100 grammes per man per day. Work varied from light (clearing out goods waggons) to heavy (quarrying, and pushing and emptying railway trucks full of hard-core). Underground factories for aircraft production were being excavated here, too; but the aim, along with getting the work done, was clearly to work the prisoners to death. The well-known expression in the mouths of the SS, 'If you don't put your back into it, you filth, we'll send you up the chimney', was new to Hacker, coming from the ghetto to the camps late, and having spent only a short time in Auschwitz; but its sense became clear as, with time, fresh transports came from Auschwitz with new labour, and took back with them those too sick to work, to be gassed. Meanwhile the treatment of the labourers by the kapos and *Organisation Todt* officials was so brutal that Hacker actually remembers occasions when the SS stepped in to put a stop to it – not out of concern for the victim, of course, but so that the work should not be too much delayed. 'I remember, too, that my colleague, the lawyer Dr Schleiffer, one day was unable to carry a double-thickness railway sleeper up a slight incline alone. He was beaten up for this so violently with a shovel, that by the time we were allowed to carry him back to camp he had lost a lot of blood from his head-wounds. They took him to the "hospital" *Block*, and a few days later he was taken back to Auschwitz and "turned into smoke".'

To maintain any kind of hope or self-esteem was inestimably difficult: the more so since these were two special targets for SS attack. In Kaufering III, as in other camps, there was a special *Scheisskommando* (latrine-detail). 'This was exclusively made up of intellectual and cultured prisoners: university professors, doctors, rabbis, priests – the last because in my experience the SS was almost as violently anti-Christian as they were anti-Jewish. Lawyers formed part of this *Kommando*, too, and I was privileged to be a member. We had to empty the latrine ditches into a soil-waggon, but they didn't give us buckets to do the job, just flat wooden spades. Of course that was on purpose, so that the mess would spill on to us and on to our clothes as we worked, and we smelt of excreta day and night. The *Kommando* worked from dawn until dusk. We had to do something to keep sane, so we invented diversions: the members of the team would take turns in whistling melodies, and the others would then guess where they were from – what opera, or what symphony. Or we would recite poetry to each other – Goethe, Schiller, Heine, Lessing – or quiz each other about Greek mythology. I remember very well someone reciting from the *Iliad* to us, and we did all this, played these games, just to keep our minds on an even keel. And certainly culture proved stronger than guns, bravado and barbed wire. They could make our bodies shovel shit, but they couldn't make our minds do it.

'One last thing about Kaufering. I was there again late in October 1957. I went to the town hall and talked to one or two of the officials there and, do you know, not one of them seemed to know anything about a camp that had been there. It was hard for me not to lose control of myself. After all, it was a bare 12 years since I'd left the place. I told them that I could show them exactly where it had been, where the kitchen *Block* stood, where the kapos' *Block* was. Old and young looked at me askance. No, they said; there had never been a camp at Kaufering. I asked after the chimney-sweep, the plumber, locals who had helped us in the camp – they offered a number of names I didn't know. They were blocking me, and I knew it. They were purposely burying that piece of the town's history, lying to me, to the people and to themselves, for they looked at me as if they genuinely believed that I was mad, or a liar. I encountered precisely the same reaction in Landsberg.'

He lives in a spacious old flat, typically Viennese, with high double doors in dark wood, walnut furniture and Turkish rugs, in an early-nineteenth-century apartment building by the side of the Danube Canal. There is a policeman at the street door, who escorts me to the first floor when I tell him whom I wish to visit – Hacker's name is not against any bell. Hacker greets me warmly and explains the policeman: 'one of the courtesies extended to me by the city'. He was made a Privy Councillor by the Austrian President in 1983. 'We decided as soon as we were free never to consider revenge, but equally never to forget. I come from one of the oldest families in Austria – we lived in the Burgenland for 300 years, and had landed property there; and on my mother's side the family has lived near Vienna since 1500. My father became director of the Hungarian Bank in Steinamanger, and I attended the Catholic *Gy.nnasium* there. In that school, which was attended by Catholics and the children of the Hungarian aristocracy, we Jews were on completely equal terms, and those times were among the happiest of my life. The monks were excellent teachers, and I made many good friends. In my opinion, the people who behaved best towards the Jews when the trouble began were the workers and peasants, and the aristocracy – the top 10,000. It was the middle classes who let us down and who, deliberately or not, sided with the Germans.'

His wife Liesl also comes from Steinamanger, and they were together in the ghetto there, before they were taken to Auschwitz. She was sent to work in the cement factories in Bremen, where the prisoners were relatively decently treated, and subsequently deported to Bergen-Belsen. In the course of the war her entire family was killed, either in the camps or in actions against the Jews. She will not talk of those times at all.

'I think it was very bad that after the war the Austrian schools didn't strictly teach the truth about what happened between '38 and '45 – "Austria was an occupied country that had no choice in what happened, so let's forget about it as quickly as possible" was the quasi-official line; but the youth of the country wanted to get at the truth, and thus it was that it came out. Every house has a family album, and the son leafs through it and sees a picture of his father in SS uniform – they can't bear to throw such things away – and he says to his father, "You were in the SS." And what can the father answer? He could say, "Yes I was, and I regret it," but on the whole the answer was: "Yes I was, but it wasn't that serious. Auschwitz was just a labour camp and the gas chambers didn't exist." They wanted to suppress the truth about those days. They couldn't say to their sons: "Yes, I was a murderer too."'

The sad fact is that very few of the young of Austria and Germany will have met a Jew, so small are the communities. There were more than 200,000 in Austria before the war. Registered with the community now are about 6,500, to which can be added another 2,000 predominantly Russian Jews who entered the country immediately after the war when the frontiers were open. Of the old Viennese community, very few remain.

Immediately after the war he returned to his home town in what was now Hungary, but although both he and his wife spoke fluent Hungarian as well as German, he didn't want to live under Communist rule, and none of the family or the family property was left. It was worse for Liesl who discovered only then that she had lost everyone, and consequently did not want to remain in a place that held so many memories. It was not easy to leave, nor could it be achieved immediately. 'Things got very difficult for us there, and so when the frontiers were open for a very short time after the revolution in 1956 I came across into Austria. There were no difficulties in terms of nationality-change. I'd been born in the Austro-Hungarian Empire; my parents had been born in the Austrian Empire. We became Hungarians only later, when Hungary became a separate state. You could say that we were chased away from home twice – first by the Nazis, then by the Communists. I couldn't get out earlier than '56 because I'd been lamed in the camps and wasn't up to skipping across the border illegally; we just had to seize the opportunity when it came. It was very difficult to work in Hungary. We'd had some help from the JOINT, and it might have been possible to get help through a political party if I had belonged to one. It was certainly possible that we might have been given extra help if I had declared myself for the Communist Party in Hungary; but we were in an unfortunate position *vis-à-vis* the Hungarian authorities. We were Jews; I was a lawyer, the son of a bank director, and my wife was the daughter of landowners. They didn't look on us very favourably. Luckily I did have a couple of friends who helped me, but there were times when we didn't know what we were going to do for clothes, even. On the other hand they did allow me to practise law, and with time I built up a clientele; and I still had some contacts in the profession and in the Lawyers' Society. Of course later, in Vienna, I had to start more or less from scratch, but I was able to join a colleague and work myself in quite happily. However, I had to sit legal exams and qualify under Austrian law, which was no picnic as I was 50 by then – because hitherto I had only been qualified under Hungarian law.'[21]

He has never felt bitter about the time he lost or the frustrations that fate placed in his way. 'Although I'm nearly 78 now[22] I feel as if there is still a lot to do. My attitude has always been optimistic and positive towards life: that is my nature. One occupies oneself with the present and the future, and one doesn't waste time crying over spilt milk – there's nothing to be gained by that, and a lot to be lost. Whether I've been happy in life, I don't know; but I've certainly been contented.'

Austrian and German
'Red Triangles'

The political situation in Austria in the years leading up to the *Anschluss* is relatively complex, and a very short summary may be helpful. At the beginning of the Thirties, Austria's economy was in a state of collapse and confusion. Two forces predominated: the *Heimwehr*, which amounted to a private army under Prinz von Starhemberg, and the less powerful and ideologically opposed *Schutzbund* of the Social Democrats. The youth wings of the *Schutzbund* were the *Rote Falken* (Red Falcons) for 12–18-year-olds (a kind of boy scout organization with similar uniforms) and the older *Wehrsport*, which was a quasi-military reserve for the *Schutzbund*. Each political party had its own military organization, each of which bore arms.

A third force was the Austrian Nazi Party, initially small in numbers but made powerful by its close links with the German NSDAP.[1] The Austrian Nazis made dramatic gains in municipal elections in 1932, and it looked as if the country might disintegrate into anarchy – something which presumably would not have displeased Hitler. Over all this chaos the conservative Engelbert Dollfuss, aged 40, formed a ministry, backed by the *Heimwehr* and by a new political group based on it called the 'Fatherland Front'. Dollfuss, a would-be dictator like Hitler and Mussolini – though not as successful as either of them – enjoyed financial backing from Italy and was opposed to the German *Führer*. His aim was to set up a one-party conservative state in Austria. To this end, he banned the Socialist, Social Democrat, and even the Nazi parties, finally abolishing parliament altogether by the constitution of 1 May 1934. (The last general election, held in 1930, resulted in 72 Social Democrat MPs being returned, 66 Christian Democrats, only eight *Heimat Bloc (Heimwehr)*, and no Nazis, though they had polled 112,000 votes.) This 1934 constitution had been preceded by mass arrests of political opponents of all colours, who made strange bedfellows in prison (which common experience led to curiously understanding relationships in the KZ between Nazi guards and left-wing

Austrian political inmates); and by a workers' uprising on behalf of democracy in the week of 12–18 February, which was put down with extreme violence by the *Heimwehr*: on the night of 12–13 February, 1,000 workers were killed. The uprising occurred throughout the workers' districts of Favoriten, Floridsdorf and Ottakring: 'in . . . the Karl-Marx Hof, the *Arbeiterheim*, in Ottakring, the beautiful sun-bathed workers' garden-city block of Sandleiten . . .'[2] Meanwhile, the ultra-right Austrian Legion, financed by Germany, began a terror campaign in Austria from its German bases.

Dollfuss clung on somehow in this near-hysterical atmosphere, but finally Hitler ran out of what little patience he had. In fact he moved too soon. Members of *SS-Standarte 89*, dressed in Austrian army uniforms, made their way to Vienna, and in a staged putsch assassinated Dollfuss (who was left to bleed to death) on 25 July 1934. But the attempted coup was too hastily planned, and mistimed. There was time for the Austrian civil and military authorities to regroup and reunite under Dollfuss' colleague, Kurt von Schuschnigg, who became Chancellor. To make sure that there would be no more trouble-making from Germany, Mussolini mobilized four divisions on the Brenner Pass. Hitler was not yet in a secure enough position to respond to this, and so dropped his plans for an immediate annexation of Austria.

I

Kurt Schmidt is an active member of the League of Socialist Freedom Fighters and Victims of Fascism, one of the three party-affiliated political survivor organizations.[3] It represents the Social Democrats.

Schmidt has been a convinced Socialist from an early age, influenced first by his father, and then by his schoolfriends. In 1927 at the age of 14 he joined the Socialist Workers' Youth League, and went on to join the League of Socialist Students. He studied to be an actor and went to the Max Reinhardt School, and as a student took part in the fighting in the Karl Marx Hof in his native Vienna in February 1934 – the so-called Bloody February days. After Dollfuss had declared all political opposition illegal, Schmidt was a member of the underground Revolutionary Socialists, until 1938. He has been a convinced atheist since the age of 16, and formally withdrew from the Church at 18. Nothing in his experience has made him doubt the validity of that conviction since.

He is a small man, with a cadaverous face, but a hunched, barrel-chested torso. He smokes heavily. His face is full of suffering, but full of strength too. Again there is a sense of burning vitality.

'In December 1938 I learnt from an old schoolfriend that I was on the SD's investigations list, and I decided to get out of Austria. I was able to slip across the border without too much difficulty and made my way to Belgium. I found a place to stay in Antwerp and remained there until Belgium fell to the Germans. By then I'd already been arrested by the Belgians as a potential fifth-columnist, as were all the Germans and Austrians in Belgium, and now I was handed over to the French authorities. I was interned in two camps – first St-Cyprien, and, later, Gurs; but in 1942 the Vichy French handed me over to the Germans, and inevitably the Gestapo dug up my file, and I and some others in the same boat were taken first to Drancy, and from there to Sosnowice, and thence to Birkenau. I was in Auschwitz from 1942 until January 1945.

'They asked us our professions when we arrived at Birkenau and I told them I was an actor. Three months later I was transferred to the sub-camp of Fürstengrube where there was a proper theatre building. There was a theatre company, too, and our job was to put on three shows a week for the SS and the civilian engineers who worked at the Farben Industries works at Buna-Monowice. There was nothing to do in that neck of the woods, miles from anywhere, and they were all bored stiff when they weren't drunk. The other four nights a week we were permitted to perform for the prisoners. That was some consolation, for it enabled us to make a small contribution at least to moral resistance, and to distract the prisoners from thoughts of their present fate. In the beginning, being in the theatre *Kommando* was a full-time job; we didn't have any other work. We were made up partly of professionals like me, and partly of amateurs. Living conditions for us were marginally better than they were for the other prisoners, and we had slightly better food, at least up until mid-1944; after that there was no food left. And from mid-'43, when they started to need prisoner labour, until January '45, we had to work in the coal-mines. We worked nights; then we could get a little rest in the mornings. After that we rehearsed, and gave our usual performances in the evenings.

'What we performed was mainly operettas. I remember that we did *La Belle Hélène*, and of course we had to keep Offenbach's name out of it, but the SS were just too ignorant to realize that what they were listening to with such pleasure had been written by a Jew. We had a good orchestra leader who'd been a band leader before the war, and there was an arranger too – we had to orchestrate the scores from piano parts, or even half-invent, half-remember whole chunks. And we slipped in bits here and there that satirized the Germans; but they never noticed. We did poetry readings occasionally, and put in some Heine – though of course we didn't mention his name, and once again the SS never knew that it was "Jewish" poetry. It was all we could do for the sake of our self-respect and to make our work a little useful to our fellow-prisoners. However, since that time I have only once set foot on a stage again. I felt that I had been forced to become a kind of prostitute in terms of my art. I do still do poetry recitals, and readings, things like that, for the SPÖ,[4] but that is all.

'At the end of January 1945 we were evacuated from the Auschwitz complex along with everyone else, and went on one of their notorious death-marches. There were 1,300 of us from Fürstengrube, and 10,000 in the whole transport. The idea was to get us to Mauthausen. After marching for some distance, they loaded us on to a huge train[5] of open coal-waggons, 100 to a waggon, and the journey on that train lasted ten days and ten nights. The winter of '44 to '45 was the coldest of the war. You can imagine what it was like. When we finally arrived at Mauthausen, they couldn't accept us because the camp was already filled to overflowing, so they took us on to Nordhausen in the Harz mountains, and thence to Dora, where the V-2s were being manufactured in underground factories. We were there nearly three months and then were evacuated once more. Dora was pure hell: and obviously there were no more advantages for us – the theatre *Kommando* had been disbanded on leaving Auschwitz. There was no food. People ate grass, earth, just to have something in their stomachs. They moved us to a small holding camp in North Germany. On 29 April we were handed over to the Swedish Red Cross. We were taken to Trelleborg. There were only 48 of us left of the 1,300 who'd been in the camp at Fürstengrube.

'During the whole period of imprisonment there was no conscious decision to survive. Indeed, one accepted that the chances of dying were very high; but as long as one retained the will to live, so I think the chances of dying were reduced. The minute you lost the will to live, you were dead. We Socialist prisoners were lucky too because we had a political motivation for staying alive: we had to stay alive, to tell the world exactly what fascism was, and what it did. I know, too, that I am glad I had the "apprenticeship" of the two French camps before they took me to Auschwitz: at least I was prepared to a certain extent for what was to come, and I'd learned how to organize, and so forth. The actual psychological shock of arriving at Auschwitz was less for those of us who were hardened than for those who came directly from home.

'I couldn't believe it when we were freed. We were put in quarantine in Sweden – given paper sheets on our beds to reduce the risk of infection to the Swedes. It took a week or more for the whole thing to sink in. The first thing you noticed was that the pressure of "will I still be alive tomorrow morning?" was gone. You see, despite our privileged position, we were still subject to the whims of the SS, and they had no sense of logic. They would shoot you as soon as look at you if they were in that kind of mood. I got four bayonet stabs from a drunken SS during a performance once. There were a few, a very few, who had traces of humanity in them. The best requested transfer to the front; others just became brutalized by habit and exposure to the way of the camp. But there are no excuses for those bastards.

'I didn't come home here after the war. I stayed in Sweden for 20 years. It wasn't too hard to learn the language. I already had English and French, and even a little Italian; but if you know German and English, Swedish isn't too hard. I could read the newspaper after three weeks, and I was fluent by the end of 18 months. And we were helped by the fact that the Swedish authorities and people were very generous. I arrived there on 2 May with the first male group into the country. We were given a hero's welcome, which was not unmixed with curiosity; but there was nothing the Swedish Red Cross wouldn't do for us. We were given complete outfits of clothing, all new; and during the time we were in quarantine we were excellently looked after; we wanted for nothing. I remember that the Swedish military catering was excellent. What was lacking was psychological help, but that was understandable; people really had no idea what we had been through, and obviously the British and the Americans knew more about the KZ than the Swedes – they had at least actually seen the places. In quarantine we were a mish-mash of Dutch, Norwegians and Danes, and the war wasn't quite over when we arrived, so that psychological help was a case of do-it-yourself. And naturally we tended to move into groups: the Communists together, the Social Democrats together, the Conservatives together, and so on. But there was great friendliness between the groups; our recent common experience had united us. The spirit of the camp united us. In the camp, people didn't ask each other first of all, "Are you a Conservative? Are you a Communist?" or whatever. We had extraordinary solidarity in the camp. If someone managed to organize a cigarette, it'd be shared between the four or five members of a group without question. And the friendships across political differences have remained strong, right up to today. We call it *Der Geist der Lagerstrasse*; what matters and unites us is anti-fascism.

'I only returned to Vienna in 1965. I met my wife in Sweden; she was a German, but, like me, a refugee. We were married in 1948. I expect I would have come home earlier, but my wife wanted to stay in Sweden; she absolutely wouldn't come back to Austria or Germany. She was one-quarter Jewish, though luckily she had not had to go through the camps; she managed to get to Sweden in 1939. Neither of us ever felt tempted to go to America, and after my wife's death and my illness I came back to Vienna because it is home. I wept when I saw the Danube again. It was good to come back, to make a break. We had two children, but neither of them lives in Sweden any more. My

son is here, he's a doctor of cybernetics, and my daughter runs a
boutique in Hamburg. My wife died in August 1960 – she was only 37
– when my daughter was five and my son eight. I had to send them to
my mother-in-law in Hamburg. By then I was in such pain from my
own illness that I could think of nothing else – I was too ill to mourn
my wife properly. Much, much later, my mother-in-law told me that
the doctors had said I'd be lucky if I lived another year. The crisis came
in February 1961. It was a disease of the pancreas, and my legacy from
the camps. It had to be operated on, and I was the first person in Sweden
to undergo such an operation and survive it; surgery of the pancreas
was in its early days in 1961. In the end I was in hospital for 18 months
and had to undergo five operations. At the end of that, my health was
pretty much permanently broken. I took early retirement in 1965,
which I was sorry about, because I enjoyed my job. I'd gone into the
catering trade. I was based in Gothenburg, where I lived all the time I
was in Sweden, and I'd become head buyer for a chain of hotels. There
was never a moment that I regretted the theatre; I felt nothing but
relief after I had made the decision to give it up for good.

'My wife was a great help to me in getting over the KZ experience,
and in the first years after the war I found it very difficult. A new job,
a new country, a new language – all that had to be adapted to; and then
there were the psychological problems. I had nightmares, and I often
woke up in the middle of the night bathed in sweat. I relived the horrors
of the camp in my dreams, and although in waking life I could do my
best to shut out the grim memories and try to think of the few funny
or happy occasions instead, I had no defence against the unselected
memories when I went to sleep. I was subject to bad dreams a great
deal in those first years after the war. Then they let up; but in the last
three or four years they have returned. I have no idea why.

'It is true, though, that the memory of that time never fades, not for
a moment. I do tours of duty as a guide to various camps now – for
groups of young people, mainly, but also for adults. I've done 146 guided
tours of Mauthausen, for example, in the last couple of years, and at
least twice a year I take groups to Auschwitz, and to Dachau, Buchenwald and Ravensbrück. It is my life's work, now, towards the end: to
show the young what fascism is and what it does. I don't try to angle
my talks in the direction of my own Socialist beliefs; I try to treat the
whole episode purely in a humanitarian way. And it is not easy. It does
not become easier with the number of times I do it. Each tour costs me
a little bit more of my heart. But I must find the strength to do it; those
of us here in the League who do the guiding regard the work as a duty
for life – to pass on our experience, and to do all we can to ensure that
such a thing can never happen again. But though I live with pain, I do
not think that I would ever have said that life after the camps was – or

could be – worse than life in them, for the simple reason that the terrible question of not knowing if you'd live through another day was gone. It took me two years to get totally free of that pressure: to really believe that it was off me.

'However, I am sure that the experience has made me spiritually stronger. One thing that it teaches is that, whatever situation you come across, you have to find a way through or out of it; and it taught me how to do that, how to be adaptable, how to think on my feet. It's an unconsciously acquired skill that one isn't aware one has until one needs it, I think. Because in the camp if you didn't find a way out of or around a bad situation, you were dead. It's impossible to describe how the mind works to defend itself from the constant risk of death; and don't forget either that we were defenceless, apart from quickness of mind. Ironically, those who were able to survive and rebuild their lives had been strengthened by the treatment the Nazis handed out to them; the opposite effect to that which the Nazis had wanted; but in saying that, one must not forget that there is a large number of survivors whom you will not meet, because they are permanently damaged by it; and all of us are in some way broken for good.

'The KZ didn't disturb my views and beliefs – it strengthened them. And it may sound funny, but it also strengthened my love of humanity; and not only my love, but my sympathy for people who are in trouble – those who die of famine in Africa, for example – is stronger. Our League helps financially to the best of its ability such charities as famine relief. Of course there are survivors who are still filled with a boundless hatred, and I can understand that; but they lose by it. I can honestly tell you that if I were confronted by an ordinary rank-and-file SS-man today, I couldn't hate him; though it would be a different matter if he were one of the top brass. As for revenge, I certainly felt vengeful for a few weeks after liberation; but it was a general sort of feeling, and never strong enough to make me actually want to do anything about it.

'Apart from the dreams, I am not aware of any other circumstances that trigger memories of the camps. The dreams started again in the early Eighties, and I've been doing the guiding since the late Seventies; but I do not believe there is a connection. The dreams aren't necessarily specific – they are about the KZ, but about experiences I may not actually have had. But last night, for example, I dreamt very vividly about something which did happen: they hanged five of our good friends one day. What triggered that dream last night I cannot say.

'I don't think it could happen again, certainly not in Europe. And the death-factory system that the Nazis set up – quite coldly and deliberately, based on economic principles, in that you killed the people as cleanly and as swiftly and as cheaply as possible, and took from them whatever was of value, down to their gold fillings and their hair, even down to the fat from their bodies for soap and their ashes for fertilizer – I don't see that happening again; but then, who could have seen it happening *ever*? As to the question *why?* – that's something we've been breaking our heads over for years: we few survivors discuss it pretty constantly. Why did the German people, the Austrian people, the Polish people, allow the Nazis to get away with it for so long? My own view is that it derived from people brainwashing children. If you take a child of three to a KZ and you say, look, this is terrible, this is inhuman, this shouldn't be done, and if you say that to him five times, he will learn the lesson. But if you take him there and tell him the opposite: yes, this is right; these people are simply worse than animals, and it is a good thing to get rid of them . . . Well, a hell of a lot of the SS were little more than children: in their teens and early twenties. The Nazis even had special schools – *Ordensburgen* – to groom the most promising pupils to be the SS of the future.[6]

'I have discussed the KZ with my own children. My son was born in 1950, and started to ask what I'd call proper questions when he was nine. My daughter was 12 or 13 before she showed an interest, but both reacted with sympathy to what had happened to me. I was astonished that my son was able to ask specific questions at nine, and I was worried about him; although they were certainly shocked, I am sure that no harm was done them, rather the opposite. I think my son, who was very precocious, had picked up more from overheard conversations than I'd imagined possible for one so young. I started doing the tours with very young people – with school classes – kids of about 17, so, I suppose, adult already; and I noticed that they wanted to know less about my personal experiences than about what a concentration camp was exactly, and what exactly went on. Nowadays I barely think about, let alone refer to, my own experiences when I do a tour. I describe the camps historically, and the fact that I have had personal experience of them lends authority to what I have to say. I have learnt too that you must be dispassionate in doing such a guided tour; if you get emotional, or try to put yourself in the spotlight, you actually put the truth you want to get across into question.

'They ask a handful of personal questions, of course, but mainly it's How was it done? How could it be? Why did the SS behave like that? And unfortunately it happens too that from time to time you get a school party, or elements in a school party, for whom it's just a duty to come, or a bit of a lark, a day off regular school. Not just children, either. I've known groups at Mauthausen – you could almost say coach-tours – who treat the visit rather like a trip on a ghost train at a fair, or a visit to a horror film. But I have to say this, and you mustn't think me conceited: I am very highly thought of as a guide – everybody here in the League thinks so – and I believe that at least some of the truth gets through to every group I take round. Sometimes I've been up at Mauthausen three times in a week. But, as I've said, each tour takes away a little bit of my heart. The advantage for me is that working with young people helps me master the guilt I feel at having survived at all; I fulfil a duty to the next generation by trying to be a representative of all those who died – irrespective of their politics or religion or race.

'It is very difficult to say whether there has been any positive effect on me from the suffering. I think I would say yes, there has. I know that it gave me a broader and deeper view of the world, and made me someone who feels things more deeply than I would otherwise have done. Also, a by-product of survival is to make something positive out of what is negative: to try to turn wasted years to good effect. I don't *regret* the experience, given that it was my fate to have it; but on the other hand I am bitter that my career was destroyed by it: you may say that I have only myself to blame, that it was my decision to give up the theatre, but I simply couldn't do it after the KZ, and I still can't. A kind of built-in aversion was born in me, and that was the fault of the Nazis. And I had a career. I'd been working a year already at the Deutsches Theater in Brunn. The sense of prostitution came from the fact that I was forced to do it by the Nazis. It had nothing to do with the work in itself, but after that I simply didn't want to go on stage any more. I cannot rationalize it. I did try once, in Sweden, with an amateur group of German refugees. I made my entrance on the first night, and as I stared out into the auditorium I saw the faces of the SS rabble who had been my audience in the KZ; and that was a shock. The "fourth wall" that had existed for me before the war was gone for ever. I got through that performance, but I never went on stage again.'

II

Just beyond the Prater on the Lassallestrasse are the offices of the KZ-Verband. Their chairman, Dr Ludwig Soswinski, is a lawyer, born in Vienna in 1904.

'I grew up with the Social Democrats. My father was an old Social Democrat from before 1905, and I grew up with the party, and was heavily involved with it before it was declared illegal along with all the other parties in 1934; but it was in 1934 that I joined the Communist Party, which of course was also illegal by then. I was arrested first in 1937 by the Austrian authorities, and my name was put on a list in Berlin, which meant that with the *Anschluss* in March 1938 the Germans took charge of me, and I was sent on the first transport of Austrian politicals to Dachau – the so-called *Prominententransport*

239

because everyone on it was of high standing in Austrian society. So I was a prisoner of the Nazis from 11 March 1938 until 5 May 1945. During that time I was in five different concentration camps: Dachau, Flossenburg, Lublin-Majdanek, Auschwitz and Mauthausen.

'There were three direct advantages that I had that helped my survival, for I knew that as an unregenerate and leading Communist there was no hope of my leaving the KZ until the Nazi regime was brought down: I was relatively young, I belonged to the group of German-speakers, and I was lucky enough to get into "soft" *Kommandos*: that is, always under cover and not doing strenuous physical work. I spent most of my time doing clerical work, except for the four months I spent at Flossenburg, when I had to work in the quarry; but even then the quarry was closed for two of those months, owing to a typhus epidemic. It's important to stress that the "standard of living" as well as the chances of survival for a non-German speaker, and especially a Jew or a Gypsy, were substantially lower. We politicals were interned; we were not the objects of genocide.

'I went to Lublin-Majdanek voluntarily, as it were. On 4 November 1943 they'd declared the district of Lublin *judenrein*.[7] All the businesses in the ghetto had closed down,[8] and the Germans wanted to get them going again. Many German-speaking prisoners, from Dachau, from Sachsenhausen and Buchenwald, were sent to Lublin: carpenters, electricians, every necessary trade, in order to set the moribund businesses necessary for Germany going again. Thus a sub-camp of Majdanek was established in Lublin town, so we spent only one night in the camp itself before being delivered to the "new" camp. The *Lagerälteste*[9] was a criminal, but not a bad one – he was a fraudster. I was delegated to be *Lagerschreiber*,[10] since I was a lawyer. There were. four *Blocks* there which had been used by the Jews when they were in the ghetto, and here we 300 men were lodged, and the conditions there weren't bad, as the *Blocks* were each designed for about 70 men, so there was no overcrowding; but we weren't in Lublin for long, as the Russians were advancing quickly, and in fact liberated Majdanek on 24 July 1944. We were evacuated and marched south-west to Auschwitz, at a rate of 50 kilometres a day, but we managed it because we were well-fed. The Polish peasantry gave us bacon when we were sent to them by the SS for vodka. In return for the food, we were able to give the Poles some information about the retreat movements of the SS, which they passed on to their own partisans. We were able to do this because, over the years we politicals had been together, we had woven together a network if not of resistance then at least of solidarity, and we were able to help each other collect and pass on information about the enemy. And there was some connection with the SS which, as a senior clerical prisoner [he was *Lagerschreiber* of Auschwitz-I] and an upper-class Austrian, was not too difficult for me to establish and try to exploit for the good of my fellow-prisoners. Early in January 1945, when I was in Auschwitz, I wrote a letter to *Obersturmbannführer* Dr Eduard Wirths,[11] head physician at Auschwitz, asking him to discuss the fate of the sick in the face of the camp's being evacuated. I was able to use my own name to sign the letter, not my number, and when he saw it Wirths agreed to a meeting. At it I said to him, "Look, I was at Majdanek; I know the war can't be won. When we evacuate Auschwitz, at least let the sick remain behind for the Russians to look after." He agreed to think it over, and I was then summoned to the *Politische Abteilung*,[12] to be interviewed by Kirschner, a fellow-countryman who'd taken over the SD department from Grabner some time before. To be summoned to the SD, even after Grabner had gone, was tantamount to a death sentence, and the *Lagerälteste* and my wife-to-be were trembling.[13] Anyway, I had to go. "So you don't think we'll win the war?" Kirschner said to me as soon as I arrived in his office. Of course I wondered what the hell he'd do. I could see my file open on his desk, and I didn't have any defence except argument. To my surprise, he was willing to discuss the pros and cons, and finally, after three-quarters of an hour, he flipped the file closed and said, "All right, you can go; but next time you want something, come to me direct." I was lucky; but I was also lucky that I was able to read the situation correctly.

'Another thing that helped the long-term political prisoners establish some kind of loosely knit network of contacts was that the camps had a constantly shifting population, and it wasn't unusual to come across the same people again in different camps. Actual resistance, such as it was, was organized by a much smaller group of people. In any case the whole network became more and more difficult to sustain, especially towards the end, in Mauthausen, where there was a large proportion of German-speaking criminals, and you didn't know whom you could trust.

'In general terms, too, the political solidarity was a tremendously helpful element in survival. Just the sense of comradeship was helpful, and I stress again that we weren't being hounded to death. There's another point, too: the SS didn't care about the Austrian Communists once they were prisoners, because before the war when Nazism had been outlawed along with communism, Nazis had frequently shared cells with Communists as fellow political prisoners. They were put in cells together because, as they belonged to separate ideologies, they would be unlikely to plot together.

'After the war, the solidarity that existed in the KZ even between the Austrian political prisoners of different persuasions formed the foundation for us to be able to rebuild Austria as a new republic.

'I never gave up hope during imprisonment; firstly, I'm not the type; secondly, because I was never in a position to be tempted to give up hope. Certainly I was upset by the sights that I saw, what I saw happening to the Jews, but that only made me more determined to get through and help ensure that such things never happened again; it didn't make me want to give in to despair. Liberation, when it came, was no surprise. I was liberated from Mauthausen, and we knew that the arrival of the Americans was inevitable. The SS, afraid of being killed, had fled a few days earlier and left us in the care of a few elderly *Volkssturm* and some members of the Vienna Fire Brigade.[14] I didn't feel any great emotion when it happened. I wasn't exhausted or ill. I'd been a clerk at Mauthausen; and now I had party work to do in Vienna that required immediate attention if a new administration was to be formed as soon as possible. But you see I had always been in privileged positions in the camps; I had always been within reach of news of the world outside, and I had a pretty realistic grasp of the state of play. I returned to Vienna with an American transport on 17 May. There was never any question of going to live in America, or anywhere else. I was born here, and there was a job to do here, a new Austria to build. Three weeks after my return I was a member of a commission to reconstitute the Austrian *schilling*. Subsequently I became a municipal councillor in Vienna, work I continued until 1957, when I became a member of the regional government. After that I retired from politics and returned to my original career of business consultant, which had been interrupted in 1934 because of my membership of an illegal political party. I felt that I had done my share towards the reconstruction of Austria. I have of course continued to be involved with the KZ-Verband, and there was the whole question of reparation to be worked out, which was never satisfactory. Apart from the sums that disappeared, some of those who had been persecuted could get tax relief as a kind of reparation, but of course the people who benefited from that most were the highest earners, and therefore arguably those least in need.

'I should add that my children are half-Jewish. Both my wives, in fact, were Jewesses. My first managed to get out of the country before the war and went to England. Through the separation of all those prison years, we grew apart, and in the camps I met and fell in love with my present wife, who comes from Czechoslovakia. She was originally sent on a transport to Auschwitz from Ravensbrück to be gassed; but the administration needed five typists, and my wife was a trained stenographer. Actually, they'd already selected their five, but my wife is small, and they said, "Oh well, we'll take the little one as well." She worked in the buildings administration office of the camp, which is where I met her. We were separated when Auschwitz was evacuated, but we decided to meet in Vienna after the war if we could. She managed to escape from a death-march and made her way to Prague, and from there to Vienna where we were reunited.

'I do not have dreams, nor do I find that there are events in everyday life that trigger memories; but I think the reason for that is that my work for the KZ-Verband brings me to think about those times consciously every day. The KZ has never ceased to be a conscious presence for me, and so perhaps that is why I do not suffer from bad dreams. However, again you would have to say that it depends on the individual. I've never been tempted to let it all go, to forget it; but it hasn't been a question of choice: I cannot forget it because I cannot forget it. There are people who have tried to, but I do not believe that anyone really succeeds. I don't dream about it because when I go to bed my thoughts are always filled with what work I have to do tomorrow. The past cannot get at me because the present is too busy. But we do have comrades who wake in the night bathed in sweat, when they unexpectedly think of the KZ, and very few survivors are up to the task of lecturing, or taking tours round the camps, because they cannot master the emotions that such work inevitably evokes, cannot develop the necessary sense of detachment. My wife dreams. She dreams of the *selections* – but she had a worse time in the camps than I did. I was never even in a *selection*; she was, and what's more she was selected for death. She tells me that she would never have survived without me, for she had terrible liver problems, and I managed to organize medicines for her, and extra food, and to keep her in a "soft" *Kommando*. And, you know, now the two of us don't need to talk about the KZ because not only do we know what it was like but we actually lived some of it close together. You remember those times in such detail: exact dates, times of day! I could tell you very little about my life with my first wife, but that's a lifetime away; yet I could tell you almost every detail of every day in the KZ, and that's a lifetime away, too. And I didn't have a bad time. For example, I am well aware of what happened on the death-marches. I was on the illegal camp committee in Auschwitz and we knew what was going on during the first evacuations, and how many were dying. And yet I tell you that on the march from Majdanek to Auschwitz I made, of the 300 politicals, not one died. We even had good shoes to walk in.'

III

The VVN (*Vereinigung der Verfolgten des Nazi-Regims* – the Union of Those Persecuted by the Nazis) is a left-wing and Communist West German survivor group. Many of its members served sentences in

Dachau in the pre-war years, and spent the war in probation-battalions on the Eastern Front. Those who were taken prisoner by the Russians did not see their homes again until the late Forties. Some of the former inmates of Dachau, who live in Munich or the Dachau region, continue to work in the camp as guides or in the museum there.[15] Richard Titze does not come from Bavaria, but since being a prisoner in Dachau he has never moved away.

He was born in Silesia but his family moved to Essen when he was two and he spent his early years there. 'I became politically aware when I saw how the workers in the *Ruhrgebiet* were put down when they struck for better working conditions in 1923–4. We lived near the police headquarters, which abutted a rich quarter of Essen; and when the police returned from their battle with the workers I saw how the rich people fed the horses chocolate – chocolate was something that the working classes couldn't think of having for themselves. I was about 16 at the time and that had a profound effect on me, which was strengthened when I saw the Red Front leaders brought to the police HQ in manacles. My father was already active within his own union, and in May 1926 I joined the Communist Youth League. In time I became its leader for the Essen region. When the Communist Party became illegal we set up underground cells to try to organize a resistance movement, and we listened to foreign radio stations, printed leaflets, and established contact with Catholic and Jewish youth groups. The idea was to build up some concerted agitprop against the Hitler regime, and to spread counter-propaganda. I remember one of our illegal presses for leaflets was concealed behind the altar of a church. I was sent on a course in Amsterdam in 1933 to learn about underground work and, once back home, passed this instruction on to the other members of my cell. We had an advantage in that I was a skilled worker and so got much better housing than the unskilled, among whom the authorities generally expected to unearth Communists. My flat became a safe house, and we used it too to hold meetings – discussion groups and talks. But they tumbled to it at last and I was arrested on 17 November 1933 and sentenced along with a mixed group of 48 others, including some Jews and Social Democrats, to eight years' hard labour. They sent me to Munster, where I arrived on Christmas Eve, and, just to show that they weren't fooling around, gave me a week's "dark" cell, followed by one year's solitary.

'I served my eight years and then I was set free. My mother came to collect me. We were immediately confronted by two Gestapo officials who said that I was owed some money in recompense for my eight years' hard labour. It came to 65 marks. My mother took the money and threw it in their faces. I was able to spend Christmas at home in Essen, and then in January 1942 they rearrested me, and sent me to

Dachau. They were afraid I would start working for the underground again.'

He was employed in the camp as a bricklayer – his trade – and built kilns for the pottery factory and, later, air-raid bunkers. Solidarity among the political groups was a great boon, since comrades were often able to help each other on to 'soft' *Kommandos*, and the living conditions were better for politicals than for Jews and Gypsies: *Blocks* were less crowded. However, when he was in *Block* 30, they slept six to a bunk and the *Blockälteste* was a 'green triangle' and a sadist, 'so that it was not always a picnic. The death-rate in *Block* 30 was 30 per cent.' He succumbed to dysentery but was taken to the camp hospital and cured; later he moved to *Block* 2 – the *Prominents' Block*. This privilege was accorded him because he was a well-known 'red triangle', and because the politicals looked after their own in order to continue the struggle. *Blocks* were designed to hold 200 men, but overcrowding was so dire that at Dachau even the *Prominentenblock* had 900 inhabitants. The very worst *Blocks*, in which the Russians, the Gypsies and the Jews were kept, housed 2,000.

We were talking first of all in the Dachau museum's administrative offices, and then in the camp itself, as we walked round it. He spoke obsessively, but also with a certain theatricality. At one stage, in the restored *Block* we were surrounded by a large group of teenage schoolchildren, who simply stopped and listened to our conversation. Without for a moment acknowledging their presence, he gave them a performance, knowing full well how awed they were to be in the presence of someone who had actually been a prisoner in the camp.

Effectively he has never left it. As soon as he was liberated, he and a number of comrades immediately involved themselves with organizing documentation about the camp, and preserving what the SS had not destroyed. 'One of the first things we did upon liberation was to erect a stage at the end of one of the *Blocks*, and then we had the captured SS mount it, one by one, and answer questions put to them by their former prisoners.'

He helped to compile a complete list of all the prisoners who had been killed in Dachau, and he was in the forefront of those who worked to have the camp restored and designated a national monument. 'I have never felt tempted to forget about it, or to go and live elsewhere. I have never felt that the work is a burden; it is a duty – more than a duty, something I have to do. I was a prisoner here for three years, and took part in the uprising two days before the Americans liberated us, and I was a prisoner of the Third Reich for eight years before that. Such an experience changes your life. You cannot help becoming obsessed by it. But I have no bitter feelings. During a television interview once I was asked if I felt bitter and I said that I can't help feeling a good deal of sympathy with the DDR although I'm too committed here to go there to live; but I feel a certain sense of philosophical irony when I see old comrades whom I worked with illegally in the early Thirties who've now got big administrative jobs over there; whereas here a lot of those jobs are still in the hands of former Nazis. Needless to say, they cut that bit out when they televised the interview! Bitter feelings are the result of self-pity, I think. Anyway, we were resistance fighters, and we had to accept imprisonment and even death as a consequence of fighting for what we believed in. So we don't have any right to bitter feelings. Our strength was and remains the knowledge of the rectitude of what we were doing: fighting fascism; so the feelings, if anything, are of pride.

'There are advantages too. I still suffer from bad dreams about the camp, and they are a real threat; but the comfort of still being amongst old comrades who went through the same experience is that they help you keep self-pity at bay. I think that is something which you have to fight hard to resist, and if you give in to it you are in real trouble – that is just as true now as it was then. The most important thing to realize in the circumstances under which we were prisoners was that we were not the wrongdoers. We were innocent, and it was our gaolers who were the wrongdoers. Armed with that conscious knowledge, one's attitude to imprisonment changed. One didn't start to feel guilty just because one was a prisoner. That may sound paradoxical, but take it from me that merely the situation of being a prisoner can make you think you are wrong – because you are on the wrong side of those in authority. The thing to realize was that the authority was wrong, was criminal. We knew that we were German patriots, not the cowards and subversives we were told we were – traitors, even, for one of the favourite charges made against us was "conspiracy to commit an act of treason" – and we were armed with an ideological strength that was actually deepened and hardened by the KZ experience, the more so since Nazism had no ideological foundations at all, but merely brute force. The camaraderie we had then remains, and it is as important to me now as it was then. It is my life, you might say. I took an oath: "Never again fascism"; and I must be true to that oath and fight for it until I die.'

But don't you want to get away from here? Isn't it wearing?

'Certainly it is, but on the other hand it is also interesting and it keeps me alert and brings me into contact with young people, which in turn keeps me young. If I sat at home and twiddled my thumbs, or just bummed around in the garden, I'd have gone under long ago. I know that it helps me to keep confronting the past, which I can never escape anyway. And, I say again, there is the camaraderie. Our relationship to one another is far stronger than any blood tie.

'My best relationships outside those with my comrades are with young people – what I'd call the third generation. Here in Germany, people of my generation and their children, born in the Forties and Fifties, suppressed thoughts of the war and German responsibility; they wanted to deny the Nazi episode, cut it out of our history. But we simply cannot do that, and now, with the interest of students and schoolchildren, the situation has changed. Young people really have been born into a totally different world from that of their parents and grandparents, and hopefully they have a freer outlook too, because travel and communications are so much easier and cheaper. It may be unduly optimistic of me to say this, but I think young people here feel less German, in the old nationalistic sense, than European. They are interested in the Nazi period as history, and are curious to find out why it happened. With that interest a lot of what has been suppressed must come out, and finally it will be learnt from. I want to be part of that process. My hope is that the Germans will learn never to be sabre-rattling nationalists again, and I am glad that when I take kids round the camp they are really interested – it's not just a boring obligatory day-trip from school – and they ask questions. They don't just look on the place as a museum and me as a museum piece!

'Generally, too, there have been rewarding reactions as time has passed. In the last few years the German sense of sympathy for our own resistance fighters has increased 100 per cent, and nowadays we see not only foreign tourists visiting Dachau, but also Germans. There was a time when the town was made to feel ashamed of its name, too – and people didn't like to drive around with Dachau plates on their cars – but those days are past. By coming to terms with the past rather than trying to pretend it didn't exist, everyone can breathe easier. It is good, too, that all the military have to visit a camp as part of their training programme. None of that must ever happen again. We survivors must go on shouting that until we drop, even though we know we can't ever communicate completely the horror of the KZ to those who didn't experience it for themselves.'

He takes you round the camp with a kind of familiar formality. In another context, he might be a proprietor showing you round an estate. It is a good day to see the camp: a cold weekday in December. A thin carpet of snow lies over the bleak rectangle where the blocks stood, and a few dirty flakes swirl in the air. There are not many other visitors: the party of schoolchildren, whom I had seen earlier chastened by the film in the museum's cinema, and a knot of very young soldiers with moustaches and blue faces.

Titze is very much at home here. He shows me Niemoeller's cell, and takes me to the little wooded glade beyond which the crematoria lie. 'The firm of J. A. Topf still exists, you know – they're still in business.' Then we go to the adjoining gas chamber, and stand in it. It is not large. It has whitewashed walls. It is cold. The voice echoes in it. 'They never used the gas chamber here. But they burned the bodies of the dead in the crematoria. One of my jobs was to rake out the ashes and dig them into the vegetable plots.'[16]

One of the most striking things about the camp is how *new* it is: the crematoria are built of modern red-brick, and the whole place could be a light industrial complex of the kind you see in bleak outer suburbs all over Europe. The newness brings home to one how recently the concentration camps existed. They belong to our own time.

Another member of the VVN in Munich is Hans Heiss, a retired trade union official. Like Titze, his political coming-of-age was occasioned by the strikes and unemployment of the early Twenties, which he himself experienced as a young worker. He was born in Munich in 1906. His father was an official and a convinced Social Democrat.

In 1920, Heiss started work as an apprentice with Rodenstock, the optical firm. 'I was one of the first apprentices after the war; at that time it was customary to learn your trade before you started worrying about the state of the world, but I began to feel quite strongly about the social injustices that were apparent and joined the Social Democratic Party in 1925. There was a general strike in 1924 and, following that, lockouts. We were on strike ourselves for nine months, and then in 1926 there was great unemployment. I too was unemployed. Then in 1929 there was the Crash, and of course all that led to the rise of the Nazis, amidst all the panic and the directionlessness, and I was already opposed to the Nazis. After 1933 we had to organize ourselves illegally. It was a difficult time. All the foreign powers seemed to be nodding approval at Hitler, or at least letting him get away with it. We thought about getting out, emigrating, but that seemed to be more of an escape than an answer, and at the same time we were confused by the reaction of the outside world to Nazism. Didn't they know what was going on? It was because of this confusion that in 1934 I decided to get hold of photographs taken illegally inside Dachau. The plan was to get the photographs out of Germany via the Mitropa train network – they were still running trains internationally and we had people working on the sleepers and the restaurant cars – there was the *Rheingold*, for example, which ran from Amsterdam to Switzerland, and there was another that ran from Nuremberg through to Czechoslovakia. Through the train network people were able to smuggle material in and out of Germany.

'The photographs were actually taken by the SS, and we got hold of them in the following way: women in our movement made friends with the girlfriends of the SS in the various bars. Now, the SS-men were so vain and sure of themselves that they used to take dozens of snapshots of the interior of the camp and what was going on there, and they'd give copies of their snaps to their girlfriends on request, and the girls would pass them on to our girls who pretended to be admiring. Really proud of them, they were.

'But we were rumbled. One of our couriers was a waiter in the restaurant car on the Hamburg–Munich–Prague run. He was betrayed by his brother, who was in the SA.[17] The SD arrested him, and "persuaded" him to carry on – thus the material he was carrying from Hamburg to Prague was intercepted by the Gestapo in Munich, photocopied, and sent on. This went on for three months, and they were able thereby to build up a picture of a whole network of resistance fighters. When they were sure they had the whole picture, they moved in. A lot of us were arrested. We were convicted, not because it could be proved that we had conspired to commit high treason, but because the defence was unable to prove that we had acted otherwise. Even at the time I thought that was an amusing way to carry out justice. After that I spent three years at *Sanatorium Dachau* – from July 1935 until September 1938.

'All newcomers had to work in the infamous gravel-pits. It was early days at Dachau still. All the buildings, from the commandant's lodge to the prisoners' latrines, were built by KZlers. I graduated from quarryman to track-layer to plasterer. There was already a complicated pecking order and organization among the prisoners themselves: we were a mish-mash of so-called asocials, criminals and politicals, all mixed together at that time; but even then there were illegal political groups within the prison population, though all the kapos who weren't master craftsmen were "green triangles".

'Conditions in the camp were grim, but I was helped by fellow politicals and got a job as an orderly in the camp hospital, which incidentally saved my life because the Gestapo within the camp wanted to nail me on suspicion of illegal political activity, but they couldn't find me since by then I'd left the *Kommando* they thought I was in. I suppose they assumed I'd died. It never occurred to me personally that I might not survive. From the first moment I said to myself, I'll get out of this.

'When I was released I was declared *wehrunwürdig* [unworthy to do military service]; because of having been sentenced for high treason I was unworthy of serving my country. And so I remained until 1944 when I was given service duty as printer working on – would you believe it? – the *Völkische Beobachter*. You see, I was not allowed to work anywhere that directly serviced the Military, and so I was not the only dissident to work on the Nazi Party paper! However, later in '44 came the so-called *Aktion Goebbels*, whereby any man with two feet to stand on was sent to the front. I was declared kv [*kriegsverwendungsfähig*] fit for active service; but then a confusion arose, because my papers still stated that I was *wehrunwürdig* – it was all quite dotty. The head printer, Schwarz, who was quite a Nazi, was furious, because there were barely any men left to print the paper. He said, if you take Heiss away from me too, there won't be any *Beobachter* any more! Of course my feelings on the whole newspaper issue were highly ironical, and it goes without saying that if it hadn't been for my efforts and those of my comrades, the whole production line might have been a good deal more efficient. But we had the sword of Damocles hanging over our heads all the time.

'They resolved the problem of my being "fit-but-unworthy" by letting me continue at my job, but making me join the ridiculous and sad *Volkssturm*. My fellow workers were now POWs, but they knew I was no Nazi. When the Americans arrived and took over the printworks, they engaged me to help produce a new newspaper. I was one of the two shift leaders by then – day and night – there was simply no one else left. I ran the American-produced paper for a year, and then I rejoined my old union. I went to Frankfurt for a year to study, and in 1948 I became an official of my union, and that was my work until I was pensioned off.

'On 17 December 1985 I was honoured with the Diamond Order – 60 years' SPD membership. But I also work with the VVN, even though it is too far left for me, because I agree with its principles; and I lived shoulder to shoulder with Communists in the KZ. We must keep dialogue open between all groups of political parties, or there will be prejudice. That is self-evident, but what a lot it takes to teach people the truth of it.'

IV

Karl Ibach is Federal Chairman of the *Zentralverband Demokratischer Widerstandskämpfer und Verfolgtenorganisationen* (ZDWV) and of the *Fédération Internationale Libre des Déportés et Internés de la Résistance*.[18] He was born in Wuppertal on 3 April 1915, and lives there still.

ZDWV was formed in the following way: as the post-war political parties established themselves after the collapse of Nazi Germany, so also a group of political survivors of the concentration camps was founded – this was the VVN. The Communists were very heavily involved with the VVN, and if one wanted to belong to a politically neutral survivors' organization, one had to create it. This came into being with the regionally based BVN – the *Bund der Verfolgten des Naziregims* (Association of Victims of the Nazi Regime) – and in 1954 its various regional units decided to unite in Bonn under a Central

Association. The *Zentralverband*, of which Ibach is Chairman, is a union of all the regional BVNs – of Berlin, of North Rhein-Westphalia, and so on.

Ibach has held a salaried position with the ZDWV since that time, and his work with it and as editor of the quarterly magazine *Freiheit und Recht* ('Freedom and Justice') have constituted his post-war career. Prior to that he was involved with survivor welfare work, which he began soon after his return home in 1947 from Russian prisoner-of-war camp. At first he worked for the VVN in Wuppertal as local secretary, a salaried position. With the schism of 1950 he became one of the co-founders of the BVN Nordrhein-Westfalen; and later became regional secretary (chief executive officer) – a job he did for many years, alongside an honorary position as a member of the national committee. The post of Chairman, which he has held since his predecessor's retirement in 1969, is an honorary one. 'Formerly, we had a paid staff, but of course the organization is shrinking, as our members are naturally becoming fewer.'

Freiheit und Recht covers subjects related to political oppression in the world today. It does not just perform the function of being a 'veterans'' magazine, but is news-reactive. It arose out of a need for a central source of information and news for all the member organizations of ZDWV, and also – and most importantly – to begin with, it provided information about the reparation arrangements, and how to go about claiming. Originally it came out monthly, then six times a year; now four – 'Everything in our organization is reducing now.'

Ibach is very much involved with schools. 'I am living history for those kids; I think that makes it more alive for them, and the exercise seems to be successful. I'm mainly dealing with 15–18-year-olds; talking about it with me is certainly more stimulating than just reading about the Third Reich in books. It becomes part of their own experience.

'The principal questions I get asked are: "Was it really as bad in the KZs and the extermination camps – and was it really so terrible for the Jews?" The reason they ask is I believe that very often their parents – or perhaps I should say their grandparents – the Germans who lived through it as adults and were a part of it – have tended to suppress the memories in their own minds, or to belittle the importance of what was going on; and indeed I have heard such people say things like: "Well, it wasn't as bad as all that." The other thing the children have commonly heard said is, "We didn't know anything about it." When I tell them that as an 18-year-old I was sent to the local concentration camp, Kemna,[19] with 1,000 other politicals, they realize of course that people knew what was happening from the very first. Kemna was opened on 5 July 1933, and it is right in town, not hidden away. People came for walks on Sundays to catch a glimpse of us – though of course they were not all rubberneckers; they were people who came hoping to catch a glimpse of their loved ones. And you have to take into account that by that time the SA, who ran it, had quasi-official status. They conducted a reign of terror in the town, too, so you can't blame people for wanting to keep their heads down. The fact remains that everybody who was around then knew much more than they pretend – even to themselves – today. Of course that doesn't apply just to us politicals. How could the good people of Wuppertal, for example, pretend that they didn't notice the disappearance of a Jewish community of 3,000 people, and those mainly lawyers, doctors and businessmen? It's the old human question of suppressing the bad memories and the sense of guilt. People can do it to the extent that they really believe they weren't aware of the degree of tyranny the Nazis perpetrated.

'The best way to combat a recurrence of what happened is to encourage the young to think freely and independently; I work not only with school students but with youth groups affiliated to trade unions and political parties. I am a Social Democrat, but my lectures and discussions are not politically angled, unless you argue that my recollections could provoke a certain political reaction in any thinking person! At all events, it is a history lesson that needs to be given as often as possible; its memory mustn't become blurred, and excuses mustn't be found for it. On the other hand, if we can try to understand it better, that is good. The design for the monument to the camp which was erected in 1983 was the winning entry in a competition for schools and youth groups, and it is children who look after the monument.

'I was influenced at quite an early age by two experiences. The first was in 1930 when I was at the *Gymnasium*. There were three Jews in the school – older boys than me. There were also one or two students who were Nazis, who disseminated Nazi propaganda, among it anti-Semitic material. I was simply appalled at that, and at the language in which it was couched. At the time the Nazis were just beginning to get into their stride, to develop from a small, noisy party into something to be taken seriously, and they were obviously gaining support. So I decided that I had better find out more about them, and at the age of 15 or so sat down to read *Mein Kampf*. I was especially interested in Hitler's foreign policy, his desire for *Lebensraum* in the east, the so-called *Ostpolitik*. And because I was really still a child I saw the future with a kind of awful simplicity: there would have to be a war, for how else would Hitler create this *Lebensraum*? He'd have to get rid of the people who were living in Poland and all the other countries he wanted to colonize first. This was my second revelation: for I saw that he could achieve this only by suppressing freedom at home. So we were faced with a future Germany dominated by a man who wanted to crush the Jews, and other minorities, and to suppress anyone who didn't agree with him – political opponents. His foreign policies were to be summed up in one word: war. In view of this I became a political animal. People had to stand up to this man; anti-fascism was born in me. Of course it is true to say that many people of liberal views knuckled under as soon as it became clear how political opponents would be treated, but I have to say that I was far from alone in sticking to my guns. It wasn't in my character to give in to the Nazis – so it wasn't a question of making a brave decision or anything like that; but there were not enough of us and we didn't organize or encourage popular support in time: the Nazis were extremely energetic and politically aggressive – not only politically aggressive, of course – and very quick to seize and exploit power.

'I joined the Socialist Workers' Youth League in 1931. We demonstrated against the Nazis while there was still a semblance of democracy, and there were street battles with the SA, and we worked quite openly against the NSDAP. Meanwhile, after my own political stirrings, I was making friends with the editor of the local Social Democrat newspaper, who introduced me to his collection of books – especially books on political thought – and this was wonderful, because books didn't figure largely at home, and he had a huge number of them, on all subjects, because he was always being sent review copies. Access to them was some consolation to me for another reason: my father had been made redundant and as a result I'd had to leave school after taking only *Mittlere Reife*.[20] But I was training to be a bookseller.

'With the help of the editor, I was able to develop my thinking, political and otherwise. I remember reading Engels with great interest – not least because Engels was a Wuppertaler! The drawback to all these activities was that by the time Hitler became Chancellor in January 1933, I was already on the list of political enemies of the state drawn up by the local Nazis.

'My arrest came as a great shock to my parents, who tried in vain to get me out of Kemna – I was their only child – but in vain. My father was just a little businessman in a big company here. I wasn't influenced by my parents at all. I think it is important to remember that in those three years up to 1933 when I was so wrapped up in politics, I was one of many. People were vastly interested in what was going on. We'd lost a war, we were at an economic nadir; and Wuppertal, as an important and long-established industrial centre, had its own Nazi faction very early on.

'They came for me one morning. It's interesting, because it shows clearly how oddly justice was carried out in those days. A car came for me with three SA men in their brown uniforms, and one regular policeman. It was pointless to resist them. As soon as they had picked me up and the car had turned the corner of our street, the chief SA man said to the policeman: "OK, you can get out now." Then they drove me to Kemna. Overhearing them as we drove along, I learnt that they'd come to arrest me alone but had picked up a cop on the beat whom they'd passed by chance, to give their action a veneer of respectability. The SA still didn't have absolute power at that time. I was arrested on 8 August 1933 and kept at Kemna for three months.

'It was a dreadful place. We were set useless tasks to do, like taking stones out of the freezing water of the River Wupper, and hunting for concealed weapons in the sewers. The camp was run by the SA, but they had all the basic ingredients of the KZ already worked out – right down to the diet. If they wanted more information out of you, they would lock you in a metal locker and then kick it, turn it upside down, blow cigarette smoke through its ventilation holes – or worse, before they put you in, they'd make you eat a "Kemna-cut", which was salt herring smeared with cup-grease. Those who refused to eat them were beaten bloody. Those who ate them and then vomited were forced to eat their vomit. They even had kennel cells in which you could only crouch, and where people were left for days without food or water.

'I was released on 23 October. By luck, I was able to continue my training as a bookseller; I was lucky to have such a sympathetic boss, because I'd been officially declared an enemy of the state and he didn't have to have me back at all, especially at a time when there were plenty of so-called "veterans" of the NSDAP unemployed and hungry for the jobs which Hitler had promised them as their reward. My luck didn't last long. I was rearrested – which was hardly surprising, since I had joined a resistance group. We had set up a very primitive printing unit in an allotment shed and produced anti-fascist leaflets – though only a few, maybe 100 at a time, because our facilities were so poor.

'Throughout my new imprisonment my fellow politicals and I were mixed in with ordinary criminals who were serving ordinary sentences. Our guards were ordinary regular prison guards, so that our treatment was vastly better than that which we'd received at Kemna. We had been lucky in that the camps we were sent to now had been allocated away from RHSA administration. Officially we were under protective custody – the camps were under the jurisdiction of the Justice Department, instead of the RHSA, which ran the KZs proper. I was sent first to prison in Munster, and then, as I was young and fit for work, to Esterwegen and Börgermoor – where the famous *Moorsoldaten* prisoners' song comes from. They established a lot of camps in that area [south of a line drawn between Emden and Wilhelmshaven] – the idea was that the moor should be made cultivable through prisoner labour. It was marshy ground and the main job was drainage. I worked there for four years.

'In 1940, when the war took hold, all political prisoners from the moor camps were sent back to prison for greater security. I was returned to Munster, where I remained until 1943 – my eight-year sentence was almost over. But then I was transferred to Probationary Military Unit 999 – popularly known as Punishment Battalion 999.

'The 999 was big. It was actually composed of 23 battalions, and I ought to point out that none of them were "punishment" battalions. I was with the VII/999 Battalion. We were sent to Greece, but because they didn't trust us we weren't used as combat so much as occupation troops, and that on islands. We were detailed to occupy Levkas and Cephalonia in the Ionian Islands. From there we moved on to the Balkans, where we were taken prisoner by the Russian forces, and sent ultimately to a POW camp called Mariupol (near Zhdanov). The great Azov Steelworks were situated there, and they had been totally destroyed by the retreating German army. Our job was to try to shift the rubble and tidy the place up. We noticed that acres and acres of fruit trees had been destroyed too – for no military reason; only to leave chaos behind for the Russians, and starvation. I was very surprised at how relatively little animosity we experienced from the Russians, in view of what our countrymen had done to them.

'There were three liberation days for me: the first was 9 November 1944, when I was freed from the Nazi-*Wehrmacht* and became a POW of the Bulgarians, to be exact; we were taken in Montenegro. They handed us over to the Russians soon after. There was a feeling of relief to be out of the hands of the Nazis. The first thing I did was rip the swastika badge off my uniform, and I felt a deep sense of peace. I felt freed, odd though it sounds. My liberation came in stages. The second date was 8 May 1945, when the war ended. I was still a prisoner, but Hitler's Reich was over. Again a sense of peace and relief pervaded me. I felt that now there was hope for Germany, and the worst was well and truly over. The third liberation day was the one on which I arrived home – 30 November 1947 – and could finally shake off 13 years' imprisonment.

'I wasn't tempted to go and live elsewhere after the war – in the USA, for example. I was born here, and this is my home. And I felt that I could do more good by staying at home, though I can't really take credit for that, since my future was determined by circumstances, and by fate, as much as anything. But a lot of us who came back wanted to do our bit for the new, democratic Germany. We saw ourselves as "freemen" of the new nation: Adenauer described all us returned deportees as such. However, we "freemen" had our work cut out for us re-establishing ourselves in society, and it wasn't advisable to tell just anybody that you were a former freedom fighter. There were people who might take the view that you hadn't been properly patriotic, and it might have made the difference between getting a job and not getting one. Reparation was a long time coming, too – 11 years at least for some of us. Nowadays, though, it's different. Now there's no question that people in our position are respected for what they did – especially by the young.

'The question of forgiveness is a hard one to answer. Can I forgive? Yes and no. I have no personal hatred; but I cannot forgive in the Christian sense because I am not a Christian. You see, my world-view is always coloured by considerations which are political and realistic: those people created untold misery; they are a danger to society; they must therefore be put apart from society, isolated, defused, so to speak. That is a quite rational feeling in me, not an emotional one.

'In recent years the leniency of the sentences handed down to former Nazis has been nothing short of scandalous. The Wuppertal trials were the first and in my opinion the best; at them, the only death sentence passed on a Nazi by a West German court was handed down, and there were several life-sentences: real life-sentences, that is, not ones that only last ten years or so.

'No survivor's memories of those times fade, though his attitude to his memories may change. For me, there is no trauma. I don't dream about being pursued, and I do not feel persecuted; but I think about those times a lot – always, every day. Partly, of course, that is because of my work. The KZ experience has formed my whole life – it never stopped, because when I got home I was immediately occupied in work connected with it. Because it has stayed with me at a very conscious and even social level, and because I've been able to apply its lessons in a wider context, it has never been repressed and I have never been isolated by it. I have never felt any bitterness towards those who robbed me of the opportunity to have another career – the career I might have chosen for myself; but against that I have to add that my career has been fulfilling. Had it not been, I might feel otherwise.

'The most urgent need I had on returning was to form and found a family, after such a long time of loneliness, of lack of intimacy. Of course there were friendships in the camps, but however great camaraderie is, it is no substitute for a wife and child; and naturally after such a very long time deprived of an outlet, that group of emotions carried a very strong drive! I never found it necessary, in the sense of making a confession, to talk to my wife about what I had been through. Although my imprisonment was long and hard and unjust, I was not alone in that situation; and nothing happened to me to cause me permanent mental damage: I never had my family murdered before my eyes, for example, and I was able to come home to a town that was still my home town, even though it had been bombed half flat, and pick up the threads of my life in familiar surroundings. Naturally there are scars. I am registered as 50 per cent disabled owing to damaged health, and for the past 30 years I have been obliged to make regular visits to the doctor. In the moor camps I had pneumonia twice, which permanently damaged my lungs, and I also suffer from a chronic weakness in concentration.

'I don't know if I could say that the experience of my imprisonment equipped me better to weather life subsequently. In some ways the opposite is true, because right up to today every so often I am aware of holes in my overall experience and education. I have done my damnedest to recover and make up for those 13 lost years, but I haven't succeeded to my satisfaction, though I don't wish to appear to complain. I haven't come off too badly; I have a happy marriage and I have enjoyed a happy family life. Materially, too, I am well-off, not least because owing to my long imprisonment I got a very good settlement. I own my house, and I've never been unemployed. I've never felt lonely or isolated – I am always busy, and with people.'

V

One of the earliest books about life in the Nazi prisons and camps was written by Lina Haag and first published in Germany in 1947,[21] when she was 40 years old. It describes not only an imprisonment, but a whole life; one dedicated to the fight against fascism and to her husband, whom she loved as selflessly as he loved his cause. The book is also a love story, taking the form of a series of letters to Alfred Haag during the long period of their separation, and written at a time when she was not even sure that he was still alive. He returned from a Russian POW camp in 1948.

She was born in Schwäbisch-Gmünd, the eldest of five children. She joined the Communist Youth League because the weekly meetings represented more of a social occasion for her than anything. At one meeting a lecture was to be given about Communists in prison. The lecturer was Alfred Haag.

What she learnt from the lecture shocked her. 'When it was over I went up to Fred and said, if I'm likely to be locked up for my beliefs I'm not coming any more. He replied, but you must, to help prevent this sort of thing happening at all. And so I stayed.' They were married soon after, and their daughter Kätle was born in 1927. At the time they met, Haag was also the youngest Communist MP in the Württemberg Regional Government. He was well-known as a prominent enemy of Nazism, and he was arrested the day after Hitler came to power. There followed seven and a half years of prison for him, in Kühberg, Dachau and Mauthausen.

They could have got away. She had a relative in Buenos Aires who was willing to pay her fare over there. As the clouds gathered, in 1929, they made the decision to go. She would travel first, and Fred and Kätle would follow. Once she was there, however, Haag began to have second thoughts, to worry about abandoning the party at a time when it most needed him. Finally, he wrote to her to say he was not going to join her. Lina was alone, and had no money. Her relatives could not afford to pay her fare back home. She worked as a housemaid and saved. After two and a half years she was able to return to Germany, and did so.

They were not reunited for long. Almost as soon as she was back, he left her to travel on party business. Her faith and loyalty were unshaken. Then he was arrested. 'That night I heard the neighbours shouting, "At last they've picked up that bloody drunkard." I couldn't understand it. Ours was a small town; everyone knew everyone else, and knew that Fred was all but teetotal. How blind people could become to the truth, and how fast – it was staggering.'

Her own arrest followed soon after. She was imprisoned in Gotteszell, in Stuttgart, and finally in the women's concentration camp of Lichtenburg-Torgau. Her crime was that she was Haag's wife and had acted as his secretary, since at the time he couldn't afford to employ one. 'That was the extent of my political work – arrest and persecution politicized me.' In all, she was arrested and released three times; an attempt was made to trick her into collaboration; she was threatened with death, subjected to imprisonment in a 'dark' cell, and to two years' solitary confinement. During the whole period, she had two major concerns: for her husband's safety, and that she should not lose contact completely with her daughter, who lived with her parents. In her cell once she was served buckling; she kept and dried the smoked fish-skin, and with it made a pair of golden shoes for her daughter's doll.

Following her release, her first job was to see what could be done about freeing her husband. She had found out that Haag had been transferred to Mauthausen, and that his arch-enemy, the Nazi *Reichs-statthalter* of Württemberg, Murr, had sworn that he would never leave the KZ alive. Lina made her way to Berlin and managed to find herself a humble job in a metalworks.

She rented a room for herself and her daughter, and managed to get something for them both to eat almost every day. By then she had started to pay visits to SS headquarters in the Prinz-Albrecht-Strasse, patiently filling in a request form to see Himmler every day, no matter how regularly the request was refused. 'They must have thought I was quite mad – I'd been to SS HQ nine or ten times and filled in the request form each time – everything was frightfully correct – but of course they laughed in my face. They actually called me the Madwoman.

'Finally my luck changed. One of Himmler's adjutants, a Major Suchanek, decided to put in a word for me. I don't know why. Perhaps he sensed that I was fighting for my life, or perhaps he had enough imagination to see what the interview meant to me – perhaps he even had a human heart under that loathsome uniform. But he told me he'd ask the *Reichsführer* if he'd see me. I waited, heart in mouth, unable to believe it and trying to organize my thoughts in case the unthinkable happened. Suchanek emerged from the inner office and said, "The *Reichsführer* will see you."

'A moment later I was seated opposite Himmler. Suchanek stood by the desk. The *Reichsführer* was a wretched little man – he looked like a weak little clerk. I suppose he must have been 39 years old at the time. He gave me a small, polite smile as the major briefly filled him in on my request. "I want you to set my husband free," I blurted out, baldly. I wondered if he could read in my eyes how anxious I was for Fred. "I remember," said Himmler. "It's that business concerning Murr and the Communist MP, isn't it?" "Exactly, *Reichsführer*," said the major. Himmler kept looking at me; his look was not unfriendly. "Are you a Communist too?" he asked me. "Yes," I said. He smiled briefly and exchanged a quick glance with Suchanek. "At least you're honest," he said, "I'll give you that." I didn't know what I was saying. I rather heard myself say: "We're as honest as everyone else. Being a Communist doesn't automatically mean one's a yob." "We have found differently," said Himmler. "And how, *Reichsführer*!" added the major. I felt as if I were in a dream. "We fought for an ideal," I said. "Well, I hope that now you see that it was a false ideal," replied Himmler. "I fought for what I believed was right and good, as did my husband." Himmler looked at me sharply now. "I see, and now you want me to let him go, so that you can go on fighting for what you believe is right and good, eh?" I didn't answer, but I met his gaze.

'He stood up, and I did too. His manner was distinctly cooler. "Good," he said briefly. "I'll look into it." "Thank you," I said, stupidly. I knew I had made a complete mess of things. I'd be lucky not to end up in the camps again myself.

'But once we were outside, Suchanek said to me: "You made a good impression on him." "And the rest," I said.'

Eight days later, Lina Haag had a phone-call at work. Fred had been released and brought to Berlin. She should go at once to the Prinz-Albrecht-Strasse and collect him.

There followed a year together, almost the first uninterrupted year they had had since they were married. During it, Lina studied to be a physiotherapist. She completed a two-year course in six months and qualified. Then Germany attacked Russia, and Fred was called up – not to a fighting regiment but, because of his dubious past, to a pioneer corps. Nevertheless they were separated again. They were not to be together again permanently until 1948.

She continued to work as a physiotherapist in Berlin until towards the end of the war, when the city began to be heavily bombed, and after having temporarily lost Kätle in an air-raid she became frightened for her daughter's safety and applied for a posting away from the capital. She was detailed to a hospital for wounded soldiers at Garmisch-Partenkirchen, not far from Munich. There she was to remain for the rest of the war, and there she wrote her book, secretly, at night, to keep her loneliness at bay.

Liberation came on 2 May 1945.

'I moved from Garmisch to Munich as soon as I could. I didn't have the courage to go back to Schwäbisch-Gmünd. It was a little town and I'd seen how under the Nazis people turned into monsters overnight: in their attitude to the Jews, to political opponents of Nazism, and anyone else who didn't conform. People practically spat at me in the streets – until the tide of the war turned, when they began to smile again. But in one way I was lucky: Kätle never turned against me, and we are still very close. I remember a comrade in the KZ crying most bitterly. I asked her what the matter was, and she said she'd had a letter from her son, cursing her for being a political prisoner. Because of her, he couldn't join the SA, and so he said that he wouldn't be seeing her again. It would be better if she died, he wrote. But that was the way children were encouraged to behave in those days.

'I was greatly tempted to leave Germany after the war, but my parents were still here, and I couldn't leave them. They were old, and they had looked after Kätle all the time. At least I never went back to Schwäbisch-Gmünd, not to live. I am a small-town woman, but since the war I have always felt better in a biggish city like Munich, where it is possible to lose oneself in the crowd. So I stayed here, still working as a physiotherapist in private practice. My first clients were American officers, who paid me in cocoa, lard, sugar, things like that. I also started work with the VVN immediately – there was much practical and moral help to be given to comrades. Then there was the heavenly day when Fred came home.

'In the meantime my book had come out, and at the 1948 Frankfurt Writers' Congress I was asked to make a speech – something I had never done in my life before; but I didn't duck out of it, because I really thought people ought to know what went on in the Third Reich. My theme was "Women and Pacifism". The thought of another war that could start today or tomorrow fills me with horror, I said; but every writer has a powerful weapon: the means to write a book and, through it, to denounce war and persuade people against it. I remember sitting helpless outside the cell door of my friend Lilo Hermann after she had been condemned to death; but now I can write, speak, cry out.'

She and Alfred were lucky in their relationship. They found that they had not grown apart despite all the years of separation. 'We were all right in every aspect of our relationship; even in bed we were fine. It was as if being apart had made us even keener to be together. Since his return in 1948 we were never apart again, and we had a strong and happy relationship. He died in 1983. Every day since he died hurts as much as the first, now that I am working alone [for the first and only time during our conversation she cries hard]. It doesn't matter . . . It's life.

'I am an absolute realist, and I live with both feet firmly on the ground, so I seek no mystical explanation for what happened, and I try to live in the present and for the future. But when I hear some thug today on the tram crack a joke like, "How many Jews can you get into a Volkswagen? – You can get 30 into the ashtray . . ." then I stand up and hit him in the face. If no one else objects, then *I* do it, because normally absolutely no one objects. They just bury their heads in their papers, like people do the world over. The swine who cracks jokes like that was never in a KZ, doesn't know what a KZ was, and deserves to be hit so that he never tells a joke like that again. Apart from that reaction, I live a normal, quiet life. I talk about the KZ when people show an interest in it and ask me about it, and I try to discuss it in a positive way. There is no sense in negativity: that is letting *them* win. But the memory never fades, not ever, and one becomes more vulnerable and more suspicious of any kind of joke, like when someone sees an obvious Jew in the street and says loudly, "There goes one they forgot to gas." They say it without knowing what they're saying, just to be clever; but I hear it and my stomach knots.

'I know what jokes like that can lead to. I have seen so much. I knew a Jewess, Olga Benario-Prestes, a wonderful girl, who was pregnant when they arrested her, and she had her baby in the prison in Moabit in Berlin, and the SS said to her, "You can keep it as long as you have milk to give it." That was their idea of a joke. And she knew that that wouldn't be long because they gave her so little to eat; and they knew it too, and kept threatening her, and she managed for ages to plead that she still had milk, and every time they wanted proof that she had.

'People don't believe that kind of story when I tell them, and so I am tempted to stop; but I go on. When I'm invited to go and meet people – often women teachers from state schools – I accept, and I tell them, I can't make a speech; I don't give lectures; but if you've read my book you know my life, and as long as I am alive I will answer your questions. And I answer every question, whatever it is, however hard, honestly.'

A Home in Israel

While Israel provided a new home for many tens of thousands of refugees from the wreckage of the Jewish communities in Europe after the war, there was no question of their finding, in this new land with its wholly un-European language, landscape and climate, a way to resurrect the way of life they had left, whether as sophisticated urban assimilated Jew or as little *shtetl* tradesman.

Many of the survivors I spoke to in Israel did miss their native language, and missed the European climate and European scenery – especially mountains and snow, and the colour green – more than any broader cultural aspects. My impression was that although they saw themselves as Israelis, they also remembered themselves as Europeans.

I

Hadassa Modlinger is now Custodian of Testimonies at Yad Vashem, the museum, memorial and research centre devoted to the Holocaust in Jerusalem. She was born in 1930 in Zdunska Wola, about 30 kilometres south-west of Lodz in Poland, where her parents ran a small shoe factory. She was the middle one of three sisters. Her elder sister went through the camps with her and survived. Her younger sister perished at Chelmno, aged six.

The family remained in the Zdunska Wola ghetto until 1942. 'In the ghetto *Hashomer Hatzair* [a left-wing Zionist youth organization] were active, and there were lectures on Palestine. I was about ten at the time, and was very deeply influenced by it. After the war I simply knew that the only place for us was Palestine, and I didn't even consider anywhere else. If I'd had the chance of going to the USA I would have turned it down. I always wanted to come here and I don't regret it.'

In 1942 the two older sisters and their parents were transferred to the ghetto in Lodz by train. Though the distance was short, the journey was so dreadful that Hadassa's mother died of suffocation during it. They stayed together in the ghetto until it was liquidated in 1944 and they were sent to Auschwitz, where the girls were separated from their father.

'We were there for two weeks only, because by then the fortunes of war had turned against Germany, and they needed labour. My sister and I were sent to a munitions factory near Berlin.'

They worked in the factory until February 1945, when they were sent to Sachsenhausen, and then on to Ravensbrück. Liberation came on 28 April 1945, as the sisters joined the first white bus transport of Count Folke Bernadotte. After a two-day break-of-journey in Denmark, they were taken on to Sweden, where they were examined for typhoid, typhus and other illnesses, and sent to hospitals for treatment. Thereafter they spent six months convalescing, though no psychological help was given them. 'It certainly wasn't necessary for us. You see, we were so young still that we quickly adapted back when people were kind to us. At least, we thought we did. My feeling is that we were too young at the time to really understand what had happened to us. It was only later, with time, that we began to understand it. At the time we were just happy that we were alive, that we'd got through.

'Not long after our arrival in Sweden we were approached by one of the Zionist youth organizations. They were working with all the survivor groups, doing welfare work and organizing schooling. We were taken to a DP camp near Stockholm, where we started school. It was then that the truth of what had happened to us and to our family started to sink in. A little later we heard that our father had survived and was back in Poland, but we didn't want to go back there. We didn't see any future for us there, and we were already under the influence of the Zionists: our aim was to come here. Most of our youth group made the illegal *aliyah*, but my sister and I moved to Lund in the south and stayed another year. Our father had moved to Belgium by then, and there was a chance that we might at least see him. In the meantime my sister had met a Jewish boy and we moved to Landskrona so that she could be near him. We worked in a factory there, but neither of us had any intention of settling in Sweden permanently. I never wanted to stay there. They were very kind to us but they never really made us feel that we belonged. I was there for five years, and I learnt the language and absorbed the culture; but I never felt at home there. Also, the reception by the Jewish community was as frosty as I've heard it was in the United Kingdom. They didn't even give us charity. The Gentile Swedes were much nicer to us than the Swedish Jews. Why? They're in the Diaspora and they've got a complex about being Jewish. They are always on the defensive.

'My decision to come here wasn't coloured by faith, or even by politics. It was a reaction purely of the heart. I wanted to live with my people, to be at home. I didn't want to live in the Diaspora any more. How the country was here, what it was like, didn't matter. I had to come here and help build it. I didn't want to be anywhere where people would call me a Jew and take the attitude that I wasn't one of their nation because of that, but merely a guest.'

They came to Israel in November 1949 via Marseilles and Monte Carlo.

'When we arrived in Jerusalem it was much better than I'd imagined it, much less primitive; but you know how it is when you are 20; nothing frightens you. The first thing to do was find work and get money to live on. We rented a room for ourselves – it was very difficult to get accommodation in those days, and worse since we didn't speak the language, but I got a job in a cafeteria and went to Hebrew classes in the evenings. Time passed, I met my husband, who had come over here as a student in 1935, and I got a job with the Post Office. Then in 1955 I came to work at Yad Vashem, and I've been here ever since.

'I've never talked about the KZ with my husband. I've never felt the need. I do dream though, and certain things can trigger memories. I was very ill when I first arrived here, but I had to overcome it simply because I couldn't afford to be sick. The result of that was that after I'd married, in 1951, and I could afford to relax a little because there wasn't such a pressing need to work, I got sick in earnest. It was my lungs – a legacy of the camps. In fact they had discovered that I was ill in Sweden, but they decided to let me go. Maybe they thought the climate here would help. It was TB, not dangerous, but it needed attention. It lasted two years, and I couldn't work for three. It was during that time that the nightmares and bad feelings came, probably because I was physically so weak. I didn't think about it during the day, but at night, all the thoughts which I had kept at bay for so long – not perhaps consciously, but because I had been so busy – came crowding in upon me. And it is still the same if I am unwell today.

'When I was ten they killed ten people in our town. It wasn't far from the house and I saw it. The picture is always with me, because one of the ones they hanged was the father of my best friend. I happened to be looking out of the kitchen window of my house here once and glimpsed something, maybe a piece of washing, hanging out on a roof across the way; but I saw that man hanging there; and now, every time I look out of my kitchen window, I see him again. Despite the good life we have now, we can't forget it. It's not logical, but there is nothing we can do about it. On the other hand, working here at Yad Vashem doesn't bother me, even though I am surrounded by constant reminders. One is so steeped in the subject, one's soul is so imbued with the KZ, that working here makes no difference. Certainly you come into contact with things that hurt you, often; but you can't stop the hurt, and in a way you don't want to. People went through so much, so many people died, my family died; what does it matter if I have to suffer a bit because I work at Yad Vashem? In a sense you could say that I am trying to make something positive out of the sadness: if positive is the word. I don't know if you can use such a word in relation to the Holocaust.

'I am not so much worried as energized by Israel's position. We know that we have to do everything necessary to survive and to confirm our position here. I have certainly never been afraid to live here, though when they did their military service I was afraid for my children. For myself, never. Death comes to us all, and it will come to me, too. Why should I be afraid of that? Survivors in the Diaspora have sometimes been frightened when anti-Semitism has raised its head again and they have wondered where to run to next. At least I don't have that problem! I think people in the Diaspora cannot have the sense of belonging that I have here. Only Jews who live in Israel can really say, "This is my country." I'm not criticizing the Jews who still live in the Diaspora, if that's what they want; I am just saying that I would not want to any more, and I have just said why. Israel is my home. What it was before doesn't matter, and what I was before doesn't matter. I go back to Poland pretty regularly to consult and collect documentation, and the language comes back and I think in Polish, but it seems like a strange land; or, rather, just another country that I visit in the course of my work. I didn't have good feelings at being back there, if I had any feelings at all.'

II

The Jews did not go passively to their fate. They attempted by every means born of long experience of persecution to escape it, and where they could, with virtually no outside help, they fought it.

Dov Levin was born Berl Levin in Kovno (Kaunas), Lithuania, in 1925, where he grew up and was given a Jewish education. His family were convinced Zionists, and he grew up speaking Hebrew and Yiddish. He took to the national language quickly and by the age of nine was writing postcards in Hebrew to relatives in Tel Aviv.

He finished his school studies on 21 June 1941, the day before Hitler invaded the USSR. Following the German advance and the establishment of a ghetto in Kovno, he and his family were immured there. 'We were together until the end of October 1943, when my parents and my twin sister, Bakia, were rounded up in a *selection*. I'd managed to hide because I'd been warned, but not in time to warn them. I never saw my family again. Later I learned that they had all died in the camps; my mother and sister in Stutthof.'

He took refuge with the underground, in a cell organized by *Hashomer Hatzair,* and remained with them until January 1944, when he escaped into the forests around Kovno and successfully joined the partisan group *'Death to the Invaders',* which was made up of a mixed group of Lithuanian resistance fighters, both Jewish and Gentile, and escaped Russian POWs. He fought with the partisans until July, when the Russian army advanced into their area of activity, and their group was absorbed into it. In Russian uniform, he was able to join in sweeping the Germans out of his homeland. But his thoughts were on another homeland by then. Already prepared by his Zionist upbringing, his purpose to go to Israel was sharpened by the Jewish commander of his partisan group, Abba Kovner, who not only inspired but effectively ordered the young Jews in his unit to make the *aliyah* once it became possible to do so.

Returning to Kovno as victors, they found little to tempt them to remain. 'When we heard of the liberation of the town, we rushed there as soon as we could. Each of us went to his house with a pounding heart. Mine was at Mildos 7. All that was left was a pile of rubble and burnt brick, and the house-number on its white enamel plaque, lying shining among the ruins like a memorial.' In his diary, he wrote: 'Who will release us from this pain in our hearts, from the loneliness and destruction that cry out to us from every street-corner, every stone?'

In mid-January 1945, Levin began his long journey south to Palestine. It would take him ten months.[1]

Armed with documents declaring him to be on his way to Rumania to buy dried fruit, and with the names of a number of contacts *en route* together with identifying passwords, he left Vilno (Vilnius) on 17 January in his Russian uniform, which he discarded soon after. His plan was to cross Rumania and pick up a boat on the Black Sea coast, and he reached Cluj *en route* for Bucharest on 10 March. 'I couldn't find a seat on the train to the capital, but when a Rumanian army colonel left his seat to go to the lavatory, I took it. Of course he wasn't very pleased when he got back, but I thought as a former Axis soldier he was fair game. Then he started to swear at me for being Jewish, and I wasn't having any more of that. I called to some Russian soldiers along the carriage for help, and together we threw the colonel out of the window.'

He arrived in Bucharest to find a thriving Jewish community which made him most welcome; despite several months of effort, however, he was unable to continue his journey to the Black Sea. He retraced his steps to Cluj and from there travelled by train (including one 48-hour stage of the journey huddled on a carriage roof) to Budapest.

He then made his way west and south to Italy, smuggling himself across the final frontier out of Austria, and made contact with the Jewish Brigade,[2] getting himself registered as a potential emigrant. While he waited for further orders, he wrote an article describing the fate of the Kovno ghetto for the Palestinian paper *Al HaMishmar*.

He was in Italy for three months, and at the beginning of October was transferred to the secret camp operated by the *Haganah* – the (initially secret) Jewish nationalist army of defence – at Dror near the south-eastern port of Bari. There, under strict military conditions, 180 Jews were prepared to make the *aliyah* as *maapilim* (illegal immigrants). On 15 October Levin boarded the tiny *Pietro II* – 'she was about four times the size of an average room' – with 170 others, and set sail for Eretz Israel.

'I had an image of being reborn in the belly of the ship. She anchored on the night of 23 October off the coast near Rishpon [Herzlia Pituach] and we waited for the signal from the shore that it was safe to disembark. When it came, we were taken off in groups of ten in small boats, which rowed us to about 50 metres from the shore, where a reception committee were waiting to carry us to the beach. I was carried by a young woman – and she insisted, despite my embarrassed assurances that I could perfectly easily swim! Once ashore, we were registered. We'd been terribly thirsty on the *Pietro*, and I remember plucking a grapefruit and eating it whole – my first food grown in Israel. It was a small moment, but for me it was symbolic.

'We were taken to Givat Han, a *moshav*[3] near Raanana, where a family named Fruchter put me up for what remained of the night. They gave me fresh clothes and a chance to wash away the dirt of our voyage which had been exciting, but hardly pleasant. Later, on 24 October, we all had to assemble at *Haganah* headquarters, and I was assigned to *kibbutz* Maanit as I had been a member of *Hashomer Hatzair*. That night the *kibbutz* held a welcoming party for the new arrivals. It really felt like a homecoming.'

Two days later he was moved to *kibbutz* Beit Zera, where he worked as a watchman for a year. For the six months following that, he travelled, looking up friends made in Europe and establishing links with those of his family who already lived in Palestine. He arrived in Jerusalem in April 1947, and once again took a job as a watchman. In the autumn he enrolled at the Hebrew University, and during the siege of Jerusalem the following spring he was among those who guarded the university campus on Mount Scopus. In July 1948 he joined a fighting unit of the *Palmach* (the 'commando' arm of the *Haganah*), in which he served until the end of the War of Independence, starting as a private and ending as a sergeant-major with a scout unit. When he was demobbed at the end of 1949, he completed his studies, and in 1951 qualified as a social worker, a job he worked at for 20 years. He married in 1951, and now has three children and a grandchild. When he left the social service, he entered academic life and is now a historian specializing in the recent history of Lithuanian Jewry.

'I think one of the most important elements of my survival was that from the moment my family was taken away when I was 16 to the moment I arrived in Palestine I was with a small, united group – what we call a primary group in sociology. This helped me to get through, to overcome my sorrow, and through all the hard times that were to come. All of us in the group came from the same cultural, class and political background. There was no time to brood, either. We had to stay on our toes every minute in the resistance, and when it was over we had to get busy organizing the forged documents we would need to cross Europe and come here. Coming from such a convinced Zionist background, there was virtually no decision for me to make. I would almost certainly have come here even if the war hadn't happened. Even so, I have to say that everything seemed like paradise after the Germans had gone. At the time, I don't think I'd even have minded being arrested by the Russians. Of course, they were saviours, and I didn't know about the *Gulag* then.

'During the occupation, the Lithuanians behaved very badly. A very few helped us, but they were a tiny minority; most collaborated happily with the Germans, though I must say that after Stalingrad there was a change in attitude. That is why it became much easier for those in hiding and with the partisans after 1943. The most hellish time was during 1941. The Lithuanians were collaborating very fully with the Germans then because they thought Germany would give Lithuania its independence back, and they were angry with the Jews, many of whom had worked in the Russian administration of the country.

'It was a tremendous thing to be a partisan, in that you could really express your resistance to German tyranny. I think being able to express that, and the knowledge that you didn't have to take their treatment lying down, gave us all a tremendous psychological boost. But it wasn't easy, and such a course was not open to every Jew by any means. To operate successfully, partisans needed the tacit support of the villages in the countryside where they operated, so that a food supply was assured and they could be more or less confident of not being betrayed.

'Adapting to living in Israel after the war was not a problem, and I was still very young, only 20, with a whole life ahead of me. And I was convinced that here was where I wanted to be. Don't forget, too, that I still had the support of my primary group. We all came here together, and we were allocated to the same *kibbutzim*. It was two years before the last of us went our own ways, and of course we stayed in close touch. We were like a small tribe, if you like; but we weren't surrounded by enemies any more – on the contrary, people here could not have been kinder to us. Everything was laid on for us, right down to toothpaste! We were treated like refugees from hell, and greeted like old friends – everybody wanted to hear our story. That was very reassuring and made us forget that it was a new country. It never felt "new" in that sense, or strange. Also, everything was organized for us – we were sent on induction courses about the country, and we had counsellors who looked after us. The other great advantage our small group had was that we could all speak Hebrew already. I took to this country like a duck to water. We knew many things about Israel from the Zionist groups in Lithuania, and we had seen postcards and photographs, so there wasn't a great difference between what I had visualized and what it was really like. It was better, if anything – certainly more advanced agriculturally than I had imagined; and, even though people were still living in tents, things seemed more civilized here than in Lithuania, and more modern – the city buildings, the buses, the telephone system – everything! I remember how clean and modern the *kibbutz* dining-room was, and I remember people dancing *horas* around bonfires at night! Of course we had no papers when we arrived: no papers, no past. They gave us *Haganah* registration papers. Official Israeli nationality came after independence, but it came automatically for us; I had already fought for independence, and then against the Arabs. The main thing is that Israel exists, and I am confident that she will continue to exist. I am an old fighter and my country's embattled situation does not make me anxious for her future.

'I think I have managed to make up for my missing years, certainly as far as education is concerned – I was lucky to have the opportunities that were offered me here. If I feel bitter at all, it is about the atrocities which were committed against us, and I still haven't forgiven the Lithuanian collaborators. In fact, my anger against them is greater than my anger against the Germans. I do not go to Germany myself, but I could conceive of going there. However, I certainly won't until the generation of the Third Reich has died out: I wouldn't like to run the risk, which is theoretically possible, of meeting the killers of my family. But the Lithuanians are worse, because the Germans couldn't have managed without them. For every German, back there and back then, there were 100 Lithuanians. Even before the *Einsatzgruppen* arrived, the Lithuanians were carrying out their own "actions" against the Jews.

'But I do not carry my hostility beyond the generation that did it: the children of the killers, even, would be welcome as my guests here in Jerusalem. They are not guilty of their parents' crimes. The revisionists worry me, which is why in my own studies I concentrate on facts before theories: names, places, dates; these must be unequivocally documented. It is hard, though, for the victims to have the onus of proof placed upon them.

'Immediately after the war I thought that all the good people in the world would never allow anything remotely similar to happen again, but since that time, with Vietnam, Biafra, Kampuchea . . . and Stalin's *Gulag* . . . How do we educate our children? I am a Jew, and I do not know how to educate my own students or my own children: must I tell them that they have to be soldiers and learn how to use guns, how to kill people? At the same time, of course, I do not want to see Israel overrun by the Arabs, for the very obvious reason that a new Holocaust might follow. But I don't hate the Arabs like I hate the Lithuanians. It would be nice to foresee peaceful co-existence and even mutual aid in the future. As for younger Israelis, ones who have grown up in an independent state, I think there is a tendency for them to be too militaristic – it's certainly true of my three children, and I have to remind them that their grandparents were devoted to internationalism, not nationalism.'

III

Feliciya Karay was born in Cracow in the late 1920s.

'I was the youngest of six children. My parents weren't especially rich, they ran a small business – we were *Kleinbürger*: a simple, happy family living in peace despite the strong anti-Semitism that existed in Poland. At home we spoke Yiddish and German – in Galicia a lot of German was still spoken because it had been part of the old Austro-Hungarian Empire. Some of the older Jews spoke only German, and my father had been in the Austrian army in the First World War. We were an assimilated family; we went to the Polish schools and we spoke Polish to the people. We weren't terribly religious, though we celebrated the main Holy Days, and we were exceptional really because Cracow had a Jewish population of about 60,000 and most of them were very observant. There was a Jewish quarter, though it wasn't a ghetto, and we didn't live in it or even near it, but in the city centre. We kids thought ourselves as much Polish as Jewish, and the only problem we had as Jews was with the *numerus clausus*; my older brother and sister could only be admitted to the Jagellonian University to read law.

'I was in my sixth class at school when the war broke out. For the first year we were still in Cracow, but then Hans Frank established a ghetto. Later it was decreed that some Jews should be deported away from the town, and we found ourselves sent to Brzesko Nowe, on the Vistula, about 45 kilometres from Cracow. It was made into a kind of overspill ghetto, with a *Judenrat* and an *Ordnungsdienst*; but it was not big. There might have been slightly more than 5,000 Jews there. We children had to work, but our parents couldn't, because they were too old. They managed to get by doing a little business on the side, selling some bolts of cloth they had brought with them; but of course there was a finite amount to sell, and when everything was gone there was even less to eat. We were sealed off until spring 1942, and had no idea what was happening in the *Generalgouvernement*. That spring, the first transports of Jews left District Cracow.[4] The transports went to Belzec. After a time we began to hear whispers through the grapevine of what was going on, originating with those very few people who managed to get away. But no one believed the tales we heard, and it was the same story in every ghetto: who could believe such horrors? There was no precedent for it in history either.

'But something was going on, and whatever it was wasn't pleasant. The question was, what to do? It was possible to buy Aryan certificate papers; but they cost a fortune, and we hadn't much money; also we had no contacts with the underworld sellers or the resistance, because we were just ordinary people. But other Jews were much worse off. They looked very Jewish, or they spoke only Yiddish, or Polish with a strong Yiddish accent.

'As for running away to the woods, that was impossible because the whole area was treeless – there was no cover; and in such a small place as Brzesko Nowe it was impossible to build a hide-out without someone knowing about it. At least for the time being we could count ourselves lucky. The whole family was still together, except for a sister who had gone to the Cracow ghetto, and my brother. He had bought false papers from a Pole, and with them he later managed to go to Germany with his wife and small daughter as an ordinary Polish workman. The family all looked like pure Gentile Poles, and spoke the language perfectly. At the time they were living as Gentile Poles, waiting to be recruited for labour in Germany.

'At the end of November came the *Aussiedlung* [compulsory evacuation]. The SS came with a list and rooted out the Jews. But we fled. We had contacts among the Polish farmers in the locality through my father's work. One took my parents in, and the children scattered like birds – I went with two older sisters to an old barracks near the Vistula where a number of kids were already holing up, and we stayed a week. We couldn't stay longer because Poland in November is very cold, and we had nothing to eat. We decided to split up and I set off alone.'

She asks for a word – *Bricha* (meaning the flight of the Jews to Palestine) – and explains that as she still thinks in a mixture of Polish and German, together with Hebrew, it's a bit difficult sometimes: the right word in the right language just won't dovetail. She explains that the book she is currently writing is in Hebrew, from Polish sources.

'During my flight I stayed with a succession of Polish families – a night here and a night there, for to stay would have been to compromise them, even if they'd let me . . . I finally made my way to where my brother was staying – he had not yet left for Germany – where I spent a week hiding in a chest. There were some tense moments; they had little furniture, and the chest doubled as a seat; so that when the neighbours dropped in, they might well sit on my hiding-place. By a long route I managed to reach the Cracow ghetto in December, and I joined my sister there. We stayed until the following March, when the ghetto was liquidated. The younger ones among us were transported to the KZ Plaszow, and there my sister and I were united with a third sister; having that sense of family was terribly important to us and, I think, a major factor in our ability to survive. I had some more luck, too: I got a job in the kitchens. "In the pub", as we used to say! The food wasn't good but at least I could organize a little more of it for my sisters.

'We stayed in Plaszow until 16 November 1943, when they took 4,000 Jews from the main and sub-camps to District Radom. 1,500 of us were sent to the Forced-Labour Camp (*Zwangsarbeitslager*) Skarzysko-Kamienna. The concern we were working for was HASAG – Hugo Schneider AG, of Leipzig. In 1939, HASAG took over the former Polish munitions factories at Skarzysko-Kamienna. There had only been Polish workers there until 1941, apart from a few Jewish craftsmen. Only in 1942 were Jews put on the production line, and by then Germany needed all the labour she could muster: most of her own able-bodied men were in the armed forces. At HASAG 12,000 Jews were employed, of whom 6,000 died.

'We stayed until the end of June 1944, and we were then evacuated to Leipzig, Schönefeld. It was impossible to sabotage the work. All the stuff you read in Polish memoirs about the great amount of sabotage that went on is wishful thinking, I'm afraid. HASAG was also the only firm out of all of them that kept on exploiting Jews right to the bitter end. Do you know that at the end of the war there were seven and a half million foreign workers in Germany? Every fourth bullet was made by such a worker, and there was no organized resistance. People were too terrified.

'We were in Leipzig in a women's camp until April 1945. Women make better munitions workers than men because their hands are finer for the fiddly work. We were all mixed up together, women from all over Europe. 13,000 of us. At least we had water to wash in – there was no such luxury in Skarzysko-Kamienna. And actually in the factory camp in Leipzig there was a very strong cultural life. The Germans tolerated it, and it did a lot to keep our morale up.

'That all came to an end when we were evacuated. We were

force-marched south for two weeks, during which time we ate once, although from time to time we were able to dig the odd potato or turnip out of a field. I don't want to tell you too much about it though, because I want to sleep tonight. Our SS-guards were exhausted too, and the Russians and the Americans were on our heels. We arrived at a barn. The SS said that if we didn't get up and keep going in the morning, they would burn the place down with us inside; but in fact they ran away in the night. By then they were more frightened than we were, and their main concern was to get rid of their uniforms before the Russians caught them. We stayed in our barn until we were sure the coast was clear, and then we came out in search of food. There was a village nearby, but it was deserted, and there was no food there. Most of the Germans had fled towards the Americans because they were so terrified of what the Russians would do to them. One thing I'll never forget is that a friend of mine and I managed to crawl into what we thought was a deserted farmhouse in search of bread. There was an elderly German peasant there – a sort of grandfather-type; and do you know what he did? He picked up a bit of wood and started to beat us.

'After 8 May, we decided we'd better try to get home to Poland. We didn't know what had happened to our parents and the rest of our family, though we three sisters were still together. It was especially difficult for girls travelling on their own; but we got a lift on a waggon, paying our fare with lard, and then on the roof of a passenger train – inside would have been too dangerous: Russians soldiers in the wrong mood would rape girls indiscriminately.

'We got back to Cracow in May, where we found my two other sisters; and we learnt that our parents had died in the camps. We also learnt that my brother who managed to get away to Germany had gone on the first ship to America with his family. He wrote to me later that I should join him, but I refused – I wanted to come here to *Palestina*.

'There were tough times in Cracow then. We sisters were still together, but we'd lost our old flat for ever, and the Poles were far from welcoming. We found a room about the size of a large wardrobe, and sought help from UNRRA and the JOINT. We got castoffs to wear and food from them.

'My first job was to finish my education. I went back to my old *Gymnasium*, where my old teachers still were, and managed to do a two-year course compressed into one, so I did my *matura* in one year. I couldn't have done it without the help of my older sisters. It was during that year though that I joined *Hashomer Hatzair* and came under the influence of Zionism.

'The most important thing emotionally for me about *Hashomer Hatzair* was that in it I found a second family. My sisters were much older than me, and they were busy getting married and moving away.

There were plenty of us – young orphans in their late teens, essentially, with nowhere to go. *Hashomer Hatzair* organized camping trips for us into the countryside, and on those trips we talked a lot about *Palestina* ... But at the same time I wanted to continue my education. I was book-hungry. I wanted to go to university and do French and History, but after completing my *matura* I became very ill, and I was laid up for six months – problems with my lungs, blood-clots – the legacy of the camps. But I was young, and they put me in a sanatorium, and I recovered. I was ill from November 1946 until May 1947, by which time the university had closed its doors. So one way was blocked.

'My sisters wondered if I wouldn't like to try for a career in the theatre; I'd done a lot of amateur stuff, reciting and so forth, in the camps, especially in Leipzig. The Germans liked our concerts and came to them. *Why* they did is another question. Bored? Unable to see that the sub-human vermin that had to be destroyed were the same as the human beings who entertained them so well?

'I had done theatre with *Hashomer Hatzair*, too, and I thought my sisters might be on to something. I got a place in the drama school and studied there for a year, but during that time I did not lose my links with *Hashomer*, and in time I was put in charge of all its cultural activities in Poland. To complicate matters a little, I had married in the meantime, and was sharing the work with my husband. He was also a Polish Jew, who had lost all his family in the camps. So many of us were young and alone – and wanted families. Marriages happened very fast, although for us it was hardly family life, since as soon as I'd finished my year's course at drama school we had to travel around. We moved to Lodz in 1948 and used it as our base until 1949. By then we'd had enough of living out of suitcases. We decided that the time had come to emigrate to Palestine, my husband arriving there six months before I could.

'I must say Israel seemed very foreign to me at first, though I knew a lot about it in theory from *Hashomer Hatzair* and from my husband's letters. But I didn't feel completely at sea. I didn't come alone. A very large number of *Hashomer Hatzair* came at the same time, and we are still in touch. In fact we live in a very close-knit group. We have reunions at least three times a year – a party, so that we can catch up, and keep tabs on each other. It's like an extended family, and it's important for all of us, since few of us have any real family left. Of my own sisters, one is here, one is in Sweden. The oldest is now dead, and one lives, like my brother, in America.

'The worst thing in Israel was learning Hebrew. My husband had learnt it in Jewish schools in Poland, so it went better for him. We didn't have any money, but my husband had already established himself in a *kibbutz* in the north. I joined him there, but we only stayed a year;

he had a PhD in chemistry and in those days there was no work for a man with his qualifications in a *kibbutz*; today of course it would be different. He wanted to do what he was trained for and I wanted to go on learning. The *kibbutz* was a little limiting.

'So we moved to Haifa for a short time. Life was very hard; often we had only bread to eat, and we rented one small room with a family. I went to the *ulpan*, which was a special school for crash Hebrew courses for the *olim*. I didn't learn much! I found a job in a library in Haifa which I loved.

'We stayed about 18 months, but we had no money to buy or even rent a proper flat. Then my husband found a new job teaching chemistry at the Mikve Israel Agricultural College, near Tel Aviv. We moved there, and two years later I gave birth to girl twins. We had no refrigerator, no washing machine; but we did have our own little flat with its own garden. I had to stay at home for three years, but when the girls were old enough to go to kindergarten I suggested to my husband that we'd be better off with a second income. I wanted to work anyway; I'm not a natural housewife; if you came to visit me, you'd be sure of getting some biscuits, but as for a meal . . .! I went to university, to Tel Aviv, and studied for three years, History and Bible Studies – that was really Greek to me, unbelievably hard – but not as hard as Hebrew Studies would have been, for at least I'd read the Bible. All the courses were in Hebrew, just to make life more difficult; but I got my BA and then I started work as a schoolteacher in secondary school, and I worked as a teacher for 28 years.

'I've been to Sweden, but never to America. I've never regretted coming here. I'll tell you frankly, too, that I love to go back to Europe, because the weather and the landscape remind me of childhood; but I would never go back there to live. I am very patriotic. Very patriotic. I know there is a lot wrong here, but it is *our* country.

'My first husband died of cancer, and I was left with my two daughters. Two years later I remarried. My second husband comes from Poland too, except that his part of Poland is now Russia. I spoke to neither of them about my wartime experiences. You see, I thought they'd know all about it anyway, but they didn't – they both spent the war in Russia – they'd got out. And then I didn't want to disturb my family life by introducing the subject. I haven't spoken to my daughters about it either, not at all, though they are both very conscious of the Holocaust. They were curious, and of course they learnt about it at school, and they asked me questions, but I couldn't talk about it and I didn't want to.

'For a long time I didn't dream, though there were dreams in the first years after the war. Then I saw Claude Lanzmann's documentary film *Shoah*, and that triggered a whole succession of new dreams. And there are trains. When I first returned to Europe, I couldn't travel by train. I'm OK now, but then . . . And when I saw the trains in *Shoah* – he uses them as a leitmotif – it brought it all back to me. I couldn't watch the trains.

'I've been back to Germany a couple of times. It's this way with me, and I'm sure most survivors are the same: I'm uncomfortable with Germans of my generation, but I don't mind the young ones. I meet a lot who come to Yad Vashem to study, and I have a little story to tell. I was going through some film material with a young German, and I mentioned to him conversationally that whenever I viewed that kind of material I became worried in case I recognized any of my relatives in it. And he brought me up short by saying, "I know what you mean; I have the same feeling."'

IV

Aviva Unger lives in a beautiful flat in north Tel Aviv.

'I was born in Warsaw, but the family moved to Danzig [Gdansk] because we exported wood to the United Kingdom, in the form of ships' masts in the early days. I come from a Russian background. My grandfather was a timber merchant from Belorussia; my father was born in Kiev. My mother was a Socialist, convinced that mankind could be redeemed only through the dissemination of knowledge. I too have always held the belief that knowledge was important, and that its acquisition for its own sake made you a complete person.

'At home we spoke German, French and Russian in addition to Polish and Yiddish. My grandmother was a very powerful figure who insisted that we speak these three languages purely, with no trace of a Yiddish accent. She was an observant Jewess but, to get on, she felt that her family should keep its Jewish profile low. Later, when she was old and sick, she used to say that God was now punishing her for taking that line.

'Poland is the wasteland where I grew up. I remember lunching after the war at a Polish restaurant in South Kensington, and they caught on that I was originally from Poland when I ordered *kasza*, and pronounced it correctly. I have the impression that all those émigré Poles in London live well and truly in the past. They still use their old titles, though they have ceased to have any meaning for over 40 years, and they continue to dance the mazurka, as it were. I recently revisited Poland and Austria and, coming from Israel where I have lived through five wars since 1945, it was like going into a darkened room – because those countries – especially Poland – haven't moved out of the atmosphere of the war years. It's as if time had stood still. They've never got back to normal life there. But all we survivors are prisoners of our experiences, and if a journalist or a psychiatrist says that any of us has achieved objectivity about our past, then it's bullshit: none of us has . . .

'Poland has always been effectively part of Russia or part of Germany. They find a solidarity in their proud nationalism, however, and they are also bound together by their strong adherence to Roman Catholicism. It's an uncompromising belief, very conservative, passionate and humourless. I fell under the spell of the Roman Catholic Church when I was little. We had brought a servant-girl with us from Russia, and she was very devout. I had the most tremendous crush on her, and she taught me all about the Catholic Church and all the prayers and forms which I learnt in a kind of passionate, uncaring way, because I so loved and admired this girl; and I used to enjoy going to the services. I find the Roman Catholic rite beautiful to this day, and I still love the smell of incense; but my attraction to it was emotional, superstitious, never intellectual. However, my knowledge of it was to be very useful later.

'There was always tension between the Poles and the Jews. The Poles are like the Scots or the Irish – like Celts: proud, a bit unpredictable, emotional, not very good at business, and great drinkers. The Jews didn't drink, and were good at business. Jews employed Polish servants. Jews saved their money and bought houses, did better than Poles, lived in the better streets, had better clothes, and so on. And they made up ten per cent of the population. Also, Jews were Socialists, and supported agrarian reform – don't forget that they weren't allowed to own land. Jews were intellectuals; the only Polish intellectuals were landowners, who were politically unsympathetic to Jewish opinions. In society, the Jews contributed the most successful doctors, lawyers and writers. The most important pre-war poet, Julian Tovin, was a Communist and a Jew. It really wasn't surprising that Poland was such fertile ground for anti-Semitism.

'When the war broke out I was an 11-year-old Warsaw schoolgirl. I was already an orphan, since my father died just before I was born. We were moved to the ghetto a year after Poland's defeat. My mother had given up spiritually: if this was the conclusion of all the culture and education that had made Germany such a country to admire, then what were her own life's beliefs worth? When we came to the ghetto, matters got worse for her, and she had a stroke which left her half-paralysed. She had lost the will to fight. As for me, I continued to go to school in the ghetto, and to the *Gymnasium* there.

'Then one day they shot my mother.

'In 1942 I was able to escape, through the kind action of a Gentile friend of my mother's who had heard what had happened. She smuggled in 100 *zlotys* with which I was able to pay a guide to take me out through the sewers. I was taken to a teaching order of nuns in Warsaw, at the Sacré Coeur convent. I became a pupil of the convent school, and stayed there until Easter 1943 – about the time of the Warsaw Ghetto Uprising. Then, coincidentally, I was recognized on a tram by a Jew who was a police spy, and betrayed to the Gestapo. I then spent four days in the Gestapo HQ where they hit and kicked me ceaselessly to get information out of me about the Jewish resistance. I wasn't yet quite 15. They weren't human, those Gestapo. And don't make the mistake of differentiating between the Germans and the Nazis: all Germans were Nazis.

'I was saved by the Polish priest attached to the convent who came to the HQ and swore that he had personally baptized me as a baby, that he had known my parents, that I came from a long line of Catholics; that I was now an orphan in the convent's care. All this he swore on the Cross, and eventually the Gestapo let me go. But I knew it would be too hot for me to remain in Poland, so I arranged to have myself transported for war work to Germany. However, that was another problem, because a lot of Jews tried to save themselves in that way. On the way I was saved by a Polish prostitute who was on the same transport. We were travelling by ordinary passenger train, and two men – German sailors, I think – started looking at me. I knew they suspected I was a Jewess: two minutes earlier a couple of Jewish girls had been picked off the train and shot. This prostitute said to the sailors, "What are you gawping at my cousin like that for?" "She's your cousin?" "Sure, and she's a virgin. She's no good for you; but if it's a fuck you want, I'm your girl." The sailors left it at that. The prostitute didn't say a word to me directly. Only I could tell by her eyes that she knew.

'When we arrived in Germany, we had to spend four weeks in a transit camp waiting to be allocated work. I had the first serious attacks of TB which I'd contracted in the ghetto. I was frightened that they'd send me back, but I managed to cover up. They sent me to work for a farmer's wife near Stettin [Szczecin], who needed someone to do clerical work for her.

'This lasted from May 1943 until March 1944. The couple had no children, and the husband was a bigwig among the local Nazis. They intended to leave the property to a schoolteacher nephew, and as time went on it became clear that their plan was that I should marry this nephew, since they had become fond of me. But they were all good little *Volksdeutsche* Nazis, and there was a problem: I was an ethnic Pole, and therefore an *Untermensch*. However, they were still very fond of me and of course my German was fluent, which was helpful to them, so the wife went off on a little round of bribery, with geese, eggs and bacon, and the upshot of that was that I was sent to a race commission, where I had my head measured, and my nose, and it was determined that I was a "bona fide member of the Germanic Race with slight Slavic influence". They decided that maybe one of my great-great-grandmothers must have been raped by a Slav – perfectly understandable, nobody's fault, certainly not mine: what could you expect from Slavs anyway?

'There seemed to be no escape for me. You can imagine how I felt. If I tried to get away, they would put two and two together and I would be doomed; but if I stayed . . . I had no choice. I went along with their plan, sure that something would save me from such a grotesque fate as the one that awaited me.

'It did. I was liberated on my birthday, 7 March 1945, in a little village in Pomerania. A Kalmuk scout rode into the village on his motorbike and I just threw myself at him, embraced him. It's a miracle that he didn't shoot me. Once I was sure I was safe, I went back to the farmer's wife and told her that the Russians were here, that I'd been liberated by them; that there was no reason to hide anything any more, and that I was a Jewess. And I asked her for my papers. She told me she didn't believe me: all Russians were Jews, sure; and all dirty, grasping subhumans: but I was clean and pretty and honest. It stood to reason: how could I be Jewish?

'I wasn't out of the woods yet, for the Russians hadn't quite believed yet that I was a Jew, either. After all, I didn't have a Jewish accent – and they were getting ready to rape me. It wasn't until I ran through some Jewish prayers which my grandfather had made me learn by heart that they believed me.

'I became a translator for them, and continued with them as they advanced westwards, so that I was with them when they took Berlin. I will never forget seeing Berlin in flames; but that was as far as I got. I was wounded in Potsdam and taken back to hospital in Warsaw. At that time I knew nothing of the camps, but I knew about the ghettos, and I knew that Mother had been murdered. I wanted revenge. Illness and events overtook that desire.

'Once I was sufficiently recovered, I resumed and completed my schooling, under the auspices of the Jewish community. My ambition was to become a journalist. Becoming a journalist, however, wasn't easy. The Poles had become very nationalistic after the war and started to insist that people in such key positions as journalists should prefer-ably be of pure Polish stock. This so angered me that I wrote a satirical, even bitter, essay on The Love of My Country for the entrance examin-ation to the School of Journalism. My Polish teacher at school who would have to submit the essay summoned me and told me that he couldn't. I told him that it didn't matter because I would be leaving the country anyway in a couple of days – I was still living at the orphanage in Warsaw where I'd been sent after hospital, and there many of us had been contacted by Zionists recruiting people to make the *aliyah*. I had volunteered as soon as it became apparent that I was not going to be able to fulfil my career ambitions in Poland.

'But my journey south was interrupted. I had been equipped with false papers in the Gentile name of Janina Kowalska. The Russians stopped the train at the Czech border and seemed to be checking very thoroughly. I decided not to take the risk of being found out and jumped the train with a friend. Or maybe that was just an excuse not to go on with the voyage to Palestine. Using the papers we had, we made our way to Prague, and from there we took another train to Pilsen [Plzen], which was in the American zone. I can still taste the white bread and the condensed milk today!

'There followed a period of wandering in Europe, enjoying the feeling of being free, and perhaps trying to decide what to do next; but I succumbed to TB badly again and had to be put in hospital in Munich. There I met a German Jew who had survived the KZ. He was kind and gentle, but weak; what he needed was someone to cook for him and wash his shirts. I was never a "little woman" in that sense. But I got pregnant by him and married him. I had a daughter. I wasn't ready for marriage or motherhood, and I'd let myself in for both. This was 1946. But I stuck it in Munich until 1948. I found a certain warmth, and rediscovered family life among those of my husband's relations who had survived. But I was still somehow uneasy. Then one day in 1948 I went to the Viktualienmarkt to buy a goose, and I overheard one of the peasant women market traders remark, "Look, the Jews are able to buy geese again." I went straight home and packed. Like that. It was the deciding factor. And I came to Israel, with my husband and daughter. He raised no objection to coming. His was a Zionist family, and two sisters were living here already. We arrived in December 1948.

'Our first home was a terrible flat in Kefar Gallim – one leaky room and an outside loo that sometimes worked. Soon after, we moved to Nahariyyah, where my husband took a job with the Post Office, and we took a crash course in Hebrew. I was still not 100 per cent fit, and was unsure of what career to follow, though I was convinced of the need for one. I couldn't just sit at home, and I needed to earn money. Someone suggested social work, and I said fine. Pure chance again, but I've been at it now for well over 30 years, and I would say that for someone who had had my experiences and background it was the best career I could possibly have chosen.

'For the past 28 years I have been working with children, in the field of rehabilitation, latterly with children with cerebral palsy. I've built up an entire new department to deal with the problem in Israel, and I think probably it's the best thing I could possibly have done with my life.

'Marriage was not a success. I got a divorce after 13 years, which is to say, 12 years too late. I delayed because I wanted to get on with family life, with my husband's family too, and I felt so guilty that it wasn't working. I wanted so much to be like other people. I wanted so much to be an ordinary Jewish housewife and mother. I wanted to have a dirty apron on and chat with my neighbour about what the neighbour on the other side was cooking for dinner. And I wanted it so much, and it didn't work, and I didn't want to admit it . . .

'If you look at this flat, you'll see a flat which is loved; but for the 13 years of my marriage I totally neglected my home. I wouldn't buy furniture, even. You see, really from the moment I entered the ghetto, I mentally packed a suitcase, which I never unpacked right through that first marriage. I was always *unterwegs*. In a sense too I was rebelling at 30, because I hadn't been able to rebel at 15. I wanted to shake off the small-town, ghetto-Jew mentality . . . Only much later did I come to realize what I was doing, did I come to accept that I was a member of my own original family; and I noticed then that increasingly I was adopting attitudes and opinions my parents had.

'The worst thing about coming here was the welcome. That I'd been in the Warsaw ghetto was a kind of scandal: no one wanted to talk about it. It was just like a family which has one member in a mental hospital. They're looked after there, but no one mentions it. On the surface, things were looked after; spiritually, there was no help at all. The reason isn't far to seek: many of the people here left parents behind in central Europe. It was tough here too to begin with, and to survive at all they had to develop a tough chauvinism and build an emotion-proof wall around themselves. Add to that the general sense of guilt of the Jews who escaped the Holocaust when they are confronted with the question: "Why did you do nothing collectively to save your brothers and sisters in the Holocaust? Why didn't you demonstrate, petition, publicize? Why did you keep your heads down when your people were dying?" They wanted to avoid facing up to all that as far as possible.

'There was the problem of understanding us on an entirely personal level too, for we were quite different from normal people. People of my generation had had their youth stolen, or their development arrested. In some ways you grew up fast, in others, not at all; thus I found myself here aged 26 with an eight-year-old daughter; but inside me, to all intents and purposes, I was still a 15-year-old girl. You have to have a very broad heart to understand someone like I was in 1954. We made them scared. You know the expression, *tout comprendre, c'est tout pardonner*? Well, they neither understood us nor forgave us. For what we had been through.

'But in spite of everything I feel that I am an Israeli now, because in spite of everything it is my country, the Jews' country. I also have to say that I found much greater personal stability through my second marriage, which came hard on the heels of the end of my first, since my second husband and I have been together now since 1960. He wasn't in the Holocaust, he came to Israel from Switzerland; but he listened to me; he understood.

'As I get older, I go more and more frequently to Europe. I think I still have a sense of roots there, which I cannot be rid of. I am European and I am not European. My daughter and son-in-law lived in Hampstead for many years before coming out here. One of the things that made me quite sad was seeing my grandson change from being a polite little English schoolboy into a rude little Israeli. It does make me sad that Israel will inevitably become an increasingly non-European country, and I find myself strangely isolated as a representative of European culture here. In Israel, if my grandson wanted to marry a non-Jew it wouldn't be tolerated; we hold land by force that doesn't belong to us, and we rule over another race, and that is bad too. On the other hand, it is Israel that gave me back my pride, allowed me to develop my career, provided a home for my family. For years I didn't dare go back to Europe, and when I finally did, I made sure I knew the addresses of Israeli embassies and consulates in every town I would pass through, so that at the slightest sign of trouble I could run there and get out.

'My argument turns back on itself. I don't belong to Europe, and I probably do belong here. At the time of the Six Day War, my husband and son-in-law were in the army. My daughter was pregnant; my other daughter was at home with me. Then I got my instructions to go and work for the army as a psychologist. And I went and sat outside on the verandah and wept. An old man was sitting just across from me and he noticed that I was crying and asked me why. I told him about my anxieties. I knew he had lost everybody in the Holocaust. He said, "Do you think it was any better in Warsaw?"

'Perhaps we will be able to sort something out with the Arabs, to avoid a final confrontation. One does what one can. In the kindergarten I run, there are two Arab helpers. Through them and with them we work towards an understanding of each other's cultures and we teach the children in our care about the different cultures, too – the children celebrate each other's religious feast-days. Perhaps a generation brought up understanding each other will not immediately reach for the machine-gun and the bomb. We may have a historical right to be here, but technically we are the newcomers. I am all for integration, of all of us. Eighty per cent of my relatives in America have intermarried and I think that is wonderful.

'But in the past, Jews have felt themselves to be integrated and even assimilated, when in fact they have not been so at all. Look at Heine. He was baptized, saw himself as a German, was one of their great poets;

yet in the minds of the Gentile Germans he was a Jew. Look at the way we use language: we don't say a Jewish Pole, but a Polish Jew. I think we must try to move along with history and not try synthetically to keep the Jewish race separate. As for protecting Jewish culture, the bulk of that went up the chimneys of Auschwitz. The Jews are a different race, differently disposed, from what they were up to 1938. There has been a great change and it is no good pretending it hasn't happened. I chose to live here because I felt secure here; not because I wanted to shut myself away from the rest of the world.

'The price a survivor pays is loneliness, I think. A survivor is a solitary figure; but so is a fighter. It's the inability ever to feel completely secure, completely rooted, that makes you lonely. But I cannot say how much such feelings are my own, or how much instilled in me by the war. I think original feelings have simply been emphasized by the experience. Similarly, it is hard to speak of any positive effect to come out of the suffering, because the negative side is so big and so oppressive, that whatever may have emerged that was positive is somehow lost. I wish it were possible to make a mathematical balance between such qualities as positive and negative effects, but it cannot be done. You have to come to terms with the memory, and find a way of fitting it into your future life; and you have to decide that you are going to have a future life. My second husband has been such a help to me just by listening. He doesn't make comments of his own and he doesn't judge. He says, "I wasn't there, I didn't have that experience; it is for you to tell me about it."'

13

A Home in America

I

More Jewish survivors found a new home in the United States after liberation than in any other country except Israel. Many of them had relatives in the US, who had managed to escape before the war, or branches of the family which had emigrated westwards as a result of the pogroms at the end of the nineteenth and beginning of the twentieth century. They came from all over Europe, but predominantly and inevitably from the eastern part of the continent.

Those who were lucky enough to qualify for affidavits to emigrate to America did so with mixed feelings. Some genuinely looked forward to leading a new life in a country that was at the same time far away from their roots yet, in certain areas such as New York City and its environs, already imbued with Jewish culture for at least a century; others saw their new home as a necessary temporary refuge, which became a permanent dwelling as hopes of their real homes emerging from behind the Iron Curtain faded. Many took to the United States with great enthusiasm, believing it to be the country which – of all those in the West – practises democracy in its purest form. Others live there because they have no choice; others still because they do not wish to be anywhere near the old world where such evil took place. Some clearly feel guilty that they did not go to live in Israel; some express the positive view that they did not wish to live in what would effectively be an exclusively Jewish society. There are survivors who feel doubtful about certain aspects of US foreign policy and who at the same time aggressively defend it if they feel their adopted country is being criticized – however mildly. Others (as in certain cases in England and West Germany) lived cocooned from the new homeland, staying in social circles from their own country and forming of them little replicas of Poland, or Czechoslovakia, or Hungary. There are people who have lived for over 40 years in the English-speaking world and have mastered only enough of the language to do the shopping; crossing the threshold of some houses and flats, one travels 3,000 miles, and often 50 years back in time too. 'I'd like living here more if I'd come here really from free choice; it's being like a victim of circumstances that irritates,' one survivor said to me. Another, who has adapted much better, says that if someone asks him about his tattoo and he doesn't want to tell them the truth about it, he tells them it's his girlfriend's telephone number. Another tells me she had her tattoo removed because she got so tired of misinformed remarks: 'Is it your phone number? Is it your medical insurance number? Why don't you write it on a piece of paper and carry it in your pocket-book? – When I first came here the most ignorant people in the whole country about the Holocaust were the Jews.' Conversely, one survivor remembers that in the early Sixties he very reluctantly gave a lecture to some students, telling them about his tattoo. Recently, he met some of those students again, now middle-aged people, and they told him how graphically they recalled his lecture. That experience inspired him to volunteer once again to talk to youth groups and anyone else who expresses an interest. His initial doubts and reluctance were caused by the apparent indifference of those around him to what he had been through – 'But I guess they were just trying to spare my feelings.'

Benjamin Miedzyrsecki spent much of the war hiding in Warsaw, where he was active in the Jewish resistance[1] and in helping those Jews who had escaped or avoided the ghetto. He was an expert constructor of 'priests' holes'.

He met his future wife, Vladka, in the resistance. 'We were married in Warsaw and came over to the USA together – and of those survivors who were not married, within three years 90 per cent had, because they couldn't bear to be alone; and of those marriages, 90 per cent were to other survivors. It is easier to be married to someone who has been through it too.'

They were among the first immigrants to America, arriving in New York in 1946, partly as a result of their activities in the resistance, news of which had preceded them. The long Polish surname was changed to Meed. He has not been back to Europe at all, and does not wish to, though in his official capacity as President of the American Gathering of Jewish Holocaust Survivors he has met the West German Chancellor. In the course of their conversation, the Chancellor asked Meed not to hold him personally responsible for the KZ, since 'I was only 17 at the time'. Meed replied: 'You are collectively responsible. The whole German nation is.' He feels that the Germans should continue to feel a sense of shame at what was done and not be allowed to forget too soon or too easily. He is an angry and zealous guardian of the flame of remembrance.

II

The large, light office of Ernest Michel overlooks East 59th Street. Michel himself is elegant and charming, and you have to listen very hard to detect the slightest trace of a German accent behind the American. There are three indications of his past in the room. On the wall behind his desk, beautifully framed or cased, hang not diplomas or citations or hunting prints, but his Star of David, the battered leather belt he wore with his uniform at Auschwitz, and a photograph of him sitting on the railway track on a return visit to the KZ in 1983.

He was born in Mannheim in 1923, the son of a middle-class Jewish family which had lived in Germany for 300 years. They saw the danger coming, but were unable to arrange the necessary affidavits to escape. They had few relatives in the USA, and direct appeals to the US authorities went unanswered. Michel was deported to his first camp in 1939. He was not to be free until he escaped in April 1945.

'I was in a sub-camp of Buchenwald called Belgar, and on 11 April we were evacuated. The next day Roosevelt died; the SS march commander told us the news, and said that it meant the war would turn again in Germany's favour, and that to celebrate he would shoot ten of us every day from now on. This went on until 17 April, by which time our numbers were down to 1,000. My group thought we hadn't survived six years of KZ just to be shot on the road, with liberation so close. We could hear the Allied guns. And on 18 April, which I celebrate today as my birthday, we escaped.

'We were marching through a young wood, and at a given signal the three of us just broke away and ran. They fired after us – I have the scar of a bullet that grazed my scalp – but they didn't follow. I was bleeding heavily, but we all managed to get away for the present. One of my companions is still alive and also lives in New York; but we lost track of the other guy, and I don't think he made it.'

He managed to hide by passing himself off as a farmworker until the Americans arrived; but then he found himself in further trouble, as the Americans took him for a German deserter. However, he was able to prove to them otherwise, after which they 'adopted' him as a kind of company mascot. Michel had not formulated any plans to emigrate at that stage, however. He wanted to return home, to see if there were any pieces to pick up, and he wanted to pursue his original career-plan to become a journalist. He managed to get a job with DANA – the *Deutscher Allgemeiner Nachrichtenagentur* (or German News Agency, now called DENA), and they delegated him to cover the Nuremberg Trials, which he did from beginning to end, as their first correspondent.

A memento of those days also hangs on his wall: a framed paper with the autographs of the defendants. 'See those? They are obviously very rare, and I obtained them at the trial.

'It was a quite extraordinary feeling. Just over six months earlier, I had been a prisoner in a concentration camp, not knowing if I would live another day. I got to be quite well-known during the trials; but the Russians decided that they couldn't use my testimony because I was an employed German national, though of course they questioned me about Auschwitz in great detail.' During this period he came to the conclusion that he no longer wanted to live in Germany, not least because the life he had known there before the war had been destroyed, the continuity broken with the murder of his family. He had a sister in Palestine, and for a time vacillated between the possibility of joining her there and trying again for the United States. Finally, 'I felt that I would have more of an opportunity here than I would in Palestine. I was quite a Zionist, but I made my decision, if I'm honest, for selfish reasons. I felt there'd be more of a future for me here. It wasn't a question of doubting the likelihood of the emergence of a Jewish state; I was convinced that there would be. But I came here.'

Michel was one of the first to emigrate to the USA, in 1946, taking advantage of the Truman Displaced Persons Act.[2] When he arrived in New York, he had six or seven dollars in his pocket and the clothes he stood up in. He sensed immediately that he didn't like New York, and asked the National Refugee Service to transfer him to Chicago. They told him that they could pay his fare, and no more.

'I spoke very little English when I came here, and I wanted very much to learn it, but most of the Jews I met spoke mostly German or Yiddish, and I felt that if I truly wanted to become an American I would have to get out of that milieu. I went to Chicago because there was an army officer there who had befriended me in Germany when he was working for the Allied Military Government. He was the only indigenous US citizen I knew. I called him from New York and he invited me to come. He even offered to put me through school, but I didn't want him to do that. I wanted to start a job, to start earning my own money. So I have had no formal education whatsoever. I was kicked out of school when I was 13 and that was it.

'I started looking for a newspaper job in Chicago, which was ridiculous, of course, because I spoke very broken English, and people would laugh me out of their offices. But one man listened – he was the General Manager of UPI. I told him what I'd done, and he told me I'd have to start on a small local paper. He sent me to Port Huron, in Michigan. I packed my bags and spent my last few dollars on a train ticket.

'I'd never heard of the town before, and the publisher of the local paper there looked at me as if I'd come from the moon; but I told him my background, and he agreed to make me a copy-boy, at least for a week or two until I got myself sorted out. Then he expected to see the back of me, I guess; and maybe I didn't hold out too much hope. But I worked like hell, and I stayed on the paper a year, eventually becoming a columnist with a regular spot. I learnt English just by picking it up in Port Huron, and I had an American Gentile girlfriend there too, which helped – though as things became more serious her father decided that if we were to marry I should become a Catholic. We didn't marry – for other reasons; but I certainly never had any intention of converting.

'I had no trouble adapting to life here, but I think it was a lot easier to do so within a very small, friendly community than it would have been in a big city. There, I might well have been driven back to my own people just for company. In Port Huron, there were no other immigrants to speak of, and the population was pure American.

'It is possible that the fact that I had lost all my family but was still young and unattached helped me, firstly to make the move to the USA at all, and secondly to adapt to life here. In that connection, I had a fascinating experience in Port Huron, which I think helped me to overcome some of the problems of isolation and of coming to terms with what I had been through. I wrote a little autobiographical piece for the paper, and the result of it was that the local Junior College approached me and asked if I'd meet their Foreign Relations Club and talk to them about my experiences. I told them that I couldn't, because I was nervous about my spoken English, which still wasn't too hot; but they said, "Don't worry, it'll just be a small group." What they didn't tell me was that they'd advertised the meeting in the college newspaper under the dramatic banner, FROM AUSCHWITZ TO PORT HURON, and most of the college turned up. Had I known beforehand, I would have cried off and sunk through a hole in the floor, but by the time I arrived it was too late to do that. I'd never given a speech before in my life, in any language, but I started to speak, and I have to say that it was a catharsis for me, because for the first time I was speaking about my experience, and to people of my age, about what it meant to be totally deprived of everything you had: of school, family, livelihood, home, even language. I spoke for I don't know how long – something just took over in me. And finally I stopped, because I couldn't go on any more, my throat was bone dry. Later I was told that I'd spoken non-stop for 90 minutes. I had talked the experience out of me and, even more importantly, I realized that that was possible. There really and truly hadn't been a chance to talk about it before; I'd been so busy since liberation, and there had been so many new things happening. This was the first time that I had had an opportunity to open up, and I realized how much I needed to.

'The lecture led to a turning point in my career. Port Huron is a tiny town – the population then must have been about 25,000 – and word got around. I received invitations to speak for local service clubs, the Rotary, and churches. I spoke in every church in Port Huron. One day someone told me that there would be a United Jewish Appeal meeting in a nearby community, and would I be willing to speak there?[3] I was willing, not least because it was on a UJA affidavit that I had been able to come here in the first place. And at the meeting there was an official of the UJA who was very enthusiastic about my lecture. In turn, that led to a regular speaking engagement on behalf of the UJA in many parts of the USA. My newspaper agreed that I should take the work on, with the condition that I should phone in my column every night – my column was called 'My New Home'. In it I was given *carte blanche* to write anything that occurred to me about life in this country. It was a terrific opportunity; but it was out of the speaking engagements that I finally became professionally involved with the UJA, whom I have been with since 1948.'

He moved from Port Huron to Detroit, where he had friends; but he didn't stay long because he won a car in a short-story competition, and with it decided to drive to California 'to see what it was like'. It was there that he started his lectures for the UJA and began to get seriously involved in work for the Jewish community. Today he is the chief executive of the largest fund-raising organization in the world. The UJA raises funds for Jewish needs internationally. Michel has a staff of 500, and says, 'I am very proud to play a role in this effort.'

He met his wife in California, after he had been in the USA four years. 'By then I was established and well on the road to recovery, if not wholly recovered. My wife is an American girl, who probably did love me a little for "the dangers I had passed", and was impressed by me. I talked to her about the KZ, but it was simply to let her know what had happened, since she was interested. It wasn't to get things off my chest. That wasn't necessary any more, because of the lectures. At the same time I think I would have been hurt if she had shown no interest; but that would have been unlikely since I was well involved with the UJA by 1950. Marriage was the next logical step in my development, too. I don't think there was a conscious or urgent desire to recreate the lost family – more just to have one of my own.'

Despite his early feelings, the family settled in New York, and their three children were born and brought up there. 'I wanted my children to know what I had been through, and to learn about the camps as soon as they were old enough to understand. I took them to Germany, and I took them to Dachau, to show them a camp. Today, my son and one of my daughters live in Israel – what happened to me made a profound impression on her. The other daughter lives in California and is very involved with the Jewish community. Sometimes I regret that I seem to have few contacts outside the Jewish world; but it's a fact of my life and I have to accept it. I have never been a religious man, though I did have a brief, almost mystical experience of belief when I was working as a farm labourer after my escape. It passed. I wasn't brought up to be strictly observant, and although I have always been very aware that I am a Jew, I have never been observant, and the KZ didn't affect that either way.'[4]

Of the nightmare, nothing remains in terms of bad dreams and haunting thoughts. There are no 'triggers' either. 'I think I am unusual in this, but I have totally shed any sort of demons from that time. I have used my work today to overcome, to compensate for all the horrors that I lived through. So I have adjusted totally. I have an ordinary, loving family, and I feel at home here. I love the work I do, too – though I'll never make a lot of money, it is tremendously fulfilling, and I believe in it totally. There has never been any temptation to get away from the memory of the Holocaust, either. I believe that the three most important events in Jewish history are the destruction of the first temple, the Holocaust, and the establishment of the State of Israel. Two of those events have taken place in my lifetime, and have directly involved me, for Israel was born out of the ashes of European Jewry. Thus I must be actively involved; I must dedicate the life that was given back to me to ensuring that such a thing never happens again. And equally to ensure Jewish survival, internationally, and especially in Israel. I have never tried to conceal my past from anyone and my past is very much part of me. I am proud of it, and I am proud to have survived the Holocaust, and to have come out of it physically and mentally in good shape.'

Michel was the moving spirit behind the World Gathering of Jewish Victims of the Holocaust in Israel in 1981. 'That is where I met Hugo Gryn, incidentally. It was my thought that the time had come, after almost 40 years, for the survivors to get together, perhaps to make contact again with lost relatives from whom they'd been swept away. It is all part of the catharsis process, I believe. The gathering was my idea and my brainchild. When I started planning it in 1977 people thought I was crazy, that no one would want to remember, but I said, "No; this isn't going to be a *kaddish*; this is going to be a celebration of life. We will gather to celebrate the fact that we have survived." It snowballed and became a worldwide and unique event. It is the most important thing I have done in my life.

'No one has ever criticized me for keeping a memory alive that some might think better forgotten; but when people ask me why I do it, I say to them: I do this on purpose. I owe it to those who did not survive. I owe it to my parents, to my relatives, to my friends who died in the

KZ, that the memory of what happened to us should never die, that such a thing should never happen again. Especially today, when there are people who set out to prove that it never happened at all. Of course the revisionists and the neo-Nazis are in a small minority, but they are there, and we can't ignore anyone who stands up and says that six million Jews didn't die – that it was a hoax. If we are quiet, they may increasingly get a hold on people's minds; which is why we must speak out until we die.'

I ask what made him go back to Auschwitz.

'That's a good question. I'd never been back. The national chairman of the UJA asked me to lead a group of regional chairmen from all over the USA on a visit to the camp. "If you can bring yourself to go with them, it would mean a hell of a lot to them," he said. I was very doubtful and hesitated. No one pushed me, but in the end I decided that I would go, and by a coincidence I returned there on my 60th birthday, 1 July 1983. The photo you see on the wall over there was taken on that day. Friends thought I was crazy to go back to the place of horror on such an important birthday, but I was glad I did it, for I had survived whole. It was a very great celebration. That night I spoke to the whole group about my life in Auschwitz, and for me it was a very emotional and a very significant day.

'What surprised me was that it was a beautiful day too. The sun was shining, and there was grass growing, and flowers, and I couldn't understand that in that place, where all hell had been when I was last there, there could now be such quiet, such peace. I sat on the railroad tracks and looked at the grass growing between them.

'I hope that the memory of what happened will not die with the deaths of us survivors. I do everything possible to ensure that it doesn't. That is why I support what you are doing, and that is why we are building up tape libraries, video testimonials, and stressing the importance of educating young people in Holocaust studies. But it is true that the impact of the Holocaust will be reduced once there is no one left alive with direct experience of it, because the actual experience is hard enough to communicate even directly from a survivor to a non-survivor, so terrible was it. Let me say again that I am a rarity: I am one of the few who has been able to put the memory aside, or rather turn it to positive use. Most of the survivors are still living under the direct impact of what happened to them; and maybe you won't meet those survivors who have survived physically, but who are deeply and terribly scarred; whose lives are permanently spoiled – you won't meet them because they won't talk to you. Maybe they wouldn't help you. But do not forget that they are there. Surviving the KZ is not necessarily a success story, ever.

'After the war, and my stint at Nuremberg, I worked on in Germany for a while, and came into contact with some of the people who went on to be powerful figures in post-war Germany, such as Theodor Heuss, who became the first president of the Federal Republic. He was the editor of the first German newspaper that I worked on. After Nuremberg, I was offered the directorship of the Berlin office of DANA, which wasn't bad for a man of 22, but by then I had decided that I could not live in Germany. And for the next 25 years I never spoke a word of German, never read German, used German products, or had anything to do with anything or anyone from that country. I've changed latterly. There's a whole new generation now – it's a democratic European country too – at least, half of it is, and the other half is just another Russian satellite. The old Germany simply doesn't exist any more, and I decided that in any case I could not go on hating all my life. And I had an interesting experience recently. I was invited to a luncheon, and the speaker was Johannes Rau, the Chief Minister of North Rhine-Westphalia.[5] He's in his fifties now, so he was in his teens then. I went over to him afterwards and shook him by the hand, and I said to him, "Herr Rau, this is the first time I have ever shaken hands with a German government official, and I never thought that I would see the day when I did – but I'm doing it now because I recognize that history has moved on and that you represent a different country from the one I knew." I doubt if the whole episode meant a thing to him, but it was a significant private moment for me, and an important gesture for me to make.'

III

In the testimony given to the William E. Wiener Oral History Library some years ago, Ernest Michel pays tribute to a friend he made in Auschwitz, Norbert Wollheim. 'In 1960 there was an Auschwitz memorial dinner. Among those who were in the camp was Norbert Wollheim, a Jew who decided to file a suit against I. G. Farben, our employer in the camps. I. G. Farben agreed to settle out of court if Norbert Wollheim was willing to represent all the other survivors of the camp and if they would be willing to accept a one-time settlement. The offer resulted in a payment of $5,000 to every inmate of the Auschwitz-Buna concentration camp who could prove he had been there at any time during World War II. The list amounted to several thousand people living in the United States, Canada, Israel and other countries. Once they agreed to the settlement, a few of us decided that we could not take the money for personal use. We decided to create the Auschwitz Buna Memorial Scholarship Fund, dedicated to the memory of those who died but created to give scholarships to the children of survivors who had no parents to pay for their education. The money was turned over to Bar Ilan University. The scholarship was announced at that dinner.'

Like Michel, Wollheim is a German Jew. He was born in Berlin in 1914 and after school went on to study law and political science at Berlin University. His older sister was an accountant. The family was 'typically Berlin *Kleinbürger*' – non-assimilated Jews who traced their roots back to Posen. When he was 14, Wollheim joined the non-Zionist youth movement and there enjoyed the benefits of the influence of both German and Jewish culture. Following a Jewish communal tradition he immersed himself in voluntary social work – to such an extent that he later abandoned his studies to do social work full-time. He also learnt a trade – spot-welding, a skill which was to save his life in Auschwitz, since it meant selection for Buna-Monowice.

By 1935 it was clear to him that he should try to get out of Germany, but by then he was married, starting a family, and his parents depended on him, so he hung on, and helped others get away. After *Kristallnacht* he was the organizer of transports of several thousand Jewish children aged between 12 and 18 to England, and he himself accompanied one, arriving with it in London in February 1939. A transport consisted of about 500 children, from all over Germany. He describes the work as exhausting but stimulating.

'Despite being well aware of the gathering storm, we nevertheless felt at the time that the Germans might still come to their senses. Looking back, it's hard to imagine how we could have taken that attitude, but don't forget that we didn't know – we had no idea at all – what we Jews were actually in for. However, we didn't want to take any unnecessary risks and we worked like beavers to get the children out. By the time the war broke out, my own family was just ready to leave, and then of course couldn't. Instead, I went into the administration of Jewish vocational training schools, which continued through until 1941 in Germany, but by then the net was closing, and I volunteered for what was effectively forced labour. Jewish teams were delegated to various factories to work for the Reich, but at least they could live at home. Conditions were hard, but we continued to keep our heads above water until 1943. Then, after Stalingrad, they decided to bring the Final Solution to Berlin. My parents had already been deported in 1942, and we were arrested in March. They sent us to Auschwitz three days later. When we arrived I was immediately separated from my wife, my little boy and my sister, and I never saw them again. Naturally we didn't realize at once what was happening – we thought there was a camp for women and children; and even when we found out the truth, it was hard to believe it – it was so alien to our experience, so alien to our concept of what man can do to man.'

He was in Buna from March 1943, when the plant was still in the process of being built, until 18 January 1945, when he was evacuated with a transport and sent on the death-march away from the Russians. 'That afternoon, 18 January 1945, at 4pm, Auschwitz ceased to exist for us. It was cold, −18°C. Those of us who are still alive still get together on that day to remember.

'We walked for two and a half days to Gleiwitz. There, somehow they put a train of open cattle-cars together and we were taken first to Mauthausen, which was too full to receive us, and then to Sachsenhausen, where we arrived on 31 January. The whole journey was on these open cattle-cars, and we were given almost nothing to eat or drink. Out of 6,000 people, 4,000 died in those ten days on the train.

'We were in Sachsenhausen still when the Allies launched their massive air-raid on Berlin on Hitler's birthday, 20 April 1945. By then we had illegal access to radio news and we had already begun to form committees to deal with the situation after the end of the war; but after that attack we were marched out towards Mecklenburg. The battle was raging nearby. On 2 May a motorcycle patrol arrived with the news that the American forces were just ahead. The SS pushed us into a nearby wood for the night; and all night the Russians pummelled the place with their artillery. Three of us decided to make a run for it. The SS fired at us but didn't follow. We made for the American lines. They had taken Schwerin and dug in. We reached them: the advance corps of the Eighth Division. That was my moment of liberation.

'When we saw the American flag that morning – it was 3 May – we embraced each other, and laughed, and cried; but after I had calmed down my first thoughts were of my family who hadn't made it, and I decided then, at that moment, that whatever else I did I would try to help other people for the rest of my days as a repayment for the gift of life which had been given back to me. However, there wasn't too much time for noble thoughts, since suddenly a young Texan officer appeared, and he was pointing his pistol at us. We weren't easily identifiable, as we were dressed in civilian clothes which we'd organized before leaving Sachsenhausen – the camp was in total administrative chaos by then – but he accepted our story, given in broken English, that we were escaped KZ prisoners, and he told us to help ourselves to food and whatever else we needed from the occupied area we were now in. Fortunately we had the sense to know not to eat too much too soon. We billeted ourselves with a German woman in Schwerin as my friends were very ill, and I paid her 20 *Reichsmarks* saved from Auschwitz for the two rooms she let us. Her husband was an air force major who hadn't come back yet, and she was terribly worried about him. She had a young daughter and a baby which cried all the time because there wasn't enough milk for it. I was sorry for her, and managed to organize some milk for the baby. No, I never thought about revenge. I didn't feel too sympathetic about her husband, but we were all just human beings together, and if a baby is crying for lack of milk you don't think that, just because it's a German baby, you'll do nothing for it.

'When we were originally deported we were made to sign a form which stated that as Jewish racial criminals we were denied our German citizenship. I had to sign such a form for my 3½-year-old son too, so that after liberation I swore that I would never again accept German citizenship. However, this created problems for a number of us German Jews, since the Allies wanted to classify us as Germans pure and simple and "repatriate" us as soon as possible. After a friendly US Intelligence officer told us that Schwerin was to be handed over to the Russians as part of their zone, a group of us moved on to Lübeck. There I heard the name Bergen-Belsen for the first time, and I also learnt that there was a strong Jewish community building up in the DP camp that had been established there.

'I spoke some schoolboy English at the time, and I'd been able to brush it up a bit by talking to some of the British POWs who had been conscripted to work at Buna.[6] I went first to the UNRRA offices to appeal against being forced to accept German nationality again, but they couldn't help us, because technically we were Germans, and therefore undesirable aliens. Next, I applied to the Military Government, and they were sympathetic, but bound by their bureaucracy, and it began to look as if we'd be thrust willy-nilly back into Germany. I had no papers and no official authority to travel, but I managed to get my group smuggled to Bergen-Belsen in a Red Cross lorry, and made contact with Josef Rosensaft.'[7]

Norbert Wollheim worked very closely with Rosensaft from then on, one of their main and most important aims being to get the Allied authorities to recognize their right to be treated as Jews first, and as citizens of their respective countries of origin second; and thus not be repatriated against their will. It was as Jews that they had suffered, not as Poles, Czechs or Germans; and their suffering had altered their concept of nationality. They demanded that they be treated collectively as Allied victims of the Third Reich – including the German Jews – since the Nazis had declared war on all Jews, including their own nationals, and this stand was finally accepted. 'I felt more comfortable stateless than German. The British issued us with very impressive passports.' (The passport says 'indeterminate' on it under 'Nationality'. It is actually called a 'Certificate of Identity', and is a large piece of folded vellum, issued by the Home Office.)

'When I arrived at Bergen-Belsen I got in touch with the Committee of Liberated Jews. I met Josef, who looked starved and worn, but whose eyes burned. He spoke Yiddish, I German. His aims and the aims of the CLJ appealed to me, and we hit it off. Naturally there were differences but the things we had in common were stronger, and united us. We developed a central committee of which I was vice-chairman, and a council; we organized ourselves from our beginnings as a self-help group right up to having the administrative capability of a mini-state, with schools, welfare and hospitals.'

He stayed until 1950, by which time the state of Israel was already two years old, the *aliyah* was legal, and it was considerably easier to emigrate to the UK or the USA.

In the five years he had stayed at Belsen, Wollheim had worked tirelessly alongside Rosensaft to help their fellow-Jews make the *aliyah*, to establish their rights, and to fight for reparation. There had been many lengthy, wearing meetings and negotiations with the British authorities in the course of that time. Now at last there was a moment when he was able to think about his own future.

He had met his second wife in the DP camp and they married in 1946. Both their children were born in the DP camp, his son in 1948 and his daughter in 1950. The principal reason he chose to go to America and not to Israel had to do with his domestic situation, since his wife's brother and sister, also survivors, had already emigrated to the USA, and she was particularly close to her sister, the more so since they had lost the rest of their family. Subsequently his sister-in-law moved to Los Angeles, where she lives today. His second wife died in 1977, and he has since remarried; though he still lives in the same New York house he moved into shortly after his arrival in 1952.

Once in America there was the problem, after five years spent helping others, of establishing himself in a new career. 'I decided to go for accountancy, which I had had some experience of. I took a bachelor's degree at New York University, which allowed me 58 points' advanced credit on the strength of the studies I had done at Berlin University before the war. At the same time I was involved in bringing the action against I. G. Farben, and I was becoming active in survivor organizations.'

The I. G. Farben action came about in the following way. Shortly after the war, the company announced in the press that all their shareholders should re-register. 'When I saw that, I had a kind of brainstorm, because I thought: what about us, who were literally their slaves? Don't we have an interest in the company too? I had befriended another German Jew who'd fled to the United Kingdom and who worked for the British after the war, but who thereafter, retaining his British passport, set up in legal practice in Frankfurt and became pretty successful. I put my idea of suing Farben to him, but he was doubtful. However, he was friendly with another lawyer, not Jewish, Gerhard Kramer, who was an expert in commercial law, and he was excited by the proposal – even if it didn't work, what political and public-interest dynamite there was in it.

'What disappointed me most in the Farben action was the attitude of the new representatives of the company. They still made us fight to get the pittance of compensation that was our right. They didn't have the decency or dignity to assume responsibility for their fathers' deeds, and in the end they gave in only because they were forced to compromise their stance.'

In addition to his other post-war activities, Wollheim was one of the founding members of the Jewish Trust Corporation in the British zone; this was empowered to claim from Germany for communally owned Jewish property and so-called heirless property, and he needed all the experience that work brought him in his battle with Farben. In the event, he is not satisfied with the final settlement: 'DM35 million: very little indeed; but it was enough to let them say that they'd wiped the slate clean. I'm not discounting the value of some restitution – after all, you don't leave a thief in possession of his booty – but I regret their being let off the hook morally, and I don't think they are off the hook morally.'

We talk about his daughter's wedding and the reaffirmation of life at its celebration.

'We survivors stick together because we share a common experience, and it's easier to communicate. You can be sitting round the table with friends, and let's say you're eating something nice. One of us will say: "From this I would like to have *Nachschlag*." Well, nobody else will understand this expression, but in the KZ it meant an extra little helping of food – a bit of bread, a spoonful of soup. It was given as a bonus, for extra work, for example. It's not something you can easily explain to the outside world. Then there are the moments of joy, like the morning of our liberation. That feeling of rebirth is something unique – special to our experience. It is a sensation quite literally of having one's life anew, of moving from a world of death to a world of life: there is no way adequately to communicate this feeling.

'I think that we must live neither with the past nor without it. Many of us talk about rebirth, but life didn't really start on liberation day, and the new life is bound to be coloured by the old. There are controlled and uncontrolled reactions to that past. An example of the uncontrolled reaction is the kind of buried memory which suddenly emerges in your dreams, and that can sometimes happen even without a trigger. Now and then I ask myself, what could have sparked that off – something I saw on TV? But I can't necessarily find a rational answer.

'More obvious setters-off of reactions are anti-Semitic remarks. Before the war there was an expression current in Germany that if cash was low, the thing to do was knock off a rich Jew and balance the books that way. Now, the use of an expression like that pre-Auschwitz was bad; but after Auschwitz it seems impermissible. And yet only recently a mayor in North Rhine-Westphalia (Graf Widerich von Spee) made precisely that suggestion – facetiously, in all probability, though that does not excuse him. The thing that horrifies us is that the spectre of Nazism is present in that remark, and for a German of all people to make it is even more appalling. About the same time, in January 1986, a CSU MP (Hermann Fellner) said publicly that Jews who seek reparation from German firms who'd used them as slave labour during the Second World War are "quick to show up whenever money jingles in German cash registers" – another pre-war expression rearing its dangerous head. Worst of all, he was not even censured for the remark. It makes you wonder about people who can shrug off such a crime so quickly and so easily; but they couldn't if they were not allowed to.[8]

'There are ways in which you can take precautions – I avoid watching films on television which involve violence – rather a difficult thing to do here – but one is always liable to be affected. I saw a letter in *Der Spiegel* not long ago comparing the Israeli camps in the Lebanon with Auschwitz, and concluding that therefore the Jews no longer had a right to feel morally superior to the Germans. That of course made one's blood boil. But as far as the Germans are concerned, apart from not wanting that nationality back after it had been stripped from me in the way that it was, you could almost call my feelings neutral. I never felt tempted not to use the German language. Why should I forgo the pleasure of reading Heine or Thomas Mann in German? It is still my mother-tongue, and I wouldn't want to read Germany's literature in any other language. The language didn't sin – just the people. In 1985 I was back there for the first time in a long while, with my wife, who comes from Germany too but had never been back since coming to the USA just before the war. She comes from Aschaffenburg, and the occasion was the renaming of a town square after a member of her family: Wolfsthalplatz. Afterwards we went to Berlin, and over to the eastern part of the city, which is where I grew up; and I wanted to show her all the places associated with my youth, my past; and I couldn't, because none of it is there any more. That is almost symbolic: the chapter is closed. When we went to the Jewish cemetery where my grandparents are buried, the place was so overgrown that we couldn't get to the tomb. Tombstones have been uprooted by trees, trees have fallen. Only the "honour row" of tombs of prominent artists and thinkers is preserved, and the First World War memorial. No, the chapter is closed . . .'

Norbert Wollheim was several times a witness at Nazi war trials.

'I was a witness against I. G. Farben at Nuremberg in 1946, and already the process of the trial was coloured by the Cold War – US politicians would come over and urge the prosecution to go easy, especially on German industry in case it was needed in the new Allied campaign against the Russians. And indeed the majority of the industrialists implicated got lenient sentences if they got any at all. Later, I was a witness in three cases, one of which was against the maker of the anti-Semitic film of *Jud Süss*, whose name was Veit Harlan. He was accused of crimes against humanity – the film was played to SS guards to inflame them. I saw the film after the war, and frankly it was so violent, and portrayed the Jews in so vicious and terrifying a light, that I am surprised that any of us is still alive. The trial was in Hamburg and the chief judge, who had been a supporter of the Nazi regime but who had been reappointed as a simple civil service functionary, was so biased that Harlan got off.[9] The prosecutor appealed against the decision and there was a second trial, but it was under the same judge. I consulted with the prosecution and wrote the judge a letter simply saying that I would not appear in his court again because I did not believe in his justice – and I gave the letter to the press. One was quite brave in those days. The judge could have had me for contempt, for I was still technically a German citizen then, as this was very early on; but he didn't dare.

'Much later, when I was already living here, I appeared at the trial in Osnabrück against a prominent SS-man who had been a murderer both in Auschwitz and during the death-march I was on. The president of that court had been a political persecutee; but he was so afraid of his own shadow, and of appearing to be biased against the SS, that he leant too far in the other direction and handed down a very light sentence.

'The third experience was when I was a witness at the second Auschwitz trial in Frankfurt in the early Seventies. The president of this court was a former member of the Legion Condor in the Spanish Civil War, the unit that bombed Guernica in 1936. The accused was Neubert, who had actively participated in selections at Auschwitz. In the course of the trial the judge had the temerity to ask me if I couldn't think of one good word to say for the accused. I was an American citizen by then, of course. After I'd recovered a bit, I lashed out – there were American pressmen there, so it was for their benefit too. The result was that in the summing-up I was referred to as an unfriendly witness. I refused to appear at a West German court again after that. Of course it wasn't always possible to assemble the right accused, the right witnesses, even; and the witnesses, maybe ill-prepared and unused to being in a court of law, could be tied in knots by defence counsel who were, after all, only doing their job. But that doesn't entirely excuse the Germans. One of the worst examples of that kind of behaviour was at the Majdanek trials, where the witnesses were made to feel like the accused.'

However, where moral turpitude was concerned, the Germans were not alone. 'Any moral judgments and actions relating to people like von Braun were swept aside because of the *Realpolitik* of the immediate post-war enmity between East and West, and matters were very delicate – many people flooded west before the frontiers closed, including a number of people from the former Baltic republics, some of whom had been Nazi sympathizers and active collaborators, who now mingled with the rest of us in the DP camps. And when we pointed these people out to the US Intelligence services, what we effectively got was: "If you are interested in emigrating to the USA, drop it – as long as these people are good anti-Communists, we'll overlook their past." Only now are some of these people being rooted out.

'I have to say that, much as I love this country and grateful as I am to her, the Americans were very naïve after the war. The excuse is that they were unprepared for the vast administrative burden the war would put on them, and the post-war period. The soldiers are a good example of this. The combat troops who saw us first never forgot; but when they were relieved, it was by fresh troops who had seen nothing at first hand and who therefore saw, effectively, nothing; but at least they listened, and tried to understand. The third wave of input troops preferred the Germans, who by then were already putting on a very pleasant face, which was only natural, and the girls were clean and pretty, and of course nobody knew a thing about the camps . . . But the sheer human and warm reaction of the American troops who liberated us overwhelmed me.'

IV

Max Garcia, who recently retired from full-time architectural practice in San Francisco, is a survivor of Buna, Auschwitz I, Mauthausen, Melk and Ebensee. He was born in Amsterdam into a Sephardic Jewish family. His father was a diamond polisher, and that was the career for which Max was, unwillingly at first, destined. He lost his family in the KZ and was himself arrested after a period of hiding in Amsterdam in June 1943 when he was 19 years old.

Deported immediately to Auschwitz, he was selected for Buna-Monowice, but after a month he crushed the middle finger of his left hand when setting down a heavy load. He managed to wrap it in a bit of rag and tried to forget about it, but the wound festered and he was forced to report it. Because he was still fit and well-fed, he was sent to the hospital at the main camp, where he was treated, rather than left to die. Once the infection was sufficiently healed for him to return to work, he was sent to *Kommandos* within Auschwitz-I and not returned to Buna. Early on, he realized the importance of taking as much care of himself physically as possible. In Auschwitz, the smallest cut could spell death, through abscessing, tetanus, or septicaemia. The most vulnerable parts of the body were the feet. 'Fortunately, I knew how to keep my feet warm in clogs by wrapping them, for I had had plenty of practice in Holland during the lean years. I looked about me constantly on the work-site and in the camp for scraps of paper or rags with which to keep my feet warm and dry. The protection of my feet, I was learning and observing, was the key to my survival. I saw the feet and ankles of many a prisoner swell up with malnutrition, and observed that death generally followed. I saw the wet and frozen toes of some of my fellow-prisoners rot from gangrene . . . Taking good care of my feet became an obsession.'[10] He was hospitalized twice more – for pneumonia and, incredibly, for appendicitis, which he survived only because a junior SS surgeon who wished to see an appendectomy happened to be in camp. Thus it was that he remained alive in Auschwitz and, with time, his tattooed number became an 'old' number, and was accordingly respected. He was detailed to the *Paketstelle* – the *Kommando* whose job it was to sort out the food parcels which were sent to the camp. He became a *Prominent*.

He remained in the *Kommando* until Auschwitz was evacuated in January 1945, and on the death-march he observed an extraordinary piece of SS behaviour. 'The *Paketstelle Kommando* controlled incoming food gifts until the day we left camp. The guards who marched out with us carried only the meagre rations issued to them. Access to our better food depended on the goodwill of the *Paket* workers. Our SS guards walked on either side of us with their guns, but they made no effort to shoot or overpower us for our supplies. For them the writing was on the wall. The Russians were not far behind. Our guards hastened us along. They seemed intent on delivering us to an ordered destination while there was still time. If the Russians caught up with us, the guards could do worse than surrender some well-fed prisoners pulling carts of food.'

The food was not to last, and over the next hard months – for Garcia as for many the hardest months of all to survive – stripped him of any advantages that his months on the *Paketstelle Kommando* had given him, except that he started on the calvary of Mauthausen, Melk and Ebensee fed and healthy. 'I ate grass at Melk – but furtively, because they would have shot me at once if they had caught me.'

Ebensee was liberated on 6 May by the 3rd Cavalry, 3rd US Army. The prisoners and the soldiers stared at each other mutely through the wire for some moments, and then the gates were opened and the KZ-inmates drew back to allow the American tanks access to the *Appellplatz*. Then, as the engines of the vehicles were switched off, prisoners swarmed round, uneasily and in silence, for there were not many who could speak English. 'The soldiers in and on the tanks seemed afraid. They looked as if they did not care to come down among us. They may have been fresh from the latest battles, but we appeared to be too much for them. These hungry eyes. These sunken faces and skeletal bodies. These stinking subhumans. Us!

'Some of us tried to climb on to the tanks, but were politely rebuffed with hand-gestures. Standing among the crowd of prisoners around the tanks, I watched a soldier take out a packet of Lucky Strikes and light a cigarette. Now these were American cigarettes, I knew, for I had seen just such cigarettes back in Holland, and even advertised in English-language papers and magazines my father had brought me, insisting that I learn some English. So these were American forces!'

He dredged his memory for the English that he knew, and found it flooding back to him. Over the hubbub the prisoners had broken into in five or six different languages, he yelled to the soldier with the cigarette: 'It's been a long time since I had a Lucky Strike!'

The soldier looked at him in surprise: 'You speak English?'

'Yes.'

'Well, come up here!' The soldier hauled him up and gave him a cigarette.

The ice was broken, and the course of Garcia's life was changed. Within a very short time the Americans had adopted him, given him a uniform, and employed him as an interpreter. 'I was not quite 21. I knew two things: that I didn't want to go back to Holland to live, for there would be nothing left for me there; and that I didn't want to go to Palestine, as I didn't want to live only among Jews.' His American saviours were the people he turned to, and wanted to stay with. Beyond that, he didn't think. Once his original adopted unit was ordered to Trieste and had to leave him behind, he managed to get himself attached as an interpreter to the First Battalion, 319th Infantry Regiment Headquarters Company, 80th Infantry Division, whose commander, Lieutenant Colonel Arthur H. Clark, would later befriend him and be his sponsor for emigration to the USA.

It seems that Garcia, once he had 'adopted' the American army, had no serious thoughts of ever going anywhere else to live but the USA. Apart from one reluctantly made visit back to Amsterdam, where he arrived on VJ-Day, and where he found his worst fears confirmed, the 319th became home. However, he belonged and yet he did not belong: his future was insecure.

It became less so when Colonel Clark, just before he returned to America from his tour of duty, promised Garcia that he would do what he could to help him emigrate. He proved as good as his word, although the process took time. Meanwhile Garcia spent 1946 on attachment to the Counter-Intelligence Corps, after six weeks' training in Bamberg – work which involved him principally in helping to track down former Nazis and Nazi sympathizers posing as DPs. There was also a number of Soviet agents infiltrating the DP camps in order to get to America as legal emigrants.

Finally an affidavit came through from America, but at the same time a blow fell. For the affidavit to be valid, he would have to have a visa as well from his country of origin; but he had not returned to the Netherlands after the war and registered, nor had he ever registered at any DP camp. There was a moment when it looked as if he would be unable to use the precious affidavit. Fortunately, his work for CIC had made him valuable to them, and they did not want to see him, as a stateless person, fall into Russian hands knowing what he knew about their operations. The bureaucratic objections to his departure were smoothed out, and with a fellow ex-agent in a similar situation, Garcia set sail for the USA on the SS *Ernie Pyle*, a converted liberty-ship, on 19 September 1946.

His original plan was to enlist in the army, since at that time under wartime law anyone so doing was granted automatic citizenship after 90 days. However, when he joined the Clarks in Buffalo, his sponsor wouldn't hear of it, and suggested instead that he take a job in the family chemical factory. It was not a success; he loathed the production-line work he had to start with, and his extremely coarse English and army manners did not go down well in a provincial American town. Relations became mildly strained, and Garcia decided to seek his own fortune. After several miserable weeks looking for work in New York City, he became a door-to-door magazine salesman ('"You're a natural," the boss told me. "Just tell your prisoner story and you'll sell hundreds of magazines and earn big commissions."') He got no commissions, all he got was come-ons from the lonely women in the New Jersey apartment-blocks that were his 'beat'. He gave up the job. The ambition to become an architect, which he had formed at school, seemed remote. He was uneducated and penniless, a stranger in a strange land. In desperation he joined the army, enlisting for 18 months, and was inducted in March 1947 – three months after the expiry of the law granting automatic citizenship within 90 days.

The army was a joyless place. There was little to do, and a posting to South Carolina brought him into shocking contact with racial segregation and discrimination again. After much frustration, he managed to get an attachment to the Army Medical library. As he had enlisted under the GI Bill, which extended educational benefits to servicemen based on length of service, he enrolled in the US Armed Forces Institute and started high-school diploma classes. It began to look as if he were on the road. In September 1948 he turned down offers of promotion if he re-enlisted, and took his discharge from the army as a private, first-class. Five days later he received his high-school equivalency diploma, and that same month began as a student at George Washington University, benefiting from the GI Bill once more. There was no architecture course at the University, so Garcia enrolled in adult night school to study residential design. Through his course teacher he was able to transfer to a full-time architectural course at North Carolina State University in the autumn of 1949. From then on, his life began to come together, with one nervous moment on the eve of his becoming an American citizen in April 1952. He was pulled up by a policeman for speeding. 'As he started to write me a ticket I pleaded with him not to. I explained that even one arrest on any count would automatically disqualify me for eligibility as a citizen. The cop accused me of being an artist at ingenious excuses, but enough doubt crossed his mind that he put his ticket-book away and commanded me to follow him to a police station. There the police put their heads together to read ordinances and debate my point. They had not heard of any such law. A phone-call to an attorney of the Justice Department confirmed what I had told them. The cop tore up the citation. "It's my gift," he told me, "for becoming a citizen, but if I catch you speeding tomorrow, you're going to be one sorry citizen."'

He moved to California in the early Fifties, met his Protestant wife there, and married in 1957. By 1961 they had three children. Although he does not describe himself as devout or even consciously Jewish, his children were brought up in his faith; and later, of her own volition, his wife converted to Judaism.

Garcia has had a busy and successful post-war life, lived (in the early days at least) away from the Jewish community. Yet he acknowledges that the long shadow of the KZ is still over him. He suffers from migraines, and wakes up occasionally at night, bathed in sweat. There are still nightmares, and sometimes he will wake up screaming. Although his family have criticized him now and then for talking too much about the Holocaust, there have never been any tensions arising from it, and he knows that they have helped him considerably. In 1971, they all returned to Europe with him and visited, among other places, Amsterdam and Ebensee.

In 1975 he returned to Auschwitz with his wife. They did not stay long, to watch the SS film, to see the piles of hair, of shoes, of spectacles that still lie piled where the SS left them, waiting for ever to be turned into material for a vanished Third Reich. He says that as they left he could not resist buying a small plastic Auschwitz pennant from a souvenir booth before getting into their car and setting off on the road home.

French Resistance Fighters

I

The camp at Flossenburg was built in May 1938 to house a mixture of political, criminal and asocial prisoners, but it was not long before the 'red triangles' were in the majority. The first transport of foreign prisoners arrived on 5 April 1940.

The SS had chosen to site the camp deep in the countryside near the Bavarian frontier with Czechoslovakia in order to ensure maximum isolation for the prisoners, and at the same time to employ them as forced labourers in the granite quarries nearby. The camp consisted of 24 large wooden *Blocks*, together with a kitchen *Block*, a *Bunker* (punishment block, or camp prison), and a crematorium. Originally designed to hold 1,600 prisoners, the main camp ultimately held double that number.

After the outbreak of war, the prisoners who, by then, had built the camp were used more frequently in the quarries, and then in the armaments factories which sprang up around the camp, to form sub-camps. In the end there were 85 of these, 60 for men and 25 for women, collectively occupied by a further 5,000 people. In the course of its seven-year life, Flossenburg and its sub-camps held 111,400 people: 95,400 men, and 16,000 women.

Mortality in the complex was high, especially during the last years of the war, typhus claiming many victims whose capacity to resist had already been eroded by hard labour. The International Tracing Service at Arolsen has estimated the number at 22,334, a number which covers only recorded and registered deaths and does not, therefore, include fatalities among Russian POWs in the camp, or the many deaths which occurred in the last weeks.

Flossenburg was liberated by the Americans on 23 April 1945. By that time the majority of the prisoners, about 14,000, had been evacuated and taken on the death-march in three columns, each sent in a different direction. Each was intercepted and liberated by the Americans within a few days, but Arolsen estimates that the march cost a further 4,000 lives in that short time.

The annual general assembly of the *Association de Flossenbürg et Kommandos* takes place in a different part of France each year, but the meeting that marked the 40th anniversary of liberation took place in Paris, beginning with speeches and a lunch at the Hôtel Lutétia. In 1945, this hotel was the clearing-house for returning deportees. In its foyer and reception rooms, great boards with photographs and messages were erected as mothers sought sons, husbands wives, lovers each other – or at least news of them. A plaque at the hotel's main entrance commemorates this. Up to a million French men and women were sent to the KZ – some as pure 'politicals', others, who also wore the red triangle, as resistance fighters.

France has been the most generous country of all to its returning deportees. If, broadly speaking, one identifies three types of payment (the lump-sum, the pension reflecting time lost in the camps, and the pension in recognition of suffering), then it is to the last that France adheres. Many government ministers, such as Simone Veil, were in the camps; and there would have been no question of a Franco-German rapprochement without first coming to an agreement about reparation for those who suffered in the KZ. By 1960, the average monthly tax-free pension was about FF.10,000. Additionally, the French government introduced financial aid to survivors who wished either to resume or to commence higher education. One of the survivors at the assembly had studied to be a doctor under such a scheme. There were also extra payments for permanent injury.

The status of the survivor in France is high, too. On the evening of the first day of the assembly, it fell to the Association to relight the Flame of the Unknown Soldier at the Arc de Triomphe. For a survivor group with relatively few members left, its finances are significantly high, too. It organizes pilgrimages to the site of the camp, and one of its objectives is to maintain pressure on West Germany to keep the camp in good order as a memorial.[1]

The luncheon was held in the Trianon Room of the Lutétia. 'These meetings are important; all of us, I think, have to go on reliving the experience we went through, because we are condemned always to try to get it out of our systems, but we never quite succeed. That we are aware of this makes little difference, and does not release us from the treadmill. So that when we are reunited with comrades who know exactly how we feel, and we see that some of us at least are still here, we celebrate.' Everyone looks well, which is an illusion; but everyone is well dressed, elegantly dressed. They have come from all over France, and some are unsure of themselves in Paris. What other kind of gathering could this be, of apparently quite ordinary, well-to-do bourgeois French people, enjoying the lunch and discussing its merits animatedly? But the careful eyes remind you of what these people have been through, and what they still go through.

Many express their lack of trust in people now. One says that he keeps two loaded guns in his house still, always ready, just in case.

Mme le T, who is not a survivor herself, tells me that she has never felt completely taken into her husband's confidence, and this is borne out by two others, a wife and a widow, whom I speak to later. 'His only safety-valve is this reunion. Even now he won't talk to me about it really, though I've tried and tried to persuade him to. I think it may help him stop the dreams . . . But he won't.' Later, after lunch, on the steps of the hotel, I am talking to the husband. Suddenly he breaks down and cries. I try to comfort him. His wife has walked on a little ahead, and now turns. Neither of us can reach his grief.

'One of the Rothschilds died at Flossenburg,' a frail man tells me, as he might mention a distinguished former school-fellow. 'The Count of Moët et Chandon was in the resistance. He concealed weapons in his caves. They caught him and he was sent to Auschwitz; but he survived. He died in 1970.'

The woman sitting next to me is tall and lean, tanned. Next to her cutlery she places a large, single-bladed penknife, which she uses to eat with (she will do the same at dinner). It has to be there. On the raffle that is organized, she wins a bottle of pudding wine and a man's tie. Immediately, with the generosity of every survivor that I met, she opens the wine for everyone at her table to share, and gives me the tie. 'I had that knife right through the camps. My whole family were in the resistance. When the Gestapo came to our house they shot my parents and my two brothers in front of me. All they did to me was torture me. With the result that I need never wear oven-gloves.'

She invites me to touch the dish of vegetables in front of us. It has just been put there by the waiter and it is red-hot. She picks it up and holds it, looking at me. The others grin; they have seen the party-trick before. One of them says: 'There is no sensitivity in the tips of Madeleine's fingers any more. They made her handle newly-baked bricks at Flossenburg.'

She continues: 'They put me in an *Aussenkommando* of Flossenburg. I suppose they didn't kill me because I was so young. We were liberated on the death-march by Czech partisans.' Shortly afterwards she had a horrible experience: a group of them came across a shed in which there were sacks of what they took to be flour. Starving, they threw themselves on the food and gorged, only to discover, after they had filled their mouths and swallowed, that it was powdered glue. 'We all felt our throats seizing up – by the grace of God the store also contained some cherries pickling in jars of alcohol. We smashed them open and forced the cherries down our throats – and the alcohol dissolved the glue enough to enable us to breathe and vomit.'

The following day there was early mass at Notre-Dame at which both Catholic and Protestant priests officiated, and afterwards a ceremony at the memorial to the Unknown Deportee, just behind the cathedral. On the way, M. Kuntz tells me: 'When I returned home, I trained myself to climb Mont Blanc. I did it because I have always loved the mountains. I decided that I would give myself two years, within which time I would have made myself fit enough to climb.'

The memorial, designed by Pingusson and dedicated in 1962, is impressive. One descends by steps through a narrow entranceway in a thick wall to a courtyard surrounded by high grey walls. In one of them is another narrow chasm-like entrance, which leads to a round room with a circular brass plaque in the centre of its floor. Round it is inscribed: *Ils sont allés au bout de la terre et ils ne sont pas revenus.* Beyond the room and opposite the entrance is a false corridor – a blank corridor into whose grey walls pearls of white glass light are embedded – symbolizing the 200,000 French men and women who died in the KZ. And at the end of the corridor shines a small, solitary light – symbolizing help. In front of it lies a black slab beneath which is the body of the Unknown Deportee. In the wings off the corridor, deep triangular niches are cut in which poems are inscribed. The monument is designed to weigh on the soul, to enclose. There is a private museum beyond it containing terrible photographs of life in the KZ. My companions were not awed; they chatted, pointed things out; a right they had earned.

II

Robert Deneri, the son of Corsican parents, was born in Paris in 1922. He took his *baccalauréat* in mathematics and philosophy, and was on the point of commencing a course in mathematics at the Ecole Polytechnique when he was arrested, for 'the manifestation of sentiments hostile to Germany'. He remained in prison under Gestapo interrogation for several months until, on 31 July 1944, he was informed that he had been sentenced to death and would be taken to Leipzig for execution.

He ended up not at Leipzig but at Potsdam, and was placed with a group of others condemned to death in a huge death-cell. There followed weeks of waiting, every day of which saw one or two taken out, never to return. At last only two people remained in the cell. Somewhere the orders concerning their fate had got lost, and they could not be executed without them. 'Not quite knowing what to do with us, the SS attached us to a transport bound for Sachsenhausen. We arrived there with such broad grins on our faces that the prisoners already there must have taken us for madmen. But we felt that our escape from execution was such a good omen that we were determined to fight for life from now on.'

He was sent to a sub-camp on the Polish border, where he stayed until January 1945. The Russian advanced forces actually passed their camp, but the SS were able to force-march their small group of prisoners through to their own lines at night. After days on the road, under battle conditions, they regained Berlin. They arrived in time to be attached to a transport of Jewish prisoners destined for *produktive Vernichtung* at Flossenburg, and arrived at the camp on 5 February, staying there until the evacuation of 20 April.

'During the whole period of my imprisonment there was never a moment when I said to myself consciously: "I will survive." I was 22, and all I knew was that I wanted to see my family again. The rest followed naturally. I might add that in my experience the moment a comrade started to ask himself whether the struggle for life was really worth while, we all knew that he'd be dead within a week, if not within a day. They did their best to break us down. Useless work was their favourite trick: we had to carry enormous blocks of granite from A to B, and then back again. Two other slightly more useful jobs I had were cleaning out the latrine ditches and dragging corpses to the crematorium. I think the cold would have killed me, but one day when they were asking if anyone was an electrician, I volunteered. I wasn't one, of course, but I am a bit of a handyman, and I thought, why not? I had to install the power points in a new wooden SS barrack, and I did the job so well that the German civilian foreman who took part in the selection of slaves for work duty every morning asked that I be attached to his team.

'Friendships helped one's morale, and practically, too. In Sachsenhausen I remember that the *Blockälteste* really didn't like my face. He thought I was a soft little pen-pusher, and he was right, I wasn't used to hard physical work; so he kept giving me far more to do than I could possibly manage and, when I failed to complete it, packed me off to the punishment squad. But there were seven British prisoners there – airmen, I think. They would obey the orders only of their senior officer. For example, when we were marched back into camp, and the kapos gave the order to stop, they just went on marching until their senior officer halted them. Then they cheered. The kapos and the SS were a bit frightened of them, possibly. They certainly inspired us enormously.

They were allowed food-parcels, and shared what they had with the Russians, who were treated like dirt, and starving.

'Friendship was determined by nationality as well, because of the language question. At Sachsenhausen, in my *Block* of 1,500 people, there was one other Frenchman, a Belgian, a Dutchman, a dozen Norwegians, a few Germans – though fewer than 50 of them were civilized people. The rest were mainly Russians. I always tried to get on to the same *Kommando* as the other Frenchman. He was a lawyer, and we were able to chat a little, when the SS weren't looking. We recited verses to each other, in Latin and Greek, to keep our minds bright, and we talked of our studies, and about Paris. We'd go for imagined strolls down the Champs Elysées, trying to remember all the shops, cafés and cinemas in order. And we talked about our families.

'He didn't make it, nor did the Belgian, nor the Dutchman . . .

'By the time I got to Flossenburg, it was a place of perpetual battle – you had to fight to get a place to sleep, even. But I came across some fellow-students from the polytechnic there, and they helped – and not only morally. I was able through them to avoid being sent on one of the *Kommandos* that worked on the V-1 and V-2 rockets in the underground factories. The mortality rate among the prisoners working there was touching 100 per cent at the time. Sadly, my friends were in a different *Block* from mine, and we saw one another only rarely.

'I would say that in the end it was less a question of friendships than of alliances. It may sound odd, but in the world of the camps we were divided into two main groups, just as if Yalta had already taken place. The West Europeans closed ranks, even with the German prisoners, when it came to mass fights with the hordes of Russians, Czechs and Poles.

'Kapos, in my experience, were nearly all dishonourable people, and, by the way, I never knew of a Frenchman or any West European accept a kapo's job. They were really the creatures of the SS. In our camp, kapos were mainly drawn from the ranks of the green, pink and purple triangles. The best kapos were the German red triangles, most of whom had been in the KZ since 1934 or 1935; they knew the ropes, they saw which way things were going, and they knew what precautions to take to see it through. I never knew any kapos personally, though, and I don't know anyone who did. Most of them only communicated through the bludgeon, the whip and the knife. With my own eyes I saw one kill a prisoner by driving a pickaxe into his stomach. People would run on to the wire and electrocute themselves rather than submit to the sadistic punishments of the kapos.

'We had even less contact with the SS, who remained aloof most of the time. The German SS, the real ones, were tough types, but the SS from the conquered eastern areas, like the Ukraine, were even worse.

Towards the end, though, they started to draft in much older men to keep up the numbers – veterans of the First World War.

'I remember that once we were guarded by a military unit of SS who had seen action in Normandy – I think they were from the *Reich* division – and, instead of leave, had to come and attend to us. They sought me out, since I was French, and had me light a fire. Then they invited me to sit at it with them. They told me news of the front and told me to keep my chin up, since the war was lost and the Allies would soon be here. They had been stupefied by the amount and quality of the armaments found on Allied soldiers they'd taken prisoner. They told me that now they realized, too late, what folly it had been to follow Hitler, that all his vainglorious ambitions had ended in nothing but ruin for Germany. That was in January. I had to hang on for another three months.

'Food became scarcer and scarcer. I know that the KZ proved that people could go on living without food – or, rather, at a certain level of semi-starvation – for far longer than had ever previously been believed possible; again it was a problem of how one came to terms with having little or nothing to eat. It was easier for an intellectual who would be able to distract his mind from thoughts of food than for a manual worker who might torture himself every mealtime with thoughts of steak-and-chips. I think the hardest thing to cope with was the injustice of the food distribution. To see a kapo rifle the food-packages and treat himself to piles of delicacies, and then the same day to see a man killed for trying to get an extra portion of soup: that was very hard to support. Physically, for myself I find that even today I can go for a long time without food or drink without any ill-effects.

'When it came, liberation was a slaughterhouse. The Americans had followed our death-march column but weren't able to attack it because they had sent only a small unit after us, and we were guarded by something like 800 SS. They knew they were finished, and finally – as a parting gesture, you might say – they just opened fire on the column. The only hope was to break from the road and run to one of the farmhouses already flying the white flag, and hide. I was with a group of 15. Two of us made it.'

Deneri returned home to a hero's welcome. While indemnification didn't come through from Germany until the Sixties, the French government covered his keep and fees, enabling him to finish his education. 'There was no problem with my family: everyone had survived, and there was great joy in France at having thrown off the German yoke. I wasn't yet 23 and life was ahead of me. I felt good. The worst thing was encountering the parents of those comrades who had not survived: they wanted to know exactly how and when their children had died. It was hard to tell them. Religious faith never played any role, one way or the other. I would describe myself as a non-practising Catholic. That's what I have always been.

'I had to convalesce until the autumn. I spent my convalescence in a little village in Brittany, and there I met my future wife – the only indirect effect of the deportation upon my private life. In October, I was able to resume my studies. I had two years to go. But immediately there were difficulties. I found it hard to memorize things, and over and above that I just didn't have the urge to study, to concentrate. Life seemed dull, and I increasingly occupied myself with extra-mural activities. I did a lot of sport, and became social welfare officer for my student year, involved in finding work in the private sector for those of my comrades who, on leaving, didn't want to take up jobs in the civil service or the armed forces. And there were other duties. I needed to be active, to stick my neck out, to keep away from routine.

'My own career followed this pattern: I'd originally intended to go into the army, but the disappearance of France's colonies meant that I no longer found that an attractive option. I therefore went into the private sector myself and, ironically, after having found so many jobs for others, had my father to thank for finding the job I finally settled in, as an engineer. I started work on 1 October 1947, and remained with the same company until my retirement, at 60, in 1982. During that time I became engineer-in-chief, and ended up as Technical and Research Director. It hasn't been a humdrum life. I worked for an international concern, and I visited over 60 countries in my time with them.

'I don't dream at all; at least, I'm not aware of dreaming, so that there are no nightmares for me in that strict sense. But if you want to speak of a feeling of "sad remembrance", then yes, that is with me always. You cannot help making constant comparisons between what happens now and what happened then. Always you think: this is bad, but that was worse. It isn't necessarily a good feeling. There have been times since the camp when I have experienced real fear: once, at Havana airport, our flight out was delayed for hours, and the customs hadn't give us our passports back, and there was no explanation of what was going on; and once, coming back through Checkpoint Charlie into West Berlin, the sense of relief was extraordinary. That may be the result of something that happened. One of my best comrades was liberated in hospital; he was alive, and he was well on the mend. Allied medics saw him and brought back some letters for his family which he'd written in his sick-bed. And then the hospital came into the Russian zone. Since when, nothing. Is my friend Paul still alive?

'I am convinced that the camps taught me to be a survivor. I was 21 when I was arrested and I had experienced nothing terrifying in my life other than the bombardments of Paris, which were pretty light and rare up until 1943, and the retreat west away from the German advance –

eight days on the road, constantly attacked by Stukas and Italian planes; it was then that I saw my first corpses. But that was nothing to what the camps would have in store. What armed me for life in them was, firstly, that my mind had been sharpened by the study of advanced mathematics; and, secondly, that I was very fit: I was a long-distance runner. The experience itself made me a harder man, sadly, in two senses of the word "hard". In the first sense, which applied to work, I see the hardness as a positive quality. I could drive myself, which earned me respect, which in turn brought cooperation. I built and started up factories in many countries, and never encountered serious professional problems ever, anywhere. I have survived earthquakes and revolutions. The only thing that I have never been able to accept with equanimity is the re-routing of a flight!

'However, hardness in its second guise, in personal life, is negative. I always expected absolute obedience from my children, and I was a severe father to them. I would never tolerate complaints or moaning from them. When he was only two, if my son fell and hurt himself, even if he did so quite seriously, I would always say to him: "Boys never cry." He swallowed his tears, and became hard, tough. He still remembers how I treated him. If either of my daughters cried, I would order them to go to their rooms until they had finished. I am perfectly aware of this disagreeably harsh streak in my character, and I believe it is common to many survivors of my acquaintance. But it shuts me off, because now no one ever tells me if there's anything bothering them, or takes me into their confidence; and likewise no one asks me if everything is all right with me.

'It has affected my choice of friends, too. I am very particular about whom I befriend, and seek out in a person I am getting to know any possible marks of weakness. If I find them, I withdraw. This trait in my character has increased as I have grown older, and I have become more exigent, so naturally the circle of my true friends is small. That doesn't mean that I am unsociable, or that I do not have many acquaintances. But friends are something different, something more. In my mid-sixties I find myself still hard, and still very intolerant; but I have neither the desire nor the hope of changing now . . .

'I am an optimist, though, and I bounce back. Only very rarely does a bad setback affect me for more than a few minutes, or prevent me from sleeping. But I don't deserve any credit for that, since my automatic reflex has always been: "It's happened before and I'm still here." I know that I am one of the privileged ones, since few of us are still alive; but I also know that I won't see real old age, because one year in a camp gave the equivalent of several years' stress to mind and body. Still, if I've only got a short time left, there's all the more reason to live it joyfully.'

III

Because his little brother was so frightened by the bombing raids, Gilbert Coquempot's parents moved the family out of Boulogne-sur-Mer to the little village of La Capelle, not far away. Gilbert continued to travel into town to attend school; but in 1940, when the war reached them, he had to abandon his studies and go to work. He was 16.

There was still an opportunity to study music at the conservatoire in the evenings. He played the clarinet and the tenor saxophone well; but there was no question of his taking music up professionally, whatever his private ambitions might have been. 'If I'd been born 20 or 30 years later, maybe; but at that time there really wasn't any question or much possibility. Of course, it all came to an end when I was arrested, and there was a big gap between then and returning from the camps. Not so long in time, perhaps, but an age in experience, and something that set me apart from my fellow-men for ever. It was very strange to see my clarinet again at the end of the war, in my room at my parents'. Nothing had changed and yet everything in that room seemed to belong to a different person. I don't play any more, because my health won't permit it, but I am still interested – classical and jazz – and I tinker away at the piano a bit. Music's been a great help. There was even an orchestra at Flossenburg, many of whose Jewish members were professional players. It gave concerts in the shower-rooms, and you had to be careful if you attended them. The SS thought it quite a joke to round up the audience afterwards and detail them to the hard-labour squad. Even at the *Aussenkommando* I was sent to, the Russians sang songs for the SS.'

He went to work with Petit Frères, a large hardware and metalworking concern, which also did plumbing and central-heating installation, where he remained until 1942. Then he was drafted by the Germans to work for the army of occupation at Neufchâtel-Hardelot, a small town a few miles along the coast and slightly inland, to the south of Boulogne. 'Because I had at least a working knowledge of German from school, I used to act as an interpreter for Petit Frères – who had to undertake work for the Germany navy. I understood the technical terms needed, and I translated the invoices from French to German and did the conversions from francs to *Reichsmarks*, which meant that I had a pass which permitted me to go freely to the port, to take the invoices to the German naval people. I felt that I was in a strong position to help the resistance, but although I was in contact with a cell, it was difficult to get accepted. They were fearful of infiltrators.

'The Germans weren't bad in themselves. They were regular military, not SS, but the mere fact that they were there, occupying our country, made us hate them. We refused to have more to do with them than we absolutely had to. From the moment they crossed our frontiers I personally decided to resist them.

'There was a three-day siege before they took Boulogne. When they finally occupied the town I went to the baker's – we hadn't had any bread during the siege – but the Germans wouldn't allow us to buy it. That made me very angry, right from the start.

'Four days after they arrived, they ordered that we should all give up our radios, which we had to hand over in a big room at the town hall. I had a row with my father about giving up the radio, but a day or so later my Uncle Jean said he'd got something which would interest me: it was his radio, which he'd hidden behind a gas-fire that didn't work. I used to go and listen to the BBC broadcasts at 8.15 in the evening. That was our little breath of liberty, and de Gaulle's call to arms of 18 June 1940 really inspired me. Before Boulogne fell I wanted to get on a boat for England and join the Free French forces, but all available boats were reserved for departing troops. I should have left earlier. My parents supported me in that ambition, but I did not let them know that I was now trying to involve myself with the resistance.

'My chance came in 1942 when I was sent to Neufchâtel. By chance I met a boy called René Milon – he was a lieutenant in the resistance. We sounded each other out, and finally he offered me a job as an information-gatherer, which I took, though sadly it didn't last long. Our group was betrayed by a French double-agent posing as a resistance liaison officer.

'We didn't have to commit any "act of faith" when we enlisted, since we were only an information-gathering cell, not a fighting one. My job was to monitor troop- and supply-train movements, especially ammunition trains. I gave the information to René. That was all I knew. Of course each one of us had only very limited information, in case we were caught. I don't know what effect my modest contribution had, but Neufchâtel was a busy junction, so my job was relatively easy to do unnoticed. I started work, but shortly afterwards the Belgian officer who led our cell was arrested by the Gestapo for the second time, and the "liaison officer" disappeared. We knew matters would come to a head soon.

'My turn came on 5 December 1943. I was still living at La Capelle with my parents, but we were rehearsing in Boulogne that Sunday morning for a concert to be given the same evening for the benefit of the local fire brigade. I was arrested at the rehearsal at the Music School. They'd been to my house first and arrested my father and brought him with them: two SS and two gendarmes. When I saw him with them I knew that there was no question of my escaping. They'd taken him hostage to ensure that I wouldn't. To reassure my father I told him that they were probably rounding me up for forced labour in Germany – they were doing that with young people at the time. But they held me in the prison at Boulogne for three days; from that he knew that I was actually under arrest.

'They interrogated me, and broke a tooth – in Boulogne already! They asked me if I knew why I'd been arrested; if I was a Catholic or a Communist – all sorts of useless questions. Then at one session the interrogator pointed to a gun, a revolver that was lying on the table, and asked me, "Do you know what this is?" And I could see that this was going to be some kind of game, and so I said, "Well, it's a pistol." He said, "And I don't suppose you know anything else, like all you lying Frenchmen." And he hit me with the gun across the face so that I fell down. "We know it's your gun," he said. They picked me up and put me on a chair. They interrogated us all like that, one after another; they'd got most of us, including René Milon.

'I was transferred to the prison at Loos-Lille. They put us in solitary, windowless cells. I had one interrogation there at the beginning and the people were more courteous, but the questions were more detailed. I remember that I had to go down a long sombre corridor to the interrogation room. Off it were interrogation cells and from them you could hear the cries of the tortured. That made quite an impression.

'My interrogator was called Pfeffer. He was very polite, but probing. I made my replies as vague as I could, and acted the sincere innocent. When that session was over, he said quite gently that he would have to check my statement, then he would recall me. So I went back to my cell and waited . . . two or three weeks. Then I was taken back to Pfeffer's room and immediately I noticed that there were three coshes, of different size, laid out on the table. He told me that my statement didn't check out at all against those made by the others. I continued to act the innocent. So they beat me up: 20 or 30 blows with one or other of the coshes.

'In the course of time we were able to build up a *téléphone arabe* – by tapping morse signals on the pipes. Every day at fixed times the Germans shut off the water supply. What you did was open the tap in your cell and suck out the water to empty the pipe; then you could communicate with people up to three cells distant . . . At my third interrogation I was confronted with René. We told them we were work-mates. At least over the pipes Milon had been able to let me know that we had been betrayed, and that we would have to walk on eggs.

'The great thing in our favour was that we had not been armed when we were caught. If we had been, they'd have accused us of terrorism, and I think we would have been executed out of hand. As it was, all they could level against us was "attempting to give aid to the enemy". By now it was February 1944. One fine day I was recalled to the interrogation room, greeted with an immediate blow across the shoulders, and they were back on the question of the revolver again. They said, "We know it's yours; Gaston Lambert gave it to you – and he is one of our agents." That much was true – Lambert was the name of the double-agent. I refused to fall in with their suggestion; it was foolish anyway, because Lambert hadn't given me a gun, even if he'd told Pfeffer that he had; but I had to say something, for I actually did have a revolver at home, picked up at the time of the siege, when anyone could get hold of small-arms. I told Pfeffer that I had had a gun in 1940, that I'd kept it with a vague idea of shooting myself if the worst came to the worst, but that I'd thrown it away. I even told him exactly where I'd thrown it, to give my story verisimilitude, hoping against hope that he wouldn't check ... After the war, when I was liberated and reunited with my father, he told me that he'd found my gun in my bedroom at home, and had hung on to it for a couple of months; but that it had worried him to have it in the house, so he'd thrown it away – in exactly the same place I'd told the interrogator that he'd find it, and at about the same time!

'On 1 July they condemned us to death – Milon, three others, and me. The executions started on the 14th. On the 20th they came for us, at 5am; but they didn't take us down to be shot. Instead, we were taken to Germany and put into a prison for condemned men at Ebrach, near Bayreuth, and there we stayed until the beginning of December. It appeared that our case had been reopened for some mysterious reason by the Gestapo in Berlin, and after some desultory further examination we were told we would be transported to a labour camp.'

They arrived at Flossenburg later in the month. It was cruelly cold already, and they were subjected to all the psychological assault of arrival common to all the camps: the screamed orders to do everything at the double, the snarling dogs, the blows on the head, the curses, the bewildering floodlights. And there were refinements. 'An SS-man asked our group if any of us were boxers; and almost without waiting for a reply he started to hit some of us with clenched fists. Then we were forced to run up the hill to the camp, a distance of about three kilometres, harassed all the time by the SS and their dogs. At least one of us died on the way up that hill; and I know that one of my friends lost hope the moment he got off the train and saw those bestial creatures called SS. The shock of arrival was appalling – seeing the Mussulmen, naked walking corpses – it was unimaginable. Though it was snowing, we were forced to strip naked for disinfection. At the same time we had to give up our wedding rings, our watches, anything else of value that we had – and still all at the double, though it was so cold I think we would have moved fast anyway. As we showered – one scalding, one freezing – an SS-man accompanied us mockingly on an accordion.

It was pure madness from the word go. People died within the first two hours of arrival – from pure shock, I am sure.

'We were immediately selected for *Kommandos* and we had a 1, 2 or 3 painted on our foreheads: 1 for heavy work; 2 for medium, and 3 for light – though light was worse than many could stand. I got a 2. They took us next to the quarantine *Block*, and gave us our numbers.[2] Mine was 48017. Actually, I've forgotten if it was 48017 or 48170 – I'll have to check.

'I lay down next to a comrade and wept; I thought it was all over.'

The next morning revealed fresh horrors. When they were allowed to go to the latrines they saw that the ditch over which they squatted was full of corpses. Every detail is remembered with awful clarity, and has to be described. Nothing can be skirted, or excised. He was allocated to *Block* 5, where they slept four to a bunk, 70 centimetres wide. Though the few Jews and Gypsies at the main camp were housed separately, he was not aware that, by this stage in the war, they were treated any worse than the other prisoners. In his own *Block*, all nationalities were thrust together. Small alliances and friendship groups tended to be based on nationality, and even on region. The *Block*, designed for 200 people, held 1,200. Each *Block* had two wings, and people in one never met people in the other. The building was like a crowded town. Sharing Coquempot's *Block* somewhere was the man who later became President of the *Association de Flossenbürg*, Henri Lerognon; but they never met, either in the camp or the *Block*.

'They came in at 5am and started yelling, "*Los! Aufstehen! Aufstehen!*" – maybe they blew whistles, too, rang bells. The word *aufstehen* is the worst in any language. I still cannot hear it without a sense of panic, of the stomach falling away. Then roll-call, then work.'

In Flossenburg main camp he was sent briefly to the quarries but worked mainly on snow-clearing. After two months, he was selected for the sub-camp of Ganackur, 130 kilometres away. The journey was made, as usual, in filthy goods-waggons, into which they were crammed 90 to a car. As usual, many died on the way. No one could lie down. 'But when I consider that they also transported the Jews in this way – old people, mothers and little children . . .'

Ganackur was a secondary Messerschmitt factory, where aircraft fuselages were made; but when the prisoners arrived, a camp had yet to be established. They slept on the floor of the hangars, just as they were – there was nothing at all. All they were given to eat was one piece of bread every day – for drink, they had to eat snow. The work, initially, was to make a clearing in the woods in which the camp was to be built. It was March, and the temperature was −25°C. Their only hope lay in liberation through Allied victory, but they were so totally cut off that they didn't know how close that might be.

'No one single thing made me decide to survive. There was no conscious decision. Comradeship helped. We formed little groups: that helped a lot; morally and practically, especially for me at the very end, because I had developed an eye infection, which meant that I could barely see. My comrades guided me. I would have been killed without their help. And there was a big Russian POW there. I reminded him of his son, and he helped me in my work whenever it was too heavy, too much for me. I remember that when we were liberated he said to me, "Yes, it's liberty for you – but what will it be for me?" And we went westwards, and the Russians eastwards.

'I never for a moment felt tempted to give up. Once you had got through one month, you thought, let's try to get through another one, and so on. And we'd talk together whenever we could, and try to keep our spirits up. Mostly we talked about food – but we tried to keep it under control because you ran a great risk of going mad if your fantasies ran away with you.'

He is sure that his youthfulness helped him get through. 'The older men went down more quickly, because of what they'd lost; maybe too because they simply didn't have the animal strength of a 20-year-old, who had his life in front of him and everything to live for. But there were comrades of my age who survived everything, only to die or be shot on the death-march, like my friend Paul Coquereau. And there were those who couldn't take it, who committed suicide soon after. And there were those who made it home, who had just that amount of strength left, like my friend Philippe Borrego, from Bordeaux. A month after our return home I contacted his family, and his father told me that he'd died – he had just faded away, there was no strength left to carry him into a new life. There doesn't seem to be any rhyme or reason for it. I think I was helped by finding everything intact when I got home, and by the support I got from my friends.'

During his time in Ganackur he was beaten appallingly by kapos using rubber truncheons simply because he tripped and fell during a roll-call. The truncheons were designed to curl round the kidneys as the blows fell on the back. He would have been beaten to death if his comrades had not managed to pull him clear. 'One final blow caught me across the small of my back and cut my breath off.' The whole episode lasted only a few seconds, but its effect later was to cut deeply into his life.

'As the end came, we were evacuated from Ganackur. For a week or so beforehand we saw American aeroplanes flying over to bomb the Messerschmitt factory. During the raids the Germans made us lie stretched out in the open to prevent the Allies from coming back and strafing the area.

'The SS marched us out and kept us marching for five days or so. On the last day we met an SS lorry coming the other way and the two groups of SS talked. Then our SS turned to us and shouted: "The war's over! Get lost!" We were frightened and suspected a trap. We stayed where we were. The SS became furious. "Get lost!" they shouted. I said to Philippe Borrego, "We might as well die walking as standing," and off we went. Into the forest. The next day we kept moving cautiously through the forest – and then we came across a group of regular German soldiers. They were bivouacked. We put our hands up, expecting the worst, but they told us to relax, and they gave us bread and soup. After we'd rested for a bit, they said: "You'd better get going. There're still SS around, and if they catch you here, we'll all cop it – you and us both; and it's not quite over yet."

'We wandered on and finally we reached an American unit. A soldier took my photograph, and the only thing I regret from the moment of my liberation is that I was too tired to get his name and address. I was only interested in food and sleep. But there is a photo of me at that moment somewhere in the USA. I'd like a copy.

'Every day in the KZ is imprinted upon one's mind for ever. One can run through it like a film. It's indelible. If I live to be 90, I know it won't have faded at all – no matter how much events since may have.

'Things get burnt into your mind. For example, when I was still at Flossenburg I was on a fatigue duty which took me into the *Block* which was filled with little children – yes, I know, but there was a children's *Block* at Flossenburg. And I won't describe it to you; I don't think I need to. There were little children there, three years old. Of all the atrocities I encountered, this was the worst. Hearing their cries from outside was bad enough: seeing their condition was something that haunts me still, though I can't have been in the *Block* for more than a few minutes. I still dream about it, and waken shattered. I used to dream about it frequently, during the years that I was paralysed . . . But you see, it's so difficult to communicate what it was like to someone who wasn't there.

'I got back home at the end of May or the beginning of June. I didn't have the courage to do anything; I was totally dispirited. I had nightmares all the time; there was nothing I could do, could turn my hand to. I weighed 40 kilogrammes when I got back to Boulogne. I started work again in December . . . and at the same time, music came back into my life: it was still the time of post-war celebrations, there were lots of dances. A group of old friends from the Music School and I formed a group. It was through that that I found an interest in life again. We played jazz, dance-music, on Saturday and Sunday nights, and Sunday lunchtimes.

'But little by little the back-trouble started. I moved out here to Condette for the good of my health. It was here that I met Madeleine, my wife. Although, thanks to her, my spiritual strength grew, physically I declined.

'I got in touch with the Association because, in order to qualify for reparation, you had to be registered with such an organization, through which funds were distributed, and through which representations were made. But at the time I didn't want to be involved at a personal level. I thought a great deal by myself about those friends who had died, who stayed down there at Flossenburg. And of course the fact that I was paralysed for 15 years in any case prevented me from taking an active part in the work of the Association. But I made the pilgrimage to Flossenburg, stretched out on a board in the car while Madeleine drove. That was in 1973. We did the journey in stages, two to go down there and three to come back, for I was uncomfortable both in a lying and in a sitting position. I had to keep changing from one to the other.'

He was paralysed from 1964 until 1979, the result of the beating he received at Ganackur. There is a bench, covered with green cushions, not long enough to stretch full length, but wide, in a sunny corner of the sitting room where two windows meet. That is where he spent most of his life between the ages of 40 and 55.

'As soon as I regained the ability to walk, I had a keen desire to travel, to participate, to make up for lost time. But there were lots of very simple things that were pure joy: to go for a walk with my wife; to sit down together at table and eat.

'I think my mental attitude depends upon my state of health. If I have the smallest twinge in my back these days, I have such fear that the paralysis will return that I lie awake, and many ghosts come to haunt me; except that the memories are far too real, too immediate, to be called ghosts. And all the time that I was paralysed, it was very hard to get away from the thoughts, to distract myself. At the beginning, when the paralysis was total, I was able even to read only with difficulty. I used to be terrified of going to sleep, because of the nightmares – Madeleine used to calm me when I woke. It could be grim. I had to be strapped into bed. I would throw myself out otherwise. But even if I had been tempted to try to forget it all, how could I? It isn't a question of temptation. Given the choice, I wouldn't want to. I think I would regard that as a form of cowardice. But I have an optimistic nature. Maybe it is better for some people to bury the memory.

'Certainly I picked up in spirits from the moment I met Madeleine, whatever happened to me physically. As the illness progressed, though, I became depressed, and had more bad dreams. I felt bitter, too. But it's funny how people react to things. My brother-in-law makes a great point of telling us how much he suffered too in the war, running his farm; and he says he can't even bear winter sports because snow has such terrible connotations for him. For myself, icicles trigger memories, especially the ones you see formed in tractor ruts when you go for a walk in winter. I have the taste in my mouth of the icicles we broke from the ruts made by the German lorries in Ganackur, when there was no other way of getting anything to drink.'

They have five children, the oldest born in 1952 and the youngest in 1964. The oldest is the one most affected by his father's past, since he was 12 when Gilbert fell ill. He so turned in upon himself that he would frequently refuse to speak for days on end during the first year. Gilbert says that what he regrets most about his illness is not having been able to play with his younger children when they were little.

It was inevitable that the whole family should talk about Gilbert's past, since the evidence of what it had done to him was there before them. 'The kids wanted to know what was wrong with me and why; and it was very important to make sure that they didn't automatically start to hate *all* Germans because of what *some* Germans did to me. Conversation about the camps arose naturally from the children's questions, and from that, when I recovered, I started to give talks to schoolchildren. My daughter Cathérine was given a school project to do on the deportation and the resistance, and she told her teacher that I had been involved, and she made me the subject of her project. She was proud and pleased to do it, which did me good. The teacher thought her work excellent and got her to read it to the whole class, and congratulated me, too! That is how I started.

'There's an annual inter-school essay competition on the theme of the resistance, and the last Thursday of April is consecrated to the memory of the martyrs of the deportation. All the same, when I have gone to schools to lecture on the resistance I have to admit that, out of a class of 30 15- or 16-year-olds, in general only two or three even know what the resistance was. It's a bit disappointing; you'd think their families would tell them something about it. After all, it's an important period of recent history, and most French families were affected by it one way or another. But the students do show an interest quite quickly – most of them – though of course there are those who think the whole resistance fight was rather like the Wild West: *bam! bam!*

'There are two politically opposed groups of associations of former deportees in France. I belong to both. I find it absurd that we should commemorate our dead, and try to promote harmony on account of our suffering, on party political lines. We fought a common enemy, and put our political differences aside. In terms of our associations, it seems to me that that is how it should still be. [UNADIF is Gaullist; FTP (Francs-Tireurs Partisans) is Communist.]

'Since liberation I have lived my life not just for myself but also for my dead comrades: any pleasure I feel I also feel for them – in fact I think I feel it more for them than for myself. I think of the life that they have missed. I came home, fell in love, married, had children. I do not feel guilty that I survived, but I do ask myself, why was I spared and not Paul, or Philippe? There is a kind of permanent communion with them – a contact with those who were left behind down there . . .'

Gilbert Coquempot was awarded the *Légion d'Honneur* – as a bona fide invalided member of the resistance. The *Croix Militaire* was also awarded to him later for services to France. He says that he wears them on behalf of his dead comrades. 'Materially, in terms of pensions, France paid us in relation to the degree of our invalidity. There is a special statute relating to deportees. From Germany I got two very small lump-sum payments.

'It is difficult to say how it has affected me spiritually, overall. I was born into an observant Roman Catholic family. When I was arrested I found refuge in prayer at first, but in the KZ I had a real crisis of faith – of belief. I found I couldn't believe in God any more; and yet I was spared. But that didn't bring my faith back; so I still don't know why I was spared. There were Jews in Ganackur and towards the end we found ourselves barracked together. When we couldn't sleep, when there was time for conversation at all, they might say: "Look at what is happening. Look at the children's *Block* alone, and can you then still say to us that you believe in a Christ who was sent into the world to save us all?" And I had no answer to give them . . . Only much later did my faith return – at least formally. I can't say that I'm very observant any more.

'As for being a natural survivor – well, I was born under Leo, so I'm a fighter! Seriously, it's hard to talk of oneself in such a context. When it was all over, I might well have given up. I seem fine to you today, because I feel good. But come another day, after I've had trouble with my legs or my back, and you will see a very different person.

'I don't think the camps make one stronger, either. Things were so different. Down there, I could and would be surrounded by heaps of dead bodies every day and wouldn't give them a glance: it was normal. One sat on a pile of them to eat one's soup. Today, if there's a funeral of a friend or neighbour, I won't go and look at the body. I don't want to see a dead body. But that is nothing to do with the KZ; that is just my normal nature. There may be a psychical relationship between the KZ experience and its application in life afterwards. It's debatable; I'm not convinced even of that; but I don't think the KZ affects our deportment in normal life, because the KZ is a totally different world from the one we live in normally.

'It is possible that I am more mistrustful of people than I might otherwise have been; and there is certainly a lack of confidence in a new person. There is little desire in me normally to open up to a new person. I think I operate amiably with most people, but it is also true to say that certain people set warning lights flashing, and I go into my shell. I don't know why. It is possible that I am more cautious than I was before; but I was very young. How can I tell? I certainly don't place people in the context of the KZ and then ask myself what they'd have been like there.'

IV

When the Germans entered Paris, Denise McAdam Clark had just started her career as a barrister. 'I joined the resistance in the winter of 1941/2. I had wanted to join from the moment the Germans invaded. As I have got older, I can see how some people were forced to compromise, to collaborate with the Germans – but for some years I could find no excuse for them. The desire to resist was automatic for me. There was no question of acting otherwise; the only question was how and when to contact them: they didn't exactly advertise! By luck, though, a close friend turned out to be the head of a resistance *réseau* whose work was to look after Allied flyers who'd been shot down and get them back to England – important work, when you consider how much it costs in time and money to train an airman – and also to arrange reception for Allied soldiers who were flown in to help the resistance. We weren't all that well organized.[3]

'Our main area of operation was Brittany and western France, though another escape-route led across the Pyrenees to Spain – a route which my friend Andrée de Jongh was involved in. Later I found out that our organization had the codename "Comet"; it was started in Belgium.'[4]

She continued to work as a barrister while pursuing her resistance activities, but her legal work took second place. She has a letter written in 1942 from the French Bar Association bringing her to book for not practising enough. 'I replied to them to the effect that I was *momentanément instable*,' she says with a laugh. Her job involved helping install the Allied airmen in safe-houses until it was time to take them out on one of the escape-routes. 'Sometimes they had to be concealed for months, cooped up, unable to leave the flat where they were staying. It could lead to some tension; but worse, when the time came for them to escape, they were physically unfit. If their route took them across the Pyrenees – which might mean crossing a high pass in winter, at night and on foot, some of them simply didn't have the stamina for it; and resting increased the risk of betrayal. Indeed, that was how Andrée de Jongh got caught.'[5]

By the early summer of 1943 the line was running into difficulties, and they had 25 British and Allied airmen waiting in Paris to be sent down it. 'They had no sense of real danger, and they didn't understand the risks the resistance were running for them. They complained about the quality of the civilian clothes they were given, and some of them even wanted to leave their safe-houses to go to the swimming pool! But they were very young, some no more than 19, and often from little provincial towns in the Midwest of America. They hadn't a clue what it was like in occupied Europe.

'We had collected all the airmen together – foolishly, but we often did foolish things – in one flat. It was 18 June 1943. I left them there to go to the Palais de Justice, but as soon as all the resistance people had gone, the Gestapo moved in and occupied the flat. When we returned, we walked straight into a trap and were arrested, one by one. Of course all our airmen were sent straight to POW camps. We'd been betrayed by a member of the *réseau*. I'm pretty sure who it was. A girl who was going out with a collaborator.

'I was interrogated and sent to Fresnes prison, where I spent four months in solitary. There followed another three months in a shared cell, and then, early in 1944, I was one of a 1,000-woman-strong transport to Ravensbrück. De Gaulle's daughter Geneviève was with us.'[6]

Many of the women prisoners under arrest with Mme McAdam Clark were kept in solitary at Fresnes, and their only contact with each other was by talking to each other via the water-pipes and grilles in the cells. 'You made friends without ever seeing them. There was one friend I made in that way, and she was taken away from Fresnes, and I was desolate – she was my best friend. Later, I "met" her for the first time – in Ravensbrück. We were talking to each other, and suddenly we realized that we had been "invisible" friends at Fresnes. There was a similar experience when we were transferred to Compiègne camp for a few days, *en route* for Ravensbrück – we thought it was heaven because we were all together again; we saw old friends, members of the resistance, and other people whom we'd known only by their voices at Fresnes. That is why we call the magazine of our association *Voix et Visages*.'

They arrived at Ravensbrück at night, after a six-day rail journey, to the standard SS reception. 'The conditions in the camp were as bad as you could expect. It was appallingly overcrowded, and it was a shock to see the state of the women prisoners. We couldn't imagine what we were doing there. I was wearing a ski-suit my cousin had been allowed to bring me because of the winter cold, but we were soon all stripped, shaved, and dressed in striped prison dresses like everyone else – and we looked like everyone else, immediately. You ceased to be a person and became a prisoner. Conditions in the reception *Block* were so crowded that you could not lie or sit down, and in the quarantine *Block* we were two to a lice-ridden bunk. We were lucky. I think *Block* 27 was the worst, after the Gypsies' *Block*. In *Block* 27 they'd put the Jewish women and children, and for good measure they'd put the French criminals and asocials in there, too – prostitutes and so on. There was a certain amount of lesbianism. The "males" were called "Jules", and they would carve a cross into the foreheads of their "steadies" – we called it a *croix des vaches*. The Germans erected a "tent" – a kind of marquee – between *Blocks* 24 and 26 – to cope with the overcrowding. Conditions there were quite unspeakable. They used it to house women from Warsaw, mainly, and whole convents of nuns.

'To my relief I wasn't sent to work in munition factories but at *Planierung*, which was flattening the sand-dunes which surrounded the camp. I remember local children spat at us as we marched out to the work-sites.'

In Ravensbrück the *Blockälteste* were known as *Blockovas* and were usually criminals. 'In *Block* 36 they delighted in forcing women who still had a shred of self-respect or dignity to bunk with *Schmutzstücke*[7] or madwomen. Anything to break you. But still we were lucky. Over the course of several months they took about 60 Polish girls for medical experiments – always choosing the youngest, prettiest ones. At least one had her leg muscles removed and thus became a permanent cripple. They used Gypsies and their children for medical experiments in the autumn of 1944. They took them to the hospital. We never saw what went on, but the screams that came from the *Revier* were terrible to hear. And that last winter a transport of Hungarian Jewesses arrived from Auschwitz. It was −25°C, and for some reason they were dressed in summer frocks and evening dresses. The KZ was another world – no wonder so many found refuge in madness.

'I managed to get off the *Planierung Kommando* and transfer to the painting *Kommando*, with two other French girls. The rest of the team were German green triangles and we were not made to feel welcome, but we stuck it out, and being on a relatively soft *Kommando* helped. For some extraordinary reason I never fell ill until the end, and on the *Kommando* we were given a litre of milk a day to counteract the effect of the paint-fumes. That was important. We would save some of the milk to give to our starving comrades in the *Block*. Life was so much in the balance that even a couple of spoonfuls of milk could make the difference between life and death. Being on the painting *Kommando* enabled us to avoid transports, too.

'Initially, the solidarity of the large group of Frenchwomen with which I arrived there helped – that was eroded as the group was broken up, and as people died, but we were all of roughly the same age, political outlook and social background: all of which made life marginally less unbearable. Most of the women in the camp were red or green triangles.

There were relatively few Jews and Gypsies. The worst fellow-prisoners, of course, were the German criminals. Thus friendship was essential to survival, especially within the little groups which were constituted – groups of three or four people – our "families", as we called them. There were a few people who remained isolated, and they died. You simply couldn't survive alone.

'We had striped uniforms for the first winter, and when they gave out, which was soon, they were replaced by civilian clothes with a red stripe painted down the back. Ravensbrück was the biggest women's camp. There was a men's camp, too, not far away, with the same name; but we never saw any of the inmates. We were isolated. I don't know how we got through. Nietzsche says something like, "What doesn't kill you makes you stronger."

'When I wrote my book, my feelings towards the Germans were implacable. One shouldn't exaggerate: the SS were a special bunch, not representative of the nation; but even so, the whole time I was a prisoner I experienced only one gesture of humanity from a German – and that was from the little man who was in charge of our painting *Kommando*. Towards the end I was very ill, and one day he took me out of the *Kommando* and into his hut, and gave me two potatoes. He was just a little man, harmless, a civilian who had lost two sons on the eastern front. The SS who worked in the camps were drawn from the lowest social strata. As for their mentality, it was incomprehensible. There was an *Oberaufseherin* [chief wardress] nicknamed La Binz. She was a petite blonde with rather an ingenuous face, quite pretty; but whenever she appeared, silence fell. She had a big dog, and she always carried a riding crop. The ones she delighted in picking on most were the Mussulmen. She was officially in charge of the punishment *Block*, too, and few people ever came back from there. She lived in a little house outside the camp with one of the male guards, so she must have had some kind of human existence, but in the camp, well, she'd kick a woman to death as soon as look at her. It's impossible to rationalize. There's no explanation, beyond the psychological one of what happens if you take someone – especially someone not very bright from a downtrodden background – and give them *carte blanche* power over other people who in normal life may be richer and more intelligent than they are. It's a strategy based upon revenge and jealousy.

'The dogs they used at Ravensbrück were boxers. I loved boxers – my family had always kept them – and to see them trained to be so vicious was very upsetting. I saw them tear people apart. In winter, the SS had little dog-coats embroidered with swastikas to put on them.'

Ravensbrück provides another example of how the KZ system was maintained until the bitter end. In February 1945, its gas chamber was constructed. *Selections* for it took place under the direction of male SS officers Flaum and Winkelmann, in order to solve the problem of overcrowding, since the camp was filling up with prisoners from evacuated camps in the East. Thus a month after Auschwitz was liberated, a new gas chamber went into operation. It worked ceaselessly until the camp was liberated on 30 April by soldiers of the 2nd Belorussian Front.

'One never thought about survival – one never really had time to think about anything at all. Anything could kill you. The day started at 3am – women had to go and collect the morning coffee cauldrons for the *Blocks* – two women to a cauldron, for they were huge, and the coffee when it left the kitchens was scalding hot. If you slipped on the ice and the cauldron tipped over you ... That kind of thing wasn't unusual; it wouldn't even make you turn your head. Or you died of starvation. I was lucky, we had the milk on the painting *Kommando*, and I kept my health. Nowadays, I have no special attitude to food and drink. I am the worst cook you could imagine, but I hate to see food wasted, and I find I still make comparisons: what one might eat at an average lunch, for example, would be more than enough to keep one going for two days and more in the camps.'

Liberation, when it came, was unexpected. 'They suddenly ordered a roll-call for all the Frenchwomen. It was Good Friday. Of course we knew there would be a *selection*, and that was confirmed as soon as we were ordered to strip. We were scared. SS Flaum picked 200 of us – half the total number. There was a rumour that we were to be "exchanged". Nothing was said, but we suspected a trap. We tried to prepare ourselves mentally for the gas chamber. There was nothing we could do to avoid it. We had run out of tricks, and run out of steam. I know I couldn't have lasted another month; I would certainly have been dead by Whitsun. But instead of the gas chamber, we were taken to the disinfection *Block*, and for once thoroughly deloused. They took our camp clothes away and gave us fresh outfits, taken from others of their victims. The clothes were bizarrely unsuitable. I was given a sheer black silk evening dress, deeply décolletée. As I was nut-brown with jaundice, I cannot have looked too wonderful in my new outfit. It didn't strike me as anything other than a little odd at the time, but of course it was surreal. The surreal had become the normal for us – and maybe for the SS, too. None of us lived in the real world; but now it looked as if we might at last really be going back to it.

'They marched us through the woods; and then, suddenly, we saw Red Cross buses. Until I die I shall never forget the feeling I had when I saw those four big white vehicles: "It is true; they are going to set us free." It was so impossible to believe. We never thought we would really be saved. And now the truth made us shudder – really shudder. There was a little car with two Red Cross officials, and another vehicle with a handful of SS who were evidently going to accompany us. The drivers of the buses had different uniforms, and we could see the word

"Canada" on their shoulder-badges. Later we learnt that they were prisoners-of-war put at the disposal of the Red Cross by the Germans. It was the day following Easter Monday.

'And then something else happened. The SS – the very ones who had been our guards in the camp, though no SS-women were present – presented each of us with half a pound of butter, a box of cakes, and a huge sausage. The commandant stepped forward. "We hope you won't take too unhappy a memory of the camp away with you," he said. We looked at the food – enough to kill us – at him – at each other. We were dazed. I think we said, "Thank you very much."

'The first 500-kilometre stretch took us to Ingolstadt, and we spent the first night in a little village near the town. The SS who had come with us were full of little attentions, lighting fires for us and requisitioning food. On Thursday we drove via Ulm to Lake Constance, and crossed into Switzerland at Kreuzlingen. They made us form fives for the last time, and counted us. That was the only formality there was to mark the end of our strange and wonderful trip across Germany. We all thought we were dreaming, of course.

'Someone gave us an apple each. I shall never forget that Swiss apple. We hadn't seen fruit for two years. They took us to Geneva, and the Red Cross couldn't believe it when they saw us – we were the first released concentration camp prisoners they had encountered. They wanted to examine us, of course, but none of us would agree to that. Seeing a doctor in the KZ meant death, and the association was far too strong to break just like that. They didn't want me to go on to Paris with the others because of my jaundice, but my comrades insisted so violently that they gave in.

'It took about two days from Geneva to Paris, with a short break at Annemasse. We arrived at the Gare de l'Est. There was a big reception for us: huge crowds, and de Gaulle was there. It didn't occur to us that this was all on our account; we thought we were lucky to be arriving coincidentally with such a festive gathering. But leaving the train very quickly became a horrible, sad experience, because there were thousands of people there, and they were asking us for news of their loved ones, many of whom we didn't know; but also there were many whom we knew to be dead.

'It is impossible, even now, to describe my feelings. I knew my brother would be there to meet me because the French ambassador in Switzerland had contacted our relatives on our behalf. The fact that he was there was the main thing for me. Funnily enough, I was in a filthy temper. I think it was because I was so ill. My brother was certainly shocked when he saw me – he knew that I'd been a prisoner, but he had no conception of how we'd been treated. We were the first returning KZ prisoners to be seen in France. I think the general reaction of my other relatives was surprise and horror – but also, and mostly, relief to see me safe and fundamentally all right. But they asked me the most ridiculous questions, in ignorance – and I'm being unfair because how could they conceive what we had been through? It was without precedent. And we, who had been living in a different world for so long, spoke a different language. The values of the camps even gave a different value to words – not greater: different. Communication was impossible; and I still feel that, especially in England and Scotland – even more than in France, because those countries weren't occupied. I still feel that I live in a different world from those who were not in the camps. It is my fate, and it is the fate of every former inmate. And that is why survivor associations like ours are important. ADIR[8] is a lifeline for those especially who are not just isolated by the concentration camp experience, but because they actually have no one. Our meetings are not like any other reunions: they are a time when you can talk to people who understand your language, the values of your words. And the solidarity is still tremendous: without it, half of us wouldn't have survived. Helping each other was the key, morally and materially, in the camps and afterwards. But giving help helped you too.

'Every year, ADIR holds a big reunion and it is wonderful – everyone is so pleased to see each other. What makes one sad is that every year we are fewer. It's only to be expected, but it is still sad, for the deaths are so significant for us – because of the effort that was taken to save those lives in the camps. And so it is a great honour, a great feeling, to belong to such a group of people.

'ADIR was founded immediately after the return home to look after fellow-survivors who had nowhere to go. They rented two large flats in Paris for these people to stay until they had sorted themselves out. It operated like that for as long as necessary. There is still a meeting every Monday afternoon in Paris, and members come to it from all over France. It is moving to go to such meetings, and they are very important for those of us who are lonely.

'I did not become involved in the work until later, because I was so ill, but I admire those survivors who set the association up so quickly. They had tremendous will, and tremendous humanity. I think ADIR is the expression of the continuing solidarity of the French women survivors; it helped with every aspect of life after liberation, from reparation to housing. Now, it is subsidized by the state, and it still carries out important functions. It arranges social visiting, and owns and operates rest-homes in the country. It is still very active.

'My personal homecoming could not have been better, and I think that one's recovery from the camps and from that experience was wholly influenced by the reception one got on returning, and by the conditions one found on returning. A friend discovered that the Nazis had shot her little sister in the street one day during the war. People returned to find that their whole families had died in air-raids; such discoveries, on top of what they had been through, was too much to bear.

'I was able to go and convalesce in the old family house in the country near Angers for three months, and everyone was kind and solicitous. I was looked after perfectly and was able to make at least a partial physical recovery, though I had to go on to a sanatorium in Switzerland; and all in all it was ten years before I was completely well again. But there was always plenty of support, and my family were able to give me the right kind of sympathy. I felt loved, and cared for.

'I never resumed my career. I was never tempted to – I was too ill, and too disfigured, morally and mentally. I couldn't have applied my mind to the Bar. What I wanted above all was "earth" things: a home, a family. I had no special ambitions any more: what there had been before had ceased to be important. And then after I was married, we were moving about abroad a lot. Life began to take over.

'I had met my husband – who comes from Scotland – just before the war when I was on holiday in the UK, and he came to see me soon after my return from the KZ – as soon as he got back from the fighting. He was in Africa for most of the war, and as my brother was on the diplomatic staff of the Free French Bureau in Algiers, the two of them were able to keep in touch, and at least he had occasional news of me. He managed to come and see me as early as August 1945, which gave me an enormous boost – I was so lucky.

'I don't think that at first one had any great thoughts about what one had been through. One was still young, and life was still ahead; there was a world of things to look forward to. But one did gradually become aware of the vast gulf that from now on would exist between oneself and others. I think my husband understands – within the limits that must exist for everyone who didn't go through it. He certainly didn't take the attitude that he didn't want to know, and he'd been through quite a lot himself in a different way. We were both pretty battered!'

They married in 1946, and she speaks with great pride of the birth of their first daughter in 1947. 'There was a need to have a family, but I wouldn't read more into it than normal instinct.' Her husband was a career diplomat and they had several foreign postings. Now, they live part of the time in Paris (where they have a flat, so that she can continue with her activities with ADIR), and most of the time in Aldeburgh. 'We went there because we had old friends who had a house in the town and we knew it before the war. Then I went there again to rest with my daughters when they were small, and I was getting a little tired. I just fell in love with the place.'

Owing to her involvement with ADIR, consciousness of the period of deportation remained strong; and in time she also talked to her daughters about Ravensbrück, not so much for her own sake as to recount it as an element of modern history. ADIR encourages young people's interest in the times, and Mme McAdam Clark and her comrades share with the majority of survivors the need and the responsibility to bear witness. She regrets that some of the survivors she knows still cannot bring themselves to talk about the KZ with their own families – 'After all, if we are going to encourage it to be studied in schools, why not start at home? I don't think it's harmed my children to know about the KZ – they've been very interested, in fact, and they know several of my old comrades – one of them acted as godmother. There's no tension, no embarrassment. Again I have been lucky, for I know that some people have met with a very unsympathetic response from their families, and that has made them withdraw from speaking about the subject altogether. I think too that to talk or not to talk is a matter for the individual to decide: there should be no imposition of a sense of duty to do so. But the experience remains bad, even a threat, to those survivors who cannot get it outside themselves, out into the open. Once there, I believe it can be converted into a positive, rather than a negative, force. With my children it all came out very naturally. I didn't sit them down one day and tell them all about it formally; and they had the book I wrote about it. Talking to them helped me too, in so far as I now give lectures quite regularly to schoolchildren and students in England and France. I remember one English boy knew more about Comet than I did, and it turned out that his father had escaped through it, and had even taken his son along his old escape-route.

'The memory of the camps never fades, not even slightly, not for any of us . . . and no matter how fortunate one has been in having another, busy and fulfilled life afterwards. The thing is totally imprinted upon one, and one remembers always the friends who survived, but whose minds were destroyed. What world do they live in still, and for the rest of their lives?

'I don't think I ever felt a desire for revenge, because only I was involved: no one else that I loved was put through that ordeal; no one I loved was being maltreated. If I had had the experience of a friend of mine who saw her mother sent to the gas, then I think I might have liked to kill an SS in revenge. Of course I felt a great sense of personal outrage – even more so when the SS gave us that food at parting and effectively said, "no hard feelings". That really took one's breath away!

'I'm not aware of any inborn talent to survive. I was in generally good health and good heart. But you know, when the new transports arrived, we could always tell who would survive and who would go under. There's something else. I had a happy childhood but I was rather a difficult kind of person. I lost my parents when I was very young and became independent early. Perhaps having to fend for myself, at least mentally, gave me a kind of strength. And, to my surprise, I found that in the camp I was good at dealing with people, at getting on with them. Also, all the thoughts I had were practical ones – there was very little time or inclination for reflection – I was concerned with how to get away with doing the minimum amount of work in order to conserve energy; how to get extra food. But I don't think any of us really believed that we would survive completely, that we would be free again. It was something you didn't even talk to yourself about. You kept going as best you could, from moment to moment, and hoped you'd stay lucky. Survival was very much an instinctive battle: conscious thought didn't play a great role.

'Parallel with that, a strong sense of religious belief existed within me; probably the extreme hunger and deprivation made that sense more acute – but I was aware almost of the physical presence of a protector.

'There are things which trigger the memory. Smells are the worst. I remember the smell of rotting bodies – we had to clear them up, and the last two months were unspeakable. The camp was overcrowded, disorganized – a true hell. I don't know what brings that smell back to me – I have occasionally smelt meat that has gone off, and that is certainly reminiscent of the smell of putrescent corpses. We had to store the bodies in the washrooms. If you needed water you had to clamber over them to get to the tap.

'I dream, too. After this conversation, I know that I will have bad dreams tonight; but that is something one lives with.'

Poland:
Resistance and 'Red Triangles'

I

He wasn't a spy; he was only suspected of being one. He worked as a foreign exchange clerk at the main station at Posen (Poznan) and his job meant that he had to pass to and fro across the frontier with Germany frequently – sometimes several times a day.

Stefan Przybylski had just passed his 25th birthday when the SD arrested him on 2 September 1939. He remained in German custody from then until the liberation of Mauthausen. The first year was spent in Gestapo prisons, where he underwent interrogation at Bialosliwie and Bydgoszcz. Then he was taken to Stutthof where prisoners from Bydgoszcz were automatically given 25 lashes on arrival. His progress through the camps continued with a period at Sachsenhausen – where during the 'quarantine' period following arrival the prisoners in his group were subjected to terrible beatings and *Sport* – and, finally, Mauthausen. 'There are 148 steps at the quarry at Mauthausen. We had to carry stones up the steps from the quarry to the camp. If a man took too small a stone, in their opinion, they would beat him to death. It was a hideous, confusing place. Prisoners would kill themselves by jumping from the top of the quarry on to the broken stones below. And the commandant, Ziereis, used to let his little son, who was about 11, shoot at prisoners for sport.'

After a short period at the main camp, he was transferred to the sub-camp, Gusen. There he had the luck to encounter SS *Obersturmführer*[1] Vanek, with whom he was acquainted, because his fiancée's widowed mother had lent Vanek's widowed mother money to start a restaurant in the two women's home-town of Stettin. Because of this, the SS officer promised to keep an eye on Przybylski, and he was able to alleviate the prisoner's lot now and then. The commandant was called Seidler and, like the infamous Ilse Koch,[2] he would have people with decorative tattoos killed in order to have lampshades and even wallets made out of their skins. Seidler offered Przybylski the chance of becoming *Volksdeutsch*. When he refused, and stood by his Polish nationality, Seidler kicked him in the face, breaking his nose, and ordered him to be hung up by his thumbs until he died. 'But if I had accepted honorary German nationality, they could have sent me to the front.' He was rescued by Vanek, and sent instead to a punishment squad. While working on it, he dropped a rock on his foot and smashed it. He had to go on working, and managed to drag himself back to camp that night. His disability was noticed, however, and he was sent to a *Block* where prisoners too sick to be useful were left to die. Fortunately, a prisoner-doctor (*Häftlingsarzt*) who was a compatriot found out that he was there and managed to get him out by exchanging him for the dead body of a Spanish prisoner, whose number he also inherited. Then he saved Przybylski's life by cutting off the smashed part of his toe and giving the wound a proper dressing.[3] He recovered, but there was a drawback: his former number had been an 'old' one, earning him respect. The number he inherited was 'new', and he knew that with it he would risk being selected for the hard *Kommandos*. Fortunately his ally, Vanek, came to his rescue and took him into an extraordinary *Kommando* for which he had responsibility. This was the *Kaninchenzucht* (rabbit-breeding centre). 'There were two of these that I knew of, one at Mauthausen, and the other at Stutthof.' White angora rabbits were farmed for their fur, which was used to line Luftwaffe jackets. 'There were 1,500 of them at Mauthausen. My job was to keep them clean and fed, and to comb their fur out three times a day. There were three or four of us on the *Kommando*, and a prisoner-vet. It was while I was on the *Kommando* that I met Himmler.

'There was one particular rabbit – number 724. He was a beauty, and he did whatever I liked! I taught him tricks. Of course, Vanek knew that. Himmler visited the camp and was shown the rabbits. Vanek asked me to get 724 to do one or two of his tricks for the *Reichsführer-SS* – he would beg, and find bits of bread I hid about his cage, things like that. Himmler was delighted, and laughed and clapped. And all his entourage clapped. He asked me where I came from, and I told him West Prussia – calling my part of Poland by its new Nazi name. I knew enough to do that.

'As the war progressed, Vanek became more and more depressed. He was devoted to his mother – her photo was on his desk – and she had always disapproved of his joining the SS. By that time I was his orderly, so we talked from time to time, coming from the same part of the country and effectively being countrymen. One day I noticed that he was crying. He said, "Stefan, what can I do? This is not a war – this is murder." And after we had talked for a while, I told him that he should try to escape.

'He took my advice. He destroyed the portrait of Hitler in his office, and he cut his uniform to shreds. He put on civilian clothes, and he just disappeared. After the war I tried to trace him, but without success. My guess is that they caught him and shot him.

'By this stage in the war, transports were arriving every day from the eastern camps. They killed all the women straight away; and when there was no room or time to deal with people, they simply left them sealed up in the goods-waggons until they died. At Gusen they killed 3,000 prisoners just before we were liberated. At the end there was chaos. There had been a revolt on 2 May at Mauthausen. I had got hold of a gun, too. And this is very important. I had an SS-man in my sights. But then I saw his eyes. He was terrified. I can still see his eyes today. At that moment an inner voice said to me: "Don't do it, it will make you just like them." From that moment I have been a different person; and I will never forget it. I will never allow myself to hate anybody again, though sometimes it is very difficult.

'After liberation I was sent to a hospital in France to recuperate, but as soon as I was well enough I wanted to do something positive to help – to try to make good come out of the bad. I think you have to try to do that, or there is no progress. I joined the Polish 2nd Corps[4] in Italy as a welfare officer, and later I was attached to the Red Cross. My wish was to return to Austria and help the people I had left behind. I managed to get an attachment to the 42nd Infantry Division, US Army, and found myself based in Salzburg. I was put in charge of food distribution, which meant that I had to organize and prepare 150,000 food rations twice weekly for DPs. Food had to be foraged from all around Salzburg, and distribution centres were set up in Innsbruck, Wels and Linz. At about the same time I became involved in the group making plans to set up a memorial at Ebensee, which later came about.'

In one of the DP camps he came across a little Polish girl whose parents had been shot by the Germans and who had subsequently been given to Austrian foster-parents as part of the *Lebensborn* programme of the Third Reich.[5] Having met this little girl, he started to investigate the plight of other children in a similar situation, and in his research he was able to count on the full cooperation of the US forces' administration. Throughout Austria and Bavaria he was ultimately able to trace 187 children – some of them deeply traumatized by their experience, including one little girl of nine whose parents had been killed before her eyes. Most of the children he found were aged about eight or nine, and he organized a Christmas party for them at the end of 1945. 'Contact with them gave me hope for myself, and the courage to continue.' Despite objections from the new communist Polish government, he was able to accept an invitation from Spain to give temporary homes to his orphans – those with no close living relatives at all were allowed to go. They finally found permanent adopted families in the USA, and he is still in touch with most of them.

He chose to come to England because he no longer wished to live in a Poland controlled by the Communists, and saw every sign that the regime would be long-lived. His judgment was confirmed by a letter from his father warning him not to return. They never met again. His fiancée had tried to escape from German-occupied Poland to the Russian-occupied zone, and she was seen in the eastern sector; but after the war Przybylski was unable to trace her, and has never heard of her again. He had retained his job as welfare officer with the Polish 2nd Corps, and when they were recalled to Great Britain he came with them, originally to Scotland.[6]

After rehabilitation in England, and retraining for civilian life, he went into the plastics business, and has worked and lived in London all his life since 1946.

He met his Polish wife, who spent the war in Russia, in England. 'Has he told you all about Gehenna?' she asks me, holding his hand.

'I think the most important thing the KZ taught me was determination – you had to fight for life every minute: there was no respite; and you had to be strong, in public and in private. The memory of those times remains very strong; and I am deeply affected by the suffering of others. If I see starving African children on television, it moves me very deeply. And violence, too – despite everything, I still cannot understand how people can behave so badly. I still dream, and since the war I have not slept a single night right through. Sleeping-pills don't help, and there is nothing I could do about it that I haven't tried; so now I live with it. Most of my dreams hark back to when I was in Gestapo prison – I dream of how they beat me up – and worse, when they set dogs on to me.

'I think I am still warm-hearted, and I would try to trust people. Certainly I am always willing to give them the benefit of the doubt; but I am very hurt when people let me down. It doesn't happen often. It seems to me that I have developed an intuitive ability to size people up. Warning lights flash quickly in the brain, and I would say that 99 times out of 100 I am right in my assessment. My rule of thumb is simple: I never trust anyone who doesn't keep his word – over no matter how small a thing.

'In coming to terms with it, I owe much to my wife. She had been through a lot as well, in the East; but she was also the first person I met who, I knew, would understand what I told her. For a long time I was disinclined to talk about the camps to anyone who had no experience of them, because I was afraid of being thought a liar, or at least one who exaggerated wildly. Later, I talked to my daughter, too – when she was old enough, but I told her only as much as she wanted to know, and as much as I thought she could take. In her upbringing we never forced her to do anything, but only ever used reason, because I have learnt the hardest way that nothing whatever is gained – or at least, created – by the use of force. I was delighted to find, when she was grown up, that she was very deeply involved in a charity concerned with helping handicapped children – she had never mentioned it to me. That was like getting fruit from a tree you'd planted.'

II

In his book *Fighting Auschwitz*, Jozef Garlinski writes: 'The site, which was soon to become the greatest cemetery in the history of the world, was at first of modest appearance. There were some old Austrian artillery barracks consisting of 20 brick buildings, mainly single-storeyed, dilapidated and filthy. They stood on the left bank of the River Sola in a suburb called Zasole. Next to the barracks stood several buildings belonging to the Polish Tobacco Monopoly, which were also within the perimeter of the proposed camp.

'Höss [commandant of Auschwitz] chose five SS-men and arrived at Auschwitz on 29 April 1940. On 20 May, SS NCO Gerhard Palitzsch brought 30 Germans from Sachsenhausen, almost all of them criminals. These were the first "trusties" of the new camp, and they were given numbers from 1 to 30. In charge of them was No. 1, Bruno Brodniewicz, a German with a Polish surname, who became the camp's Senior Prisoner. The second newcomer to attain equal rank (an exceptional arrangement) was another German with a Polish surname, Leo Wierczorek, No. 30. Palitzsch was appointed *Rapportführer*, responsible for discipline. These three names have gone down in the history of Auschwitz.

'The Town Council drafted 300 local Jews to the camp, and the cleaning-up of the neglected buildings began. They were guarded by 15 SS cavalrymen, sent from Cracow. Even the most elementary tasks had not been completed when an enquiry came from the Department of Police and Security in Wroclaw as to how soon the camp would be ready to receive the first consignments of prisoners. Before a reply could be sent, a train (for once a passenger train) arrived at the station in Auschwitz. It brought 728 Poles, all of them political prisoners, from a prison in Tarnow. They were mainly young men, caught on the frontier as they were attempting to reach Hungary *en route* to France, where the Polish Army was re-forming (and they were therefore called "tourists" in the camp). In addition there were a number of priests and schoolteachers, and several dozen Jews. The members of this transport were given the numbers 31 to 758, and they were put into quarantine in a building which had belonged to the Tobacco Monopoly.

'This first transport arrived in Auschwitz on 14 June 1940, and this date is accepted as the official beginning of the camp.'[7]

Zenon Frank, Auschwitz number 156, was born in the little spa-town of Krynica, in the far south of Poland, in 1913. He finished his studies in chemical engineering at the Technical University in Lvov in June 1939 and returned to Cracow, where he was then living. 'I'd left all my stuff in Lvov because I was expecting to go back there, but of course in the event I never did, ever again. When the war broke out I rejoined my parents in Krynica.' He was arrested soon after – he is not sure why, but suspects that it was because he was acting as a guide across the Zachod mountains for Polish officers escaping into Czechoslovakia. His younger brother had been in the army but was now recovering at home from a shrapnel wound in the leg, which was healing badly. Subsequently suspected of resistance activities, he too was arrested and sent to Auschwitz, where he died.

Throughout his time in Auschwitz-I, Frank was involved more or less continuously in building work and maintenance. 'The first winter was not so easy, though. We had the job of standing in the Sola and draining it by dredging the sand out with our bare hands. When we got back to the *Block*, we would take a piece of wood and knock the ice off our legs.

'It never crossed my mind that I wouldn't survive. I just couldn't visualize myself on the heaps of dead bodies, nor as a Mussulman, who were, if anything, more worrying than the corpses. But there was nothing you could do about them. I remember one odd thing about them: I don't think any doctor has yet been able to explain it: when they were on the brink of death, walking back from work, their heads would tilt right back, so that they were looking at the sky. Normally, when you are exhausted, your head droops forward.

'It was hard when my brother died. I was in the *Revier Block* with him at the time. I was there to have my buttocks treated – I had been given 25 lashes and they were flayed open. I'd been caught with two others smoking a cigarette in the *Block*. The punishment was three days' punishment squad, and then Palitzsch[8] tied us to the *Bock* [whipping-horse]; he gave us the 25. The only reason I got decent treatment in the *Revier* was because the doctor was Polish and did what he could to help me,[9] but bandages were made of toilet-paper which we had to buy in the canteen. We were allowed a few *zlotys* a month from home, and the canteen sold toilet-paper and mineral water. My brother was in the *Revier* at the same time as I was; he had pneumonia, which he contracted working in the winter in the *Bauhof*, organizing materials to build the camp itself. Somebody told me that he'd just died. I could barely walk, but I went across to his bed – and already two other prisoners were fighting over his clothes. I beat them off. But I felt very little. Certainly not despair.

'And I never felt like giving in, nor did such thoughts ever cross my mind. I was lucky: I wasn't selected for hard *Kommandos*.

'I never gave much serious consideration to religious belief. I thought about it, but not deeply. I worked alongside Father Kolbe for a time, on a gardening *Kommando*. I remember that, when a prisoner escaped, one in every ten of us was selected to go to *Block* 11 to be shot at the Black Wall. Father Kolbe exchanged places with a family man who'd been selected for this. I admired him for what he did, and I don't want to denigrate it; but, you know, I was in that camp for nearly five years, and I saw plenty of people choose death deliberately as a means of escape. Neither suicide nor thoughts of escape ever crossed my mind. All I could think of was how to get through each day. I myself survived three *selections* of the type where they took every tenth man and shot him in reprisal for an escape.

'I made a few friends. Our main topic of conversation was how to make tomorrow easier than today! One of my best friends died in '82 – he went back to Poland, but he visited us here once or twice. We worked together in the painting *Kommando* at Auschwitz, where my nickname was "Curly"! [He lost all his hair through a chemical accident when he was 21.] There was no room for hope. You just had to think, every minute, how to survive. You were on your toes all the time: how to get a softer job, shorter hours, a job under cover – and then how to keep it: what to bribe whom with. How to organize cigarettes for barter. How to get a decent pair of shoes, and then how to hang on to them. There was no room in one's mind for any kind of abstract thought . . . We were fortunate in one sense: those few of us who survived had such old numbers that even the SS respected us. I remember in '44 the paint *Kommando* had to go about seven kilometres away from the main camp to do some work on houses near the fish-ponds: Auschwitz was very famous before the war for its carp farms. One of the older SS came with us, instead of the young one we'd been expecting, and when we had our meal-break, one of us asked him if we could supplement our soup with a carp from the ponds. "Go ahead," he said; and we took a couple of carp out and baked them on a fire – and he ate with us. We asked him why the young SS-man hadn't been put in charge of us, and he said that it was because it wasn't felt that the young SS-man had enough experience to deal with us "old" numbers.

'As far as I could see over those five years, the majority of SS were very simple people, and I think there is nothing worse than to give simple people power. But because the SS were simple, you could, if you were careful, get round them and even manipulate them. In one or two cases, you know, it was good to start shouting at them. You see, they were so accustomed to having orders shouted at them! For example, one day I'd just organized myself a good pair of shoes through friends who were working in *Kanada*, in Birkenau. There was a young SS-man who said to me, "Give me those shoes." He wanted them for himself. "Give me those shoes," he said. "Not on your life," I said. He looked quite surprised. "I'll shoot you if you don't," he said. "Then you'll have to shoot all five of us," I said. My friends and I were thin, but we were bigger than the SS-man. He looked embarrassed, and then he put his gun away, and shouted, *"Los, marsch!"* Of course there were many times when one's heart was in one's mouth, but at moments like the one I've just described, instinct takes over. I think that one's instinct was trained and sharpened every day by what was going on around you – by the changing circumstances.

'There are people I remember with undying hatred. Palitzsch, for example, was a real degenerate. But there were a very few SS whom one felt sorry for. There was an architect there, with the rank of *Rottenführer* [Corporal]. I met him towards the very end. He'd been forced into the SS because they needed architects to help plan the extensions to the camp.[10] That's why he had such a low rank; but they couldn't make him a mere *SS-mann* because of the status of his profession. He came from Munich. Actually I met up with him there after the war and we went on a three-day binge together. He hated Hitler, hated the SS, the whole thing. He was the only one who was completely exonerated during the Auschwitz trials in Poland after the war. His name was Martin Gierisch. I think he's dead now; he was quite old then.

'Then there were the kapos. There were 30 of them to begin with, and they were all German green triangles. Later there were Polish kapos, too. Some of them were "promoted" because they were experts in the work-field of the *Kommando* they were assigned to. I was a kapo myself in the painting *Kommando* at the end. You know what the Germans are like for bureaucracy: at the end the painting *Kommando* was split into *Malerei-Bauleitung* and *Malerei-Verwaltung*.[11] Before, there'd been two kapos; one a political like me, only a Communist rather than a resistance man, and the other a criminal. There was a power struggle, as there nearly always was between politicals and criminals, for control. The politicals were better "masters", though they tended to favour their own. The criminals were nearly all terrible. The upshot of this struggle was that the "green" was sent to Birkenau, the *Kommando* was split into two sections, and I was promoted to lead *Bauleitung* – the Communist took the other detail. It was a good *Kommando* to be on, but all this only happened in the last month we were there, and you could hardly call us collaborators – just works foremen; and anyway I wasn't given the choice – I didn't actually *want* the job – I was ordered to do it by our SS *Kommandoführer* – a young chap called Dengler. Actually he wasn't so bad. We called him "Bicycle", because he used to go everywhere by bike.

'The main reason the painting *Kommando* was so good was that it gave you considerable freedom of movement. You had plenty of opportunities to organize extra food, even from the SS kitchens if you happened to be painting there. But if you stole food, the best plan was to eat it immediately – it was too risky to take it with you. Vital as it was, I have retained no sense of the value of food and drink: my wife is always complaining: "Auschwitz hasn't taught you anything!" But I like food – I enjoy good food.'

In October 1944 he was selected for a transport to Sachsenhausen. 'There were 10,000 of us; we didn't have a clue where we were going, but we thought, anyway, it's away from Auschwitz. The journey took three days in the usual cattle-trucks, and they gave us nothing to eat or drink. When we got there, there was nothing. They put us in aircraft hangars in Oranienburg, where they used to build the Heinkels – the place was nicknamed Heinkel-Oranienburg.[12] For the first few days we just sat around on the three-tiered bunks they had installed for us. Then they held a kind of slave-market – the local industrialists came along to "buy" us from the SS. I got a job in an aluminium workshop within the Heinkel works. By that time there were air-raids every night, and one day there was an uninterrupted two-hour bombing session. I felt no fear at all – only pleasure at seeing the bastards scuttle at last – despite the fact that some of my friends died in those raids.

'After the raids it was impossible to go on working at Heinkel, so they transferred us to the KZ, where we were set to manufacturing *Panzerfäuste*; but the factory was bombed, and so they left us to sit around all day again, until the order came to evacuate us. We were issued with a small ration: a tin of some kind of spam – there was no label on the tin – and half a loaf each. And they marched us towards Schwerin. It was early April 1945. Luckily the weather wasn't too bad, just a little rain. I managed to eke out my ration for three days, but the first night someone stole my coat. The second night, the SS put us all in a clay-pit, about five metres deep, and they stood all round the top of it; but they didn't shoot. In the morning, they had disappeared – run away. Two friends of mine and I kept marching on towards the Elbe. They're still alive – eventually they went back to live in Poland. Three days later we saw a tank with a white star on it, so we waved; and the Americans gave us some chocolate and some cigarettes, and off they went. We carried on until we reached a place called Ludwigs-lust, where there was a big Allied unit and a kind of temporary camp for people like us. And four days later a British officer came and told us that the next day a transport would be leaving for those wanting to return to Poland. The following morning, six or seven big Russian lorries arrived – and nobody went! Not one person. The lorries went back empty. We knew enough about Russia – we knew her of old. We knew about Katyn, too.[13]

'So then the Americans had to transport us west, and we were found homes in the various DP camps – a few of us from Auschwitz were still together, and we and some others were taken to a small deserted village on the Elbe, not too far from Luneburg, and it was given to us – we had food supplies, and we spent all of May and June there.

'We didn't know what we were going to do and we didn't even do much thinking. We were just enjoying being free, eating enough, not having to work. It was quite a good summer. I remember that there was an eclipse of the sun – we didn't know anything about it in advance. We were lying in the sun when suddenly it got darker and darker!

'I know that we talked about the past quite a lot, but I remember that we didn't talk much about the future. Oh, and I had a chance to weigh myself: 45 kilogrammes. We didn't have anything to do, so we organized games for the children – things like that.

'I wasn't tempted to join the 2nd Corps, and I came to the UK by accident. I was trying to get to the USA, or Australia or New Zealand, but from the point of view of emigration I had a drawback: I had a wife and son. My son was born in Germany in 1946, where I met my wife, at a DP camp at Bardovick, near Luneburg – we married there on 7 February 1946. I'd known her about six months. She had been in Belsen for a year. I remember when we were still in Germany after the war, a German woman came up to her and said, "I know you; but from where?" And my wife replied: "Warsaw, or Belsen?" The German woman gave her a look, and ran away.

'It certainly helped us both that we each knew what it was to go through a concentration camp, but I think my five years made a deeper impression on me than her one year did on her. One thing we don't share is sympathy. I have lost the ability to feel it. The sight of suffering makes no impression on me – I have always seen worse with my own eyes. And there is another thing, which may be the cause of my death in the end: I am indifferent to pain. I can know I am unwell, even be in pain; and I ignore it. I can't be bothered to have it seen to.

'Perhaps I have become too hard; I am certainly cynical, but my experience has made me so. Even in the DP camps we were cheated and swindled. The English commander of Bardovick had the incoming Red Cross parcels opened and removed the coffee, soap and cigarettes to sell on the black market. I am sure similar things happen with famine aid today. There are still too many jackals alive.

'We came to England by a roundabout route. First of all, we were transferred to a DP camp in the Harz mountains, where we stayed for some time. There I met a friend who was organizing a primary school for DP children in a village near Munster, and he asked me to join him as a teacher there. At first I was reluctant, because I had no experience at all of primary-school teaching; but finally I agreed. I taught every subject under the sun for a year, and then I moved to Lippstadt to teach physics and chemistry in a similar secondary school. I stayed there from 1947 until 1949. By then the education programme was winding down, but we spent a further three years drifting through the DP camps, wondering where fate might take us, not wanting to return to a communist Poland. We were finally able to come to England through the good offices of the director of the school in Lippstadt.

'Once I was here, I neither expected help nor looked for it, though I was given some aid by the Polish community while I was looking for work. After 18 months I found a job with Vidor's in Erith – a job I located through the Polish Ex-Combattants' Association. I worked first in the technical department, then as a chemist.

'Certainly to begin with the change of environment involved a good deal of stress; but I think it was alleviated by the fact that I had a family. The major problem was that I didn't speak English – my interview with Vidor's was conducted in broken German, and I got through it and held down the job because the technical division was based on the international language of maths and graphs. Now, although I know I still have a Polish accent, I am proud that I can speak fluent English – and I have never had a formal lesson in my life! As my career progressed, which it did very rapidly, I became a chemical trouble-shooter for the company, and that meant that I had to write reports. I did my best, and I got my Welsh second-in-command to vet my first one. It was disastrous, mainly because the nuances of English escaped me. But after six months I was promoted to the post of deputy chief chemist for Vidor.'

He now holds 13 British chemical patents, mainly in chemistry applied to batteries and electronics, but one is in the field of photography – his hobby and his great passion since childhood. He is a member of the Polish Photographic Society, and is closely involved with the Polish community in London. 'I would go back to Poland if she were free, but as things are I have no regrets about being here. My mother tried to put pressure on me to return after the war, but I had heard about the forced-labour camps for dissidents, and I remember writing to her, "Auschwitz you can survive only once."

'It hurt me a lot to be separated from my parents, and I never saw them again. The move and the war did not affect my romantic life: there had been one or two girlfriends before my arrest, but never anything serious. My wife was the first real woman in my life, and I am sure – it is natural – that the suddenness of our romance had a lot to do with my having been five years without female company.

'I do have nightmares – dreams of being pursued – but they are not specifically related to the camps. And I don't think there are any more triggers. When I see films about the KZ, however, I get very angry, because they are nonsense; they are nowhere near the truth – even those that have been made or presented by people who actually were inmates. They talk nonsense – not a word about basic things, about what basically happened there. I can't explain the day-to-day life of Auschwitz just like that, but if I went to Auschwitz with a film-crew, then they would really see something, and hear something.

'I don't think you become a survivor by accident or by magic. I think there has to be something inside you that enables you to learn the tricks and skills of survival, so that you increase your chances. Everything being equal, the longer you managed to live, the greater your chances were; though you were never free of being a pawn of luck. But Auschwitz taught me the biggest lessons of my life – and you will think me mad for saying this – but I am not sorry that I was there. What I learnt there about human nature cannot and could not be learnt anywhere else. In normal life you do not see more than a tiny corner of what people are. But in Auschwitz everybody threw away his mask.

'Those who gave up simply couldn't take it. It wasn't necessarily a question of brooding. It might have been simply that their constitution couldn't stand it. And in many people their constitution improved, because they were hungry. Just on the physical plane, I think hunger is a good cure for many ills. There's no doubt that we all eat four times as much as we need, or even should, to be healthy. Having said that, don't let me give you the impression that Auschwitz was a health farm. I have arthritis, and my back is very bad. I slept on concrete or wet stone for five years. That leaves a legacy. It was only while you were there that your body fought for you, if it could. It's afterwards that the debts to nature have to be paid.

'My relationships with other people have been affected by my experience in so far as I can see behind the mask. In the camp I had a good friend – he survived and became a racing car builder back in Poland after the war. In Auschwitz we had a game: when there were new arrivals, we'd look at them after they'd been shaved and stripped, and try to guess their professions. After a year, we made no more than ten per cent of mistakes; and I still find that acquired skill helpful today, when I meet someone and need to size him up. It's not even something I do consciously any more – but I know.

'I've never seen any reason to look back; but occasionally, at a party or a reunion if the subject crops up, I'll talk about it. I know very few people here who were in the camps. Occasionally I would talk to my son about it, but it was my daughter who was the more interested; neither of them was significantly affected by it. To them, the whole episode is part of past history. My son runs a wine-bar in south London, and my daughter is a computer consultant. It doesn't worry me. I don't want to live in or glorify the past. Much has been made about the resistance movement in the camps – which as far as I could see in Auschwitz consisted of a handful of older politicals sitting in a corner nattering. I am much more interested in what happened to Polish Jewry – the people who really took the brunt of the KZ. I'm reading a book about the Warsaw ghetto now, based on diaries that were written there. It was all happening while I was in Auschwitz.

'The experience has changed me to some extent, but not radically. It has simply become part of my wisdom, now, and I'm grateful for that. People have asked me to write down my experiences; but I'm not a writer, and anyway I don't want to. I want to get on with the next thing; you should look where you're going, not where you've been, but in the knowledge that the past illuminates the future. Then ordinary troubles – the kind of things that may loom quite large in normal people's lives – can be shrugged off. More, I barely even notice them.'

III

Before the war, Kielce was an agricultural centre which, because the soil was poor, had begun to build up some industry. The town was set in picturesque scenery, surrounded by mountains. It was there that Eugeniusz Konecki's parents had their principal jewellery and watch-maker's shop. Konecki grew up in the town. He studied German at school (which was to stand him in good stead later) and went in for a variety of obligatory scout activities and military training. 'In Poland, everybody is always preparing for the next war – it's part of our history – semi-military training involved learning to shoot, and riding, swimming, and general keep-fit.'

When he was 16, as a member of the PW (*Przysposobienie Wojskowe* – roughly equivalent to the British Combined Cadet Force at school), he was on air-raid patrol. 'We used to fire our ancient rifles at the German planes – it did no good whatsoever, but it relieved our feelings.' Returning home from duty one day, he found that the Germans had occupied Kielce.

The family moved away to Warsaw and Konecki was sent to the Liceum Budowlane to study civil engineering. In Warsaw, he made contact with the resistance. The job initially involved basic training, and collecting and hiding weapons. 'When the Gestapo finally came to arrest me, I had an almost complete armoury in the flat – some weapons had been hidden prior to invasion in case of need, but others had been acquired from the Germans – you would occasionally be able to exchange a bottle of vodka for a Luger, for example. I also went in for minor acts of sabotage. My personal contribution was a poster campaign: everywhere, on the best restaurants, and so on, a notice was appearing that said FOR GERMAN USE ONLY. We printed our own and stuck them on lamp-posts. At the same time, unknown to me, my father was involved in the underground press.

'My arrest came on 3 July 1942. I was in the middle of sitting my final exams, and I had a break, so I went home to relax a little, and to play the piano – I'd been out to buy myself some new music. As I was playing, concentrating on the music, I was suddenly aware that someone had come into the room – and there were two Gestapo, standing by the door. I didn't stop playing – I carried on to the end of the piece, and they waited. It was a popular piece called *Sag' zum Abschied Leise "Servus"* – I still play it sometimes – then I got up and said to them, "What can I do for you?" I was playing the fool, because they were in uniform, with all the trappings, death's heads and SD-tags on their collars. "Are you from the Inland Revenue?" They took me seriously and said, "No, we are looking for Jozef Konecki." That was my father. I told them he wasn't at home, he was at work. Then they asked to see my room, and I took them to it, but I was shaking in my boots because in my room was a marble clock, and concealed in its base were four hand-grenades. In the false ceiling of the cupboard were my automatic and ammunition, and in the false architrave of the doorway was a rifle and – worst of all – a supply of dum-dum bullets. We used them against the Germans because we hated them so. If they'd found those, they'd have skinned me alive. The Germans searched the room – one sitting on the bed to watch my reactions. The other first went through the papers in the cupboard, and I could see that he was concentrating on them. Relief! But then he turned his attention to the clock: he could see that its case was much larger than its mechanism could require – there was obviously room to hide something inside. I think that was the worst moment of my life. If I had had a gun on me (like a fool, I normally carried it around), I'd have shot them; if they found the grenades, they'd take the room apart, and if they found the dum-dum bullets, we'd all be for it. And the other guy was still watching me, so I had to act calmly – I think he must have been a bloody fool to sense nothing.

'By the grace of God I was standing next to a small cabinet which was crammed with school papers and jottings – all impressive-looking technical stuff. The other man had his hands on the clock, was turning it round to open the door at the back. I managed to open the door of the cabinet first, and released an avalanche of papers. This distracted him. He left the clock, actually pulled an armchair up to the papers, and said comfortably: "Aha, what have we here?" Now I could afford to look nervous.'

Despite the innocence of the papers, he and his father were arrested and taken to Pawiak prison. On occasion the Gestapo had been known to take bribes in order to let people go, and his mother tried this; but she was told that in this case it was impossible, since Konecki and his father had already been condemned to death – something which they themselves did not know at the time. All the Gestapo could arrange to do, in return for money, was rearrange the official papers so that, instead of being shot, father and son would be sent to a concentration camp. Mr Konecki was sent to Majdanek in January 1943, and the family learnt later that he had been killed there two months later.

Konecki remained in Pawiak right through 1942 and up until May 1943. Then he was transferred to Auschwitz. He describes it as 'a scene from Gogol: it was just like, actually like, you imagine an arrival at the gates of hell. The flames from the chimneys rose five metres above them. At their worst, they were burning 10,000 people a day. The bricks inside the chimneys cracked and exploded from the heat.' He was selected for Birkenau, where he spent 13 months.

After the period of quarantine he was given a skilled job, working as a bricklayer. This in turn led to his being given a privileged position: that of *Stubendienst*.

'Being a minor "Prominent" didn't protect you from all danger, however. In front of our *Block* stood part of the so-called hospital, two wooden barracks, and on one particular day in February 1944 there was a *selection*. This one was conducted by Dr Mengele who arrived with his cronies. All the numbers he'd selected were noted, and all the people were collected together, and the lorries drove up to take them to the gas. Mengele ordered all the *Stubendienste* to come out and help load these people on to the lorries. The tailgates were lowered, and two of us jumped up, while two more stood on the ground at the back, ready to bundle the people aboard. They were stripped of their uniforms and driven from the hospital naked to the gas chambers – and they were all very sick. The guys on the ground grabbed them and hurled them up to us. We caught them, and flung them to the front of the lorry: it was like loading wood, or sacks of potatoes. You almost had to think of it like that. And Mengele stood there watching, and as usual it was all at the double – and sweat was pouring off us. Finally the order came to shut the flap, and they shut it immediately, and I was still aboard. I was wedged in among those living skeletons, and I couldn't get off because I was wedged in tight; and the lorry started to move off. I tried to disengage myself and jump off. The lorry started to pick up speed. I frantically pulled myself over the bodies of the Mussulmen and threw myself off the back of the lorry, falling into the mud. Of course, Dr Mengele was killing himself with laughter. He knew what I must have felt.

'On 12 April 1944 we left Auschwitz for Buchenwald – two days before my 21st birthday. The transport was not unpleasant. It was amazing. We had ordinary carriages – although the windows were boarded up – and normal seats. It was fairly cramped, but that didn't matter as they managed to get us from one camp to the other in the course of one night's uninterrupted travel. In one sense I was lucky that I had been a "good" kapo, because in Buchenwald I saw justice meted out to a former Auschwitz kapo, who I am sorry to say was a former Polish army officer, for he was a cruel bastard when he had power. His name was Zabierski. At Buchenwald it was customary for the senior inmates already there to weed out former kapos on arriving transports. We were kept in a quarantine *Block* for a few days after arrival, and Zabierski was sitting playing chess with another prisoner when the door suddenly burst open and in came three or four quite burly Buchenwalders. "Where is Zabierski?" "Here I am." The group approached him. "Do you remember, when you were *Blockälteste* of *Block* 2 at Auschwitz, you killed my brother?" "No, I didn't do anything of the sort." "You've got until the evening. Think about what you have done, and pray." That evening, after *Appell* I saw a huge crowd of prisoners gathered round something, and as I watched, something long – like a sack, but longer – was thrown out of the crowd and fell to the ground, and the crowd dispersed – ran off in all directions. But I went over, and the thing on the ground was Zabierski. There was blood coming from his mouth and his ears – pouring out. And I knelt over him. But his eyelids just flickered, three or four times, and he died.

'At the end of the war, as I could speak German, I was put in charge of a *Kommando* which used to go into the woods to cut trees to use as props below ground. It was not a bad *Kommando* – the woods were attractive, you were in the fresh air, and even the SS were more relaxed – they'd allow you to pick wild berries to eat. In my position as interpreter I was able to walk between the groups of tree-fellers, translating, so I avoided the hard physical work. I thought that if I could stick it out I could survive fairly easily until liberation, which I think we all knew by then was only a short time away. But one morning at roll-call I was called out and reassigned to the boilerhouse – my skills as a building technician, such as they were then, were needed there. It was no good trying to argue my way out of it, so I swallowed my disappointment and went to the boilerhouse. That evening, the woodland *Kommando* didn't return: a felled tree had struck an SS man and killed him, with the result that all the prisoners were shot dead. I was beginning to feel like a cat with nine lives.

'The death-march, when the time came to evacuate us, was fairly short. On 12 April – exactly a year after I had left Auschwitz – the order came for us to form fives and make ready to march out. We did so under heavy SS guard, but we could hear the US artillery quite near and that kept our spirits up. It didn't help many of us. They marched us late into the night and shot stragglers without hesitation. But two days later, the artillery was all round us, and the SS realized that they were walking straight into the jaws of the enemy. They marched us towards a small wood. But suddenly above us there was a US spotter-plane – a small, slow one-engined machine. We were made to lie down. The plane circled low, and the pilot must have recognized who we were. He flew off, and we were ordered to continue, but shortly afterwards we saw clouds of dust – a column of vehicles. As soon as the SS realized that it was a US column, they ran away. We, left alone, still weren't sure; but as they didn't shoot us, we knew we were free. This was my 22nd birthday, 14 April 1945.

'The response to liberation is one of the hardest things to describe. Exhilaration I certainly felt. Everyone was jumping for joy, embracing, embracing the US troops. I picked up a gun one of the SS had dropped and there was a moment when I nearly shot a kapo – but he was small-fry: I really wanted to kill an SS. The US troops were rounding the Germans up in a big walled garden nearby. Our SS commander was pedalling away on his bike – pedalling like mad. One of the American tank gunners was taking pot-shots at him with a small gun, standing on his tank, trying to knock him off his bike. When he succeeded, a great crowd of prisoners ran over to the fallen man and surrounded him. All they had were their red metal mess-bowls from the KZ, and you could see those bowls going up and down – all you could see was those bowls going up and down – and they were killing him with those bowls. I took the magazine out of the gun I was holding and gave the gun to an American soldier. It was a Bergman sub-machine gun with a wooden stock. I regret giving it away; it would have made a good souvenir, but I didn't want to risk using it. We were ordered to gather in a village nearby to await the military police, so we started off. At that moment some German fighters flew over, low, and started to strafe the US column. But after one pass they didn't come back.

'The little German village turned into Dante's Inferno soon after our arrival. We had a lot of Russian ex-prisoners among us and they really started taking revenge on the Germans. They looted, turfed the people out of their homes, beat them up – everyone was running everywhere. I was caught up in the exhilaration of the moment. I ran into a house – I later discovered that it was the pastor's house – I ran through the rooms – the place was empty. Suddenly in a room I saw a radio, a beautiful big thing, in a walnut case, and I went to it and I picked it up and I smashed it, right down on the floor! And even as I smashed it, it was as if someone had thrown a bucket of cold water over me. I stood there and I thought, what have I done? What am I doing? The Russians were smashing everything – beautiful shelves full of beautiful books – all around me, in fury. But after I had smashed the radio I thought, what am I doing? I am behaving like an animal.

'We stayed in the village for a few days, and there was a fair amount of food available, but there was more drinking done than eating, and that proved fatal, because there was a cistern on a truck abandoned nearby that was full of industrial methylene. We got buckets of it – people started drinking it. Six or seven died. I drank about half a glass of it – I woke up in the night and found that I couldn't see. I had a headache that was like nails going through my eyes from my brain. That was another close shave – this time by my own hand.'

He travelled to the south of France and joined a Polish army unit stationed at Avignon. While there, he visited Nice and Cannes, and took up the piano again. 'In Nice one night I played before an audience of 500. I'd met a number of Polish Americans in the US forces, and I had become very friendly with one of them, a big sergeant. I was in US army uniform too, though without insignia – and one night he took me to an elegant club on the esplanade at Nice, and said that I should take over from the pianist. We'd both had a bit to drink. I said I couldn't but he told me I had to, and started to shove me towards the stage. The little rumpus attracted the attention of two MPs, since we'd been talking pretty loudly in Polish. My sergeant explained the situation to the policemen – one of whom was also a Pole: "We want to show this audience how a Polish boy can play." The MPs waved us on, and I climbed up on to the stage and sat down at the piano.

'It was a kind of arrival.'

He came to the UK after serving with the Second Corps in Italy. He worked for years in menial jobs, and in the meantime he studied civil engineering at evening classes at Westminster Polytechnic. In 1956 he joined British Railways for four years as a draughtsman, and later went on to specialize in structural dynamics, a field in which he is now a consultant.

He is a quiet and neat man who smiles apologetically at some of the experiences he relates. The camps have left him with a weak heart, but he feels that the experiences he went through crystallized his own character. 'The compassion that I had to suppress in the KZ can emerge now, and although I think I have come to terms with the horrors of the camps, for years immediately after the liberation I would faint – literally – at the sight of blood. Now, I can even enjoy reading material about the camps – if "enjoy" is the word; at least I can say to myself, "You've been through that and you are alive and you have done all right." It gives me a boost just being able to think that.'

IV

Alec was born in Starogard (Starogard Gdanski) in Pomerania, in the Polish Corridor, in 1922. In that part of Poland, the influence of Germany upon both lifestyle and thinking was great, and Alec's father had been in the Imperial German Navy during the First World War. Alec was the youngest son (there were three half-brothers from an earlier marriage of his father). He grew up speaking Polish, but learnt German in the *Gymnasium*. In addition to his ordinary schooling, Alec studied the violin at the conservatoire in Danzig.

'When the war started I was absolutely convinced, there was no doubt in me, that we would win. I was 16. It was a shattering blow when we were invaded. I joined the PW, but when our units were evacuated I went to Warsaw to fight the Germans, only returning home after the capital had fallen. My way home lay through Bydgoszcz, where the Germans had shot 150 Boy Scouts as a reprisal for the deaths of German natives of the town killed in fighting with the Poles when the invasion started.' The atrocity had taken place only days before he passed through the town, and when he arrived home his parents were fearful for his safety. They told him that the regular German troops had not been bad, but they had been followed by an *Einsatzgruppe* unit which had confiscated all radios and then rounded up the Jews, the priests, and as many schoolteachers as they could find, had taken them into the forest, and shot them.

As locals, the family was left alone, and Alec was able to work, first as a housepainter and later as a draughtsman in a sawmill, where he also played in the works orchestra. 'But in 1940 or early 1941, one of my half-brothers was arrested – he was a member of *Jaszczorka* ['Lizard'] – an organization which at that stage just held clandestine discussion groups, but which nevertheless voiced resistance to the Nazi regime. They took him to Stutthof on the Vistula delta. Two months later the Germans sent us a certificate of his death: heart disease. He was 20. He'd been a housepainter too, and I can remember my mother crying, cuddling his painter's overalls. After that, the hatred got into me.

'When they decided to move against Russia, the Germans needed cannon-fodder, and they graciously declared that all the cities in western Poland (or West Prussia, as they liked to call it) were henceforward German cities – and we duly got call-up papers. I had no desire to join the *Wehrmacht*, so I ran away. I managed to get some forged papers and made my way to Warsaw, where I already had contacts in the resistance. I worked under the codename "Jankowski".

'Because I could speak German pretty well by then, and because I hated them so much, I was attached to an execution squad: our rule was that you didn't just shoot a German; you had to tell him first that he was going to die, that he'd been sentenced to death, and why. Then you carried it out. I was only prepared to kill Germans, though our units also executed Poles who betrayed Jews. I think they were first given two warnings to desist, but the temptation to earn easy money was very great.

'We all knew what we were risking, and it was impossible to keep absolutely watertight security. My turn to be arrested came when we were in the midst of preparations to assassinate the Jewish traitor, Lolek Skosowski[14] – the Jews had already tried to shoot him in the ghetto but, though they hit him twice, they were both grazing shots – one on either side of the head. I was actually arrested at the Hotel Polski; luckily I didn't have a gun on me at the time or they would have shot me immediately.

'They kept me in Pawiak for about two months. Pawiak was a good training school for Auschwitz: it hardened you up. But the mental attitude was important too. In our minds, we were at war; we weren't going to give up just because we were prisoners.

'They sent me on a transport to Auschwitz-Birkenau, and there I had to become a different animal altogether from what I had been in the free world. Here, there was no question of fighting for survival, in an active sense. You became like a threatened rabbit: you kept still, crouched, ears flat, and you hoped the danger would pass, that they wouldn't notice you. There was something else: I remember some advice an "old" prisoner gave me shortly after my arrival: never hit anybody. If you do, you'll hit another, and another, and eventually you'll start to enjoy it – and before you know where you are, you'll be a kapo, and you'll start killing people then.

'After quarantine, the first *Kommando* I was put on was detailed to dig drainage trenches: we would dig a fairly narrow channel, lay water-pipes in them, and then turf them over. Our kapo wasn't bad – he pretended to be brutal when the SS were nearby, but he wasn't. With time, I started to get parcels, which weren't big, but they contained important food: onions, fats, garlic. You'd always divide your parcel with your friends: most of us formed alliances of about four men who stuck together and helped one another. And you could supplement your diet. From the French Jews on our *Kommando* we learnt how to eat frogs' legs. There were plenty of frogs around where we were working on the canalization, and we caught them and killed them, and then just put their legs into the hot soup – the flesh was so delicate that it cooked straight away, and then you skinned them and ate them. Frogs' legs in Auschwitz!

'Nearly all the time I was with the *Kommando* we were working not far from one of the crematoria. When we were returning to the camp one evening, we passed closer than usual to the gas chambers, and we suddenly saw a crowd of naked skeletons, crowded outside it, and they were wailing or, rather, moaning. A low moan. In such circumstances it was hard to keep sane, to keep strong; but above all was the urge to live through it and tell. I can remember seeing the SS helping little children down from the lorries that took them to the gas – almost lovingly; and I knew that some of those buggers had three or four kids of their own at home.

'I know some people back in Cracow who remember everything, but I have had to get rid of a lot to keep sane. Sometimes of course it comes back to me, and then I have problems; but if my friends talk too much, or go into too much detail, I have to ask them to shut up.

'Cold was the worst thing for me. At *Appell*, for example – they would have delousing sessions and make you stand naked for hours. It was good if you could get a bit of stick, or some twigs, to stand on, to keep your feet off the icy ground. Through all of it somehow you hung on to hope – without it you were finished. But hope alone couldn't keep you healthy, and in the end I succumbed. I got typhus, and I was sent to the HKB [Häftlingskrankenbau], the camp hospital.'

Recovering, Alec became a *Blockschreiber* in the HKB. While being a relatively protected job, it was not without danger: 'On one occasion after a selection I was ordered to carry a Dutchman who was too ill to walk to Crematorium Four. I had to carry him right into the gas chamber; and as I was coming out the SS officer said to me jokingly, "*Du bleibst dort* [Stay there]." And I thought: My God; because I knew they wouldn't shoot me – why waste bullets when they could gas me? And I was dithering, really, because I didn't know if they were being serious or not, as they stood there with their dogs. Then they started guffawing, and said, "*Raus, Idiot*," and kicked me out of the chamber.'

As a prisoner working officially in the camp hospital, he was deputed to work with the famous French pathologist, Dr Levy, himself a prisoner because he was a Jew. Levy would be obliged to give lectures and perform post-mortems for the SS surgeons in the hospital mortuary. Most of the corpses were people who had been shot or who had electrocuted themselves on the wire. Under Levy's direction, Alec would have to perform the dissections; he remembers having to skin the top of a head, cut the top of the skull off, and then place it like a shallow bowl; he would next remove the brain and place it into the container provided by the top of the skull. 'And if it was someone who had been shot, I would have to describe to those buggers how prisoner number so-and-so had received seven bullets, or however many it was, and the points of entry and exit, and what parts of the body they had passed through, or lodged in; translating it all for the benefit of the SS: "And bullet number five, which passed through the left ventricle of the heart, was probably the principal cause of death" – crap like that. I had to deal with the corpses of both men and women. And the SS doctors would consult with Levy in the most professional way. And I would be standing to attention nearby, immaculately clean, because I was near them.' He performed such duties four times.

'As the Russians approached Auschwitz, we were evacuated – firstly to Sachsenhausen; but we were experienced KZ-inmates when we got there, and so when they sent us to the showers we sent two of our number ahead of us to see if the windows were hermetically sealed with tape. If they had been, the rest of us were going to put up a fight; we'd decided that no one was going to gas us just like that, as they'd gassed the poor bewildered creatures who got off the trains at Birkenau. In the event, of course, they still needed us for war work, and the shower was a shower, nothing more.

'I had become good at handiwork – I was always quite good with my hands – but two of my friends were hopeless. The Germans tested us by setting us to file a piece of metal to see if we knew how. Luckily there were great crowds of people doing this test, so I was able to take it three times – once for myself and once for each of my two friends. We all looked the same, bald and thin – it's astounding how quickly individual characteristics disappear when you starve. So the three of us got into an engineering *Kommando*, and we were sent to a sub-camp of Buchenwald to work on making pumps for aeroplanes in an underground factory built in an old salt-mine.

'I was getting terrible blisters on my feet because of the wooden clogs we wore. Finally, I think because of those bloody blisters, I'd had enough. With my two comrades, I simply dived into the woods one day on the march from the factory to the camp. The SS gave chase, but they had the rest of the column to look after, and they soon gave up. We found a graveyard and hid in a large tomb – some big pompous thing about the size of a small house built in the last century for some great Weimar family. A few days later we heard some workers outside whistling Polish songs and we were about to go out to them; but some instinct stopped us. We were right: the Poles were slave-labourers and they had German guards with them.

'We held out for one more night in the tomb, and the next day we emerged cautiously and began to scout along the road. We found it crowded with tanks and jeeps. Of course we had never seen a jeep before, and we were rather fascinated. There were lots of soldiers too – but so different from the Germans; relaxed, in brown uniforms, smoking cigarettes; and it so happened that a great many of them were Polish-speaking. I later met an American general, who spoke real peasant Polish – it was very amusing.

'And so we were liberated. For three days there was anarchy: we could do what we liked, take whatever revenge we chose. SS were captured and made to hang each other. But after three days, that was the end, and the Americans established some kind of order. I never felt tempted to take revenge personally. There seems to be a mark of civilization in most of us which one's training forbids one to overstep. It's nothing especially virtuous; it is just that you can't contemplate taking that step; if you do, you become a moral bankrupt. But perhaps there was a simpler reason still why so few of us wanted to take revenge: we were weak, and we were tired.

'My main sensations were that I was happy to be alive, and happy to be able to be alone. I wanted sex, too, really desperately, and a couple of weeks later I got my chance, in a holding camp for released Polish prisoners. But when I lay down with the woman – nothing. I was impotent. I just wasn't strong enough.

'After a month we began to put on weight, but at first it was just fat – the muscle hadn't redeveloped yet.

'We heard that people were going to join the Polish 2nd Corps in Italy, and we decided to go along too, but it wasn't easy. The first thing we had to do was acquire some papers, and we found a German who was able to forge some. They said that we were Polish officers on our way to Rome to take part in an education programme. We had to hitch-hike, and in order to get lifts more easily we organized some American army jackets and trousers, and a few miscellaneous pseudo-military badges, including a handful of Boy Scout fleurs-de-lys, which we sewed on to the uniforms to make them look more convincing. All this we did quite instinctively – our behaviour was based on the training we'd had in the underground and at Auschwitz; survival courses *par excellence*, really, where the price of failure was death.

'I think the British were beginning to worry about the number of Poles they had promised their protection to, but Anders was taking as many men as he could into the Corps. Already in Rome, courses were being started in architecture, art and so on.

'Originally, I wanted to come to live in the UK, rather than farther afield, because I was still hoping to get home to Poland. We weren't sure how long the Russians would stay in power in our country, and we even wondered to begin with if the Western powers would push them back to their pre-war frontiers. But also it was easy to come to the UK with the 2nd Corps because Great Britain had extended her protection to all members of the Polish Free Forces who wanted to make their home here. By 1946 I had met my wife and our first son was born in Italy. I spent some time with a drama group in Rome and even had some small professional film roles; but when we arrived in England a year later, in 1947, I realized I wasn't going to be able to earn my living as an actor!

'Under the retraining schemes that were available to us, I got a grant to study at the Sir John Cass College in Aldgate; it was an art course in modelling, stone-carving, wood-carving, and life-drawing. The courses were designed to complete our education and equip us with a skill, as well as to prepare us to an extent for life in England. By then it was becoming clear that there would be no question of returning to a free Poland. He set up in business as a wood-carver, and is now a master of his craft.

'Rehabilitation was not that easy on a personal level. For a long time any kind of difficulty, any kind of quarrel, was a matter of life and death. If, for example, someone wanted me to do a job on a pay-later basis, I became disproportionately anxious; but that was because every little thing that went awry in the KZ was really a matter of life and death: one lived unimaginably close to the edge, and all my thoughts were formed in the framework of a constant fight for life. In the same way, if anyone tried to con me, or the slightest question of trouble arose from any official source, I immediately felt persecuted. I didn't have the mellowness of attitude that I think I have today. Now, I think I can switch off; I can put any problem out of my mind, especially if there's nothing I can do about it. But at the heart of things for me is the pleasure I take in being able to create something, and to have to do with great carvers like Grinling Gibbons whose lives were dedicated to making beautiful things, like mirrors, console tables, candelabra . . .'

We are sitting in his workshop, an airy room crowded with his work, the ceiling festooned with angel's wings in walnut, grapes and pears and knots and wreaths of leaves in great swags of cedar and oak, violins and clarinets and trumpets and hunting horns and shy, nude girls rising out of sea-foam; pedestals and looking-glass frames, candle-holders and chair-legs, chimney-pieces and picture frames. Alec works as a restorer and in his own right.

'This is my pleasure and my pain. This is a connection with the past, and that knowledge somehow mellows death, which is coming to us all. I feel part of a flow of craftsmen. They were here, and I have been one of them, and I will go, and then there will be others to do this work. It is a good feeling. Otherwise it's terrible, isn't it – life? It's so short. I am lucky to have found something real to do with it, and beautiful.'

Alec's wife Maria was born in Zakopane, in the Tatra Mountains near the Czech border.

'I come from a very strict family, a very religious home. We were comfortably off, and my childhood was secure, even sheltered. In 1943, a distant relative asked me if I would deliver a letter or a package for him from time to time, and I agreed. He used to hand the package over to me whenever he came into town, bringing produce, and the arrangement lasted three months. I was simply a messenger, a courier; I never knew any members of the resistance myself.

'I was working in a large, communal kitchen when they arrested me. Altogether, they rounded up 100 of us. 50 they shot immediately, and the rest were sent in due course to Auschwitz. You see, the cell I was such a small part of was communist – Red Faction. I know who betrayed us. She was a year younger than I was – 16. Not that it did her much good, for they sent her to Auschwitz with the rest of us. She survived, and she is still alive, in Poland.

'Because I was in the Red Faction, I would be treated like a heroine now if I returned to Poland to live; but at that time not a soul had the power to help me. They took me to Pawiak, where I was held for two months. I was a complete innocent. When I was called to my preliminary interrogation, I was so naïve that I told the SD that my auntie would be very worried at home, not knowing where I was; and that I had a very important document that my auntie would need; and would they at least see to it that she got it. And they said they would. It wasn't brave of me; I was just completely green. I think my naïveté is what flummoxed those killers: but my guess is that they left me alone too because they could see there wasn't much I could tell them.

'I was in Pawiak during the ghetto uprising – and that was really terrible. You could see people jumping from burning buildings. I was given the job of cleaning up the ash and smuts that blew in from the burning ghetto, which at least gave me the freedom of the prison. Of course I got very dirty, and so I went to one of the chief SS officers – we called him Popeye because he had protruding eyes – and asked him if I could wash. At first he told me that there were no facilities, but then he relented; and once a day for the duration of that cleaning job – about a week – he opened the washrooms personally, just for me, and ran the water, and stood guard with his dog – his back turned to me, very proper. And I am sure I only got away with it because I was so innocent. I expected normal behaviour from him, and that shocked him into behaving normally. Later I found out that he was a killer, and that he used the dog to kill people too.

'There was definitely a moment when I decided to survive. Like most people, we arrived at Birkenau at night – you couldn't really see anything. But the next morning, when they let us out of the quarantine *Block* and I looked around, I remember quite distinctly saying to myself, "I don't like it here and I am not going to die here." But when I got my first ration of food, I threw it out of the window – "I'm not going to eat this muck," I said. I remember it was a horrible-looking piece of cheese. I really was childish. I just sat on my bunk and threw it out of the window. And then there was the most horrifying commotion. Hungry, terrifying Jews were fighting for it. I grew up quickly.

'While we were in quarantine, we were allowed no letters and no food-parcels, and we were not allocated to *Kommandos*. Instead, they made us do useless work: for example, we would have to carry heavy bricks at the double from one pile to another and then back again. After the first month, really heavy physical labour was organized for us, though we looked forward to just being outside the camp. It was still spring, and in that part of Poland the springs are long and wet. It was very muddy, too – you would work up to your knees in mud. But by June, because the place was getting so overcrowded, we were transferred from what they called the former men's camp to a new women's camp. It was crazy, because everything was so disorganized. There was nowhere for us to sleep, and there were endless roll-calls to keep a tally of us. We exchanged brick-built *Blocks* for wooden ones; they don't exist any more, except for one or two, the first ones to be erected. But I remember where I was.

'Later on, that autumn, I became very ill – I had typhoid, TB, avitaminosis, all at once. One day I collapsed and they took me to the HKB, which we all dreaded, but somehow I survived. I'd got hold of one aspirin, I remember; and I was pleased because I was terrified of getting 'flu – which seems funny now, considering what else I had wrong with me already; but that one aspirin was the sum of my medication for my entire illness. I must have been an extremely healthy person underneath. But I think I was sensible: I never foraged among the rubbish for food, and when I got dysentery, which of course was a killer, I went to the kitchens and gathered charcoal and ate only that for two days. That not only cured me, but I never got even diarrhoea again for as long as I was a prisoner.

'I kept to a ritual of washing, too – although they made water available in the *Block* washroom only at midnight. All through the summer of 1943 I remember getting up at midnight, which was an effort, and going to wash myself. That was my toughness – don't ask me why I did it, but it was in me.

'I know that having a self-imposed routine was a tremendous help; but having a good mental attitude didn't help a lot of people: they died or were killed just the same. I never felt that the longer I survived, the greater were my chances of seeing it through to the end, because the whole thing was getting progressively worse – not least my health. I'd been lucky to have been in Pawiak for only two months. People came to Auschwitz who had been in prison and under torture for years, so naturally they had fewer resources with which to fight. And we were supported by food-parcels, proper food-parcels with important things in them: onions, garlic and lard.[15]

'I think my religious training had made me a fundamentally decent person. I would share what I had. I wouldn't take advantage of anyone, and I think from a perfectly practical point of view that behaving decently increased your chances of getting through – not least because you could live with yourself better. It is quite common knowledge that the people who had no tenets to live by – of whatever nature – generally succumbed, even if they were ruthless in their struggle to survive. Of course at school we had all prayed in the normal way, and even in the KZ I remember praying. Once when it had been raining remorselessly for days and we were all soaked through and through and the rain was eating into us, I begged Him at least to take this extra punishment away from us. And the next day the weather cleared. But that hardly proves anything, and a day did come when I said to Him in my heart, I spit on Your face for allowing this; and with that my faith died within me. This was on account of one incident: the death of a Greek Jewess. The Greeks were in a terrible state: they couldn't survive the climate, first of all. They'd been days and days on transports from the warm south, to be dumped in the KZ, already in ruined health, in a climate which they were totally unused to.

'We were on an outside *Kommando*, digging trenches for pipes. When we returned from work one day it appeared that one of the Greek girls hadn't come back with us. It was assumed that she had escaped. We had to stand on the *Appellplatz* all night. Meanwhile they were searching for her, and they found her not far from where her *Kommando* had been working – she'd curled up in a hollow and gone to sleep. She was exhausted. And they brought her back to camp, and they set dogs on to her, and we had to watch . . .

'Later, I went to church, I had my sons christened, I went through the motions; but it wasn't until 1970 that I went to confession again. Someone very dear to us died and it seemed to me that I wanted my prayers at the funeral to really mean something for the sake of the departed. But maybe too it's because I'm getting older myself.

'You have to understand that the girl in the camp and I are two different people. I have her memories, but not the motivation she had. The KZ separated me for ever from the person I was born, and for the period that I was in the camp I was a different person again. Although I could skip over the years since 1945 with my husband and sons, in my memory, I remember the years in the camp in such detail that to relive a day would take a day. But a German lady doctor – you must understand that I had some mental problems after the war – told me that I had to come to terms with the fact that the KZ was *the* most important and traumatic event in my life, and would probably always be. And I was crying, and asking her, wasn't giving birth to my children more significant? And she said, I think not.

'Late in the war we were moved westwards, ultimately to a Buchenwald *Aussenkommando* in Leipzig. One of our jobs was cleaning the

SS barracks there. This was in early April, and everything was collapsing around the Germans' ears. As we were going to work, suddenly we were aware of American planes which were flying over and bombing the city. Everybody ran madly for the shelters, because the bombs were already falling. There had been no sirens, there were no anti-aircraft guns; the town was defenceless. The bombs were exploding around us, and there was a woman pushing a pram down some steps which led towards a shelter under a house, but she was stuck and obviously she just couldn't think that it would be easier to take the child out of the pram. And I didn't, either; I just ran to help her carry the pram down the steps. And in the shelter the German people began to talk to us as if we were one with them. There was conversation – normal, human, helpful conversation – about us, about them. We were just people together, during the hour or so that the raid lasted. And when the planes had gone and we went up to the street, we became prisoners again. But the point is that in the street, only our house still stood. That's the only reason we could get out, why we weren't buried under the rubble. Everywhere around, for as far as you could see, was flattened. Only our house stood. And I swear this is true, on the heads of my children.

'But they were still determined to move us prisoners on, and so we were to be sent east, into the Sudetenland, where a Panzer division was still holding out against the Russians. We found ourselves walking east, passing close by Dresden. After three days we were out of food – we'd only had a little sugar – and we'd had no sleep. The SS were on horses and carts, and could sleep on them in shifts. They walked us three days and two nights without stopping, five abreast. We started to have hallucinations; but we were still *compos mentis* enough to realize that we couldn't go on, so we had to do something. Only four of our line of five moved – the fifth girl was too frightened: we hurled ourselves into the thick woods that came right up to the road on one side. We were lucky: the dogs didn't sniff us out, and the SS obviously didn't want to waste time on too extensive a search. We lay there for quite some time after they had gone, and then we made our way deeper into the forest, until we came to a glade, and there we stayed – for two weeks. We fed on young nettles, and wood sorrel, and wild rape, which is full of goodness because of the oil it yields. Finally, some Polish slave-labourers who were working on nearby farms found us and gave us a little proper food and some extra clothes, and we joined them and went to work on the farms, but we didn't let on that we had escaped from the KZ, and we kept our sleeves rolled down to hide our tattoos.

'It wasn't so long before the Russians arrived. Of the Soviet unit that liberated us, only the two officers were Russians. The men were Mongolians. It was like something out of the history of Genghis Khan, for the vengeance those troops took upon the Germans was appalling to watch. The men were killed brutally and wholesale; the women were raped, sometimes to death. I managed to save one young German soldier who had been wounded and was sheltering in a hayloft. I told the Mongolians that he was just a farm boy and had had nothing to do with the army. The only reason I did this was that I had seen what they did to the German soldiers they caught.

'I wanted to stay with two of my friends who aimed to head north-west, towards Lübeck and Bremen. The feeling of togetherness, of solidarity, was very strong. We teamed up with a couple of liberated prisoners-of-war from the camps that had been around Dresden – an Englishman and a big, black American, who used to get our food for us. This is how he did it: when we approached a village, he'd strip naked and march into the village with a huge kitchen-knife clenched between his big white teeth – and he'd march into a farmhouse and shout COCORI-COO! – meaning that he wanted a chicken. We were always given food – more than enough. The Germans were quite terrified. And we were just dying of laughter. It was just incredible, the way we laughed then. I know I will never be able to laugh like that again.

'We got to the Grimma bridge over the Mulde, between Dresden and Leipzig, and we made ourselves a tricolour, and spoke French to each other, and bluffed our way past the Russians – at that time the bridge divided eastern and western zones, and I heard later that the day after we crossed the Russians closed it because too many people were getting away. We were now in the American zone, but they were eager to move us on to Leipzig, in the British sector, where a big DP camp had been established. I think they already knew that the whole area would cede to Russian control, and wanted to keep people moving westwards as fast as possible.'

Something has happened in the course of the conversation, which I have noticed several times before, with other survivors. Maria has become much more animated and relaxed since we left the concentration camp behind. Liberation continues to have its effect, but she looks tired. 'Yes, I am tired; but I want to get it over and finished.

'By the time we reached Leipzig it was late May or early June. They gave us clothes – until then we had been dressed in the remnants of the clothes we were in when we escaped from the death-march, and we were taken to a DP camp at Northeim, just to the north of Göttingen. From there I finally made my way to Italy.

'I became an actress in the Polish Dramatic Theatre which had been formed under the auspices of the 2nd Corps, and I remained an actress, in Italy and later in England, with the same troupe, for seven years. But I didn't particularly want to make a career out of being an actress. You see, when I was first arrested, the first night in Pawiak, my heart froze;

and I know now that it didn't unfreeze until the late Sixties, when I had to go through a terrible breakdown. It was triggered, I think, by meeting someone from the camps, and had nothing to do with my family life; my family helped me through it. It was very hard, but through it I realized consciously for the first time that my heart was frozen and, when I did, I knew why I had never had any strong feelings about being an actress; I did not want to release feelings.

'The legacy is still there, and always will be. I have bad dreams, and there are moments when a memory is triggered; there are certain smells, certain situations, and what is frightening is that you can never know for sure when it will happen. I can't read books about the camps, and when we meet other survivors we don't want to talk about Auschwitz. It's not necessary to go over facts that everybody knows; everybody was beaten, everybody was starved, humiliated, worked half to death. I can only tell the story for myself, from my point of view.

'There was one very vivid reaction after the war. My second son was born here after the war, in 1949. In the maternity hospital he was taken away from me briefly after having been born, and I asked where he was going. They told me he'd been taken away to be circumcised – at that time it was medically in vogue to circumcise babies. Of course that sent me into a total panic, because to be circumcised in Poland was the death-penalty. I rushed from my bed and down the corridor and almost had a tug-of-war snatching him back from the doctor. I refused to have him circumcised. All my instincts were awake: I was back in the camp.

'You may think that nothing could happen to me in life more terrible than what I have already lived through, but there is one thing: it would be to see something happen to my children: to see them die. I would live through the KZ again to avoid that.

'There are relationships, even momentary ones, that remain with me. I remember when I was in the HKB there was a *selection*, and the girls chosen for the gas chambers were put on one side of the aisle between the bunks, separated from us. They left them there overnight and you could sneak across to them. There was one girl who was my age, about 17, and I went to her and I gave her my onion and my garlic, and we talked, like sisters, not about anything spectacular, not about Life, or anything; just about this and that: kid's stuff. I had the need to be with her, and she responded; we knew each other a little already. She was a Polish Jewess. She would have survived if they hadn't selected her, for she was over the crisis in her illness.

'And there was one lovely morning, and we were called out to *Zählappell*, and I was looking out of the *Block* window, and the air was so clear that I could see right across to the mountains in the Sudetenland. I had been born in the High Tatra, and I was lost in a dream, when suddenly somebody pinched me – not spitefully, playfully; and I jumped, and turned round, and there was an SS-girl, about the same age as me, who had been sent in to clear the *Block*. And we both started to laugh; and for a moment we were just kids, laughing; and then we were serious again, and we went back to our roles, and she marched me out to *Appell*.'

Healers

I

Elie Cohen was a country doctor in the north of the Netherlands when the war started. His later experiences in the Dutch concentration camps, and in Auschwitz, led to his publishing one of the first books to attempt to analyse their function and the behaviour of those involved with them, on both sides of the wire, scientifically.[1]

He was born in Groningen in 1909. 'My parents were both observant Jews, and we lived in the Jewish quarter of town – it was a little like the old East End of London, with streets of little merchants. Our street was the kind with so many different shops that you could start at one end naked and come out at the other fully equipped for life! My father had many different jobs, but most of the time he was a waiter.

'I went through school in the normal way and was considered good enough to go to university. My father was delighted. He was greatly envied among his friends on account of the social standing I had acquired, but I myself was caught between two worlds. I was raised to a social level which I didn't really belong to. I remember once that I cut my father dead in the street when I passed him with some student friends, and the memory of that still makes me feel ashamed.' He adds that he still feels like an outsider, a Jew, in Arnhem, where he has lived since the war. 'Not that I am made to, in any way – the feeling comes from within. When I was a student, I didn't know how to behave at middle-class dinner-parties, for example – though again, no one made me feel ill at ease. I had only myself to blame for my lack of confidence.'

He graduated from Groningen in 1935 and was confronted by the immediate problem of finding a practice, which was not easy. 'But the head of the medical faculty was also a regular customer in the café where my father worked, and he phoned one day to ask if I'd be willing to do a locum for an elderly doctor who was himself unwell. I did, and subsequently inherited the practice, since the doctor took a liking to me. The surgery was in a little village not far from Groningen called Aduard.

'I was in practice at Aduard from 1936 until 1941. It was a good practice, and I was sorry to leave it; but on 8 February 1941 the Aryan Declaration was publicly enforced, and Jews had to make themselves known publicly as such. I was also the community doctor for the poor of the Aduard district at the time, and I remember the mayor coming to see me, very distressed and embarrassed. "I know what you are going to ask me," I told him: "You are going to ask me how many Jewish grandparents I have." "That is so," he replied. I said: "I have four." "Then I am afraid you may no longer be community doctor," he said. Jews were stripped of their public functions: I was allowed to continue in private practice for the time being. I could have lied, I suppose, but why? Why apologize for what I am, or cover it up? I felt Jewish, just as you feel British or another man feels American. It was important, but it was also no big deal: it was simply natural; though I should add that I was a quite ardent Zionist then, owing to influences when I was a student. My wife was a Zionist too and we had been considering going to Palestine, because we had seen the clouds gathering and because we felt that that was where our destiny, and that of our young son, lay. But we didn't get around to it. Our parents were in Groningen; I was just starting up in my career. I wasn't brave enough to go.

'The deadline for me to abandon my job was 1 May 1941 – by then the practice was moribund anyway, so we packed our bags and returned to Groningen – and it was because of this move, which we did not notify to the authorities through some oversight or other, that I didn't get a draft notice about a year later to go to the labour camps along with all the other Jewish men aged between 15 and 60, on 15 July 1942.

'At that time I was practising, more or less undercover, in the beleaguered Jewish community in Groningen, along with a handful of colleagues in the same position. After 15 July we went into hiding in our own house, but I knew I couldn't stay cooped up in one room indefinitely, so when a chance presented itself to get away to Sweden by boat from Delfzijl, we jumped at it. The cost was high – Dfl.13,000 – but I could just about manage it. A date was set for Thursday, 13 August. My contact told me we'd be hidden in a boat taking timber to Sweden. You can see how deluded I'd become by wishful thinking: timber to Sweden is worse than coals to Newcastle! But we went along with it, and of course it was a trap, and we were betrayed to the Gestapo who arrested us at Groningen station.'

In one sense, the family was lucky, for a friend of theirs, Jo Cohen, was a member of the local *Judenrat* and managed to get the Germans to let him take the Cohens' little boy (who was about two at the time) home with him. Under arrest, Elie Cohen had his first encounter with the physiological effects of fear: his legs gave way and he had to drag himself up the steps of the police station. In his despair, he tried to hang himself in his cell, but was interrupted by the police. This was the only time in the entire period of his imprisonment that he was tempted by suicide.

'They took us to prison in Amsterdam to interrogate us about diamonds, because my wife's family was in the diamond business, and the Gestapo suspected us of trying to smuggle diamonds out of Holland. Obviously they got nothing out of us because we were innocent. They took me alone and sent me to the camp at Amersfoort, which was very bad. They put me on a bricklaying *Kommando* – my job was carrying the bricks to the skilled workmen, under a constant hail of blows. However, I had a lucky break. Through the wire separating us I met a girl I had known in Groningen, where she had been a nurse. She was looking after injured American POWs at an adjacent camp, and she was able to get me a job there too – I was allowed to work in my capacity as a doctor at this new job only in the evenings, but it did mean extra food, and it led to a different job at Amersfoort. I was put in charge of the burial detail. I was not beaten any more, and I think that saved me.'

He remained at Amersfoort until 8 December 1942, when he was transferred to the second camp established in the Netherlands: Westerbork. 'Transfer from Amersfoort to Westerbork was like going from hell to heaven. There was no work to do, and at the beginning only a very small proportion of the Jews there were being transported east. It was more like a transit camp than a proper concentration camp. I had an "S" designation[2] for having tried to flee Holland without permission, and prisoners so designated were slated for immediate transport; but once again I had luck on my side, because one of the German Jews who made up the *Prominent* class of prisoners at Westerbork wanted me to remain there to work as a doctor; it was arranged by the local Nazi functionary, a Dr Harster. I met him in Munich after the war, in 1978, when I was researching my book about Sobibor.[3] He was responsible for sending the Jews east, and I simply wanted to ask him when it was that he found out where he was really sending them. He told me he thought he was merely sending them to labour camps, and of course I cannot prove that he didn't know otherwise at the time.

'Harster was astonished that I had no personally unfriendly feelings towards him; but, as I told him, I could have none since he had been indirectly merciful to me: I was able to stay eight months at Westerbork, during which time a crucial change occurred at Auschwitz: Jewish doctors became needed to work as prisoner-doctors. That was to be my salvation: at a cost, even a terrible cost, but still it is why I am alive.

'Unlike Amersfoort, there was no abuse at Westerbork – no one even called you a *Saujude* [Jewish pig]. At Amersfoort you were vermin and made to feel like it. The way I was able to withstand this was through understanding within myself that the only things that gave the SS the power to boss me around were accident and a uniform; whereas I was a doctor. I was somebody in my own right. That gave me a sense of superiority over them, which helped. Another advantage I had was that I could speak German (of course they couldn't speak Dutch), and I behaved like a German – correct to a fault, and shouting a lot. That was defensive.

'At Westerbork, the whole administration was Jewish. The only German was the commandant, Gemmeker. I am afraid that, in my view, the Jews, especially the Jewish councils, were all too willing to abet the Germans, and Hannah Arendt's condemnation of them is correct. I am guilty of it, too.

'As a doctor in Westerbork I didn't have to live in the barracks. I had been reunited with my wife and we shared a small flat with a German Jewish couple.[4] Favoured prisoners like us lived in families in private accommodation. Rank-and-file lived in segregated barracks, but they were not wholly separated as at Auschwitz. In addition, I had a red stamp on my identity card which meant I was on the *Stammliste* – exempted from transportation. However, there arose a severe difficulty which was to bring me into conflict with myself. I became the transport doctor. On one hand, it meant that when transports of Jews arrived in the camp I had to examine them and refer the sick to the hospital, which was not a bad hospital at all. But I also had duties concerning those transports made up to go to the east. I had the power to declare a person "unfit for transport"; and if I stated that someone was *transportunfähig*, it meant that his family was also spared. It was quite some power that I had, and I made good use of it: I faked high temperatures to save people, and so on, and I am proud to say that I did it in a disinterested way.

'However, I overstepped the mark in my fake diagnoses and the senior camp doctor, Spanier, double-checked. He warned me that if I continued to behave in this way, he would make sure that my wife and I were put on the next transport ourselves. And I knuckled under. I collaborated.

'It is a terrible word, but I cannot escape it, although my situation was impossible; just as I cannot escape the guilt that I feel. We did the Germans' job for them. It is impossible for me to say whether I would have done the job if I had known the truth about their destination, if I had thought for a moment that they were going anywhere other than work-camps, even with brutal treatment as at Amersfoort. As things were, it was unavoidable to send people on the transports, provided they fulfilled the Germans' criteria – and these included women with tiny children. I remember at least one pleading with me that, if she were sent with her six-week-old baby to the east, it would die of the cold; which was true, but there was nothing to be done. Of course now and then you could still manage to keep people off the transport, but I was no longer able to save people to a significant extent. I gave in to pressure and became the victim of my own selfishness.

'What made it worse was that when I saw people off, they said goodbye to me cheerfully, even gratefully, if I'd been able to be of any help to them at all in the camp: no one held my work against me. And when my work was done and the transport had gone, I'd have a shower and a nap, and in the evening we might go to the cabaret in the camp, and laugh and joke and have a good time. I buried my feelings; I had a good life, and I didn't have to go east myself. My only excuse is that we didn't know about the gas chambers. 19 trains went to Sobibor, and we didn't know what went on there; we didn't even know the name Sobibor. Auschwitz we had heard of: we knew it was a destination, but not what it really was.

'I put a friend – the same Jo Cohen who had looked after my son and taken him back to my parents after our arrest – on to one of the transports that I later found out was destined for Sobibor, and as I did so, even *as* I did so, I was weeping, and he said to me: "Why are you weeping? They want us to work for them, don't they? Well, they'll have to feed us and clothe us."

'There are many matters of deep regret: you could say that I was to blame for my own sister's death. She looked like a Gentile and she was living as one in Amsterdam; but I advised her through a cousin who was in the Jewish Police to declare herself and come to Westerbork. She was terrified that she'd be killed if she was discovered as a Jew in hiding, and I thought I would be able to protect her. As it was, I condemned her to death in Auschwitz – a much more certain death than she would have faced if she'd stayed in Amsterdam, where the chances of her survival would have been relatively high – at least 50 per cent. She was astonished when she was selected for transport and there was nothing I could do to stop it. I remember how she looked at me, bewildered . . .'

I ask what made him write his book on Sobibor.

'Nearly 100,000 Dutch Jews were killed in the extermination camps, but here in Holland that is little known; all anyone knows about is Auschwitz. Now I am the last person to belittle the importance of Auschwitz. I was in Auschwitz-I for 18 months. But I wanted to make a memorial and a *kaddish* for those Jews who died in the extermination camps. A third of those 100,000 died in Sobibor: 34,294 Dutch Jews were sent there, and 19 came back, of whom only two survived the camp proper – the others are survivors of outside work details.

'The book taught me things about myself. I made an appointment with the former SS-man, Gomerski, to interview him in Frankfurt. He was agreeable, but when the time came to go, I fell ill. I made a new appointment, and the same thing happened. I couldn't bring myself to meet the man.

'I put my problem to a German psychiatrist friend of mine. Willi Schumacher had been the forensic psychiatrist at Gomerski's trial, and he offered to go with me to meet him. This time there was no illness. Gomerski and his wife were pleasant; they lived in a nice house. He looks quite normal, behaves quite normally; and it was impossible to get at any kind of truth. She stoutly denied that she'd ever known the nature of her husband's work; and he took refuge behind the old *Befehl ist Befehl* (Orders are orders) excuse. "Anyway," he added, "I had a wife and two children and if I had refused to obey orders I would have been put into a camp myself. What would you have done in my place?" I have to say that I couldn't honestly answer that question. Would I have been brave enough to refuse? To have said No, whatever the cost or the personal consequences, simply because it was the right thing to do. It is the easiest excuse in the world to say to yourself: I'll do it, because if I don't someone else will, and it'll make no difference. So few of us have the courage to say No, and that is why the generals and the dictators thrive. My answer to him was silence. I had no answer. I try to be honest at all costs, with myself as much as with anyone else; and it is hard, because now I have to try to face some of the things I did in the KZ which I had to do, but which I can't help feeling guilty about; and ask myself: might there not after all have been another way?

'They asked me to be a witness at the Eichmann trial. I wouldn't do it. I regret it now, but at the time I couldn't face it; I couldn't face confronting what I imagined would be such a monster; and I wasn't sure what it would do to me emotionally . . . But I have in fact sat five metres away from Eichmann, because I covered the trial for a Dutch newspaper, *Het Parool*; and although he certainly didn't give the impression of being a man you'd want to know, just taking his personality and leaving his history aside, I couldn't read the enormity of his crimes in his face. One of the things about him was that he just sat there in his glass box, and he wasn't so important any more – though, oddly, he seemed to make out that he was, writing down notes and so forth, as if he were pretending to himself that the whole thing concerned another man. He was trying to make himself appear less guilty.

The disturbing side of the affair for me was the question of our complicity in our fate, which was an accusation thrown at us by the *sabras*, and which I found hard to answer, again. It made me think about who I was, though: was I a Dutchman first, or a Jew? The distinction between a Jewish Dutchman and a Dutch Jew is important:

the first is totally assimilated, whereas the second puts the stress on his Jewishness, which is the internationally linking thing between us all. As a Zionist I belong to the second category, and I felt that the first line of defence for the Jewish race was the foundation of the State of Israel. It was disturbing to be accused by the heirs of that state of not fighting sufficiently for their race.

'Many of the SS – look at Höss's memoir – saw themselves as soldiers doing their duty, and most have no concept of having committed a great moral wrong as individuals. They have drawn a veil over their own past, or they are not sufficiently sensitive to be affected by it. They won't, or can't, take the responsibility personally. It's not cowardice: their brains just aren't capable of it: *I obeyed orders*; that was and is the most important thing for them. Without such behaviour there can be no structure. You or I might be weak enough to conform, but I think we'd feel guilty for the rest of our lives. These people simply don't. And once they'd started, it became a process like any other factory process. After a while, you don't think about it any more. It's a job that has to be done, and they found it by and large a very dull and unattractive job, I think. In *Human Behaviour in the Concentration Camp* I refer to the absence of hatred on the part of the SS. I don't think emotions played a great role in the process. We prisoners were even referred to habitually, not as people, but as "merchandise" or "blocks of wood" – absurd and frightening euphemisms.

'On 9 April 1943, all the Jews outside Amsterdam were to be rounded up. My little boy was staying with a mixed-marriage couple at the time – good friends – and there was a choice: should we leave him there or have him with us? The kind of monstrous decision one has to make. Well, I was a *Prominent* at Westerbork, I thought we were safe, I didn't yet know that German promises were valueless; and I couldn't predict what fate had in store for us. So we had Ronnie join us. Soon after, my wife had a quarrel with the husband of the German Jewish couple we were sharing with – over, of all things, a misplaced spoon. He made a great fuss about it and she told him he was being very German to make such a big noise about such a little thing. Someone overheard, and reported her (and, by extension, us) to Dr Spanier, for making anti-German remarks. Spanier summoned me. My "red stamp" status was revoked, and a fortnight later we were sent on the transport. My parents-in-law came with us. My own parents had been sent on an earlier transport to Auschwitz and, as I later learnt, were gassed there.

'There are certain pivotal moments in anyone's concentration camp experience. The incident with the spoon was one for me. The next followed soon after. On the goods-waggon transport to Auschwitz my little boy wanted to look at the passing countryside through a

372

ventilation hole; but he'd had an infection of the middle ear and I was worried that the draught might bring it on again, so I took him away from his "window". Two days later he was killed. I didn't even allow him his last pleasure in life: to see the fields, and the cows and the horses in them as we travelled past . . .'

But you couldn't possibly have known . . .

'No! I didn't know! And that is the proof of it – I absolutely didn't know what was happening at Auschwitz, in which I had participated by sending so many people. I have to reassure myself that it is *true* that I didn't know.

'The *selection* was made immediately we arrived. Of course we didn't know that that was what it was. There was nothing panicky in my waving goodbye to my wife and Ronnie and my mother-in-law. I had no premonition. I found out the truth an hour, or two hours, later . . . We were marched to the *Stammlager* [Auschwitz-I], stripped, divested of everything – but still there was no anxiety because we were not being treated brutally, and I had no reason to suspect that the shower might be a disguised gas chamber: I had not heard of such a thing! After that, we were clothed and sent to the *Ringallee* where we were served soup which none of us could eat, it was so disgusting. And then a Dutch Jew came up to us and said, "Congratulations." And I said, "Why? We're in a KZ." "That's true," he said; "but you are alive. The others are dead." And then I knew. The strange thing is that I believed it at once – I accepted it. And I wanted to survive. There was no question.

'I knew that my best chance was to get work as a doctor, and I applied my mind to that. I had no thoughts of giving up, of not trying to get through it all. I was probably in a state of shock; but you see from the moment you enter a camp your reactions have to change: you are using a different set from the ones you use in normal life. The proper reaction – the mourning – came only after the war. At the time, normal human reactions were suspended immediately and instinctively. Besides, I wasn't alone: many, many of us had the same experience at the same time. One had to get on or go under: there was no other choice. I was to spend nearly two years in the realm of death – it was quite accurately that – and one got used to it, awful as that sounds. No respect was shown to the dead, and bodies came to mean very little more than sacks. One developed techniques for survival. It was important to be in good shape physically – the best you could manage. It was important not to be squeamish about the conditions, and not to be too proud if, for example, your duties as a doctor involved latrine-cleaning. If you couldn't adapt, if you didn't realize that any dignity attaching to your profession (whatever it was) was out of the window here, you would go under.

'They called out the doctors among our transport, but I was not one of the three chosen by the SS – later I learnt that two of the volunteers selected were not in fact doctors at all. Later on that same day of my arrival, some of us were transferred to Buna-Monowice, and put into tents. It was September, and cold at night. I mentioned to the SS in charge that I was a doctor, and before long I was transferred back to the medical *Blocks* at Auschwitz-I. I was fortunate; I was working indoors, and I did not have to stand roll-call. I think that was the most important privilege of all.

'But although we were privileged, our work brought us up against terrible moral dilemmas. Doctors must learn to be philosophical in the face of death; but, normally, if they lose a patient they can take comfort from the knowledge that they have done all they can for him; they have not deliberately killed him. My work at the time of which I will now speak was in *Block* 9, one of the medical *Blocks* in Auschwitz-I. I was assigned to the ward for Gentile prisoners who were psychotic. A Jew with the slightest illness would be selected for the gas; but these Gentiles were spared. I worked with the senior doctor, Erwin Valentin, a German Jew who was about 60 at the time. He was a former naval officer, and he was "the heart of the *Block*" – I had the greatest respect for him. On one occasion we had a particularly intractable patient – he was raving and violent, and his behaviour was attracting the attention of the SS. We realized that, unless something was done, they might clear the ward, Gentiles or not, and send all the patients to the gas chamber. At Dr Valentin's instigation, I injected the man with insulin, and he died. It was done to save others, but it is something that is very hard to live with.

'It was not the only occasion when I behaved against the tenets of mercy. There was a Dutch university professor who had been selected for the gas. Knowing the fate that was in store for him, he begged me to let him have something to render him unconscious at the moment he entered the chamber. I could tell you that I didn't give him anything, because we had so few drugs that they had to be kept strictly for use where they could do most good; but the truth is that I refused him because I was scared of the consequences to myself if I were found out. The legacy of that one decision is a lifetime of remorse.

'But I was able to be of help to people on occasion, and I think that is my only justification. One did what one could. For example, there was an "old" number with erysipelas who came to me for help. He was scared of going into the HKB because of the *selections* that were made from them. I managed to beg some sulphur tablets for him, which were like gold but which, washed down with about five litres of camp "tea", made him well enough to pass for fit, and saved his life. The point about that incident, one among many, is that I have to keep reminding myself of it because it counterbalances the things which I did that were bad.

'The sense of guilt that I suffer at having survived is made all the more acute by the memories of those things. The things we did were insane by any standards. We had to keep records of medicines administered, though in fact none were – there were none to be had. Perhaps the SS sought to cover their tracks, in case there should ever be a Red Cross inspection, or should they be unable to destroy their records in the event of defeat.

'I was forced to assist the Rumanian SS doctor, Klein, in his selections. Klein's manner to me was always courteous and professional, though that condones nothing. He would come and choose those among the Jewish patients whom he deemed no longer worthy of medical treatment, and condemned them to the gas chamber. I had to hold each one's medical card, and Klein would ask me my opinion of the patient's condition. Of course any attempt to cover up was doomed, because Klein could see for himself what sort of state the patient was in, but the charade had to be played out. Anyone who was thought to need more than ten days' recuperation before being sent out to work again was sent to the gas. But I participated, because I wanted to live . . .

'I think that to get through I had to undergo a period of adaptation to a completely different standard of behaviour – call it rather an anti-standard. I certainly didn't do it by an intellectual process. But what could I do if an SS ordered me to do this, or this? Nothing! Or I could refuse, and be killed on the spot. You couldn't even disobey a *Blockälteste*. There was a pecking-order for survival, too. I was ordered to take food for a prisoner in *Block* 11 – the *Bunker*. My seniors were afraid to go there, so they passed the job to me. I went, and I was lucky – they didn't take me in on a whim, as they might have done. And I knuckled under to avoid a fight because a fight would lead to death.

'*Block* 9 of course was next door to *Block* 10, and I took food in there three times a day. It was said that there was an unofficial brothel in *Block* 10 too, but I never saw any evidence of it. People from the *Sonderkommando* were supposed to take advantage of it – brothel isn't actually the word, because the sex was casual and not part of a formal transaction. The SK men had everything they wanted, for as long as they were alive. My own feeling is that there were romantic attachments formed between men prisoners outside *Block* 10 and the women prisoners inside. The women had nothing to do; they were laboratory animals; but they could flirt through the windows with men who might bring them extra food or articles of warm clothing.'

How could the women be so cool under such circumstances?

'You cannot judge what happened in Auschwitz by any normal circumstances. Women were especially persecuted in the camps, sent to Birkenau, condemned to hard labour; the Birkenau women's camp was far more overcrowded than the men's, and the conditions were worse, I believe. Whereas in *Block* 10 you could rest, you had no work to do, you were sheltered, and there was always a chance that you would not in fact be used for experimental purposes. Added to which they had no precise idea what kind of experiments would be performed on them. One of the hardest things to explain is that death was the normal thing. Its consideration wasn't important. We expected that we would die. We lived in an atmosphere of death, as usual for us as life is usual for, say, Mr Average living in Arnhem today.[5]

'Hope was important and unimportant. It was a basic constituent of the character, an instinctive trait, and probably important in that it kept you going. Pessimists died fast. But though we hoped, whether we rationally believed that we would live is another question. From my entire extended family of 80, only two survived. About 80 per cent of Dutch Jews died. There are maybe 25,000 Jews here now; in 1939 there were 150,000.

'Our conversation was invested with hope: the progress of the war, rumours of Russian victories; and food; Sabbath dinners, the soup our mothers made. We talked about work, too – our careers in the real world. And there was the so-called resistance movement. I was a member of a cell in Auschwitz-I, and I have to tell you that it was completely meaningless.

'What we almost never talked about was sex, though we were well enough fed to be capable of it, I suppose. And there was little or no masturbation – except for "stomach masturbation". Our actual diet had improved, and by the time I was working in medical *Block* 28 as quite a senior prisoner we were eating bread and soup and cheese, and now and then sausage and marmalade. At Christmas we got goulash. There was considerable relief in the very last couple of months before we were evacuated because they had stopped the gassing. I remember New Year's Eve 1944 – one of the doctors could play the saxophone and he'd got hold of one from somewhere and he was playing jazz with a couple of medical orderlies who'd got mouth-organs or something, and we'd rather dangerously made vodka out of pure alcohol. A couple of SS chanced upon our celebration, and wished us well: "Happy New Year," they said. "This will be your last one here. Some time in 1945 you'll be in our shoes and we'll be in yours."

'I was liberated from Ebensee on 6 May. One jeep arrived first, with four Americans aboard. Others followed soon after. They were wonderful. They'd erected tents and showers, food parcels were distributed, and three meals a day were provided – all within 24 hours. They asked doctors to identify themselves, and so I did. "Have you lice?" they asked me. "If I put my blanket on the ground, the lice will walk away with it," I replied. We were all totally infested. The Americans arranged a two-day treatment. We thought they were crazy, but they dusted us with a white powder and on the first night we didn't itch so much. The next day – another dose of DDT – and the lice were gone. And I cannot tell you what losing those lice meant in terms of morale. We began to feel like human beings again, and the Americans were our great heroes.

'At the moment of liberation I was laughing and crying. Immediately. The moment I saw the American jeep.

'Everyone was looting the camp. I took a typewriter. God knows why! The only thing I regret is that I didn't feel the urge to take revenge, to kill someone. I think I should have taken revenge, but later I did. My revenge was to write *Human Behaviour in the Concentration Camp*.

'It was difficult to write. It is an emotional problem and an emotional subject; it will never leave me. But the only way I could begin to write about it was by adopting a scientific attitude. And I had to do it. We who lived through it have to bear witness: to show that we are still here, and to represent the dead.

'After two or three weeks, the possibility arose of being flown to Western Europe under the auspices of the French or Belgian Red Cross who had arrived by now. I was reluctant to leave, and above all reluctant to leave the Americans, but I knew there would probably be a limit to the time that I could spend with them.

'So I flew back to the north of France, and from there we were put on trucks to take us to Holland. The Belgians were wonderful to us as we passed through – and supplies were plentiful. Finally we were billeted in a clearing centre in a castle at Maastricht. The great thing that sank in during the two or three weeks that we were in Maastricht was that we were free – able to do anything, go anywhere. It is amazing how quickly life can change and how quickly one can adapt to those changes. A month earlier, I had been fighting for my life. I was caught up in the euphoria of being free.

'I made my way back to Groningen, where I had the address of a friend – the only address I had. But when I arrived, he had left. Then I remembered the family who had sheltered my son. I managed to borrow a bicycle and rode to their village, and they were still there; but they were frightened when they saw me – they thought I was a ghost, and I probably still looked like one! I looked up former patients, and took up lodgings on a farm belonging to the sister of one of them. She was a nurse, and she took such good care of me that every day I put on a pound. Of course much of it was liquid; I drank masses of milk.

'Thoughts of revenge in the crude sense began to recede. Looking back, I cannot express my feelings. What I can say is that when I lecture I tell my audience that for me to be here, and to be able to talk to them, is my victory. But what haunts me is the sense of guilt that I carry with me. I cannot rid myself of the feeling that I was a collaborator.

'If I hadn't done it, I wouldn't be sitting here now. But there must be a limit in collaboration!'

But you did what you thought was right.

'At that moment I did what I was told. I wanted to live; I didn't think any more about it. But afterwards, when I repudiated other people for collaboration – did I have any right to do that? People say I'm *meshuggah* to think like that; but there's no comfort in the thought that if I hadn't done what I did someone else would. That's not an excuse. I should have set myself some kind of limit – some point of collaboration I wouldn't go beyond. But I feel that in order to survive I would have done anything. I hate to admit it, but I must try to be as honest as I can. And that's not easy for me to accept, you see.

'I never speak about it with my children, not really. When I wrote my books, I didn't mention the names of my first wife or my son, because it was too painful and because I didn't want to impinge upon my present family by doing so. Now that I have come further along the road, perhaps I will mention their names in my next book, which will be more broadly autobiographical.

'Although my wife tries hard to understand, she cannot comprehend my feelings as a survivor. It is, perhaps, not fair on her. I am restless, I want to travel. In the winters I would like to go to Israel for a few months, for example. But she is happy to stay here in Arnhem. She has her social circle, and she teaches Hebrew.

'I think the KZ made me outgrow what I was happy with before. In Aduard I was one of the three local dignitaries: the doctor, the priest and the mayor. People called my wife "Madame"; and I was perfectly happy with that. Had it not been for the war I might be there still.'

He has two children, both born in the early Fifties. His daughter is a career lawyer, his son a psychiatrist. His daughter doesn't object to his continuing interest in the concentration camps, though she has not involved herself with his interest. His son told him only very recently, 'I'm just a replacement, aren't I?' – and it seems to Cohen that for all these years his son has been feeling like an understudy for Ronnie; that if Ronnie had lived, he would never have been born. 'Which is untrue; so untrue. After my daughter was born, I was reluctant at first to have another child, but my wife wanted one, and then the son of a patient of mine was killed in a car crash, and I was terrified at the thought of losing my only child, as had happened before, at Auschwitz. I couldn't have borne to repeat that nightmare. My son's accusation hurt me very deeply, and I am sorry that I cannot talk to my children about what I went through – above all else, I would like to talk to them. I think at least that my daughter is a little bit proud of me.

'Of course my suffering must influence the children. It is very difficult for me, too. It is difficult for me to make friends, especially with those people, and there are plenty of them, who boast about what they did in the war. They make me laugh – they are disgusting. It reminds me of the joke: Moshe and Sarah were visiting cousins who'd been in hiding. And the whole evening the cousins were telling them what a terrible time they'd had in hiding. Moshe and Sarah couldn't get a word in edgeways. And on the way home Moshe turns to Sarah and says, "Boy, are we lucky that we were in Auschwitz!" I size people up in the light of their war record; this upsets my son, he can't understand why the war occupies such a central position in my life.

'I don't think of my first wife with any sense of comparison, and I don't think that my present wife feels that she is merely a replacement for my first; she has certainly never spoken of it. But the death of my first wife is still hard to accept, and even harder to accept is the meanness of those who could take away a little boy of four and gas him . . . That I shall never forget. Here are their photos, by my desk. I look at them and I think, did those people really have something to do with me? I cannot adjust to it inside myself.'

Since *Human Behaviour in the Concentration Camp* earned him his full doctorate, he has practised as a psychotherapist, specializing in helping fellow survivors. He stresses how important it is for them to have someone to talk to who literally speaks their language, who will understand their frame of reference, who is, in a sense, a member of their club, and above all who will believe them. 'Maybe I am a little bit jealous of some of my colleagues, but I have nothing but praise for Eitinger, who was in the camps, and Elie Wiesel; but where Wiesel is a great popularist, Eitinger is a great scientist, and his work towards defining and locating the KZ-related syndromes is second to none. I think he is right that they derive from a combination of psychiatric and somatic ills, and not, as Bastiaans supposes, from a purely psychiatric source. The other person who agreed with that from the start was my good friend Shamai Davidson, who was always very careful to point out in his work that he had not been in the concentration camps himself, which showed humility, and sensitivity towards those of us who were. And that is what I want from people: that they should recognize that there is a difference between them and us KZ-inmates who were in hell – and I do not exaggerate. When I was preparing recently for a lecture I was to give in California, I came across a subject I had not given much thought to before: that of the Jews who lived in liberty. What did they care about us? Nothing! When Karski[6] was about to leave Poland with the tale of what he had seen, the Jewish leaders there said to him: "You will start telling them what you have seen at 11, and at 1 they will ask you to pause so that they can lunch." They would go on lunching at their regular hour at their favourite restaurant; they could not understand what was going on in Poland. Normal life was going on. Business as usual. I find it so difficult to understand how they of all people could not do more for us.

'As for the Germans, perhaps my attitude has mellowed a little. We have a little house in Italy. Whenever we went there, I used to pick a route through Belgium, France and Switzerland; but since about 1980 I have thought, to hell with it, I'll take the *Autobahn*. On the other hand, I couldn't bring myself to own a German car. Nowadays of course Russia is so powerful that it would be better to have a united Germany allied to the West; but it won't happen. Effectively those two countries have nothing in common any more but a language and a name. One would like to see freedom of choice restored to all the countries of Eastern Europe that were swamped by Stalin. People think that if Germany were united again, the Germans might try again. Maybe. But I think the initiative for that sort of thing has gone from Europe and, as far as West Germany is concerned, she is so prosperous now and has such wide market interests in the world that crude military power wouldn't be in her interests any more.

'I think for many of the survivors, self-awareness returned only after liberation, as the mind had more leisure to think about other things than just getting through the day. I was never scared of becoming a Mussulman, for example, though I weighed 35 kilogrammes when I was liberated, which was about half my normal body-weight; but when I recently saw some film of starving Africans on television, I had a shock, because suddenly I saw myself standing among them. I cannot believe that I really weighed that little and looked like that. In Belsen they had difficulties putting a stethoscope to people's chests, because it bridged the ribs and wouldn't come into contact with the sunken skin. But I was not a Mussulman, I think, because I did not die inside. They did, and once that happened only a miracle or a superhumanly faithful friend could bring you back. I remember at Ebensee one day I had had enough. Nearing the end is always the most dangerous time. I let my shovel drop. An SS-man came up and told me to get on. Shoot me, I said; I cannot go on. And he asked me what my real job was. I'm a doctor, I said. He left me alone. Another slice of luck. I recovered a bit, and went on. It was all you could do.[7]

'The most significant thing following liberation was the conditions the survivor encountered when he returned home.[8] There could be a terrible sense of abandonment, for people did not know that you were coming back from a cemetery. I knew that my beloved ones were dead; and I was fortunate that I was helped by the van Dams, the couple who had looked after Ronnie, and by former patients.

'I started work at the Sonnenstrahl Hospital in Hilversum in January

1946, treating TB cases. It was a claustrophobic job and, although we were now able to treat our patients with streptomycin, the work gave me little satisfaction. In the course of the year, however, romance had blossomed between my wife and me, and I began to look into the possibility of a practice in Rotterdam. Quite by chance I ran into a friend whom I'd thought dead. It turned out that he was living in Arnhem. We came here to visit him and discovered that there was a vacant practice for sale. I took it over. We got married in 1947 and moved into this house the same year.

'Buying the practice was quite amusing. When I was first arrested I had Dfl.11,000 with me, which the Gestapo took; but later, in Westerbork, I was given a bank receipt for the money. The Germans were very correct in some ways! After the war I actually tracked this money down and used it towards buying my practice. I was lucky in another sense: before I left on my abortive escape, I left my valuables with former patients, and not one of them behaved dishonourably. This desk I bought in 1936; and the cutlery we've been eating with is family silver I had hidden for me while I was away. They were polished every week . . .

'As soon as we were settled I began to write *Human Behaviour*. I was very conscious of the fact that I was one of the very few who survived, and I wanted to provide a memorial for my loved ones. As a scientist I thought that a research document about the KZ would be the best. It took three drafts to reduce the emotional slant I had unwittingly given the book. I didn't want to write a personal book at that stage – I did that later with *The Abyss*. It took four years to write and research, and it was pure research, bar one or two consultations. I was one of 150 Groningen Jews who came back, out of a pre-war population of 3,000, and of those 150 only ten returned from the camps (as opposed to hiding or exile), so I was one of a very small group. About 60,000 Dutch Jews were sent to Auschwitz, of whom 1,052 returned. I had the feeling that my luck at having survived had to be turned to some effect, and I felt an obligation to be a witness and to tell the world of the crimes the Germans were capable of – but also to try to find an explanation for the behaviour of both the inmates and the SS. But to do this I needed a foundation on which to proceed, and I found this in Freud's theories, because of his work on the subconscious; I had the feeling that subconscious motives played a significant role in the life of the camps. My work grew out of testimony I had given, over several weeks in 1947, to the *Rijksinstitut voor Oorlogsdokumentatie*, and research that I had also done there. Reviewing those papers and the transcript of my testimony, I wondered if they might form the basis for a thesis. I went to the Professor of Psychiatry at Utrecht, Rümke, for advice. He looked at my notes. At least, I think he did. I didn't hear from him for six months and then when I phoned him he asked me rather hurriedly to come and see him in a month. I think his wife, who was also a psychiatrist, must have read them for him in that time. But he did encourage me, so I started writing. At the time I was establishing my practice here, so it was hard work; I had only the evenings and nights to work in. And I had to study a lot, to teach myself Freud, if you like, as I went along. However, I presented my finished work in 1952, and was duly awarded my doctorate in psychiatry.

'Then came the problem of finding a publisher for it. "It's ancient history," everyone said. "No one wants to hear any more about that now." So I published it privately myself, and when it came out it created a storm. Everyone wanted a copy; it ran to four editions and could have done more. Jonathan Cape published it in London in 1954, and later Norton did so in the USA, where it became a best-seller. I felt triumphant. It was my revenge, and it was also an exorcism. And as the book brought me fame, so it helped the practice! In its wake came many invitations to give lectures and contribute articles; and I was under pressure to write another book; but it wasn't until I gave a series of interviews to a weekly magazine here that *The Abyss* emerged in 1970.

'I no longer suffer from nightmares. My wife tells me she has to wake me now and then, but I don't think it happens more than twice a year, and I'm not conscious of any anxiety in that direction. Until about the mid-Seventies I was aware of dreams, mainly of pursuit.

'There are triggers: as far as food and drink are concerned, I don't like to see them thrown away – especially bones; I calculate how much food is left clinging to the bones and think how grateful I would have been for that once. But when I eat a meal I always leave a little – just to show that I can.

'If someone shouts at me, I succumb; I don't stand up for myself. And there are a handful of mundane triggers. The most common is this: when I am trimming my fingernails and throw the cut nails into the fire, the smell takes me back to Auschwitz. And burning. You know how evocative of memory the sense of smell is. But the memories are not accompanied by pain; they just return. Not that they have ever really gone away. They are always there, and I live with them.

'When survivors meet together, we always seem to talk about the KZ, though I have to say that I don't need to, therapeutically. But it gives pleasure to talk about it, and to lecture about it gives satisfaction. If I am honest about the memories, I would say that mine are selective. Those that remain are acute, but much has faded away.

'Certainly there was a mental safety-net at the time, too. I think mine came into play at Amersfoort. I was looking through a screen. I saw a man there beaten to death in front of me and it was almost as if I were watching a film; either it wasn't really happening, or I wasn't really there. The reaction was instinctive and immediate; one was pitched into a situation where one saw things without precedent in one's imagination, let alone in one's experience. But as I watched I knew it was real, and another part of me was glad that it was that man and not I who was being beaten to death – that the pressure was off me for the moment . . . And I remember those feelings with grief; but I suspect that I was not the only one to feel them. Man is egoistic under those circumstances where life is at risk, and that is not a reaction which is exclusive to the KZ . . . But if you survive you have to pay for it. I gave a woman who had been in Auschwitz psychotherapy for some time, and she finally told me that she could never forgive her husband for taking the opportunity to escape the police, leaving her in the lurch when their hiding place was discovered. After the war they were reunited, but there was always a deep feeling of resentment, which for a long time she repressed. The best thing to do is hope that you are never put into that kind of situation, for then you act not as you have been taught to, but as you naturally would.

'I lost God in Auschwitz. It must be very nice to have religious belief, to have a fixed point, but I have not. I met very few religious people in Auschwitz; but there were some – some who even fasted on Yom Kippur, some who tried to keep to a kosher diet. Maybe the ritual discipline helped, just as the ritual discipline of keeping clean was important. I think that a spiritual life could give one a feeling of superiority to the SS, which might also be fortified by one's social and educational superiority to them. They came from lower-middle-class backgrounds on the whole. Fränzel had been an assistant stage manager in a theatre, for example; there were short-order cooks, waiters, clerks, shopkeepers; Stangl had been a policeman. There were a few actors. But on the other hand Kremer and Mengele were highly educated professional men, as was Ohlendorf. That only makes it the more frightening. I have written of the identification by prisoners with the SS. I think most victims will at least for a time identify with the aggressor, as the Stockholm syndrome suggests, but it is something that affects the super-ego, and if the super-ego is no longer subject to that stimulus, then in all but extreme cases the identification atrophies. On the return to normal life I think that was the case with any identification with the SS, who were no longer there. After the war I thought the SS were inferior people.

'Being in the camps has not made me either harder or more philosophical vis-à-vis problems encountered in later life; and that is a pity, because ideally having been through that one deserves to and perhaps should take things easier; certainly one should not get so excited about things any more. I had a heart-attack in 1966 for the following reason:

the marriage of Princess Beatrix to Prince Klaus. I made a fuss about it as great as if it had been my daughter who had made such a marriage. That that woman, who would become Queen of the Netherlands, could have forgotten so soon what the Germans had done to her people as to marry one . . .! I was beside myself, and I worked myself up so much that a heart-attack was the consequence. As a result of it, I did later learn to adopt a sense of detachment, and in one way it was a blessing in disguise, for it forced me to give up general practice and thus gave me more time to develop my psychotherapeutic work.

'But I hadn't quite learnt my lesson, for I had a second heart-attack later, arising from a disagreement I had in the religious community here. I think both were caused indirectly by my KZ experience. Now I do take it easy, and I have lived a long life, especially by the standards of survivors. I have also found that helping others has helped me. I worked with the Advisory Committee on Assistance to Concentration Camp Victims, and the fact that I too went through the camps is an advantage there, because through cross-questioning I can weed out fraudulent claims. On the other hand, survivors will confide in me more, because they know that I know. In my psychotherapy sessions with patients, I think that having to go through the experience while holding someone else's hand helps me grow stronger in my confrontation with my own past.

'For a time, after I had finished the first book, I was tempted to forget all about it – to push it to the back of my mind. But I couldn't, and I don't think in the end I would have chosen to forget it. There is a part of me that has to admit that I was grateful, retrospectively, to have been in Auschwitz, for without that experience I would never have written the book. My work and my books in turn have helped me to come to terms, and it has all happened naturally. I wouldn't say that there had been a deliberate plan. Another good thing which has come out of it is that I have defeated the inferiority complex which was implanted in me as a poor student and which the Germans reinforced. My work, which I would never have come to if it had not been for my wartime experience, has ensured me a place in society and given me social confidence.

'I wish it were easier to communicate what it was like to all those people who are not survivors. I met a colleague here after the war who had also been through the camps and who helped me with personal details and theories when I was writing *Human Behaviour*. Now, whenever we met we talked of the camps in the language of the camps, and I was never aware of the effect of this on his wife. Some years later they were divorced, and I didn't see her again, but I do remember being struck by an autobiographical note in one of her own books: "Whenever Elie came to see my husband, I withdrew, because I had the feeling of being excluded from their conversation, from their circle." Of course, one didn't know at the time that one was committing such a solecism.

'But now, finally, looking back over half my life to the time when it happened, I have to say that it was the most important thing that ever happened to me, and the most important element of the rest of my life has been trying to understand it and to live with it. When you reach a certain age, you look back and you draw up a balance sheet. When I look back and think of what I did to my sister . . . I cannot forgive myself . . . Although I did it for the best reasons. When they sent her away on the transport she said to me, "But you advised me to come here because it would be safer . . ." And it's no good saying it's no use crying over spilt milk; if the milk weren't spilt, there'd be no reason to cry.'

II

'My interest in unemployment, redundancy and stagnation goes back a long time. After the Nazis gained increasing influence in Hungary in the early 1940s, my father was not allowed to practise law, nor could he take part in political activities as an elected member of the County Council. In modern terms he became redundant. *My father was the first redundant person I ever came across in my life.* Within a year he acted, behaved and thought as if he were at least 20 years older. He also lost interest in practically everything, became very depressed, and sat all day by the window, oblivious of what was going on around him.

'I believe that my concern with unemployment started when I impotently had to witness the totally useless existence thus imposed on my father by the National Socialists. Later, after the war, when I made my home in England, my interest in the unemployed re-awakened when I saw in my professional work so many men who, as a result of their wartime experiences, had received injuries (visible and invisible), and could not find work without considerable assistance. Like my father, they seemed to have lost interest in life and were often anxious and depressed. By helping them to find new meaning in their lives, I could at last do something; I could heal at least *their* apathy, even if I could not help my father any more. Today, having reached the age my father was then, I am still involved in trying to find new roads for the unemployed, the redundant, and those who feel they are "stuck" in a bad job.'[9]

Professor Eugene Heimler has dedicated his life since the war to helping others – the socially insecure and those troubled profoundly by the mental problems adhering to unemployment – through a technique developed by him as a psychiatric social worker and now taught throughout the world: human social functioning. He was born in Szombathely, Hungary, in 1922, the son of a prominent lawyer and liberal politician. Very early, he found fame as a poet, publishing two collections by the time he was 20. 'I was a very well-known poet in western Hungary in those days, but more because my work referred to the current situation than for any intrinsic quality it had – though I don't think it was too bad! Both editions sold out – maybe only 1,500 copies, but that's quite a lot for a book of poetry. The strange thing was that these poems were revolutionary from a Jewish point of view, but the censor had known my father from earlier days, and let them pass. I think that they were popular because they spoke a language that was not allowed any more. And at that time, when thousands were already being slaughtered in the camps, we were having literary evenings. It wasn't that we were unaware of what was happening – my father was a politician with good connections and he had certainly known about Dachau for a long time – what we didn't know anything about was Auschwitz.

'Meanwhile, as the storm broke in Hungary's neighbouring countries, I continued with my studies and graduated from Budapest University in 1943. For me there was no sense of being under any particular pressure at that time – indeed, the atmosphere in Hungary was beginning to ease. I read widely, for no books were forbidden, and in fact there was more freedom in Hungary in 1942 and 1943 than there had been before the war. When it hit us, therefore, it hit us hard, though there was some minor conditioning to the change of temperature through my father's enforced "redundancy". When the Germans invaded in March 1944, my father was taken away immediately, along with other leading liberals, and I later discovered that he died in Auschwitz. I myself was able to avoid even the ghetto for a time, because I was hidden by a friend of my father who was the supervisor of a mental hospital[10] – a curious episode, a prelude to what was to come. However, soon afterwards I went voluntarily into the ghetto. I could not be comfortable in safety when my fellow-Jews were suffering and, even more urgently, I had discovered that my wife of only a few months was also there – I had to rejoin her.

'It was not long before the inevitable selections started, and under hellish conditions we were taken to Auschwitz, where I was separated from my wife. Though she was not sent to the gas chambers, Eva died of hunger and disease.

'I was barely 22, and in common with all the Jews of Hungary was totally unprepared for this alien planet on to which I had been pitched. One of the most crucial things was the ability to absorb the truth of where one was very quickly: in a place you were not expected to emerge from alive; where people were gassed and burned wholesale. It was not easy for the mind to accept.'

Being young and healthy, after a few weeks at Auschwitz he was selected to go and work for the German war effort in the Buchenwald sub-camps. The first was at Troeglitz, where there was an I. G. Farben plant manufacturing synthetic petrol, though the work of the *Kommando* was to clear up bomb damage. Later, after an unsuccessful escape attempt for which he was lucky to receive only the standard punishment for minor 'crimes' – 25 lashes – he was sent to another factory sub-camp at Berga-Elster, where he arrived in mid-December 1944. There he remained until the spring when, with the approach of the Allies, his camp was evacuated and the prisoners sent on the death-march towards Mauthausen. The SS conducted them as far as the village of Manetin. By this time their captors were thoroughly demoralized and had ripped their death's-head insignia from their uniforms. Heimler and four companions broke away from the column and fled.

Although ill with jaundice, he made his way back to Hungary, hoping to pick up the threads of his life.

'When I got home, nothing was waiting for me. Nevertheless I started work and, as writing had been my original ambition, I became a journalist. I made a success of it, and became well-known, but I saw that what was going on now under a different colour was the same thing as ever: the Communists and the secret police were tracking down and arresting former Nazis and torturing them, and I thought: "I can't have that." I am very proud of taking that attitude, though I was attacked for it at the time. I felt that to carry on taking the same measures immediately after the war, just changing the roles, was a continuation of the same story. I was finding adaptation to post-war life difficult, the more so since all my close family had gone; but at least I had an interesting job, I could write, and I felt that I was making a contribution to my country's future. It was an illusion, however, and it was smashed within a year or so of my return home. Like my father, I was a Social Democrat; as soon as I saw unequivocally how closely aligned our Communist Party was with Russia, I understood what was coming and I decided to get out. And that was a correct decision, not least because my public criticism of the administration was not making me very popular. I caught the trans-Europe express via Paris and, after spending a few days there, arrived in London on 11 February 1947.

'I chose the UK because two remaining relatives were here, an elderly uncle and my sister, who was to teach me English; but I also chose to come here because my father was a complete Anglophile. I knew more about Hyde Park Corner and Piccadilly Circus when I was a little boy than I knew about anywhere else in the world. I never thought of living anywhere else, and even though half my professional life has been spent in the USA and Canada, I have always regarded London as my home.

'When I arrived, I couldn't speak a word of English, and that was another mountain to climb – there were so many mountains to climb. I expect that is why I am not always entirely able to understand those people who complain to me socially of insurmountable difficulties in their lives. Basically there are no difficulties that you cannot overcome – it's only a question of time. My own attitude then was a simple one: if the camps hadn't got me, why on earth should a few problems to do with getting started in a new country do so? I was scarred, mentally and physically, but I had enough energy and enough self-confidence to come here, nursing my ambition to become a writer, even though I didn't know enough English to order my lunch. But *Night of the Mist* came out in 1959 – so at least I was being published in English by then, and my second book, *A Link in the Chain*, was the first that I actually wrote in English.

'I think that in all probability I was a fighter when I went into the camps, and that they developed that ability. Ever since, of course, I have reacted quite differently from most people to setbacks or misfortune. I can withstand much more – and not only mentally. As a result of a very severe beating I received in the camps, I got cancer in my back after the war, and had to be operated on. I made a complete recovery.

'It is hard to say, but I probably knew I was a fighter, too; I certainly had the feeling that I could survive. Without that inner conviction I would have gone under, without a doubt. You had to have confidence and purpose; without them you were lost; it was no longer even a matter of chance.

'Today, the memory of those times is not so constantly with me, but a number of chance occurrences can plunge one back into the emotions of the time without warning. I do occasionally have dreams, but they are not dreams of persecution. In fact in most of my dreams I seem to be eating, and if they are dreams which take place in the KZ, they are dreams of achievement: for example, that I am able to get a bit more bread than the others ... The most important thing for me, what dominated my thinking about the problem, is that one must try to turn the negative concentration camp experience into something positive – to transmute it somehow, though one cannot forget the pain. The pain is still within me, but it has been a source of regeneration for me. And this is a crucial point in my work: the problem is not that one has pain, but what you do with it. As a man, as an individual, I can never deny the pain, the horror; but for me it is no longer a threat because I have done something with it: I have used it to inform my work in helping others. And I have never liked to talk about the concentration camp experience publicly myself – or even to individuals, unless they specifically want to know. I have not made it the focus of my life, as some have. To my mind, that is living in the past, and is something to be avoided if possible.

'I might add that the way people behaved in the camps has a very important bearing on their subsequent lives – and on their self-respect. There is not much that I did in order to survive that I can be ashamed of. I made love to a Gypsy woman in order to get some food in Auschwitz; and, still in that camp, I managed to get myself the job of kitchen orderly, so maybe I didn't find myself in situations where I had to do something I'd consider bad in order to survive. And through my job in the kitchens I was able to help others by smuggling extra food out to those who really needed it. I did what I could, although it was risky, and the memory of that gives me a tremendous feeling of pride – whereas if I'd survived by being a kapo, I don't think I, personally, could live with the memory. The retention of self-respect is a bridge to successful adaptation after the experience. In other words, it is not just survival, but the quality of survival that is important: the question is, did one survive without abandoning a sense of morality, ethics, humanity? If one survived by jettisoning that sense, one didn't survive at all. But I must immediately add a rider to that, for a question that bothers me is that if I had had to hold out longer, would I have tried to do so at any cost – does there come a point at which you decide to cross, or not to cross, the moral boundary? And how conscious is the individual of that decision? I thank God I was spared it.

'Nevertheless, for a long time I hated the Germans for what they put us all through. Losing that hatred came about by an interesting chain of events. There was an American professor who very recently introduced the subject I teach into West Germany, and I went over there to lecture. I'm not a great drinker, but on the flight I got so drunk from fear that they wouldn't serve me any more. The lecture itself was not too bad, though it was daunting to face an audience of 800. But they were mainly young Germans and, as I got to know them as individuals, I found my attitude changing. There is something else. My second wife sadly died a few years ago now; but I have remarried, and my present wife is German. Although she is Jewish, she is a convert to my religion – something she had done before she met me; and she was born after the war. But I do not know how I would have survived the grief of Lily's death without the help and support that Brigitte gave me. So I now owe my survival to a German.

'I do not believe in chance, but I do believe in something – call it predestination, if you will; but there has to be more to life than blind chance. My own experience is, I believe, proof of that. And three times in my life I have had very vivid and entirely accurate precognitive visions, which I cannot deny, although I am a rational man and a scientist. The first was a dream I had the night before the Germans invaded Hungary.[11] The second was in Auschwitz, where I heard, quite definitely, a voice telling me not to return to my *Block* after roll-call. I obeyed it, and laid low. And the entire *Block* was cleared and taken to the gas chamber. The third happened after the war, when I was about 30. Out of nowhere I had a perfectly clear vision of a young woman. It was so vivid that I described it in detail to my friend Andrezj. And three decades later, when I met Brigitte, I knew who she was, and when I introduced her to Andrezj, he knew too. I must have had the vision at about the time she was born. These things are beyond human comprehension – but after such experiences I cannot believe in mere chance.

'For me, the stress of the years immediately following liberation was not as great as it had been during the time I had been in the camps. Physically I was very weak and took several months to recover. Emotionally, it really didn't hit me until the late Sixties or the early Seventies – I had been so busy until then. It may be significant that I collapsed only when I had time to draw breath. Then, it took me four and a half years to recover. To this day I do not know what actually triggered the breakdown, and though on the surface I am sure it had nothing to do with the KZ, I am equally sure, in my heart of hearts, that the KZ lay at its core.

'I didn't come to England as a journalist, I came here to study. I wanted to learn about England, and the only courses available to me were sociology, combined with trade union studies at LSE. I was at LSE for three years, financed initially by the settlement I'd got on leaving my job in Hungary, by payment for some broadcasting for the Hungarian section of the BBC's World Service, and by loans, in the very early Fifties, from one or two of the Jewish organizations here – which, as far as I was concerned, were most helpful, both then and later when I requested a further loan to buy a house. However, I didn't need any help other than practical financial aid.'

From 1953 until 1960, Heimler worked as a psychiatric social worker for Middlesex County Council, and in 1960 he was promoted to a newly created post, what nowadays would be called Director of Social Work. In 1965 he started to give courses on human relations and social functioning at London University as evening classes for civil servants and other public functionaries, a job which he continued to do for 20 years, and in the same year he founded his own project to help the unemployed and to develop social functioning skills.

In 1964 the US government invited him to be their consultant on unemployment matters; during the period he was so employed, he was also invited by the University of Calgary to take a specially created

Chair for one half of each academic year. He was thus able to teach his methods there without abandoning his projects in London, and he held the professorship for 18 years. The Heimler Foundation, which promulgates his methods, is now internationally based.

He has also played a major role in the establishment of the Jewish community in Harlow New Town, near London – a job which was partly dictated by the practical necessity of earning money, but which also, much more importantly, symbolized a sowing of new seed – at least one of the communities destroyed in the Holocaust would be reborn. 'I was brought up as a Jew, but I was also very much in contact with the non-Jewish world, and I am grateful for the balance that provided me with. There didn't seem to be any division between myself and others when I was a boy, and Judaism affected me as a culture far more than as a religion. But irrespective of my Jewishness I have since childhood had an awareness that there is something else. After the camps came a denial of belief in religion; but as the years went by, I retrieved my belief. Whatever I believe in – call it God, if you will – is not specifically related to Judaism, though my sense of being a Jew gives me comfort and security. My God is not exclusive; and I don't think that my belief now is directly attributable to the concentration camp experience. In the sense of my relationship with my belief, the KZ experience is just one of many that have shaped it. The God that I have inside me is far beyond what I understand by the religion of my fathers, or even by religion itself. It is not so clearly definable. I just know that at a very crucial time I was aided by something – or someone. I don't know what it was; I only know that it was there.'

III

In a letter of attestation on behalf of Dr Hadassah Rosensaft dated 23 July 1945, Lt. Col. James Johnston, RAMC, wrote: 'I first entered Belsen Concentration Camp with my unit on 17 April 1945 and was Senior Medical Officer of that camp for two months. The conditions that were found there are known to the world.

'Dr Ada Hadasa [sic] Bimko was imprisoned in this camp. She had been there since 23 November 1944, and was interned for two years [sic] in Auschwitz prior to this.

'Dr Bimko was one [of] the very few people amongst the 50,000 interned in Belsen who, in spite of all the horrors she had undergone, was still capable and was doing a magnificent job amongst the thousands of sick and dying. I cannot speak too highly of her work in this camp against difficulties which no doctor can have experienced before – a complete lack of instruments and medicaments, even of the absolute essentials – beds, blankets, clothing. She had organized her own staff of nurses and was quite outstanding amongst all the other doctors in this camp.

'I therefore appointed her to be Senior Internees doctor in Belsen, in the new hospital areas which we established there – this task she is still carrying out today. Her duties were manifold and included the drafting up of suitable doctors and nurses from the Horror Camp to the new hospital areas, the organization and control of this work in these areas and, in general, to administer the very large non-British medical staff. This task she has carried out at all times most magnificently. I have already represented Dr Bimko's work in this camp to British Authority. I am convinced that whatever medical task is undertaken by Dr Bimko, that task will be undertaken superbly.'

Dr Hadassah Rosensaft was born Ada Bimko in Sosnowiec in 1910. She came from a large observant family, and before the war studied dentistry in France, at Nancy – as a Jewess there was no possibility of her studying in her native Poland, though she was allowed to practise there and returned upon completion of her studies in 1935.

She grew up speaking several languages, including French and German, which were to stand her in good stead later. She is the widow of Josef Rosensaft,[12] and the mother of Menachem Z. Rosensaft, who is one of the most prominent members of the Second Generation movement in the USA. She is the godmother of Elie Wiesel's son Elisha; her official posts include membership of the US Holocaust Council and honorary presidency of the World Federation of Bergen-Belsen Associations. For five years, as Chairperson of the Archive Committee of the Holocaust Council, she worked on the Belsen Papers, which were presented to Yad Vashem in 1984, in memory of her late husband, Josef, the chairman of the DP camp established at Belsen.

'When we arrived in Birkenau on 4 August 1943, we came with a transport of 5,000 from our town ghetto, but only 500 of us were selected for work. The rest were sent to the gas chambers. I did what I could to survive; and by 1944 I was working on the prisoner medical staff. We had slightly better conditions – beds to ourselves, and of course we were working under cover; but the hospital – such as it was – was more of a casualty ward. I found myself mainly involved with treating wounds made by the dogs, or the SS, or just by accidents at work. Later that year, Mengele arrived one morning and asked which of us had had the full list of common children's illnesses: mumps, measles, and so on . . . I said that I had, because I was very afraid that sooner or later I might be rounded up for *Block* 10; but in the event I was sent to the new section of camp they were building called *Mexiko*, to look after a transport of Hungarian girls who had just arrived and who were suffering from scarlet fever.

'I was convinced that I would never leave the camp alive, and that I would die of one or other of the illnesses I was exposed to in the course of my work; I was determined to see the gas chambers before I died. I wanted to see the place where my family had been killed.[13] One was filled with a sense of death, of the inevitability of it. I certainly didn't develop any unconscious drive to survive. Later, when I was in Belsen, I used to reassure the little children in my care by saying, "One day you'll be free, one day you'll go to Palestine" – but not for a moment did I believe it.

'In November '44, seven of us medics were detailed for transport. We all thought at first that it meant the gas, but the truck took us to the main camp at Auschwitz-I, and from there we were brought to the town railway station, where we were given a loaf of bread each. It reminded me of the Last Supper, and I thought, what do I need bread for? But we were put on to a passenger train, in our own compartment, with two heavily armed SS-men as escorts, and left Auschwitz.

'We changed trains several times, and finally got to Berlin. The station had been bombed, and we had to cross the city; Berlin had already been pretty badly hit, and we enjoyed looking at the ruins, I must say. When we arrived at our onward station, there was a train all right, but no private compartment for us. Our SS got very angry with the conductor, who was an elderly man. He wagged his finger at the SS and said, "Young man, don't you know there's a war on?" So we had to get on to the train and find seats where we could among the German civilians. We didn't look too grotesque, I suppose, as we had ordinary coats on, with a red stripe painted down the back, but our heads were shaved. I found myself sitting next to a young man, and after a while, as we got under way, he looked around and then whispered to me: "I have got two postcards. Take them and write to whomever you want. I promise I'll send them for you." But sadly I had nobody to write to, and I couldn't bring myself to trust the young man – it might have been a trap. I'll never know whether or not he was genuinely kind-hearted, and that hurts me still.'

They arrived in Belsen on 23 November and remained there until liberation, the following April. 'No British or American or Russian soldier who liberated a camp will ever forget the experience. I can only speak for the British, and they were wonderful. As far as I could see, there was no reaction of fear or disgust, though either would have been understandable; but their reaction was one of spontaneous compassion. They cried, too – but of course they were just kids, many of them still in their teens. And for us, these were the first ordinary, decent, normal people we had seen in years. They cried tears of humanity and disbelief. Humanity is such a normal thing – but when it's not there, the absence is terrifying.

'The transition from the concentration camp to the DP camp which we established had its own difficulties. We all wanted to get away as soon as possible. Leaving Bergen-Belsen itself wouldn't have been difficult, if we'd wanted to make new homes for ourselves in Germany or had wanted to return to Poland. But few of us from Germany or Eastern Europe wanted to go home – and the *aliyah* was still illegal. Affidavits to other Western countries were not handed out very generously to begin with. In the meantime, we had problems in the DP camp itself with 800 or so Gentile Poles who were hostile to the Jews and wanted to have control over them. It took some time for the Jewish administration of the camp to persuade the British authorities to move them elsewhere. However, with time, the DP camp became effectively self-administering and self-maintaining, with all its own facilities, and Josef, and Norbert Wollheim, were able to travel, and represent our interests internationally. Finally we were granted 300 official certificates for Palestine per year, up to Independence, and they were distributed throughout the British, American and some French zones. In the midst of this, in the autumn of 1945 at Lüneburg, the British held the trials of Kramer and 44 others involved in running the camp, among them Dr Fritz Klein (who had also been in Auschwitz), Hössler, and Irma Grese. I was the principal survivor witness.

'My husband was very much involved in negotiating the reparation to be paid to Israel, but one of the first gestures both of us made was to decide that we would not accept individual reparation, for it could never be commensurate with the loss, nor should we seem to be accepting it as such; then a delegation came to us and made the practical point that, if we didn't accept it, no one in the camp would. And there would be people forgoing it who would really have need of it. So we accepted it – not as payment for the suffering, nor to cancel the debt to Jewry; but in the sense that Germany should pay back what she had stolen. And I have to say that Adenauer was very sympathetic, and that substantial restitution was paid to Israel – though it was not commensurate with what was taken, and I think it's important to remember that. Overall, reparation is a legal issue, not a moral one: the payment of money can never be viewed as the payment of a moral debt.'

After liberation, there were many children in her care – as there had been during her time as a medical practitioner in the concentration camp of Belsen. The culmination of her work was to accompany a group of orphaned girls and boys to new homes provided for them in Palestine in 1946.[14]

'I think it would have been hard to abandon any of my charges after liberation. At the end of 1945 there was a party to bid farewell to Brigadier Glyn Hughes, the chief Medical Officer of the 2nd Army, and he had a surprise for me: he had organized papers which would enable me to go to London and work. I had the papers in my hands and I could sense that everyone was about to start clapping; but then I knew that I had to say no, and I did so, and apologized. It hurt me very much to have to turn down such an opportunity. But how could I go and have a better life for myself when there were still so many thousands in Bergen-Belsen who needed my help? When I took the children to Israel in 1946, I was not tempted to stay there. My duty still lay with my work at Belsen. Accompanying the children was just part of my job; there was no question of staying, nor was my mind in any kind of gear to stay.

'I have to say that right after liberation a team of 100 British medical students under an Irish doctor called Michaelson came over to us and helped devotedly. I daresay it was good practice for them, too, because, especially with regard to typhus, it was a rare opportunity actually to see the disease; but there was no question of their kindness and valuable help, and I cannot praise the British army doctors and nurses too highly, who together saved thousands of lives. On the other hand we made an appeal to Britain and the USA, asking for volunteer doctors, but not one came, Jewish or non-Jewish. They started to come only when the JOINT and the Jewish Relief Agency sent them as salaried workers. We were obliged to take in German military doctors and nurses. They were in *Wehrmacht* uniforms, not SS, but the psychological effect was bad enough on me – imagine what it was like on the severely ill. I remember saying to Colonel Johnston: "Johnny, I just can't take these people." It took me a week to bring myself to work with them; but I had to, for the sake of my patients.

'I remember good things, too. One of the British officers, a Dr Smith, suddenly arrived at the children's barracks with two trucks loaded to the brim with toys – and at that time you couldn't get toys anywhere. He had taken the trucks and an interpreter and gone around all the neighbouring villages, and asked the children in them to volunteer to give up some of their toys for the Jewish children in the DP camp. And that's how he collected them. That's the kind of thing that gives you your faith back.

'I was always a Zionist, and my intention originally was to live in Israel. This was also Josef's wish, and dream, as it was for the majority of the Jews at Belsen. We didn't go, for a variety of reasons; and now I can't honestly say whether I regret it or not. I have many friends in Israel, and where I have friends I feel good; so maybe I could still live there, if fate dictated that I should. But I couldn't live in Europe any more. I have been back to Poland and to Auschwitz; but unless Menachem wanted me to go with him I would not go again. I wish I hadn't gone back to Sosnowiec because that visit robbed me of an illusion of roots which have been so thoroughly torn out that, although my old house still stands, it's as if I had never had anything to do with it. Is it a ghost, or am I? I wasn't even angry – there was just this terrible feeling of emptiness.

'I married Josef in August 1946. Ours was one of hundreds of marriages that took place in the DP camp Belsen. Menachem was born there on 1 May 1948. When the camp was closed, early in August 1950, there were still 1,000 Jews who were still waiting for visas to the USA, so the British moved them to another camp called Jever. I was exhausted, and I told my husband that I really couldn't face another camp; and what's more I didn't want Menachem to grow up in any more DP camps. By then he was 2½ and he had known no other kind of life.

'In 1948 the World Jewish Congress had had a conference in Montreux, and Josef had been a delegate. He'd been taken with Montreux, so that is where we decided we would settle. We went there on 14 August 1950, after Josef had supervised the move to the new camp for the remaining Jewish DPs. In fact he stayed with them until it, too, was closed down; and I commuted from the two rooms we had in Montreux to help there, although it was a long way. I didn't like leaving Menachem but I couldn't abandon my fellow-survivors either.

'Josef started to do business, dealing in investments and to a certain extent in real estate. We settled down, and although we came to the USA on a visit in 1952 and quite liked what we saw, we returned to Switzerland because of business commitments, and didn't finally make the move until 1959. Switzerland is a beautiful country, and I know it backwards, but I never felt that I was more than a visitor there. Although I lived there for nine years or so, for me it was always a temporary halt.

'When we moved to New York, I sent Menachem to an ethical culture school – it's a private school where they try to achieve a good balance of many disparate nations and cultures; I wanted him to go there in order to experience as many different peoples as possible, to ward off prejudice, or even the danger of it. He was exposed to talk of the Holocaust from an early age and saw its effects, because he grew up with it naturally. Some people were horrified at us for allowing him to be so exposed, but it wasn't as if we sat him down and told him stories to horrify him. He absorbed naturally what had happened to us, which I think enabled him to come to terms with our past and what had happened to his own immediate ancestors and family in a way that, although it was deeply affecting, was not traumatic.'

Once in New York City, it was Dr Rosensaft's intention to take up medicine again, 'but it was difficult for Menachem. My husband was away on business a lot. I had friends here and could speak English, but for Menachem, who was 10 or 11 at the time, it wasn't so easy. He had a new language and a new culture to get used to, and I thought that if I went back to university to re-do my medical exams I'd have to leave him with strangers to look after him, and he'd be coming home from a strange new school and finding neither Papa nor Mama at home. So I made my choice. I'd postpone my studies and look after my son; but, you know, when you postpone things they have a habit of not happening at all!

'There were many things I had to adjust to both in Switzerland and in America. But I am equipped to cope with change. Over the years, I would say that my assimilation in the USA has been to the people, but not to the culture. I like it here, I like the people. I feel at home here and I feel good when I get on the plane to come home from Europe. I am an American citizen, and I hope I am a good one; but I still have a European heart and mind.

'I don't want to forget. I think it would be a crime to forget; and I am sorry for those survivors who have tried to do so. I have lived many lives, but they have added up to one rich life. Even so, I feel that the strongest years were those between 1939–45 and 1945–50, and I don't think a day passes during which the Holocaust doesn't come into our minds, into our conversation. It affects every part of your life, whether you like it or not.

'I've never felt resentful about people asking me about it, but I must add that I've never met anyone who has hurt me by their questions. In such a case I would certainly back away from the subject. Of course one encounters great ignorance of the subject, and that makes me angry. When I took the children to Israel in 1946, I remember a woman there asked me how many bananas a week the children in the KZ were given. I told her 100 each. She said, "It's impossible; they'd get sick." "As you see," I replied, pointing to the children I'd brought with me. But she didn't cotton on. And the same year, after the ceremony at which the Yad Vashem project was announced, Golda Meir said to me, "Did you have many people come out of the camps abnormal?" And I said, "All of us who came out normal are the abnormal ones." And she used to quote that often. She said to my husband later, "Your Hadassah taught me a lesson."

'I don't know if I have nightmares; but waking dreams, yes . . . I get terrible headaches, and my sleeping habits are dreadful. I can easily be awake all night and not feel tired in the morning. Nobody will ever be able to tell you the whole story, to describe all the emotions: the fears, the anger, the shame – or the Germans' efforts to dehumanize you. All of that is very hard for me to be able to express in words; I am neither a poet nor a writer, and I don't try to make the suffering beautiful – it wasn't. But if I told you every detail of every moment from 1939 right up to now, I would not have told you the whole story.

'We can't tell the whole truth because it hurts so much. That's what it is.

'For us, I think survival was a question of luck and a question of time. If the war had gone on for another three or four months, there would have been no survivors of the KZ. In Belsen for the last six weeks there was no water-supply and no electricity. For those last six weeks all we got to eat was bread once a week and soup three times a week. That was all. Even the strongest couldn't survive long on that. And in addition, of course, elsewhere there were the death-marches. And even the elements were against us, because if ever there was a hot April, it was April 1945. You died for lack of a drop of water. I am not a suicidal person, and I don't even know, under those circumstances, whether it was courage or cowardice to do it. Any of us could have done it in the KZ, but there were very few cases of suicide overall, which I think proved that most of us believed that our personal suffering would come to an end if only we could hold out. But all that would have been irrelevant if the war had gone on until September 1945: none of us would be alive to tell you about it.

'There was no meaning to the Holocaust: it was horrible and pointless; but if you want to look for something positive that can come out of it, and you must, then it is for us who went through it to talk about it as a warning, a dire warning, of what happens if indifference is taken to the extreme that it was in the Thirties; and then the only positive effect of the Holocaust will be if the world learns from it.'

A Musician and a Dancer

I

Modern maps of Poland on sale in that country do not show the former names of those of its towns which belonged to Germany. For the German Jews of Breslau, for example, the name and German identity of the town no longer exist. It is called Wroclaw today.

A, a professional cellist based in London, grew up there. Her family background she describes as 'semi-musical' – her mother played the violin to a professional standard, but in an amateur orchestra which was nevertheless good enough to accompany professional soloists.

On the eve of war, Leo, the cellist brother of the famous violinist Max Rostal, came to Breslau to play with the orchestra. While he was there, he listened to A; after he had heard her, he offered to take her to Berlin to teach her, promising that in four years' time she would be a wonderful cellist. For A, not quite into her teens, this was a marvellous opportunity. Arrangements were made for her to leave school and take private tuition in Berlin, and she left in great heart; but she had not been there long before Nazi measures against the Jews began to make themselves very palpably felt. A returned home.

No ghetto was established in Breslau, and the Nuremberg Laws had been introduced so insidiously that it was possible almost to ignore them, or to tell oneself that one could accommodate the hardships and humiliations they subjected one to. A's father convinced himself of the normality of what was going on; but in the end he could not escape deportation, with his wife. A was left behind with an older sister.

Before her parents had departed, the family had been forced to leave their own flat and to move in with her mother's sister. This flat was filled with other unfortunate people, also lodgers. Gradually all were summoned for deportation, with the exception of an 82-year-old grandmother and two elderly South African Jews who had been in Breslau since the Boer War.

In time A and her sister, Renate, found work in a paper factory. Life was very hard and food difficult to get; but their situation was alleviated slightly by the fact that Renate looked Aryan and could therefore get away with shopping outside the Jews' restricted shopping hours.

By the end of 1941, news had percolated through about gas chambers to the east. 'We knew enough by then to realize that whatever we did would neither increase or decrease the eventual risk to our lives, and I had never accepted the idea that, as a Jew, I was simply a louse to be squashed by the Nazis. We felt that we wanted to do something positive before they got us. Some people today take the view that the Jews went to their deaths like lambs to the slaughter, but that isn't strictly fair or true. People did what they could; but the means of resistance were very restricted.'

The sisters became involved in forging travel documents for those wishing to escape west: the forged travel papers were based on those issued to French impressed labourers, who were allowed home leave; in the paper factory, the workforce was made up of French civilians and POWs, together with Aryan Poles and Jews. Since she had had a German education, A was able to fill in the forms in the special style of handwritten German in use then. One of the forms she forged was later used by an escaping British POW called Eric Williams, whose book, *The Wooden Horse*, became one of the best-known post-war escape memoirs. 'Well after the war, in 1973, when I had already been living in London for a long time, I visited an exhibition at the Imperial War Museum based on the "Wooden Horse" story and I noticed the document I had forged in Breslau in my teens. It gave me the most extraordinary sense of *déjà vu*. I contacted Williams through his publisher, and he was baffled, for he had been under the impression that the provenance of the document had been MI9.'

The girls had been forging documents for some time when, in 1942, they decided they had better forge some on their own behalf and try to make their escape. Their elderly relatives had been deported and they were living in an orphanage. 'But we had to go on fighting as best we could. We were on a kind of high of terror – but we just had to keep on going.' They got as far as the railway station, but there they were arrested with a number of others. 'I was on the platform, Renate was already on the train: it was cut that fine.'

They were taken to the local prison for interrogation. 'We knew that every day in prison was a day saved from the KZ. Luckily, we weren't separated. Germans have always paid attention to detail but they can also be remarkably dull-witted. They were quite unable to perceive that keeping us together helped our morale and enabled us to fabricate useful stories, which tallied, for interrogation. There was a "practical" reason for keeping us together though: it was standard practice to keep

Jews away from Gentile prisoners in case they contaminated them. Since Renate was slightly older than me, we decided that the best way to play it would be for her to take the role of the "baddie", and for me to act the silly little sister who just followed along. The consequence of this was that she received a harder sentence than I did in the end.'

They were finally sentenced in September 1943, and now for the first time they were separated. Her sister was sent to a hard labour camp. A was sent directly to Birkenau, where the sisters were later reunited.

The circumstances by which they found each other were these: 'When I was sent from prison to Auschwitz I was given back my civilian clothes, what was left of them, and among them was a pair of shoes that had started their lives light tan pigskin, but they had got stained and had had to be dyed black. To cheer them up I'd put red laces with pompoms on them. I arrived in Birkenau wearing them. Of course they were taken away from me on arrival there, but when my sister arrived a week or so later and saw these very recognizable shoes, she was able to ask the girl who was wearing them where the original owner was, and she was told that I was in the orchestra. Otherwise she'd never have found me.

'Another piece of luck that we had was that we both arrived as Karteihäftlinge – we were convicted criminals, complete with a case-history on file. Because of that file, we were not selected straight away for the gas. We were people with a past acknowledged by the Gestapo. This did not guarantee our survival. Renate became a Mussulman, and only getting her a job as a Läuferin, or camp messenger, because of her languages, enabled her to survive. As for me, it was lucky that I was a cellist.

'One of the reception Kommando asked me what I did and I said I played the cello; she got very excited and asked me to stand to one side, and bustled off. I wondered what I'd said. Time passed, and I waited, naked, shaven and tattooed in the shower room, thinking, "When will they turn the gas on?" – because by that stage we had heard enough rumours to know what went on. But nothing happened until a lady came up to me, very elegant, in a camel-hair coat and a headscarf, and she said, "My name is Alma Rosé,[1] and I hear you play the cello. How wonderful." They didn't have a cellist, you see; they were just forming the women's orchestra at the time, and I was the first bass-instrument player to arrive, so I was heralded with great enthusiasm. Of course if it had happened that another cellist had arrived the day before, I would already in all probability have been of no interest to them. She asked me whom I'd studied with. It seemed crazy, surreal somehow, to be having that kind of conversation under those kind of conditions at Auschwitz.

'The SS wanted an orchestra, I am sure, because they were bored; but also perhaps because it was good for the camp's image: after all, anywhere where music is played can't be all bad. But one thing we must get out of the way immediately is the idea of a full concert or even chamber orchestra pumping out Beethoven and Mozart with tears in our eyes in the midst of hell. We were a motley bunch of whatever instruments and players could be cobbled together into an ensemble – mandolins, guitars, violins, accordion and piano – and the music that we played reflected the taste of the SS: a mixed bag of popular stuff, Strauss waltzes, Suppé, Peter Kreuder. Often the repertoire depended upon what was available. Most of it came in the form of piano parts which were then orchestrated by Alma Rosé and Fania Fénélon, with "clerks" under them. One of the aims of the orchestra was to save as many people as possible by getting them into it, so that people with the most tenuous connection with music were recruited – even if all they could do was write out notes.

'The orchestra was a haven, with its own *Block*, divided into living accommodation at one end and rehearsal room-cum-concert hall at the other. It was the only *Block* in which there was a mixture of Jews and non-Jews. Our main job was to play marches for the work *Kommandos* leaving and returning to the camp, and we had the great benefit of having *Appell* indoors. We also gave formal concerts – not necessarily only for the SS – in the *Revier* and in our own *Block*. Our food was marginally better, and it was occasionally possible to get food-parcels from the *Paketkammer*. With extra food, we were able to organize warmer clothes. Alma was always well dressed because she was friendly with the kapo of *Kanada*, and all of us had something. I had a red jumper which started life as a really expensive garment. I still have it – totally in shreds from being worn night and day for months and months.

'For reasons which are probably obvious, it was easier to get instruments – from the people who'd brought them with them but were selected for the gas – than paper and pencils to write out the scores, but what we couldn't organize the SS would occasionally supply.'

In the orchestra *Block* the people formed a more civilized cross-section than might be found in an average *Block*, but that did not mean that they were either happier or safer. Their lot depended completely upon the whims of the SS, and they were in close and direct contact with these dangerous and unpredictable people. 'Hardly any of us were professionals; only Alma, that I can think of at the time, and the flautist. Hélène, the Belgian girl who led the orchestra, was only 16 or 17 years old, and was a most gifted student. She survived, and continued her studies after the war, but she didn't become a professional musician.

'My feeling is that you didn't reflect on the nature of your position, or the ethics or the morality of playing for the Germans. You were bloody glad that you were in the orchestra *Block*, and not with the kind of work *Kommando* Renate found herself on when she arrived. But perhaps the most important difference was that one had an identity. I wasn't one of the grey mass of people condemned anonymously. I was the cellist. Thus I had some small shred of dignity left, which I think helped my morale. And Alma was a tremendous lady, in that she forbade us to look anywhere other than at the music. She isolated us in a capsule; anyone who cried would be brought to book, but she wasn't the cruel martinet that has been described. Most ex-members of the orchestra – nearly all – remember her as our saviour, pure and simple, because she was so single-minded about our music, and that in turn concentrated our minds and saved us from despair. She used to punish us for playing a wrong note: I was once made to scrub the orchestra-room floor. But we didn't brood. Either she achieved this instinctively, or she knew what she was doing, but its effect was brilliant.

'There would have been no point in thinking, "Tomorrow, I may be going up the chimney"; but it happened that the SS did not make *selections* from the orchestra. I came close myself, though, when I succumbed to typhus. I had headaches, and my eyes and hearing were affected. I couldn't even get up. It would have been the end for anybody else, but I was the cellist. They gave me medical treatment and I recovered.

'I think it is impossible to define what makes a survivor. What helps survival *per se* is a group existence: companions who help you are more important than your own individual nature, and there was a tremendous camaraderie in the orchestra. We bullied each other, and Alma bullied us, if somebody gave up washing, for example. We hustled each other to stay alive, to stay on course, and to stay disciplined. But it is dangerous to generalize. I would always qualify what I say by adding "in my opinion", and "in my experience".'

She continued in the orchestra until December 1944. 'Then one day the SS entered our *Block* and ordered Jews to one side and Aryans to the other. That was never a good sign in Auschwitz; but the selection was not for death – it was for transportation to Belsen. By good fortune, my sister was able to get on to the same transport. Belsen was described to us as an *Erholungslager* – a recuperation camp[2] – which of course none of us believed – but there was something else: we were leaving Auschwitz alive, and we never thought that would happen.

'There was no orchestra at Belsen, of course, nor did we enjoy any further privileges; but somehow we survived until liberation. I can remember only scenes, moments. That we heard the rumbling of tanks; that suddenly there were no SS any more. Everything was void; there was no water, no food, nothing – for days. I think it was Sunday afternoon, at about five o'clock. I was very sick at the time, I didn't want to acknowledge anything – but my sister finally persuaded me to come out of the *Block*. And I saw the British arriving. It was a terribly hot day – the whole of that April had been like midsummer.

'On 21 May the old camp was burnt down, and the population of the camp was moved up the road to the old German barracks, which became the basis of the DP camp. The British were desperate for interpreters. Renate was already working for them as one and, as I was recovering and getting rather bored with myself, she encouraged me to do the same, even though my English was virtually non-existent. I got a job in an office, copying letters and reports; but I don't find languages too hard and I picked English up very fast. Of course, it was far from perfect, and when I finally reached England I had to clean it up – because, as I had learnt it from the British army, I had acquired some quite decorative phrases and expressions.

'Soon, people started to be repatriated. We had always wanted to go to England, because our older sister was there, as well as a number of other relatives. The question of *how* was more difficult. At that time there was still no category under which we could go to England, despite representations made by my family to the Home Office.

'Meanwhile I had acquired a cello again, and I was trying to play. In the camp I met up with an Italian cellist, also an ex-prisoner, though a former POW. We played a bit together in Belsen – nothing grand, of course, no double-cello concertos or anything – and we stayed in touch by letter after the war.

'Finally people under 21 with bona fide relatives there were allowed into Britain. Renate didn't qualify, but a bribe of 50 cigarettes enabled us both to lower our ages slightly. Of course neither of us had any papers relating to our past lives, and I still have no birth certificate.'

Getting to England was still something to be achieved, in the midst of the post-war chaos of Europe. What the sisters had to do was report to the nearest British Passport Office. The snag was that it was in Brussels. 'It was a problem to get there without papers and without money, but we managed it.

'We went to the Passport Office, thinking that from now on it would just be a formality; but in the event we had to stay in Brussels for three months. This was because one of the officers at Belsen, thinking to help us, had written ahead to the office explaining who we were and stating that we were the nieces of the chess grandmaster, Edward L. That scuppered us, because he lived in America, and to qualify for Britain we were supposed only to have relatives there. Uncle Edward had lived in the States since 1913, and in fact he would have loved to have had us go there, but neither of us wanted to live in the USA. Our father had been a great Anglophile and that had rubbed off on us profoundly.

'We had to malign our poor uncle dreadfully and say that he'd never take us in. Then we had to write to him quickly and tell him what we'd done and ask him to support our slander when the British authorities double-checked with him – otherwise our chances of getting to England would be ruined. Then we waited for the outcome.

'Finally we got our way. Once in England we stayed with a cousin in London. When we were more or less established, my first job was to find a cello teacher. My ambition to become a cellist had not wavered; I had just been kept from it for eight years.

'I'd seen William Pleeth playing at lunchtime concerts at the National Gallery, and I became his first pupil – though that was something I only found out at his 70th-birthday celebration in 1985. I owe it to him that I got back to cello playing, for I was old for the standard I had reached. One further problem was to get hold of a decent cello. A friend of Bill lent me one to begin with; and, later, my cousin bought me one of my own. I had it for many years after that.

'Although our adopted London family had been very welcoming to us, inevitably there was some friction. We were many people in a small space, and Renate and I were scarcely "normal" girls: we were neither young nor old; we were both. Renate solved the problem by getting married and moving out – she lives in France now. I realized that the time would soon come for me to leave too, but I hung on for a while longer. I was scared of being on my own, and yet in a way I was isolated in any case. No one asked us about what we had been through, and I think at the time we both would have welcomed the opportunity to talk about it. I am sure that the apparent lack of interest was in reality either reticence or a fear of hurting us – but it hurt more to have our experience seemingly ignored. Then somehow the magic moment passed and we didn't want to talk about it any longer. The KZ is a very difficult subject. If people want to know, I always say to them, ask me questions. I can answer those; but just to talk, in general, is impossible. Either it will take hours and hours to explain the detail, or you get the impression that the people you are talking to think you are lying or exaggerating. It's because the whole thing is foreign to other people's experience, even imagination. The KZ is essentially incommunicable.'

The next battle that had to be fought was over reparation. 'The German administration send two forms a year. One you have to fill in to confirm that you are still alive, for the pension ceases with your death. The second form requires you to fill in details of your earnings, investments and your husband's income.

'As far as form one is concerned, there's no point in telling lies; and as far as form two is concerned, I don't feel I need to, and so I have always filled in everything correctly. The upshot of this was that in 1985 I had a letter from the *Amt* responsible, telling me that they had decided that I was earning too much money and that they would therefore cut my pension by half. Retrospectively they proposed to deduct a further £2,000 which they argued they had overpaid me in the light of my earnings. I think they gave me a three-month period in which to appeal against the decision. So, after I had recovered, I rang up the West German Embassy and asked for an appointment with a lawyer who was versed in the reparation law. I went to see a young German, who was very scared and started off by saying, "*Bitte, seien Sie nicht böse* [Please don't be angry]," – so I vented my anger anyway, and then he explained that they always try to adjust the pension downwards with people of about my age, that is, in their late fifties, because what is fixed with regard to the pension at the age of 60 then remains unassailable for the rest of the recipient's life. I imagined that there would be a lot of furious people around, but he told me that I'd be surprised at how few people had protested about this testament.'

She thereupon proposed that she would go to the European Court in Strasbourg about it. The law is complex, but the relevant paragraph in her case states that monies invested from sources other than reparation payment (in the sense of a lump-sum originally paid, as distinct from a pension) yielding investment income would be offset against the value of the pension. She had not known this at the time of the receipt of the original lump-sum she was paid, or of the pension.

She referred her predicament, without comment, to a lawyer acquaintance in Bonn; he was appalled, and took up the case. In late May 1986, she heard that she had won her case, and that the *Amt* withdrew all objections, and in fact withdrew their case. 'But only because I fought back.'

She is not afraid of the memories of the camps, but cannot identify specific triggers for them. 'People always think that there might be a compartment in your mind that can be opened by some trigger, but in reality the KZ memory is with you all the time. I do dream about the past, but the dreams are not directly about the camps. I dream of my home town, and having to leave it – that sort of thing. That experience was deeply depressing for a young person – having to leave home, and what was pleasant and familiar, for no reason at all.

'I have been back – to what is now Wroclaw. It was coincidental; the orchestra I play with gave a concert there. I was curious to see the town again. But it was all like a dream, and I was pressed for time, which perhaps wasn't such a bad thing. During the same visit, in 1978, because we did only two concerts in Poland, I took the opportunity to fly down to Katowice with two colleagues, and from there . . . visited Auschwitz.

'I was very pushed for time there too, because there'd been a mix-up

over the hire car, and it was November, and the *soi-disant* museum –
I call it that because for me the place isn't a museum at all – shuts
when it gets dark. I got into trouble there. They had conducted tours,
and the guide told me to be quiet, and also reprimanded me for smoking
in the restored crematorium. And I thought to myself, here I am again,
being told off in Auschwitz! . . . Birkenau was a curious experience,
because there's really nothing there; it's just been left as it was, and
the buildings seem to be collapsing by themselves: they've just kept
one up so that people can see how it was. The others just have the
skeletal brickwork where the heating was – the wood has all rotted
away. I found it hard to orientate myself.

'The main camp of Auschwitz was stone barracks anyway. That has
all been preserved, and it is horrifying. The heaps of spectacles; the
piles of suitcases with people's names on them; the hair store. It's all
still there, and when you see the spectacles, and the piles of artificial
limbs – you see the people they belonged to, the people who died there.
There is a problem, too: the signs are all in Polish, and it is kept very
much as a Polish memorial. The Jews are mentioned incidentally. It's
unjust; but many, many Poles were slaughtered there too, so what can
you expect? I don't regret going back; but at the same time I don't think
I ever would have returned expressly to see Auschwitz. I am glad to
have had the chance: it helped me chase away a few ghosts.'

II

'I wanted to be a dancer since I was six. I never wavered from that.
Dancing is in me. All the family were musical, but it was my mother,
especially, who encouraged me and who got me to listen to good music,
from the very start. She was a good guide. When I was ten, she told me
that dance cannot always be pretty, and she made me do a grotesque
dance. She made me dance to poetry as well; I can remember she got
me to dance to Chinese poetry when I was 12 or 13. Her ideas were far
ahead of their time. When we arrived in Prague, later, I soon found out
that I had yet to learn technique. I was frustrated and I used to come
home from classes crying; but my mother was paying for the classes
and on the doorstep I would wipe away my tears, because I would never
allow her to see that I was unhappy.'

Helen Lewis's Auschwitz number is a late one: A-4772. Today she
lives in a quiet street in Belfast with her husband, who comes from the
same town in the Sudetenland, Trutnov. She went to German schools
and grew up speaking better German than Czech, but after her parents
separated she went to live in Prague with her mother. Studying dance

there, she was plunged into the middle of Czech culture, which was unfamiliar to her; but she felt at home with it immediately.

There had been a brief romance with Harry in Trutnov, but she was still a schoolgirl then, and he went off to study in Vienna, Paris and Florence. Just before the annexation of the Sudetenland, she married a glover called Paul, but she did meet Harry again. For a very short time after the occupation of Bohemia and Moravia on 15 March 1939 it was still possible to leave for Britain without a visa. The possibility ceased on 1 April. 'He was all by himself, so it was easy for him to pack a suitcase and go; so that is what he did.

'Harry was based in Manchester for a short time, but virtually ever since he came to Great Britain his work has been with the Irish linen industry, and that is why we are in Belfast. Harry has been here since 1940. I did not come here until six years later.'

Restrictive measures against the Jews began gradually ('all the things that were helpful but not essential to living – all the cultural things – were taken away') but escalated rapidly after the outbreak of world war. 'It became quite intolerable, and one realized that the net was closing in on all sides. I remember a particularly sadistic decree: that no Jews were allowed to have pets any more. I can still see the old people, the old women, with their little pets – hamsters, canaries, even goldfish – in the trams, holding on to these little creatures, taking them to the collection-points with tears streaming down their faces, and trying to say goodbye to their little friends.

'My own studies were more or less completed, and until 1941 I managed to teach and even perform in a very restricted way – not of course in grand productions or theatres, but in little tucked-away places, or at matinees. I came and went quietly and my name wasn't mentioned. I had to be careful in my classes, too. Once a little girl tripped and hurt herself, and started crying for her mother. Luckily it was nothing serious at all, but if it had been, and if the mother had taken it into her head to kick up a fuss, the fact that I was Jewish would inevitably have emerged and that would have meant that everyone at the dance school would have had hell to pay. Of course I was dreadfully frustrated in my career; but such horrible things were happening around me, and so fast, that to fret over dancing ambitions seemed very petty indeed, and they decreased in importance in any case because we all knew we were under threat of deportation; the only question was, when?'

The first deportations were to the Lodz ghetto, but October saw the foundation of the ghetto-camp town of Theresienstadt, and from then on all deportations from Prague went there.

'For us, to go on the transport was almost a relief, because life in Prague had become so impoverished, in every sense of the word. At least in Theresienstadt one would be among one's own, and able to think aloud again.' Theresienstadt was a garrison town which had formerly had a population of 3,000. The Nazis had turned it into one huge ghetto and 'model' camp; but in August 1942 its exclusively Jewish prisoner-population was touching 70,000. 'It was a very hot summer, so you can imagine the living conditions. The place was an inferno. There was little to eat, and disease was rife. The Jewish administration within the town were very efficient in trying to improve our lot, but it was an almost impossible task. The German solution to the overcrowding was to transport people wholesale to Auschwitz and Treblinka.

'Theresienstadt had a rich cultural life, and as we were left to manage ourselves to a large extent, we enjoyed relatively great freedom of expression. I even danced. We did a piece called *The Big Shadow*, about a totally assimilated Jewish child who doesn't know what it means to be Jewish. She grows up, marries a Gentile, but finally falls victim to the Germans and finds herself in the end as an old woman sitting with her bundle of belongings in Theresienstadt and asking herself: Why? The piece was written for a musician, an actress and a dancer, and took the form of a series of flashbacks in which answers to that question were suggested. It was very controversial because it sniped at the assimilated Jews, but it was very successful. To be able to work on it gave me an enormous uplift and for those few weeks I was on a different plane – I even forgot about my hunger. And we did political cabaret, in Czech; and we put on operas: *Rigoletto, Carmen, The Bartered Bride*. There were concerts all the time, and in any little room you might hear a string quartet playing Beethoven – which was odd, because we Jews had long since been forbidden to perform German composers' music; but there were different rules once you were inside the world of the KZ.

'The flourishing arts were the plus side. The minus side was the privation, the loss of freedom, the disease. There was also the lie we had to live, and be a party to. When the Swiss Red Cross paid a visit to the camp in May 1944 there were huge transports to Auschwitz beforehand so that the place wouldn't appear overcrowded, and everything got a lick of paint, and they set up fake shops and fake kindergartens, even a bank – the SS called it a "beautification" exercise. The Swiss came and poked around but not very deeply; after they'd gone away, satisfied that the Jews were being well treated, everything went back to normal again. About the same time, when the camp was "beautified", the SS made a propaganda film about Theresienstadt, in which I had to dance. Of course the film didn't show the *Mala Pevnost* – the "little fortress" where they sent those of us who wouldn't toe the line. Nobody came back from there.

'At the end of the year I fell very seriously ill. By the time anyone paid any attention to me, I had peritonitis. Luckily prisoner medical facilities in Theresienstadt were excellent in terms of staff, because the best Jewish doctors in the country were imprisoned here. Medicaments were virtually non-existent, and there were barely any bandages or cotton wool; but they managed to operate on me and save me – though I don't think anyone seriously expected me to live. I was in the hospital for a year, during which time I was given morphine only twice.'

Her survival made her the pride and joy of the surgical department; when she had fully recovered, she remained in the hospital as secretary to the chief surgeon. 'By then I knew so much about medicine that I was able to look after his files. I worked for him from the end of 1943 until May 1944. Later that month, Paul and I were finally transported to Auschwitz. I remember my doctor saying to me, "If only I hadn't treated you so successfully; then you might be able to remain here still, as a patient."'

They were sent to the Second Czech Family Camp, in sector B II b. The first, established in September 1943, had been liquidated in March 1944 and all its inmates gassed. The same fate was planned for the second camp, which had been established in December 1943; but by that time the younger and more able-bodied were needed for labour, and *selections* were held. 'I had dreadful scars from my operations in Theresienstadt and I was sure that I would be sent to the gas, or worse, if Mengele saw them. Three times I managed to slip through the *selections* without being slated for death. The first time the process was taking too long, and Mengele ordered us just to strip to the waist, so I could hide my operation scars. The second time I was queueing up to be inspected by him, and I could see that there was no escape; so, in a moment when the SS had their attention elsewhere, I simply leapt out of line and joined the group to one side who had escaped with their lives. The others were sent out through a side-door. I was within six feet of Mengele when this happened, but the room was crowded and there was the usual confusion, so he didn't notice me at all. It wasn't a brave thing to do. It was a purely instinctive act of self-preservation which was as likely to fail as to succeed. The third time there was no way I could avoid the *selection*, but I managed to hold my bundle of clothes in front of me in such a way as to cover the scars. I couldn't look at him, and I knew I mustn't let him catch my eye, or he would have known. As soon as I knew I had got past him and was all right, I collapsed in a faint; I couldn't go on.'

'On 1 July the first transport of able-bodied young men left Birkenau. I know it was the first because my husband was on it. They sent him to Schwarzheide, near Oranienburg. When Paul and I said goodbye we were laughing because for the first time there seemed to be hope. The healthy women, including me, went to join the main women's camp at Birkenau shortly afterwards. And that left the old people, the sick, the pregnant, and the children in the Family Camp. On the night of 12 July, the sky was red from dusk to dawn. The Germans killed them all. Among them was my mother-in-law, who had come on an earlier transport with her husband. He had died of pneumonia several weeks before, but she had hung on. She refused to believe in the gas chambers to the last.

'The women's camp at Birkenau was and remains beyond description. It was dominated by Polish prisoners, some of whom had become completely brutalized with the years they had been there, and who were more frightening and dangerous than the SS. We were tattooed, but our heads were not shaved when we were transferred. I felt frozen. There was not anybody in the whole world who knew where I was. I do not know where my resilience came from and I still don't understand it; but the rumours that went around were always hopeful and always positive. You didn't really believe them but you repeated them: they helped keep your spirits up. And that took some doing. While we were in quarantine, the SS-women and the kapos found ways to amuse themselves with us. We had to carry rough-cut, heavy bricks at the double from one pile to another – and then back again. I remember doing this on the day an enormous transport arrived from Hungary; we were being "exercised" not far from the ramp. There were streams and streams of people coming off the trains – an endless flow – and there was no selection, they were all sent straight to the gas chambers, all of them, in their thousands. We went on carrying our bricks. If anyone fell down, she was simply shot. Well, if she was lucky, they just lashed her. It was the end for me; it was only six months after my last operation, and I had had it.

'But for the first time fate made it clear that my time had not yet come. As I reached the pile of bricks I staggered; seeing this, a red triangle kapo yelled at me not to go back for another load. "Start building these bricks into a wall," she shouted. I began the new job, which was easier, and soon the kapo got another prisoner working with me. This same kapo managed to save quite a few of us by making us build this ridiculous wall out of the bricks. Whenever she saw someone who was on their last legs, she'd order her to join the wall-builders; and when it was big enough, she saw to it that we took turns to sit behind it and catch our breath, snatch a few moments' rest. Her name was Käthe, this kapo, and she was a German. She was very clever at making the wall-building look like just another part of the sadistic game they were having with us. But behind the wall she talked to us. We thanked her. "There's nothing more I can do," she said. "But at least this will have helped a few of you."

'In August I was selected for a transport to go to work at Stutthof. By then I was a member of a small group of girls who looked after each other, and although the rail journey north was unspeakable, our spirits were high – at least for the first day of it. We were leaving Auschwitz. Whatever awaited us had to be better.

'Stutthof itself was a halfway house for us. We just waited there until work was allocated. We were sent to a labour-camp satellite of Stutthof called Kochstädt. We travelled there by open train, and that was actually bliss. It may sound crazy, but just to feel the wind on your face, and see the countryside, was a pleasure beyond price.

'Our work was to level ground for an airstrip. We were close to the Baltic, and the earth was composed of sand-dunes. We had to work fast because the concrete-laying machinery was hot on our heels. We were equipped with shovels with which we loaded the sand on to open trucks. It was back-breaking. I found it bearable as long as the sun shone, but the heat made it worse for some of the other girls, who couldn't take it and fell ill. The SS didn't give us much water.

'None of the 800 men and women at Kochstädt died at work because every second counted. Prisoners who couldn't make it were loaded on to lorries and taken to the gas chambers at Stutthof. The lorries brought fresh people back the same day as replacements. The work we were doing was of actual and urgent importance to the Germans, so we were always kept topped up to 800.

'Life was not made any easier by the SS. There was an *Oberaufseherin* called Emma. She was about 35, I should think. She greeted us when she first met us with the information that prior to Stutthof she had been at Riga, where she had personally been responsible for the deaths of several thousand Jewish children. That was so we'd be under no illusion about what sort of woman she was.

'One evening at roll-call I happened to be standing next to a Hungarian girl who casually mentioned that she hoped it wouldn't last long because it would cut down their rehearsal-time if it did. It transpired that Emma was keen on culture and had encouraged a group of prisoners to put a Christmas show together: music, poetry and dance. I thought they were mad to devote precious rest-hours to rehearsing, but later when I had another conversation with the same girl, it turned out that they were weak on the dance side of their programme. They were trying to do *Coppélia*, and I rashly told her not only that I knew the ballet but that I was a trained dancer.

'The next thing I knew was that I was summoned from my barrack to the barrack where they held their rehearsals. I cursed my big mouth, but when I arrived I found that the barrack was warm and well lit. It was a huge room, and different girls were rehearsing different things in various corners. I saw some half a dozen girls prancing around appallingly to an accordionist who was, sure enough, playing *Coppélia*. No one paid any attention to me, and I sat down, furious that I was losing sleeping time. I watched the dancers until I could stand it no more and then I stood up again and said to them: "You got me to this damned rehearsal; now, do you want me to show you what to do or not?" They were all Hungarian girls and a bit shy, but we soon got over that, bridging the language barrier with German and Czech and French, and I started to choreograph them; and while I was doing it, the old energies took hold of me and I really got to work and the thing began to get pushed into shape. I forgot where I was – and then I realized that everyone else had stopped and they were all watching us. So I told my girls to try the dance from the top again, and it still looked pretty awful, but it had shape. I was high. The girl on the accordion, who was very good, started to play a tango. "Dance!" she called to me. And I started improvising to the tango, right there, in my striped uniform; and I got completely carried away. The Hungarians loved it and they hugged me and kissed me and said, "You are a star! We have a big, big star in our midst!" And someone who worked in the kitchens rushed off and brought me back margarine and a slice of bread. I took the food back to my barracks and woke up my friends to share it with them, and of course I wasn't exhausted any more; I was more alive than I had been in years.

'The next day brought me back to reality harshly and suddenly. The tiredness caught up with me, and it had snowed on the site, and the work was hellish. I knew it was going badly with me, and our overseer that day was one of the most unpleasant SS-men. I could feel him watching me, and finally approaching. I will never forget his words: "*Du bist auch schon reif für Stutthof.* [You look just about ready for Stutthof.]" The death-sentence. But nothing came of it, and my number wasn't called that evening at roll-call. Instead, I was summoned to the rehearsals again. The others had told Emma that they had found a brilliant dancing star, and she should come and see! I remember she sat on a chair and they ran through the whole programme for her – she sat like a block of wood, arms crossed, terrifying, with eyes like slits. They left me until last.

'When I had finished, there was a dreadful silence, and during it she just stood up and walked out. And I thought, oh God, and everyone was terribly depressed. Emma was displeased. I was dismissed with none of my former glory.

'I passed one of the worst nights of my life. Next morning, at roll-call, I was as usual asleep on my feet, vaguely listening to the usual announcements being made over the loudspeaker system, when suddenly I was wide awake – my number had been called.

'I was not kept in suspense long. By order of the *Oberaufseherin*, who had clearly thought it beneath her dignity the night before to indulge in any public display of enthusiasm – or maybe she just acted tough for effect – I was excused all other duties in order to take charge of rehearsals full-time until the day of the performance. Which meant I would be warm and indoors. There would be little physical labour, and what there was would be enjoyable. I was given an extra soup ration. Because it was dry in the rehearsal barrack, I would be able to wash some of my clothes. The other performers had to go out and work during the day as usual, so rehearsals didn't start until 5pm; until then I was free to do as I chose – which meant resting and sleeping. It was like a holiday; the only thing that marred it was that the performance would just be for the SS, but even that objection was taken away. In the spirit of Christmas, the SS decided to let the whole camp see it.[3] And Emma became very enthusiastic, and organized make-up and costumes.

'When it came, the evening was a great success. I had prepared two dances to do myself – the tango and a slow waltz – and everything else went like clockwork. Everyone applauded like mad and Emma's face was wreathed in smiles – she was barely recognizable, and as proud as Punch to be Little Miss Culture. In the enthusiasm of the moment, she ordered goulash to be made for the whole cast of 30 – though when it came it was very hard to eat it with 770 hungry pairs of eyes watching you. Mind you, it wasn't so rich that it would do us any harm, but it was warm, and there was a bit of meat and potato swimming around in it. We had to earn it again though, because Emma was so delighted that she ordered a New Year's Eve programme. The entire cast was taken off work to knock it together in a week. I shudder to think today what it looked like, but in the circumstances it was considered to be high art. Anyway, it too was thought a great success and Emma once again was very pleased – a fact which led to a horrible moment afterwards, for she decided that there would be a post-performance party dance for the cast. We all danced with each other, of course, but Emma danced, too. Of course she chose her partners, and of course she chose me. And I danced with her. The tango. The foxtrot. I can remember how I felt when she put her arms around me . . .

'But I felt that I had turned a corner. I'd had three weeks indoors, with extra soup, and I was that much stronger. I might even have put on a bit of weight. Now that I had to go into the cold again, I thought I could manage a while longer; but it didn't last long, because the Russians were getting closer.

'We were evacuated on the morning of 27 January. I would certainly not have survived what was to follow without the reprieve my knowledge of dancing had earned me. Dance saved my life.

'At least we were not simply marched into the sea and drowned, as happened to one column. We were on the road to begin with for a fortnight. It was indescribably cold, and the only food we got was from villagers – the Poles gave us some, the Germans, later, none at all. At least I had a coat over my prison stripes. We slept in barns and abandoned churches. Our escort seemed to have no fixed plan of where to take us. Our clogs cut our feet and most of us had frostbite before long.

'We marched on, sometimes at night, and the only things that the cold did not kill were the lice and the typhus. The sky by now was red with the battle not far away. We marched five abreast, and if any one of us so much as stumbled, she was shot. By that time the law of the jungle had taken hold of all of us, but still if in a line one person could be supported, the others did so. In our line I was certainly the weakest, and the others were looking after me, but one of our line was a girl who was a newcomer to the group, not one of the original "team", and I heard her say, as if in a dream, "We can't go on like this . . . We can't save Helen. If she goes down and we try to help her she'll drag us all down." Objectively this girl – Mimi – was right. The road was icy.

'I was edged to the end of the line, so I was only supported on one side. I kept hearing *bang, bang, bang, bang* as they shot people, all the time. And from the corner of your eye you could sometimes see a shadow disappearing somewhere – someone trying to escape . . . I couldn't go on; they couldn't hold me any longer. I felt their grip on me loosening. I had no choice. Soon the whole column ground to a halt. For some reason we were marching in the opposite direction to everyone else, and we were far from alone on the road. There were hordes of German civilians, fleeing in confusion from the Russians, driving their cows ahead of them. In the congestion I saw my last chance. Dimly I saw a ditch by the side of the road, and a house behind it from which light seemed to be coming. In one movement I threw myself into the ditch, into deep snow. At that moment the door of the house opened and the column leader – an *Obersturmführer* – came out and almost stepped on me as he crossed the ditch and shouted, "*Los, marsch!*" And I was left in the ditch by myself.

'As soon as I knew I was on my own, I managed to generate a little energy and tore off the number tag sewn on to my uniform. I got up and knocked on the door of the house. Some German regular army soldiers were billeted there. I talked in German with them and tried to tell them that I was from among the German refugees. I'd lost my family on the road, I said, and could I rest there for the night? They joked, and said they could well imagine what kind of family I'd lost – they knew damn well what I was – apart from anything else, I spoke German with a Sudeten Czech accent. But they said, "You can stay here.'' They threw me some straw to make up a bed on the floor, and a woman brought me some boiled potatoes and some soup.

'In the morning, they saw me off with a chunk of bread. I walked for a while until I came to a big Polish farmhouse. I spoke to the family in Czech and told them what had happened to me, and they took me in and said I could stay until the Russians came. I remember there was an old grandfather sitting by the stove who told me to take off my coat and join him. Under it was the striped uniform. They brought me food, and we tried to talk. Luckily I couldn't eat, because the rich salami would have killed me, but I managed a little milk. My comfort was short-lived. Not long afterwards the door flew open and there stood an SS-officer.

'There was no time to put my coat on, and when he saw my uniform he drew his gun and started waving it about. "Raus!" he screamed at me. "If you're not out of here in ten seconds, I'll shoot the lot of you!" So I went out with him, and he marched me all the way back to the road, where he left me with orders to join the next column that came along. I don't know if he thought I'd obey him. As soon as he was gone I made quickly for a little shed I'd noticed, and hid in it for a while, until the owner arrived. She was a Polish peasant, and she told me I could stay with her. "If the Germans win the battle for the village, I'll turn you over to them; if the Russians do, I'll keep them from wrecking my property by showing them that I've saved a KZler." She was an old witch, but she took me in and let me sit by her stove. She lived alone with her son, who was a simpleton. We sat there and listened while outside the Russians approached and battle was joined. The son kept darting in and out to report on its course.

'It went on for hours, and then suddenly the shooting stopped and there was a long silence. It was broken by the sound of someone in boots approaching. I thought I could distinguish that they were jackboots. But then the door was flung open and there stood the smallest, youngest Russian soldier I have ever seen. He might have been 17, and he shouted, "Germania kaputt!" I knew I was saved.

'Once I had recovered and was clean and in fresh clothes, I remained with the peasant woman as an unwelcome guest, sleeping on a bench by the stove. On the third or fourth day a high-ranking officer arrived, who asked me to join him at dinner.

'He was very sorry that he couldn't do more to help me, but he had to press on with his unit. What he did do was produce from his pocket a piece of pink paper on which he wrote something in Russian, and he said, "Don't let this go, whatever happens. Whenever you come across someone in the Russian army, show them this and they will help you." But no more Russians came to the house after my guardian had left and, once the peasant woman realized that, she started to abuse me;

she thought I was going to die, and she didn't want me to die in her house. All this she told me, in her straightforward way. But the officer had extracted a promise from her son to take me to the nearest established Russian unit as soon as I was well enough, and when the peasant woman was out, I reminded him of his promise. He half dragged, half carried me to where the Russians were billeted. A Russian doctor arrived, and she examined my legs, which had turned blue, treating them with an ointment which brought immediate relief; the Russians are so familiar with frostbite that they know very well how to treat it. They made up a bed for me and I stayed with them for some days before they transferred me to a hospital.

'While I was there – the place was called Lauenberg – I became obsessed with taking baths. I really couldn't keep out of the bathroom. This obsession may have led to a bad skin ailment later.

'I discharged myself from the Lauenberg hospital because rumours were starting to circulate with enough consistency to be believed that that part of Poland would be annexed by Russia, and I didn't want to be caught in the Eastern Bloc. I had to observe all the medical formalities and sign a paper stating that I was discharging myself against medical advice. Then, together with two other Czech girls, I set off for Prague. It took us five nights and six days. Whenever there was a train that went south-westwards however vaguely, we took it, though we began with a considerable diversion. It was a ghastly journey. They drove us from the hospital to Bromberg [Bydgoszcz], gave us a little money and some kind of identity paper, and left us to it. There was no question of travelling with tickets, but we were covered by our papers. Every train was overcrowded; but when we got to the Czech border one evening, there was nothing except a very dead-looking line of carriages on a siding, without a locomotive. We ran into a family of Yugoslavian refugees who were camping on the train in the hope that sooner or later it would be coupled up and travel into Czechoslovakia, so we joined them on the train and curled up in corners and slept and slept.

'The train was duly coupled up, and set off westwards. As we journeyed home, we passed other trains – of cattle-waggons. Their ventilation-slots were covered with barbed-wire entanglements, and they looked horribly familiar. They were transports of German POWs being sent home.

'We had to change trains pretty well immediately, in Ostrava. We were actually home, but of course we knew nothing. There were news-sheets stuck to lamp-posts, reporting the bombing of Germany in glowing terms. We saw the Czech flag flying again; we joined in the mood of victory, sang patriotic songs. And I was crying at last, but somehow, at the same time, I had a feeling that none of all this celebration was for me. Perhaps it was just because I was still so sick: I couldn't think straight . . . Finally we found a train that was going to Prague – with luck. I think it was on that one that I noticed the name Truman in big letters in a man's newspaper, and I asked him who Truman was. The man looked at me as if I were daft and said, "He's the President of the United States." "I thought that was Roosevelt," I replied, and the man looked at me more closely, and said more gently, "Of course, how could you know?" And he explained.

'I remember that we arrived at the familiar old main railway station of Prague at midnight after a long, hard journey. There was a Red Cross kitchen there, which was just closing. We were exhausted and thirsty, and so we hurried over to see if they would give us a cup of tea. The woman in charge asked us where we came from, and we told her, "From the KZ." "I see. How long were you there?" "Three years." And she looked at us and she said, "Well, if you have lasted for three years, you can last one more night. We are closed." A Red Cross official. We bedded down on the station floor for the night.

'And that was our homecoming.

'There were shower-rooms in the basement of the station hall, and we took a shower and smartened ourselves up as best we could before we ventured into the city the next morning. And we said goodbye and went to look for our relatives. I had an uncle and aunt who lived not far from the station, so I caught a tram – we were allowed to travel free – and found their block of flats without any trouble, and their name was still on the bell, so I rang it.

'My uncle had been in Theresienstadt for six months, and the experience had left him a shattered man; but they cared for me as best they could, although we were not close. At the flat were two postcards from my husband. They were both official postcards, written from Schwarzheide. The second one was dated 15 March 1945. He wrote the usual basic stuff that one was allowed to write, but his handwriting was firm, and he asked after me, had there been any news? I was moved and delighted to see these cards. If he was alive and apparently well on 15 March – well, it was only 5 June now: he had probably survived.

'There was a big repatriation office in the centre of Prague. It was quite a long way from my uncle's flat but, ill as I was, I went there every day. One day, not long after I had started paying my daily visits to the repatriation office, I ran into a young fellow whom I'd vaguely known at Theresienstadt. He greeted me warmly, and we exchanged bits of news; and then he said, out of a clear blue sky, "You know I was with Paul until the end?" And I said, "What do you mean?" "Oh, you know, he was perfectly all right in the evening; we were all chatting. But the next morning we found him dead . . ."

'He looked at me and at that moment he must have realized that I hadn't known. He was only a young chap, and he must have panicked, for at that moment his tram arrived, and he blurted out, "I'm sorry, I must go," and he left me there. I later learnt that Paul had just faded away. He died of hunger and exhaustion in his labour camp, ten days before it was evacuated.

'I had written a couple of times to another aunt and uncle who lived in Mlada Boleslav. I was very fond of them, and had confided in them in my letters. I was so low now that I wrote to them again, and they came immediately, packed my bags, and took me back with them. They knew how I must feel, for my aunt had also spent six months in Theresienstadt, though her response to it had been more resilient than that of my Prague uncle.

'As soon as I was in their care, doctors were summoned. The reason no one had paid any attention to me before, apart from simple ignorance of what might be wrong, was that I was just one of hundreds wandering around town in a similar state, trying to patch up our lives again. I had actually met doctor friends in Prague who had offered to get me into a rehabilitation unit, but I'd refused because I didn't want to be shut up with a lot of people like myself again – it was the last thing I wanted.'

She was sent to hospital to have operations on abscesses which had developed under her arms, and was discharged, but soon after she had to return for further operations. The third time this happened, the surgeon said that she would have to stay in for a considerable time: clearly she was septic all over. Her doctors thought of consulting a colleague in town who had also been a prisoner in the KZ. He examined Helen and diagnosed tertiary scabies immediately. They gave her a mercury bath treatment which arrested the scabies after two sessions.

She was discharged at the end of October, and on the same day she had a letter from Harry in Belfast. It had been written in August and was addressed to the Red Cross in Prague. 'My aunt remembered the old romance in Trutnov and prophesied what would happen.

'All I wanted to be was normal. I just wanted to merge into the crowd, and be just like anyone else, not to be distinguished by my experience. But it was difficult, there were little incidents that reminded you. For example, I was on a tram, with a survivor friend, in 1946: there was no room to sit, and so we were hanging on to the straps, and of course our cuffs pulled down and exposed our tattoos. Suddenly we heard a man say, very loudly and distinctly, "Isn't it funny how only the young and pretty ones have come back." The implication was clear. I will never forget that. It hurt as much as anything we had survived. More.

'I never wanted to have the tattoo removed – that would have been a kind of betrayal of the past – and it is the Germans' shame, not mine, that I carry. Funnily enough, I am more sensitive about it now than I was then, but I would never show it if I could avoid it, and I still wear long sleeves whenever I can. If I'm anywhere – on holiday in Yugoslavia, for example – and I'm likely to meet Germans, I put a strip of sticking plaster over it. I just don't want them to stare at it. If I'm somewhere where I don't think there will be Germans around, I don't bother, of course.'

She corresponded warmly with Harry, and they arranged that he should come over and visit later in the year. 'We got married almost immediately, in Prague, and because Harry was already a naturalized British citizen, I became one too; overnight I became an alien in Czechoslovakia, and had to stop work, and report to the police once a fortnight. Filling in their alien registration forms made everybody laugh: born in . . . educated at . . . and so on!'

Dancing went into abeyance for ten years, but she has been very actively involved in choreography in Northern Ireland since 1956. She has also choreographed dance sequences for several operas. 'I couldn't have done any of it without Harry's support: he has always been wonderfully warm and understanding and kind. He provided the security I needed to learn to walk again, as it were.

'I was very disappointed and unhappy when I found that I could no longer dance – I knew I could never do it again as a professional performer, so I gave up altogether for some time. I used to watch rehearsals occasionally, with the proverbial bleeding heart! My world had been taken away from me. I was very bitter, but at the same time I wasn't going to fight to try to get it back, because I knew that it would be a losing battle, and I couldn't face the humiliation. My pride forbade me to try again, and for some time I needed to build myself up physically – it was a long process.

'However, I was very lucky when I came to Belfast – I had arrived in the right place at the right time, because there wasn't much in the way of choreography going on, and I had a lot of success. I couldn't believe it.

'My marriage was and always has been happy. Maybe some of Harry's friends in Belfast looked at me askance to begin with, and maybe they suggested to him that he was mad to marry me – after all, I was just debris from the concentration camps, and they suspected me, I think, of all sorts of things, from physical debility to moral corruption. But I was happy to be married, and marriage put me well and truly on the road to complete recovery. Sex was wonderful, it was just what I needed, and it was such a positive reaffirmation of life. To my surprise, for I did not think of myself as especially maternal, having children was very important. Perhaps not just to me; it proved to those Job's comforters among Harry's acquaintances that I was all right; that I was a real woman.

'Settling down here was difficult. People had no real idea of what had happened to me, and they thought the best line to take was to keep quiet about it. In any case it was beyond their imaginations and, to be fair to them, in 1947 I was very far from having worked it out of my system: that process had barely begun and it will never finish. But people didn't only display a lack of interest from a misplaced sense of tact; there were some who, if the subject did crop up, were stupid enough to say, "Oh, don't talk about it or I shan't be able to sleep all night," and my unspoken reaction to that was, "So what?" To me the apparent lack of interest seemed like rejection, but with Harry it was fine right from the start.

'My main desire after the war was to shed my KZ persona; but it was impossible, and one had to learn to accept that, just as one has to learn to live with any permanent physical wound: it's no good pretending that it isn't there. I wasn't alone, of course, but different survivors manifested their legacy in different ways. I knew a lady in Boleslav, for example, who was the wife of the writer, Josef Bor [the author of *Terezin Requiem*]; she had been liberated from Bergen-Belsen. She was part of a circle of comfortably-off intelligent people, and gave dinner-parties relatively often. Whenever I was there, I noticed that she always had a loaf by her plate. It was never touched, it was just there. My curiosity eventually got the better of me and I asked her about it. She replied, "Don't laugh; but I have this feeling that if for any reason I should have to get up and run, at least I would have a loaf of bread to take with me. I wouldn't be without." I think it's interesting that when I met her again in 1967, I noticed that the bread was no longer on the table; when I asked about it again, not only did she not remember, but she suggested that I must have imagined it.

'The term "normal" has a different meaning for KZ survivors from the one it has for other people – their normality is related to different things and different values. I don't know why I survived. I know of so many decent people who didn't, and I know of some bad people who survived and rebuilt their lives very happily. But what was the deciding factor? It brings us to moral questions: why should somebody be more deserving than another? What have I done to deserve survival and, if it is a question of deserving it, what must I do with the rest of my life to go on deserving it? I think it places a certain moral obligation on you. You aren't consciously aware of it all the time, but from time to time the thought strikes you afresh: you are a survivor. What does that mean? – That you are a person with enormous physical and moral strength? That you are lucky? Or that you were cunning enough to get through by any means? What made one person a survivor when another person, under the same conditions, regardless of physical strength, went under?

'It is not easy to have survived.'

Three Artists

I

Edith Birkin started painting in the early Seventies, and a few years later
met an art teacher who taught her to look at pictures, to understand the
history of art, and to broaden her own range and feeling. But, perhaps
more importantly still, he also understood what she needed to express
within herself of the Holocaust she had lived through as a young
teenager – in the Lodz ghetto, briefly in Birkenau, in the work-camp
of Christianstadt and, finally, in the last days of Belsen.

She had first tried to express herself through writing and, in the
early Fifties, soon after her arrival in Great Britain, completed a long
autobiography covering her years in hell. At the time she presented it
for publication interest in the subject was minimal; but as therapy, the
book was (as she thought then) important – and it is now a source-work
for her painting, whose subject-matter, though not exclusively the KZ,
returns again and again to it.

She lives in a modern house on the outskirts of Hereford. Her studio
is a heated shed in the garden, and one of the bedrooms is crammed
with paintings. Four are with the Imperial War Museum, and another
is at the Wiener Library. The paintings are hard, primitive, garish in
their use of colour to deal with a subject which, in fact as well as in
the imagination, was predominantly grey. Red and purple predominate,
and it is not hard to see the influence of her two principal mentors:
Rouault and Munch.

She was born in Prague, the daughter of a banker, and has one sister,
seven years older, who managed to escape to Britain just before the
war. Edith joined her – in Londonderry – early in 1946. 'I was due
to follow my sister but I was too young to travel on my own, and
the war broke out two weeks before my transport was due to leave.
Perhaps if I had managed to leave then, I might have adapted to
Londonderry, but in 1946 it was a dismal place – and the Jewish

community was narrow-minded to a degree. It was very painful to go there when one's last memories of civilized life had been of a cultural centre, and a modern, liberal Jewish community. Added to which, I had acquired a completely new set of values from the camps: there was no one who understood those values, and I felt desolately lonely.

'My sister didn't want to know at all. I think she was frightened to hear about what had happened to our parents – she knew, because I had written her a letter from the DP camp at Belsen, but when I joined her it was never mentioned: she couldn't face it. She's seen the paintings but she hasn't read the book, and now I think she suffers more than I do from the effects of the Holocaust – because she didn't live through it. But it hurt me at the time, and the memory still hurts; I didn't want sympathy – in any case there wasn't anything anyone could do – but I wanted someone to listen. Kitty Hart opened the first exhibition of my paintings, at Coventry Cathedral in 1984, and I know how she feels when she speaks of her reception in Birmingham. The mental suffering for me in those years immediately after the war was worse than it had been in the camps. The Jews in London, later, weren't so bad – they were of great practical help, they saw to it that I was afloat financially and put me through college – but in Londonderry they were awful. They had a collection for me and they thought they had bought my soul with it.

'I had never intended to settle here. I wanted to join my sister, learn English perhaps, and then return home; but the communist revolution put a stop to that. I had in fact returned to Prague from Belsen, but was unable to find anywhere to live, and there was no one left alive that I knew. I stuck Londonderry for 18 months before I moved to London, where the Jewish National Fund paid for me to do a teacher's diploma. I worked desperately hard on the course, but it was a great release: my education had been interrupted and frustrated – something I will never be able to make up completely – and I was like a sponge for knowledge. I learnt English from trying to follow *Julius Caesar* in class – it is still my favourite play.

'But my experience of those post-war years, and conversations with fellow-survivors, led me to conclude that the main problem to resolve in terms of keeping your mind on an even keel was not that posed by getting through the camps, but that posed by afterwards – because of the loneliness. I had all those experiences inside me, and I needed to get them out of my system – just by sharing them – and no one would let me do it. Looking back after more than 40 years, I can still sense how horrible it was, however I may have come to terms with it now, and found other helpers along the way. Then, you felt that you were supposed just to close the door on the past and be normal, and it made you sick. There weren't even doctors or psychiatrists who might have reassured us by simply saying, "Look, you're bound to feel abnormal, sickened, mad – and to see the world differently from other people." I don't think even the men who went through the Japanese camps had quite as dreadful an experience as we did: they didn't see their parents, wives, children, shot and burnt in front of them. The Japanese may have been cruel gaolers and torturers; but they didn't have gas chambers in which they killed pregnant women and little children in filthy, crowded darkness. The SS used to pack the people in and then shove the children in above their heads! And the filthy, greasy smoke from the crematorium chimneys, and the smell . . . To have all that bottled up inside your mind, having seen your loved ones die, and not to be allowed to talk about it in case it might upset other people, seemed unjust.

'Both my parents died in the Lodz ghetto, and I was alone there. Everybody was out for themselves. People needed bread, and fought for it; but at least many of them had someone left to love. And you knew that all the suffering was deliberately imposed – it wasn't an accident, a natural disaster, an act of God – it could have been relieved, all of it, by one order, overnight. That, too, made it harder to come to terms with afterwards.

'Now there are few triggers, perhaps because I am living with it in my conscious mind through painting; but I do constantly compare values. People here talk of deprivation, but they don't know what it means: deprivation to them means being without a TV, without a car; they don't know what the word means, and I find their values, their materialism, extraordinary. Immediately after liberation I had dreams, and one has persisted and still recurs every three or four years, that the Germans are chasing me. There was another which disappeared when I started painting; but before that it came to me every night: there was an intruder in the house and I'd try to switch the light on but the darkness would remain, no matter how often I pressed the switch.

'I can feel great sympathy with the suffering of others – those who are really deprived. The Africans who are ravaged by famine, and the children who are the innocent victims of war. And no government does anything to help, every country stands by and wrings its hands briefly and then gets on with the job of overproducing food for itself, because that is the lunacy of this world. I have painted those starving children because I have been a starving child. My husband says that I shouldn't judge people's sense of deprivation in this country now by the standards of the KZ; but I can't help seeing life through a different window. My benefit from this is that I can enjoy little simple comforts that other people can't. I've got a warm house, and food in the refrigerator; I can even get a glass of water from the tap when I'm thirsty. That is important. That gives me pleasure. I never take anything that I have for granted – I am glad to have however much of it there is for as long as it is available, but if it all went I would not die of grief. The only shadow over me is that something should happen to someone in the family; but as long as that doesn't happen, I am quite happy. But I have reached this state only after a long time, and it has been achieved only since I started painting.'

Edith spent her career teaching maladjusted adolescent children. 'It wasn't so hard because I think I could understand them, and I think that is why I wanted to work with them. Early on, of course, these were kids born in the Forties – war babies – their fathers had been in the army, and some of them had come home and they and their wives found that they had grown apart. I got on very well with those children, especially the girls.'

Her nervous breakdown occurred shortly after her marriage. 'I had held on for so long, and I suppose I thought, now I am safe, now I can let go. I'd wanted to share my life with someone for so long, and now that it had actually happened . . .' In the early Sixties she was teaching in a primary school, where she had to deal with particularly unruly children. 'Despite my experience, I couldn't take it and I reached a point when I couldn't bring myself to get out of the train when it arrived at the station for school.' She contracted pneumonia, which meant that she had to give up work. Afterwards, she went into deep depression, which her doctor thought was a reaction to the antibiotics she had been on, though she knew that it was due to 'all the poison coming out, now that I could let it out. I wasn't alone any more; I didn't have to be so mercilessly strong. Not many people would have put up with me like my husband did. But at least we share something which I think is as vital to any relationship as it was to survival in the KZ: a sense of humour.'

There are three children in her family: two boys and a girl. She has a very close relationship with her daughter, who has learnt to paint alongside her and whose nature, in which compassion and level-headedness are blended, she admires. 'She has read my book, and wants to do a collection of paintings herself under the title "What my mother told me". I take comfort in the thought that she will carry on where I leave off – that she will take charge of the paintings I leave behind. I always enjoyed talking to her about my experiences, not just because it was of any therapeutic value to me, but because it was pleasant to talk to her about the deeper things in life anyway. What triggered my daughter's interest was the film Kitty Hart made for television about going back to Auschwitz. I thought it was a wonderful film. At last, I thought. She peopled the camp.

'What kept me going in the KZ was the dream of and the desire to start another family, because the family I lost was so wonderful; it had to be replaced. That was my conscious motive for survival. I was 13 when I went in and 17 when I got out, but you grow up very quickly when your life depends on it . . . I had it all mapped out: after war I'd go home to Prague and rebuild everything. And everything would be as it had been.'

The family was rounded up and sent on the third transport from Prague to the Lodz ghetto, on 26 October 1941 – the so-called Transport of Professional People, because most of the family men had academic titles. They wore ski-suits because they were weatherproof and warm, and they were allowed only 50 kilogrammes of luggage per family. The transportation notices were pink cards, and from now on – as they were gathered in the Exhibition Hall in Letna – they would have to get used to the German habit of numbering everyone off in fives. To a certain extent, Edith was already hardened. The yellow star was a target for other children to spit and throw stones at; and the worst humiliations she had undergone so far were at the hands of adolescent boys who used her, as a Jewish girl, as an object for their first, clumsy and sadistic, nascent sexual feelings.

The ghetto, however, still came as a shock. It had been in existence for two years when they arrived, and the signs of starvation and disease were firmly stamped on its inmates. Two images from Edith's unpublished book well indicate the degree of shock: '[She] looked him up and down, and her gaze became fixed on a pale grey louse taking a stroll up and down the black coat. A shudder passed through her, and a feeling of terror and disgust overwhelmed her. She made an attempt to conceal these feelings. It was the first time she had seen a real louse. Once, a long time ago, during a hygiene lesson at school, they had been shown an enlarged picture of this gruesome creature. How it horrified her! For the rest of the conversation, she did not let the crawling object out of her sight.' And in the ghetto kitchens, where gas-rings could be rented for a small fee: 'Women, men and children bent over their pots mixing up concoctions true to ghetto style. Lice crawled freely up and down their dark garments and criss-crossed the tangled hair that was falling in their faces. Their skinny hands clutched old spoons with which they were stirring a soup of some kind. When they finished, they wrapped the saucepan into a rag to keep it hot, paid for their time, and hurried home.' One is reminded of how, in these nightmare societies where hunger is enforced, people become unable to share their food, particularly 'special', extra-to-ration food, even with friends or relations. Etiquette, and important social bonds which involve sharing, are thereby destroyed or at least seriously eroded. Such decay among the Jews in the ghettos only aided the Nazis' unspeakable plan.

'My parents died in Lodz, within the first year. My father died first, and then my mother just gave up, though it was typhoid that killed her. They died in bed, and were buried in the cemetery, and it is important to me that I know where they died and where they are buried. That at least is better than to have seen them sent to the gas chambers. For a time after their death I felt like giving up, and I just lay in bed, fading away; but then I must have decided that I would pull myself together after all, and try to see it through. I had contracted typhoid through my mother and was in the ghetto hospital when she died, but I wasn't told by anyone until a bachelor friend of my father – they had been colleagues at the bank in Prague where he worked – came and broke the news to me. Later, he looked after me like a second father.

'There were other friends of my family who rejected me as soon as I was alone, and that taught me a good lesson for life, too: that you expect nothing from anybody ever, and when you get something then it's a welcome surprise, and a big bonus. Even today when I am getting to know a new person, I put him or her into the ghetto and wonder how they would have made out there. I remember people who stole from their nearest and dearest: who fought for life at any cost; but it is possible to buy life too dearly.

'My job was sewing military uniforms together, and I did that for most of the time I was at Lodz. We talked while we worked, and our conversation was about food, about what we'd eat when we got out – you might think that that would be the wrong thing to do but, you know, talking about food you kind of experienced eating it. And we had day-dreams about our lives. Friendships were bonded, and I became part of a small group that was to stay together for the rest of the war – through the camps. We were all Czech girls, we were good friends, and we trusted each other. We also helped each other through the bad days. At Lodz the worst times were when they took away the children. It's something I've tried to paint many, many times and I still haven't got it right. People may not have behaved perfectly in the ghetto, but they did love their children. And the SS came and tore those children out of their arms.

'Our group went on transport soon after. We were told that volunteers were needed for labour camps elsewhere, and we thought anywhere would be better than the ghetto. They didn't say they were sending us via the Auschwitz selection procedure.

'The Germans were beginning to close the ghetto because the Russians were coming closer, and there were more and more transports to Auschwitz. Luckily we only spent ten days there, on a timber *Kommando*, before we were selected for war work. We were lucky not to be split up, too, for there was great comradeship between us, and that helped enormously.

'My father's friend was on the same transport to Auschwitz; but they took him immediately to the gas.

'We were sent to Christianstadt near Gross-Rosen where they had set up underground munitions factories. The camp was actually a converted holiday-camp for German children, in a beautiful forest setting, but sufficiently remote to be safe from Allied air-raids. We were a strange work-team: Jewish girls mixed up with an assortment of Gentile men. Our job was making hand-grenades: we had to fill them with explosive, but we often managed to take them off the machine when they were insufficiently full to work, so I hope we saved a few lives. This tiny act of sabotage was possible because we had only one overseer: by that stage most of the German manpower was at the front. It was the end of 1944.

'When Christianstadt was evacuated, we were force-marched to Flossenburg where we stayed only two weeks before being sent on to Belsen. It may sound crazy, but I didn't mind the march. It was January, but I loved winter weather, and we had not been too badly treated at Christianstadt, so I was well enough to be able to appreciate being in the open air and not being surrounded by barbed wire. The countryside was beautiful, too. I was young, and I had had to recover from my losses quickly in order to keep going myself.

'But as the march went on, our feet started to bleed, and we had to concentrate just on putting one in front of the other. All feeling, all thought, focused on that; but I knew that I would survive.

'We had been at Belsen only a month before the British liberated us. It seemed like an eternity, though we knew the end was in sight, because we had to struggle against the worst privations yet. There was no food or water, and because so many of us were at the end of our strength, death was having a last orgy. My immediate response to the arrival of the British forces was, thank God I don't have to stand through roll-call any more, because I had typhus by then. I would have died if the British had arrived even two days later, because if you couldn't stand through roll-call, you were finished.

'I remember that the British troops were very young – about the same age as me, some of them. They were horrified at the sight of us, and frightened of us at first, and who could blame them? But the older men were immediately compassionate and helpful, and by luck they gave us the right sort of food – things like milk pudding.[1] A strange thing happened. None of us could speak English, but one of the girls in our group got herself an English boyfriend, and he gave her things like corned beef and bags of sugar. Up until then, right through, we'd shared everything, but for some reason she wouldn't share with us any more, and she died of the food.

'The first food I got was macaroni milk pudding, and that's what I feed my family with every year on 15 April. After liberation, the simplest things were the most marvellous: sitting on a chair. Having a cloth on the table; eating from a china plate. Walking on a carpet; switching on a radio; seeing an egg. Having flowers on the table; a toothbrush; reading a book. Money; washing one's hands before eating; ironing clothes; having a bath. Shall I go on?

'We decorated the cattle-waggons of our homebound train with flowers; but I don't really miss Czechoslovakia, because of the experiences I had in Prague after I returned there from Belsen. You will have heard variations of this story: when I got back, the Gentile friends my parents had left valuables with when we were deported refused to return them or denied all knowledge of them. I'd spent three months getting over typhus at Belsen DP camp before returning home, but I was still pretty weak; I didn't have much fight left in me, and certainly not as much as I needed. I think the worst day of my life was the day I got back to Prague, because for all those years I had lived just for that day and, when it dawned, I realized that there was nothing but ashes; I was in a strange town; no one I knew lived there any more. At the same time there was a host of memories of happy times. With the realization that I was alone the troubles of readjustment began. I needed to be with someone, and the only person I had was my sister.'

Attempting to adjust to life in Londonderry, and the sense of being uprooted, led to illness, palpitations and dizziness, the causes of which were partly psychosomatic and partly due to anaemia. 'It was as if my body suddenly had a chance to let go – and to release all the badness that was in it.' After her escape to London, she shared a flat with two Czech girls who were former comrades from Belsen. 'That was a great help, because it countered the loneliness, and we had the KZ experience in common, though when we talked about it we laughed about it more often than anything. Still, our flat-sharing wasn't a permanent answer. We each wanted to be settled in a family of our own, and all our instincts were geared to forming one. But it was very difficult to meet the right people; there was no forum then for meeting nice people in public, and we had no entrée into English society on any level. My illnesses continued, too; and although I was under treatment continuously from 1946, it wasn't until I started painting in 1972 that they finally receded. During all those years that the palpitations, dizziness and heart-anguish continued, I was afraid to go out alone, for fear of what might happen. It wasn't until I met my art teacher in the mid-Seventies that I began to improve substantially. He told me what I needed so much to hear: that I needn't feel that I had to push the concentration camp experience away, and that I had to learn to live with it. I had earned the right to do so, he told me, and it was nothing to be ashamed of. In any case, I couldn't push it away or keep it under – it had to come out. And it wasn't abnormal in a bad sense. Nobody after the war could see that, because nobody understood the magnitude of it. When I went to the dedication of the Holocaust memorial in Hyde Park, I looked around at the other survivors there and I couldn't believe that there could be so many of us. You can't forget something which for better or worse becomes part of your life in the same way that any experience does – however horrible. Whatever it is, it is with you for ever, and you might as well acknowledge its presence and learn to live with it. Confront it, and it ceases to be a threat; but it can take forever to realize that – and even then perhaps you have to be lucky enough to have the right kind of help.

'My two friends who shared the flat in London also married non-Jews, but I think that is a coincidence. Although religion has no meaning for me, ideally I would have liked to have married a Jew, because I should have liked to bring Jewish children into the world. Fate decided otherwise, but I am sorry that I am not passing on any of my own Jewish roots and traditions.

'When I started painting, it was like a kind of arrival. I had something to think about other than myself and, because I stopped worrying about myself, I got better. I love colour, and it gives me a lot of joy to create with it, so every evening now I look forward to the next day. And when I do my war paintings, I am back there with my comrades who never came home. I'm not running away from them any more. The people in my paintings are real, and until I am sure that they are real, the painting isn't finished. It can take a long time to prepare, six months of thinking and sketching sometimes. As I have said, my book enlivens my memories, and I also use photographs of the time. One of the main ideas is that of the head shrinking less in proportion to the body as a person starves. Heads, hands and feet are huge in proportion to the body, arms and legs. That is even more evident in children. I had never seen death, and suddenly I was seeing nothing but death.'

The paintings' titles tell their own story: 'The Death Waggon', 'The Separation of Children from Parents'. Above all, perhaps, is her 'Liberation Day', which expresses bewilderment, anxiety, mistrust – anything but joy.

'I have tried beyond my book to express it in writing too – in poetry; but I am not satisfied with what I have done yet. What I really cannot do is express my post-war sufferings. Even London was so grey in the Fifties. I would like to write a collection of stories from the ghetto – vignettes of life there. That part of my life is much easier for me to face now than London in the Fifties. In the camps, rightly or wrongly, you lived on hope, and day-dreams about how lovely life would be if only you were free. But once I was free, I realized that all my past was gone for ever, that even my country had ceased to exist for me – or had I ceased to exist for it? – and that there was no more hope. I think the essential difference for me is that in the camps I may have been broken down physically, but I never was, in the end, mentally. In Northern Ireland and England after the war, I was broken down mentally, and I am frightened to go over that ground again.'

II

All Valerie's paintings of the KZ are in grey and black. The central event of her experience, when she spent the night with her mother under guard in a freezing cabbage-field, waiting for death, is repeated again and again. Figures with swollen heads and stomachs stare emptily at you, standing against a sky dotted with tattoo numbers. There are charcoal drawings of huge-eyed people, split in two; and sculptures: an agonized head split in two; another head, its long neck encircled by barbed wire; an eyeless bust behind a target, pierced by black arrows. There is no colour here either; she works in bonded aluminium – grey, hard metal.

Her apartment is large and airy, and overlooks the East River on two sides from broad windows; but it is crowded with the KZ. An aluminium starving man pushes with the last of his strength against a perspex wall; four famished heads rise from a black base.

'My paintings and sculptures are only a tiny fragment of my feelings, and of the pictures I have in my head. My memories are full of the faces of my comrades who perished; I would like to paint six million of them. As I work on my pictures, they talk back to me, and I learn more about myself, about how deeply I have been affected by the experience, and about human mortality. We who survived the Holocaust will all be dead soon, so I have a great sense of urgency: I must do all I can to convey to the future what this great scar across human progress means. I find painting more of a struggle than sculpting, though I do both with equal pleasure. I sculpt in wood as well as aluminium; but I do my sculpting in the studio I have at our weekend house in Westchester.'

Today, her paintings are in the Yad Vashem collection and in the Ghetto Fighters' Museum near Haifa. I wonder that she is happy to live surrounded by such images. 'It took some time; I didn't bring them home for a long time, and then, little by little . . . I think I have come to grips with a lot of things through my work, and I am able to live with my memories through having created works of art out of them. In fact, when the pieces are out on a show, I miss them.'

She was born in Munkacs in 1926. The town passed to Hungary when it was annexed with the rest of Ruthenia in 1939. It is now called Mukachevo, and is part of the Ukrainian SSR. It was a poor area, but her father was a prosperous timber-merchant who tended to spoil Valerie, the youngest of his four children. Her best friend was the daughter of their neighbours, a family of impecunious Hungarian aristocrats. 'We had wonderful times together, and my father's timber-yard was the best place in the world to play. The only difference that I was aware of between us was that I was not allowed to go and eat with her, because my family was reasonably observant.' There was anti-Semitism in the air, however, and Valerie's parents warned her not to provoke it. Although Ruthenia was made a part of Czechoslovakia after the Treaty of Versailles, its mixed population was dominated by Hungarians, and Valerie's mother-tongue is Hungarian, not Czech. She went to a mixed school, but learnt Jewish culture and traditions within the family, and grew up aware and proud of them.

The annexation of Ruthenia did not affect the family at first, although they were aware that Hungary was aligned with the Third Reich; but in due course inevitably the licence given to anti-Semitism made itself felt. Valerie's Christian friend became aloof; her older brothers were sent as labourers to the Eastern Front. After the invasion of Poland, Jewish refugees from that country began to filter into Munkacs, and with them came the first news of the systematic persecution of the Jews. Valerie found her education blocked because of the *numerus clausus*, and switched to a private Hebrew *Gymnasium*. However, apart from a dangerous moment when her father was temporarily placed under arrest, the family, in common with most Hungarian Jews, lived relatively unaffected by the war, until Germany invaded in 1944.

A ghetto was established immediately and, within four weeks, the entire family found itself uprooted and transported to Auschwitz. 'I retain the most vivid memory of my grandmother, who was 84 at the time, lying in the cattle-car, wrinkled, old, nearly blind; and just praying, praying.' Upon arrival at the KZ, all the older relatives and the children, together with several aunts and uncles, were selected immediately for extermination. 'We hadn't known about Auschwitz before; but within hours we knew everything. My brother, who had returned home to his own new family from the labour camps only a short time before, must have known, though; because as we arrived he took his 3½-year-old son out of his wife's arms and gave him to her mother. They were both sent to the gas. My brother was later to perish at Dachau, though his wife survived the war.'

After the men and the women had been separated, Valerie's female relatives found that, by a miracle, 14 of them had been selected for the camp, including her mother.

Her mother had hitherto been an aloof figure whose praise she had sought but never enjoyed; now they were going to be thrown into a much closer relationship than they had ever had. They both survived, as did her other brother and sister, her father, and 10 of the other 12 female relatives. Valerie is in no doubt that being part of such a large family-group contributed enormously to the survival of each member. 'We were indeed a fortunate family in that respect, though survival can taint the rest of your days; and adaptation to life in the USA was very difficult for my parents. I never returned to Munkacs, but my father, who was left behind at Auschwitz when the camp was evacuated as being too sick to travel, and was therefore liberated by the Russians a few days later, walked home. He was back in Munkacs by early April 1945.'

Shortly after their arrival in the camp, their *Block* was cleared and taken to the crematoria. 'This was the occasion of the night in the cabbage-field. Part of me died that night. I remember how we were selected in the morning, and we were driven to the "showers". I remember the geraniums the SS planted around them: the colours a mockery in all that grey. We were put in a stable and ordered to wait there. We knew what was happening, we could see the smoke and smell the burning flesh. We were made to strip, and then we waited, for hours. No one spoke. Then they ordered us to dress again. I don't know why; either they changed their minds, or there was no room for us that day. We were marched out of the stable in the late afternoon. I was slow and an SS-man hit me and broke my tooth. They drove us into a cabbage-field, where we had to spend the night; and I vividly remember the cabbages and the very strong, bright moon. And the way I remember, 40 years later, there was one beam coming down from it, and that beam was like a signal: live, it said to me. It was like a rebirth. Part of me died that night, but what was left was new. That is why I paint myself in two halves: the dark-grey half, with the head of a skull, and the other . . .

'We remained there for another three months, until there was another large *selection* – the very young and the very old were taken, including my mother. The rest of us were locked into our *Blocks* – *Blocksperre* was standard practice during *selections*, and I knew that I would never see my mother again. I begged the kapo to allow me to go along to the kitchen as part of the detail which picked up our daily food-ration, in the hope that I might just see my mother once more. In the food queue by the kitchen *Block*, I saw my mother among the group of women selected for the gas chambers, standing about 100 yards away, but still our side of the wire. Only one guard was watching them from a lookout tower.

'Before I was able to think about what I was doing, I was crossing the space between us. She looked paralysed, and her eyes were glazed. When she saw me, she said, simply: "Oh, good; you are here. We will go together." I said, "We'll go back to the others." And I pulled her out of the crowd after me. She followed me like a child, and we rejoined the kitchen detail.

'We were in Auschwitz for another two long months, before Mengele arrived in our *Block* to weed more of us out. He was accompanied by a group of SS-women who marked those whom he slated for death with a painted red cross on the forehead – like cattle. My mother was close to being a Mussulman by that time, but I managed to guide her past the Angel of Death.

'It was fall by then, and the weather had turned cold – the bitter cold of central Europe, when the ground freezes so hard you can't get a spade into it. Cold and hunger are my main memories, vivid enough to feel as if they were real again today. I was fairly certain that my mother would not survive the winter after all that she had been through; and I was unsure of my own chances. By the kind of luck that has enabled me to reach today, there was a *selection* for transport to labour camps, and we managed to get on to it. We were taken to Unterluss, about 30 kilometres from Belsen, where there was a Farben munitions factory. Our work was to make a clearing in the woods – felling trees – we were used for the hardest work because I think the SS considered women even more expendable than men – and we had to dig foundations for further buildings. There was also a 15-kilometre march to and from the camp every day. But we were away from the gas chambers. A kind of timid hope crept into our souls. We could hear Allied planes. We sensed that if only we could hold out, we would be saved; and it seemed a pity to give in now, after so much, and being so close.

'On 12 April we awoke to find the SS gone. It should have been the day of our liberation but before we could leave a group of what appeared to be armed civilians rounded us up and marched us to Belsen. Within hours of arrival there, we were crawling with lice, and I am certain that we would have died if the British had not arrived as soon as they did. Our strength was not sufficient to cope with the conditions in that camp. As it was, upon liberation I had contracted typhoid, diphtheria and jaundice. Of the original group of 800 out of Auschwitz, perhaps 500 were left alive. The 300 who died, died in Belsen, not Unterluss.

'How did we react to liberation? We cried. I don't remember crying once in Auschwitz, though before the war I was a spoilt little girl and I cried often to get what I wanted. I cry easily now, too, for different reasons. I am an emotional person, even moody; but in the KZ I was not. I think I had a mission to get through, and to bring my mother through with me.

'I cannot analyse the precise feelings I had at liberation despite the considerable time and energy I have devoted to thinking about the KZ in my attempts to confront it. I do a lecture, using 80 slides of the Holocaust pictures I have done; but I only started working with the subject in 1980. I hadn't touched it before, except for a little drawing I did unconsciously ten years earlier, and which disturbed me so much that I put it away – though I wasn't aware that the KZ was behind the inspiration for it. It was just a five-minute sketch done as an exercise – draw the first thing that comes into your head. Looking back now, I suppose it was the first breakthrough. I had suppressed my memories until 1980, though after liberation, when the family moved to New York City, I would talk to my mother daily on the telephone, and almost always the subject would come up. But after her death in 1955, I buried it.

'I didn't know what to do about going home because my mother had phlebitis and was too ill to move from Belsen, and there was no question of leaving her to go on the early repatriation trains to Prague. When I heard that the Swedish Red Cross were running a recuperation programme, I decided to apply for that with my mother. We went to Sweden for three months. They separated us in Malmö, and that was terrible, because we had never been separated, and even in Sweden, where the rational part of our minds knew we were safe, we panicked; we couldn't adapt so fast from the habits acquired in the KZ. I was convinced that if we were separated she would die, and I became very angry. The Swedes were bureaucratic, but I pestered them until they told me where they had sent my mother – to a convalescent home near Gothenburg. Through the Red Cross, we heard from cousins who were already in the USA that my father was in Prague and was waiting there for us. As soon as my mother was well enough, we set off to join him. In the meantime, I had taken up art lessons at the suggestion of a fellow refugee.'

Living in Prague presented a new set of problems, because the family were not Czech-speakers, and the Czechs were inclined to view any Hungarian-speaker with an unfriendly eye. She took six months to learn the language. Meanwhile, her father was trying to organize the family's emigration to America, where a branch of the family had been established for some years, and where a number of relatives were prepared to sponsor them. The process, however, took two years. 'I managed to get trained as a beautician in Prague, thinking that I'd need some practical skill to earn money by, and I paid for my training with coffee and cocoa which I'd brought with me in quantity from Sweden, since they were the black-market currency of post-war Czechoslovakia. Luckily our relatives in America had sent us $200 when we were still in Gothenburg. I also managed to have some dental work done – the

SS had not been kind to my teeth in the course of the various beatings they had given me.

'It was my parents who decided on going to America. I think if I had been alone I would have gone to Palestine. I had a strong Zionist background through my older brother – the one who did not survive – and through the Jewish schooling I received after I was unable to continue in mainstream Hungarian education. Palestine would have been no good for my parents, though. They were in late middle age, and in any case were facing all the problems of starting again at a time when they would have preferred to be looking forward to retirement. My father, too, was faced with a quite dramatic drop in status and needed as much family support as he could get. After the war, my parents became my children. I had to look after them, and I had to find some way of making a living immediately. As soon as we arrived in New York, I took a job on the Lower East Side doing manicures, and despite my training I didn't know how – fortunately one of the customers taught me! Then a little later I moved to a Hungarian beautician's on Lexington, where I worked for nine months. Then I got married. This was 1949. I'd been introduced to Frank by a cousin who I think had had me in mind for him – once we'd met, things certainly seemed to work out! And it was due to him that I was able to adapt to life here with less difficulty than I would have encountered otherwise.

'Frank was very understanding. I used to have very bad nightmares and grind my teeth in my sleep; then he would wake me and comfort me. But I didn't talk about what I had been through much, even to him; in fact he has only learnt about it recently, since I decided to break my silence. It helped that he knew very well what I had been through. He comes from Hungary originally, and he lost his parents in the camps, though he came to America before the war. He served in the army and fought the Japanese in the Pacific for four years. I look back on his patience with gratitude, because it took some time to adjust and, especially at the beginning, there were some bad moments, which arose from the simplest incidents. I remember that one day in the fall of 1948 we were watching a soccer match in Central Park, which is a game I enjoy because it reminds me of Europe, and suddenly I saw a policeman. I seized Frank's arm in panic. Of course he couldn't understand what the matter could be, though he tried to reassure me; but it was a very long time before I could see a policeman without feeling immediate and involuntary panic. It wasn't helped by the fact that New York Police uniforms are superficially reminiscent of those the SS wore.

'In general, though, there wasn't too much difficulty for me at the beginning, nor did memories of the Holocaust put our relationship under any kind of strain. I was young and happy, and happily married, and I just wanted to be normal, like everyone else, and forget that I had ever been in Auschwitz. We started a family almost immediately and had two sons.

'Nevertheless we lived in a closed world. For many years our close friends were exclusively from the family, from fellow refugees, and survivors – though we seldom spoke of the Holocaust. We were like a secret society – in fact that is my nickname for all survivors collectively – because only we know. For myself, I neither denied the Holocaust nor would I dwell on it. I didn't seek out opportunities to talk about it. When the Eichmann trial took place, my older son was ten. He was a TV bug, but very bright. I wanted him to watch the trial on TV. He knew a little about what had gone on by then, and about my background. But he got fed up with it and by the third day of watching it he had had enough. So I sat him down and told him all about what had happened to me, and he became very interested, and asked questions, and we sorted it out together. It was a heavy responsibility in a sense, because it was difficult to judge how much to burden him with; but the next generation must not be left in ignorance of what happened to us. I don't know how much my younger son remembers, but he does say that the three things he remembers as vivid historical events of his childhood are the Eichmann trial, Kennedy's assassination, and the moon-landing.

'Apart from the trial, the Holocaust was something I kept at arm's length between 1955 and 1980. I know that it was hard work, keeping it at bay. I had to be active all the time; I painted bright, geometric abstracts; I smoked 60 a day and drank gallons of coffee.

'One of the things that triggered my thinking about the Holocaust again was that it began to become a focus for public and historical and even popular attention again at the end of the Seventies and in the early Eighties. I must say that through the years of neglect I had forgotten much of it. Frank would protect me from whatever films and books I saw if they had too drastic an effect on me, but it was difficult for him, too. He didn't like to talk about it much, because he had lost his parents, added to which he felt guilty because he had escaped their fate and had not shared the suffering with them. Guilt is something I feel too, when I think of all the good people who died for no reason, who had just as much right to life as me, and probably more. It was very painful for both of us when I started to paint, because the process started to open doors inside that we had both kept closed.

'There always were triggers for my memories, though. I have been operated on for cancer of the sinus, and since that time I have had no sense of smell; but earlier in my life the smell of burning leaves in fall bonfires was enough to take me back to the KZ – immediately. Or the sound of a firehouse siren. Or even the sight of smoke from a fire, or a dreary day. A November day – that is Auschwitz, somehow.

'There was a time, too, when Frank made a business trip to Germany. I was going with him, but in the end I had to stay in London and wait for him there. I don't go to Germany or Austria because I get angry and insecure; I cannot forgive them, and it does me no good. I was in Vienna once for a week, and I hated it. Hearing the language, and the very atmosphere – it was all too upsetting. And I was afraid. The problem is that anti-Semitism is still with us. I was horrified at the attitude of the Polish peasants interviewed in *Shoah*. I can remember, too, a survivor who visited friends here and was horrified that they had the candles lit in the window at Hannukah, for all to see. "You mean you don't mind your neighbours knowing you're Jewish?" she said.'

After their marriage, Valerie gave up work and went back to school to learn English properly.

'I hadn't pursued drawing since Sweden, but now a fellow-survivor, who had married an uncle of Frank, asked me to sit for her. When I saw the result, I was encouraged to start again myself. Frank gave me a box of paints and a sketch-book. I took a course at the 92nd Street "Y" and followed it with a course in ceramics at City. Then, a little over two years after my first son was born, we moved out to Great Neck because of the schools – it's a solid, suburban community up there. The bonus was that there were also good adult education pro- grammes. I signed up for a sculpture course and studied with Louise Nevelson for three years. She used to bang on at me to break loose, because I was just doing naturalistic work. "You have talent," she'd say; "but if you want to get anywhere you'll have to leave your family!" So I had to make a choice; and I chose to be a wife and mother instead of a professional artist. Maybe I should add that I don't think Louise had any idea that I was a survivor.

'I had ambitions to become a designer, and in the mid-Fifties I took a dress design course back in the city, commuting up to it two or three times a week; but when the nanny I'd organized for the kids left, I had to abandon it. Another choice, not too hard to make. Then I started a boutique in Great Neck with a friend, but it flopped because we never had enough backing to see it up and running. Life seemed becalmed and, to make matters worse, the spice-importing business which Frank runs was going through a bad patch. The boys became adolescents, and there was I, treading water, a suburban housewife. It wasn't the life I had wanted. But then the business got better and the boys went off to university. It was time for me to get out of my rut.'

This was the process that led to her breaking her silence. 'When I started to go to therapy, it was not because of my experiences in the KZ, but it emerged through the sessions that the Holocaust was at the root of the problems which had sent me to see a therapist in the first place. Several things happened. First of all, I took my father's death very hard, because we were very close.

'At about the same time, there were two other deaths: one of my best friends, who had been through the camps with me and who now also lived in Great Neck, died of cancer; and a cousin of Frank committed suicide. All this hit me broadside on. In the course of my therapy sessions, my own pain began to come out. After two months or so I felt better, and I said goodbye to the therapist; however, he urged me to continue to keep my Holocaust memories in the open. He said, "It's like the roots of a weed. Leave them hidden in the ground, and the weed will keep coming back; dig them up, and the weed will die." I couldn't afford to continue treatment at that time, so there the matter rested.

'At about the same time, Frank's business recovered and we even managed a vacation in Jamaica. But when we came home from that, I started to have pains in my arms, and in my throat at night. Not long after they began, when Frank was away on a business trip in California, I had some cousins from Montreal to stay. I insisted on carrying heavy luggage downstairs for them when they left, and when I'd seen them off I suddenly felt terrible. I managed to get to the doctor, and he told me I'd had a mild heart-attack. I was 40. Frank came back that day, luckily, and rushed over to the hospital. It was all quite dramatic, but looking back I can see how I was paying the price for all that hyper-activity, all those cigarettes and all that coffee. I've slowed down a bit now, but I've always been an active person, and I don't think I can blame it all on the KZ. I always wanted to gobble up the whole world!

'After the boys had gone to university in the early Seventies, I wanted to go back to Manhattan. Frank was against it because the place was getting such a bad reputation; but I'd had enough of the suburbs, so I persuaded him to rent an apartment for the winter and see how it went. We still have the apartment – it's now my studio. Three years later we bought this place, and it turned out to be a great way to change our lives. We both loved it. To be near theatres and museums again was marvellous.

'But the KZ was only buried skin-deep, and matters were brought to a head again when my younger son became very serious about a Catholic girl. The blow came when he announced that he was going to marry her. I felt a deep sense of pain and guilt – it had never occurred to me that our sons would marry outside our faith, and I wondered whether I hadn't told him enough of what his people had been through in the Holocaust. More selfishly, I was disappointed in my own ambitions to see a Jewish line established, descended from me. As I

440

have said, the sense of race is very strong, and naturally it has been heightened by the KZ. We had terrible rows, and I did not attend the wedding, though we are friends now. Three years later, my older son also married a Christian girl. These events forced me to dig deeper into myself to seek for reasons.

'I was also unwell. I had started to get sick with cancer of the sinus before my sons' marriages. During a flight to Arizona I had appalling earache, and when I had myself examined by a specialist later, he told me that there were polyps in my nose. An operation had to be scheduled. That went fine, but in the course of it they discovered that I had cancer. I had to undergo further surgery which changed my face to some extent, but I am lucky that I have no scars.

'There were further operations over the next few years, and also radiation therapy, which is devastating, especially in a sensitive area. My mouth was burnt; I had difficulty swallowing. It all made me very depressed; but I had opted for the treatment. The young doctor who was my radiologist told me after he'd examined me that he'd use radiation treatment on me only if I twisted his arm. Sinus cancer is rare and no one knew quite how to deal with it. On the other hand, they were virtually giving me six months to live if I didn't have treatment. I remember I went home and went to the window, and thought, right, shall I throw myself out now, or shall I wait until it starts to hurt? I really didn't know what to do; but in the end, all I could do was make the best of it. Now they all think it's a medical miracle that ten years later I am still here. But at the time . . .

'Everything crumbled. My resistance was low, the radiation really brought me down. The great compensation was getting this apartment and moving in, and I tried to take my mind off things by decorating it. And then someone suggested I might try therapy again. I went to a comic-strip therapist with a Viennese accent and an abusive manner. I thought: my life is a wreck; my face is changed, it doesn't look like my face any more, and I do not need this guy shouting at me. So I left. Luckily I found a sympathetic analyst through a friend and then, at last and very slowly, I started to let the poison come out. It took two and a half years, and they were the most difficult of my life. I would walk the streets for hours after each session, because nearly every session took me back to Auschwitz, to the cabbage-field, reliving it all after so long. I couldn't manage it all the time. And then one night I was in the den here. I couldn't sleep, and I picked up a pad and some charcoal, and I started to draw. And what came out of my unconscious was faces, faces from the Holocaust – and I drew them: many, many faces. And that is how it started.

'By then our rented apartment had become my studio, and I re-equipped it, and painted and painted and painted. I couldn't stop myself;

it was pouring out of me. And sometimes nothing would come and I would cry. And then I would start again and I would cry; because the pictures upset me. What was I creating? All this black and grey – the room was filled with it; the world was filled with it. It hurt and hurt and hurt, but the more I did, the more I stayed with it, and gradually the pain started to ease.

'I know that I will never extirpate the memory; but now I can recognize it and live with it. Also, I know and I accept what I fought against for so long: that I cannot be like everybody else. There is a tattoo on my soul.'

III

Yehuda Bacon was born in Ostrava. He lives in Jerusalem now, where he teaches at the Bezalel School of Art. His work is on view at Yad Vashem and the Ghetto Fighters' Museum, and he has had exhibitions internationally.

'I was about ten when the war broke out. My family was a conventional one, and my father ran a small leatherworks. We tried to escape, but circumstances were against us. One of my two older sisters managed to get away to Palestine, but I wasn't old enough to make the Youth Aliyah. Ostrava was the first place from which deportations were made, though the very first selections of young men were sent to forced-labour camps. My own family was sent to Theresienstadt in 1942, and I was placed in a *Jugendheim*.[2] We spent a year in the ghetto-camp and then, in December 1943, the family was transferred to Auschwitz – to the Second Czech Family Camp in Birkenau B II b. When we got there we were made to write postdated cards back to Theresienstadt to say that we were fine and that all was well – probably the Germans had it in mind to allay the fears of those left behind, should they be sent after us. The family camp was unbelievable – we even had a school for the children, which was mad when you consider that the Nazis had discontinued education in the normal way long before for Jewish children. But Auschwitz was another world, with its own laws.

'*Block* 31 was the children's *Block*, and we even had our own kapo, Fredy Hirsch.[3] I was the *Block* cook. Of course we were relatively better off than the Polish Jews because we had arrived that much later, and for the first few months we remained with our families intact. But we knew enough about what was going on – and I think perhaps we felt it, too. I got all the boys who had been in the Theresienstadt *Jugendheim* who had come on the transport to Auschwitz to sign their postdated cards: "and with this, my dear death, I finish". The word *death* we wrote in Hebrew, and the SS were too stupid to check – no doubt they assumed it was a proper name, which was our intention. In this way we hoped at least to warn those left behind in Theresienstadt.

'The family camp was designed to show to the Red Cross when they visited Auschwitz, but in June or July 1944, after precisely six months, they proposed to gas us in the same way as they had gassed the first family transport from Theresienstadt, but instead there was a *selection*. Now the families were split up, and parents separated from their children. My father was sent to the gas chambers; but my mother and sister were sent to work at Stutthof, as I later discovered, for I never saw them again. I was in a group of 89 children, aged between 13 and 16, selected by Mengele. We were Dutch, German and Czech children. It is probable that they wanted to keep us either to show the Red Cross if they should revisit the camp or to hold us for eventual use in exchange for captured Germans.

'To isolate us from the rest of the camp, and with typical SS craziness, we were lodged in the same *Block* as the punishment *Kommando*, and witnessed the brutal treatment and torture handed out to the people in it. But in Auschwitz you had to take everything in your stride; the abnormal became the normal. And we children had barely known a life other than that of the camps: the KZ was our reality. In the *Block*, we continued to enjoy the better treatment that we had had in the Family Camp. We were brought better food from *Kanada*, and the SS would come and play table-tennis with us. I can remember, years later at the Auschwitz trial at Frankfurt where I was a witness, seeing some of these men again. Some of them had committed the most heinous crimes. To us, they were very nice. I remember one who said to a group of ten of us one day, "Come with me"; and we were very frightened because we thought he wanted to take us to the gas chambers; but he just took us for a walk and shared a big salami among us.[4] I saw the same SS-man quite calmly shoot other prisoners dead. Maybe they were nicer to us because we looked like real children. We had had our heads shaved in Theresienstadt as a hygiene measure; but since then our hair had been allowed to grow again; and we weren't quite walking skeletons. But I also knew that a German could be nice to you today and shoot you tomorrow, without thinking twice.

'One of the hardest things to get to grips with was that life was totally paradoxical. I can remember a prisoner in the punishment *Kommando* who made friends with me. He was a French Jew from Paris, arrested as a criminal. I don't know what his crimes had been, but he was also an intellectual, and he taught me not only how to pick a kapo's pocket of a fountain pen without the kapo noticing at all, but also about Spinoza. However, he was exceptional, and not everybody had the luck to meet such people. Most of the prisoners were in a dreadful state, mentally and physically. They weren't aware of the paradoxes of life in Auschwitz: they were only aware of the daily struggle with death.

'Because by this stage of the war Pohl's WVHA needed manpower, everyone who usefully could be was pressed into the service of the Reich on one level or another. We were put in charge of a cart which we had to drag around, sometimes distributing the bread rations, and sometimes hauling clothes from the gas chambers to *Kanada* for sorting. I remember that one cold day the kapo on guard at the gas chamber said, "Look, children, it's a cold day and there's nobody in there at the moment; why don't you pop in for a couple of minutes? It's warm in there." Well, I was a curious child, and when I was inside the building I asked one or two of the prisoners on duty there what this or that was used for, how things worked, and so on. Of course you weren't supposed to talk to *Sonderkommando* people; if they caught you doing that, they'd kill you. All the gassing was supposed to be secret.

'I got to know one of the SK people quite well though, and he had the job of burning the documents of those who went straight from the ramp to the gas. Can you imagine it – one day he turned up a photo of me – he found it by chance among a pile of papers belonging to a transport of maybe 10,000 people, and from it I knew that an uncle of mine who had been with us in Theresienstadt had now gone up the chimney. The whole place was crazy. I think it is impossible for anyone who wasn't there to grasp quite how crazy: there wasn't a consistent value in the place. Rationally, I think I accepted that there was no hope of getting out; but one still had a child's mind, and it was interested in the mechanics of the gas chamber, in just how the whole process worked. But maybe there was also nascent in me the unconscious artistic feeling which needs to absorb whatever it sees. Some people preferred not to know; that is a mentality I have never understood. You can't turn your back on anything. I memorized everything I saw.

'I knew I wanted to be an artist, and I had even had some lessons at Theresienstadt. More or less immediately after liberation, I started to draw what I remembered seeing. And after the war came the greatest disappointment of all, because nobody wanted to know, nobody wanted to hear our story; so we withdrew from the people who didn't want to listen, and we divided the world between us and them – largely because one of the main motivations for surviving at all was to tell of what had happened – for the sake of our dead parents.

'There was a tremendous solidarity among us children, and I think that was also a factor in helping each individual through, at least indirectly, because with fellow-feeling one's spirits are kept up. When our parents were taken away from us, for example, we knew what was going on. And not one of us could cry. But from that moment, though nothing was said, we helped each other in every way that we could.

We sold our last bits of saved bread to buy charcoal pills to help those with dysentery, for example. But the mutual help only extended within our group, although we helped another group of children brought in from Lodz who were separated from us by a barbed-wire fence and who were not so well treated. We were able to push a bowl of soup through to them now and then, if we were careful. I think our total solidarity was an attempt by all of us to replace our lost families with each other; and the loss of loved ones was a general, not an isolated thing: it happened to all of us. As I have said, too, as young children we had so little experience of any other kind of life. In Theresienstadt I used to yearn for home, and in Auschwitz I used to yearn for Theresienstadt, for it seemed like a kind of home by then. The thought of sleeping in a bed, for example, seemed almost too far-fetched to allow. Or even sitting in a chair. I couldn't grasp the memory of such a sensation any more. I had forgotten what it was like . . . I didn't see myself in a mirror for many years. The first time I did so again was after liberation; I had been ill with typhoid, and there was a mirror on the wall of the ward. I finally managed to crawl to it. What I saw made me feel sick, quite literally: I wanted to vomit. Of course I had seen other people who looked like that – I'd been surrounded by them. But it had never occurred to me that I looked like that too.

'On the one hand we were half-starved children in the camp; probably physically much younger than our years because of malnutrition; on the other, we were like a species of animal – tremendously alert, because life depended on it. I don't think the SS had any real concept of what they had turned us into. Can you imagine how I felt when I saw my father beaten up in front of me and I couldn't express my rage, because to have done so would have meant death there and then for us both?

'We had our own moral code: you could steal from the SS, or from kapos, but not from women with children [in the Family Camp]. I remember that one of our boys was so down that he did steal some bread from a mother. We ostracized him, and that was so terrible for him that he was driven to sell himself to a homosexual German in return for a piece of bread to make up for the one he'd stolen. But our code was among ourselves. There was no moral code in Auschwitz generally. How could there be? I remember when we arrived, we were waiting to be tattooed, and there were some Russian prisoners there as well. The SS wanted us all to give up what food we'd brought in with us. One of the Russians had a piece of salami, which he put in his mouth. An SS-man saw him and started to beat him, really savagely, just to make him spit out the salami; if he'd done so, the SS-man would have stopped, but he didn't. He was like an animal in his desperation. He needed the salami more than he needed to be free of pain.

'One saw the greatest moral strength too, though, and it was often shown by simple people. In Auschwitz you learnt that education and status mean nothing: the soul was stripped naked and showed itself for what it was, better or worse. There was no acting; we were past that.'

On 18 January 1945 they were evacuated from Auschwitz and marched to Mauthausen from where, some time later, they were transferred to Günskirchen. There they were liberated on 5 May.

'My friend Hugo Gryn was in Günskirchen too. It was a hard camp, and it was there that I witnessed cannibalism, though to say that makes it sound much more dreadful than it was. If anything, at the time it seemed natural, and the friend who'd eaten, who told me about it, was a simple creature from a little village: "Yehuda, you won't believe my luck. I went into the *Lazarett* just after the bombing raid, and it was unguarded, and there was a dead body in there, and I managed to cut off some thigh where there was most meat before the others came up and tore up the rest between them." Again, it's very complicated; whom do you blame? Not the cannibals. The machine that made them like that, that dehumanized them? But it hadn't dehumanized me, or indeed many of us, to that extent. The thing about cannibalism is not the action of eating human flesh in itself so much as the decay of moral and ethical civilization that it represents.

'I contracted spotted typhus in Günskirchen, and the illness ate up the last of my strength. If liberation had come ten days later, I would not have lived to see it. As it was, I weighed 33 kilogrammes when the Allies arrived. I was hardly alive physically any more.

'After our liberation, however, two of us had the crazy idea that we would walk to Switzerland. Of course we couldn't walk half a mile, but we started. Everything was confusion. We'd taken some bread from a store in Günskirchen, but we were waylaid by some liberated Russian POWs who took it from us. It was just as well – later we learnt that the SS had poisoned the bread in the store before abandoning the camp. We passed an American patrol and begged them for bread. And they apologized and said that they hadn't any to give us – only cookies – would they do? And they had a tiny tin of cheese, which we opened and bit into, but we couldn't eat it – it was too rich for us to stomach. In fact we were lucky because, although the American troops weren't allowed to give lifts to former KZ-inmates on account of the diseases we carried, we were the only two on this road – all the others had opted for Wels. When the GIs heard our crazy plan to get to Switzerland, they took pity on us and arranged for us to have accommodation in a nearby house; and so for the first time in three years we slept in beds, with pillows and linen: it was beyond our dreams, and it can never be conveyed. But in the morning it was obvious that we were too ill to carry on, so the GIs took us to the hospital in Steyr, which was nearby, and forced the local doctors to accept us. In fact they took very good care of us there, and the nurses were all nuns.

'Later we were repatriated to Czechoslovakia and taken to Prague. The Jewish organizations had not yet developed any programme on behalf of the children returning alone from the KZ; but there was one man in the town, a saintly man called Premysl Pitter, who had made preparations precisely for the reception of child survivors. I think people believed what we told them about what had happened, but then they pushed it away – except for this one very wonderful man. He was a true Christian, and it is right that he should be commemorated in the Avenue of the Righteous at Yad Vashem. I later dedicated a drawing to him, which is in the Yad Vashem collection. He gave me back my faith in human beings.

'The principal emotional reaction to liberation was endless sadness. Do you know the sculpture by Michelangelo in the Uffizi of "The Victor"? He doesn't look glad. He only looks into the future with sadness. No one enjoys victory – it's over as soon as it's achieved. Suddenly you can stop working, and you see your real situation. For us it was this: no one else had come back; we were alone, and the outside world didn't care. There was a world of habits to unlearn, too. Do you know when I first saw a funeral after liberation I burst out laughing! "People are crazy; for one person they make a casket and play solemn music? A few weeks ago I saw thousands of bodies piled up to be burnt like so much junk." And I remember when I went to a theatre, I found myself calculating how long it would take to gas the audience, and which of their clothes would be salvageable, and how much gold their teeth would yield, how many sackfuls of hair they were worth. These thoughts just came automatically; they even seemed funny, for if you weren't able to laugh you just didn't stay alive for a moment.

'But the underlying emotion was sadness. We didn't speak the same language as the outsiders, it seemed. We were isolated by our experience and it looked as if it would go on being like that. We were 16, and we felt like old men. I went back to school, but of course I was so much older than my teachers: what could they teach us? What was the point of sitting there? And people told us how they had also suffered: "We had ration cards," they said. "We only got two eggs a week." I was very sad for a long period after the war – for years – but I was not exhausted, and I had a goal in my life, which counted for a lot. And I could express my bad feelings through my drawings and get them out of my system.

'My education as an artist had begun with some lessons in Theresienstadt, and I even had a few in Auschwitz. That was odd. You could be hanged for owning a pencil in Auschwitz, but the huge transports of

447

Hungarians in the summer of 1944 brought with them some artists, and they were retained by the SS to do family portraits and so forth for them. One of these men ended up in the punishment *Kommando* and thus I came to meet him and he gave me a few "private lessons". I resumed my studies in Prague, with an anti-Fascist German who had been a friend of Kafka and Max Brod. His name was Willi Novak. I had no state help, or anything. I got an introduction to Novak through Hans Günther Adler, who was a friend of his. I was still staying in the castle the state had given to Premysl Pitter just outside Prague to use as his hostel for children, and they gave me bread and eggs as my food for the day when I went into Prague to study, and I used them to pay Novak. It was a gesture. He didn't need money and he didn't take private students, apart from me.

'There was no real reason to choose Israel as the place to live after the war – at least, there was no political reason. As long as I was allowed to draw, I didn't care if I was in Jerusalem or at the Prague Academy. I had no family left in Europe, and when they suggested Israel to me, I said, "Fine, as long as I can go to art school." It was all I cared about. I stayed in Prague longer than most of the others – I didn't get here until March 1946, and I came quite legally. There were so few orphan children in Czechoslovakia that it wasn't necessary to come any other way. Of course my older sister was here – all that remained of my family. I remember I had vague hopes that she would be like a mother to me, but she was about to marry and she was living on a *kibbutz*. She had her own life to lead, so I lived on my own in Jerusalem and studied. I had a tiny scholarship which didn't allow me to die! At that time, things were as austere here as they were in Europe, and there were so many new immigrants that individuals didn't matter. I had a vague sense of looking for roots, or establishing some, at any rate; but I'd missed three years of education, and I lacked self-confidence; so I studied and studied, and read a lot – and caught up as best I could. In the course of time I became a graduate of the Bezalel School here, and later I studied abroad – at the Central School in London. I was lucky, I had arrived in Jerusalem armed with letters of recommendation from Willi Novak and Max Brod; but I was isolated, for at that time most young immigrants were taken up by Youth Aliyah, which was only interested in very practical things like agriculture. I starved again and, in some ways, life was as horrible as it had been in Auschwitz: especially as there I starved for only one year. Here, to begin with, I starved for four! But don't let me exaggerate. There were a few other students who had been in the camps, and when you're a student you don't really feel too bad; you might even feel that a little hunger is good for the soul! I had enough friends, and plenty to occupy my mind. Those were the main things. Then later, by a miracle, I discovered some other relatives, and they took me to South Africa, where I had my first foreign exhibition.

'After the war, people came here from the USA and South Africa to look for relatives who might have survived the Holocaust. The relatives of mine from South Africa tracked me down, and it transpired that they had no children of their own, and that there was a lost younger brother who had been artistically inclined. At the time I was living in a little room with no water and no electricity: one really had nothing. My relatives were very eager to help, and I gave them some drawings to take back with them. They managed to get an exhibition organized for me in Johannesburg, and sent me an air-ticket. Getting a ticket to Africa was like a dream. I was so poor that I could afford only one shirt a year. Now my life was developing like a kitsch romance. I was going to Africa! And there I experienced for the first time in my adult life what it was like to be in a real family. There were other advantages: I could eat as much as I liked! I went for three months, the first time. I had set out with my worldly wealth in my pocket: $5.

'That trip to South Africa marked the beginning of three years of travel and study. I was mainly concentrating on portraits and life drawings, and working on woodcuts and in oils. I studied lithography for a year in Paris, and etching in London. The voyage to London was financed – just – by the sale of work at my exhibition in South Africa. And after my time away I returned to Jerusalem and started my career proper – teaching at Bezalel, and beginning to have my own exhibitions.

'I was never really tempted to live anywhere else but here – I had established my home here, and made friends. Maybe if I had been a good businessman I could have made it somewhere else, but I lack talent in that direction! During my time abroad, however, I was developing my own art. Like every student, I wanted to draw as much as possible, and to visit all the world's art-centres, and I managed to make many very low-budget trips in Europe! I got to Florence and Rome and Naples, and to see all the other main collections. And many artists were very close to me then – especially Rembrandt and Breughel and Bosch and Goya. And of the moderns, Picasso, Braque and Matisse.

'I only painted the Holocaust as a subject during the very first years after the war. There was a need to get it out of my system. I wanted to record remembered impressions too – of the gas chambers, of a Mussulman; and to express the suffering of the poor people imprisoned with me. Through the work I developed psychologically in my approach to the suffering: first of all, it was blind suffering and then it changed, became refined and moved towards compassion. Later it moved beyond that still, and then suffering began to transmute into beauty – but this took a long time; and all of it, even the last phase, was infused with sadness. None of this development was conscious; but the minute I was strong enough to hold a pencil I started to draw the Holocaust. I cannot rationalize why – I could say that I did it in order to record while the memory was still fresh – though that isn't a satisfactory, or even accurate, answer. I was still a child. I was 16. I wasn't thinking. I picked up a pencil and drew: if I was hungry I would pick up a piece of bread and eat.

'I never felt the slightest desire for personal revenge. I went back to Ostrava, once, in 1945, just to see our old house, and the window I'd looked out of as a child. It was all a world away. But they had Germans out in the street, shovelling snow: old men, too – doing to them as they had done to us. And people said to me: "Look, throw a stone at them, you can, you know." And given that opportunity, I didn't want to. Would throwing a stone at the head of an old man bring my father's ashes back out of the Vistula? It would only make the old man hate me; and the hate would continue then, and go on and on. I had had enough of that.

'But I understand the feelings of those who did find it necessary to take revenge, to relieve their feelings that way. And I thought about it very deeply, and considered how much it might solve. The Czechs expelled the Sudeten Germans after the war with great cruelty; and Premysl Pitter, as well as looking after the survivor children, also took care of the German children orphaned in those times. So that we were placed in close proximity with German children, and some of them had been in the Hitler Youth. The interesting thing is that we got on, because the more you suffer, the more likely you are to end up by overcoming your hate; and Premysl Pitter provided a tremendous example for us. Only he and Leo Baeck, in my opinion, in the whole of Europe, had that breadth of vision in the early post-war days. The fact that he let us alone politically, unlike some of the Zionist groups at work with survivors after the war, was great therapy for us. He gave us room to draw breath.

'I wanted to find out for myself how I would react personally to Germans, and so, at a time when nobody was going to Germany – we didn't even have diplomatic relations with them then – I applied for a visa. It wasn't easy, but I succeeded. I needed to confront the Germans, and through that confront myself. I went back to Mauthausen, too. I hadn't seen it since I was a boy of 16. Now I was a man of 28. I went alone. It was necessary. Of course, when I talked to the Austrians in the town, none of them knew anything about a concentration camp, so I invented a little cover-story for myself: I told them I was an American studying the atrocities the *Germans* had committed during the war. Then their faces cleared and they pointed out the camp where the Germans had committed their atrocities; it was, of course, nothing to do with the Austrians!

'Mauthausen seemed much smaller than I remembered it, and it was indeed small. Only the thousands who had been crammed into it made it seem large. What hadn't changed was the beautiful landscape it is set in. I remember that even when I arrived there at the end of the death-march I was overwhelmed by the beauty of the scenery surrounding it.

'In Germany, I was very lucky; I met people with whom I became good friends, and I have remained so with them to this day – we are even on *Du* terms! One of the things which I think compelled me to make this journey was the common desire of the artist to make something out of suffering and thereby to give suffering purpose. I remember that when I was a witness at Eichmann's trial I was asked by the BBC and by CBS whether I had learnt anything from my suffering; and I said that I thought I had because the pain had been shattering enough to enable me to reach my soul. And when you reach the base of your soul, I think you learn not only about yourself, but about all men; and thus you grow; and that is positive. I am not saying that my experience is universal; I am saying that I have been fortunate that the experience has turned out this way for me.

'But it is also true that the degree of suffering, once experienced and survived, does not inure you to any further suffering in the future. I used to think that it would, but I have since come to realize that that is merely a comfortable thought. Each new misery demands a new battle. Nothing is sure. It is like God: the minute you think you have Him in your grasp, He is gone again. I think that setbacks sustained by a survivor in his post-war existence can cause him twice as much pain as an ordinary person, because he is so vulnerable to it. On the other hand, one knows for a certainty that the pain will pass. One of the very simple things that helped me in the KZ was this: "Today I was hit 20 times; but I wasn't hit 30 times. Therefore I am happy. As long as you aren't dead, things could always be worse than they are." That is such a cliché. But unfortunately it is true: and believe me, in the camps you learnt just how true.

'One of the aspects of the relationship of the survivor to the Germans is that coloured by reparation. It was a very complicated question. There was a tremendous furore when Ben Gurion accepted the large payments from Adenauer – some people didn't want anything from Germany, didn't want to become involved with the question of forgiveness, and didn't want to recognize Germany at all. I get a pension, but it took years and years to come through, and the file my lawyer built up was six inches thick. The whole process is a nightmare of bureaucracy; a lot of people couldn't bear to go through with it and preferred to go without a pension completely rather than face the medical examinations and so on that were involved, together with cross-examination about one's time in the camps, and generally being treated much more like a criminal than a victim. I went to Berlin from London, where I was at the time, for my medical examinations, because they told me that in that way my application would be processed more quickly; and I have to say that the doctors were not unpleasant to me personally. But of course the X-rays reminded me of the experiments Clauberg and the others did in *Block* 10 – trying to sterilize people by burning their genitals with X-rays.

'I've never thought about whether the pension was adequate or not, and in any case I don't touch it – it goes into a trust for my children. What struck me as unfair was that the people who got reparation earliest, and who were most generously treated, were the claimants from Germany who hadn't even been in the camps; and I do get outraged by the bureaucratic letters I get from the German authorities enquiring rudely into my financial affairs.

'I don't feel bitter. Bureaucracy makes me angry, as does the irony of the very word *Wiedergutmachung*. Making good *again*. Again. What nonsense! And I feel very angry that we are made to think that we should be falling over backwards with gratitude for this money they are giving us out of the goodness of their hearts. I sometimes think they wish we had all died so as not to be an embarrassment to them. But what the hell, we don't live in Utopia, and if the bureaucrats in charge of reparation really cared, they'd go mad; because the details on the files are horrible. After reading ten case-histories you would have to switch your feelings off. It comes down to the old question of how difficult it is to be a human being 24 hours a day!

'The question of forgiveness is equally complex. Quite early on, in the mid-Sixties, when no one would speak to Germans, I invited a German social worker to dinner with me. He was taken aback, but accepted. When he got here, he told me how his taxi-driver, discovering his nationality, had thrown him out of his cab. That doesn't solve anything.

'I come from a conventionally, not especially strict, religious background, but I think that I have developed my own religious philosophy, and that the experience of the concentration camps is just one contributory factor to it. I cannot believe, with some people, that God does not exist, on the grounds that, if He did, he wouldn't have allowed Auschwitz; nor can I believe that He does exist because He saved me. For me it is not true belief to argue that God is good only when He is good to me. And even if He isn't good as I conceive morality, does that mean that He is no longer God? We are hampered because we can only judge God with human minds. There are a thousand theories, and none answers the question satisfactorily. I'd rather be quiet. I cannot define my feelings about God. I cannot say I believe in Him in the same way that I believe in a table, because it is palpably there: that belief doesn't change me; it isn't mystical belief. Perhaps there should be no belief in God more than a search for Him. Or, to put it another way, perhaps faith should be a search. It depends on the individual's need for a commitment to something; and on how far one is prepared to go before one is satisfied with the answers to one's questions. People can easily, and happily, spend their lives committed to one country, or one political party. I can't even feel homesick for my homeland, because there was nothing left for me there. I had been uprooted like a flower, and replanted in the soil of Israel, and the problem for me here was that it was a long time before the roots took. I wasn't a committed Zionist. It was hard to learn a new language which had no personal connection with me. And I have never been committed to anything but my painting and my students, because that is where I think I can give something.

'Adapting to life here seemed endless, though getting into the way of being an art student helped. In 1948 or 1949, one of my teachers – a man I was very fond of – died. And at his funeral I cried, before I knew what I was doing, and I said to myself, "Yehuda, how wonderful – now you are a human being again." It was a revelation to me to have human feelings again. The road back was an enormously long one, because it had to do with rejoining humanity, not just getting used to a new physical environment. The question of language is important. What language do I think in? Many. I was brought up speaking Czech and German. We talked German at home, and Czech at school. Here, I learnt Hebrew and English. But if I had to say, I would say that I think in Czech and German, though I talk English very much with my wife, who is American. I met her here, but it is my second marriage. My first wife, from whom I am divorced, is English. I don't think personal relationships such as these helped me adapt, in that sense. I didn't marry at all until I was 30, since I devoted all the early years to study, and by the time I did, there was less urgent need to talk about the KZ, which in any case I had been able to externalize successfully through my work.

'None of us get back completely. I think that all of us dream. I used to dream that I was in the gas chambers again, but in the dream Mengele caught me and said to me, "This time you won't get out again." I had that dream often. And recently there was a little exhibition here – organized by some young Germans who do a form of overseas voluntary aid as moral reparation – about the camps, and it contained a text by a member of the *Sonderkommando* – one of the texts they wrote and buried in tins in the ground, which were discovered years later. I knew the text already, but I hadn't read it for years. It described the killing of a transport of 1,000 children. The night following my visit to the exhibition I dreamt again. A dream of fire in the chimneys; and we were in the camp, watching, and I turned to someone and said, "Why don't we have weapons, why don't we go and help the children?" But we stood helpless, and after a time the fire ceased and the chimney was dark.

'That is another trigger: seeing factory chimneys. There's a brick factory on the road from Jerusalem to Tel Aviv. It looks exactly like a crematorium, and has the same flames, the same smoke. But, you see, quite often our reaction is to laugh, and to get on with our lives. It depends on how one is feeling. There are times when I can read a good deal of concentration camp literature without any ill-effect; but at other times I cannot cope with it. And I know people who have never read one book on the subject, and who not only won't discuss the Holocaust at all – they won't even discuss unpleasant matters in general. Many of my friends won't speak about it, even to their wives and children, but I never for a moment wanted to keep the KZ experience buried, so I spoke openly about it always – that was never a problem for me. In general, here, it was little spoken of until Eichmann's trial. That trial was in many ways a deliberate historical object-lesson for the new generation, and opened the subject up considerably. Now, there is a kind of Holocaust-industry, with all the in-fighting and political jockeying that that implies.

'For me, the fact that I could talk about it freely kept me sane; but I also accepted the KZ as an integral part of my life, just as I accept the suffering that it has made me heir to, since it seems to me that there is little that I can do about it anyway, and I certainly can't pretend that it didn't happen or that it hasn't affected me, because it has, profoundly and for ever. For years, I couldn't enjoy all kinds of pleasures, though. I couldn't listen to popular music; I couldn't go anywhere where people were happy or dancing. I felt, "Knowing what has happened in the world, how do these people dare to be happy?" I was alienated from them, though I wasn't a loner. I wasn't abnormal and I didn't stand outside society. I had girlfriends, and I could take moderate pleasure in things – but too much seemed to be a crime and a betrayal. I think I was fortunate, finally, because I was naturally equipped with the ability to see things as an artist does, and that enabled me to do something with the experience I had had which others, less lucky, were not able to do. They were changed by it but they were not articulate enough to identify or utilize the change, or come to terms with it. Those are the people upon whom the KZ has had its most damaging effect.

'When we former concentration camp children get together, we tend to laugh about shared experiences if we reminisce. I've noticed that older survivors – those who were born nearer the beginning of the century – tend to be more serious when they talk together. We laugh, I think, because humour was a great preserver, literally, of sanity –

then and now. It could be quite cruel. When we were crowded into the cattle-waggons to go part of the way from Auschwitz to Mauthausen, someone would say, "There're too many of us in here – some of you will have to go up the chimney." Or if there was an old man around – and I am referring to someone of perhaps 30 or 40 (because at 30 you were old, and at 40 you no longer had the right to be alive) – we might say, "You old fool, you've already got one foot in the crematorium, what're you cluttering the place up here for?" It was difficult to adapt from that atmosphere to normal life; and for years after the war, one couldn't help having immediate KZ reactions to normal things: that man's old, what on earth is he doing alive? And one would size people up by KZ standards: what would they have been like in the camp? What would their chances of survival have been?

'But I think it is harder for the older survivors. Their lives were messed up; they lost wives and children. They can't look back to the camps without remembering that. It was easier for us; with the KZ behind us, we still had all our lives in front of us: a clean sheet; and because we had been children, we were quicker to recover – and we were able to recover, as children often can, with a laugh. Children are very speedy adapters – and that is a great key not only to survival but to getting away from the influence of hell. But I think that anyone who was in the KZ has a permanent trauma, and thus you are fundamentally changed, for better or worse. You can never go back to being the person you were before. It's like Adam after being sent out of the Garden of Eden. Or, to put it another way: we survivors are like people whose house roofs have blown off, and the winds can blow all sorts of terrors and ghosts in; our security is gone, and nothing is or can be comfortable any more. Even people who have been mugged, or who have had their houses burgled, lose their sense of security; how much more when your senses have been raped, and raped systematically for years?

'I have talked to my own children about it, but only in response to questions, and only told them what they have wanted to know. One son's first question was, "How did they burn the Jews?" That was the first question he ever asked – and virtually the first words he ever spoke – so he was very young, and he must have absorbed the atmosphere about him. There had been TV crews in the house at the time quite often, interviewing me about Eichmann, and so on. Some time before the Eichmann trial, Yad Vashem asked all of us to write a few pages of testimony. I hate to write: I have never had any formal training beyond very early schooling. And in what language should I write? In any case I write very badly in all languages – my grammar is terrible and I make dozens of spelling mistakes. So I said I would do a taped interview, and this made a document of about 70 pages. Now, when they caught Eichmann they went through the archive of testimonies, and it was from that that they asked me to be a witness. I appeared for about two or three hours altogether at the trial. Confronting Eichmann was not a problem. He was a remote figure. And they only asked me questions about the conditions in the camp, and about one or two specific cases that were known to me.

'All in all, I am not sure that I have adjusted well. The memory is always with me, by my side. I don't even know if "memory" is the right word, so vivid is the impression it makes. If I'd adjusted well, perhaps I'd be rich, a go-getter, aggressive. But I don't care about things beyond my art – material things. Maybe it's just that I don't have the guts to be ambitious. What I think is most important in life is to be able to establish real relationships on an individual level which involve sharing what you have. You don't always succeed, but you have to keep on trying. If we all tried to do that more, we would be far more effectively on the way to peace than we are with all the great sentimental organizations of international brotherhood, or the vainglory of politics which changes the surface, but never the soul. And the memory of the Holocaust should be kept alive, not so much as a memorial, but as a lesson. This thing happened, and it could happen again, anywhere.

'The memories are so strong that they can annihilate the present, and that is a grave danger. I wouldn't say in my own case that has ever happened, because the reality of living life is strong for me, and there is much in life to interest me, so that the horrors of the past have to share my mind with a host of other, pleasanter, diffuse experiences. However, the memories can still make what is happening now seem insignificant, and I believe that all of us suffer from depression. I have a friend in Germany who tells me that it can hit him out of nowhere. He can be driving along and then have to stop the car because he has begun to cry; because it has become too much for him to bear. Again, I am fortunate in that I can use my depression. It is my job as an artist to make myself channel it into creativity; and coping with the very technical problems of resolving the relationship between *Dichtung* and *Wahrheit* – expression and the truth behind it – itself helps one to be strong, because it forces one to be disciplined. Do you know the little story of Freud's? That both the madman and the artist can experience what it is like to be one with the ocean – but the madman dissolves in it like a grain of salt; the artist comes back and describes what it is like.

'I trust people now, and I think it is better to risk trusting them and to be disappointed sometimes than not to trust anyone at all, because I believe that the act of trust in itself can bring out good. Sometimes you get abused, but you must never yourself transmit negative feelings. Who knows, you may have left a seed of something in the person who's abused you. I think all one can do is find one's sphere of influence and try to be as good and as positive and as creative as one can within it, and hope that the effect of this will spread. You create a microcosm – I leave trying to do something about the macrocosm to the politicians, who must be great optimists. But they won't change anything – and they might, finally, destroy us. Power is the worst thing. We children in Auschwitz had such power over the other prisoners. If they did anything to harm us, they would be killed, because of our special status. And how did we react? Some of us stole bread and gave it to the less fortunate prisoners. And some of us beat them mercilessly – for no other reason than that we could. One boy struck so viciously that he broke his own hand. I know him still, we are friends. He is harmless; he's never done anything like that since; and is it so hard to understand why he did it? I don't think so, though I am sure he has never reflected upon it himself. That is the kind of memory which gets buried.

'All suffering is relative to experience; and life, while it is everything, is also not much at all. A century is nothing, and a generation is nothing. We can only enjoy our time here and cope with it on a personal level. Friends, family, love – these are the important things. These are the things that last, and with which we can – if we are lucky – rebuild.'

Epilogue

Most survivors suffer more than they show. It is an aspect of human nature in our society not to bare one's soul, and survivors are no exception to the rule which determines our behaviour in this respect. There are those, too, whose post-war lives have been blighted by further tragedies which cannot be connected to what they went through in the camps, since their behaviour has not been a determinant of those tragedies; although it is significant that they tend to seek a link, or to blame themselves for any failure in either a relationship or the way a child grows up.

However, all the survivors I met had one quality in common: generosity. They were generous with their time, in their giving of trust, and in straightforward hospitality. The giving of food and drink in some cases was an important rite, to be observed on the smallest occasion. Tola L, who spent two and a half years in Birkenau, offers refreshment to anyone who crosses her threshold. And Elie Cohen, who had never met me, immediately suggested I stay with him for the three days of our meeting, rather than have me stay at a hotel. Everybody I met was generous to me personally, and generous in spirit. Of course this trait might be coincidental, but it was so consistently present that I think it is not.

I was not able to speak to everybody who responded positively to my requests, or who wrote to me as a result of articles or notices about my research in such publications as the *Jewish Chronicle*, the *Association of Jewish Refugees Newsletter*, and the *Polish Daily*, but I was overwhelmed with the response I had. In only two or three cases was help refused, and then for reasons which were understandable. Further, survivors who had their own written material, published and unpublished, were extremely generous in not only allowing me access to it, but in permitting me to use it.

At the beginning of this book, in the dedication, I mentioned the courage that survivors have. All carry a physical and mental legacy from the KZ and, however easily some may appear to be able to talk about their time in the camps, the memories are a source of great pain; reliving them, while a necessary action, is a hard one to perform. For some, I believe I provided an outlet which until now, after so long, they had not been able to find among their own families and friends; but that is the extent to which I was able to return the favour bestowed on me. I may add that more often than not I came away from meeting a survivor far more inspirited than depressed.

'What doesn't destroy me makes me stronger,' said Nietzsche; but it would be a mistake to say that every survivor who came out of the camps necessarily changed. Myriam Pfeffer, a survivor of the Kovno ghetto and Stutthof, who now lives in Paris, was divested of any materialistic desires by her experience; but her sister, who had been materialistic before the war, emerged from the KZ if anything even more so, and cannot understand Myriam's indifference. Most survivors have acknowledged that their experience has brought about some kind of increased spiritual awareness, but equally, most would agree that the experience was not worth having, simply in terms of the greater awareness derived from it. I was struck, too, by the fact that in nearly every case there was no desire for revenge. Interestingly, but perhaps not surprisingly, it was replaced by a desire – a nagging desire – to understand why it happened, to be able to explain and rationalize the Nazis' behaviour. To understand an evil does not mean only that it is easier to forgive it; it means too that you can more easily live with the memory of it. That lack of understanding is, I think, one of the main reasons why the spirits of survivors cannot be completely still.

There are further conclusions which could be reached, but to do so in an ordered way would produce another book. In any case, it is my hope that anybody reading this one will be able to draw his or her own. For myself, I mourn those who died, and I do not forget those who were broken for ever by the experience of the KZ. But I also remember, and celebrate, those ordinary human beings who went through the ice and fire of hell and came out with their souls.

Glossary

Appellplatz roll-call square; also scene of public executions

Aufseher (Aufseherin) guard (female guard)

Aussenkommando A *Kommando* working outside the main camp; sometimes used to designate a sub-camp

Blockälteste(r) prisoner *Block* Senior

Blockschreiber prisoner *Block* Clerk

Block barrack

Bunker punishment barrack; camp prison

HKB (Lazarett, Revier) camp 'hospital'

Holocaust the destruction of the Jews in the camps

Judenrat Jewish Council in the ghetto

Kommando work-detail

Koje bunk

Lagerstrasse main road of a camp

Läufer (Läuferin) runner or messenger (female form in German)

Nachschlag a second helping

Piepl prisoner bum-boy

Priviligierte (Prominent) privileged prisoner

Pyjama ('Zebra-Suit') nicknames for the uniform of the KZ

RSHA *Reichssicherheitshauptamt*: the main security department of the Third Reich, created in 1939 and combining the Gestapo, the criminal police, and the *Sicherheitsdienst* (security service)

Selection the selection made by the camp doctors or their delegates concerning which inmates or arrivals were fit for work, and which should be gassed

Sonderkommando (SK) the work-detail responsible for the burning or other removal of the gassed bodies

Stubendienst subordinate to the *Blockälteste*

WVHA *Wirtschafts- und Verwaltungshauptamt*: the SS economic and administrative office. Under Oswald Pohl, it controlled the economic concerns of the SS and administered the KZ

Zählappell roll-call

Select Bibliography

Adler, Hans Günther:
  *Theresienstadt 1941–45: Das
  Antlitzeiner
  Zwangsgemeinschaft*
  (J.C.B. Mohr, 1960 [2nd edn])
Améry, Jean: *Jenseits von Schuld
  und Sühne* (Szczasny, 1966)
Arad, Yitzhak: *Ghetto in Flames*
  (Holocaust Library, 1982)
Arendt, Hannah: *Eichmann in
  Jerusalem* (Viking, revised edn, 1964)
Bauer, Yehuda: *Flight and Rescue,
  Brichah* (Random House, 1970); *My
  Brother's Keeper* (Jewish
  Publication Society of the USA,
  1974); *The Holocaust in
  Historical Perspective* (Washington
  UP, 1978); *American Jewry and
  the Holocaust* (Wayne State UP,
  1981)
Bayfield, Tony: *Churban* (Michael
  Goulston Educational
  Foundation, 1981)
BELSEN (Irgun Sheerit Hapleita
  Me'haezor Habriti, 1957)
Berenbaum, Michael (ed): *From
  Holocaust to New Life* (American
  Gathering of Jewish Holocaust
  Survivors, 1985)
Bergman and Jucovy (eds):
  Generations of the Holocaust
  (Basic, 1982)
Bernadac, Christian: *L'Holocauste
  Oublié – le Massacre des Tsiganes*
  (France-Empire, 1979)
Bettelheim, Bruno: *The Informed
  Heart* (Free Press, 1960)

Bezwinska and Czech (eds): *KL
  Auschwitz Seen by the SS*
  (Panstwowe Muzeum w
  Oswiecimiu, 1978)
Bloch, Sam (ed): *From Holocaust to
  Redemption* (World Gathering
  of Jewish Holocaust Survivors,
  1984)
Bor, Josef: *Terezin Requiem*
  (Heinemann, 1963)
Bower, Tom: *The Paperclip
  Conspiracy* (Michael Joseph,
  1987)
Brenner, Robert Reeve: *The Faith
  and Doubt of Holocaust
  Survivors* (Free Press, 1980)
Brewster, Eva: *Vanished in
  Darkness* (NeWest, 1984)
Brome, Vincent: *The Way Back*
  (Cassell, 1957)
Brumlik, Kiesel, Kugelmann and
  Schoeps (eds): *Jüdisches Leben in
  Deutschland seit 1945*
  (Athenäum, 1986)
*Centralkontoret for Særlige
  Anliggender for Storkøbenhavn –
  Beretning* (Copenhagen, 1947)
Cohen, Elie A.: *Human Behaviour
  in the Concentration Camp* (Cape,
  1954); *The Abyss* (Norton, 1973);
  *De negentien treinen naar
  Sobibor* (Sijthoff, 1985)
Davidoff, Lucy: *The War Against the
  Jews* (Holt, Rinehart and Winston,
  1975)
Des Près, Terrence: *The Survivor*
  (Oxford UP, New York, 1976)

Dinnerstein, Leonard: *America and the Survivors of the Holocaust* (Columbia UP, 1982)

Distel and Jakusch (eds): *Konzentrationslager Dachau 1933–1945* (Comité International de Dachau, 1978)

Donat, Alexander: *The Holocaust Kingdom* (Secker and Warburg, 1965)

Donat, Alexander (ed): *The Death Camp Treblinka* (Holocaust Library, 1977)

Döring, Hans-Joachim: *Die Zigeuner im NS-Staat* (Kriminalistik Verlag, Vol. 12, Hamburg, 1964)

Drozdzynski, Alexander (ed): *Das verspottete Tausendjährige Reich* (Droste, 1978)

Eban, Abba: *Heritage: Civilisation and the Jews* (Weidenfeld and Nicolson, 1984)

Eitinger, Leo: *Concentration Camp Survivors in Norway and Israel* (Martinus Nijhoff, 1972)

Eitinger, Leo, and Krell, Robert: *The Psychological and Medical Effects of Concentration Camps and Related Persecutions on Survivors of the Holocaust* (University of British Columbia Press, 1985)

Eitinger, Leo, and Strøm, Axel: *Mortality and Morbidity after Excessive Stress* (Oslo Universitetsforlaget/ Humanities Press, 1973)

Elkins, Michael: *Forged in Fury* (Piatkus, 1981)

Encyclopaedia Judaica (Keter, Jerusalem, 1971)

Fénélon, Fania: *Playing for Time* (Sphere, 1980)

Ferencz, Benjamin B.: *Less Than Slaves – Jewish Forced Labour and the Quest for Compensation* (Harvard UP, 1979)

Fest, Joachim: *The Face of the Third Reich* (Penguin, 1972); *Hitler* (Penguin, 1983)

Filmer and Schwan (eds): *Mensch, der Krieg ist aus!* (Econ, 1985)

Francesconi, H.:

Extremtraumatisierung und ihre Folgen für die nächste Generation (Sensen, 1983)

Frank, Anne: *Diary* (Pan, 1968)

Frankl, Viktor: *. . . trotzdem Ja zum Leben sagen: ein Psychologe erlebt das KZ* (dtv, 1982)

Friedlander, Albert: *Leo Baeck, Teacher of Theresienstadt* (Holt, Rinehart and Winston, 1968)

Friedlander, Albert (ed): *Out of the Whirlwind* (Union of American Hebrew Congregations, 1968)

Friedländer, Saul: *Counterfeit Nazi* (Weidenfeld and Nicolson, 1967); *When Memory Comes* (Avon/ Discus, 1980)

Garcia, Max: *As Long As I Remain Alive* (Portals, 1979)

Garlinski, Jozef: *Fighting Auschwitz* (Julian Friedmann, 1975)

Gilbert, Martin: *Final Journey* (Allen & Unwin, 1979); *Auschwitz and the Allies* (Michael Joseph, 1981); *Atlas of the Holocaust* (Michael Joseph, 1982); *The Holocaust: The Jewish Tragedy* (Collins, 1986)

Grof, Stanislav: *Beyond the Brain: Birth, Death and Transcendence in Psychotherapy* (State University of New York Press, 1985)

Guttmann and Rothkirchen (eds): *The Catastrophe of European Jewry* (Yad Vashem, 1976)

Haag, Lina: *Eine Handvoll Staub* (Röderberg, 1977)

Haas, Albert: *The Doctor and the Damned* (Granada, 1985)

Hammer, Gottlieb: *Good Faith and Credit* (Cornwall Books, 1985)

Hart, Kitty: *Return to Auschwitz* (Granada, 1983)

Hausner, Gideon: *Justice in Jerusalem* (Harper and Row, 1966)

Heger, Heinz: *The Men with the Pink Triangle* (Alyson/Gay Men's Press, 1980)

Helweg-Larsen, Hoffmeyer, Kieler, Hess-Thaysen, Hess-Thaysen, Thygesen and Wulff: *Famine Disease in German Concentration Camps –*

Complications and Sequels
(Acta Medica Scandinavica,
Supplementum CCLXXIV,
Copenhagen, 1952)

Herzstein, Robert Edwin: *The War
That Hitler Won* (Hamish
Hamilton, 1979); *When Nazi
Dreams Come True* (Abacus,
1982)

Hilberg, Raul: *The Destruction of
the European Jews* (Quadrangle,
1961)

Hillesum, Etty: *Etty* (Triad Panther,
1985)

Hitler, Adolf: *My Struggle*
(Paternoster Library, 1933)

Hohmann, Joachim S. (and others):
*Zigeunerleben – Beiträge zur
Sozialgeschichte einer Verfolgung*
(MS, 1980)

Ibach, Karl: *Kemna* (Hammer, 1981)

Joffo, Joseph: *Un sac de billes* (Livre
de Poche, 1973)

Joll, James: *Europe since 1870*
(Weidenfeld and Nicolson, 1973)

'Ka-Tzetnik' (Yehiel Diner): *Piepl*
(Anthony Blond, 1961)

Kedward, H.R.: *Fascism in Western
Europe, 1900–1945* (Blackie, 1969)

Kempner, Robert M.W.: *Das dritte
Reich im Kreuzverhör*
(Athenäum, 1980)

Keneally, Thomas: *Schindler's Ark*
(Hodder and Stoughton, 1982)

King, C.E.: *The Nazi State and the
New Religions* (Edwin Mellen
Press, 1982)

Kogon, Eugen: *The Theory and
Practice of Hell* (Farrar, Straus
and Co., c.1950)

Kolb, Eberhard: *Bergen-Belsen*
(Verlag für Literatur und
Zeitgeschehen, Hanover, 1962)

Kraus, Ota, and Kulka, Erich: *The
Death Factory* (Pergamon, 1966)

Krausnik, Helmut, and Broszat,
Martin: *Anatomy of the SS State*
(Paladin, 1970)

Kuznetsov, Anatoly: *Babi Yar*
(MacGibbon and Kee, 1967)

Langbein, Hermann: *Nicht wie die
Schafe zur Schlachtbank*
(Fischer, 1980)

Lanzmann, Claude: *Shoah – the
complete text of the film*
(Pantheon, 1985)

Laqueur, Renate: *Bergen-Belsen
Tagebuch* (Fackel-Täger)

Laqueur, Walter: *The Terrible Secret*
(Weidenfeld and Nicolson, 1980)

Laqueur and Rubin (eds): *The
Israel–Arab Reader* (Pelican,
1976)

Levi, Primo: *Se Questo è un Uomo*
(Einaudi, 1958)

Lévy-Hass, Hannah: *Vielleicht was
das alles erst der Anfang –
Tagebuch aus dem
KZ-Bergen-Belsen* (Rotbuch,
1979)

Lifton, Robert Jay: *The Nazi Doctors*
(Basic, 1986)

Lind, Jakov: *Counting My Steps*
(Granada, 1972)

Lorenz, Konrad: *On Aggression*
(Methuen, University paperbacks,
1967)

McEvedy, Colin: *The Penguin Atlas
of Recent History* (Penguin, 1982)

Margolius, Heda: *I Do Not Want to
Remember* (Weidenfeld and
Nicolson, 1973)

Marshall, Bruce: *The White Rabbit*
(Evans, 1952)

Meed, Vladka: *On Both Sides of the
Wall* (Holocaust Library, 1979)

Michel, Jean: *Dora* (Sphere, 1981)

Mitscherlich, Alexander: *The Death
Doctors* (Elek, 1962)

Müller, Filip: *Auschwitz Inferno*
(Routledge & Kegan Paul, 1979)

Neave, Airey: *Saturday at MI9*
(Hodder and Stoughton, 1969)

Niederland, William G.: *Folgen der
Verfolgung: Das
überlebenden-Syndrom,
Seelenmord* (Suhrkamp, 1980)

Nielsen, Henrik: *Dødelighed og
invaliditet blandt danske
modstandsfolk deportet til
nazistiske koncentrationslejre*
(FADL's Forlag, 1986)

Parkes, Colin Murray: *Bereavement*
(Pelican, 1975)

Poutrain, Louis: *La Déportation au
Cœur d'une Vie* (cerf, 1982)

Rabinowitz, Dorothy: *New Lives* (Alfred A. Knopf, 1976)

Rauschning, Hermann: *Hitler Speaks* (Thornton Butterworth, 1939)

Rothchild, Sylvia (ed): *Voices from the Holocaust* (Meridian/New American Library, 1981)

Selzer, Michael: *Deliverance Day* (Sphere, 1980)

Semprun, Jorge: *Le Grand Voyage* (Gallimard, 1963)

Senger, Valentin: *The Invisible Jew* (Sidgwick and Jackson, 1980)

Sereny, Gitta: *Into That Darkness* (André Deutsch, 1974)

Sinti und Roma in Ehemaligen KZ-Bergen-Belsen AM 27. Oktober 1979 (Gesellschaft für bedrohte Völker, Göttingen, 1980)

Speer, Albert: *Inside the Third Reich* (Weidenfeld and Nicolson, 1971)

Stephensen, Hakon: *Frihedsfonden 1945–1970* (privately published, 1970); *Et Krigsmonument – ni 4. Maj Kollegier* (privately published, no date)

Strøm, Axel (ed): *Norwegian Concentration Camp Survivors* (Oslo Universitetsforlaget/ Humanities Press, 1968)

Thomson, David: *Europe Since Napoleon* (Pelican, 1966)

Uris, Leon: *Exodus* (Alan Wingate, 1959); *QB VII* (William Kimber, 1971)

Vrba, Rudolf: *I Cannot Forgive* (Sidgwick & Jackson, 1964)

Walk, Joseph (ed): *Als Jude in Breslau 1941* (Verband ehemaliger Breslauer in Israel/ Bar-Ilan University Institute for the Research of Diaspora Jewry, 1975)

Wdowinski, David: *And We Are Not Saved* (W.H.Allen, 1964)

Weiss, Reska: *Journey Through Hell* (Valentine, Mitchell, 1961)

Die Wiedergutmachung Nationalsozialistischen unrechts durch die Bundesrepublik Deutschland (C. H. Beck)

Wiesel, Elie: *The Town beyond the Wall* (Robson, 1975); *Night* (Penguin, 1981)

Wiesenthal, Simon: *The Sunflower* (Schocken Books, 1976)

Wilson, Francesca M.: *Aftermath: France, Germany, Austria, Yugoslavia, 1945 & 1946* (Penguin, 1947)

Wiskemann, Elizabeth: *Europe of the Dictators 1919–1945* (Collins, 1966)

Zeman, Z.A.B.: *Nazi Propaganda* (Oxford UP, 1973)

Zeman, Zbynek: *Heckling Hitler – Caricatures of the Third Reich* (Orbis, 1984)

Zentner and Bedürftig: *Das grosse Lexikon des dritten Reiches* (Südwest, 1985)

Zülch, Tilman: *In Auschwitz vergast, bis heute verfolgt – zur Situation der Roma (Zigeuner) in Deutschland und Europa* (Rowohlt, 1979)

Notes

PROLOGUE

1. Albert Friedlander (ed.): *Out of the Whirlwind* (Union of Hebrew Congregations, New York, 1968) p. 18. Friedlander is quoting Hannah Vogt: *The Burden of Guilt* (Oxford UP, 1964) – in the German edition, p. 192. *The Burden of Guilt* was written as a textbook for German schools. The figures given are conservative. Research continues on precisely how many died in the Holocaust, but the true figure will never be known.
2. See: Malgorzata Niezabilowska: 'Remnants: The Last Jews of Poland', in *National Geographic Magazine*, September 1986, Vol. 170, No. 3, pp. 362–89. The article is extracted from *The Last Jews of Poland* by the same author, published by Friendly Press Inc., 1986.
3. Tony Bayfield: *Churban* (Michael Goulston Educational Foundation, 1981), pp. 61–2.
4. For an exhaustive discussion of Allied attitudes to the concentration camps, see: Martin Gilbert: *Auschwitz and the Allies* (Michael Joseph, 1981).
5. A near-complete list of specialist papers is given in the bibliographical work, *The Psychological and Medical Effects of Concentration Camps and Related Persecutions on Survivors of the Holocaust*, by Leo Eitinger and Robert Krell (University of British Columbia Press, 1985).
6. A notable exception is Dorothy Rabinowitz's *New Lives* (Alfred A. Knopf, 1976) – a book which deals exclusively with survivors now living in America. Another book which deals with survivors' lives in the USA is *Voices from the Holocaust*, edited by Sylvia Rothchild (Meridian/New American Library, 1981).
7. Those interested in former Nazis in East Germany should consult file number Gdc(5) at the Wiener Library, London.
8. *German Democratic Report*, East Berlin, 10 February 1967.
9. For example, Heinrich Hoffman (see *The German View*, Vol. 6, No. 20, 3 November 1965, p. 2).
10. Conversation with the author.
11. Bayfield, op. cit., p. 173. An aspect of the KZ too big for discussion here is the dichotomy in German thinking *vis-à-vis* the destruction of the Jews. The Nazis were always able to excise from their minds any inconsistencies between the high ideals they purported to hold for themselves and what they actually did; and the whole concept of the blond master race was made ludicrous by the physical appearance of the top Nazis themselves – a fact which Allied cartoonists were quick to seize on even before the war had started – see Alexander Drozdzynski (ed.): *Das verspottete Tausendjährige Reich* (Droste, 1978), and especially Zbynek Zeman: *Heckling Hitler – Caricatures of the Third Reich* (Orbis, 1984).

12. See for example the work of Dr Roderick Orner and the case of Trooper Tim Lynch, who saw action in the Falklands War – as reported by Celia Hall in *The Independent*, 15 September 1987, p. 13.

13. See *Acta Medica Scandinavica*, Supplementum CCLXXIV (Copenhagen, 1952). The work of Dr Ancil Keys, whose 'Minnesota Experiment' (observing the effects of semi-starvation on volunteers over a six-month period under controlled conditions at the University of Minnesota in 1945–6) must also be mentioned here.

14. The SS *St Louis* sailed from Hamburg, bound for Havana with 907 refugees in May 1939. The refugees all possessed accredited landing certificates, but the Cuban government refused to honour them. Negotiations to permit the landing, conducted between the American Jewish Joint Distribution Committee and the government, failed, and the *St Louis* was forced to set sail back to Hamburg. While she was on the high seas, the JOINT and other organizations won the consent of the governments of the Netherlands, Belgium, the UK and France to accept the refugees, the JOINT posting a cash guarantee of about $500 per refugee. (Source: *The Annotated Archive Catalogue, American Jewish Joint Distribution Committee, 1933–1944*.) The 12-year-old Friedlander was one of the 288 refugees accepted by the UK. The story of the *St Louis* has been the subject of fictionalized film accounts.

15. Professor Herbert A. Strauss, of the Technische Universität, Berlin, conversation with the author. Strauss is the founder of the Anti-Semitism Research Foundation at the university.

16. Conversation with the author.

17. Helen Epstein: *Children of the Holocaust* (Putnam's, 1979), p. 177; also quoted in Bergman and Jucovy (eds): *Generations of the Holocaust* (Basic, 1982), p. 18; but see their p. 11: 'It must . . . be emphasized that, in recovery, many survivors have shown an unusual degree of psychic strength and resilience, and have adapted to the renewal of their lives with great vitality.'

18. The examples are taken from Niederland: *Folgen der Verfolgung: Das überlebenden-Syndrom, Seelenmord* (Suhrkamp, 1980). Professor Niederland, himself a survivor (see *Freiheit und Recht*, Jahrgang 31, No. 2, for April–June 1985, p. 7), was involved in interviewing survivors in relation to reparation claims. His book covers 12 survivors who have not been as successful at reintegrating as most of those covered in this book.

19. Niederland, ibid., pp. 229ff. and (quotation) p. 235; my translation.

20. A certain amount of this section derives from ideas discussed with Saul Friedländer in Jerusalem. Professor Friedländer was born in Prague, and survived the war in hiding in France as a child; but his parents died in Auschwitz. He tells his own story in *When Memory Comes* (Avon/Discus, 1980).

21. See: Joseph Walk (ed.): *Als Jude in Breslau 1941 – (Aus den Tagebüchern von Studienrat a. D. Dr Willy Israel Cohn)* (Verband ehemaliger Breslauer und Schlesier in Israel/Bar-Ilan University Institute for the Research of Diaspora Jewry, 1975). Though a Zionist, Dr Cohn, who was born in 1888, loved Germany passionately, and saw himself absolutely as a German citizen. The diary pathetically shows how he could not accept what was really going on, what was really happening in and to his country.

22. Saul Friedländer, conversation with the author.

CHAPTER 1: THE KZ SYSTEM

1. The Bayreuth Group, founded by Richard Wagner the Younger, and dedicated to promoting racial theory.

2. Bones were turned into superphosphate by the German firm of Strem. A bone mill was actually installed at Belzec.

3. The school textbook example is quoted in Elie A. Cohen: *Human*

Behaviour in the Concentration Camp (Cape, 1954), p. 244. The children's rhyme is from H. G. Adler: *Theresienstadt 1941–45: Das Antlitz einer Zwangsgemeinschaft* (J.C.B. Mohr, Tübingen, 1960 [2nd edn]), p. 650; my translation.

4. 'In *Mein Kampf*, Hitler wrote: "If, at the beginning and during the war [the First World War], someone had only subjected about 12,000 or 15,000 of these Hebrew enemies of the people to poison gas – as was suffered by hundreds of thousands of our best workers from all walks of life and callings on the battlefield – then the sacrifice of millions at the Front would not have been in vain." When this sentence came to be printed and was seen by the author at the proof stage, it was left as it was and remained unchanged in edition after edition, without, apparently, ever rousing the reaction that might well have been expected' – Krausnik and Broszat: *Anatomy of the SS State* (Paladin, 1970), p. 38.

5. The British maintained an internment camp on Mauritius throughout the war for 2,000 European Jews who had attempted to emigrate to Palestine illegally. See: Alexander Donat (ed.): *The Death Camp Treblinka* (Holocaust Library, 1977), pp. 115 and 145.

6. See: Krausnik and Broszat, op. cit., pp. 49ff. 'Unofficial' action against the Jews had been underway for a long time already. Even if they were only 'Jewish' to the extent of having one Jewish grandparent, Jewish doctors had their right to practise severely restricted and Jewish civil servants were dismissed from office from the spring of 1933. The first official anti-Jewish action of the Nazis was the promulgation of an Act called 'The Re-establishment of the Career Civil Service' of 7 April 1933 (ibid., p. 44). In 1933, too, Hitler banned *schechita*: the Jewish ritual slaughter of animals for meat.

7. Memorandum of 5 June 1942, quoted in *Shoah, the complete text of the film* (Pantheon, 1985), pp. 103–4.

8. ibid. See Claude Lanzmann's interview with Walter Stier (p. 132ff.) and with Raul Hilberg (p. 138ff. and especially p. 142). See also Martin Gilbert: *Final Journey* (Allen & Unwin, 1979), p. 68.

9. Source: *Encyclopaedia Judaica*.

10. Krausnik and Broszat, op. cit., p. 68. See also pp. 69ff. and *Jüdisches Leben in Deutschland Seit 1945* (Athenäum, 1986) pp. 74–5 (article by Heiner Lichtenstein).

11. The *Einsatzgruppen* are estimated to have claimed two million victims, predominantly Jews.

12. A fifth, Majdanek, started as a hard-labour camp and later became an extermination camp. 'Operation Harvest Festival' took place during the days after 2 November 1943, involving the killing of 50,000 Jews. See: Martin Gilbert: *The Holocaust* (Collins, 1986), p. 627; and Rudolf Vrba: *I Cannot Forgive* (Sidgwick & Jackson, 1963), p. 67. Vrba also recalls (ibid., p. 70) the mass shooting of surviving prisoners, the men separated from the women. They were driven naked into pits they had dug themselves, to the accompaniment of dance music and marches from loudspeakers. 17,000 people were slaughtered in one day, between 6am and 5pm.

13. This and the data which follow are taken from *The Death Camp Treblinka*. A history of Belzec by Michael Tregenza is in preparation.

14. *The Death Camp Treblinka*, p. 52.

15. See the plan of Auschwitz on p. viii. In the text of this book, the three camps will generally be referred to as Auschwitz-I, Birkenau, and Buna-Monowice.

16. Jozef Garlinski: *Fighting Auschwitz* (Julian Friedmann, 1975), p. 14.

17. Zenon Frank (see Chapter 15) was on this transport.

18. Ota Kraus and Erich Kulka: *The Death Factory* (Pergamon, 1966), p. 124.

19. ibid. pp. 5–7, for precise details.

20. There were in fact two such camps, both comprising people from Theresienstadt. Both camps were liquidated despite German assurances to the contrary. The Gypsy camp was also liquidated in early August 1944.

21. Kraus and Kulka, op. cit., p. 124.

22. Vrba, op. cit., p. 77.

23. Data which follow are nearly all taken from Adler: *Antlitz einer Zwangsgemeinschaft.*

24. Adler, op. cit., p. 124. There is an illustration of the banknotes in Bayfield: *Churban*, p. 114.

25. Nazi attitudes in the camps were oddly inconsistent. Eugen Kogon, in his *Theory and Practice of Hell* (Farrar, Straus), points out that books which were banned in the Third Reich generally were freely available in Buchenwald's library.

26. From a manuscript in the Wiener Library, London:

    A sea of tears
    Endless longings –
    Never satisfied –
    Theresienstadt.

27. The other principal liberation dates are:

    Majdanek: 24 July 1944
    Auschwitz: 27 January 1945
    Stutthof: 29 January 1945
    Buchenwald: 11 April 1945
    Ravensbrück 21 April 1945
    Sachsenhausen: 22 April 1945
    Flossenburg: 23 April 1945
    Dachau: 29 April 1945
    Mauthausen: 5 May 1945
    Theresienstadt: 8 May 1945
    (but under Red Cross protection from 21 April).

CHAPTER 2: THOSE WHO SUFFERED

1. Kogon, in *The Theory and Practice of Hell*, gives the following description: 'Prisoners suspected of plans for escaping had a red and white target sewn or painted on chest and back. The SS even devised a special marking for the feeble-minded – an armband with the German word *blöd* (stupid). Sometimes these unfortunates also had to wear a sign around their necks: "I am a moron!" ... The camps were a veritable circus, as far as colours, markings, and special designations were concerned. Occasionally prisoners were decked out in nearly all colours of the rainbow. There was one Jew, for example, who was a member of the Jehovah's Witnesses,

a "race defiler", a member of the penal company, and also wore the escaper's targets!' (pp. 44–5).

2. A survivor, Witold Huml, Auschwitz number 189786, has told me that Russians were tattooed on the chest, and Gypsies on the left thigh, but I have not found other references to this. Numbers were sometimes painted on the chest.

3. One Jewish survivor of Birkenau, Kitty Hart, has the number 39934, which is 'old'.

4. The subject of the psychology of the prisoner is dealt with in depth in Cohen: *Human Behaviour in the Concentration Camp*, pp. 115–210.

5. Gilbert: *The Holocaust*, p. 551.

6. See: C.E. King: *The Nazi State and the New Religions* (Edwin Mellen Press, 1982); also Kogon, op. cit., pp. 41–3.

7. Hans-Joachim Döring: *Die Zigeuner im NS-Staat* (Kriminalistik Verlag, Vol. 12, Hamburg, 1964), pp. 153–4.

8. *Autobiography* of Rudolf Höss, taken from *KL Auschwitz Seen by the SS*, 2nd edn (revised) (Publications of Panstwowe Muzeum w Oswiecimiu, 1978), p. 63. The League of German Girls (*Bund Deutscher Mädel*) was the female equivalent of the Hitler Youth.

9. *Deutscher Bundestag*, Plenarprotokoll 10/171., 171, Sitzung, Stenographiischer Bericht, 7 November 1985.

10. The letter, dated 29 November 1985, was sent on 24 January 1986.

11. Tilman Zülch (ed.): *In Auschwitz vergast, bis heute verfolgt – zur Situation der Roma (Zigeuner) in Deutschland und Europa* (Rowohlt, 1979), p. 91, article by Jerzy Ficowski. See also *The Destiny of Europe's Gypsies* by Donald Kenrick and Grattan Puxon (London, 1972), and Christian Bernadac: *L'Holocauste Oublié – le Massacre des Tsiganes* (France-Empire, 1979).

12. José Gotovitch: *Quelques Données Relatives à l'Extermination des Tsiganes de Belgique* (Cahiers d'Histoire de la Seconde Guerre Mondiale, No. 4., December 1976), pp. 161–80; my translation. The

race law referred to specifically is the *Ehegesundheitsgesetz* (Marriage-hygiene Law) of 18 October 1935, where Gypsies and Jews are described as of 'non-human' blood.

13. Kogon, op. cit., pp. 43–4. Homosexuals in the KZ – people imprisoned for homosexuality, that is – were male. The Nazis do not appear to have made any special law against lesbians.

14. *Siegessäule*, August 1985, pp. 9–10.

15. See: Heinz Heger: *The Men With The Pink Triangle* (Alyson/Gay Men's Press, 1980). Data that follow are taken from that book. I am also grateful to Joachim Müller, of the West Berlin Homosexual Community, who has himself been unable to contact a solitary homosexual survivor of the KZ (letter to the author).

16. These observations are based upon several conversations with survivors.

17. In his introduction to Heger's book, the translator, David Fernbach, explains that Heger had been told the story by an anonymous Austrian. In fact the book is autobiographical. See: the text of Joachim Müller's address at the laying of the wreath at Sachsenhausen, 27 June 1985, pp. 1 and 2.

18. The data for the *Blocks* and the size of the bunks are taken from *Acta Medica Scandinavica, Supplementum CCLXXIV*, pp. 35–6, and are based upon observations at Neuengamme.

19. ibid., p. 37. In Birkenau, conditions were worse.

20. See: Terrence des Près: *The Survivor* (Oxford UP, New York, 1976), Chapter Three – but all KZ literature is full of examples.

21. Kogon, op. cit., describes a moderately better issue of clothes at Buchenwald, where the uniform was 'freshly laundered' (p. 70). Kogon was, however, a German political prisoner.

22. Certainly true of Jewish inmates. There was greater flexibility with non-Jews, especially *Reichs-* and *Volksdeutsche*.

23. See *Acta Medica Scandinavica*, op. cit., pp. 44–5.

24. Cohen, op. cit., p. 51ff., in his discussion of diet, mentions a substance called AVO, but when I talked to him recently he had not ascertained more about what it was. Kitty Hart, however, in her *Return to Auschwitz* (Granada, 1983) mentions AVO as a poison (p. 283). In a letter to me, she writes that AVO may have been a derivative of bromide, a white powder which 'was added to the morning liquid – so-called "coffee", also to the soup, and there was some even in the bread. The quantity was determined by the SS woman in charge of the kitchen. Prisoners who had too much soup (for example my mother who worked in the hospital *Block*) found that they could not concentrate, and it slowed down their reactions. (One way to ensure total submission!)' Dr Cohen is a survivor of, among other camps, Auschwitz-I; Mrs Hart is a survivor of the Lublin Ghetto and Birkenau.

25. Maria Ossowski, conversation with the author.

26. Cohen, op. cit., p. 53, quoting D. Rousset: *L'Univers concentrationnaire* (Paris, 1946) p. 125.

CHAPTER 3: DISPLACED PERSONS

1. Robert W. Ross, quoted by Leonard Dinnerstein in *America and the Survivors of the Holocaust* (Columbia UP, 1982), p. xvi.

2. Josef Rosensaft and the leading Jews of the community formed at the DP camp at Belsen had to insist that they be regarded as Jews first, and by their nationality second. See Rosensaft's article 'Our Belsen', in *Belsen* (Irgun Sheerit Hapleita Me'haezor Habriti, 1957) pp. 24–51, and especially pp. 35–6.

3. Dinnerstein, op. cit., p. 31; my italics.

4. This and the following quotation are from Dinnerstein, ibid., pp. 16–17.

5. Quoted in Dinnerstein, ibid., p. 53.

6. Francesca M. Wilson: *Aftermath*, pp. 40–41.

7. ibid., p. 48.

8. ibid., p. 49. The vigour of the prose attests her feelings.
9. ibid., p. 138.
10. *Army Talk*, No. 151, 30 November 1946 (US Army).
11. Dinnerstein, op. cit. p. 75.
12. ibid., p. 113.
13. ibid., pp. 189–91. The 14-point list issued by the Hebrew Sheltering and Immigrant Aid Society (HIAS) of those documents and actions required to be considered for immigration is prodigious. Dinnerstein quotes the German correspondent of the *Christian Century* as thinking it 'a miracle that *any* displaced persons have arrived in America . . .'
14. ibid., p. 176.
15. Yehuda Bauer: *My Brother's Keeper* (Jewish Publication Society of the USA, 1974) pp. 9–10.

CHAPTER 4: REPARATION

1. United States wartime quotas were not filled, though there was an escalation in emigration from Germany and Central Europe in the years leading up to the outbreak of war. That the wartime quotas were not filled was not a factor in calculating those set post-war.
2. Norbert Wollheim, conversation with the author.
3. Conversation with the author.
4. See: *Danish Medical Bulletin*, March–April 1970, Vol. 17, Nos. 3–4: *Concentration Camp Survivors in Denmark. Persecution, Disease, Disability, Compensation – A 23-Year Follow-Up – A Survey of the Long-Term Effects of Environmental Stress* by Paul Thygesen, Knud Hermann and Rolf Willanger, pp. 93–4: 'The arbitrariness in the practice of the law is illustrated by the rejection percentages in different *Länder* [i.e. regions]: e.g. 54% and 66% in Schleswig-Holstein and Baden-Württemberg, compared with 15% and 19% in West Berlin and Bremen.' The authors are citing J. v. N. Ziegler, *Einführung*, pp. 7–11, in *Extreme Lebensverhältnisse* (Manualia Nicolai, Herford, 1967).

5. See: *The Times*, 19 March 1986.
6. For much of what follows I am indebted to information and papers given me by the Bundesministerium der Finananzen, Bonn, Department VI A 4. Translations from the German are mine, although I acknowledge with gratitude help from Anthony Vivis. At the risk of editorializing, one has to make the comment that the tone of the original is at times self-righteous, even making allowance for German 'officialese'.
7. The German word is *Wiedergutmachung* – literally, 'making good again'. German commentators have discussed the semantic implications of this word at length.
8. This may be a dig at East Germany's abrogation of responsibility for National Socialism. The East Germans have shown responsibility in terms of reparation to 'victims of fascism' within their own frontiers: see main text, below.
9. Representing reparation claims provided a much-needed means of re-establishing themselves for many émigré lawyers who had resettled outside Central Europe and Germany after the war.
10. Letter to the author, 29 July 1986. Since the West German authorities were always courteous and prompt in their replies to my enquiries, I feel bound in fairness to give the original text of their letter here. My translation aims to reproduce the sense of their letter, rather than to be elegant, or to reflect the style of the original. The paragraph in German reads: '*Wiedergutmachungszahlungen konnten naturgemäss erst nach Inkrafttreten der jeweiligen Regelung und nach Durchführung eines entsprechenden Verfahrens geleistet werden. Im Einzelfall war die Auszahlung vor allem abhängig vom Zeitpunkt der Antragstellung, von der Beweislage, der Dauer des Verfahrens usw. Soweit Zahlungen – wie von Ihnen geschildert – erst relativ spät geleistet wurden, dürfte es sich*

*regelmässig um komplizierte Fälle
gehandelt haben, in denen eine
Entscheidung erst nach langwierigen
Ermittlungen möglich war.
Daneben gab es aber zB auch
zahlreiche Fälle, in denen erst sehr
spät ein Antrag gestellt wurde
oder die mangelnde Mitwirkung
des Antragstellers eine schnellere
Erledigung unmöglich machte. Zu
berücksichtigen ist hierbei auch,
dass die damit befassten
Entschädigungsbehörde der
deutschen Bundesländer vor kaum
lösbare Aufgaben stellte.'*

11. The German word is *Land* – federal
region with its own government.

12. Regional bureaus are attached to
each regional government.
According to Paragraph 185 of the
BEG, the indemnification bureaux
for victims living in Europe on 31
December 1952 are those of Cologne
and Düsseldorf in
Nordrhein-Westfalen and, for
victims living outside Europe on
that date, the offices of
Rheinland-Pfalz. Many of the
Rheinland-Pfalz offices have since
closed and their cases have been
transferred to the Amt für
Wiedergutmachung in Saarburg.

13. Or a lump-sum may be paid as a
once-and-for-all settlement; or
reparation may be made as a
combination of the two: as, for
example, a lump-sum paid in
respect of lost education, and a
pension in respect of damaged
health.

14. *Höhere Dienst,* followed by
Gehobene, Mittlere and *Einfache.*
My translations.

15. *Minderung der Erwerbsfähigkeit.*

16. Richard Saper.

17. Letter to the author from Dept VI A
4 of the Bundesministerium der
Finanzen: *'Soweit bei ihrer
Berechnung die persönlichen und
wirtschaftlichen Verhältnisse des
Empfängers zu berücksichtigen sind,
kann sich die Höhe der Rente (zB
bei Steigerung oder Minderung der
sonstige Einkünfte) im Laufe der
Jahre ändern.'*

18. For more on this, see the article by
Milton Kestenberg,
'Discriminatory Aspects of the
German Indemnification Law',

especially pp. 65–79, in Bergman
and Jucovy (eds): *Generations of the
Holocaust.*

19. As I understand the provisions of
the law, in cases of physical and/or
mental damage.

20. Article by Monika Richarz, 'Juden
in der BRD und in der DDR seit 1945',
in *Jüdisches Leben in Deutschland
seit 1945,* pp. 13–30; see especially
pp. 20–21; my translation.

21. Constituted 7–12 October 1949.

22. Otto Funke, Chairman of the
Central Administration of the
Committee of the Anti-Fascist
Resistance Fighters of the German
Democratic Republic; letter to the
author; my translation.

23. For the following information I am
grateful to the Bundesministerium
für soziale Verwaltung in Vienna.

24. See *The Voice of Auschwitz
Survivors in Israel,* No. 38, April
1987. See also Benjamin B. Ferencz:
Less Than Slaves (Harvard UP,
1979).

25. See also the article by Arnold Spitta,
'Wiedergutmachung oder wider
die Gutmachung?', in *In Auschwitz
vergast, bis heute verfolgt,*
pp. 161–71.

26. *Time,* 3 December 1979. My
personal sense is that such action
should not be seen as deliberate
deceit on the part of the West
German authorities.

27. *Köln Stadt,* 7 August 1985.

28. Spitta, op. cit., p. 161; my
translation.

29. See: *Freiheit und Recht,* Jahrgang
31, for July–September 1985 (No.
3), p. 15; my translation.

CHAPTER 5: THE SURVIVOR AND
SOCIETY, THE FAMILY,
AGE AND GRIEF

1. Yael Danieli, 'Families of Survivors
Milgram (ed.): *Stress and Anxiety*
(Hemisphere, 1982) pp. 405–21.

2. Colin Murray Parkes puts forward
the concept of 'monsterization' –
where in contrast to the idealized
dead spouse or child, the living
'replacement' will constantly find
himself or herself compared
unfavourably with the dead one.
This behaviour is not peculiar to

Colin Murray Parkes *cont.*
concentration camp survivors.
Conversation with the author.

3. Danieli, op. cit., p. 407.
4. The other attitude survivors had to contend with was that they had let the Germans do it. 'Why didn't you fight back? At least you could have taken one of the bastards with you' was a frequent challenge thrown at survivors' heads – a remark which could only be made by one with no knowledge of the KZ system or the isolation of the Jews. The effect of such remarks was to increase the survivors' own sense of guilt at having survived at all.
5. As defined by Danieli. See op. cit., above, and, *inter alia*, 'Differing Adaptational Styles in Families of Survivors of the Nazi Holocaust', in *Children Today*, Vol. 10, No. 5, September–October 1981. Danieli concerns herself exclusively with Jewish survivors. In my experience, few non-Jewish survivors married other survivors.
6. I encountered several very active survivors who admitted that they had to keep busy in order to keep unbearable retrospective thoughts away.
7. Danieli, 'Differing Adaptational Styles', p. 10.
8. See: Klaus Hoppe: 'The Master–Slave See-Saw Relationship in Psychotherapy', *Reiss-Davis Clinical Bulletin*, Vol. 8, 2, 1971, pp. 117–25.
9. Jan Bastiaans, 'Psychotherapy of War Victims Facilitated by the Use of Hallucinogenic Drugs', paper read at the Fifth World Congress of the International College of Psychosomatic Medicine, Jerusalem, 10–14 September 1979.
10. op. cit.
11. The patient was addicted to ritalin, which had been prescribed by her physician.
12. The late Professor Shamai Davidson; conversation with the author.
13. See Freud, *Totem and Taboo*, 1913, pp. 158–9: 'What are the ways and means employed by one generation in order to hand on its mental states to the next one?' No mental impulses can 'be so completely suppressed as to leave no trace

whatever behind them. Even the most ruthless suppression must leave room for distorted surrogate impulses and for reactions resulting from them. No generation is able to conceal any of its more important mental processes from its successor. For psycho-analysis has shown us that everyone possesses in his unconscious mental activity an apparatus which enables him to interpret other people's reactions, that is, to undo the distortions which other people have imposed on the expression of their feelings.'
14. For what follows I am indebted to Professor Davidson, both through conversation and correspondence before his tragically early death, and through his papers, especially 'Transgenerational Transmission in the Families of Holocaust Survivors', *International Journal of Family Psychiatry*, 1; 1, 1980, pp. 95–111.
15. Discussed in Chapter 6. This syndrome is coming to be known in its wider and more recent application by the more descriptive title of post-traumatic stress syndrome.
16. Shamai Davidson: 'Long-Term Psychosocial Sequelae in Holocaust Survivors and Their Families', from the proceedings of the Israel–Netherlands Symposium on the Impact of Persecution, Jerusalem, 1977, published by Rijswijk in 1979 (p. 64).
17. ibid., p. 65.
18. ibid., p. 106. It is not unusual for children, equally, to have felt guilt at not having suffered as much as their parents. They will therefore, especially in adolescence, have devised 'tortures' for themselves: forcing themselves to go without sleep, without food (to the point of developing anorexia nervosa), and even 'wilfully' failing examinations they could easily have passed.
19. Conversation with the author.
20. See also, *inter alia*, Yael Danieli's 'The Aging Survivor of the Holocaust', *Journal of Geriatric Psychiatry*, 14 (2), 1981, pp. 191–210.
21. Edith Sklar, conversation with the

author. The quoted remarks in what follows all stem from the same source.

22. Colin Murray Parkes, conversation with the author.

23. Parkes: *Bereavement* (Pelican, 1975), p. 158. (The quotations are from V. A. Kyval, 'Psychiatric Observations under Severe Chronic Stress', *American Journal of Psychiatry*, 108, p. 185.)

24. ibid., p. 213.

25. Davidson, 'The Survivor Syndrome Today', in *Group Analysis*, November 1980, p. 24.

CHAPTER 6: SOME EFFECTS OF
THE KZ ON THE MIND

1. One of the two concentration camps in the Netherlands. The other was Amersfoort.

2. From Westerbork, many thousands of Dutch Jews were sent by train to Auschwitz-Birkenau.

3. In the experience of this survivor, the barracks were known as such, and not as '*Blocks*'.

4. Hannah Lévy-Hass was to play an influential role in this survivor's later life. She had particularly impressed him by her caring for children in Belsen (he was not one of those in her charge). In 1986 he learned that she had left Israel for a lengthy stay in Paris, where she was undergoing medical treatment. He wanted to meet her, but she was unable to see him. At first he took this very hard, as a personal rebuff; but subsequently they corresponded. (See more, later in this chapter.) Her diary is published as *Vielleicht war das alles erst der Anfang* (Rotbuch, 1979), though Mme Lévy-Hass herself thinks that the third edition, published in 1982, is the best. The book has also been published in an English translation as *Inside Belsen* by Harvester Press in the UK and Barnes & Noble in the USA.

5. He took early retirement in 1987, but still works part-time.

6. Leyden is where the LSD treatment sessions took place.

7. Professor Bastiaans is a very tall and powerfully built man, who is clearly regarded by this patient with adoration.

8. The colours are related to the size of the dosage of LSD, and to the progress of its effect.

9. The man referred to is also physically very big.

10. The patient spoke in Dutch when reminiscing about or re-enacting childhood.

11. The expression is Eitinger's. See main text, this chapter, section II.

12. From *The Implications of the Specificity Concept for the Treatment of Psychosomatic Patients* (Psychotherapy and Psychosomatics; Karger, Basel, 1977), p. 289.

13. Not every session in such a course of treatment would normally be LSD-assisted.

14. Conversation with the author.

15. A form of analysis or therapy through dream-sleep induced by a drug such as thorium pentathol, usually of ten minutes' duration.

16. Conversation with the author. For more on this, see *Vom Menschen im KZ und vom KZ in Menschen*, and *Psychotherapy of War Victims Facilitated by the Use of Hallucinogenic Drugs* (Jelgersma-Kliniek Oegstgeest, 1979).

17. *Mental Liberation Facilitated by the Use of Hallucinogenic Drugs.*

18. These and the preceding remarks were made in conversation with the author. Bastiaans is the author of a large number of papers, many of which are listed in the Bibliography compiled by Eitinger and Krell (see Note 5 to the Prologue).

19. There is a variety of names under which this syndrome exists, and while there may be subtle distinctions between them, they refer essentially to the same condition. The survivor syndrome, the post-concentration camp syndrome, and the disaster syndrome, are three. As I have already said, the most widely used modern term is the post-traumatic stress syndrome.

20. Leo Eitinger and Finn Askevold: 'Psychiatric Aspects' (Chapter VI of *Norwegian Concentration Camp*

Eitinger and Askevold: *cont.*
Survivors, edited by Axel Strøm;
Universitetsforlaget Oslo/
Humanities Press New York,
1968), p. 59. The quotation is from
Knud Hermann and Paul Thygesen:
'KZ-syndromet', in *Ugesk. f. Læger*,
116, pp. 825–36, 1954. See also
Acta Medica Scandinavica,
Supplementum CCLXXIV, Chapter
XXII: 'Psychiatric Symptoms on
Repatriation', by H. Hoffmeyer and
M. Hertel Wulff (pp. 362–413).

21. *Acta Medica Scandinavica*, op. cit.,
p. 365.

22. The description of the
concentration camp syndrome
here is necessarily brief. See also
Bastiaans, *Life Against Life: the
Psychosomatic Consequences of
Man-Made Disasters* (University
of Leyden).

23. *Danish Medical Bulletin*, op. cit.,
p. 81.

24. The Jewish community is now
about 1,500 strong. The numbers are
made up mainly by Jews who came
to Norway from the DP camps or
from the Eastern Bloc.

25. Eitinger: 'On Being a Psychiatrist
and a Survivor', in Rosenfeld and
Greenberg (eds): *Confronting the
Holocaust: The Impact of Elie
Wiesel* (Indiana UP, 1978), p. 188.

26. Eitinger: 'Experiences in War and
During Catastrophes, and Their
Effects upon the Human Mind'.
Torstein Dale Memorial Oration,
8 May 1984. Reproduced in the
Journal of Oslo City Hospital,
1984, 34, pp. 75–84 (p. 78). As only
24 Jewish survivors of the
concentration camps lived in
Norway, the studies focused on
survivors who had been in the
Norwegian resistance, Norwegian
'politicals', and former members of
the Norwegian armed forces.

27. These and all the following
otherwise unacknowledged remarks
were made by Professor Eitinger in
conversation with the author.

28. Eitinger: *Concentration Camp
Survivors in Norway and Israel*
(Martinus Nijhoff, 1972).

29. Eitinger: *Psychological
Consequences of War
Disturbances* (Oslo).

30. 'New Investigations on the

Mortality and Morbidity of
Norwegian ex-Concentration
Camp Prisoners', *Israeli Journal
Relat, Sci.*, Vol. 18, No. 3 (1981),
pp. 173–95 (p. 185).

31. Rudolf Vrba: *I Cannot Forgive*
(Sidgwick & Jackson, 1964),
pp. 152–3.

32. Maximilian Kolbe was a Roman
Catholic priest who as a prisoner
in Auschwitz laid down his life so
that another man might live.

33. For Jews, the ability to speak the
native language of their country
without a Yiddish accent was a
considerable advantage if they were
to attempt to survive the war in
hiding in Eastern Europe.

34. Conversation with the author. It
appears that in Kiev today what
happened at Babi Yar is played
down. See: Colin Thubron: *Among
the Russians* (Penguin, 1986).

35. *Danish Medical Bulletin*, op. cit.,
p. 78.

36. In *The Theory and Practice of Hell.*

37. From *Norwegian Concentration
Camp Survivors*, Chapter III.

38. Eitinger: *Psychological
Consequences of War
Disturbances* (Oslo).

39. A speech given at the 1961 Annual
Meeting in the session 'A Generation
of World Tension', Joint Session of
the American Orthopsychiatric
Association and the World
Federation for Mental Health.
Reproduced as 'Concentration
Camp Survivors in the Postwar
World', in the *American Journal of
Orthopsychiatry*, April 1962, Vol.
32, No. 3, pp. 367–75. It should be
stressed that Eitinger is referring
to his work with former political
inmates of the concentration
camps.

40. *Danish Medical Bulletin*, op. cit.,
p. 76, citing E. Minkowski.

41. ibid.

42. *Sport* – strenuous physical jerks
imposed by the SS as a punishment
on prisoners, usually at the end of
the day's work. *Sport* could be
sustained for over an hour and
caused the death by exhaustion of
many prisoners. It was, of course,
applied to both sexes.

43. The 'special detail'. The men of this
Kommando were prisoners who

worked in the gas chambers and the crematoria, stripping the dead naked bodies of any jewellery hidden on them – in the anus, for example – and taking the gold crowns and fillings and teeth out of people's mouths; then burning the corpses. Because prisoners were not officially supposed to know of the existence of the gas chambers, members of the *SK* were periodically liquidated and replaced. Thus very few of them survived the war. See especially Filip Müller: *Auschwitz Inferno* (Routledge & Kegan Paul, 1979). Müller is a survivor of the *SK*, and his is a searing account.

44. 'New Investigations', op. cit., p. 191. Organic psycho-syndrome has more or less the same symptomatology as senile or presenile dementia but is distinguished as a disease of people under 65.

45. In relation to this, see Yael Danieli's idea of the Fourth Blow in *The Aging Survivor of the Holocaust*: 'When Freud speculated about the reasons people rejected and avoided psychoanalysis, he said that Copernicus gave the first blow to humanity's naïve self-love or narcissism, the cosmological blow, when humankind learned that it was not the center of the universe. Darwin gave the second, the biological blow, when he said that humanity's supremacy over the animal kingdom is questionable. Freud claimed that he gave the third, the psychological blow, by showing that "the ego is not [even] master in its own house" and that, indeed, we have limits to our consciousness. I believe that Nazi Germany gave humanity the fourth, the *ethical blow*, by shattering our naïve belief that the world we live in is a just place, and that human life is of value.'

46. He treated Elie Wiesel in Auschwitz, and is the doctor mentioned in *Night* (Penguin, 1981), pp. 89–92. He describes something of his experiences through Norwegian prisons to Auschwitz and Buchenwald, as well as his liberation and his personal response

to the news of the end of the war, in Filmer and Schwan (eds)— *Mensch, der Krieg ist aus!* (Econ, 1985), pp. 83–5.

CHAPTER 7: IN DENMARK. HEALERS AND FIGHTERS

1. *Acta Medica Scandinavica* and *Danish Medical Bulletin*, op. cit.
2. Kogon, op. cit., p. 46.
3. See also *Danish Medical Bulletin*, op. cit., p. 68.
4. ibid., p. 81. The Nielsen and Sørensen papers referred to are: Henrik Nielsen and Henrik Sørensen: 'KZ-syndromet i individuelle forløb', *Nordisk Psykiatrisk Tidsskrift*, 1984, pp. 305–12; and Henrik Nielsen: *Dødelighed og invaliditet blandt danske modstandsfolk deportet til nazistiske koncentrationslejre* (FADL's Forlag, 1986). Both have summaries in English.
5. See: *Acta Medica Scandinavica*, op. cit., pp. 236ff; *Danish Medical Bulletin*, op. cit., pp. 83ff.
6. Conversation with the author. All of the following section is taken from conversation with Dr Kieler in Copenhagen.
7. Kieler and Flemming were among those former KZ prisoners liberated and brought home shortly before the end of the war on the 'white buses' – transports arranged under the auspices of the Swede, Count Folke Bernadotte, who as a prominent member of a neutral country was able to enter into direct negotiations with Himmler. The white buses, supplied by Sweden, were petrol-fuelled and thus long-range enough to go as far as Leipzig to collect prisoners. The initiative, however, was Danish.
8. What follows is based on a conversation with Frode Toft which took place two months before his death.
9. Senior *Block* Prisoner. He or she would have certain privileges, such as a private room; but would be placed in a position of power over the other prisoners who lived in the *Block* – power which was nearly always abused.

CHAPTER 8: A HOME IN ENGLAND

1. Mühlhausen not far from Erfurt, now in East Germany, not the Mühlhausen just to the south of Bamberg.

2. For reparation in Great Britain. Its European office is in Frankfurt-am-Main.

3. Successor to Woburn House. A former hotel in Bloomsbury Street, London, it housed the offices of the Jewish Refugee Association.

4. Szalasi succeeded Horthy on 15 October 1944 – after the 'action' against the Jews of Hungary had taken place. Horthy had managed to halt the deportations temporarily, and the heroism of some individuals, notably Raoul Wallenberg, saved many Jews from death. Under Szalasi's regime further atrocities were committed against the Jews still in Hungary.

5. A 'selection' was made of the arrivals at Auschwitz-Birkenau immediately, usually conducted by one of the SS doctors and frequently by Mengele himself, who affected white gloves and sometimes used a baton to indicate 'left' or 'right' – one side meant life, the other, death.

6. Melk was one of the major sub-camps of Mauthausen. It was opened on 11 January 1944 inside a large Wehrmacht installation. It had a gas chamber and a crematorium, and as it was a large camp it was probably intended for future use as an extermination camp. The surrounding hills consisted of fine, sandy quartz, into which tunnels were dug. Many of them collapsed, killing the prisoner-miners. The excavation was carried out by the firm of Quartz GmbH, which paid the WVHA a 'hire-fee' for the prisoner-labour. Melk had a fluctuating population of about 8,000 inmates. See: Evelyn le Chêne: *Mauthausen* (Methuen, 1971).

7. The camp at Ebensee was begun late in 1943. It was situated in a mountainous, well-wooded region of the Salzkammergut, and is a famous beauty-spot. At the time, it provided an ideal site for concealed underground factories. The prisoners had to construct enormous underground tunnels and halls to house armaments works. 'Some of the machines were for manufacturing parts for aeroplanes, others were for the V-1 and V-2 rockets' (le Chêne, op. cit., p. 227). There was also a large benzine store. Two of the worst features of the camp were its appalling *Revier* and the ghastly, lightless galleries which were hollowed out and destined to be used to house prisoner-miners underground permanently. This nightmare plan was interrupted by the liberation.

8. See Bibliography.

9. 'Return to Auschwitz', Yorkshire Television, UK.

10. Others would not agree – but different people had different experiences. There can be no hard and fast rule. On the whole, though, my experience has been that retaining one's moral integrity actually increased one's chances of survival.

11. Terrence des Près: *The Survivor*, Chapter Three.

12. Where women prisoners in Birkenau who had been selected were left – sometimes for days – without food or water to await transport to the gas chambers.

CHAPTER 9: TWO FRIENDS

1. High school or grammar school, with the accent on the Humanities.

2. For a detailed description of Hugo Gryn's arrival at Birkenau, see Bayfield, op. cit., pp. 116–23; see also Martin Gilbert: *The Holocaust* (Collins, 1986), p. 677.

3. Hugo Gryn discovered later that his mother had not been sent to the gas chambers. She survived the KZ. See main text, below. His grandparents and his younger brother died that day.

4. Leo Baeck, the eminent German-Jewish rabbi and scholar, survived Theresienstadt and lived in England after the war. See Albert Friedlander's biography, *Leo*

Baeck – *Teacher of Theresienstadt*
(Holt, Rinehart & Winston, 1968).

5. 'Survivor guilt often stems from
feeling that lost relatives were
"better" than the survivor himself,
physically and mentally – and that
the dead therefore had a greater right
to life. There seems to be no way of
rationalizing this attitude away.'
William G. Niederland: *Folgen der
Verfolgung*; my translation.

6. The World Gathering of Jewish
Holocaust Survivors took place in
Israel in June 1981. A
commemorative book, *From
Holocaust to Redemption*, was
published in 1984 by the World
Gathering of Jewish Holocaust
Survivors, in New York. Meir
Kahane is an American-born rabbi,
and a right-wing member of the
Knesset.

7. There are many references to Hugo
Gryn's story in Gilbert, *The Holocaust*.

8. A police force of Jews operating
within the ghetto.

9. The *Armia Krajowa* was not
essentially anti-Semitic. It had
about 300,000 members, and was
organized as a conventional army,
with regular divisions, regiments,
and so on. *AK*, the 'Home Army', was
apolitical, and saw its job as
liberating Poland from Hitler while
ensuring a future free of Russian
dominance or colonialism. Also
fighting were the *Armia Ludowa*,
which was a very small
pro-Communist force, and the
Narodowe Siły Zbrojne (NSZ),
numbering about 70,000, which was
politically to the far right: their
biggest enemy after Hitler was
Stalin. They were also fanatical
fighters, and members of the *NSZ*
continued to fight against
communism after the war,
conducting their campaign from the
woods, and countryside hideouts.

10. In a *Block*, the *Stubendienste* were
the *Blockälteste*'s assistants. They
held great power over the other
prisoners in the *Block*, and the
corrupting influence of this power
could be horrific. A similar system
operated in the women's *Blocks*. As
in this case, however,
Stubendienste were not necessarily
evil.

11. The story which follows is also in
Martin Gilbert: *The Holocaust*,
pp. 813–15. I recount it here as Ben
Helfgott told it to me. There are no
dissimilarities. Gienek later
emigrated to Israel and changed his
Polish first name to Gershon.

12. The Jewish leaders of the ghettos of
Warsaw, Lodz and Vilno (Vilnius)
respectively.

CHAPTER 10: JEWS OF 'GREATER GERMANY'

1. See: Jean Michel: *Dora* (Sphere,
1981).

2. A significant number of Jews
managed to survive in this way.

3. I have noticed that in survivors'
homes there are either many books
about the KZ, or none.

4. See Martin Gilbert: *Final Journey*
(Allen & Unwin, 1979) pp. 18–22.

5. A novel by Thomas Keneally which
is set to a great extent in Plaszow
concentration camp, and in which
Amon Goeth appears as a main
character. See: Bibliography.

6. Under the provisions of the
Nuremberg Laws, Jewish doctors
were designated medical
practitioners only, and were not
allowed to have non-Jewish
patients.

7. Sarastro's aria at the end of Act II
Scene iii of *The Magic Flute*;
'Within these sacred halls / Revenge
is unknown . . .'

8. *Das Antlitz einer
Zwangsgemeinschaft* – see Note
23 to Chapter 1.

9. See: Josef Bor: *Terezin Requiem*
(Heinemann, 1963).

10. It is possible that a genuine
arrangement to send these children
to Switzerland fell through and it
was thus that they came to be killed.

11. 'Say "so long" softly when we part',
and 'Who will weep when we say
goodbye?' – well-known songs from
German operettas.

12. Himmler had been engaged in
negotiations for permitting Jews to
be ransomed since the end of 1944
– a policy he pursued without
consulting Hitler and which, when
discovered, led to his disgrace
within the by then disintegrating

Nazi Party. However, Himmler was not acting out of any change of heart. His original suggestion was that the Jews of Theresienstadt be marched to the border 'on the assumption that about 60 per cent would survive'.

13.

STEPS

The heart must always be ready to part
At every call of life and at each new start

To enter bravely, without regret,
Into such tasks it had before not met.

And each beginning bears a magic spell,
Protects, and helps us on this earth to dwell,

Serenely we should step through space and space
And should not cling to any native place.

World Spirit does not want to hem us or   chain
But lift us step by step to reach new heights again.

(translation by Edith Kramer-Freund)

14. Lists of survivors of the camps were circulated worldwide where possible.

15. Sadly Fred Kramer has since died. Dr Freund continues to travel, visiting friends and relatives around Europe.

16. See especially: Simon Wiesenthal and Joseph Wechsberg: *The Murderers Among Us* (Heinemann, 1967) and Simon Wiesenthal: *The Sunflower* (Schocken Books, 1976). Wiesenthal considers the latter book his best. In it, as a KZ prisoner, he is confronted with a dying SS-man who begs his forgiveness. He does not feel able to give it. In the latter half of the book a number of historians, writers, theologians and thinkers give their views, at his invitation, on whether he was right or not. He told me: 'The question is more important than the answer; it represents a universal human moral problem.'

17. 'A semi-military government agency (*Reichsbehörde*) established in 1933. Its main function was the construction of strategic highways and military installations. After Todt's death in 1942, Speer,

Minister of Armaments and War Production, became its chief' (Krausnik and Broszat, op. cit., p. 291). Fritz Todt was Speer's predecessor.

18. One of the commandants of Treblinka. Imprisoned for life in December 1970, he died in 1971. See Bibliography: *Into That Darkness*; Gitta Sereny conducted a number of interviews with Stangl shortly before his death. Kurt Franz, the last commandant of the camp, is still alive, serving a life sentence; but he refuses interview requests.

19. Privy-Councillor Dr Ivan Hacker-Lederer was President at the time of the interview. He was also in charge of all Austrian KZ memorials – e.g. Mauthausen – which are designated as National Monuments.

20. Grouping by fives seems to have been almost universal in the KZ.

21. Hungary became a state in the general redistribution of the Austro-Hungarian Empire at Versailles in 1919. See: David Thomson: *Europe Since Napoleon* (Pelican, 1966).

22. At the time of the interview, December 1985.

CHAPTER 11: AUSTRIAN AND GERMAN 'RED TRIANGLES'

1. For interesting detail, see G.E.R. Gedye: *Fallen Bastions* (Gollancz, 1939). Gedye was a British journalist based in Vienna, who watched things fall apart, and writes with all the immediacy one can imagine of a clear-sighted man publishing in 1939.

2. ibid., p. 104.

3. The others are the Österreichischer Volkspartei Kameradschaft der Politisch Verfolgten (conservative), and the Bundesverband Österreichischer Widerstandskämpfer und Opfer des Faschismus (KZ-Verband) (socialist). I should add that the Deputy Chairman of the KZ-Verband, Ing. K. Pordes, tells me that today the organization is no longer party political.

4. Socialist Party of Austria.
5. Prisoners were frequently transported in trains of up to 70–100 waggons.
6. The *Ordensburgen* were the highest residential academies for the training of the Nazi elite – finishing schools for the future party leadership. Four were established in castles in remote, romantic settings. They were: Crössingsee, Sonthofen, Vogelsang and Marienburg. The accent was on physical training and 'the inculcation of ruthlessness'. Those who lasted the course were sent to Marienburg for a final polish – political indoctrination. Students were in their mid-twenties and spent a year at each 'Order Castle' in turn in the order they are given here. Only one per cent of them were university graduates; the *Ordensburgen* failed to attract university students, despite the financial inducements and high status offered.
7. 'free of Jews' – though 'purged of Jews' conveys the sense more accurately. This, of course, is a Nazi-German expression, and should not be taken to be a current German word.
8. In the course of the organized massacre known as 'Operation Harvest Festival'. See: Note 12 to Chapter 1.
9. Senior Camp Prisoner.
10. Prisoner-Secretary (Clerical Officer) of the camp.
11. The SS had its own ranking system. An *Obersturmbannführer* was equivalent to a Lieutenant-Colonel. For more on Wirths, see *KL Auschwitz Seen By The SS*, inter alia. It is a measure of just how senior a prisoner Soswinski was that he was able to negotiate with the top level of Auschwitz's SS administration, and it must be understood that as *Lagerschreiber* of the camp he was in a unique position. He was also an Austrian political prisoner, and a man who enjoyed high personal standing.
12. The political department of Auschwitz, the office of the *Sicherheitsdienst* at the camp. Max Grabner had been its head until 1 December 1943, when he was

arrested by the SS on charges of corruption and removed from office.
13. Soswinski's second wife worked in the administrative offices of Auschwitz while a prisoner there. They met in the camp. See main text, below.
14. The *Volkssturm* was a kind of Home Guard created by Hitler towards the very end, consisting of old men and boys. It is perfectly possible that the Viennese Fire Brigade did guard-duty at Mauthausen during the final couple of days, since 'Towards the end of April, Ziereis [the commandant] formally handed Mauthausen over to Captain Kern of the civilian police in Vienna. Kern was now faced with the terrible task of controlling the huge death pyre which Mauthausen had become; and also of finding guards to police it, since Ziereis had joined in the general rush to escape and hide' (Le Chêne, op. cit.).
15. The former camp is now a national monument. One *Block* has been fully, almost over-, restored, and there is an excellent museum in the former administrative buildings, which contain a cinema where archive film of the camp in operation is shown, with narration spoken by former inmates.
16. Michael Selzer: *Deliverance Day* (Sphere Books, 1980), p. 35, states that the gas chamber was used.
17. SA – *Sturmabteilung*. The name was adopted in 1921. Members wore brown uniforms, and numbered 400,000 by 1932. Hitler regarded the SA as a political force, but its head, Ernst Röhm, saw it as a revolutionary army. Röhm was assassinated in 1934, and in 1935 the SA was reorganized as 'an internal peacekeeping force' (Hitler). It continued in that role as a relatively minor organization throughout the war. Membership of the SA was not regarded as criminal by Nuremberg.
18. ZDWV: Central Association of Democratic Resistance Fighters and Organizations of Persecutees. FILDIR: International Free Federation of Deportees and Internees of the Resistance.

19. See also: Karl Ibach's memoir of the camp: *Kemna, Wuppertaler Konzentrationslager 1933–1934* (Peter Hammer Verlag, 1983). The account was originally published in 1948. Ibach was the youngest prisoner of the camp, which was set up in an old factory on the edge of town.
20. A school examination similar to 'O' levels, or GCSE, in the UK.
21. *Eine Handvoll Staub*. First published by Nest-Verlag, Nuremberg, in 1947, and thus one of the very earliest accounts. Reissued by Röderberg, Frankfurt, in 1977. It has also been published in English by Gollancz (1948) as *How Long the Night?*, and has appeared in several other languages.

CHAPTER 12: A HOME IN ISRAEL

1. Levin's journey, which was made with a small group of comrades, is shown on Map 313 of Martin Gilbert: *Atlas of the Holocaust* (Michael Joseph, 1982). See also: David Geffen: *One Man's Journey – The Odyssey of Dov Levin* (WZO Department of Information, 83/4/30/970).
2. 'The only military unit to serve in the Second World War in the British Army – and in fact in all the Allied Forces – as an independent, national Jewish military formation' (*Encyclopaedia Judaica*).
3. A *moshav* differs from a *kibbutz* in that in a *moshav* each man has his own house and his own land to work – though machinery and administration are owned and conducted communally, as in a *kibbutz*.
4. The *Generalgouvernement* – a large administrative area of German-occupied Poland – was divided into four 'districts': Cracow, Lublin, Radom and Warsaw.

CHAPTER 13: A HOME IN AMERICA

1. See also: the account by Benjamin Meed's wife, Vladka, who was very much involved with the Jewish resistance in Warsaw: Vladka

Meed: *On Both Sides of the Wall* (Holocaust Library, 1979). Originally published in Yiddish in 1948, it is the earliest published account of the Warsaw ghetto and the uprising there by someone who was involved.
2. See Dinnerstein, op. cit.
3. The United Jewish Appeal was formed in late 1938 and conducted its first campaign in 1939. See also: Gottlieb Hammer: *Good Faith and Credit* (Cornwall Books, 1985), passim.
4. For the effect of the camps upon the faith of individuals, see the study by Reeve Robert Brenner: *The Faith and Doubt of Holocaust Survivors* (Free Press, 1980). His survey is conducted among survivors now in Israel.
5. Rau officiated in that capacity at the dedication of the memorial to Kemna concentration camp (see main text, above, Chapter 11).
6. These British POWs had originally been taken prisoner by Rommel after Tobruk. They were sent to camps in Italy, but after the fall of Mussolini and the invasion of that country, they were transported to Silesia. From there some of them were sent to work at the I. G. Farben works at Buna-Monowice, in contravention of the Geneva Convention. Several Jewish inmates, including Wollheim, have said how greatly the cheerful defiance of the POWs helped restore their own morale.
7. Josef (Yossel) Rosensaft: the head of the Jewish administration of Bergen-Belsen DP camp, as Chairman of the Central Committee for the Liberated Jews in the British Zone. See also: below, Chapter 16, and *Belsen*, a collection of essays, including contributions from Rosensaft and Wollheim, published by Irgun Sheerit Hapleita Me'haezor Habrizi, Israel, in 1957.
8. See also: *Freiheit und Recht*, January–March 1985, p. 4. Fellner, born 1950, was one of the German Chancellor's 'favourites'.
9. Harlan made a number of propaganda films for the Nazis, with his wife and leading lady, Kristina

Soederbaum. He continued to make films after the war, and died in 1964, aged 65. See also: Robert Edwin Herzstein: *The War That Hitler Won* (Hamish Hamilton, 1979).

10. This and some of the following passages between quotation marks are taken from Max Garcia's own account of his life: *As Long As I Remain Alive* (Portals, 1979).

CHAPTER 14: FRENCH RESISTANCE FIGHTERS

1. There is little left. Much of the camp-site was built on soon after the war. See Annexe 3 of Louis Poutrain's book, *La Déportation au Coeur d'une Vie* (Cerf, 1982).

2. They were not tattooed. This only occurred at Auschwitz.

3. Her own account, written under her maiden name, Denise Dufournier, is *La Maison des Mortes* (Hachette, 1945), which must be the earliest published account. See also: *Voix et Visages*, the magazine of ADIR, Nos. 84, 86, 87, 89, 94, 130, 140 and 146; and Mme McAdam Clark's 'Méditation sur Ravensbrück', in *La Revue des Deux Mondes*, April 1975, pp. 99–108.

4. For more on Comet, see: Airey Neave: *Saturday at MI9* (Hodder & Stoughton, 1969). One of the principal actors in the Comet drama was Albert-Marie Guérisse, whose extraordinary wartime career is described in Vincent Brome: *The Way Back* (Cassell, 1957). Guérisse was betrayed to the Gestapo by the traitor Roger le Neveu and was imprisoned first in Fresnes, and later in Mauthausen and Dachau. Although a Belgian national, his cover was that of a Lieutenant-Commander in the Royal Navy, under the name Patrick O'Leary, and it was under this cover that he was arrested. His red triangle thus had an E on it (for *Engländer* – though technically Guérisse's cover nationality was Irish). Four British and Australian SOE (Special Operations Executive) agents went through the KZ with him – Tom Groome, John Hopper, Bob Sheppard and Brian Stonehouse.

All survived, and the last-named is now a portrait-painter based in London (see *The Times*, 1 May 1987, p. 12). Guérisse became President of the International Prisoners' Committee formed in Dachau, a position he retained after the war. Upon liberation, he returned home and resumed his career as an army doctor. In 1951 he saw action in Korea as Medical Officer of the British 29th Brigade, then part of the US 3rd Division. Bravery in rescuing a wounded Belgian soldier under fire earned him the Orders of Officer of the Order of Leopold with Palm, and the *Chung Mu* (the Korean equivalent of the DSO). From France he holds the *Légion d'Honneur* and the *Croix de Guerre*; from the USA, the Medal of Freedom; from the UK the George Cross and the Distinguished Service Order; and, also from Belgium, the *Croix de Guerre*. He rose to be head of the Belgian Army Medical Corps, and was recently created a Vicomte, though he refers to himself simply as 'Dr Guérisse'. He lives in Brussels.

5. Andrée de Jongh was in fact betrayed for money by a Spanish peasant. She was taking a group of airmen across the Pyrenean route and had intended to return to fetch her father, who was too old to make the journey with her until the winter weather improved. Both had been involved in Comet and knew that the Gestapo were on their heels. Frédéric de Jongh was later arrested and shot. His daughter survived Ravensbrück and took up a nursing career in Africa after the war.

6. As Geneviève Anthonioz, she is director of ADIR (see main text, below).

7. Mussulmen. *Schmutzstücke* (literally, 'dirty pieces') seems to be a Ravensbrück variant of the common term. Prisoners were frequently referred to by the Germans simply as *Stücke* – 'pieces', or 'things'.

8. Association Nationale des Anciennes Déportées et Internées de la Résistance – the French women's survivor organization.

CHAPTER 15: POLAND:
RESISTANCE AND 'RED TRIANGLES'

1. Approximate to a lieutenant. SS ranks in the KZ administration were often quite low in relation to the responsibility of the post held.
2. Wife of the commandant of Buchenwald, who was arrested and tried for corruption by the SS during the war. She died, insane, in the Sixties.
3. The SS were concerned only that the numbers of prisoners in any given group tallied – whether the prisoners were alive or dead was of no consequence to them. All prisoners looked alike – the result of starvation removing individual characteristics from a face, coupled with shaven heads, and uniforms. Thus it was frequently possible to save someone's life by getting him out of a death *Block*, for example, and substituting a corpse. The camp numbers had to be exchanged, too, since the Germans would have checked and noted them. The Spanish prisoners in the camps were former Left-wing fighters in the Civil War who had subsequently come to France and joined the resistance. See: Jorge Semprun: *Le Grand Voyage* (Gallimard, 1963).
4. The Polish 2nd Corps was commanded by General Wladislaw Anders. When the Germans invaded Russian-occupied Poland, various Polish units were formed in Russia out of the original Polish army. These were sent to Persia to regroup and re-form, taking in people who had been below military-service age when they had originally been evacuated from Poland. Broadly speaking, the Polish 2nd Corps was formed out of these units, and later formed part of the British 8th Army. Anders had been ordered to create the Corps by the Polish Government in Exile in London. They saw action in North Africa, and their last main action was at Bologna. The battle for whose victory the Poles were directly responsible was at Monte Cassino, in May 1944.
5. A programme of selective breeding to transform the Germans into the Master Race of the race theorists; part of it included the wholesale kidnapping of 'racially acceptable' children from the occupied countries – the children were then fostered by selected German families. A number of books have been written about *Lebensborn* – 'The Fountain of Life'.
6. Ernest Bevin had issued a statement to the effect that all members of the Free Polish Forces (effectively the 1st Armoured Division, operating in northern Europe, and the Polish 2nd Corps) would be demobbed when their post-war duties were at an end, and that if they did not wish to return to Poland they would be helped to find a new home in the UK, and retrained. At the end of the war the 2nd Corps had a strength of about 100,000; but tens of thousands of Poles in the various DP camps wanted to join, to benefit from the offer contained in the Bevin statement. The 2nd Corps helped as many Poles as possible to join up, even after the war was over, but they could not take everybody (the 1st Armoured Division operated similarly on a smaller scale), and after Yalta the UK cooled in its attitude to the Polish Government in Exile. It still rankles that the Free Polish Forces were not even allowed to participate in the VE-Day parades. Nevertheless, Great Britain honoured its obligations to all members of the Polish forces who wished to make a new home there, and the Polish Resettlement Corps was responsible for rehabilitation and retraining programmes. Centres were established across the country, notably in Scotland and northern England.
7. See: Jozef Garlinski, op. cit., pp. 14–16.
8. *Hauptscharführer* (Sergeant-Major) Palitzsch was just 27 when he took up his duties at Auschwitz in 1940. He was a sadist of feared reputation even there. For more, see: *KL Auschwitz Seen by the SS*. Incidentally, it is interesting to reflect on the relative youth of many of the main Nazi and SS figures. Himmler, for example, was born as late as 1900. At the height of their

power, these men were generally in
their late twenties and early
thirties.

9. Frank was also treated for a foot
infection by Dr Wladislaw Dering,
and after the war appeared as a
witness for Dering in the libel case
the doctor brought against the
novelist Leon Uris for defamation of
character.

10. *Mexiko*, a new sector of Birkenau,
was started to house the expected
intake of Hungarian Jews. It never
approached completion.

11. Painting Detail: Supervision; and
Painting Detail: Administration.

12. The camp at Sachsenhausen, just to
the north of Berlin, is sometimes
known by the name of the nearby
town of Oranienburg, the centre of
an industrial complex at the time.

13. Scene of a Russian massacre of
Polish officers. 4,250 men were
executed in the Katyn forest near
Smolensk, after the Russian
occupation of eastern Polish
territory in 1939. The bodies were
discovered by the Germans in 1943.
The Germans and the Russians used
the atrocity to try to score
propaganda points off each other, but
it is clear that the Russians were
responsible. In the context of
propaganda, it is interesting to note
that in June 1943 SS propagandists
photographed some KZ-inmates at
Lublin on their way to the gas
chambers at Majdanek. The
photographs subsequently
appeared in a magazine with the
caption, 'Victims of British Terror
and Starvation in India' (Kraus and
Kulka, op. cit., p. 205).

14. See also: Vladka Meed, op. cit.,
pp. 176ff. Mrs Meed's book also
contains further information on the
Hotel Polski at this point.

15. These parcels were sent from
Warsaw by the *Patronat*, a welfare
organization run by Countess
Ponialowska.

CHAPTER 16: HEALERS

1. *Human Behaviour in the
Concentration Camp* was first
published in Great Britain by Cape
in 1954. Dr Cohen presented it as his

doctoral thesis on 11 March 1952.
A second, personal account, *The
Abyss*, appeared in 1973, published
by Norton.

2. *Straf* = punishment.

3. Cohen: *De negentien treinen naar
Sobibor* (Sijthoff, 1979).

4. Their son was still free. Dr Cohen's
wife's menstrual cycle, which had
ceased, recommenced as soon as
they were together again.

5. See also: Frankl: *Ein Psychologe
erlebt das KZ* (dtv, 1982), where it
is argued that the prisoner is
literally in a world of living death, a
place where life is suspended. The
camp had its own reality which was
nothing to do with normal reality.
'People have referred to it as another
planet – on it, the world beyond its
barbed-wire confines became unreal.'

6. Jan Karski served as a courier
between the underground in
Warsaw and the Polish National
Council, first in France and later in
the UK, using the code-name
'Vitold'. In the course of his work
he was smuggled into Belzec, and
into the Warsaw ghetto, in order to
be able to report on conditions
there. When he did so in the West,
his reports and his requests on
behalf of the beleaguered Jews
were ignored. In the UK it was
Anthony Eden who blocked any
intercession with Churchill.

7. Frankl, op. cit., p. 46, relates a
similar experience, in which the
SS didn't speak to him or even treat
him as human; Frankl stopped one
day to catch his breath, and in that
moment the guard noticed him
'slacking'. What distressed Frankl
was that as a result of this he didn't
even earn a curse from the guard,
who just picked up a stone and
threw it idly at him, as he might
have done at a farm beast.

8. ibid., pp. 146–7. Frankl gives a
graphic and moving description of
a survivor returning to the
dreamt-of home and friends, to
find that they have gone, and it has
passed into other hands. This cruel
revelation spelt the end for many
survivors who didn't have the
strength left to cope with it.

9. Heimler: *The Healing Echo*
(Souvenir, 1985) pp. 13–14.

10. See also Professor Heimler's personal memoir of his time in the KZ and after: *Night of the Mist* (Bodley Head, 1959).
11. See: *Night of the Mist*.
12. The story of Josef Rosensaft, who died in 1975, and the administration of the DP camp at Belsen is told in *Belsen* (Irgun Sheerit Hapleita Me'haezor Habriti, 1957).
13. See Dr Rosensaft's evidence at the Belsen Trial: Raymond Phillips (ed.): *Trial of Josef Kramer and Forty-Four Others* (William Hodge and Co.) pp. 66–7.
14. See *Belsen*, op. cit., pp. 98–116.

CHAPTER 17: A MUSICIAN AND A DANCER

1. Alma Rosé was in charge of the women's camp orchestra at Birkenau. She did not survive.
2. cp. Cohen, op. cit., p. 20 – *Vorzugslager* (= 'preference camp').
3. Vrba, op. cit., reports that at Christmas 1942 all the prisoners in Auschwitz-I were ordered to sing 'Silent Night'.

CHAPTER 18: THREE ARTISTS

1. Dr Isaac Levy told me that initially the British didn't know how to treat the prisoners and gave them too much food, including army biscuits, which the KZ-inmates described as 'cake'. Later, intravenous feeding techniques learnt in the recent famines in Bengal were applied successfully.
2. A barrack for children and adolescents. For Yehuda Bacon's account of it, see Adler, op. cit., pp. 552–7 and pp. 709–11.
3. Fredy Hirsch refused to lead an uprising of the First Camp, and committed suicide. See Adler, Kraus and Kulka, and Vrba.
4. The man involved was Stefan Baretski, born 24 March 1919. See: Bernd Naumann: *Auschwitz – Report on the Frankfurt Trial* (Pall Mall Press, 1966).

Index